THE LONE STAR SPEAKS

UNTOLD TEXAS STORIES

ABOUT THE JFK ASSASSINATION

SARA PETERSON & K.W. ZACHRY

bancroft
press

ISBN:
978-1-61088-192-0 (Hardcover)
978-1-61088-193-7 (PB)
978-1-61088-194-4 (Kindle)
978-1-61088-195-1 (Ebook)

Cover & Interior design: Tracy Copes
Author Photo:
Published by Bancroft Press "Books that Enlighten"
410-358-0658
P.O. Box 65360, Baltimore, MD 21209
www.bancroftpress.com

Printed in the United States of America

To Dr. Herbert Hogan,
who taught me the importance of dissecting, critically
analyzing, questioning, and interpreting all information
regarding political theory, political philosophy, and historical
facts. He also taught me these twin imperatives: Don't
allow others to influence your research, and draw your own
conclusions by deciphering the Truth.
—Sara Peterson

To Dr. Selma Bishop,
who taught me how to write;
and to my mother, who taught me how to think.
—K. W. Zachry

TABLE OF

CONTENTS

PROLOGUE

"There are two ways to be fooled. One is to believe
what isn't true; the other is to refuse to believe what is true."
—Soren Kierkegaard

In ancient times, marvelous sorcerers were nothing short of amazing, at least if you asked the poor gullible common folk. Such magicians "caused" fierce storms, accurately predicted rain, walked on hot coals, and summoned long dead spirits to commune with the living.

Science has taught the modern world that these tricksters had no more magical powers than anyone else had.

What they *did* have was knowledge not available to most people. They knew how to use balms and herbs, their so-called "magic potions."

They were aware of how birds and animals behave before the weather changes. They understood how the bereaved feel after losing a loved one, and how desperately they will grasp any hope of an earthly reunion. In other words, magicians had "inside information."

We 21st century sophisticates osmugly tell ourselves that we are now too intelligent, too well-educated, to be drawn in by magic. Magicians exist only in Las Vegas, and their secrets have been exposed to national audiences via television. "What fools these mortals be!"

But "real" magicians are at work every day, bewildering us just as easily as Merlin did King Arthur. They convince us there is an over-abundance of wheat, that all the homeless are minorities, that all drug addicts are from poverty-stricken areas. The hand is quicker than the eye, but the mouth is quicker than either. Promises of lower taxes flow sweetly from smiling lips while the old sleight-of-hand trick pilfers our coffers.

Yes, indeed. Just as in the days of old, we still have magicians and sorcerers. They simply have new names—"politicians" and "bureaucrats." And it is these politicians and bureaucrats who helped take away the voice of John F. Kennedy and the voices of many who were touched by his death. Even if they had nothing to do with his assassination, they altered, ignored, and hid evidence so that one man was assigned all the blame for the death of a president. Like the best magicians, they kept the public's eyes on one thing, the Warren Report, while they made sure important information and witnesses were "hidden behind the curtain" of national security. Most of the people never saw the ventriloquists's lips moving while the dummies mouthed the official story.

What the politicians and bureaucrats forgot is that the American people can handle the truth. What they can't handle are distortions, half-truths, character assassinations, and out-and-out lies. Ignorance is not bliss to most Americans. That is why some of them finally demanded to "look behind the curtain," even if their curiosity spoiled the performance or cost them their lives. These brave souls refused to sit like trained seals and applaud an "investigation" that invisibly banged nails into the coffin of truth.

Sadly, American history books devote very little space to the mystery surrounding President Kennedy's death. Many high school and college students know only that he was assassinated by someone. Perhaps that is preferable to the history books which refer to Lee Harvey Oswald as "the assassin." In a country that preaches "innocent until proven guilty," many textbook authors seem to have forgotten that Oswald was never given the opportunity to defend himself. This alone makes him innocent simply because his voice was silenced before a jury could hear his defense.

That silencing began before Oswald even reached the Dallas Police Department. Dallas reporter Hugh Aynesworth witnessed his arrest and heard him shouting, "I protest this police brutality" as local police were forcing him into the backseat of a patrol car. In Aynesworth's notes can be found a chilling observation: "A hand reached out and covered his mouth."[1] This could certainly explain why Oswald attempted to speak to news reporters every time he was in their presence. They were the only "voice" he had.

Fortunately, the voices of many other individuals are no longer silent. It has taken some of them years to tell their stories. For some, this was because they were afraid to speak or at least correct what the Warren Commission claimed they had said. Some did not realize that the information they had was important. Some had been sworn to secrecy even though what they knew might have exonerated innocent persons. Some were never even questioned, and others were never asked the appropriate questions.

Their stories may not tell the reader exactly who assassinated President John F. Kennedy in Dallas, Texas on November 22, 1963, or why and how. But they will provide information that the members of the Warren Commission and even the House Select Committee on Assassinations either did not know or chose not to share with America (for national security reasons, of course).

More importantly, their stories will raise questions which need to be answered. The "torch" to which President Kennedy referred in his Inaugural Address has already been passed to several generations since that snowy day in January 1961. That torch represents not only freedom, but freedom from ignorance and lies, *and* knowledge of the truth. June Oswald Porter, the older daughter of President Kennedy's accused assassin, once said that all she wanted to know was the truth. Surely, if she can handle it, so can the rest of the country. But truth can only be obtained if the right questions are asked. As several of our interviewees told us, "No one ever asked me that!"

If more voices speak out, perhaps their personal stories will chase away the shadows that have held the truth captive for so long.

I
SECRETS FROM
THE SHADOWS

President John F. Kennedy arrived in Dallas, Texas on November 22, 1963 appearing to be in good health; almost exactly three hours later, he left the city in a casket. Those two facts are about the only things that most Americans agree upon concerning that tragic weekend. To this day, important details and secrets about President Kennedy—his life, his administration, and his assassination—have not been brought to light. These details and secrets could help lift the murky shadows of doubt that continue to obscure the truth about what really happened in Dallas that Friday in 1963.

CHAPTER 1

THE KENNEDY FAMILY

"In reality, the Kennedys were only interested in power and politics...
They spent their money on buying votes, whether it was to get JFK into the
Oval Office or Teddy and Bobby into the Senate."—Pierre Salinger

John Kennedy, a Catholic, became a part of history the moment he was elected President of the United States. History is, after all, basically the voices of people recalling events in which they deliberately, or inadvertently, become engaged. Many of the voices that could have spoken so honestly about John F. Kennedy were sworn to secrecy by him and his family, by the government, or by other "organizations." Some voices either kept details about Kennedy to themselves out of respect for the President or because, after his death, they were afraid to speak out.

The image of America's young, vibrant, idealistic new President was just a shadow of the real man. Little did the public know that the world surrounding the Kennedy White House was like the world Alice discovered in Lewis Carroll's *Through the Looking Glass*. Very few things were as they appeared to be. But this discrepancy between reality and appearance did not begin in 1960. The members of the Kennedy family, their friends and associates, and even their staff members always kept secrets about the family and its activities. Only during the last decade or two have some of those privy to private information shared it with certain authors and historians.

If embarrassing facts might alter the public perception of any Kennedy, then they were to be swept under the rug, hidden in a closet, omitted from the record. Joe Kennedy, Sr., the family patriarch, would, for a time, hide from his own children the fact that their sister Rosemary had been institutionalized because of her mental retardation. Her siblings were told that she was teaching in a convent.[2]

Kennedy, Sr. also controlled the publicity concerning the plane crash that killed his daughter Kathleen and her Protestant lover, Peter Fitzwilliam. As grief-stricken as he was at the sudden death of his daughter, he made sure the press erroneously reported that the couple had just met prior to the flight.[3]

Thanks to friendly journalists like Ben Bradlee, David Brinkley, and Roger Mudd, to name just a few, members of the Kennedy family managed to control the image they sold to the American people. These reporters "wound up promoting the Kennedys and building false images and myths about them that became part of Kennedy history and legend."[4]

To the Kennedy family, appearances were more important than reality. When he was a young Navy lieutenant serving in the Pacific during World War II, John Kennedy's PT boat was sliced in half by a Japanese destroyer. Kennedy received a great deal of flattering and well-deserved publicity for his role in rescuing the survivors. Nevertheless, two of his crew died because of the incident. Despite this, Kennedy was awarded the Navy and Marine Corps medal for "lifesaving," though some historians still criticize him for mishandling the situation in the first place. Certain details surrounding the heroism of Kennedy were exaggerated.[5] These exaggerations led to magazine articles, a book, a song, and, eventually, a motion picture; all focused their story lines on Kennedy's heroism rather than his mistakes.

Joseph Kennedy, Sr. controlled the publicity around the incident, and instead of JFK's actions being reported as a military blunder, they became an important part of Kennedy's campaign literature. It is questionable whether American voters would have accepted Kennedy as a war hero if they had known all the facts about PT-109. In his book *A Question of Character*, Thomas Reeves refused to accept the official story of Kennedy's heroism; instead, he described the situation thusly:

By allowing the American people and his own crew members to hail him as a hero, John Kennedy demonstrated "a basic lack of integrity." The facts of the matter reveal a very young man, in bad physical condition, who performed poorly on his PT boat and exhibited some recklessness and poor judgment in the subsequent rescue efforts. The bravery was real. However, it was exaggerated in campaign literature and in authorized books."[6]

Behind closed doors, even Kennedy admitted that his heroism had been exaggerated. After the Bay of Pigs fiasco in 1961, he remarked to author Robert J. Donovan, who had created the Kennedy-approved script for the movie version of the PT-109 incident, "That whole story was more fucked up than Cuba."[7] This was not the first time that those close to Kennedy would alter historical facts; nor would it be the last.

Another example of how important details were omitted concerns Kennedy's Pulitzer Prize-winning book *Profiles in Courage*. In 1957, the Pulitzer Prize Committee and the American public did not know that JFK's future political speech writer, Theodore Sorensen, had greatly assisted him in writing the book.

Historian Herbert S. Parmet's research for his book *Jack: The Struggles of John F. Kennedy* indicated that Sorenson played a "dominant role in the creation of *Profiles in Courage*," and that he had also authored many other publications supposedly written by Kennedy. "Though Kennedy responded powerfully, even viscerally, to great prose, he had always been an awkward writer."[8]

Kennedy's notes show that it took a professional writer like Sorensen to turn his ideas and research into a well-crafted piece of non-fiction.

In addition, it's uncertain how many copies of the best-seller were sold to the public because, according to family friend Jewel Reed, "Joe Kennedy purchased thousands of copies 'to keep it on top of the best seller list.'"[9] As far as the Kennedys were concerned, the public needed to be as unaware of what occurred "behind the political curtain" as any audience that enjoys an illusionist's magic tricks. The Kennedys seemed to think what people did not know would not hurt them. History would show that John Kennedy and his associates, family, and staff would spend years convincing even those who thought they knew JFK well that he was really larger than life, almost infallible—a King Arthur-like figure surrounded by a magical kingdom. Only insiders knew that world was mythical, not magical.

This kingdom became the Kennedy administration, but it was built on sands of deception. And much of this can be blamed on Joe Kennedy, Sr.'s beliefs and actions—the way he treated his wife, the standards he set for his children, and the lies he was willing to tell to reach whatever goal he had set.

His actions affected every member of his family. For example, his wife Rose refused to be referred to as the "mistress" of her own house. "A housekeeper, I am," she said. "A mistress, I am not."[10] The word "mistress" seemed to leave a bad taste in Rose Kennedy's mouth. Chances are, she felt this way because her husband had blatantly carried on numerous extra-marital affairs, perhaps some even in his family home.

Perhaps she also preferred not to know how many female visitors her husband entertained in and out of her presence. Joe Kennedy, Sr. became a role model of infidelity for sons who carried on the family tradition. Instead of being shocked by their father's behavior, the sons seemed to be amused by it. John Kennedy would smile knowingly when he told female visitors to his family's home, "Be sure to lock the bedroom door. The Ambassador [his father] has a tendency to prowl late at night."[11]

Like her mother-in-law, Jackie Kennedy tried to ignore the fact that John F. Kennedy, the man America knew as an ideal husband and father, was an unfaithful marital partner. Numerous books published after the assassination finally revealed how unlike King Arthur John F. Kennedy really was, at least concerning his sexual conduct.

Kennedy's behavior could not be kept secret today. But in the 1960s, reporters ignored information about his extra-marital affairs, even when one was with the girlfriend of a mobster, and another was with the ex-wife of a CIA agent. The President's staff members and Secret Service agents aided and abetted him by slipping females into hotels during his out-of-town trips and even into the White House itself. One specific staff member, Evelyn Lincoln, seemed to be quite adept at preserving JFK's image.

The President's personal phone calls were taken by Lincoln, his executive secretary, so she must have known about women like Judith Campbell Exner and Marilyn Monroe. Surely, she at least suspected that the President's wife would object to her husband's immoral behavior. However, Lincoln knew that she worked for Kennedy, not his wife. When the President asked her to do things like call Frank Sinatra, whom Mrs. Kennedy hated, and invite him to a dinner at the White House, Lincoln gladly did so. For the Sinatra event itself, the President waited until his wife had gone to Virginia and his sister, Eunice Shriver, was available to act as hostess. So even the President's family members covered for him.[12] Kennedy's brother-in-law Peter Lawford admitted that he and his wife Pat, the President's sister, entertained JFK and beautiful starlets like Angie Dickenson numerous times at their Santa Monica home, and all when the President's wife was elsewhere.[13]

White House photographer Cecil Stoughton seems to have had more sympathy for Jacqueline Kennedy than Evelyn Lincoln had. He warned her that Marilyn Monroe would be performing at her husband's birthday party in Madison Square Garden in May of 1962. Consequently, the President's wife refused to attend the celebration (even though his sisters and sisters-in-law did so) and was spared what would have been humiliating—Marilyn Monroe singing a super-sultry version of "Happy Birthday" to John F. Kennedy.

Stoughton was responsible for photographing the President and his guests at Arthur Krim's New York apartment party after the official birthday celebration. He took the now famous photo of John and Robert Kennedy with Marilyn Monroe standing between them, as well as numerous other photos of famous guests like singer Harry Belafonte and actress Shirley MacLaine.

Director/producer Bill Asher, who organized the birthday event, was also pictured in a photo with Monroe; for years, this photo was displayed in his home. But Stoughton admitted that there were more photos of the President and Monroe than the one that finally surfaced.

He told filmmaker Keya Morgan, to whom he sold the original prints, that he had taken ten photos of Monroe, the President, and his brother that evening. While he was printing the tenth negative, Secret Service agents entered and removed every photo showing either of the Kennedys with Monroe—every one except the last print, which was still drying. They overlooked that one.

Stoughton took another photo of Kennedy leaving New York the morning after the birthday celebration; the uncropped version shows a group of people standing on a balcony watching the President about to enter his limousine. Among those on the balcony is a smiling Marilyn Monroe.

To spare Jacqueline Kennedy embarrassment, Stoughton did not release that photo until after her death. While he was trying to protect the First Lady's dignity, the Secret Service was protecting Kennedy's career. (Whether Monroe was sneaked into the White House, as other women were, is anyone's guess.[14])

Kennedy loyalists have gone so far as to say that Kennedy and Monroe barely knew one another. This appears not to be true at all. Doyle Whitehead was one of the military stewards who served on Air Force 1 for Presidents Eisenhower, Kennedy, and Johnson. Of the three, Whitehead preferred Kennedy. "He was the friendliest," he recalled in a telephone interview with the authors. He also recalled a fact that would have made front-page news at the time. The steward observed Marilyn Monroe aboard Air Force 1 as a guest of the President. When asked if she had been wearing any type of disguise, such as a brunette wig, Whitehead replied, "No, but she signed in as a secretary." No one has yet revealed whether the actress, like some other women, visited the White House while the First Lady was absent.

The President's paramours were not the only individuals slipped into the White House. Even though the President remained close to his father and valued his advice, he did not want the public to know how often they communicated.

Joe Kennedy, Sr.'s "ruthless and controversial reputation labeled him an undesirable associate of the President. Great caution was taken to dispel any thought that the President or his administration was under his father's influence, so much so that he was smuggled in, under wraps, whenever he visited the White House."[15]

That did not mean that the two men did not stay in close contact. Even after his father's serious stroke, the President still consulted with him on various matters. He once said, "Even if my dad had only ten percent of his brain working, I'd still feel he had more sense than anyone else I know."[16] The father and son had to devise a way to communicate privately. Evelyn Lincoln explained how the subterfuge worked:

"The Kennedy family had leased a private telephone line that ran from Joe Kennedy's office in New York directly to the Oval Office and to the President's living quarters. JFK also had a telephone installed in his private hideaway off the Oval Office. It was a little office with a couch and telephone where the President could go and rest.'" Known as the prayer room, it was a place where

Kennedy could take private phone calls. Some of these came from his father; some came from other people he preferred to talk to in private.[17]

Jacqueline Kennedy, dubbed "Jackie" by the press, was just as secretive as her in-laws and just as determined to protect the Kennedy family image. Staff members learned immediately that they were not to speak about anything that occurred in the White House or about anything connected to the Kennedy family. In fact, staff members had to sign a secrecy oath immediately upon employment. This did not keep several staff members from eventually writing memoirs about their days with the Kennedy family. However, it may have affected how much they revealed in their books.

Jackie Kennedy's personal secretary, Mary Barelli Gallagher, for example, wrote *My Life with Jacqueline Kennedy* in 1969. She revealed little-known facts that show Jackie Kennedy was a woman of contradictions. She could be generous and thoughtful but also selfish and miserly.

Gallagher spent so much time at the White House that she observed a great many things the public was unaware of, like the fact that the Kennedy children were basically cared for by their British governess, Maud Shaw. It was Shaw who dressed, fed, and tended to the children. Since Gallagher had also worked for Jackie Kennedy's mother before Gallagher worked at the White House, she realized that this type of upbringing was one with which Jackie Kennedy was familiar.

Jackie Kennedy had never been expected to perform any household chores, even before the Kennedys moved into the White House, so she certainly did not know her way around the kitchen. It was a cook who rose early to prepare the breakfast meal for her husband and their children. No middle-class American housewife could have possibly related to a woman who employed maids to perform household duties, a nanny to care for her children, even when they were sick, a butler/valet to care for her husband's clothes, and a chauffeur to drive the couple wherever they wanted to go.

"In short, Jackie was the 'director' of those who actually carried out her housewifely and motherly chores and responsibilities."[18] Typical American parents would not have understood the "hands-off" approach that Jackie Kennedy employed with her children. "Caroline did not sit at the table with her parents for meals, nor did John-John. They had their own schedule with their governess and sometimes saw her and their Secret Service men more than they saw their parents."[19]

Even on the evening after the assassination, the task of sharing the heartbreaking news of her father's death with Caroline Kennedy fell to Maud Shaw. Shaw recalled that Caroline was so astute that even as a little girl, it was difficult to deceive her. Caroline insisted on the truth instead of evasions. "It was like that when I had to break the news of her father's death to her," Shaw wrote in 1973. "That was a time for honesty—not for fairy stories."[20]

The job of handling the First Lady's finances was assigned to Mary Gallagher. She was instructed by the President himself to share with him "a complete list of all the checks written by Jackie Kennedy and exactly what they were for."[21] This was just one of Gallagher's many duties, but most of what she did was kept hidden from the public because neither Kennedy wanted Americans to know that the First Lady had a personal secretary.

For example, Gallagher learned to copy Jackie Kennedy's signature, which meant she signed numerous letters and pieces of correspondence. Eventually, she learned to sign President Kennedy's signature, too. Until Gallagher published her book, the public did not know this; in fact, the public had not known that Gallagher even existed. She was not supposed to appear in official photographs with Mrs. Kennedy, and if she did, it was her back, and not her face, that was caught by the camera.

During the presidential campaign, the press created an image of Jackie Kennedy that was so exaggerated it might as well have been false. Americans were led to believe that she only had a part-time secretary, and that the candidate's wife herself read and answered the 225 letters she received daily. Actually, Gallagher was taking these letters home to read and answer herself. Readers were also told that Jackie Kennedy did not have a nurse for Caroline. This, of course, was blatantly false. Another secret that Mary Gallagher would keep from others was that President Kennedy often slept in the Lincoln bedroom while Mrs. Kennedy slept in the Queen's room.[22]

Besides her secretarial duties, Gallagher seemed to be at Jackie Kennedy's beck-and-call for extra duties like ironing her nylons, arranging furniture, and entertaining her children. Even when at home, she was expected to answer telephone calls from Jackie Kennedy, night or day. And yet, in 1962, after seventeen years of employment, Mary Gallagher, personal secretary to the First Lady, was being paid only $4,830 a year. And Jackie Kennedy was determined not to pay any of that salary out of her own pocket. When Gallagher requested a raise to be paid by the Kennedys' New York office, the First Lady "retorted rather petulantly: 'But then the money would be coming out of our pockets.'"[23]

Even though the whole world knew that the Kennedys were multi-millionaires, Jackie Kennedy, like her mother-in-law Rose, was quite thrifty, unless she was spending money on herself. As a senator's wife, she would even resell certain dresses to resale shops, always under an assumed name. In 1961, the press somehow discovered how much money she had spent on clothing and printed the figure as $30,000. Jackie Kennedy insinuated that this amount was incorrect. Truthfully, the figure *was* incorrect; she had actually spent $40,000 that year.[24] In today's dollars (2020), this would be equivalent to $344,000. In any event, it was almost ten times the amount of Gallagher's salary.

The First Lady's thriftiness even applied to her own children. Gifts sent to the children from public admirers were sometimes used as personal Christmas gifts. Caroline and John's mother would decide whether the gifts were nice enough to be used for them or for her sister's children.[25] Only the ones she deemed ordinary were given to charitable organizations.

William Manchester, chosen by Jacqueline and Robert Kennedy to write the book, *Death of a President,* after JFK's assassination, learned how demanding Jackie Kennedy could be. Manchester had previously written *Portrait of a President*, a book so flattering that the President found it unnecessary to ask for a single change. But Jackie Kennedy was so obsessed with her public image that she threatened Manchester with legal action over details in *Death of a President.* Information not becoming to her or to the Kennedy family, or any comments that might affect Robert Kennedy's future political career, were to be excised.

In the book, Manchester had innocently enough revealed that Mrs. Kennedy smoked, a detail she had hidden from Americans, even though many of them also smoked. Manchester also revealed that the First Lady had imbibed two, tall dark tumblers of Scotch to settle her nerves on Air Force One as she returned from Dallas to Washington, D. C. with her dead husband's body.[26] Why Jackie Kennedy worried that the American public would fault her for trivial matters like these is anyone's guess. But perhaps it is because so many inconsequential pieces of information about the Kennedy family had already been hidden. Keeping Kennedy secrets had become a family tradition.

An aide close to Senator Edward Kennedy learned, like many others, that if he wished to remain employed, he should ignore certain behaviors by anyone in the family, even the Senator himself. He had just inadvertently seen Kennedy in a compromising position with a party guest while his wife slept a few rooms away. George Dalton, who had originally worked for John Kennedy and later for Edward, explained the cold, hard facts to the aide. "The Senator really likes you. You can go far here," he said. "You have to grow up. You can't be . . . judging. You can't say anything to anybody. If you want to be part of the team, you just have to shut up and go along with it."[27]

This same aide also discovered that a Kennedy family friend had requested the erasure of certain portions of various Oval Office tape recordings made during John F. Kennedy's administration. He assumed this was for national security reasons, but he questioned his reasoning when the friend announced one day: "We had to erase a couple of hours of tape 'cause Marilyn was on the phone with the President. Boy, the things they talked about!"

The aide was particularly concerned about this behavior because at the time, President Richard Nixon was being questioned about gaps in his Oval Office tapes. When the aide shared his concerns with the governess for Edward Kennedy's children, he received a response similar to the one George Dalton had given him: "Don't get into it," she advised quickly. "Forget it. Don't ever mention it to anybody. You are better off to shut up and never say anything."[28]

The aide followed this advice for years, even after he was privy to transcripts of John F. Kennedy's original, unedited tapes. From these transcripts, he learned that the President *had accepted* private calls from both Marilyn Monroe and Judith Campbell.[29] Connections to these two women would later prove embarrassing to the Kennedy family.

The advice the young aide received from insiders seemed to be standard operating procedure for Kennedy employees and even friends. They were required to understand that they should never speak negatively about the family. It was only after President Kennedy's death that his former press secretary, Pierre Salinger, publicly shared his opinion about the family. Being close to the President and to his brother Bobby, Salinger saw that the Kennedys were driven by two things. "In reality, the Kennedys were only interested in power and politics," he said. "They spent their money on buying votes, whether it was to get JFK into the Oval Office or Teddy and Bobby into the Senate."[30] Fortunately for the Kennedys, only certain insiders knew this.

CHAPTER 2
THE VOICE OF LAYTE BOWDEN

"I wasn't going to be raped, even by the President."

The media is partly to blame for foisting onto the world the false image of the Kennedys as an idyllic American family. Behind the scenes, those close to the family knew otherwise. Some even knew about the President's relationships with his closest family members, including his unusual relationship with his mother. According to a female friend of the President, Layte Bowden, "She did a number on Jack."[31] By "she," Bowden meant Rose Kennedy. Rose made sure John Kennedy, her second son, realized how close she was to his older brother Joe, Jr. For whatever reasons, she was not as close to the son nicknamed "Jack." Author Barbara Leaming revealed the following:

The first time John Kennedy may have wondered about his mother's absences came when he was just two years old. He nearly died of scarlet fever, but Rose Kennedy was not by his bedside. This was because she was giving birth to his sister and could not be near her second son, even after his sister's birth."[32]

Her lack of warmth with her offspring may not have affected all nine of her children, but it did affect Jack. He seems to have been particularly influenced by her frequent absences and her distant nature.

At the age of five, he scolded her as she was about to leave again, "Gee, you're a great mother to go away and leave your children alone." He later confided to a friend, "She was never there when we really needed her…My mother never really held me or hugged me. Never! Never!"[33]

This lack of maternal nurturing doubtless affected Kennedy's relationships with women, even his relationship with his wife.

There were few women who did not succumb to his charms. Layte Bowden, receptionist for Florida Senator George Smathers and, from time to time, a Pan American stewardess, thought highly of President Kennedy, but she did not have a sexual relationship with him. A statuesque Mary Tyler Moore look-alike, Bowden was not only among the many young women who surrounded the President, but one who seemed especially worrisome to Bobby Kennedy. She was a bright young lady with class— nothing like some of the other women Kennedy consorted with. Perhaps Bobby Kennedy thought Bowden was the type of woman for whom Kennedy might have left his wife.

Bowden recalled in her memoir *Under the Radar during Camelot* that John Kennedy pushed and pushed her for a romantic relationship. But Bowden was involved with Senator Smathers at the time. She enjoyed the President's wit and conversational skills, but she did not realize that it was difficult, if not impossible, for him to have platonic relationships with women.

She discovered this in 1962 when Kennedy, who certainly knew she was involved with his friend, George Smathers, told Smathers right in front of her: "I would trade a lot for one weekend with Layte." She admitted that this made her feel like "a stuffed ragged doll that George dragged around."[34]

This was atypical of how Kennedy had previously treated her. Bowden was shocked by his disrespectful comments. She thought she had made her feelings clear to him. As charming as she thought Kennedy was, she did not want a sexual relationship with him. Apparently, he did not realize how serious she was about this, and she did not realize how determined he was to initiate an affair. She also had no way of knowing that her words echoed similar ones that Marilyn Monroe had expressed not long before her untimely death. According to the recollection of private detective Fred Otash, who had listened to recordings of Monroe describing her relationships with John and Robert Kennedy: "I feel passed around—like a piece of meat," she had said.[35]

On June 5, 1963 Kennedy and his entourage spent the night in El Paso, Texas. Bowden had flown in on the backup press plane. That evening Kennedy telephoned her from the El Cortez Hotel's Presidential suite. He invited her and several other stewardesses to join him, Press Secretary Pierre Salinger, and other aides in his eighth-floor suite for daiquiris. The women were delighted at the invitation and thoroughly enjoyed the lively conversation that ensued. As the party broke up, Kennedy asked Bowden to wait a few moments. "… I didn't suspect what was to follow," she wrote in her memoir. "I had been alone in a room with him several times, including his bedroom in the White House. Never once was he inappropriate with me."[36] That was about to change.

Kennedy suddenly lifted her from her chair, embraced her, and kissed her with more passion than she expected. She knew immediately what would follow. "Jack, this can't go any further," she insisted. "Please let me go."[37] But he did not let her go. Instead, he backed her towards the bed and wrestled her down. Instinctively, Bowden pushed the President away from her, which threw him off balance, off the bed, and into the wall with a loud thud. On the other side of the wall, Secret Service agents were in a dilemma as to whether they should rush to the President's aid or remain where they were. The sound of love-making was not new to the agents, but the sound of the President crashing into the wall was.

Bowden admitted to the authors that she had reacted the way she did because of the thought that raced through her mind: "I'm not going to be raped, even by the President!"[38] Her next thought was that she might have seriously injured the President of the United States. The grimace on his face told her she had. Immediately, she knelt next to him, frantically asking if he was alright. Even though he was in excruciating pain, Kennedy managed to maintain his sense of humor. He groaned, "Let's not mention this little episode to George, okay?"[39]

Bowden discovered later that the "wrestling" encounter had injured the President's back more than she had realized. It was because of this injury that a stronger back brace was designed for him—one that kept him from bending forward. The President was wearing this brace the day he was killed in Dallas. Some have even speculated that the brace is what kept him from falling forward in the limousine after he was first wounded.

In fact, a former Secret Service agent close to the Kennedy family accused Bowden years later of being partially responsible for the President's death.[40] Bowden strongly disagreed with his accusation. Of course, she was terribly sorry that the man she had remained friends with until the day he died had been killed. In fact, she was there that day in Dallas on the press plane and was waiting at Love Field for the trip on to Austin when she heard over the radio about the President's death. But she still refuses to feel guilty that she did not allow the President of the United States to force himself on her that day in El Paso.

Layte Bowden was one of the few women that John F. Kennedy eventually learned to respect. He admired her intellect and her personality as much as he admired her beauty. Because she was not having an affair with the President, Bowden felt free to interact with him in public and even photograph him.

Bowden overlooked the incident in El Paso because none like it ever occurred again, and she and President Kennedy remained close friends. In fact, she had received a call from the President the night before he was killed. He had casually asked her to join him and his Assistant White House Press Secretary Malcolm Kilduff for a drink in his suite at the Hotel Texas in Ft. Worth.

Bowden was surprised at this request because she knew that Mrs. Kennedy was staying in the same suite. The President had assured her that his wife had gone to bed and would not mind if she joined him for a drink. Once again, it was Layte Bowden who showed restraint, not the President. She politely declined his invitation. She had no way of knowing that her final opportunity to chat with a man she considered a good friend would be that evening.

The next morning, Bowden and several other stewardesses waved to the President and his wife as they left Love Field Airport and headed towards downtown Dallas. She is pictured in photos taken as the Presidential motorcade began its tragic route into downtown Dallas. In fact, she snapped some photos of the President and his wife right before they departed. Instead of joining the motorcade, Bowden waited in the backup airplane for the entourage to return so they could make a short trip to Austin, Texas. Like all the others waiting near Air Force One, she had no way of knowing that Kennedy would return to the plane in a casket.

In life, Bowden's relationship with Kennedy did not harm the President's political reputation. *She* made sure of that. She was not a threat to his marriage, to his image, or to his career. That cannot be said for some of the other women the President "entertained."

CHAPTER 3
THE VOICE OF AXEL HOLM

"I'm convinced Inga Arvad was John Kennedy's major love."

John Kennedy's relationships with women began long before his marriage to Jacqueline Bouvier in 1953. Some of his women friends were nothing more than good friends, but only because the women refused to become his paramours. Others were short-termed relationships and one-night stands. The names of most of these women are still unknown. However, Inga Arvad, Gunilla von Post, Mary Meyer, Marilyn Monroe, Ellen Rometsch, and Maria Novotny were names now familiar to Kennedy historians.

Axel Holm was only a teenager when he was introduced in 1962 to an intriguing older woman once involved with a future President. Inga Arvad's past rivaled any from a Hollywood screenplay. As a globe-trotting journalist, she met and interviewed people as famous as Joseph Goebbels and Adolph Hitler.[41] However, when she and her movie-star husband, Tim McCoy, moved to Nogales, Arizona, in 1962, she hid her illustrious past from those around her. Her neighbors knew her only as Inga McCoy, not as Inga Arvad. Very few of them would have recognized her maiden name anyway. After all, Inga Arvad McCoy had decided years before to end a scandalous but passionate love affair that could have ruined the career of a young John F. Kennedy.

Arvad was probably the only woman in the world to have photos signed and personalized to her from both Adolph Hitler and John F. Kennedy. As the subject of one of her interviews, Hitler found Inga Arvad as attractive as John Kennedy later did. However, this innocent association with two important Nazi leaders led American government officials to suspect her of being a Nazi spy.[42]

In America, the beautiful blonde Danish journalist found employment in the summer of 1941 with the *Washington Times-Herald*. Though married, she fell in love with a young bachelor named John Kennedy. A co-worker who knew of her connections to both Hitler and Lt. Kennedy brought her to the attention of the FBI.[43] FBI Director J. Edgar Hoover realized how serious it would be for any enlisted man, especially one assigned to military intelligence, to be socializing with a woman previously so friendly with the Nazis. As a friend of Joseph Kennedy, Sr.'s, Hoover also knew that this situation would be extremely embarrassing for the ex-ambassador.[44]

The secrets that this woman kept about her passionate love affair with Kennedy did not come to light until after his death. But that did not mean that Arvad had forgotten the young Navy officer or that he ever forgot her. In 1941, Arvad was a gorgeous young woman who may have been the only true love of John Kennedy's life. She and Kennedy might have been the perfect example of star-crossed lovers. They met in the early 1940s when the United States was teetering on the edge of World War II. Though neither Arvad nor Kennedy realized it at the beginning, their love affair was doomed to wither, not because their feelings for each other would change, but because Kennedy decided for the very first time that his professional career, in importance, would supersede any personal or romantic relationship he would ever have.

Arvad was never the perfect "girl" for Kennedy. She had already been divorced and was married to her second husband when she met the young officer. She was not Catholic, and she was four years older than Kennedy.

To determine whether Inga Arvad was using Kennedy to solicit military secrets, Hoover bugged her apartment and the motels that the two lovers used. He also tapped her telephone. Hoover then reported back to Joe Kennedy, Sr. and let him determine how serious the romance was.[45]

It is only because Arvad and Kennedy treasured the letters they wrote to one another that researchers now know how deeply the couple cared for each other. Kennedy kept Arvad's letters, along with letters numerous other women had written to him, even after he had married Jacqueline Bouvier. Arvad kept all of Kennedy's letters and passed them down to her sons.

The letters are evidence that both Arvad and Kennedy seriously discussed marriage, as impractical as the idea was. At first, the impediments seemed trivial. But they were not trivial to Kennedy's father, who seems to have made his son realize that a marriage to this beautiful, twice-married Dane was impossible. The consequences of a union between Arvad and John Kennedy would affect not only him, but also his older brother, Joe Kennedy, Jr., and the political career his father had planned for him. But John Kennedy, like the rest of his family, was accustomed to getting everything he wanted. Why shouldn't he "have his cake and eat it, too?"[46]

Arvad soon realized that she was madly in love with Kennedy. She had never felt this strongly about either of her two husbands. In a letter written in 1942, she described her young lover as "full of enthusiasm and full of expectations, eager to make his life a huge success. He wants the fame, the money—and what rarely goes with fame—happiness."[47] Indeed, Kennedy did want the happiness that a relationship with Inga Arvad brought him. Perhaps he even considered chucking the future his father had planned for him and choosing his own path.

"Don't ever think I should be disappointed in you," Arvad wrote on April 6, 1942. "If you start growing potatoes in Ireland—or live a similar kind of life—somehow Jack I shall always not think but know for dead certain that you have done the right thing."[48] Inga Arvad was probably the only person in Kennedy's life who encouraged him to make his own decisions. He had Arvad's approval to do whatever he wanted, even if that meant leaving her behind.

Their love affair consisted of short weekends together and stolen moments in between trips that Kennedy made to and from Washington, D.C. But he was never far from her thoughts or her heart. She reminded him in a letter written hours after he had departed Washington, D.C., for Palm Beach: "When the plane took off, I said the same prayer to myself as I did in church Sunday, 'Please keep him safe, God.'"[49]

Though John F. Kennedy seemed to love Inga Arvad as much as he had ever loved anyone, he also wanted a career, and he did not want to disappoint his father. Now the woman he loved had given him permission to choose a life without her. So, with the help of his domineering father, he decided to clear his path for a political career. According to author Scott Farris in his book *Inga*, the beautiful but unattainable woman Kennedy had nicknamed "Inga Binga" was the first person to encourage Joseph Kennedy's second son to step out of his older brother's shadow and seek a political career for himself.[50] Ironically, Kennedy's desire for a political career overshadowed his desire for Inga Arvad.

The romance between Kennedy and Arvad was one of the best-kept secrets in the life of John F. Kennedy. After Arvad realized that John Kennedy was never going to marry her, the two separated. She was heartbroken; in fact, in a letter, she described to him how she reacted to their separation: "In the beginning I was just stunned darling. Then I slowly woke up. Hard to start and realize that you are a living corpse."[51]

Eventually, Inga Arvad moved to Hollywood to temporarily take over a popular newspaper column. It was here that she met and later married western movie star Tim McCoy and bore him two sons. Through newspapers and television, she followed Kennedy's life and career—his election to the House of Representatives and then to the Senate, his marriage to Jacqueline Bouvier, the birth of his children, and his final triumph—his election to the presidency.

Inga and Tim McCoy moved from Hollywood to Nogales, Arizona and soon became popular members of the community. In an interview with the authors, Axel Holm remembered her as a "warm-hearted woman with a delightful sense of humor."[52] He knew her because his parents had become good friends with the McCoys. Quite often the two couples would party together, so Holm was frequently in the McCoys' house. Holm recalled one special dinner at his parents' house. Arvad was a wonderful conversationalist, he remembered, but she usually let her husband Tim tell the stories. She preferred that the spotlight be on him.

This particular evening, however, Arvad was relating a humorous story to the other guests. "She lifted a spoonful of soup to her mouth and some of it dribbled on her. Instead of acting embarrassed," Holm remembered, "she just laughed and announced in her heavy Danish accent, 'Good heavens! My bazooms got in the way!'"[53]

Arvad seldom discussed the many famous people she had once known, but occasionally someone's remark triggered an intriguing disclosure. For instance, Holm once mentioned to her that she reminded him of Swedish actress Ingrid Bergman. Arvad answered quickly, "Dahling, I knew Ingrid Bergman well and she would be appalled at you saying that!" Despite comments like this, Arvad did not flaunt the fact that she obviously had known many, many famous individuals. "You could not impress Inga," Holm emphasized. "If you were warm and friendly, you earned her friendship no matter who you were." She used the word "dahling" often, but it was only directed at people she liked. Arvad, Holm recalled laughingly, sounded very much like the legendary actress Tallulah Bankhead, who was also famous for using the word "dahling."

In a town with a population of 8,000, Arvad soon grew to know a great many of the townfolk. She kept busy by writing articles for the small newspaper in Nogales. It became known that she had once interviewed Adolf Hitler, but because she made it clear that she had no use for the Nazis, no one held this against her. What she did not ever discuss was her affair with John F. Kennedy.

"She was not forthcoming about Kennedy," Holm explained, "even after his death." The first inkling that Axel Holm got about a connection between his neighbor and Kennedy came when he noticed a framed signed photo of the late President sitting prominently on her bedroom dressing table.

"Mrs. McCoy, I didn't know you knew John Kennedy," he commented. Arvad simply replied, "He was President of the United States, dahling. Lots of people knew him." However, this photo showed Kennedy as either a senator or as President and was inscribed, "To dearest Inga Binga" (a nickname that Holm was too young to have known about), and signed "Love, Jack." What Holm did not realize was that this sentiment alone indicated a close attachment between Arvad and Kennedy.

A few years later, he picked up on another clue. Holm's father was in the hospital at the time for back surgery. Arvad called Holm's house and expressed deep concern.

"What are they doing for his back?" she asked. All Holm could say was that his father was about to have back surgery. Arvad peppered him with questions concerning the procedures the surgeon would be using. Frustrated, Holm explained that he did not have any idea what the surgeon would be doing, and did not know anything about back surgery. Arvad, on the other hand, did. Her next statement surprised Holm.

"Dahling, I know a lot about backs," she explained. "I remember Jack's bad back."

"Jack who?" Holm asked, thoroughly confused by the turn in the conversation.

"Kennedy, dahling," she replied in exasperation. "You might remember him. He was President!"

At this point, Holm realized that this entertaining lady, who had joined his family for birthdays and attended neighborhood cocktail parties, had once been so close to President John F. Kennedy that she knew his intimate health secrets.

"Keep in mind," Holm reminded the authors during an interview, "that very little had been written about Kennedy's love affairs at this time. So, there was no way any of us could have known about this unless she had told us."

Only one person in the world observed Arvad's immediate reaction to the news that her former lover had been assassinated. The son of the editor of the local Nogales newspaper described Arvad's reaction to the report that John Kennedy had been shot on November 22, 1963. When reports came over the radio and television, she drove immediately to the newspaper's office because, as a journalist, she trusted the wire services. The radio announcer might have made a mistake; a report from the wire service, in her mind, would be more accurate. Publisher Alvin Sisk recalled later that Arvad, after entering the newspaper office, rushed to the teletype machine, grabbed the paper, and scanned it for the words she dreaded reading. There they were. Arvad let the papers slip out of her hands as she slowly turned and walked to her car.[54]

Of course, no one in Nogales and very few people in the rest of the world would have realized that Inga Arvad McCoy was personally affected by John Kennedy's death. But then, not everyone had a bundle of old love letters hidden away that detailed an intimate relationship with the President. Arvad's letters served as proof that she had known John F. Kennedy better than some of his family members. She knew, for example, that in her opinion he had "two back bones: his own and his father's."[55] She also knew him well enough to tell him this in a letter and to know that he would agree with her.

At the time of their affair, she must have seriously considered the idea of being a backstreet mistress to the future President. She wrote, only half in jest: "I have made up my mind to turn out a few stories—and when I get time, a few babies—hope illegitimacy becomes a fad after the war, as I only know one man worth reproducing a perfect copy of."[56]

John Kennedy might have accepted this arrangement, but Inga Arvad had second thoughts. Perhaps she wondered how she would explain to the child she wanted so badly that he could never know the identity of his father. So Arvad and John Kennedy went their separate ways. However, she made clear that she would always be there to help him any way she could: "…Know my dear, that anytime and day you need to talk to a person who likes you with and without faults, with and without pretenses, then stop in and see me. I will be there… always with an outstretched hand…"[57]

It is possible that Kennedy remembered this particular letter and did pay a short visit to the woman who had written these compassionate words. Alvin Sisk remembered that President Kennedy once ordered Air Force One to land at Davis-Monthan Air Force Base in Tucson for a prearranged meeting with Arvad. There were also rumors about telephone calls from the White House.[58] Holm never knew whether these rumors were true or not, or if Kennedy really stopped in Tucson to visit with Inga McCoy. He did feel strongly that if she had met with the President, it was nothing more than a visit between two old friends. "She adored her husband," he insisted.[59]

Just as she had survived the shattered love affair with Kennedy, Inga Arvad McCoy also survived his death. However, her health had already begun to deteriorate even before she and her husband had moved to Nogales. The arthritis that had plagued her while living in Washington, D. C. continued to progress, and she also developed cancer.

Inga Arvad survived John Kennedy by ten years and passed away in 1973. While he is buried in a ceremonial grave in Arlington National Cemetery that has been visited by millions of people, Inga Arvad's ashes are buried miles away in a simple cemetery in Michigan that few even know exist.[60]

If John F. Kennedy had loved Inga Arvad as much as she obviously loved him, he could have changed his career plans, confronted his father, and married the woman he affectionately called "Inga Binga." Instead, he chose fame and success but, perhaps, not happiness. Even if Arvad was Kennedy's one true love, it is questionable, based on his future behavior, whether he could have controlled his wandering eye and his desire for other women even if the two had married.

The affair between Arvad and Kennedy would have seemed even more romantic if Kennedy had not continued to add a bevy of girlfriends to his list of conquests. Oddly enough, he not only kept Inga Arvad's letters, he also kept letters from other lovers, and he continued to write letters to other lovers. For example, Gunilla von Post, a beautiful Swedish woman, met Kennedy not long before his marriage to Jacqueline Bouvier. The fact that he was engaged to another woman did not keep Kennedy from pursuing von Post. He continued to write von Post even after his marriage. He told her he missed her and suggested that they meet in the near future. A book that von Post later wrote indicates that this romantic rendezvous did eventually take place.[61]

Many of those close to Kennedy felt that he and his wife were not a happily-married couple, at least not in the traditional sense. His philandering must have had something to do with the stress that seemed to accompany the marriage. However, the death in August 1963 of an infant son brought the Kennedys closer together. In fact, this closeness is why Jackie traveled with her husband on the campaign trip to Texas in November 1963.

But, once again, as was so often true in the Kennedy family, appearances were deceiving. A letter assumed to be to Kennedy's then-mistress Mary Meyer dated October 1963 shows that the President was continuing to cheat on his wife even after the death of their child. The letter was written on White House stationery and was an amorous request for the woman to join him "at the Cape next week or in Boston." The President seemed determined that the recipient of the letter "Just say Yes" to his request.[62]

Either Kennedy planned on destroying the various letters sometime in the future, or he was unconcerned about their effect on his family and the American public. He had spent years on the brink of death, and yet, he still did not part with intimate letters from a variety of women who could have ruined the career that meant so much to him. But John Kennedy had always been a risk-taker. It was a flaw that both benefitted and harmed him.

Inga Arvad loved John Kennedy enough to keep their war-time romance a secret, but not all of the women he became involved with were as discreet while he was president. Some, in fact, became serious problems for his brother Robert Kennedy, then the Attorney General, for J. Edgar Hoover, and for the Secret Service. Actress Marilyn Monroe was so famous that it seems almost impossible that the President could have kept his affair with her a secret. And, yet, he did, at least as far as the voters were concerned. What Kennedy did not know was that the houses where the two met had been bugged by the FBI and by certain Mafia members. So, he unknowingly was placing himself and his administration in jeopardy. His behavior could easily have affected the entire Democratic Party and the political futures of his two younger brothers.

One JFK lover who caused great concern was Ellen Rometsch. A Washington party girl, Rometsch was born in Germany, and as a child was a member of the Communist Party youth group. "Kennedy did not seem to realize—or care— that if his sexual relationship with Ellen Rometsch somehow became known, she would be thought by many to be a communist spy."[63]

An affair in 1960 with Maria Novotny, an Anglo-Czech prostitute linked to a Soviet vice ring at the United Nations, returned to haunt Kennedy in 1963. Her name appeared in conjunction with a British scandal involving the British Minister of War.[64] In both cases, U.S. Attorney General Robert F. Kennedy acted swiftly to deport Rometsch and to kill the story on Novotny. But this did not curtail Kennedy's womanizing.

The fourth woman who could have destroyed his political career was Judith Campbell. When Campbell was introduced to Kennedy by singer Frank Sinatra, she knew very little about the senator. It is uncertain how much Kennedy knew about her. She was a beautiful brunette who was connected to mobsters Johnny Roselli (sometimes spelled "Rosselli") and Sam Giancana.

By March 20, 1962, the Department of Justice had already disclosed in an FBI memo that Campbell's phone calls had been traced to Evelyn Lincoln at the White House. These phone calls had occurred on November 7, 10, 13, and 15, of 1961 and on Valentine's Day of 1962. An informant whose name has been redacted from the memo advised that he had seen Campbell with mobster Johnny Roselli. He referred to her as the girl who was "shacking up with John Kennedy in the East."[65]

The above memo is proof that J. Edgar Hoover and the FBI, as well as various Mafia members, had information concerning Kennedy's extramarital affairs. This obviously made the President a target for blackmail. It also tightened the connections that John Kennedy already had to organized crime— ties that could have been as dangerous as his connections to various girlfriends and one-night stands.

CHAPTER 4

THE KENNEDYS AND THE MAFIA

"Oh, my God," my father cried. "We elected a Mafia prince
and put him in the White House!"—Chuck Helppie

O ne of the most important secrets John Kennedy was forced to hide concerned the background of some of his father's associates. Some Americans had read that the Kennedy patriarch had made his fortune bootlegging during Prohibition. But few knew of Joe Kennedy's association with Sam
Giancana, head of the Chicago organized crime family, and other mobsters, and
that was a fact that certainly had to be hidden. Sam Giancana crossed paths with
Joe Kennedy long before the 1960 presidential election.

According to Giancana's brother, Chuck, Joe, Sr.'s "ties to the underworld
intersected at a hundred points. Besides making a fortune in bootlegging,
Kennedy had made a financial killing in Hollywood in the twenties—with the
help of persuasive behind-the-scenes New York and Chicago muscle."[66]

Mobster Frank Costello revealed more evidence of Kennedy, Sr.'s links
to organized crime: "(Joe) Kennedy had been a partner in bootlegging and
rum-running in the early 1920's."[67] Even though these connections had to be
clandestine, they could also be very helpful if a man's son who happened to be
a presidential candidate needed more votes than he could legitimately collect.

Testimony from mobsters like Frank Costello and Sam Giancana's brother,
Chuck, might be considered questionable. After all, both were involved in
numerous illegal activities. However, their statements are not the only evidence
to tie John Kennedy and his family to organized crime. The FBI knew about
the connection between the presidential candidate and the mob boss. "William
F. Roemer, Jr., an FBI special agent in the Chicago office in the early 1960s,
revealed that Giancana had been overheard on a still-unreleased FBI wiretap
discussing a straight-forward election deal: mob support in return for a
commitment from the future Kennedy administration 'to back off from the FBI
investigation of Giancana.'"[68]

In the late 1950s, Joe Kennedy was forced to go to Sam Giancana to save his
own life. "Talk to Frank" (Costello) for me, he begged Giancana. "I'm a marked
man if you don't get the contract called off." Kennedy then offered Giancana
the best reason he could think of for granting him his wish: "I can help my son

get to the White House. Isn't that what we've all wanted all along?"[69]

Naturally, Giancana wanted to know specifically what he would get in return for his help. The senior Kennedy promised that Giancana would have the President's ear. "He'll be your man. I swear to that. My son...the President of the United States...will owe you his father's life. He won't refuse you, ever."[70]

During John F. Kennedy's presidential campaign, Joe Kennedy reportedly met with a variety of organized crime bosses at a restaurant in New York. "I took the reservations," said Edna Daulyton, then working as a hostess at the restaurant, 'and it was as though every gangster chief in the United States was there. I don't remember all the names now, but there was John Roselli, Carlos Marcello, from New Orleans, the two brothers from Dallas, the top men from Buffalo, California, and Colorado. They were all top people, not soldiers. I was amazed Joe Kennedy would take the risk.'"[71]

Apparently, Joe Kennedy struck a deal with certain mob bosses. What he did not know is that the various Mafia families, like any experienced gamblers, were making certain they won no matter what. Perhaps even Joe Kennedy was not aware that political contests were nothing more than horse races to the Mafia. Even though some of the Mafia were financing the Kennedy/Johnson ticket, they were also contributing to the Nixon ticket. By supporting both Kennedy and Nixon, they were "hedging their bets."[72] Chuck Giancana admitted he did not understand this strategy. "You know, I can't understand why you don't just back Nixon," he said to his brother. "He's been the Outfit's boy for years."

"A lot of bosses own a piece of Nixon...we share the influence. Jack will be all mine," Sam Giancana replied. [73] How much did John Kennedy and his brother Bobby know about their father's pact with the mob? By 1959, John Kennedy, at least, was aware that his father had asked the mob for help with the election. Sam Giancana told his brother that he had met three different times before the 1960 election with Joe Kennedy, Sr., Jack Kennedy, and Mayor Richard Daley at Chicago's Ambassador East. Here the four men had finalized their agreement concerning a victory for Jack Kennedy (and for the Mafia).[74]

Despite this agreement, the President almost immediately allowed his brother Robert, the Attorney General, to harass mob bosses Giancana, Carlos Marcello of Louisiana, and Santos Trafficante of Florida. These three men and their organizations did not always agree with each other, but they all eventually grew to feel the same way about Kennedy and his family. They wanted him out of the White House; at various times, each of them made subtle and not so subtle threats against President John F. Kennedy.

However, it must be remembered that Joe Kennedy, Sr. had made a deal with Sam Giancana, not with Marcello or Trafficante. This would explain why

Giancana was willing to assist Kennedy with campaign contributions and vote tampering. After all, if John Kennedy was not elected president, Giancana would have saved Joe Kennedy, Sr.'s life for nothing. So, the Kennedy connections to the Mafia were as top secret as any classified documents. This explains why the President used women like Judith Campbell, Marilyn Monroe, and other Hollywood starlets, as couriers between himself and Giancana.[75] He certainly could not have used his own staff members or aides.

It must have been a rude awakening for the President when J. Edgar Hoover confronted him with proof that one of his paramours was sharing Sam Giancana's bed as well as his own. President Kennedy may have known, or at least suspected, this; what shocked him was that J. Edgar Hoover also knew.

Numerous authors have speculated that these secret connections between the Kennedy White House and the Mafia resulted in Kennedy's death. According to their accounts, Joe Kennedy, Sr. had already broken the Mafia code of honor by refusing to return favors to Frank Costello. Could he also have been so arrogant as to think that the President and the Attorney General did not have to honor the agreement made between their father and Giancana? Or was the Attorney General kept in the dark about the agreement, and is that why, despite possible repercussions, he continued his war on organized crime?

The individuals that Robert Kennedy was harassing had originally supported his brother's election; however, they grew to despise the man they had helped elect. Whether they were referred to as the "Mob" in New York, the "Outfit" in Chicago, the "Mafia" in New Orleans, the "Dixie Mafia" in the South, the "Texas Mafia" in the Southwest, all these groups collectively were known as the "Commission," the "Cosa Nostra," or the "Family." These powerful men became irate when Robert Kennedy continued to prosecute members of their organizations and when the President's father did not deliver the access to the White House that he had promised.

The FBI learned via wiretaps that members of organized crime wanted the President removed from office. Conversations between mob bosses indicated that they did not care how the President "was removed," but they did not want to take a chance on him being re-elected. The voices of Sam Giancana, Santos Trafficante, Johnny Roselli, Meyer Lansky, Jimmy Hoffa, and Carlos Marcello were heard repeatedly by FBI agents. None of the bugged conversations were pleasant ones.[76]

New Orleans boss Marcello told associates that "President Kennedy had to go, but that he would have to arrange his murder in such a way that his own men would not be identified as the assassins."[77] As early as the fall of 1962, one of Marcello's underworld friends, Trafficante, shared Marcello's plans with a

Cuban exile leader, Jose Aleman Jr., who was also an FBI informant. "Mark my word: This man Kennedy is in trouble, and he will get what is coming to him… Kennedy's not going to make it to the election. He is going to be hit."[78]

Just as angry as Marcello was Sam Giancana. "My millions were good enough for 'em, weren't they? The votes I muscled for 'em were good enough to get Jack elected. Well, I'm gonna send them a message they'll never forget." According to Giancana's brother, Chuck, this was a formal declaration of war.[79]

Conversations between various members of organized crime suggest that members of the Mafia were planning on doing away with President John F. Kennedy, just as they had done away with so many other inconvenient persons. They had the motive and the means to eliminate the President of the United States. As far as anyone knew, they did not have a way to control all investigations of organized crime. Members of organized crime were known for internal wars during which one family attacked another. But when they had a common goal, they could also work as a well-oiled machine, even if this meant cooperating with members of the intelligence and political communities.

Since John Kennedy had often been described as the type of person who could compartmentalize, perhaps he could justify taking assistance from the Mafia and at the same time allow his Attorney General to prosecute them. After all, by compartmentalizing, he could successfully lead a double life as a devoted husband and father always seeking new sexual partners and experiences. This ability to compartmentalize might explain how he and his brother were able to use legal and illegal means to prosecute certain members of the Mafia and at the same time use them as assassins. John Kennedy was a pragmatist who, like Machiavelli, believed that the ends justified the means. Unfortunately, his enemies felt the same way.

Surely the President's father had qualms about his sons' war on the same people who had helped elect John Kennedy to the presidency. Robert Kennedy's determination to destroy organized crime was matched by his anger towards Fidel Castro because of the way he had humiliated the President at the Bay of Pigs. When Robert Kennedy first learned about the CIA's assassination plots against Fidel Castro, the president of neigboring Cuba, "he was mad as hell. But what he objected to was the possibility it would impede prosecution against Sam Giancana and Johnny Roselli. He was not angry about the assassination plot, but about the involvement with the Mafia."[80] He saw nothing wrong with America deposing another's country's head of state. Apparently, Robert Kennedy also managed to justify what appeared to be an ethical dilemma; eventually, he recognized the advantage of using criminals to remove Castro, who had illegally overthrown his own predecessor.

Robert Kennedy's behavior mirrored behavior that he had observed in his father. Kennedy, Sr. was known as ruthless long before his son Robert was described with that same adjective. Part of being ruthless meant winning every time. This obsession with winning affected who the Kennedys knew, how they looked at life, and how they played the game—any game. Obviously, the most important game that John Kennedy and his family played was politics. And, once again, winning was everything. If this meant the family and its associates had to distort the truth to win elections, they did so. It also meant that keeping campaign promises like the one Kennedy made concerning Fidel Castro was vitally important. He had goaded his Republican opponent Richard Nixon because the Eisenhower administration had not handled the Castro situation effectively. So, to appear to be "winners," John and Robert Kennedy secretly used the Mafia in conjunction with the CIA to attempt to eliminate Cuba's dictator.

Kennedy kept secret from the American people his plans to overthrow the leadership in Cuba. After the fiasco between the United States and Cuba, which became known as the Bay of Pigs, Kennedy was almost obsessed with Fidel Castro and continued a secret war against the dictator. His hidden agenda fused certain elements of the CIA with certain elements of the Mafia. No one knew this better than Sam Giancana. His brother Chuck recalled the mobster flipping an old Roman coin and explaining, "This coin has two faces...two sides. That's what we are, the Outfit and the CIA...two sides of the same coin...We're on the same side, we're workin' for the same things...we just look different. So... we're two sides of the same coin."[81]

The Kennedy brothers and the Giancana brothers kept this "partnership" so secret that even people like Charles Everett (Chuck) Helppie, who worked for Robert Kennedy's Department of Justice, were unaware of the ties between the U.S. government and the Mafia. A devoted Kennedy employee, Helppie finally realized after the House Select Committee on Assassinations published its report in 1978 that the rumors he had heard for years were true. His response to the committee's conclusion was almost heartbreaking. In 2017, his son Chuck recalled in an interview with the authors just how horrified and disillusioned his father had been.

"Oh, my God!" my father cried. "We elected a Mafia prince and put him in the White House!" [82]

CHAPTER 5

THE WARREN COMMISSION
AND THE CIA

**"I think it is fair to say that no major undertaking by the CIA
was done without the knowledge and/or approval of the White House."
—Nelson Rockefeller**

Joseph Kennedy, Sr.'s connections to the Mafia were just one of many secrets the family shielded from the prying eyes of the media, the public, and the Warren Commission. Robert Kennedy dared not share information with the Warren Commission about the plans his brother had authorized for the CIA and its associates to remove Fidel Castro as head of Cuba. "National security" became the justification for withholding information like that. Thus, it is unfair to totally blame the members of the Warren Commission for the errors and incompleteness of its investigation. Those who worked thousands of man-hours did the best they could with the limited time, resources, and *information* available to them. Little did they know that so many important details never reached their desks.

The answers to all the questions concerning the assassination were supposed to lie within the covers of the *Warren Report on the Assassination of President Kennedy*, or at least within the twenty-six volumes of appendices that accompanied it. The report was released to the public in September 1964.

Based on White House tapes made of Johnson's conversations with various individuals, the new President at first wanted Kennedy's assassination to be investigated by officials in Texas.[83] However, he was eventually convinced that an independent commission should review the evidence gathered by the FBI and determine the facts about the former President's death. Until Lyndon Johnson's Oval Office tapes were released after his death, many people assumed that he had initially refused to allow the state of Texas to investigate the President's death, even though his murder had taken place there.

In 1974, Chief Justice Earl Warren explained in an interview with historian Alfred Goldberg, an editor of the Warren Report, why President Johnson had not wanted his fellow Texans to investigate the assassination. "The President pointed out that one of the dangers was that the Attorney General in Texas would try to set up a hearing and have a carnival down there in Texas."[84] Apparently, even Earl Warren did not know how determined Johnson had been at first to have his home state investigate Kennedy's death. Instead of allowing Texas Attorney General Waggoner Carr to head a Court of Inquiry, Johnson named some of the most respected and powerful men in the United States to gather all the evidence to determine who had killed President Kennedy and why.

The public was told this would be an independent investigation. And, yet, the very members of the Commission were hand-picked by Johnson, who had a great deal to gain from Kennedy's death. A question which still lingers today is why former CIA Director Allen Dulles, who had been fired by President Kennedy after the Bay of Pigs fiasco, was placed on the Commission. Author Gus Russo's research led him to believe that Lyndon Johnson had named Dulles at the suggestion of Attorney General Robert Kennedy. [85] In his memoir *The Vantage Point*, Johnson stated in no uncertain terms that this was the case. However, transcripts of recordings from the White House Oval Office have the President saying, "I'm going to ask John McCloy and Allen Dulles," and on that same day he told Georgia Senator Richard Russell that he would not allow Robert Kennedy to select anyone for the Commission.[86]

So perhaps Johnson changed his mind and did allow Robert Kennedy to suggest two Commission members. If not, he lied in his own memoir, which was not written until after Robert Kennedy's assassination. Neither Robert Kennedy nor any of those close to him have mentioned that he might have placed anyone on the Commission. However, Kennedy may have *needed* Dulles on the Commission to control how much the Commisson members learned about CIA-Presential activities. Researcher-author Max Holland studied tapes made in the Oval Office after Johnson assumed the presidency. According to a memo from presidential aide Walter Jenkins to Johnson dated November 29, 1963, Johnson learned that Abe [Fortas] "talked with Katzenbach [deputy attorney general under Robert Kennedy], and Katzenbach talked with the attorney general. They recommend...." A recorded conversation between President Johnson and Fortas on December 17, 1966, available in the Johnson Presidential Library, also confirms that the new president allowed Kennedy input on the Commission.[87]

Though there is some evidence Robert Kennedy did select two of the Warren Commission members, he did not select the other members. Lyndon Johnson insisted that Chief Justice of the Supreme Court Earl Warren serve as head of the Commission. Between him and ex-CIA head Allen Dulles, the Commission should have had access to all the crucial information necessary to solve the most infamous crime of the twentieth century. J. Edgar Hoover, the Director of the FBI, assisted the Commssion with information known only to him and his agents. Put another way, the Warren Commission had to receive all its information from the FBI because it did not have investigators of its own. Would the CIA have shared confidential information with the FBI? Would individuals from *any* involved group admit they had been complicit in trying to depose a leader of another country?

When it was finally revealed years later that the CIA had worked with the Mafia to assassinate Fidel Castro (and possibly other heads of state), Kennedy loyalists immediately said that the agency had done so without the President's knowledge. It was not until 1975 that Kennedy's former Secretary of Defense, Robert McNamara, admitted to the Church Committee, which investigated alleged assassination plots involving foreign leaders, that "the CIA was a highly disciplined organization, fully under control of the government...I believe with hindsight we authorized actions that were contrary to the interest of the republic...I don't want it on the record that the CIA was uncontrolled."[88]

Richard Bissell, the CIA's foremost planner of the Cuban Bay of Pigs attack, knew better than most how closely connected President Kennedy and the CIA were. Bissell commented, "There was never anything undertaken without presidential approval."[89] Even Vice-President Nelson Rockefeller agreed. When asked about the plots to kill Castro, he answered, "I think it is fair to say that no major undertaking by the CIA was done without the knowledge and/or approval of the White House."[90] That had to have included Attorney General Robert Kennedy, who was a close confidante of the President..

Despite the so-called "in-depth" investigation of the Warren Commission, an enormous number of questions were not asked; many of those that *were* asked went unanswered. Time constraints meant that the Commission did not locate all the witnesses whose testimony might have changed the conclusions of the report. Some witnesses later told historians that their testimonies had been altered by the Commission. At least one witness who knew Jack Ruby, the man who murdered the President's accused assassin, was allowed to send a *proxy* to give his testimony. In a case involving the death of a president, one would assume that the lawyers would want to hear from the witness himself, *not a proxy*. Unorthodox behavior like this was observed and reported by Texas Assistant Attorney General, Robert T. Davis. He was so disgusted that he removed himself from the Commission. Of course, the public was kept in the dark about the way the Commission had truly functioned.

Twenty-six volumes accompanied the official Warren Report. Much of the information in these volumes was non-essential (if not worthless), but the volumes were also packed with important information that contradicted original statements from witnesses. There were also numerous errors in both the Warren Report and the twenty-six volumes. Any report that is full of errors, omissions, and discrepancies can hardly be described as "definitive." Transcripts of witness depositions indicate that it was not unusual for the Commission inquirers to ask that a discussion take place "off the record." These discussions were omitted from the transcripts, thus preventing historians from ever knowing exactly what was said.

Apparently, the Commissioners, President Johnson, and J. Edgar Hoover all thought that Americans would purchase copies of the Report but would not read them. Allen Dulles seemed sure that the Warren Report itself would go unread by most Americans. Dulles was wrong, and so were Johnson and Hoover. The Warren Report did not sit on bookshelves unread. If it had, researchers and historians would not still be discussing John F. Kennedy's assassination.

Many of those courageous enough to question the Warren Report were often criticized and even slandered for daring to ask if all the facts had been presented to the world. Since the day Kennedy was killed, numerous historical witnesses and researchers have died, some by their own hand, without knowing that others were asking the same questions they were asking. Undoubtedly, many of these researchers would have been relieved to have known that Richard Russell, one of the members of the Warren Commission, did not accept its findings and was reluctant to sign the Report. They might have felt vindicated to know that President Lyndon Johnson claimed he did not think his predecessor was killed by a single gunman. Those who sneered at and even insulted people who questioned the conclusions of the Warren Report might have been less vocal if they had known that the chief of the Dallas Police Department, Jesse Curry, had doubts about Oswald being the assassin.

Even Robert Kennedy's Deputy Attorney General Nicholas Katzenbach had doubts. He told author John H. Davis that "he thought it was a little 'fishy' at the time, that the case that developed against Oswald during the three days following the assassination was 'too good to be true.'"[91] In 1966, Robert Kennedy sent his favorite investigator, Walter Sheridan, to New Orleans to seek information about an investigation being run by District Attorney Jim Garrison. It has been suggested by some authors that Sheridan's role was to disrupt Garrison's investigation as well as to report his findings to Kennedy.

But author Evan Thomas' research indicates that Kennedy needed to know if Garrison had found evidence to support his own suspicions that mobster Carlos Marcello was behind the assassination. Sheridan would not discuss the assassination with his family members until just before his death in 1996. "Then he shocked his son, Walter Jr., by stating that he was 'convinced' that President Kennedy had been killed by a conspiracy."[92]

Critics of the Warren Report would have received much more support had the world known that Robert Kennedy himself did not really agree with the findings of the Warren Report. "In the last year of his life, RFK told his son [Joseph Kennedy III] that the full truth about the Kennedy assassination would never be known. Young Kennedy had the impression that his father knew something that others did not."[93]

Unfortunately, neither researchers nor the American public knew any of this when they first questioned the Warren Report. But many Americans did realize in the first few years following the assassination that the Warren Report did not contain all the answers concerning Kennedy's death. And many of the "answers" that the Report did provide were incorrect. Those who are most often blamed for misleading America are the members of the Warren Commission— all the members. The very men tasked with thoroughly investigating the death of the President were later blamed for covering up and ignoring inconvenient information—information that might have led to that infamous ten-letter word "C-O-N-S-P-I-R-A-C-Y." Yet, in 1966, President Johnson taped conversations with several government officials and staff members stating that right after the assassination he had "thought it was a conspiracy and I raised that question, and nearly everybody that was with me raised it."[94]

The truth is that certain members of the Commission and its staff members deserve the blame for producing an inaccurate report. As head of the Commission, Chief Justice Earl Warren, for example, controlled information about the President's autopsy that resulted in misinterpretations of what should have been the most crucial evidence. Future President Gerald Ford and future U. S. Senator Arlen Specter guaranteed that the American people would be placed on a "need to know" list, and at times, seemingly believed that the less they knew, the better. Allen Dulles kept even his fellow commissioners in the dark about CIA activities that should have been investigated. Even Lyndon Johnson referred to Senator Richard Russell of Georgia as his "man on the commission."[95] Obviously, the "independent" commission was filled with men expected to answer to other individuals, even if this meant concealing important information. However, the commissioners and their staff members hid no more than other key figures did.

According to Philip Shenon in his book *A Cruel and Shocking Act*, America's Ambassador to Mexico, Thomas Mann, admitted that President Kennedy's Secretary of State Dean Rusk had personally ordered him to stop any investigation in Mexico that would "confirm or refute rumors of Cuban involvement in the assassination."[96] Rusk denied this, but Mann never changed his statement. Of course, Dean Rusk was no longer Kennedy's Secretary of State; in a matter of minutes, he had become *Lyndon Johnson's* Secretary of

State. John Kennedy could not have ordered anyone to stop an investigation in Mexico, but the new president could have.

The director of the FBI, J. Edgar Hoover, could also make sure that not all the information available to his agents would ever reach the members of the Warren Commission. He could not guarantee, however, that every secret would remain hidden.

Only four years after the assassination, newspaper columnist Drew Pearson discovered that the CIA and former Attorney General Robert F. Kennedy had also withheld information from the Warren Commission. This information concerned the possibility that Fidel Castro might have had President Kennedy killed because he knew that John and Robert Kennedy had ordered the CIA to kill him.[97]

Other secrets that could have led to the assassination were Kennedy's duplicitous acts concerning Cuba. Anti-Castro guerrillas and certain CIA members had every right to feel that their president had abandoned them. The original battle plan had not been followed, and thousands of American allies had been slaughtered or imprisoned. When word reached family members and friends of these individuals that President Kennedy agreed to never again invade Cuba, many undoubtedly would have been angry and disgusted. They, like the rest of America, did not know that Kennedy had no intention of keeping his promise to Castro. They had no way of knowing that Kennedy was *still* secretly attempting to assassinate his Cuban counterpart. All they knew was that thousands of men had sacrificed their lives for a cause that Kennedy seemed to be abandoning.

The Kennedy brothers were adept at feeding political information to certain groups or individuals while keeping them in the dark about other projects. At times, they must have felt that they could only trust one another. Perhaps this is why they sometimes relied on people who worked for the Kennedy family long before John Kennedy became President.

These people were so close to John F. Kennedy that, though without official titles, they knew more than even his closest staff members. The Kennedy family, like other unbelievably wealthy families, used its money to "buy" people for protection, for information, and even for illegal activities.

One of these individuals was a man who used various names. Sometimes he was known as "Hugh," and other times he used the name "Jim" or "Jimmy." Even in his eighties, "Jim" has the physique of a thirty-year-old, six-pack and all. In an interview, he explained why he felt it necessary to stay physically fit and to have a bodyguard. "Jim" himself had served as a type of bodyguard for the Kennedy family. He knew personally how dangerous some people could be.

Like others, "Jim" had been recruited from the military by Joe Kennedy, Sr. Kennedy, Sr. had known all about Jim's background and that he was the type of person who would do *anything* once an agreement was made. "Jim" referred to the individuals Joe Kennedy had "bought" as the "Kennedy Group." Even as a Marine, Jim would be summoned for specific assignments by the Kennedys.

"I would use my mother's illness as a cover whenever Jack or Joe Kennedy needed me for an assignment," he explained.[98] Jim's definition of "an assignment" was rather vague, but he suggested it could include "smoothing the way for the 'boys.'" Jim preferred working for John Kennedy, but after his assassination, he felt obligated to help Robert Kennedy also.

"There was no way I was going to work for Teddy Kennedy!" he added.

The stories this former Marine shared with us were chilling. In fact, they seemed almost too dramatic to be true. However, further research showed that many of "Jim's" claims have been proven correct by investigative journalist Jim Hougan. In his book *Spooks: The Haunting of America: The Private Use of Secret Agents*, Hougan described scenarios that supported Jim's claims. Jim related stories about domestic and international assassinations, wiretapping of private citizens, and the blackmailing of public officials.

"You just think the special effects used in movies like *Mission Impossible* and *James Bond* couldn't happen in the real world," Jim laughed. "I'm telling you, they were used years before the movies were ever made. Who do you think were the consultants on those movie sets?"

Hougan spent four years researching and interviewing mercenary spies, their employers, and their victims.[99] For years, certain sectors of the American public had suspected that "Big Brother" was using whatever means it desired to gather information about American citizens, thus controlling and manipulating the American government, American businesses, and the American way of life. Suddenly, there in black and white was proof that these suspicions were accurate. Joe Kennedy could certainly use his fortune to hire numerous individuals who would assist his family in any way. But so could other wealthy individuals or even certain organizations. It is certainly possible that other individuals like "Jim"—individuals loyal to other "employers"—might have played a part in John F. Kennedy's assassination.

CHAPTER 6
THE VOICE OF LT. J. GOODE

"You can't imagine what it's like to find severed human heads lying on a blood-soaked beach. And who knew where their bodies were?"

As a young man, J. Goode never dreamed he would one day disguise himself as a Cuban insurgent, participate in a bloodbath that would become known as the Bay of Pigs, and attempt to prevent President Kennedy's assassination. He also had no idea he would become involved in government activities so secret he would be forced to use numerous aliases.

However, his motherless childhood and non-traditional background helped prepare him for Vietnam, the Bay of Pigs, and November 22, 1963. He grew up in New Mexico, where he was orphaned at a young age. In the 1950s, people in Goode's hometown took him under their wings but also allowed him to keep his independence. They had known his father, and they also knew that J. Goode knew as much about ranching as most adult men. His sense of self-confidence later served him well in the military. It also allowed him to walk away from situations that admittedly gnawed at his conscience for years.

Goode laughed during an interview as he asked, "How many people can say they know who their father was, but they're not sure who their mother was?"[100] He explained that he had been reared by his father, but Goode Sr. had never enlightened him as to who his mother had been. She had apparently disappeared, having decided that Goode's father could care for her son better than she could.

"And he did a pretty good job," Goode insisted. By the time Goode was ten years old, he knew how to break a wild horse, herd cattle, lead hunting parties, and survive in the West Texas desert and the mountains of New Mexico. Somehow, his father sensed that Goode would need survival skills. So, when his son was twelve years old, Goode Sr. left him alone, in a cabin in a New Mexico forest, to fend for himself, even though he had a broken leg.

After setting his son's leg and wrapping it tightly in bandages, Goode Sr. announced, "I've got to get back to the ranch. You come on as soon as you can." The cabin was stocked with food and water and, within a few weeks, Goode managed to mount his horse and ride bareback all the way home.

The survival skills thus acquired were vital to Goode after his father's sudden death. The townspeople checked on him weekly, and one of his father's friends even taught him how to weld. Goode received welding lessons every weekday, both before and after school. As much as he loved his father's ranch, the orphaned boy also understood that an education was important. Reading was difficult for him, but he excelled in mathematics. (Goode realized later that he had dyslexic tendencies, but no one in his hometown at the time had ever heard of the reading disability.)

J. Goode's quiet confidence came from having to be a man while still only a boy. A local teacher was impressed with the fact that Goode had asked her for reading assistance. Goode credits this unusual woman for helping him avoid illiteracy and for preparing him for college.

"If that teacher had not worked and worked with me, I would never have learned to read," he admitted. What Goode did not say was that he worked as hard as the teacher did. No one could ever say that J. Goode was unwilling to work to achieve whatever goal he set.

To earn extra money, he led hunting parties through New Mexico mountains in search of mule deer. Often, the tired and sleepy hunters dozed off while Goode scrambled through the underbrush to herd the deer towards the hunters. He realized that he was the one working while they claimed their trophies, but he grinned triumphantly as they paid him in cash. The hunters were always more generous when they left with a buck and an exaggerated story of how they had tracked him! Goode not only earned extra money; he also acquired hunting, tracking, and camouflage skills.

As a teenager, Goode joined a local Civil Air Patrol squad, where he learned to fly small planes. Despite enjoying the freedom he felt soaring across the sky, he did not join the Air Force. Instead, he joined the Navy. In 1961, he joined a group of "advisors" that were sent to Vietnam. Goode was assigned to the Underwater Detonation Unit, the forerunner to today's Navy Seals. His familiarity with guns, his childhood experiences as a hunter, and his excellent eyesight made him invaluable to the UDU team. Like a great many veterans, Goode was reluctant to talk about his time in Vietnam but did show the authors some of the medals he earned for marksmanship.

"President Kennedy presented this one to me," he said proudly as he carefully placed a medal into the hands of the authors, "and President Carter gave me this one." But he no longer had the medals he was awarded for bravery in Vietnam, nor the Purple Heart he also earned. Only after months and months of conversations with the authors did Goode finally feel comfortable enough to describe the harrowing event that led to his Purple Heart.

"One of my best friends was always sticking his head up no matter how many times I told him to stay down. One day, we were hunkered down and the [Viet] Cong were about to wipe us out." Goode paused for a few moments, seemingly weighing how much he should share.

"Skip kept looking up to see where the enemy was. I kept telling him to keep his head down. But he wouldn't listen to me. The last time he stuck his head up, a bullet caught him in the throat."

Goode glossed over how he pulled his friend to safety, only to discover he had already bled to death. "If he had just kept his head down," he repeated softly. When asked if he had been wounded while attempting to save his friend, he just nodded. He silently rolled up his sleeve to show the shrapnel scars.

Having proven himself in Vietnam, it was logical he would be needed in Cuba. His memories of that fiasco are bitter ones.

"A lot of us used makeup to make ourselves look like native Cubans." Goode had the advantage of being able to speak fluent Spanish. His perpetual tan also helped him blend in with the Cubans. Goode's experiences are evidence that some of the "anti-Castro insurgents" who were supposed to rise up against the dictator and his forces during the battle were actually American soldiers. Goode shared some of his Cuban adventures when he overheard the authors discussing a man named Robert Morrow.

"Do you mean 'Bob Morrow'," he asked. "CIA?" When the authors assented, Goode explained quickly that he had not "known" Morrow, but he had known "of him." The authors loaned Goode a copy of Morrow's book *First Hand Knowledge*, which detailed Morrow's experiences in Cuba after the Bay of Pigs. Goode had tears in his eyes when he returned the book a month later.

"I needed to read that," he explained softly. "I needed to go back." When asked if the book was realistic, he nodded, and a remark about how narrowly Morrow had escaped capture on the island brought a surprising comment from Goode.

"He wasn't the only one," he answered as he turned and walked away. It was quite some time before he would elaborate on that comment. Goode never mentioned the Mafia's involvement in the Bay of Pigs. Either he did not know about it, or more likely, he saw no reason to mention the subject. He knew first-hand that the Bay of Pigs operation had been a failure. To those captured, it was more than a political fiasco. Goode, who would eventually become a CIA asset, had become friendly with anti-Castro guerillas. He still remembers the gruesome scene a few days after the botched attack.

"You can't imagine what it's like to find severed human heads lying on a blood-soaked beach. And who knew where their bodies were?" he murmured. Those who had survived Castro's well-prepared army were captured and immediately thrown into a centuries-old prison. The conditions were so terrible that some prisoners might have envied the corpses on the beach.

Kennedy was blamed by the anti-Castro insurgents, his own military, and by some in the CIA for his refusal to supply air cover for the insurgents. For the failure of the Bay of Pigs invasion, Kennedy privately blamed the incompetence of former President Eisenhower as well as Kennedy's own Joint Chiefs of Staff and the CIA. He felt that by recalling the air cover, he had avoided a possible war with not only Cuba, but also with the Soviet Union.

In reality, "Neither the military nor the bureaucracy misled Kennedy in to the invasion."[101] But that is not what Kennedy wanted people to believe. His public relations staff led Americans to believe that Kennedy had simply inherited this military venture from his predecessor. There was some truth to this, but Kennedy had known more about the proposed invasion before his election than he admitted. He met with a Cuban leader in his Senate office as early as July 1960. "The meeting was arranged by the CIA, its purpose shrouded in secrecy."[102]

Years later, former Governor of Alabama John Patterson admitted in an Oral History for the Kennedy Library that he, too, had personally briefed Kennedy on the proposed military venture against Cuba. This had occurred right before the Kennedy debate with Richard Nixon in October 1960. Because Patterson's story did not jibe with the "official" one told by the Kennedy administration, it was censored by the library officials.[103] So, once again, those loyal to John F. Kennedy changed facts to fit the image Kennedy wanted to project.

What Kennedy and his staff did not know was that Castro was aware of their attempts to murder him. In fact, with the Mafia's help, Castro was supposed to have died during the Bay of Pigs invasion. The assassination attempts failed, and the invasion was an embarrassing and costly mistake. The Bay of Pigs was Kennedy's first political defeat, and "he spent his remaining days in office determined to make Castro pay—with his life, preferably—for staining the Kennedy honor."[104] "There is evidence that Castro's knowledge of the attempts on his life, and the Kennedys' desire to keep them secret, played a key role in the official whitewash of John Kennedy's death, if not the murder itself."[105]

Unfortunately, the ripple effect caused by the Bay of Pigs disaster created greater problems for Kennedy and the nation than mere embarrassment. Though the President survived the crisis, even experiencing a spike in popularity, his secret war against Castro led to the October Missile Crisis in 1962. When Kennedy first learned that nuclear missiles had been placed in Cuba by the Soviet Union, he kept this fact a secret from the American public. Instead of using cautious diplomacy, Kennedy issued ultimatums to the Soviet premier.

Americans reacted positively to the young President's boldness. However, they did not know that the missiles Kennedy referred to as "offensive" were actually considered by Cuba and Russia to be "defensive" because the United States already had missiles in Turkey pointed towards the Soviet Union. Both Castro and his ally, Soviet Premier Nikita Khrushchev, felt that they were the ones being threatened. The restraint credited to the American president was actually demonstrated by the Soviets,[106] for they did, indeed, "blink first." It is questionable whether Kennedy's administration would ever have blinked. No one knows whether he would he have committed the United States to a nuclear war without admitting that the U.S. had threatened the Soviet Union, and its Cuban satellite, before any Soviet missiles were sent to Cuba.

Goode, of course, knew nothing of the political games being played in Washington, D. C. He simply knew how dangerous the whole situation was for the United States military. His experiences in Vietnam and his experiences at the Bay of Pigs had been valuable. But Goode wanted to forget what he had seen and heard.

"When I finally got out of the Navy," he began, "I took those medals they had given me out to the lake and I threw them as far as I could throw them! They're still at the bottom of Crater Lake." After a few moments of silence, he continued, "So you can see why I was so glad to get back to civilian life. What I didn't know was that my uncle A.J. had told the U.S. marshals about my sharpshooting skills. So, as I was walking out of the gates of the base, U.S. Marshal Robert I. Nash was waiting for me." Goode, he said, learned that day that even though a man had Honorable Discharge papers in his hands, another branch of the military could still force him to work for it.

"So that's how I began working for the U.S. marshals," he explained simply. "And that's why I was in Dallas the day Kennedy was killed." He watched for a few moments as the authors frantically scribbled notes. "You won't find my name in any records," he commented, smiling. *"Not anywhere.* That's what they did for me in exchange for what I did for them. They expunged every document that contained my name." Before the authors could demand more, Goode walked away. The rest of his story would not be revealed until another day.

CHAPTER 7

THE VOICE OF TOM MILLS

**"If President Johnson had said anything about chest pains that day,
I would not have left the ranch."**

Because J. Goode's supervisors had promised him complete confidentiality, his name does not appear in any books or documents. Similary, the name "Tom Mills" appears in few books, and few researchers are familiar with him. This is partly because President Kennedy did not want the public to know of his existence. However, Mills himself may have deliberately stayed in the shadows as one of the few persons to witness details about the limousine in which Kennedy rode in Dallas on November 22.

He was also one of the few individuals who personally knew about the health issues afflicting Presidents Kennedy and Johnson. As a Navy medic, he worked for both men. As innocuous-sounding as his White House position was, it was kept private.

Much of the information hidden by Kennedy's staff was unimportant and, technically, none of the public's business. However, the public did have a right to know about a president's major health issues and a president's risk-taking behavior. President Kennedy's health was definitely affected by his womanizing, but some of his health problems began long before he was sexually active. He was ill throughout most of his childhood. Family members knew how much time Kennedy spent in and out of hospitals, but much of his medical history was hidden from the voters. Childhood illnesses could be overlooked by the public because so many people experienced similar illnesses. But the Addison's disease with which Kennedy was diagnosed in 1947 was a different matter. At the time, very little was understood about this unusual disease; doctors warned patients with Addison's, and their families, that there was no cure. Because of the disease, patients were more susceptible to infections, which made even the most common surgery dangerous.

Kennedy also had problems with his back, which he attributed to either a college football injury or a war injury, depending on when he told the story. The back problem was really a congenital one. He had been born with one leg shorter than the other.[107] After he aggravated the problem during his military service, Kennedy's back pain was often so excruciating that he was forced to use crutches. Like President Franklin Roosevelt, John Kennedy and anyone close to him hid these health problems from the American people. After all, a man in the prime of his life should be full of energy and "vigor," a term he used frequently. It would be difficult for a president insisting that the country "needed to get moving again" to admit that he himself could barely walk at times. Thus, such health problems were denied vehemently, and crutches hidden from public view.

This meant that most of the American public never knew that Kennedy used crutches (except immediately after his back surgery). However, some outside the President's inner circle discovered how disabled he actually was. Vice-President Lyndon Johnson's staff members knew that there were days when the President could barely walk. A Johnson aide remembers seeing President Kennedy hobbling on crutches in the privacy of the Oval Office area in 1962. She had heard rumors about his health difficulties from other Johnson staff members. Nevertheless, it was still a shock to see the President's drawn face and obvious pain that day.[108]

Tom Mills helped Kennedy deal with his back pain, but like the crutches, he, too, was hidden from most people. Official visitors to the White House sometimes saw the President in his rocking chair, but not on crutches. A rocking chair was considered acceptable, even if the President was only in his forties. What the world did not know was that this special rocking chair was not just for comfort; it was a medical necessity. It was so essential that staff members often packed up the President's rocking chair and transported it to parties held at private residences.[109]

Though the President's ailing back had been publicized as the result of a war injury, which was something no one should be ashamed of, he and his family still could not admit that he was disabled. That was because the Kennedy children had been taught that illness was a sign of weakness, not that overcoming weakness was a sign of courage—a quality John F. Kennedy admired greatly. This prevented him from complaining about the pain he suffered daily.

If the Kennedys were secretive about an unavoidable disease like Addison's and about a back injury, the fact that the President suffered from venereal disease for more than thirty years, and that he was repeatedly infected because of his continual sexual activity, was reason for even greater secrecy. His urologist, Dr. William P. Herbst, indicated that Kennedy suffered from acute postgonoccal urethritis throughout most of his adult life.[110] The results of this disease proved to be tragic. Sarah Bradford's research for her book *America's Queen* included previous research done by author Richard Reeves. Reeves's research indicates that "the underlying cause of Jackie Kennedy's miscarriages, and her subsequent history of still births, and premature births, was chlamydia, which she assumedly contracted from her husband as a result of his gonorrhea."[111] There is no record of whether President or Mrs. Kennedy ever knew this.

Kennedy basically survived through antibiotics, but he also received high dosages of amphetamines from Dr. Max Jacobson, an unorthodox physician who lost his license to practice medicine in 1975.[112] The President may have truly believed that these shots were nothing more than massive vitamins. He allowed his wife, his friends, and sexual partners to be inoculated with Jacobson's "feel-good" shots. In 2016, Layte Bowden recalled that she had received shots from Jacobson, but she assumed they contained nothing more than vitamins. But Kennedy's brother Robert, his personal physician, his aides, and even some of his Secret Service agents tried to warn the President of the dangerous side effects that could result from these injections.

Kennedy ignored these warnings, much as he had always ignored advice concerning his extra-marital affairs. He knew the press would not publish stories about his activities, and he also knew that the Secret Service agents were sworn to secrecy. He once commented to close friend Senator George Smathers, "While I'm alive, they'll never bring it out. After I'm dead, who cares?"[113] As much as Kennedy loved his children, he apparently never considered that *they* might someday care.

However, Kennedy was correct about one thing: Many of his close friends and aides, as well as fellow politicians, admired his "conquests" and envied his sexual freedom. Typical Americans knew that the President exercised in the White House swimming pool to strengthen his back. But they did not know what Secret Service agents and White House insiders quickly realized—that he also used it as a rendezvous area for extra-curricular sexual activities.

The Kennedy administration never hid the fact that two physicians were on call for any health problems President Kennedy might have, including problems with his back. But Americans did not know that at least two Navy medics were also employed to assist the President. In an interview with us, Tom Mills said, "My job was to show President Kennedy how to do the exercises Admiral Burkley had prescribed for him. I made sure he was doing them correctly, and they seemed to help his back problems."[114]

"President Kennedy," Mills remembered, "had insisted on having a Navy doctor on staff at the White House. I was associated with Dr. Burkley, so that's why I was asked to help with Kennedy, too." Tom Mills admitted that he realized at the time how lucky he was to be working at the White House during both Kennedy's and Johnson's administrations. He also admitted that the Kennedys had required him and other staff members to sign oaths of confidentiality.

Mills must have taken his oath quite seriously. Even during a casual conversation with the retired medic, he was extremely careful as he spoke about Kennedy and Lyndon Johnson. Though he had more contact with President Kennedy than with his wife, he thought highly of her. As President, Lyndon Johnson did not seem concerned about Mills' employment, but in the Kennedy White House, it was kept so secret that even Mary Gallagher, Jackie Kennedy's personal secretary, did not realize he worked there. Mills often accompanied President Kennedy on Air Force One. He recalled that he often flew with Kennedy to the family's Palm Beach winter home so that he would be available to assist with the President's back exercises. In fact, Mills was scheduled to be with Kennedy on the Dallas trip in November 1963. Instead, another medic, Chief Ellis Hendricks, travelled with the President because he had family in Texas he wanted to visit during the presidential trip.

Reclining comfortably in the living room of his house in Johnson City, Texas in 2016, Mills thought back to those heady days in the White House, and later ones on Lyndon Johnson's ranch. His demeanor seemed informal, but his words were obviously carefully chosen. He seemed more at ease speaking about Johnson than Kennedy.

He casually mentioned that Johnson had been friendly with his foreman's wife Jewell Malecek, who still lives on the Johnson ranch. In Mills' *Oral History for the LBJ Library*, Mills spoke fondly of times when he would eat lunch with ranch foreman Dale Malecek, his wife Jewell, and the President. Sue Hardy, whose husband, Red Conger, was then an assistant ranch foreman to Dale Malecek, recalled in an interview that her husband repeated gossip from Johnson's Secret Service agents about President Johnson. According to them, Johnson was *extremely* close to his foreman's wife. Randall B. Woods, author of *Architect of American Ambition*, learned of this rumor from a Johnson agent: "The boss was sleeping with Jewell Malechek."[115] If Tom Mills had heard these rumors, he was too much of a gentleman to say.

Eventually, other Johnson insiders and biographers revealed that like Kennedy, Johnson, too, had been romantically involved with numerous women. The accuracy of this gossip is debatable, but Jewell Malecek admitted in her Oral History that she drove former President Johnson around his ranch on the last day of his life (something she did almost every morning for him) while his wife was away from home. By then, the two were probably nothing more that good friends, if, indeed, they had ever been more than that. In her Oral History, Jewell Malecek also stated that she was in Fredricksburg, a small town near the ranch, when Johnson suffered his heart attack. She arrived back at the ranch in time to accompany the former President on the airplane that carried him to

Brooke Army Medical Center at Ft. Sam Houston in San Antonio.

Oddly enough, several of Johnson's staff members had been sent to Omaha, Nebraska that day to train on Valley System irrigation equipment and were not at the ranch the day Johnson died. Mills revealed this when he spoke with the authors. He smiled as he explained that Johnson was always irritated if any of his staff members, even those paid by the U.S. government, appeared to be idle. Consequently, Mills, who was serving as a medical liaison for the former President, and the ranch hands were sent away from the ranch the day Johnson died. Mills was troubled that he had not been there to help Johnson on January 22, 1973, when LBJ succumbed to a massive heart attack. Mills knew that the former President needed nitroglycerin tablets from time to time for heart pains, but, "if he had said anything about chest pains that day," Mills stated adamantly, "I would not have left the ranch."

It seems odd that Johnson would deliberately send his only medically-trained staff member out of town. Considering his declining health, perhaps he was hoping no one would be available to provide extreme medical intervention if his heart finally gave out.

Mills soon returned to more pleasant memories. One of his duties at Johnson's new ranch in Austin was to provide massages for the President, both during and after his administration. He chuckled as he admitted to the authors that he often worried because his fingerprints could have been found on numerous top-secret documents.

"Let me explain," he said. "The President would read all sorts of papers while I gave him his nightly massage. Sometimes, he would hand them to me so I could lay them aside. I knew my fingerprints were all over papers I was never supposed to have seen. But what could I do?"

When the authors visited Tom Mills and his wife Jane, the couple pointed to some of the presidential memorabilia covering the walls of their living room. Large reproductions of Kennedy and Johnson White House Christmas cards had been carefully framed and now served as unique pieces of décor. Not once did Mills say anything negative about Kennedy or Johnson. He seems to have fond memories of both Presidents and has carefully kept medical information about both men confidential. If Mills was privy to some of Kennedy's and Johnson's private activities, as so many of the Secret Service agents were, he kept those memories to himself.

An interesting detail that Tom Mills did not reveal that day is that after the Kennedy assassination, he had been directed by Admiral George Burkley to wait at the Secret Service garage in Washington, D. C. Mills' assignment was to inspect the presidential limousine.[116]Was Mills expected to look for bullet fragments or for pieces of the President's skull? If so, Secret Service Agent Sam Kinney provided him with a large skull fragment that Kinney found in the car immediately after the assassination. Obviously, Mills would have been able to observe the windshield of the Presidential limousine and any bullet holes or cracks that might have existed. He might have also seen bullet fragments. Whether Mills was sworn to secrecy concerning his examination of the car, or if he simply felt that his role should not be made public, he was undoubtedly the person Admiral Burkley trusted that evening. However, like many others, Mills has never spoken publicly about what he saw hours after President Kennedy's assassination.

He also was unable to mention a story about Johnson's final words because he had no direct knowledge of what Johnson supposedly confessed to. Indeed, if Mills had known this intriguing story, he might very well have kept it to himself. Almost all the witnesses did. Two people, however, shared what was heard the afternoon Johnson took his last breaths. In a conversation in 2000, Robert Slobens and his wife Elizabeth and their friend Bob Burnside learned some historic details that, if true, would certainly change history.

On January 22, 1973 Lyndon Johnson, obviously aware that his life was ending, began exonerating himself about the death of his predecessor. In doing so, he pointed the finger at his wife and the head of the FBI. The plans for John F. Kennedy's assassination, he claimed, were first made by J. Edgar Hoover and Lady Bird Johnson! Johnson had simply allowed them to open the door to the presidency for him.

As implausible as this scenario is, the person who claims to have witnessed this shocking event is still determined to stay anonymous, because of what still might occur and because of the death threats that began almost immediately after Johnson's death.

"They threatened our lives and followed us for years" are words that explain why the witness remains in hiding. Does "they" refer to government officials? Military personnel? Political allies? This fascinating story adds to the melodrama that the Kennedy assassination has become, but it also explains why so many people outside of the Kennedy circle are not revealing everything they know.

The secrets that enveloped John F. Kennedy and his administration could not be revealed even after the President's death. For example, Ellis Hendricks was a well-known physical therapist, but President Kennedy did not want Americans to know that his back aliment was so severe that he required the services of this highly-trained therapist. The drapes that most, if not all, politicians keep so tightly drawn on their lives could never be opened by the Kennedy family. This was partly because so many of their secrets were dark ones, and partly because, even after the assassination, the family still had political plans for Kennedy's brothers Bobby and Ted. Kennedy's plans may have extended even further to the next generation of Kennedys. How could the Kennedy family and their associates admit they had lied to American voters in 1960 and still ask for their votes in future elections?

CHAPTER 8

THE VOICE OF SHARON CALLOWAY

"Dr. Rose was livid. I remember seeing him jumping up and down. 'This is my body! This is my body.' "

Sharon Calloway observed things at Parkland Hospital in Dallas that are still controversial today. She had no way of knowing that procedural mistakes made in Dallas would lead to suspicions that more "mistakes" later occurred in Bethesda, Maryland. She did know that the scene unfolding in front of her was one she would never forget.

Like any widow, Jackie Kennedy was reluctant to have her husband's body autopsied. "It doesn't have to be done," she told the President's personal physician.[117] At first, Admiral George Burkley agreed.

"He said that since the presumed assassin, Lee Harvey Oswald, was under arrest in Dallas and that there seemed little doubt about his guilt, there was no need for procedures that might severely disfigure the President's corpse."[118] It wasn't until the Bethesda doctors insisted that the autopsy take place that Burkley convinced Jackie Kennedy that one was unavoidable.

(It is easy to imagine what kind of trial Oswald would have received when his guilt had been "established" so soon after the assassination. No explanation was given on how the President's personal physician *knew* so much about the guilt of the "assassin" only hours after the President's death.)

President Kennedy's personal Secret Service agents and aides made sure that his autopsy was not performed in Dallas, even if it meant breaking the law. Researchers still wonder if they would have dared kidnap the body of the President at gunpoint if they had not had the verbal approval from someone in authority. In his *Oral History for the Sixth Floor Museum* on November 8, 2005, Dallas Medical Examiner Earl Rose painted an entirely different picture of the infamous confrontation between himself and the Secret Service that day in November 1963. His depiction was at such odds with the testimonies of bystanders that even the interviewer seemed stunned by his comments. Witnesses that day described shouting, agents brandishing weapons, and practically a tug-of-war for the President's body. Rose simply said that he and the Secret Service agents "talked." X-ray technician Sharon Calloway, as well as ambulance driver Aubrey Rike and Dallas District Attorney Henry Wade and numerous others, all disagreed with Rose's description of the hospital scene.

After the President's body arrived at Parkland Hospital, Secret Service agent Clint Hill spoke over the telephone to Attorney General Robert Kennedy. Even William Manchester's detailed description in his Kennedy family-authorized book *Death of a President* does not relate exactly what was said between the two men. However, the behavior of the agents and Kennedy's aides after the President's death can lead one to assume that these law-abiding agents felt free to supersede state regulations concerning the President's autopsy in Texas. Author Gus Russo, in his book *Live by the Sword*, claimed that the new President, Lyndon Johnson, directed the men to bring the body to Air Force One.

"Johnson ordered the Secret Service to bring the body immediately from the hospital, local ordinances notwithstanding. Although Texas law required that an autopsy had to be performed locally in a homicide case, both Lyndon Johnson and the Kennedy entourage demanded otherwise for the dead President."[119] If Russo is correct, then the first order given by Johnson, as Kennedy's *de facto* successor, broke laws in his own home state. However, it seems logical that if the Secret Service agents were following orders, at least one of these frustrated, outraged individuals would have invoked the name of the new President when the group confronted Medical Examiner Earl Rose. Surely Rose would have stepped aside if any of the men had explained that they were merely following the new President's orders. It is possible they were following Robert Kennedy's directions; it's possible, but not likely, that Johnson demanded that his name not be used. It could be that the Secret Service agents were trying to appease the late President's widow, who had insisted she was not leaving Dallas without her husband's body. Perhaps in the aftermath of the assassination, the men who had failed to prevent the President's death were determined to hide any health secrets that they knew would embarrass his family.

Anyone who has listened to Earl Rose's *Oral History from the Sixth Floor Museum* in Dallas would assume that there had been a smooth transfer of the President's body from Parkland Hospital to Air Force One. However, anyone who has read *The Death of a President* or numerous other books describing Kennedy's death knows better.

Most people would not have described the removal of the President's body as a "transfer." A great many of them referred to it as a "kidnapping." Rose was prepared to autopsy the body of President Kennedy. He had arrived at Parkland Hospital as quickly as possible after the announcement of the President's death. He was prepared to begin immediately.

"There has been a homicide here," he said to those gathered in the hallway. "They won't be able to leave until there is an autopsy."[120] A loud argument followed between the Secret Service agents, President Kennedy's personal physician, and Dr. Rose.

"The remains stay," Rose said. "Procedures must be followed. A certificate has to be filed before any body can be shipped out of State. You can't lose the chain of evidence."[121] The arguments continued, but Rose was correct. By moving the body, the chain of evidence would be broken. The autopsy *should* have taken place in Dallas. However, Kennedy's Secret Service agents and staff members prevented this.

In a scene that might have been humorous had it had not involved so tragic an event, witnesses describe Rose and the Secret Service agents practically fighting over the President's casket. The agents made it abundantly clear that they did not care if Rose had the law on his side. They knew that Mrs. Kennedy had refused to leave the hospital as long as the President's body was there. They also knew that President Johnson had refused to leave Dallas unless Mrs. Kennedy accompanied the presidential party back to Washington. The Secret Service agents had already lost one president that day. None of them knew whether there were assassins waiting to kill Lyndon Johnson, too.

Secret Service Agent Roy Kellerman informed Dr. Rose, "My friend, this is the body of the President of the United States, and we are going to take it back to Washington."[122] Angry verbal exchanges escalated to the point where some of the bystanders feared a physical altercation would take place.

Rose cried out, "If you allow this body to be moved, it will be moved illegally."[123] Rose, however, was outnumbered. Even a Dallas police officer, Sergeant Robert Dugger, did not understand the reasons for the delay. He was sympathetic to Jacqueline Kennedy's predicament and was so angry at the medical examiner that his fists balled up like a boxer's. One of Kennedy's staff members thought to himself, "He's going to belt him. He's really going to do it."[124]

Aubrey Rike describes the scene vividly in his book *At the Door of Memory.* Standing in Trauma Room One, Rike was attempting to help move the President's casket into the hallway. A Dallas priest was blessing the casket with holy water.

"The crucifix that he had put on the casket was being jerked around so much by the ensuing tug-of-war that despite the strength of the magnetic adaptor on its back, the crucifix was sliding off; I [Rike] twice grabbed it and centered it back on the casket...We had to stop twice and get that casket put back on the truck to keep it from falling off and onto the floor."[125]

Finally, the Secret Service agents won the battle and loaded the President's casket into a hearse. Following the hearse was a convertible full of former motorcade participants. None of them realized at the time what a crucial mistake the Secret Service agents had made that day. Because the President's autopsy was not performed immediately and appropriately, questions about the wounds, the number and direction of bullets, the condition of the brain, etc., would remain for years. In fact, questions linger even today.

Dr. Rose could have consulted with Parkland doctors and examined the Governor's and the President's clothing immediately if he had been allowed to. He would have learned that a tracheotomy had been performed on the President's throat by Dallas doctors. The medical examiner would not have been hampered and controlled by the Kennedy family, and, possibly, the military. He would have been allowed to examine Kennedy's adrenal glands, something that the Kennedy family did not want done during the autopsy that took place later at Bethesda Naval Medical Center.

Dr. Rose was never even allowed to examine the President's body. What should have been a solemn, decorous moment turned into a circus of tragedy. His attempts to follow Texas law were met with nothing but hysterical resistance. Many researchers feel that this suspicious behavior was the first indication of an official cover-up. Five years later, Robert Kennedy's autopsy *was* held immediately after his death in the hospital where he had died.

From inside Parkland Hospital, Sharon Calloway had a unique perspective on the events following the assassination. Calloway, an x-ray technician at Parkland Hospital in 1963, recalled that even before the ugly scene between the Secret Service and Earl Rose, "the [hospital] hallways were pandemonium." Calloway watched from nearby as the President's body was wheeled into the emergency room. "I was about five feet from him and could see the back of his head. The top of the head was gone." A few minutes later, a doctor came down the hall and described Kennedy's head by saying, "It looked like a watermelon had been dropped on his head."[126]

Because Secret Service agents ordered all employees to remain in the hospital, Calloway explained in her *Oral History* that she and her co-workers had the opportunity to observe this historic event. "No one was allowed up on the second floor, and we weren't allowed outside of the hospital until JFK was removed." She remembers being bothered by the fact that Secret Service agents followed her and other radiology employees everywhere they went.

"I picked up a phone and got an outside line. I called my husband and asked what was going on. Secret Service were everywhere!" There was so much chaos that even with the Secret Service and FBI agents trying to guard entrances and exits, "the sister of an x-ray technician, expected from out of town, walked in the back door of the hospital with her suitcase in her hand." No one stopped her

THE LONE STAR SPEAKS

or checked her suitcase or her identification. If the young woman's suitcase had contained an explosive device, the new President could have been killed while the Secret Service wrangled over the corpse of his predecessor.

Some of Calloway's most vivid memories of the Kennedy assassination concern Dr. Rose. Everyone in the Dallas medical world knew he was fully familiar with both medical and legal procedures, and that he was adept at dealing with homicides and suicides. Calloway understood why he was so upset with the Kennedy situation.

"He was livid. I remember seeing Dr. Rose jumping up and down. 'This is my body! This is my body,'" he yelled. "He was furious and he was holding onto the gurney." According to Calloway, "Rose never got over what happened that day. He never forgave [those who forced him to release J.F.K.'s corpse]. Rose often said, 'Things would have been different if I had been in charge.'"

"Rose left his job with Parkland," Calloway continued, "because he thought he had been betrayed when the District Attorney's Office would not support him that day. Rose took that decision personally. This affected his credibility. I think he always questioned: 'Was there something else I could have done [to keep the body at the hospital]?'"

If Dr. Rose had not finally stepped aside, there is no way of knowing how violent this situation might have become. Undoubtedly, those closest to President Kennedy were overcome by grief and shock. But there is also no doubt that an official autopsy should have taken place in Dallas, Texas. Can overwrought emotions account for the desperate and unreasonable actions of Kennedy's entourage? Were there other reasons why the President's body was technically stolen from Parkland Hospital?

According to Sharon Calloway, Doris Nelson, the head nurse at Parkland Hospital, was asked by the Secret Service not to speak to anyone for security reasons. "This meant [not talking] about the 'nature of the wound.'" But Nelson said, "We had seen what had happened. The crown of his head was not there." Nelson was not the only staff member to be cautioned. Calloway remembered that after the assassination, hospital staff members received "a lot of memos... 'What you saw should be kept to yourself.'" They were told that this was because of the chance of miscommunication. Even the head of security at Parkland Hospital, O. P. Wright, "did not speak of that day" to his wife, Elizabeth, who was a nurse at the hospital. Why were medical personnel silenced almost immediately after the President's death? A "chance for miscommunication" does not seem like a valid reason.

Other reasons might explain the need for secrecy. No one was more loyal to President Kennedy than his younger brother Bobby, and no one knew better than he how embarrassing it would be for the American public to find out that the Kennedys' insistence about JFK's good health had been outright lies. Also, Jackie Kennedy would have been humiliated had it had become public knowledge that the President had been treated numerous times for sexually transmitted diseases.

Could the necessity to keep secret certain facts about the President's medical history explain why his body was forcefully removed from Parkland Hospital? Were Kennedy's security agents so angry because they were desperate to follow someone's orders? Did they realize their illegal actions would affect the type of autopsy Kennedy would eventually receive?

Could there have also been a group of individuals who wanted to control Kennedy's autopsy for other reasons? An appropriate forensic autopsy should have answered any questions about how many bullets had hit the President and Governor Connally and from which direction(s) they had come. If the autopsy had taken place immediately after the assassination, no one could have later speculated (rightly or wrongly) that the President's corpse might have been examined "unofficially" and altered before the official autopsy at Bethesda even began. Interfering with John F. Kennedy's autopsy was just one blunder that occurred that day in Dallas and later in Bethesda, Maryland.

CHAPTER 9

THE VOICES OF JAMES JENKINS AND DENNIS DAVID

"The President's spinal cord had already been cut before the official autopsy began!"—James Jenkins

J ames Jenkins was a hospital corpsman who assisted in President Kennedy's official autopsy. Though he was not a doctor, he realized that evening that the President's autopsy was different from any of the others he had participated in. His observations, along with those of other technicians, would eventually raise shocking questions about the President's wounds and whether they had been altered before the official autopsy began.

There is ample evidence from the testimony of Jenkins and other medical personnel present at the President's autopsy at the Bethesda Naval Hospital in Maryland that more than one autopsy took place. David Lifton documented numerous errors in the official autopsy reports in his 1980 bestseller *Best Evidence,* and James Jenkins shared with a small group of researchers that he had personally seen evidence in the Bethesda autopsy theatre on the evening of November 22, 1963 that contradicted the final official autopsy report.[127]

Jenkins had always been interested in medicine and eventually earned his Master's Degree in Clinical Pathology and Clinical Immunology. On the day Kennedy died, however, he was just a technician at Bethesda Naval Hospital. He and other Bethesda technicians began preparing for the President's autopsy at about 3:00 p.m. EST. He did not leave the Bethesda morgue until 9:00 a.m. the next morning. Before being dismissed, Jenkins received orders from the Department of Defense and the Secretary of the Navy to keep everything he had observed confidential. Confidentiality is something Dr. Earl Rose could not have required from those who would have assisted him at Parkland Hospital; the military, however, could.

As the President's ornate coffin was opened, Jenkins saw that the body, both head and torso, was wrapped in sheets. The two pathologists in charge of the autopsy, Dr. James Humes and Dr. Thornton Boswell, directed everyone in the room to leave except for Jenkins and another technician, Paul O'Connor. Jenkins began recording the location of scars, measurements, and weights, etc.

on a face sheet. He wrote each detail down in his own handwriting as the two pathologists fed him information.

The examination of the President's head began even before Dr. Pierre Finck, a specialist in wartime wounds, entered the autopsy theatre. As Dr. Boswell removed the bloody sheet from around the head, he dictated his observations. Beneath the sheet was a bloody towel.

According to Jenkins, on the top of the President's right ear was a small wound. It was at this point that discussions began between the various doctors, including the President's personal physician, Admiral George Burkley. Jenkins recalls that the men deliberated among themselves "all night" about the various wounds. Multiple x-rays of the body were taken before the actual autopsy began. Jenkins stated flatly that the x-rays did not show *any* bullet fragments in the body itself.

"Nothing seemed to be pleasing people in the gallery," Jenkins said, referring to the group of individuals who observed the autopsy from the viewing area. "Internal organs were removed and placed on a cork-type cutting board that also held a scale used to weigh them."

Humes probed a back wound in the President's upper right shoulder with his finger. "The wound did not go into the chest cavity. It went as far as the right top of the middle lung lobe." In Jenkins' opinion, the bullet that caused the "back wound could not have exited from the throat." If the bullet did not exit through Kennedy's throat, then it serves as evidence of at least three shots having hit the President.

The throat wound was left unexamined because the doctors assumed it was nothing more than the remnants of a tracheotomy. However, Jenkins remembers there was a discussion about the large size of the hole in the President's throat. "The hole was 6.5 centimeters, which is over two inches. At one point, we were directed away from the throat wound. Someone said it would make the job too hard for the mortician [if the hole had been probed]." If Dr. Earl Rose had performed the autopsy, he, undoubtedly, would have been in complete control, and likely would have made a different decision.

Jenkins thought carefully as members of the audience peppered him with questions. When someone asked him if he had been aware of how much time had elapsed, Jenkins just answered, "There was a huge clock in the morgue, but my attention was focused on that table."

The discussion among the researchers turned to the appearance of the President's head. Jenkins was asked if he had had any doubts that the face he was staring at on the autopsy table was the same one he had seen in newspaper and magazine photos.

"No," he answered without hesitation. "The body looked like John Kennedy."

Jenkins did remember that as Dr. Boswell examined the President's head, he asked if any surgery had been done on the head at Parkland. There appeared to be an *incision in the top of the skull*. Jenkins made a point of adding, "There was no need to remove a skull cap in order to remove the brain." The term *removing a skull cap* refers to the procedure used when the top part of a corpse's skull is sawed off so an entire brain can be removed. Apparently, there had been so much blood and brain matter on Kennedy's skull that Sharon Calloway, Doris Nelson, and others at Parkland Hospital had assumed the top of his head had been removed by a bullet.

Jenkins' comment indicated that the hole in the President's head was so large that the brain was easily accessible to the surgeons. In fact, Jenkins recalled Dr. Humes emotionally describing the President's brain matter.

"The damn thing fell out in my hands!" Jenkins remembered Humes exclaiming. The pathologists also wondered about the fact that the damage to the brain itself did not seem to correlate to the damage done to the skull. There seemed to be more damage to the *interior* of the brain than to the skull.

The doctors removed Kennedy's brain and laid it upside down in a gauze sling and then infused it with formalin. Jenkins remembered this as being particularly difficult because of the President's carotid arteries. Jenkins then made a statement that was more shocking than anything he had already said.

"The President's brain stem looked like it had been cut from each side and then from the middle." He paused dramatically and looked directly into the eyes of the opened-mouth audience members.

"I feel it had been removed before this autopsy," James Jenkins stated.

He went on to add that the spinal cord of a corpse is sliced so that the brain can be removed from the skull. In the case of President Kennedy, the spinal cord had *not* been severed by a bullet. It had been *cut* by a knife or scalpel, but not by the physicians in Dallas. Dr. Rose could not have cut the President's spinal cord because no autopsy was performed. Jenkins described the cuts made to Kennedy's spinal cord as "uneven."

"Normally, a spinal cord would be cut with one smooth motion. In this case, it had been partly cut from the right side and then completed with a cut from the left. Therefore, the two center edges did not meet exactly." Jenkins was asked if this indicated that an amateur, rather than a professional, had severed the spinal cord.

"Not necessarily," he answered. "But it does mean that someone had a difficult time getting to the spinal cord." It is possible that an unorthodox procedure was used because someone was rushed and short on time. The vitally important detail about the severed spinal cord became one more intriguing matter because it was not entered into the autopsy report.

Another discrepancy Jenkins identified was that the information he had personally recorded on the official face sheet was later changed by someone. He obtained a copy of the so-called "official" face sheet years after the assassination. The copy he was sent was not the one he helped complete on November 22, 1963. He could not identify any of the handwriting on it as his own. There were errors concerning the right and left lungs and the kidney. Data had been blacked out and replaced. Changes on the form were not initialed—a complete variance from standard military protocol. At the bottom left-hand corner was the signature of Admiral George Burkley. The signature of Dr. Boswell, which should have also appeared on the form, was nowhere to be found.

Jenkins is particularly suspicious about the data that had been obliterated. He stated adamantly, "As an ex-military man, I know that changes to official forms are made with a single straight line through the information and initials are placed next to the corrected information." Any "official" medical document from a military hospital that does not meet official protocol must be considered suspicious. Only a high-ranking military officer or government official could order the alteration of an official document.

Jerrold Custer, an x-ray technician, was also at Bethesda Naval Hospital on the evening of November 22, 1963. According to his testimony before the ARRB (Assassination Records Review Board), he observed two different coffins outside the autopsy theatre. Both were ornate, and both, according to witnesses, had arrived at Bethesda Naval Hospital on the evening of November 22, 1963. One coffin was identified as the ceremonial casket in which Kennedy's body had been placed at Parkland Hospital, the same casket that Jenkins recalled seeing. Another coffin, which had arrived earlier, supposedly contained the body of an Air Force colonel.[128]

Still another casket was observed by medical corpsman Paul O'Connor and Dennis David, Chief of the Day; it was a simple military-issue shipping casket. Jenkins admitted to the audience of researchers that he had been surprised by the fact that he was ordered to *not* record the arrival of the Air Force major's body. Not recording data concerning caskets and corpses violated all military procedures. It was years after the assassination before Bethesda employees, who had been forced to sign confidentiality statements, realized that "something fishy had gone on."[129]

Speculation about nefarious reasons for an unofficial additional autopsy arose as soon as the book *Best Evidence* was published in 1980. It is possible, however, that Robert and Jackie Kennedy had given permission for a hurried, partial autopsy before the official autopsy so that evidence of health issues could be hidden. It is presumed that Robert Kennedy would have given orders through Admiral George Burkley for the Bethesda doctors to avoid mentioning anything about the President's adrenal glands. According to Dr. J. Thornton Boswell in his AARB deposition, "...Jim (Humes) had promised George Burkley that he would not discuss Kennedy's adrenals until all the living members of the Kennedy family were dead."[130] The conditions of the adrenal glands would have provided evidence of Addison's disease.

If Kennedy family members had given permission for a partial autopsy, they would have been helpless to object if they had discovered that other alterations to the President's body had also occurred—alterations that might have changed the paths of the bullets, for example.

Like Jenkins, Lt. Commander William Bruce Pitzer was a Bethesda employee with evidence that the true facts about the President's autopsy were not revealed to the Warren Commission or to the American public. As the head of the audio-visual department at Bethesda Naval Hospital, he had films and slides in his possession that showed crucial information about the President's autopsy. Shortly after the assassination, he showed these to a friend, co-worker Dennis David. According to David, he and Pitzer saw a small entry hole in the President's upper right forehead and a large exit wound in the back of his skull. Both men concluded that the President's head and throat wounds had been the result of a shot from the front, not the back.[131]

David left Bethesda in late 1965, but he stayed in contact with Pitzer; he knew that Pitzer was about to retire and that he had been offered employment with several private audio-visual studios. Before Pitzer could retire, he allegedly committed suicide on October 29, 1966 at Bethesda. The autopsy showed that he had shot himself with a revolver; the bullet had entered his right temple and exited on the left side of his head. However, there were no powder burns on his skin, and as Dennis David pointed out, Pitzer had been left-handed. He would not have shot himself with his right hand.

Like Pitzer's family, David doubted that his friend had committed suicide. He felt that Pitzer had become a threat to someone because of the photos, slides, and films in his possession that contradicted Kennedy's official autopsy results. Pitzer was about to free himself of the military. Did government officials fear he would reveal what he knew about Kennedy's wounds? It can be assumed that, as a military man, Pitzer would have turned over any copies of the autopsy if an officer had ordered him to do so. He might have refused the directives of someone *not* part of the military, and that may have caused his death. However, his own branch of the military may have participated in covering up his death. Regardless, if the Pitzer family and friends like Dennis David were correct, Lt. Commander Pitzer might not have died if Dr. Earl Rose had handled John F. Kennedy's autopsy.

Fortunately, Dallas District Attorney Henry Wade had no control over President Kennedy's autopsy. In Wade's *Oral History for the Sixth Floor Museum* in Dallas, he stated, "You see, the only thing you had to prove by way of an autopsy was that John F. Kennedy died of a gunshot wound. It doesn't make any difference where it [the bullet] came in or where it went out." [132] Dr. Earl Rose would have, undoubtedly, disagreed with Henry Wade's opinion concerning the importance of autopsies and the vital information that can be garnered from them.

Wade's statement was a weak attempt to defend why he had allowed the President's body to be moved out of Texas without an autopsy. Wade's *Oral History* was given in 1992. By 1992, he surely knew that one of the most important controversies surrounding the President's assassination was the question about which direction the shots had been fired from. This is something Dr. Earl Rose could have determined almost immediately. So perhaps there were other reasons that some of those closest to the President insisted that his autopsy take place under controlled conditions.

Even so, the pathologists who performed Kennedy's autopsy at Bethesda Naval Hospital noticed something the Parkland doctors had overlooked: one bullet had struck the President in the upper right shoulder approximately two inches to the right of the spinal column. However, it was a shallow wound, one that Dr. James Humes probed with his finger. Humes could feel the end of the opening; the bullet had not even penetrated Kennedy's lung, much less penetrated his entire body. This wound was proof that at least one bullet had been fired from behind the motorcade.

Unfortunately for those seeking to know the complete truth about the President's injuries, the location of this particular wound was changed on diagrams so that it appeared to align with what Parkland doctors originally described as an entry wound in the President's throat. In other words, a shoulder wound that had caused very little damage became a rear entry wound at the base of Kennedy's neck. This allowed the Warren Commission to state that a single bullet from behind had struck Kennedy in the neck, exited through his throat, and then wounded Governor John Connally, who had been seated in front of the President.

This alteration was directed by Congressman Gerald R. Ford, and he eventually admitted it, but not until July 3, 1997. On that day, he explained to a reporter from the *New York Times* in a telephone interview that "the change was intended to clarify meaning, not alter history."[133]

What the *New York Times* called "a key change in Kennedy's death report" did alter history. It changed the number of bullets supposedly fired at the Presidential motorcade and the location of wounds. This made it possible for the Warren Commission to ignore evidence that Kennedy had been shot from at least two different directions, in which case Oswald, deemed the sole assassin, had not acted alone.

Ford's alteration may have also changed Presidential history. When Vice-President Spiro Agnew resigned in 1973, President Richard Nixon appointed Ford to replace him. In less than a year, Nixon would resign because of the Watergate scandal, and Ford would replace him as President of the United States. Ford's presidential pardon kept Nixon from facing a trial and possible imprisonment.

Only three years earlier, most of America had been singing along with Lynn Anderson as she warbled "I never promised you a rose garden." In 1974, some of them may have wondered whether in 1964 Ford had been promised "the Rose Garden" in exchange for altering the location of a vital wound on the body of President Kennedy. His change benefitted the Warren Commission, and possibly his own political career. However, like so many others, Ford kept this detail to himself for as long as possible.

There is no doubt that Attorney General Robert F. Kennedy kept important information to himself throughout his brother's administration. There is no reason to think he would be more forthcoming concerning his brother's death. According to an individual who worked as a personal assistant for the entire Kennedy family, Robert Kennedy was given a bullet from his brother's body— evidence that certainly should have been in the possession of authorities. In keeping with the Kennedy family's determination to reveal only what flattered them, it was the Attorney General's responsibility to keep the public unaware of information concerning the President's health issues. A typical autopsy would have revealed that Kennedy, his family, and his doctors had all lied to the American public about his health. But secrets about the President's health and his autopsy were just the tip of the iceberg. Just as important were secrets about his death and why it had occurred.

CHAPTER 10
VOICES OF WITNESSES UNKNOWN
NOVEMBER 22, 1963

"Over the phone, I heard my wife cry,
'I have had two calls saying if your husband doesn't shut his mouth,
you and your kids are dead!' "—Jerry Coley

Almost immediately after the President's assassination, certain people learned that discrepancies in the official story were not to be discussed. Connie Kritzberg, James Tague, Jerry Coley, and Jim Huggins were just four of the many individuals whose stories did not surface until after the Warren Report was safely in the hands of the American people.

Kritzberg, a reporter for the *Dallas Times Herald*, discovered right after the assassination that something was rotten in the state of Texas and especially in the city of Dallas. Kritzberg had spent the afternoon of November 22, interviewing witnesses such as Jean Hill and Mary Moorman. In a telephone interview, Kritzberg recalled that she had been fortunate enough to be available at the offices of the newspaper when one of the doctors from Parkland Hospital telephoned. Dr. Malcolm Perry and Dr. Kemp Clark had both worked frantically hours earlier to try to save President Kennedy's life. Now they wanted to discuss their efforts with a reporter. Kritzberg was more than happy to interview the two men.

In the article she wrote immediately after her conversation with the two doctors, she reported that Dr. Perry had repeatedly described the wound in the President's throat as an "entrance wound" below his Adam's apple. Dr. Clark described the President's head wound as being on the right rear side. Both doctors agreed there were two wounds. Kritzberg realized on November 23 that someone had added a sentence to her story. The sentence read, "A doctor admitted that it was possible there was only *one* wound." Kritzberg knew she had not written that statement and that neither doctor had suggested such a thing. With a typical reporter's outrage, she phoned her newspaper and demanded to know who had inserted this extra statement. An assistant editor answered promptly, "The FBI."[134]

Kritzberg was one of the first of many to realize that less than 24 hours after the President's murder, the FBI was already interfering with stories written by local reporters. For some reason, it was already important for the public to assume that all the President's wounds were caused by one bullet. That story would eventually change again and again as new evidence about the President's wounds, Governor Connally's wounds, and the wounds of a nearby spectator were discovered.

Eyewitness James Tague was observing the motorcade from the southside of Dealey Plaza between Main Street and Commerce Street near the triple underpass. He was slightly wounded by a piece of concrete that flew up and pierced his cheek during the shooting. Deputy Sheriff Buddy Walthers ventured over to Tague and noticed blood on his cheek. The two men looked at the curb and observed a scar on the curb, proof that at least one bullet had missed its target. The result was an injured bystander and a change to the original story concerning the number of shots fired at the President. Because Tague came forward with the information, Arlen Specter had to ultimately create the "single bullet theory" concerning the number of shots fired that day even though a forensic examination of Kennedy's clothing contradicted it.

Tague may not have been the only spectator injured that day in Dealey Plaza. According to Jerry Coley, who worked for the *Dallas Morning News* in advertising in 1963, after the assassination he spotted a large pool of blood on the top step of the concrete stairs between the pergola and the grassy knoll. Coley and another newspaper employee, Charlie Mulkey, had been standing on the west side of Houston Street as the President's motorcade passed. Ironically, early that morning, Coley had eaten breakfast with Jack Ruby, who would soon become notorious. However, at 12:30 p.m. on November 22, Coley had no idea that he would be dragged into the mystery that surrounded President Kennedy's death.

The first unusual event Coley witnessed that day on Houston Street was a man who appeared to be having an epileptic seizure. Coley remembers that the man fell to the ground, "and began squirming around on his back."[135] Coley had no idea who called an ambulance, but one soon appeared and removed the incapacitated spectator shortly before the presidential motorcade arrived.

Coley waited anxiously as the motorcade turned onto Houston Street and passed directly in front of him. He remembers the gunfire that soon erupted as making "an echoing noise" in Dealey Plaza. Like so many others, Coley and Mulkey did not run towards the Depository; they ran towards the picket fence behind a grassy knoll west of the Depository. The two men got as far as the fence when they were stopped by a man who appeared to be a member of law enforcement. Even at eighty-five, Coley still remembered this encounter.

"He was wearing a brownish uniform and had a shotgun. He had a typical policeman's hat on," Coley recalled. At the time, Coley assumed the man was a sheriff's deputy or what was commonly called a "county mountie."

"What do you think you're doing?" the man demanded of Coley and Mulkey, and before they could answer, he added, "Get out of here!" Coley could see that some people were already behind the fence and that others were looking at the railroad tracks behind the Depository, but he did not argue. As he turned to walk away from the grassy area, he noticed a reddish-brown circle on the sidewalk leading towards the picket fence. His first thought was that he was seeing a large pool of blood. As much as he would have liked to have taken a closer look, he was not about to antagonize the man who had ordered him away from the area. After all, he could not even claim to be a reporter; he just worked in the newspaper's advertising department.

"I hotfooted it back to the *News*; I thought, 'They'll know what's going on,'" Coley remembers. When he reached the advertising department, there sat the man he had eaten breakfast with. Jack Ruby was not a friend of Jerry Coley's, but Coley was familiar with him because Ruby advertised with the *News*. It dawned on Coley that Ruby had been sitting in this same chair before Coley had left to watch the motorcade. Coley announced that the President had been shot, and he particularly remembered Ruby's reaction.

"He jumped out and looked out of the window towards the Depository," Coley told the authors. "He began crying. Then he grabbed a telephone and called someone. He was talking excitedly and crying at the same time." Coley admitted he did not pay much attention to Ruby's reaction at the time because he was focused on finding a photographer to take a photo of the pool of blood he had just seen. Nevertheless, Ruby's reaction was an odd one, even to Coley, because that morning the night club owner had not even mentioned the President's visit to Dallas.

Coley located Jim Hood, one of the newspaper's photographers, and led him back to what became known as "the grassy knoll" area. The man who had chased Coley away was no longer present, so the two men had time to examine what Coley had assumed was blood. Hood looked closely at the stain on the concrete.

Realizing how unusal his next comment might sound, Coley prefaced it by saying, "Remember, this was a long time ago," before he added, "Jim stuck his pinkie into it, tasted it, and commented, 'It's blood alright.' You know, people didn't worry about getting contaminated back then," Coley explained. Hood then took a photo of the pool of blood, and the two men returned to the newspaper office.

There, Coley shared the story about the blood with two of his supervisors. It was not until after Sunday, November 24, that he also mentioned having eaten breakfast Friday morning with Jack Ruby. That little detail had not been important until Ruby killed Oswald. Then a small article appeared in one of the Monday editions put out by the *Dallas Morning News*. The article referred to Jerry Coley as "Coley of the *Dallas Morning News*," and it mentioned that he had seen Ruby on the morning of November 22, 1963.

While most of America was watching the President's funeral on Monday, November 25, Coley and Hood were back at Dealey Plaza. They had decided to take another look at the pool of blood. To their surprise, there was no visible proof that the blood had ever been there. Sometime between the afternoon of November 22, and the morning of November 25, all signs of a pool of blood had been eradicated. Hood had enough experience with photographic chemicals to understand what befuddled Coley.

"Jerry, it takes a strong chemical to remove that," he explained. "But with a strong enough chemical, you can take it off in a matter of seconds." What the two men did not understand was why this particular pool of blood was so important that it be erased so quickly.

On Tuesday, November 26, two men carrying green identification cards and claiming to be from the FBI approached Coley at work. They flashed their cards, but it was clear from their first question that they did not know which employee was named Jerry Coley.

"Are you Coley from the *News*? The one in the article about Ruby?" they demanded. Before admitting this, Coley excused himself and asked his supervisor to verify the identities of these two men. He wanted to make sure they were really from the FBI before he spoke with them. After a few minutes with the agents, Coley's supervisor assured him they were actually FBI agents, so Coley led them into a small office. He answered their questions about his breakfast with Ruby, and when they seemed satisfied, he decided to ask them a question.

"I would like to ask you a question," he ventured. The agents bluntly explained that *they* were the ones who asked the questions…that is, until they heard him ask about "a pool of blood." Suddenly, they were quite interested, and Coley found himself providing minute details about what he and Hood had seen. The agents were especially interested in the fact that Hood had taken a photograph of the blood stain.

In a matter of moments, Hood was summoned, and the agents demanded the one print and negative Hood had produced. As the two agents left, one turned to Coley and Hood to make a final point.

"Boys, if you know what I mean, this conversation never took place!" Coley and Hood both understood what the agent meant. They both had wives and children, and, frankly, the seriousness of the agent's voice frightened them. Coley was about to become even more frightened.

While he was being interrogated by FBI agents, his wife was trying frantically to reach him by phone. When Coley was finally able to return her calls, he learned why.

"You've got to come home," Coley heard his wife cry desperately. "I have had two calls saying if your husband doesn't shut his mouth, you and your kids are dead!" Coley assumed that the threats were the results of the small article in the newspaper that mentioned his breakfast with Jack Ruby. However, he could not think of anything Ruby had said that would cause anyone to threaten his family. He wondered if someone was upset because Coley had described Ruby as "calm" and "unconcerned about the President's visit."

Coley realized that his two FBI questioners had not previously known about his discovery of the pool of blood. Their reactions proved that. Perhaps the telephone calls to his wife had come from someone not connected to law enforcement. Perhaps someone had seen Coley examining the blood on November 22, 1963, and watched Hood take the photograph of it. Was that the information Coley and Hood were expected to keep secret?

Despite their confusion, the two men agreed that their families' lives were more important than any information they had to offer about the day Kennedy died, so neither discussed the incident. Finally, in the 1980s, the producers of a television program titled *Unsolved Mysteries* approached Coley about his breakfast with Ruby on the morning of November 22, 1963. Television personnel spent a few days filming Coley as he discussed talking to Ruby that November morning. Obviously, they had no idea he had an even more intriguing story to tell.

"I'm going to talk about the blood," Coley told his wife, and even though she had misgivings, he shared with the producers the fascinating tale of an eighteen-inch pool of fresh blood that had appeared, and then disappeared, near the grassy knoll of Dealey Plaza.

"The guys from NBC just flipped out," Coley chuckled as he recalled their excitement. "They stayed to film an extra day. They went to the exact spot in Dealey Plaza, and their last words to me were, 'We'll call you and tell you when this will air!'" There was a long pause before Coley continued.

"Three days later, they called and said they would not be airing the part about the blood because there was no way to corroborate my story." Photographer Jim Hood had died in what Coley described as a "mysterious airplane crash," and the two newspaper executives who had known about the blood, Merle and Osmond, were also dead.

Even so, Coley is philosophical about those who doubt his story. When he speaks at clubs and organizations, the response is nearly always positive. In fact, the only negative comments he has ever received were from some members of the Dallas Petroleum Club. They seemed to question his veracity.

Coley's story, which at one time was verified by photographer Jim Hood, Coley's supervisors at the Dallas Morning News, and two FBI agents, raises more questions about the top-notch "investigation" that supposedly took place following the President's death. Neither the photo nor the negative showing the pool of blood were ever returned to Hood, and they were not mentioned in the Warren Report.

What Coley and Hood never knew was that another assassination witness also spotted the pool of blood on the concrete path. Jean Hill "saw what she thought to be blood near the knoll's concrete path and she thought someone had wounded a culprit."[136] She was later convinced by authorities that she had seen nothing more than soda pop. This is why she did not mention this important detail to author Bill Sloan for his book, *The Last Dissenting Witness*.

Texas Senator Ralph Yarborough, who had been riding only two cars behind the President's, made a startling comment to reporter Mike Quinn as the two men stood at Parkland Hospital awaiting news on Kennedy's condition. He told Quinn, "When the fatal shots were fired, Secret Service men fired back at the building with a submachine gun. I could smell the smoke all the way to the hospital."[137]

On the day the President was buried, Coley and Hood realized what reporter Connie Kritzberg had discovered two days before: The FBI was already attempting to control and conceal any evidence of a *conspiracy*. Some of that evidence was not discovered until years after Kennedy's murder.

It wasn't until 1975 that Tom Johnson, the publisher of the *Dallas Times Herald*, the same paper that Kritzberg had worked for, discovered that FBI agents in Dallas in 1963 had helped orchestrate a "cover-up" of what was actually known about the President's accused assassin, Lee Harvey Oswald." Johnson discovered that in 1963, FBI agent James Hosty destroyed a threatening handwritten note from Lee Harvey Oswald. The Dallas FBI had hidden information about the note and Oswald's visit to the Dallas FBI office."[138] Obviously, this would have come as no surprise to Connie Kritzberg.

A cover-up could not have been a surprise to the President's family, either. Their *need* for both power *and* secrecy tied their hands and prevented America and the world from knowing the full truth about the assassination of

John F. Kennedy. The very family members and friends who should have been demanding an honest, thorough investigation were forced to support the Warren Report because they could not admit that so much of what they had told their fellow Americans had been untrue. They allowed those who knew the truth about the assassination to bury it with the President's body, and they hoped that the secrets they had all protected for so long would stay buried.

Researcher Christopher Fulton would probably argue with the word "allowed." He claimed in his memoir *The Inheritance* that Robert Kennedy *instigated* the disappearance of valuable assassination evidence by hiding it in President Kennedy's coffin, but that this was done to keep government agencies from eradicating it.[139] Regardless, it was buried just like the truth!

II
THE SHADOWS
OF AMBITION

What all politicians have in common is ambition, but not every politician has been willing to circumvent the law to reach his or her goal. A lifetime of ambition drove both John Kennedy and Lyndon Johnson to the point that they were willing to sacrifice ethics and morals to reach the Oval Office. Richard Nixon was also known for being extremely ambitious; he never hid the fact that he wanted the presidency, just as Lyndon Johnson did. When asked to explain the difference between himself and Johnson, Nixon responded, "I wasn't willing to kill for it."[140]

CHAPTER 11

THE VOICE OF ROBERT T. DAVIS

"...the biggest whitewash I've ever seen!"

Robert T. ("Sonny") Davis was the assistant Attorney General of Texas in 1963. Attorney General Waggoner Carr assigned him to assist with the Warren Commission interrogations in Dallas. Davis understood ambition and that John F. Kennedy was driven by it. However, he could not have known just how driven Kennedy was because that was one of many family secrets. The desire for power was ingrained in John Kennedy by both of his parents. His father blatantly pushed all his children to succeed. Kennedy's sister Eunice summed up the most important lesson her father ever taught his children. "The thing he always kept telling us was that coming in second was just no good. The important thing was to win—don't come in second or third. That doesn't count, but win, win, win."[141] However, a comment by the President to his mother indicates that he also felt pressured by her.

A friend of Kennedy's recalled a day at the Kennedys' Palm Beach house when the President's mother said sympathetically to her son, "Oh, baby, I just hate the idea of your having to go [to Washington]." The President's immediate response was: "If you hadn't pushed me to be a success, I could stay here."[142]

Once Kennedy had reached the epitome of power in America, he could not bear the thought of losing it. What became evident during the investigation of his assassination is that the former President's reputation and legacy were more important than the truth. Even more than fifty years later, Davis had no problem recalling how disillusioned he had been by the Warren Commission's so-called "investigation."

A few months after the Commission officially began its inquiries, Davis stormed into Carr's Austin office. Anger seethed through every inch of his lanky six-foot-four frame. Eyes that normally twinkled flashed as he gritted his teeth. "Waggoner," he sputtered, "it's the biggest whitewash I've ever seen!"[143]

Davis had assumed that the members of the commission would use every investigative agency and tool available to discover who had killed John F. Kennedy and why.

Originally, Carr had planned on the investigation taking place in Texas. After all, the assassination had taken place in Texas and, by all rights, it should have been investigated there. However, even after Carr had announced to news reporters that Texas officials would launch its own investigation, he was told by his fellow Texan, President Lyndon Johnson, to step aside. Powerful Washington insiders apparently did not trust Texans to investigate Kennedy's death. Perhaps Carr should have been grateful that he was even allowed to send a representative to assist the Commission.

Davis arrived in Dallas on March 24, 1964 eager to assist the attorneys who were questioning witnesses. It was no secret that the Commission had deliberately waited before actually beginning its investigation. It was important that the trial of Jack Ruby, the man who had killed the President's accused assassin, be completed before the Warren investigation began. The commissioners did not want their investigation to taint Ruby's trial. But what Davis did not realize was that certain decisions about the Warren investigation had already been made.

Deputy United States Attorney General Nicholas Katzenbach sent a memo on November 25, 1963 to President Johnson's aide, Bill Moyers, stating, "The public must be satisfied that Oswald was the assassin; that he did not have confederates who were still at large; and that the evidence was such that he would have been convicted at trial."[144]

It is especially important to note that Katzenbach's priorities were expressed less than *three* days after the President's death. Even if Oswald had confessed to the crime, this memo would have been unusual. Because the accused assassin consistently maintained his innocence, the memo is even more disturbing, having been sent twenty-four hours after the murder of Oswald himself. Another disquieting red flag? The memo originated from the Attorney General's office. If anyone in the United States should have wanted to discover every piece of evidence about the assassination, it should have been the brother of the late President.

If Davis had known about Katzenbach's memo, he might have returned to Austin even sooner than he did. After all, if it had already been decided that Oswald was the lone assassin, why was the Warren Commission even created? Perhaps its real purpose was to reassure the American public that the lone assassin, actinbg solely on his own, had been captured, and America was safe again. The Commission could thus be used to completely control a so-called "investigation" so that inconvenient facts would be ignored, altered, or hidden.

Davis explained to Carr that all the information given to the Commission had come from the FBI and its director, J. Edgar Hoover. It was common knowledge in Washington that Hoover and Lyndon Johnson were long-time political allies, and often did favors for one another. Johnson's wife Lady Bird indicated this after the deaths of Hoover and her husband. She had written gushingly of Hoover while he was alive, but proved to be more reserved in 1988.

"I wouldn't," she said, "consider him [Hoover] a friend of ours."[145]

One reason President Johnson may have placed the investigation of the assassination in the hands of the FBI was the agency's stellar reputation. Another reason was that he may have wanted to make sure no one could accuse him of controlling an investigation of a murder that had taken place in his home state of Texas. A third reason could be that he knew he could control Hoover and the FBI better than he could control an independent investigation in Texas. Regardless, the FBI made sure that no witnesses ever reached the Commissioners until they had already been interrogated by its agency. If the FBI deemed a witness unreliable or unimportant, the Commissioners never learned of his/her existence.

All official investigating was done by FBI agents; there was no money to pay independent investigators to assist the Commissioners. The members admittedly felt pressured to produce a report in a shockingly short amount of time. An investigation that did not really begin until early 1964 was due to President Lyndon Johnson by June 1, 1964.

"Besides being under pressure to produce a report at a specified time for Lyndon Johnson, the Warren Commission had to contend with Hoover's tactics, which included delaying the delivery of documents and other evidence and then, as the deadline approached, deluging the Commission with materials, knowing the staff wouldn't have the time to adequately examine everything."[146] Obviously, Hoover, for whatever reason, was controlling the flow of information to the Warren Commission.

As Carr's representative on the Commission, Davis could see and hear things that others would never know about. He soon realized that the investigation was *not* an independent one, and he convinced Carr of that, too. In an interview, he described observing depositions being taken by various attorneys. But the entire investigation focused on only four areas: motive, Dallas Police Department activities, medical aspects, and the activities of Lee Harvey Oswald *in 1963*. The committee was not supposed to investigate Oswald's activities *before* 1963 even though the whole world now knew that he had defected to Russia in 1959. No other possible assassin or assassins were investigated, and only certain witnesses were questioned.

"Most of the questions asked of these witnesses in Dallas stemmed from information already contained in FBI statements."[147] Davis wondered then why there was not more interest in uncovering facts the FBI didn't *already* know, and was still outraged about that in 2014 when we interviewed him. "They took the limo out of Texas and wouldn't let us see it," he complained. "Wouldn't do the autopsy in Texas. I told the Warren Commission, 'You need to get some Mafioso involved to find out their role in the assassination' and they said, 'No, Jack Ruby was the Mafia's representative in Dallas.'"[148]

Looking directly at the authors, Davis shook his head, still confused because the Commission had admitted knowing about Ruby's Mafia connections. Nevertheless, it had refused to thoroughly examine his connection to underworld figures, both in and out of Dallas.

Davis was particularly disgusted that the hands of everyone involved in the investigation seemed to be tied. After observing depositions and various investigators, he reported back to Carr, "By three months, most of the work was over and Lyndon was running everything anyway." Davis realized all information had been filtered through Hoover and Johnson. Most witnesses were not questioned by the seven illustrious Commission members; they were questioned by junior attorneys and clerks. Some of the techniques used by various Commission attorneys were unorthodox. Answers were left hanging, questions went unanswered, and appropriate follow-up questions were not asked.

Davis realized from his legal experience that this lack of thoroughness and incompetence was not typical in other legal investigations. In fact, he described the entire investigation as "lackadaisical." But the word "whitewash" was a better description of what he had witnessed. Oddly enough, *Whitewash* by Harold Weisberg became the title of one of the first books to question the findings of the Warren Commission.

Davis was not the only person to suspect that the Warren Commission had been created to control which facts the world would be privy to and which would be hidden for at least 75 years. Waggoner Carr trusted Davis' opinion. But despite his own misgivings about the investigation, Carr officially supported its findings, just as many others did, according to Davis, "because he needed Lyndon Johnson's political support in Texas." This, in itself, is evidence of who controlled the Warren Commission. In fact, as Davis recounted, there was a rumor floating around the Commission at the time that Arlen Specter, an attorney who worked closely with the Commission, was told by President Johnson, "You play ball with me, I'll put you in the U.S. Senate," and, eventually, Arlen Specter *was* elected to the U.S. Senate. Specter's name is well-known to researchers because he ignored crucial evidence and created a theory of how President Kennedy and Governor Connally were wounded by a single bullet.

Waggoner Carr felt obligated to accept the Warren Report findings whether he believed them or not. The bottom line was, he was as ambitious as any other politician and wanted to remain in his position of power. Surprisingly, even though Hoover and the Warren Commission had taken the investigation out of his hands, Carr was still leading his own "off the record" investigation. However, he never used any of the information he discovered for it. Carr's political ambitions kept him from revealing everything he and his investigators learned.

Davis' comments about Carr prompted him to discuss politics in general. Eventually, Davis decided that the Democratic Party was too liberal for his taste. So, he became a Republican and was pleased when the former Democratic Governor of Texas, John Connally, did likewise. Davis chuckled as he recalled the first political advice he had ever received from anyone. "My grandfather always told me, 'Sonny, don't ever sit close to a Democrat. They carry disease!'" Davis had apparently avoided the disease, but he couldn't avoid the fact that, in his opinion, the Democratic Party had changed. Some historians have suggested that the change in the Democratic Party began with the politically-controlled investigation of Kennedy's death.

Davis confessed that he had been severely disappointed because his assessment of the Warren Commission was officially ignored by Waggoner Carr. But, he admitted, his political experience did give him an inside view of Lyndon Johnson and how he operated. Years later, when in his early eighties, Davis announced loudly in an Austin restaurant that "Lyndon was the biggest damn crook you ever saw. But when Lyndon's people do something, you're not going to find any fingerprints."

As an example, Davis explained, "Lyndon controlled the Federal Communication Commission for years. He had a monopoly going with that radio station he owned in Austin." He paused to take a breath. Then, in his booming voice, he continued, "Lyndon was ruthless. But that damned 'Vulture Bird' was even worse. She just hid it better!'"

In Austin, Texas not everyone had the courage to refer to former First Lady Lady Bird Johnson as "Vulture Bird." But having worked in the Attorney General's office, Davis had access to statements and information that others did not. He knew people like Barr McClellan, who had exposed the dark side of Lyndon Johnson in his book *Blood, Money and Power*. Davis felt that McClellan expanded on what Texas author J. Evetts Haley had already shown about Johnson. Like Haley, McClellan claimed that Lyndon Johnson was behind Kennedy's death.

Kennedy's murder was just one more in a long line of mysterious deaths that Haley attributed to Johnson in his 1964 book *A Texan Looks at Lyndon*. Davis spoke with Barr McClellan a month after McClellan's book was published. Despite its incendiary accusations, Haley lived a long, full life, quite to Davis' surprise. "I told Barr, 'I would get in the Witness Protection Plan if I were you!'" But Davis agreed that everything McClellan had written was true, which would probably explain why he worried about McClellan's safety.

After Waggoner Carr's retirement from politics, he apparently had a change of heart about the "facts" that he had supported in the Warren Commission. He wrote a letter to Texas Senator Lloyd Bentsen stating,"I strongly urge the Senate of the United States, through a proper committee such as the Senate Intelligence Committee, to conduct a *thorough, independent,* and *public* investigation to determine the truth of (1) whether Oswald was connected in some way with the FBI or CIA, and (2) whether the FBI and/or CIA, and/or Secret Service had advance information that Oswald was a threat to the life of the President, yet, for whatever reasons, failed to protect the President from that known threat."[149] Without directly stating so, Carr was assuming the fact that the Warren Report was *not* thorough, independent, or fully forthcoming. But that did not change the fact that in 1964 he put his seal of approval on it and allowed the truth to remain in the shadows.

On a rainy morning in 2014, Davis sipped his coffee thoughtfully as he continued to reminisce. "I had gotten to like Kennedy. He wasn't as liberal as people said, and he was smart."[150] Davis had also grown close to Governor John Connally, though Connally was known as "Johnson's boy." The more he got to know Connally, the more he realized how conservative he was. In late 1963, Davis realized that Connally and Vice-President Johnson were not as close as they had once been. He also knew J. Edgar Hoover was "under Lyndon Johnson's thumb." Perhaps Davis understood that Johnson had as much blackmail information on various individuals as Hoover did.

Davis seemed intrigued by this question from the authors: Was Connally's death a planned part of the Kennedy assassination? Finally, rather than answer, he just raised his eyebrows and looked away. When asked who he thought had caused the death of the President, he answered seriously, "My personal thought is that LBJ got the Mafia to kill Kennedy, and anyone connected with the assassination was killed, too."

Davis was still bothered, even then, by the fact that Texas officials had not been allowed to discover the truth about the assassination and that Waggoner Carr had not stood up to Lyndon Johnson. A weary look spread over his handsome face, and he simply shrugged and said, "Politics is politics."

Davis died one year after our interview.

CHAPTER 12

THE VOICE OF GEORGE DAY

"Everyone does it. It's only politics."

Like most politicians, John F. Kennedy and Lyndon B. Johnson were surrounded by associates who ignored the two men's flaws and supported their political ambitions. The higher these two men climbed, the higher their supporters rose also. George Day, a Brownwood, Texas attorney, was heavily involved with local and state political machines from the 1950s through the 1970s. He and his friend, Groner Pitts, one of Brownwood's morticians, were campaign managers for John Connally when Connally ran for Governor of Texas in 1963. He was also good friends with Texas Speaker of the House Jim Wright and with President Lyndon Johnson's right-hand man, Cliff Carter. Day knew and rubbed elbows with major and minor Texas politicians, including Dallas assistant District Attorney Bill Alexander, and they gave him an insider's view of Texas politics.

In the spring of 2014, Day welcomed the authors to the small office in his Brownwood home, which was decorated with Texas A&M memorabilia and a large portrait of his deceased daughter. The conversation turned to political dirty tricks that always seem to pop up in politics. Day simply shrugged at the words "dirty dealings." He indicated that he knew first-hand about the way politicians got what they wanted. His attitude changed, however, when Lyndon Johnson's name was mentioned. Asked about serious accusations made by some authors against Johnson, Day responded indignantly that LBJ had never been involved in any killings.

"Where did you read that?" he demanded, but he had little to say when the authors rattled off a list of titles,[151] including J. Evetts Haley's *A Texan Looks at Lyndon*; Barr McClellan's *Blood, Money and Power;* Phil Nelson's *LBJ: Mastermind of the Kennedy Assassination* and *LBJ: From Mastermind to "The Colossus";* and Roger Stone's *Lyndon Johnson: The Man Who Killed Kennedy*. Ignoring these titles, Day once again demanded, "Who did they say Lyndon killed?" By now Day's face had reddened and his blood pressure was, undoubtedly, higher than it should have been.

Rather than mention President Kennedy's name, the authors ventured, "Well, what about Henry Marshall, the Texas Agriculture Adjustment agent?

And what about Texas Ranger Clint Peoples?" These two names silenced him immediately, and for a moment he simply stared across the desk. Perhaps his reaction was based partly upon the fact that Day's own deceased brother James, an English professor at the University of Texas at El Paso, had written a well-received biography on Clint Peoples which discussed his mysterious death. After that, any comments about other unscrupulous political activities brought nothing more from George Day than the comments, "Politics is politics" and "Everyone does it. It's only politics." There was no more mention of Johnson's connections to any untimely deaths.

Part of "Politics is politics" in Dallas, in Brownwood, and in many other places included entertaining visiting state officials and, according to Day, one of the favorite types of entertainment for many officials at the time were parties featuring lovely young women. Groner Pitts would lose his mortician's face when he collected "live party girls" for the Law Association socials.

"You know," Day snickered, "boys will be boys." He added, "Well, you know, Cliff Carter is the one who had me reserve rooms at various hotels so that young women could be invited to entertain the politicians." The girls may not have known that Carter was closely associated with Lyndon Johnson, but everyone else did. If Day was too busy to accommodate Carter, his best friend, Groner Pitts, would assist with room arrangements.

Brownwood was not close enough to the infamous "Chicken Ranch" (the subject of the motion picture *The Best Little Whorehouse in Texas*) to be used to "entertain" visiting officials, so when politicians arrived in this small town near Abilene, the "entertainment" was brought to them.

According to Day, Groner Pitts would bring in empty railroad boxcars and place them around the shores of Lake Brownwood. Rather than use lake cabins, Cliff Carter hosted parties for the visiting officials in these boxcars. One of the most sought-after attractions for such parties was the famous Texas stripper "Candy Barr." Most of the politicians knew Barr only as a beautiful dancer and stripper. Few of them knew or cared about the story of her tragic life. Even fewer knew she might have been involved with individuals connected to the Kennedy assassination.

Though born Juanita Slusher, it was as "Candy Barr" that she first gained fame, and from time to time, even fortune. What she experienced while dancing under her stage name ran the gamut from A to Z. At times, she drove a new Cadillac; other times, she borrowed money so she could eat. She was used and abused by most of the men she ever knew, including police officers, gangsters, and politicians. In Dallas, she appeared on the arm of R. D. Matthews, a man born in Aspermont, Texas who eventually became close to Louisiana's godfather, Carlos Marcello. Barr even became involved with Mickey Cohen, the notorious Mafia boss of California, possibly through her connections to Dallas nightclub owner Jack Ruby.

As part owner of the Carousel Club in Dallas, Ruby consistently made a point of knowing as many entertainers as possible and wanted to hire Candy Barr to perform at his establishment. However, Barr danced for Ruby's competitor, Abe Weinstein, at Dallas' Colony Club. Of course, this did not mean that after her workday, she could not move on to another of Ruby's establishments, the Vegas Club, and dance for pure pleasure. And that is exactly what she did.[152]

Most of Barr's audiences would never have guessed that she had been raised in the tiny south Texan town of Edna, Texas. She escaped Edna as quickly as possible, including a step-mother who resembled Cinderella's. Drawn to big cities like Dallas and Los Angeles, she eventually discovered that the bright lights exposed sordidness and corruption. So, she moved on to smaller cities in Texas like Midland and Brownwood.

The petite blonde with the heart-shaped face and knock-out figure seemed to be too trusting, but experience eventually taught her that life was a game of chance, and too often the cards were stacked against her. In Dallas, she was forced into prostitution for a time. The same men who would gladly pay for her services would then testify falsely against her rather than admit to their wives and neighbors that they had enjoyed the company of the infamous stripper.[153]

Barr always claimed that she had been set up by the Dallas police on a drug charge in the fall of 1957; she was sentenced to fifteen years in prison for possession of a small amount of marijuana. Her explanation that she was just holding the marijuana for a friend was one the police said they had heard a thousand times.[154] No one was surprised that they did not believe her. But people were shocked by the fifteen-year prison sentence she received. Fifteen years was longer than some Texas murderers had served. Could there have been another reason officials wanted the stripper safely hidden away in prison?

Perhaps Candy Barr simply had not made friends with the right individuals. Judge Joe Brown, who would eventually serve as the magistrate in Jack Ruby's murder trial, would teach Barr another lesson about the Texas justice system. It was a well-kept secret at the time that he had asked her to pose for photos in his private chambers during her trial.[155] Barr did not have a law degree, but even she thought this was a bit unusual. If Candy Barr had any illusions about life being fair, she lost them in Dallas.

Another politician to cross paths with Candy Barr was George Day's friend, John Connally, Texas' Governor. George Day had supported Connally for Governor. Sympathetic to Barr's situation, Connally ordered her release from prison in March 1963, and in 1967 he fully pardoned her. She was fortunate to have served only three years of her fifteen-year sentence. On probation and disillusioned with big cities, she followed her closest friend, Gloria Carver, to Midland, Texas, where she met Judge Bill Morrow who, along with Connally, restored some of her faith in humanity.

Recognizing that she had a talent for writing, Judge Morrow helped her publish a small book of poems. The book, *A Gentle Mind...Confused* is difficult to find today, but the poems tell as much about Barr's feelings as any autobiography could. During the time when she and Morrow worked together, Morrow made audio tapes of Barr discussing her life. Exactly what was on these tapes and where they are now is anyone's guess.[156]

Barr's friend, Gloria Carver, married and moved to Brownwood, Texas and encouraged Barr to come to the small, picturesque town, too. Carver even allowed her friend to live in a small lake cabin that she owned. Barr, of course, remembered Brownwood from her days of dancing in boxcars for well-known politicians. Certain people in Brownwood remembered her, too. Some displayed a "forgive and forget" attitude, but others referred to her as a "$100 prostitute." This last comment was particularly insulting to Barr, who would joke that it was more like "$100 an hour."[157]

Perhaps the residents of Brownwood were unable to accept that Candy Barr was trying to live a new life under her birth name of Juanita Slusher. This meant she was no longer "available" or "for sale." According to close friends, this may be why, even in Brownwood, she was set up and almost sent back to prison for a crime she did not commit.

In 1969, Brownwood police officers searched her cabin, either without a warrant or with an improper warrant, and found a small amount of marijuana. Barr was immediately placed under arrest. It did not take long for this news to reach Dallas. One newspaper headline there read, *"Candy Barr: Last 'Queen of Burlesque' in Trouble Again."*[158] George Day, a man Barr remembered from her days of entertaining in boxcars on the banks of Lake Brownwood, was now the District Attorney who would be prosecuting her case.

Barr was terrified of returning to prison. Only her closest friends knew about the atrocities she had suffered there, including sexual favors the beautiful dancer had been forced to bestow on numerous cell mates. They understood why she was so determined to keep her freedom. She was also outraged that she had been set-up again.[159]

"I'm not going back to Goree," the Texas prison unit where she had spent three years, she said adamantly. "This is a great error, and I will fight it, and fight it until any and all things that need to be exploited are exploited, unless I am destroyed, and they will have to destroy me physically."[160]

This time the judge was sympathetic to Barr's dilemma. Judge Joe Dibrell would not allow the evidence obtained from an improper search to be used. Little did he realize that his decision would affect his future political career; he was not re-elected the following year and soon left Brownwood. He had also learned that "politics is politics."

However, thanks to him, the charges against Barr were dropped. Had the judge ruled differently, George Day would have been the prosecuting attorney who would have returned her to prison. When asked by the authors if he felt guilty about prosecuting someone who had probably been set-up, he simply shook his head and said, "No."[161] He did not volunteer any explanation for why someone in Brownwood had wanted Candy Barr back in prison. It is possible that Brownwood officials did not want Barr sharing the stories about the politicians she had met in the railroad boxcars years before.

The incident helped Barr realize that she was no longer safe living in Brownwood, so even though she had once practically sold her soul to get away from Edna, Texas, she was forced to return to a place she despised. George Day kept in contact with her because he felt her story would someday make a fascinating book. He also knew she had been close to the infamous Jack Ruby. Day was acquainted with Dallas lawyer Joe Tonahill, who had helped defend Ruby for killing Lee Harvey Oswald. In fact, Day admitted that he had suggested to Melvin Belli, Ruby's famous lead attorney, that he use an unusual defense strategy. Ruby was found guilty, but enough errors had occurred during the trial that, following appeal, he was granted a new trial and a change of venue.

According to Day, his advice led to Ruby's new trial. Besides the notoriety that Ruby's trial brought Belli, he may have represented him because he was connected to gangster Mickey Cohen, with whom Candy Barr once had an affair. It was common knowledge that Belli also represented Cohen in legal matters. What is known by only a few Brownwood insiders is that Cohen spent at least six weeks in Brownwood, Texas with girlfriend Candy Barr. However, Cohen was not her only male companion; in Dallas, she was seen on the arm of mobster R. D. Matthews.[162]

Day became privy to information that would have led to the disbarment of Tonahill if it had become public knowledge. While Ruby was sitting in a Dallas jail awaiting trial, Tonahill secretly delivered handwritten letters from Oswald's killer to Candy Barr. It is unclear why these letters were so important that Tonahill was willing to risk his career to deliver them. Perhaps Candy Barr was supposed to pass them on to her ex-boyfriend, Mickey Cohen, a man Jack Ruby revered.

Barr had always insisted that she knew Jack Ruby only as a personal friend. In fact, she considered him one of the few men who had ever been decent to her. It is true that Ruby made a specific trip to Edna, Texas not long after Barr was released from prison and placed on parole. The official reason for this visit was to deliver two registered dachshunds, a male and a female, that he encouraged Barr to breed so she would have a means of support.[163]

Though this did fulfill part of her parole requirements, it is difficult to imagine that two litters of puppies a year would have earned Barr enough income to survive.

Jack Ruby's phone records indicate that he made several calls to Edna, Texas not long before Kennedy's assassination. Perhaps he was checking on Barr's puppy business. It is also possible he was using her as a link to Mickey Cohen or other organized crime members. It has been suggested that Cohen was supposed to assist Ruby after he killed Oswald.

Shortly before Barr's death on December 30, 2005, George Day and his wife made a trip to Edna to visit her. Day was about to complete a biography he was writing on the notorious stripper. Barr, at seventy years old, still looked beautiful for her age. But abuse, prison, and prostitution had taken a toll on her health. The Brownwood attorney remembered that day in December—the last time he was ever to speak to or see the woman who would eventually be named one of Texas' most famous women.

Barr dressed up for the visit and seemed in good spirits, though her health problems were obvious. According to Day, he, his wife, and the former stripper talked and laughed and reminisced about their younger days. Barr shared a little more information with Day that he was able to use in her biography. This included a comment about the letters that Jack Ruby had written to her from his jail cell in Dallas. Barr told Day that she had burned all those letters just as soon as she received them.

She also made a point of winking when she told the couple goodbye. Day remembered that as he and his wife walked back to their car, his wife commented wryly, "You do know she was flirting with *me*, don't you?" Day, like most men, insisted the famous stripper had eyes only for him.

Juanita Slusher died not long after the visit. For whatever reason, Day did not mention in his Barr biography that he and his wife had visited her in the hospital shortly before her death,[164] or that he learned then that she had destroyed the letters connecting her to Jack Ruby. Why he omitted this final interview from his book is something that even his wife could not explain.

Slusher may have died in 2005, and "Candy Barr" years before, but her legend lives on. Part of that legend includes her connection to Jack Ruby and the Kennedy assassination. No one knows what Ruby shared with her, and no one ever will. Apparently, she learned that keeping secrets was the way to play the game of politics. Day's biography of Candy Barr was published in 2009. Unfortunately, Juanita Slusher did not live long enough to even read the manuscript.

CHAPTER 13

THE VOICE OF IRIS CAMPBELL

"I would have gone to prison for Lyndon."

Politicians and elected officials seem to surround themselves with those who supply them with plausible deniability. The names and photos of most such assistants (press secretaries, chiefs of staff, speech writers, and other aides) usually appear in newspapers and magazines at some time or another. But, there are people like Iris Campbell who assist the politicians best by quietly and anonymously blending in with the woodwork. Such individuals are the eyes and the ears of the elected official, and they can only fulfill their responsibilities by remaining invisible.

Iris Campbell was one of those "invisible" persons who observed the political machines of both John F. Kennedy and Lyndon B. Johnson. Although the media often contrasted the two policians, which the Kennedy camp encouraged, the two men and their political organizations were more alike than different. Campbell knew that both men craved power, that they had personal secrets that could be used against them, and that both men had underlings to smoothe out any "problems" these secrets might cause. As a Johnson insider, she had an unusal perspective as the lives and careers of Kennedy and Johnson intertwined and, subsequently, changed American history.

Campbell was one of those striking young women who was too smart to be a secretary or a receptionist. As a very young graduate of the University of Texas, she had an interest in politics and a desire to be close to the powerful. In her case, the most powerful person in Texas was Lyndon B. Johnson. A "yellow-dog Democrat," Campbell was fascinated by the political *process*. She was intelligent, a good conversationalist, and an even better listener. She was a quick study and loved the excitement of the political arena. She also understood what Sonny Davis and George Day both knew: "Politics is politics." Campbell quickly learned how much valuable information could be acquired by someone with an excellent memory, especially someone who knew what to remember and what to forget.

In the 1950s, Campbell became connected to Johnson through Cliff Carter. Carter was so close to Johnson that he was known as Johnson's "man in Texas." LBJ had become so powerful politically that, even as a Texas Congressman, he had his own county chairman—normally, a county chairman worked for an entire party, not for an individual.

Years after the deaths of Lyndon and Lady Bird Johnson, Campbell discussed her early exciting days in Texas politics. She was a natural politician at a time before women could be much more than aides or secretaries, even if they were really *"the power behind the throne."*[165] She admitted that she had been a "bagman" for Johnson both before and after he became president. This term meant that Campbell delivered money from donors to the candidate and his aides, but she quickly explained that this was "not illegal at that time." The future governor of Texas, John Connally, had also worked for Johnson in a similar capacity. Neither Connally nor Campbell worried about repercussions because delivering dollars from donors was so common among politicians.

Campbell did not reveal to us how much money she delivered for Lyndon Johnson and his associates, but she explained that she learned the political ropes by accompanying Carter as he travelled through every hamlet and rural town in Texas. The two of them would stop to buy gas, visit with the owner of the gas station, and then write a letter to the owner about how nicely the gas station attendant had treated them. LBJ would then write his own letter to the owner of the gas station thanking him for being so friendly to *his* representatives (Carter and Campbell). At the young age of twenty, Campbell was learning how the world of politics worked.

Campbell quickly realized how important Cliff Carter was to Lyndon Johnson. But Carter's mother either did not understand this, or she understood Johnson better than Carter did. Carter once showed his mother a beautiful pocket watch that Johnson had given him.

"Look," he said, "I got the prettiest watch from the Senator." The back of the watch was engraved with the words *Lyndon Johnson*. Carter's mother looked at the watch and sniffed, "Couldn't he have given you one that wasn't used?"[166] Cliff Carter may have been impressed with a second-hand gift that Johnson passed down to him, but his mother was not.

Iris Campbell had begun making connections with important people the day she became Cliff Carter's aide. In the small town of Campbell, Carter's wife, Mary Jane, met twenty-year-old Iris Campbell in a local beauty shop. She overheard the young woman discussing politics with a group of men and was impressed with Campbell's incisive comments. She also noticed Campbell's confident manner. Mrs. Carter did not know that Iris Campbell had begun her college career at the University of Texas at the tender age of fourteen. However, she instinctively knew that Campbell could be very helpful to her husband.

Mrs. Carter's prediction proved to be an accurate one. Cliff Carter recognized that Campbell was extremely intelligent. Under his tutelage, she became so knowledgeable about political strategy that she was able to assume all his responsibilities when he suffered a serious heart attack in 1954. She became a female "advance man." This meant she arranged the logistics for any trips that Johnson made to Texas. One of Johnson's staff members would call Campbell to report that "the Man's making a trip to Texas and you get to advance it." Advancing a trip involved a great deal of work, but Campbell was paid $450 a month, and in 1954 that made her one of the highest paid employees in Campbell. She was also one of the youngest "advance men" in the nation and certainly one of the prettiest, even if she did not think so herself. Photos of Campbell at the time show a striking brunette, but she seemed unaware of how attractive she was.

"I was never a pretty girl," Campbell explained, "but I was wholesome-looking, and I could talk, and I had so much energy." All of this made her a "people person." One of the most important facets of Campbell's personality was that she did not insist on being in the spotlight. She learned that that quality was extremely important to Lyndon Johnson. Out of the spotlight, she began to make connections with powerful people in the government and the military, and with wealthy donors who supported various candidates.

Obviously, Campbell knew that other individuals like herself existed in both parties. After all, someone had to shuffle the money from the donors to the candidates. "Everyone did this, Democrats *and* Republicans," she commented casually. Campbell greatly admired John Connally and seemed to know things about him that were not public knowledge. She lowered her voice to share with the authors that "John and Nellie [Connally's wife] were not happily married. I know that for a fact."

She elaborated that this marital unhappiness continued even after Connally's near death in Dallas in 1963. Once again, she shook her head contemptuously. "They were *not* happily married," she repeated. Eventually, she admitted that she and Connally had been involved in a two-year love affair. "Pillow talk" had convinced her that he and his wife were not the contented couple they pretended to be. Johnson had known about the affair between Connally and Campbell but had not approved, so as punishment, he assigned Campbell to assist Connally's wife when she accompanied her husband on political trips. In Campbell's eyes, this was the worst punishment Johnson could have imposed.

Another interesting tidbit that Campbell shared with us was that she had known a woman named Madeleine Brown, a Dallasite who wrote a tell-all book in 1997 about her affair with Lyndon Johnson. Campbell insisted there was no proof that Brown had ever been LBJ's mistress. According to Campbell, having mistresses was not unusual because all powerful men had mistresses and girlfriends, and this was just a fact of life. Various researchers agreed. They discovered that Johnson had affairs with women like Alice Glass, Helen G. Douglas, and numerous other women. Perhaps this explains why LBJ was unimpressed with Kennedy's romantic affairs. However, there are numerous researchers who disagree with Campbell and her doubts about Madeleine Brown. Most accept that she was his long-time mistress and that she even bore him a son.

Jan Jarboe Russell revealed in her book *Lady Bird* that Johnson even had an affair with a young woman with whom his wife, Lady Bird, had attended college. This long-term affair was also mentioned in Robert Caro's book *The Path to Power* and in Governor John Connally's book *In History's Shadow: An American Odyssey*. Because historians have recognized that Johnson, like many other powerful men, had an "official wife" and many lovers on the side, there is no real reason why Madeleine Brown's story would be considered suspect. Of course, Brown broke one of the cardinal rules of politics by daring to publicize her affair with Lyndon Johnson. After all, ladies in the South were not supposed to kiss and tell.

Iris Campbell did not work for Johnson during the early part of his career, so any stories she may have heard about like voting irregularities would have been hearsay. However, if she had had access to Johnson's FBI files, she would have realized that the FBI was quite concerned about voting irregularities in the Texas counties of Webb, Duval, Starr, Zapata, and Jim Wells. One FBI document dealt with irregularities in Webb County, particularly in Laredo. It stated that a Laredo attorney, Truman S. Phelps, advised the FBI that "the FBI could do nothing in this situation because Mr. Lyndon Johnson (U.S. Senator, D-Texas) considers Laredo his private county...If the FBI started any kind of inquiry in Laredo, Texas, Mr. Johnson would immediately have that investigation stopped...If an FBI agent talked to any official...or checked any record at the Clerk's office regarding alleged irregularities, Mr. Lyndon Johnson would be advised of this matter within six hours and would have the investigation stopped."[167]

Iris Campbell did know two of the most controversial politicians connected to Johnson. Archie and George Parr were the infamous controllers of Duvall and Jim Wells counties. In Texas beginning in the 1940s, the father and son were known for their unorthodox political maneuvers. They were decidedly corrupt, even by then-current Texas standards. The Parrs secured votes for the Democratic Party, both legally and illegally, targeting the Hispanic population in southeast Texas. They bribed them, offered them jobs, committed fraud, and stuffed ballot boxes.[168] Of course, they were not the only ones. Campbell explained what she quickly learned about Texas politics: "One party couldn't rat on the other party because they had both done illegal and unethical things."[169]

Campbell threw back her head and her red hair shook as she laughed heartily about her adventures with the Parrs. "I got so many tickets speeding through Duval county that Judge Parr got tired of seeing me in court. He was continuously scolding me for driving too fast. But that was when I was selling guns to the anti-Castro Cubans, you see," she added, as if this was something everyone did. In fact, Campbell added that in the early sixties, this was very common, almost like teenagers out for a joyride. "It was sort of the 'thing to do' back then," she chuckled. "I only did it once—for the money and because I didn't like Castro."

This fascinating woman was obviously a treasure trove of memories, and most of them involved her political escapades. Campbell explained, however, that she and certain other Johnson aides were to "fade into the woodwork and never be photographed. If your connections to Johnson became obvious, you lost your job," she added. This explains why no photos of Iris Campbell have surfaced in any books about Johnson and his administration. It also explains why photos of people like Jim Huggins do not appear in books about John or Robert Kennedy.

The same strategies that Johnson used to win his Congressional and Senatorial seats also helped John Kennedy and the Democratic Party in 1960. Despite Johnson having assured Bobby Kennedy in 1959 that he would not be a presidential candidate in 1960, he decided to toss his hat into the ring, after all. The only surprise for his staff was that he waited so long to do so. In fact, he waited too long.

Campbell worked closely with other Johnson staff members on Johnson's 1960 presidential campaign. She knew the Johnson political machine to be better organized than Kennedy's. "But they [the Kennedys] had more money, and they also had those mob connections," she said. She also admitted, "Kennedy had extraordinary charisma, but he wasn't as handsome in person as he looked in photos. He had freckles and reddish-brown hair." She laughed. "In black and white photos, the freckles didn't show, and his hair looked darker. Personally, I always thought Bobby was nicer looking than Jack."

Campbell was present during the 1960 Democratic Convention, and she remembered Johnson's frantic, last-minute drive to wrestle the presidential nomination away from John Kennedy. Gossip and rumors abounded about Kennedy, and they did not all concern politics. Campbell's eyes lit up as she related a rumor someone had shared with her. "I did hear a story about a party during the convention at Peter Lawford's beach house [in Los Angeles]." She blushed as she continued, "All I know is, I was *told* that some sort of sex game involving a chicken was played."

If Campbell knew other behind-the-scene stories about non-political activities, and chances are she did, she kept them to herself and focused on her memories of the Democratic Convention. What Johnson had not realized in July of 1960 was that John Kennedy practically had the Democratic nomination in his pocket before the convention even began.

The drama behind Kennedy's choice for vice-president was far more exciting than Kennedy's first-ballot nomination. John Kennedy's father seemed to think that Johnson would make the difference in whether Kennedy was elected or not. Johnson was caught in a Catch-22 situation when Kennedy offered him the vice-presidency. He did not want it because it was a powerless position. Everyone knew that. At first, he and his associates were outraged at the offer. "Lyndon did not want the vice-president slot in 1960," Campbell insisted, "but Sam Rayburn [the Texas-based Speaker of the House of Representatives], who had been his mentor, influenced him into taking it."

Campbell paused for a moment. "I understood," she said thoughtfully, "that Rayburn told him that if the party offered it to him, he was obligated to take it." Apparently, no one was more surprised than John F. Kennedy and his brother Bobby when Johnson accepted the position. Campbell speculated that Rayburn, one of Johnson's closest friends and allies, might have questioned whether Kennedy's health issues would keep him from completing a full term.

The same thought struck Lyndon Johnson. When asked why he had agreed to accept the vice-presidential slot, he answered, "I looked it up. One out of every four presidents has died in office. I'm a gambling man, and this is the only chance I got."[170]

According to Dallas attorney John Curington, Joe Kennedy, Sr. contacted Dallas millionaire H. L. Hunt during the 1960 Democratic Convention and asked him to convince Lyndon Johnson to accept the vice-presidential offer. Kennedy, Sr. felt that his son would not win without Johnson on the ticket. Hunt agreed to pressure Johnson, but not just because Kennedy, Sr. asked him. Curington knew that Hunt "badly wanted Lyndon Johnson in the second position—ready to step up."[171]

Regardless of why Johnson accepted the vice-presidential position, his staff, including Campbell, worked night and day to make sure a Democrat ended up in the Oval Office in 1960. As a Johnson aide, Campbell inevitably met both John and Jackie Kennedy.

Though Kennedy was known as charming and sophisticated, according to Campbell, it was Johnson who expected the women who worked for him to "act like ladies." He personally could be crude and uncouth, but the women who surrounded him could not. Campbell remembered that "he made sure we knew how to sit properly with our legs crossed. Women staff members could not even be alone in a room with a man."[172] Campbell's memory is supported by a statement in Jan Jarboe Russell's biography of Lady Bird Johnson.

Johnson's first private secretary was Mary Rather. "As he did with others, Johnson set about making Rather according to his own idea of what constituted the perfect female. He encouraged her to lose weight and bought her new clothes. He also expected her to work eighteen hours a day, to serve him drinks, to guard his door, and to befriend his wife."[173]

Though both Kennedy and Johnson were involved in extramarital affairs, people seemed more interested in Kennedy's, and rumors about them surfaced during the 1960 convention, and continued even afterward. Of course, these were closely guarded secrets, just like the details about the President's health. As a Johnson staff member, Campbell was only in the White House two or three times during the Kennedy administration. On one of these occastions, she noticed that Kennedy at times was almost physically disabled. She was probably one of the few people in America who ever saw the President walking with the aid of crutches.

Though Campbell deliberately stayed out of sight, she was able to learn important government secrets. Close friends like Walt Rostow, Kennedy's Assistant National Security Advisor, and Captain Theodore Freeman shared information with her that she passed on to Vice-President Johnson. Rostow allowed her to tour the inside of a missile silo; Freeman broke protocol by allowing her to enter top-secret hangars at Edwards Air Force Base, where highly guarded U.S. aircraft were stored. Thanks to friends like these, Campbell was able to share with Johnson certain pieces of valuable, classified information. So even though Kennedy staff members may have assumed that Johnson knew little ahead of the Cuban Missile Crisis, for example, thanks to this little-known woman, he sometimes received information before the President did.

Campbell's "adventures" are also an indication that powerful men will sometimes share very private government information with friends, especially female friends. Hence the oft-reported comments of actress Marilyn Monroe's concerning secret government information in her diary, which she learned from the Kennedy brothers, seem more plausible than they did in 1962.[174]

Campbell was quick to say that she felt fortunate to work with Cliff Carter. Carter had been a respected businessman before he began working for Johnson. Because Campbell worked so closely with him, she knew him better than most. She also knew that because of him, she had a front row seat to history, especially after Johnson became president.

She described the first months of Johnson's administration after Kennedy's assassination as "hectic." She at first had a small office in the White House. "I think my title was 'Political Organizational Coordinator.' But the White House is not as large as you would think," she told us. "*Offices* are more like cubicles, everyone can hear what everyone else is saying, and too many people are listening. Contributors would call for favors, and other people could hear our conversations. I was dealing with fundraising, so I needed some privacy."

Eventually, Johnson had Campbell's office moved to the Sam Rayburn Building. From there, she continued to work in organizational management and was also sent out of town a great deal—to make hotel arrangements for meetings, meet with donors, etc. When she was not on some Democratic politician's campaign trail, she moved from city to city, finding unimportant odd tasks to do, sometimes at military bases, just so she "could keep her ear to the ground and gather information."

Some of this information came from senators, congressmen, and other Johnson staff members. One of the most interesting characters associated with Johnson was Bobby Baker, a man who began his political career as a page boy in the Senate. In a very brief time, Baker became secretary to Lyndon Johnson, the Democratic Majority Leader of the U.S. Senate, but he was also a business associate and confidante of mobster Ben ("Bugsy") Siegel.[175] Baker was so valued by Johnson and other senators that the media referred to him as the "101st Senator."

In time, Baker's financial and political problems became Johnson's too. The man LBJ once referred as his "right arm" became a liability, at which time Johnson pretended to barely know him. As Baker said himself, "Friendship with Lyndon was a oneway street."[176] Baker was eventually found guilty of seven counts of theft, fraud, and income tax evasion and was sent to prison.

Though Johnson would not commit political suicide to get Baker out of prison, there is evidence that he controlled incriminating information about his friend. An FBI memo dated February 13, 1964, from Special Agent Rosen to Special Agent Belmont, shows that the FBI realized this. The heavily redacted memo reads: "There is attached hereto information received from the Washington Field Office that [name redacted] advised the Washington Field Office that President Lyndon B. Johnson had confiscated the Robert G. Baker file from the U. S. Department of Justice while Attorney General Robert Kennedy was on his recent peace mission trip."

The memo also stated that this information had been given to the informant by Senator John Williams of Delaware. "The informant stated that as a result of this action, the Senate Rules Committee investigating the Baker matter was at a complete standstill because it was not receiving any further information from the Justice Department." [177]

Perhaps Johnson had "helped" by removing any connections Baker had to him! It is reasonable to assume that Iris Campbell knew nothing about something this confidential. Nevertheless, she did travel as part of Johnson's staff and overheard conversations and observed activities that the public never knew about. When the authors raised the subject of Bobby Baker and the fact that he, in retaliation, could have incriminated Johnson but did not, Iris Campbell made a surprising statement. "*I* would have gone to prison for Lyndon," she said proudly.[178] Obviously, Mary Jane Carter had been correct when recommending Iris Campbell to her husband Cliff. Campbell *was* as loyal to Cliff Carter and Lyndon Johnson as Mrs. Carter had thought she would be.

An interesting point that Campbell made concerned one key development after Kennedy's assassination. Johnson not only asked many of JFK's aides to stay on, but solicited *their* advice rather than take that of his own White House staff. "That hurt so bad," she recalled, the sorrow still evident in her voice. "We didn't understand why he was treating us like this. But Cliff told me to just go on and do the job I was supposed to do and do it better than I'd ever done it before."

Campbell described Lyndon Johnson as a "pragmatist," certainly not a liberal. Part of being a pragmatist meant having a lot of derogatory information about everyone. "Lyndon knew where every single body was buried, and if he didn't, his friend J. Edgar Hoover told him. They both loved power and gossip."

By the same token, Johnson's Texas constituents must have thought he had a phenomenal memory, recalling, as he invariably did, personal but insignificant details about themselves and their families. He could do so only because staff members like Campbell kept a Rolodex of information about contributors and anyone connected to Johnson.

In receiving lines, Campbell or another staff member would stand at Johnson's elbow and whisper, "His daughter is at A&M" or "His son recently got married." When Johnson's booming voice called out, "How's that daughter of yours at A&M?" the recipient of this personal comment would float away on cloud nine, thinking "the Man" had truly remembered him and his family. This is how Johnson's political machine continued to increase financial donations and gain loyal followers. Campbell may or may not have known that the Kennedy political machine had a similar way of cataloguing supporters.

She was close enough to Johnson to realize he had many sides to his personality, and she also noticed how that personality eventually changed.

Questions about his mental stability and his erratic behavior during the last years of his administration did not surprise her at all. She nodded thoughtfully as she looked back on the last year or so of his administration.

"He reached a point where he did not trust hardly anyone. If any staff member wanted to leave his position, Lyndon took it as a personal insult." She then added, "He expected complete loyalty from others." Campbell, like Navy medic Tom Mills, *was* completely loyal—so loyal that, from time to time, she even took menial jobs on military bases because it helped her keep Johnson apprised of military information.

Campbell and staff members were not the only ones to notice a change in Johnson's personality during his final months as president. Reporters recognized his manic behavior and the fact that, like Kennedy, he was tormented by his own dark secrets. Well-known White House correspondent Helen Thomas wrote this: "Reporters spent much time psychoanalyzing Lyndon B. Johnson, especially his mania for secrecy and his feeling of inferiority which he could not overcome."[179] D. Jablow Hershman used everything ever written about Johnson to reach the conclusion that the 36th President was manic depressive.[180] If Hershman's diagnosis was correct, it explained Johnson's mood swings throughout his lifetime, his paranoia, and the fact that some people remember him fondly while others still cringe when they recall some of his behavior.

Lyndon Johnson's life-long desire for power and his constant fear of losing it might explain why numerous researchers have reached the conclusion that he either planned Kennedy's assassination, or at least played a significant role by protecting the actual murderer or murderers, and, thereby, obstructed justice. There is evidence that he was connected to illegal activities involving associates like Bobby Baker and Billie Sol Estes. The public exposure of their activities could have negatively affected him and his career—maybe even ended it.

Campbell, however, believes that Johnson's career was never truly threatened by these associates. However, she was aware of rumors that, had JFK lived, Johnson might not be his running-mate on the 1964 Democratic ticket. She smiled as she explained that Johnson's staff members already had a contingency plan in place.

"Lyndon was going to be recalled to Texas because the State and the Democratic Party needed his expertise."[181] This maneuver would have helped him save face if Kennedy had preferred a new vice-presidential candidate. Such a plan was not common knowledge at the time. However, campaign buttons reading "*Bring Back Lyndon*" had already been made and were ready for distribution before the assassination.

Another close Johnson associate also admitted that in 1963 the Vice-

President had talked of removing *himself* from the 1964 Kennedy ticket. Horace Busby recalled that Johnson had "expected to to talk with President Kennedy on Friday night, November 22, 1963 to tell him that he didn't believe he wanted to run for vice president again in 1964."[182] However, in Busby's opinion, John F. Kennedy would not have accepted his vice-president's resignation. Others, who were closer to Kennedy, believe he would have. Regardless, fate intervened, and Johnson never had to address the possibility of being replaced on the 1964 Democratic ticket.

One of the best indications that President Kennedy may have been severing his ties with Lyndon Johnson can be found in the office records of Kennedy's secretary. According to Evelyn Lincoln, in the first year of the Kennedy-Johnson administration, the two men conferred privately for a total of ten hours and nineteen minutes. Between January 1 and November 22, 1963, the private conferences totaled only one hour and fifty-three minutes.[183]

The media well knew that he was not a Kennedy confidant, and made sure the American public knew too. For example, in November 1962, comedian Jonathan Winters appeared on the *Jack Paar Show* and imitated President Kennedy. In his best Harvard accent, Winters commented on the Cuban situation, "... I tried to get Congress to go along with me ... My friend Lyndon, who I saw about a year ago..."[184] Parr buckled over in laughter. That, and the loud audience guffaws, spoke volumes. Lyndon Johnson, who had once been the powerful Senate Majority Leader, was now the butt of jokes on national television.

Not only were Americans laughing at Lyndon Johnson, they were also hearing more and more about the illegal dealings of some of his associates. Johnson publicly distanced himself from Bobby Baker and Billie Sol Estes, even after he became president. Nevertheless, Washington insiders knew how close he had been to Baker, and they also knew that Estes had been invited to Kennedy's first presidential anniversary celebration. In fact, he had been seated next to Lyndon Johnson.[185] So, it was becoming more difficult for Johnson to deny the access that these two men obviously had to him.

Although some researchers feel sure Johnson would have eventually been indicted for various illegal activities, and might have even served time in prison, Campbell does not think Johnson would have ever been indicted for anything. Perhaps she knew what eventually became apparent to the American public— Johnson associates might go to prison, but "the Man" himself would *not*. After all, there was never anything in writing.

That does not mean Lyndon Johnson was willing to "go gentle into that good night"[186] and end his career as an impotent vice-president. Very few people who knew him well thought that would happen. Some of his detractors believe that Johnson was so desperate to become president and fulfill Sam Rayburn's dreams for him that he could no longer wait for John Kennedy to die a natural death. Some have wondered why Johnson did not simply let friendly journalists reveal some of Kennedy's indiscretions. That, of course, would have wounded not only Kennedy; it would have affected his entire administration, including his vice-president *and* the Democratic party. Lyndon Johnson would have never hurt himself or his party!

It has been suggested that if Johnson had been involved in Kennedy's death, he might have arranged for the President to die of poison or from an induced heart attack. Under that scenario, a complete autopsy would have been controlled by the family, staff members, and the Secret Service (as, apparently, it eventually was) so that Kennedy's secret health issues would never be revealed. Johnson could have stepped up, and Kennedy would never have become a martyr and, therefore, the millstone which Johnson could never lose. An assassination in Johnson's home state would not have occurred, and suspicions about the Vice-President's involvement might never have arisen. For these reasons, some have argued that Lyndon Johnson did not plan or implement the plot to kill his predecessor.

Whether he was involved in the assassination or not, Johnson did use the excuse of "national security" to control the official investigation of Kennedy's death, even though he admitted to some that he did not believe Oswald was the only assassin.

During our interview of Campbell, we raised the subject of President Kennedy's fatal trip to Texas. Many reasons have been suggested for the visit to the Lone Star State. Kennedy staff members felt that the President had been maneuvered into making the political trip to Texas. The main reason was to drum up support for the 1964 re-election campaign. Another reason, according to some, was to heal a split in the Democratic Party; Governor John Connally and Senator Ralph Yarborough were political enemies, and Kennedy was determined that their disagreements would not divide the Democratic Party. For whatever reason, Vice-President Lyndon Johnson, who was close friends with Connally, had not been able to smoothe over the differences between the two men.

But this is not the way Johnson staff members remembered the situation. According to Campbell, Johnson did not particularly want Kennedy to come to Texas. In fact, he and his aides were furious that funds raised in Houston, Dallas, and Austin would help retire Yarborough's campaign debts.

"We didn't understand why we managed to pay our debts, but Ralph Yarborough didn't mind asking the President to help pay off his," she recalled, still indignant after all these years. Obviously, there were several reasons for Kennedy's trip to Texas; the most important to the President was his re-election. He certainly understood that the 1964 election could be as close as the 1960 election had been. He did not live long enough to see the headline on the December 17, 1963 issue of *LOOK* magazine, but the words would not have shocked him. The headline read: *"Preview Poll: Kennedy Could Lose."*[187] President Kennedy knew this better than anyone, so the trip to Texas was an opportunity to use his wife to garner votes.

Campbell, who was living in San Antonio at the time of Kennedy's assassination, was fortunate enough to be seated on the second row of the audience that heard the President speak at Lackland Air Force Base on November 21, 1963. She told us that, earlier in the fall of 1963, she had been approached by certain officials from Johnson's staff to help plan Kennedy's motorcade through downtown San Antonio. They knew she had been trained as an advance man by Cliff Carter, so she seemed like the logical choice.

Campbell refused the assignment because she was "horrified by the fact that they would be taking President Kennedy's motorcade downtown through all those tall [San Antonio] buildings," exactly the way they did in Dallas on November 22. "The Secret Service had let him ride down the main streets of San Antonio with all of those tall buildings. I couldn't believe it," she exclaimed. "Somehow, it just didn't seem safe." Campbell's comment about being asked to help plan Kennedy's San Antonio motorcade raises questions about whether someone else connected to Johnson helped plan the Texas motorcades instead of Campbell.

Sadly enough, her concern about tall buildings and presidential safety was a valid one. On the day of the assassination, she was waiting in San Antonio for a friend flying in from Alaska. He was to escort her to the presidential dinner in Austin that evening. After they heard the news of the assassination, he and Campbell drove frantically to Austin. Her explanation for this sudden road trip was that she had to pack clothes for Cliff Carter so he could fly with Johnson to Washington, D.C. (Carter had moved back to Austin from Washington so he could organize the Kennedy-Johnson 1964 election campaign).

According to Campbell, Carter contacted her from Parkland Hospital in Dallas. She remembered him telling her, "I want you to go to Dallas and try to get in with the Dallas police." Campbell understood that Cliff Carter's orders actually originated with Lyndon Johnson, and there was no question that she would do whatever was asked of her. That evening in Dallas, in her room at the Adolphus Hotel, the shock and adrenaline that had accompanied her all afternoon finally wore off. Suddenly, she was shaking with fright.

"If they could kill the President, they could certainly kill me," she remembered thinking. She curled up in a fetal position in the middle of the luxurious bed, sobbing uncontrollably. After all, John Connally, the man she had had a two-year love affair with, had been seriously wounded that day. She also realized that if the assassination had occurred the day before in San Antonio, and if she had agreed to help with the motorcade route, she would have felt partially responsible for Kennedy's death. And though her allegiance was to Lyndon Johnson, she had liked John Kennedy, and his death had a larger impact on her than she expected.

"So, I was in Dallas when Oswald got himself shot," she continued matter-of-factly. Stunned, the authors asked her to clarify her comment; Campbell refused to explain how Oswald "got *himself* shot." After a moment, she added, "In fact, I was upstairs on the third floor, at the police station, visiting with some police officers when it happened."

Campbell was obviously hinting at a crucial detail about Oswald's death. Oswald had used every opportunity to speak to the media, and that may be why he did not survive long enough for a trial. Most of the statements he made were ones that any innocent man would make, but perhaps he had been expected to remain silent.

Instead, he insisted, "I didn't shoot anybody. I want to get in touch with a lawyer...in New York City...I never killed anybody...I really don't know what the situation is about. Nobody has told me anything except that I am accused of murdering a policeman. I know nothing more than that, and I do request someone to come forward to give me legal assistance." When asked by reporters whether he had killed the President, Oswald had answered, "No. I have not been charged with that. In fact, nobody has said that to me yet. The first thing I heard about it was when the newspaper reporters in the hall asked me that question...I did not do it. I did not do it...I did not shoot anyone."[188]

Perhaps the mistake Oswald made was to tell reporters and the world, "I am only a patsy."[189] The term "patsy" suggested Oswald's realization that he had been framed by others. That knowledge may have led to his demise. A completely innocent man probably would have said, "You have arrested the wrong man." However, a man who knew nothing about a plot to kill the President would not have referred to himself as a "patsy." This verbal slip may have convinced the conspirators that Oswald could not be trusted to be the "fall guy." They may have also realized that he knew more than they thought he did and that, eventually, he would share this information with authorities or, at least, with his lawyers.

Oswald was not intimidated by a photo shown to him by the Dallas police in which he is holding a rifle and a pistol. Instead of cringing at the sight of himself with such incriminating "evidence," he quickly asserted:

"That picture is not mine, but the face is mine. The picture has been made by superimposing my face. The other part of the picture is not me at all, and I have never seen this picture before. I understand photography real well, and that, in time, I will be able to show you that is not my picture and that it has been made by someone else. . . . It is entirely possible that the Police Dept. has superimposed this part of the photograph over the body of someone else. . . . The Dallas Police were the culprits. . . . The small picture was reduced from the larger one, made by some persons unknown to me. . .[190]

Perhaps someone feared that Oswald could prove the photographs fake. This would have helped his defense, but it would have been a black eye for the Dallas police and the prosecution.

Still another mistake Oswald may have made concerns a telephone call he attempted to make to Raleigh, North Carolina.

On the evening of November 23, Oswald asked to make a long-distance call to Raleigh, North Carolina. The party he was trying to reach was a man named John Hurt. Switchboard operator Alveeta Treon was a witness to what happened that evening. Her supervisor, Louise Swinney, allowed two men in suits to enter the switchboard room and listen to Oswald. Oswald gave Swinney the name of the party he wished to reach and two numbers to call. The operator wrote down the information but did not place the call. However, she told Oswald, "I'm sorry. The number doesn't answer," and immediately disconnected him. The two men in suits promptly left the room, apparently satisfied that Oswald had not been able to reach out to the man named "John Hurt." Researchers discovered that a John Hurt in Raleigh was a former Special Agent in the U. S. Army Counterintelligence department, and his telephone number was available to the public in 1963.[191]

Just attempting to reach a man with a military intelligence background may have been enough to get Oswald killed. Like most Americans, he probably assumed that his phone call would be private and that no one would dare prevent him from reaching someone who might help him. After all, he wasn't in Russia anymore!

Campbell made only one or two more comments about Oswald, but she shared more memories about the assassination. She paused and seemed to think a moment before she continued discussing that weekend in Dallas. "I was the one who called the White House to tell them Oswald had been shot." It was years before New Orleans District Attorney Jim Garrison discovered that Jim Martin, the man assigned to assist Marina Oswald after her husband's death, had a private telephone line to the White House. This meant that someone close to the new President was in frequent contact with the man closest to Marina Oswald at that time. Since Iris Campbell admitted that she had been the eyes and ears of Lyndon Johnson in Dallas immediately after the assassination, it is possible that she continued this role for the first few weeks of Johnson's administration. She may have been Jim Martin's contact at the White House, and she may have worried that the others near her cubicle might overhear conversations they shouldn't have.

Because Campbell had been close to John Connally, she knew details concerning his surgery—information that was kept secret. Bill Stinson, one of John Connally's administrative assistants, had been allowed to remain in the operating room while surgeons worked on Connally. He shared private information with Campbell.

"Bill Stinson was in Connally's operating room," she explained. "He swears he heard pieces of pellets hit a pan as Connally was operated on." Dr. Robert Shaw, who operated on the Texas governor, reported that *no* fragments were removed from Connally's body. This meant that it was impossible to determine if the bullet that hit Connally had originated from Oswald's rifle or from somewhere else. There would also be no way of determining if the bullet which hit Connally had also hit the President.

But the statement that Stinson made to Campbell changes the story. As a witness in the operating room, he knew that there *were* fragments removed from the Governor's body that certainly should have been tested for trace evidence. If he knew *why* the information about the fragments was kept secret, he never told Campbell.

When asked who Lyndon Johnson thought had killed President Kennedy, Iris Campbell answered firmly, "The Mafia." It is ironic that Johnson would point a finger at organized crime because he had been the recipient of Mafia contributions himself. Mob boss Carlos Marcello of New Orleans had used his Texas bagman, John Halfen, to funnel "a percentage of Marcello's illegal Texas profits to the political campaigns of Houston Congressman Albert Thomas, Associate Justice of the Supreme Court Tom Clark, and U.S. Senator Lyndon

B. Johnson."[192] President Kennedy had honored Congressman Albert Thomas at a dinner the evening before the assassination in Houston, Texas. Less than twenty-four hours later, Thomas was photographed in Air Force One winking at his friend Lyndon Johnson as Johnson completed his oath of office.

"Of all the Texas politicans the Marcello-Halfen interests supported, the most powerful was Johnson," wrote John H. Davis. In fact, in his book *Mafia Kingfish,* he wrote that "thanks partly to the influence of Vice President Lyndon Johnson, Carlos Marcello was able to operate freely in Dallas in 1963."[193]

Later, Campbell elaborated. She personally understood that "Mafia" included not only individuals like Lucky Luciano and Sam Giancana, but also Mafia bosses who had dealings with Kennedy's father Joe Kennedy, Sr. and with the Dixie Mafia, a loosely organized group of gamblers, thieves, and hitmen scattered from New Orleans to Houston and from San Antonio to far West Texas.

Campbell made a point of stating that Johnson seldom went to Dallas. "Dallas wasn't Johnson people," she stated.[194] She meant that the majority of the voters there supported Richard Nixon for President in 1960. She explained, however, that Johnson had been in Dallas three days before the assassination; he had spoken on November 19 at the Bottlers Convention. She added that Lady Bird Johnson supported numerous Texas retailers and would fly to Dallas to shop at the exclusive Neiman-Marcus department store. Stanley Marcus, one of the original owners, would continue to dress Mrs. Johnson throughout her White House years. So, perhaps the Johnsons were more familiar with Dallas than Iris Campbell realized. Whether they were welcomed by most of the Dallas citizens is another question.

Campbell may not have known about the support that Johnson enjoyed from Carlos Marcello, but she herself believed the Mafia were involved in the Kennedy assassination only because of how "Bobby [Kennedy] had hounded them." She also thought Oswald *had been involved* in the assassination, but perhaps only as an unwitting patsy. She believed that his New Orleans connections were probably evidence that he was connected to the Mafia.

Campbell may have known what FBI officials soon learned after the assassination—Dutz Murret, Oswald's uncle by marriage and his surrogate father, was a mid-level bookie in the Marcello gambling network. Oswald's mother Marguerite "had been friendly with a New Orleans underworld figure by the name of Sam Termine, who had once served as a chauffeur and body guard to Carlos Marcello."[195] So whether Campbell had learned inside information about Oswald from the Dallas police or from those associated with LBJ, she was probably very close to the truth.

When asked if Johnson had ever worried about the Mafia killing him, too, Campbell simply waved her hand as if this was the silliest comment ever made and responded, "Oh, no."[196] With this simple answer, she reinforced the possibility that Johnson's connections *to* Carlos Marcello may have protected him *from* the Mafia.

There were certain questions about the Kennedy assassination that Campbell seemingly wished to avoid. The reason for this became apparent when the documentary *The Men Who Killed Kennedy* was shown on the History Channel on the thirtieth anniversary of Kennedy's assassination. One episode contained a black and white photograph of a small group of people sitting in a restaurant. One of the women in the photo strongly resembled the person known to the authors as "Iris Campbell." Standing behind and to the right of Campbell and smiling at the photographer was none other than the notorious Jack Ruby, the killer of Kennedy's accused assassin. Campbell had never mentioned knowing Jack Ruby.

A question about this surprising revelation caused Campbell to shake her head and quickly respond, "That wasn't me. That was a woman named Iris Cassavettes. She died a mysterious death like a lot of other people associated with the Kennedy assassination." Campbell seemed to be fumbling for an explanation, but she did admit that, even though she had not seen the documentary herself, someone else had mentioned the program to her.

"I thought I'd only told two people about working for Lyndon....," she said, her voice trailing off. "And both happened to see that documentary. I didn't think anyone would remember," she murmured. Campbell would not admit to knowing Jack Ruby even though he was easily identifiable in the photo. Other intriguing individuals were also spotlighted in the documentary. Campbell did admit to knowing a woman identified as "Lois Liggett." Liggett was the ex-wife of John Liggett. According to his ex-wife, her well-known Dallas mortician husband had been called to Parkland Hospital shortly after Kennedy's assassination. He telephoned his wife from the hospital not long afterwards and told her not to expect him home for a while. That is all he would tell her.[197]

One of the most interesting facts about John Liggett was that he was not the average mortician. He had a stellar reputation as one of the top cosmetic morticians in the nation and he was known for being able to make any corpse, no matter how disfigured, presentable. In fact, four years later in 1967, he prepared the corpse of actress Jayne Mansfield after her horrific car accident.[198]

THE LONE STAR SPEAKS

According to Lois Liggett, when her husband finally returned home the day after the assassination, he offered no explanation of where he had been or what he had been doing. If he had been preparing a corpse during that time, he refused to tell his wife about it. She did not know if he had been sworn to secrecy about his activities during those hours or if he was simply afraid to talk about his experiences. Lois Liggett never discovered where her husband had been during part of that much-remembered weekend.

However, she and her daughter Debra distinctly recalled that on that Saturday, Liggett insisted that they immediately pack their suitcases and drive to Corpus Christi, a city in South Texas. Still with no explanation, Liggett checked his family into a motel and spent that evening and the next morning watching the assassination coverage on television. Lois Liggett recalled: "The minute he saw Jack Ruby shoot Oswald, he jumped up from the bed and said, 'We can go home now.'" Once again there was no explanation for the sudden trip to South Texas or the sudden return trip to Dallas.[199]

Iris Campbell claimed not to know John Liggett, but she did seem familiar with his story. She swore that she had been misidentified in the photograph on the History Channel documentary, and that she had never met Jack Ruby. "No, I never met him," she insisted. Nevertheless, she averted her eyes when his name was mentioned, and she seemed familiar with some interesting details about him. Ruby once owned a "safe house" in Kemah, Texas, near Galveston Bay, where he supposedly stored weapons to be sent to Cuba to fight Castro, she said.

If Campbell knew more about Jack Ruby, she refused to admit it. But she did not seem to mind talking about her personal secrets—stories she had not shared even with her parents. For example, she mentioned that she knew Texas had its own version of the Mafia.

"I knew people in the Dixie Mafia," she added. "Wrecking yards and vending machine companies were usually owned by mob members because they were easy to launder money through." Campbell's memories of the Dixie Mafia reminded her of a story concerning an intriguing character well-known to assassination researchers.

"I was always getting into trouble," Campbell went on. "Why, just a few weeks after Kennedy's assassination, I was in San Antonio and a friend of mine, an extremely over-weight woman, was catering a party and she asked me to go with her to deliver the food." Her eyes widened at the memory of that night. "The minute we walked into the apartment, I recognized David Ferrie and nearly panicked. I knew I had to get out of there!"

Campbell seemed to assume that anyone who knew anything about the Kennedy assassination would know who David Ferrie was, and she was correct.

He is one of the most fascinating figures associated with the assassination, but even more fascinating is the fact that Iris Campbell knew who he was.

Almost immediately after Kennedy's death, authorities in New Orleans began looking for Ferrie. He would not have been difficult to recognize, simply because of his strange appearance. Having lost all of his body hair from alopecia, he wore inexpensive toupees and either pasted on false eyebrows or drew them on with a makeup pencil. He either had no idea how outlandish his appearance was or he chose to draw attention to himself, at least at certain times.

Ferrie had at one time been a leader in the Civil Air Patrol in Louisiana. He had also been a pilot for Eastern Airlines and even a personal pilot for Carlos Marcello. He claimed to be unfamiliar with Lee Harvey Oswald, but a photo finally surfaced which showed a teenaged Oswald standing with a small group of Civil Air Patrol members—and their leader was none other than David Ferrie.

Ferrie had been at the courthouse in New Orleans the day Kennedy was killed. He was assisting Carlos Marcello in a deportation trial that Attorney General Robert Kennedy had instigated. His travel immediately after the assassination was difficult for him to explain to FBI agents. He suddenly left New Orleans with two friends to check out a skating rink in Houston, Texas. The three drove all night through severe thunderstorms so they could do nothing more than make numerous phone calls from the Winterland Skating Rink.[200]

In December of 1963, Ferrie's name and his strange activities were unfamiliar to most of the people in the United States. Those who did know him were more apt to speak of his freakish appearance. In 1967, Ferrie was accused by Jim Garrison, the District Attorney of New Orleans, of being involved in a plot to kill President Kennedy. It is noteworthy that Iris Campbell recognized him long before Garrison brought him to the nation's attention. Campbell's explanation was, "Well, I recognized him because of those weird-looking eyebrows he had pasted on!"

She swallowed before elaborating. "Uh, I think I had seen his picture in a FBI file," she added rather lamely. "So, I made an excuse and told my friend I had to leave. I literally ran to the closest pay phone and called Lyndon's ranch. Someone put me through to him, and I said, 'Lyndon, I've been a bad girl again.' Before I could explain the situation, he told me not to worry about it. 'The FBI knows where you've been, and they know exactly what time you went in there and exactly what time you left. They have the place under surveillance,'" he assured her.

This fascinating story only raised more questions concerning why Campbell, who was "just Cliff Carter's assistant," would have been allowed to see a photo of an assassination suspect, David Ferrie, in an FBI file only weeks after the

President's assassination. The answer to this question Campbell kept to herself.

Her encounter with suspect David Ferrie wasn't the only time Iris Campbell caused problems for herself. She mentioned that she had also been part of the Sharpstown Savings and Loan scandal in the early 1970s, and that even though Johnson was no longer president, she called "The Man" for legal assistance. His "assistance" amounted to advising her to leave the state and to "not tell me where you're going."

"But, Lyndon," she protested, "I feel safer in Texas because you're here." The former president again suggested she leave the state.

"Well, I guess I could go to New Mexico," Campbell began. "I have a boyfriend there."

"I told you not to tell me where you're going," Johnson repeated firmly.

Johnson's response was not what Campbell had expected. "I am a little bitter about how I was treated," Campbell admitted. "After all, I was on the payroll and helped Lyndon. I mean, I procured prostitutes for some very powerful men. So, I guess I expected more help." She should have known "the Man" would not come to her aid. Campbell once made a simple request for a reference from Johnson so she could obtain employment as a caterer. Johnson refused her request. He informed her that the fact that she had worked for him should be reference enough.

Johnson may have refused Campbell's request, according to his Press Secretary George Reedy, partly because Johnson "had no respect for the political intelligence of any woman except his wife."[201] This may not have been the only reason Johnson refused the request. Campbell may not have realized that Johnson probably had a practical reason for refusing to put his name and signature on a reference. Always the politician, even after he was no longer President, he was still guarding information about his associates. Like a great many politicians, he never put anything in writing. He certainly would not have wanted his name on a reference for someone who had procured prostitutes for his associates.

The stories Iris Campbell has shared are probably just the tip of the iceberg. Besides her intimate knowledge of Johnson's life and his administration, the only evidence that proves she was ever associated with Lyndon B. Johnson are letters from Johnson's aide, Cliff Carter. Filed carefully in the LBJ Library, they thank her for trivial deeds like bringing a sombrero back to someone from Mexico. Campbell's eyes danced as she recalled that the "sombrero" she had brought back for a political friend of Johnson's was really a bottle of tequila with a worm in it.

If all the memories and experiences of Iris Campbell were ever published, they would make fascinating reading. However, despite living to the age of 85, she never kept copious notes, not ever wrote a memoir. At first, she said, this was because she did not want her elderly mother to know about some of her escapades. After her mother's death, Campbell said there were certain things she did not want Lady Bird Johnson to know. "I wouldn't want to hurt Lady Bird," she once explained.[202]

After Lady Bird Johnson's death, Campbell still had a good reason for staying in the shadows. "I haven't forgotten what happened to Bobby Baker's secretary," she added. Baker had been accused of accepting large amounts of campaign donations which should have been used to influence various senators; supposedly, he kept at least part of the money for himself. Campbell remembered that Nancy Carole Tyler, Baker's secretary, was killed in May 1965 in a plane crash. She also remembered that Tyler's roommate, Mary Jo Kopechne, secretary to Florida Senator George Smathers, also met an untimely death in July 1969 while a passenger in a car driven by Senator Ted Kennedy. Those events may have occurred years ago, but they were still fresh in Campbell's memory.

After Kennedy's murder, she admitted, the FBI did question her several times. She would not elaborate on why the agency was interested in her or how they even knew she existed. Agents may have wanted to know why she had been allowed to visit with Dallas police as early as November 23, 1963. Regardless, the agents left with no more information from her than they had when they found her. Her standard response to any and all of their questions was always a wide-eyed "How could *I* know anything about *that*?"

Iris Campbell was very careful about the information she shared with the authors about Johnson and his associates, even though she outlived most of them, never wrote a "kiss and tell" book, or publicized her connection to President Lyndon Johnson. The authors are the only ones who know that Vice-President Johnson sent her to his ranch during the Cuban Missile crisis. She would not elaborate on why, and if we had pressed her for more details, her response would have surely been, "Well, how could *I* know anything about *that*?"

However, Iris Campbell worked so closely with so many powerful men, and she learned how the "government" really works. She was not shocked by the dirty tricks and dealings associated with political machines, even if those dealings resulted in someone's death. She also knew how to protect herself, even if she occasionally slipped and unintentionally revealed interesting details about her life.

For example, when she identified the woman in the photo with Jack Ruby as "Iris Cassevettes," she had no explanation for how she knew someone who was to soon die "a mysterious death" or why the woman resembled her and had a name with the same initials. When the authors explained that Dallas mortician John Liggett had been seen alive by his ex-wife Lois years after officially being shot by a Dallas police officer, she interjected, "He's dead," but refused to elaborate on how she knew this.

She also would not explain why she moved to Lubbock, Texas shortly after Lois Liggett moved there or why she quickly made Liggett's acquaintance. Apparently, Campbell became close to the woman because it was Lois Liggett and her daughter Debra who identified Iris Campbell as the woman in the photo with Jack Ruby!

It would be fair to assume that "Iris Cassevettes" was an alias that Iris Campbell sometimes used, and perhaps Campbell was being quite truthful when she said Cassavettes died. If she stopped using this particular alias after the Kennedy assassination, then Cassevettes would have "died." Of course, this raises the obvious question: Why would Iris Campbell use an alias? Had she sold weapons to anti-Castro Cubans more than once? Investigative journalist Gary Cartwright discovered that Jack Ruby had been involved in gun-running; in fact, he was the "bagman" for this endeavor. Could this be why Iris Campbell was photographed with him sometime before the assassination? Would Lyndon Johnson have distanced himself from Campbell if her connection to Jack Ruby and gun-running had become known, just as LBJ lied about his connections to Bobby Baker and Billie Sol Estes?

And the most fascinating question is: As loyal as Iris Campbell was to Lyndon Johnson, would she have ever admitted, if, indeed she knew, that Johnson might have been connected to the assassination? The answer to that question died with Iris Campbell in 2016, unless the notes she kept for her memoir ever surface. And chances are, that is one topic she would not have discussed in such notes!

Cliff Carter would have known whether Johnson was involved in Kennedy's death, but he did not live long after Johnson left office. As close as Iris Campbell was to Cliff Carter, she may not have ever known the truth about Carter's unexpected death. If she did know the entire story, she was still protecting him decades after his demise, just as she had protected Lyndon Johnson for so many years. Chances are, Campbell had no way of knowing that Carter may have signed his own death warrant on a warm autumn afternoon in Abilene, Texas, when he shared memories about Lyndon Johnson with Billie Sol Estes and Kyle Brown.

CHAPTER 14

THE VOICE OF KYLE BROWN

"You have to have a conscience to be bothered by one. Johnson was so egocentric that he actually thought Divine Providence intended for him to be President of the United States."

O ne person had a ringside seat to a historic conversation between two of Johnson's closest associates—Kyle Brown, a man who can discuss Billie Sol Estes, Cliff Carter, Lyndon Johnson, and Texas' infamous "Chicken Ranch" in a single breath. He grew up in Brady, Texas, about 95 miles from Johnson City, which is near Lyndon Johnson's ranch. Brown explained that he was personally familiar with Billie Sol Estes and Cliff Carter, both of whom were closely associated with the 36th President.

"My father ran the agricultural farm CO-OP in Brady, Texas, so I knew both Billie Sol Estes and Cliff Carter. I met them when I was seven, I guess," Brown explained.[203] He went on to say that his father did not have a high opinion of Lyndon Johnson, but he liked Estes and Carter. Brown met the two men during the 1950s, before Estes' legal troubles with the government began. He also knew Lyndon Johnson. "In fact," he added, "LBJ gave me a silver dollar once. My father could hardly stand him, but it did not bother him when Lyndon came around Brady and the CO-OP." Apparently, Brown's father understood the necessity of politicking as well as the importance of high-level politicians' support for farmers and ranchers.

Brown, with a grin in his voice, admitted that "Cliff and Lyndon inadvertently got me into a lot of trouble when I was a little boy. They brought their big donors to Brady for entertainment. My dad and other Bradyites took the donors to La Grange, to the Chicken Ranch." The "Chicken Ranch" was the house of prostitution which became famous worldwide because of the Broadway play (and movie) *The Best Little Whorehouse in Texas*.

"My mother had gone somewhere, so my dad had to take me along with him to the Chicken Ranch. I was just about seven or so. When we got there, the donors went upstairs, and Cliff and my dad and his friends stood around drinking beer. I got tired and wandered off into the kitchen part of the house. Inside was this pretty, big-bosomed lady. She asked me what I wanted, and I answered, 'I want some hot chocolate and some toast.' So, she made me some, and after that, I got even more tired, so I sat down on a couch next to her and leaned against her until I fell asleep.

"My dad found me there later and took me home and put me to bed." Brown paused and then continued with a chuckle. "But the next morning, my mother came in to kiss me and wake me up, and I guess she smelled that woman's perfume on me. She demanded to know where I'd been, and I just said, 'I don't know,' but the next thing I knew, she launched into my dad." Apparently, Mrs. Brown had realized exactly where her little boy had spent part of the previous evening, and she was anything but happy about it.

Brown said he did not know if all the stories about the "Chicken Ranch" from *The Best Little Whorehouse in Texas* were true or not. "It was *expensive*," he said, "and I don't know if the Aggie football players were rewarded with trips there, but I do know the UT [University of Texas at Austin] players were. When I was a teenager, I made extra money by taking other teens to Acuna, Mexico, to visit prostitutes. I charged them $10 a head. One time, one got put in a Mexican jail, and I had to call my dad for help." The jails in Mexico had horrendous reputations, but the trips must have been worth the risk because the "adventures" in Mexico did not cost as much as the much safer "Chicken Ranch." Another plus was that the prostitutes in Mexico did not care how young a customer was.

One of Kyle Brown's good friends was Madeleine Brown—"no relation," he said hurriedly—who claimed in her book *Texas In the Morning* that she had been Lyndon Johnson's mistress and mother of his illegitimate son. "I think Lady Bird found out about this son while they were in the White House," Brown recalled. "She threw such a fit that the Secret Service had to push her into a closet and leave her a while to cool down."

After Madeline Brown completed her book, she showed it to Kyle Brown. He read her first draft and suggested she get a professional writer to edit it. She turned to author-educator Ed Tatro, a highly qualified historical researcher on the Kennedy assassination. That Madeleine Brown had an affair with LBJ is supported by numerous people who knew of their relationship.

In her book *Faustian Bargains,* Joan Mellen acknowledges that Madeline Brown bore Lyndon Johnson a son in 1950. Evidence that Johnson unofficially recognized the boy as his son comes from a letter from Johnson's lawyer Jerome T. Ragsdale. It guaranteed Madeleine Brown that Johnson would financially support her and her child.[204] Evidence indicates that he did so until his death.

Kyle Brown's tales about Lyndon Johnson's affairs and his wife's reaction to them were surpassed by one particular story which was anything but humorous. It concerned a secret meeting between Brown, Billie Sol Estes, and Johnson's aide Cliff Carter. In 1971, Estes had been paroled and was once again living in Abilene, Texas. Kyle Brown was a student at Abilene Christian College and still close to the notorious "wheeler dealer." Driving through Texas on his way home to Campbell, Carter made a point of stopping in Abilene to visit with Estes. The two men knew so much about Johnson and his political activities that it was not surprising for them to sit and reminisce. But what Kyle Brown heard that day was a story that would have outraged Lyndon Johnson because he would have been furious that Estes and Carter would share this type of information with a third party.

"I was invited to participate in this conversation at Estes' home in Abilene on September 20, 1971," Brown stated. "Cliff Carter and Billie Sol Estes thought that they did not have long to live." [205] Brown was twenty-two at the time; he speculated later that he was included in the conversation because "I think Cliff Carter wanted to clear his conscience and wanted me to know these things."

Estes' house sat on a small lake southeast of Abilene. On the afternoon of September 20, Estes and Carter and their young college friend sat casually under an umbrella that covered part of a pier extending forty feet into Lytle Lake. Carter and Estes wanted to make sure that no one overheard this particular conversation. Estes' house might very well have been bugged, but surely the pier was not. Estes had been criticized by a great many people because, even after serving time in prison, he lived in an expensive home on Lytle Lake. What others did not know was that the home had been purchased by his brother John, and it was not a mansion, contrary to how some people described it.

Though Kyle Brown was just a college student, he realized the historical importance of what he was hearing that day. He listened intently as Estes and Carter discussed various murders that had involved President Lyndon Johnson and his "chosen few." If Brown had been a typical college student, he might not have believed what he was hearing. But he did believe it because he had grown up around politicians.

"Well, I wasn't shocked," Brown admitted, "because I had heard some of these stories from James Norvill already." Norvill was a graduate of the U.S. Naval Academy and an attorney who at one time represented Billie Sol Estes. Later, Norvill authored a "fictional" account of the Kennedy assassination and Johnson's connection to it.

J. Evetts Haley of Midland would not have been shocked, either, for he had described in 1964 several murderous situations involving associates of Billie Sol Estes. Associates of Estes were often associates of Johnson, whether they knew it or not.

Chances are, though, the American public would have been appalled by the stories Carter and Estes told that day, especially when the topic turned to Lyndon Johnson's infamous, so-called henchman, Malcolm (Mac) Wallace.

Like so many of Johnson's followers, Wallace was connected like a tentacle to "the Man" who controlled the people and events around him. He was a convicted killer who was fortunate enough to have been defended by one of Johnson's personal attorneys. The trial took place in Austin, which everyone knew was controlled by Lyndon Johnson.

In an Austin police report dated October 22, 1951, Wallace confessed to the murder, and he also inadvertently admitted "he worked for Lyndon Johnson."[206] Despite being defended by Johnson's attorney, Wallace was found guilty of murder with malice aforethought in a state that was well-known for sending killers to the electric chair. But, for murder in the first degree, he received nothing more than a five-year suspended sentence. Malcolm Everett Wallace walked out of the court room blatantly guilty of murder, but a free man. Obviously, he had contacts with powerful individuals.

Two of them were Cliff Carter and Lyndon Johnson's sister, Josefa. Perhaps Wallace's connection to Carter and to Johnson explains the fortuitous direction that his life took.

The story of Malcolm Wallace and his miraculous escape from the electric chair grew even stranger. He moved to Dallas in 1952 and went to work for TEMCO in 1954. Somehow or another, he received a security clearance at the level of SECRET. Someone with a great deal of influence must have recommended Wallace. TEMCO merged with Ling Electronics Company in 1961, and Wallace was employed by the company. Coincidentally, James Ling, the owner, was a Johnson supporter. This company was connected to the defense industry.[207]

But the strangest detail that could have linked Malcolm Wallace to the Kennedy assassination, and, thus, to Lyndon Johnson, was not discovered until years after the assassination. A partial fingerprint from a cardboard carton found on the sixth floor near the "sniper's nest" in the Texas School Book Depository on November 22, 1963, had intrigued law enforcement and researchers for years. It did not belong to Oswald or to any other School Book Depository employee. Dallas police officer J. Harrison was determined to identify the bearer of this mysterious fingerprint. After all, it was evidence that a non-employee had recently been on the sixth floor of the Depository. In 1998, he was finally able to compare the mysterious fingerprint to a fingerprint on Malcolm Wallace's official fingerprint card—a fingerprint which had been taken when he was arrested for murder in 1951.

Two fingerprint experts, Nathan Darby and E. H. Hoffmeister, separately compared the two fingerprints. They agreed that the mysterious fingerprint matched the print of Wallace. For years, this seemed to prove that a convicted killer with connections to Lyndon Johnson had been on the sixth floor of the Depository on November 22, 1963.

However, in 2016, a book by Joan Mellen introduced new evidence showing that Nathan Darby and E. H. Hoffmeister were incorrect in their findings concerning the mysterious fingerprint. In *Faustian Bargains,* Mellen explained that she had located a fingerprint specialist in 2013 named Robert Garrett. Garrett had been trained at FBI headquarters in Washington, D.C., and Quantico, Virginia. Garrett insisted on working from a negative or a first generation of the print. The other experts had worked from photocopies. Mellen was also able to provide Garrett with Wallace's fingerprints from his Navy record. After his examination of Wallace's print and the print from the sixth floor of the Depository, Garrett determined that the mysterious print was still mysterious. It did not match Malcom Wallace's print.[208]

That does not mean that Malcolm Wallace was not in Dallas on November 22, 1963, but his son Michael feels sure, according to Mellen, that his father was home that evening in Anaheim, California.[209] Of course, it is very possible that Wallace *was* in Dallas until 12:30 p.m., that he then caught a flight for California and arrive home in time to greet his son. Furthermore, Wallace never had to prove his whereabouts on that day to anyone. He was never considered a suspect, so he was never questioned. Kyle Brown stated that Cliff Carter and Billie Sol Estes thought Wallace *was* one of Kennedy's assassins.

"Mac Wallace was in on *all* of Lyndon's doings," Brown commented. Throughout Wallace's lifetime, he was charged with only one murder, for which he served no time. But according to Carter and Estes, he committed numerous other murders, all for Lyndon Johnson. When asked if this included the President's assassination, Brown assented, but he did not mean that Wallace was on the sixth floor of the School Book Depository building at the time of Kennedy's assassination. Brown was told that Wallace was firing at the presidential motorcade from what became known as the grassy knoll next to the Depository Building. He stated that Lee Harvey Oswald was "was in the wrong place at the wrong time. I think he was scared when he realized what had happened and knew he would be used as a patsy."

Wallace may or may not have been involved in the Kennedy assassination. Regardless, like many others, he did not live long after November 22, 1963. He died less than eight years later at the age of forty-nine in what was determined to be a car accident. Brown was told about the accident. He was also told that "accident" was an erroneous term.

"Lyndon killed Wallace himself." He then elaborated, "The two of them had a meeting at the ranch [Johnson's home]. Wallace got into his car and drove off." When asked how he obtained information that no one else seemed to have, Brown replied, "Everything I know about Lyndon came from either Lyndon himself, Cliff Carter, or Billie Sol Estes." The story Brown heard differs considerably from the official story concerning Wallace's death.

"Lyndon ordered his helicopter pilot to follow Mac's car." Brown paused and then quietly dropped a bombshell: According to what he heard, Johnson's pilot somehow managed to control Wallace's car. Whether he disabled the brakes and/or the steering mechanism, or hovered so closely over the car that Wallace overreacted, is speculation because there were no known eye-witnesses to the crash. For some unknown reason, Wallace's car left the road and slammed into a stone fence. Wallace supposedly suffered severe head injuries and died immediately. There is some question about where the accident occurred; officially, it happened outside of Pittsburg, Texas. When Brown was asked how Johnson could turn on Wallace after everything he had supposedly done for him, he replied, "You have to have a conscience to be bothered by one. Johnson was so egocentric that he actually thought Divine Providence intended for him to be President of the United States."

Brown's father's connections to Carter and LBJ were strong enough that his son was invited several times to Johnson's ranch. "I was only there twice after LBJ left office," Brown commented. "But I know there was a meeting in August of 1962 at the ranch with Lyndon Johnson, John Kennedy, and Bobby Kennedy. JFK and Bobby were there to say that Lyndon's services would no longer be needed in 1964."

This startling tale is partly verified. Johnson's Vice-Presidential Daily Diary shows that on August 9, 1962, Johnson, his wife, his daughter Lynda, and one of his secretaries flew to Austin, Texas, and then on to his ranch "to stay several days in Texas without staff or secret service."[210] The diary indicates no recorded activities for August 13-15, 1962. In fact, the page for August 14 has been entirely removed from the diary. It is possible that Attorney General Robert Kennedy may have visited the Vice-President during this time. Because the Attorney General was the President's most trusted advisor, Kennedy often used him to deliver private messages to others. If Johnson did not want a record of a meeting with Robert Kennedy, this could explain why Johnson's calendar page for August 14, 1962, is missing. President Kennedy's diary indicates he was in Maine at the time. A photo of him sailing with brother-in-law Peter Lawford is evidence of his whereabouts that day.

Brown learned from Billie Sol Estes that Estes had known Joe Kennedy, Sr. as well as mobsters Sam Giancana and Carlos Marcello. He also learned during the years he knew Johnson, Estes, and Carter, that Carlos Marcello had financially backed Lyndon Johnson's campaigns. During Johnson's administration, he made a point of distancing himself from Estes and downplayed their association and Estes' influence. But Kyle Brown knew how influential Estes could be. He explained, "Bobby Kennedy learned early on how powerful Billie Sol really was. Jackie Kennedy wanted to remodel part of the White House, which was going to take money. JFK told Lyndon they needed money so she could do this."[211]

"'I can get it for you tomorrow,'" Lyndon told him. To prove his point, Lyndon called up Billie Sol and said, "I need a half million dollars in Washington tomorrow." Lyndon knew that Billie Sol practically owned one of the banks in Pecos, Texas. So, Billie Sol went down to the bank that night with the bank president and got Lyndon his money. The next day, Lyndon marched into the Oval Office with a briefcase full of cash. He pointed to the briefcase and then said to the President of the United States, "There's my half. Where's yours?"[212]

When the subject of Johnson being "dumped" from the 1964 ticket arose again, Brown indicated that Johnson appeared to have ignored the rumors that he was not going to be Kennedy's vice-presidential choice in his re-election bid. Saving face was vital to Lyndon Johnson; only his closest advisors would have known that "the Man" was agonizing over the rumors and was setting up a back-up plan in case Kennedy chose a new vice-presidential ticket-mate.

The meeting in 1971 between Brown and the two older men made a lasting impression on the young college student. During the telephone interview, his voice softened as he returned to the subject of September 20, 1971. Carter and Estes recalled that afternoon how many deaths Lyndon Johnson had ordered because knowledge of certain events could threaten his career. One of the last comments made to Kyle Brown on September 20 was one that he took lightly at the time.

"Kyle, you realize you'll be the last man standing," Billie Sol Estes said quietly. But neither Billie Sol Estes nor Kyle Brown realized how soon the trio would lose one of its members.

"Cliff Carter died 36 hours later," Brown explained. "He died in a Texas hotel." Brown is quick to mention that no one could have overheard what the three of them had discussed that day in Abilene. So perhaps Carter simply died of a heart attack, or perhaps someone hidden across the road from Estes' house, as men often were, observed Brown and Carter entering Estes' domain. Mere speculation about what was discussed may have been enough to cause Carter's sudden death.

Brown remembered that he was with Estes when he received the phone call from Campbell, Texas, concerning Carter's death. Both were shocked at the suddenness of their friend's demise. "Billie Sol is who arranged for the mortician to go pick up Cliff's body. Billie Sol had owned a mortuary in Pecos," Brown explained, "so he had connections to morticians all over the state."

There are numerous discrepancies about when and where Carter died. One version of Carter's death stated that was in an Alexandria, Virginia, hospital with pneumonia and that no penicillin was available in other area hospitals.[213] But there is also Iris Campbell's version of Carter's death. She heard that Carter had a heart attack on the steps of the State Department in Washington. This makes more sense than the story about Washington hospitals lacking penicillin.

There is still another story, which Phil Nelson included in his book *LBJ: From Mastermind to Colossus*. Carter's secretary said that Carter disappeared such that no one was able to locate him, including her. According to her, his body was eventually found in a Virginia motel.[214] .

"This [Carter's death] really got my attention," Brown commented quietly. "Billie Sol and I had visited Clint Peoples [a well-known Texas Ranger] about a week before Cliff died. Peoples had a separate house in his backyard full of Billie Sol memorabilia and Texas Ranger memorabilia." Peoples is the person who convinced Estes to reveal what he knew about Lyndon Johnson's connections to the untimely deaths of several individuals. He had no way of knowing that he himself would die in a mysterious one-car accident. Kyle Brown shared with the authors that the idea of Peoples dying in such a manner "was ridiculous." Brown believed that the only thing that kept Billie Sol from being killed, like so many other people "in the know," was pure luck.

"Stupid luck kept Billie Sol from getting murdered. He and I would go to Las Vegas between Thanksgiving and Christmas. He introduced me to some of the mob members out there who would have just as soon killed you as look at you. But I got a pretty good job out of meeting these people." Brown was referring to a job with Brown and Root Industrial Services, one of the largest companies in the nation; its headquarters were in Texas.

"George Brown knew I was a friend of Billie Sol's. George was a charismatic character, and you would never meet him and question his ethics. But his brother Herman was the most corrupt person ever." Both these men, ethical or not, were closely associated with Lyndon Johnson.

Kyle Brown is one of the few who has shared some of the information that people like Cliff Carter kept to themselves, even though it could have shed light on the Kennedy assassination. All of what he heard that day at Billie Sol Estes' house would certainly be considered hearsay in a court of law. However, Brown feels certain that the stories he heard were true. In fact, he regards Cliff Carter's statements as almost a deathbed confession.

CHAPTER 15

THE VOICES OF TOMMY WRIGHT AND JAN AMOS

"No wonder LBJ had JFK killed!"
—Brigadier General Joseph J. Cappucci

Long before Kyle Brown heard Cliff Carter's and Billy Sol Estes' confessions, rumors spread throughout Texas and the rest of the nation that Vice-President Lyndon B. Johnson might have been connected to the death of John F. Kennedy. Tommy Wright, a Fort Worth police officer in 1963, was quite open about rumors that had reached the Fort Worth police department. Fifty-one years after the assassination, he stated bluntly, "LBJ had JFK murdered. Kennedy wanted everyone to like him. He knew LBJ had a lot of pull vote-wise. Apparently, he didn't know what kind of guy Johnson was."[215] Wright was not the only person in the Fort Worth police department to feel this way. He recalled that many of his fellow officers held similar opinions about Lyndon Johnson.

Wright was strongly affected by President Kennedy's death. He had liked John Kennedy. He knew about Johnson's reputation in Texas as a manipulator and as a corrupt politician. "It was well-known in Johnson City that dead people had voted for Johnson." Wright's disapproval did not end with Lyndon Johnson. "Lady Bird owned a radio station in Austin that at one time was the only one allowed. They had a monopoly," he said, unknowingly echoing the words of Sonny Davis.

Wright never knew Kyle Brown, but he agreed with Brown's comments concerning Johnson's lack of conscience. According to Wright, "LBJ *had* no conscience. The first thing he did after the assassination was to tell all local officers to get out of the way. He even sent his own FBI agents to Dallas to handle things." The more Wright remembered that terrible weekend in 1963, the more animated he became. He repeated that there was no "question in the Fort Worth police department's mind that LBJ had Kennedy killed. JFK and Johnson were as different as day and dark." Wright then added, "It was well-known that LBJ would not be JFK's vice-president in 1964." Wright's comment may have been based upon an article in the *Dallas Morning News* which had appeared the morning of November 22, 1963. It quoted former Vice-President Nixon as suggesting that Kennedy would have a different running mate in 1964. All these comments led to a final summation. In Tommy Wright's opinion, "When the Warren Commission investigated the assassination, they found what Lyndon wanted them to find."

Though Wright and numerous other individuals in the Dallas/Ft. Worth area immediately suspected Johnson's involvment in the assassination, people were very careful about repeating such an opinion in the wrong circles. Johnson's temper and his ability to retaliate were legendary, especially after he became President. Wright had heard from others how Johnson could respond to criticism; Jan Amos found out directly.

Amos' daughter Gail admitted in a telephone conversation that she had no idea that her parents had been told confidential information about the Kennedy family and about Lyndon Johnson, at least until her mother showed her the book *LBJ: From Mastermind to Colossus* by Phil Nelson.

"I could not believe my mother had never told me this," Amos confided.[216] Amos' mother Jan had shared her story with Nelson and as an *Oral History for the Sixth Floor Museum* in 2014. Years before, she had promised her husband Bill that she would never reveal the conversation that the two of them had had with Air Force Brig. Gen. Joseph J. Cappucci in September of 1969. This was about two months after Senator Edward (Ted) Kennedy had been involved in the Chappaquiddick scandal resulting from the death of Mary Jo Kopechne, a former female campaign worker of Robert Kennedy.

Lt. Colonel William Amos and his family were stationed in Rome, Italy, in the late 1960s. It was here that Amos and his wife heard a startling comment from Gen. Joseph Cappucci, who happened to be one of J. Edgar Hoover's best friends. At a dinner one evening, the discussion turned to the tragedy involving Edward Kennedy and Kopechne. Kopechne had been found in Kennedy's submerged car in Massachusetts during the same weekend that Americans were celebrating Neil Armstrong's and Buzz Aldrin's walks on the moon. The so-called "investigation" of the young woman's death had been mocked by people in almost every state except Massachusetts. Apparently, General Cappucci knew Hoover well enough to know that he had a dossier on the Kennedy family, on several Dallas millionaires, and on anyone else who caught his attention.

It is likely that the information that Cappucci shared with Bill and Jan Amos came from J. Edgar Hoover. As the Amoses and the General were eating and drinking, Cappucci began making derogatory remarks about the late President Kennedy and his family. He looked squarely at his dinner companions and blurted out, "Ted Kennedy paid one million dollars to Mary Jo Kopechne's family to avoid an autopsy." His next comment was even more shocking. "No wonder LBJ had JFK killed!" he said disgustedly.

Jan Amos recalled in her *Oral History* that her husband, on hearing this, became frightened, realizing that General Cappucci's outburst could put him and his family in danger. Lt. Colonel Amos knew, according to his wife, that there were actually "two FBIs. J. Edgar Hoover had his personal squad." Amos meant that the official FBI was not the *only* FBI. Some of those unofficial FBI agents eventually admitted this.

A special group of trained agents were at Hoover's beck and call. According to one of those agents, who used the alias Michael Milan, "J. Edgar Hoover had recruited a band of professional killers for his private execution squad. He found them in organized crime families, the armed forces, and in other intelligence services. He called them the Unknowns, and they did jobs so dirty even the CIA was afraid of them."[217]

"On the way home that evening," Jan Amos remembered, "my husband said, 'Don't *ever* repeat what the General said!'" Until she spoke with Phil Nelson and with the staff of the Sixth Floor Museum in Dallas, Texas in 2014, Amos had never shared this story with anyone, not even with her daughters. But she must have realized that the General's information had come from the Director of the FBI, and that the General had trusted her husband enough to confide in him. The General had no way of foreseeing that the Lieutenant Colonel and his wife would eventually divorce and that Jan Amos would finally feel obligated to share what she had been told.[218]

Gen. Joseph Cappucci was not the only high-ranking individual who showed utter disdain for President Kennedy and his family. The widow of William King Harvey, one of the CIA's most valued agents, related to Scott and Andy Alderton in 1999 that her husband had referred to the Kennedys as "scum." His opinion was based on personal experiences.

"When Jack [Kennedy] was in Rome visiting the embassy, my husband, being head of the CIA there, had to assign two men along with his group of service men who were protecting him—these two men were required to get Italian prostitutes into Jack's bed, two at a time. And it was a sorry thing." Mrs. Harvey, a CIA agent herself, also recalled that her husband had personal knowledge concerning Jackie Kennedy's immoral behavior. She added, "Jackie carried on with Onassis on his yacht" [while Kennedy was President].[219]

Bill Amos may not have been as surprised by Cappucci's comment as his wife had been, because his position as an Air Force lieutenant colonel and as an Air Intelligence officer had already allowed him to see firsthand how Lyndon Johnson had reacted to J. Evetts Haley's book *A Texan Looks at Lyndon*. In 1964, Amos told his wife in confidence something he had learned about Kennedy's successor.

Lt. Colonel Amos was stationed in Little Rock, Arkansas at the time. Haley's book, which was privately published, was nonetheless distributed to individuals and to various military bases. It's possible that Haley's friend, Gen. Edwin Walker, helped him deliver copies of the book to various military bases. Haley's research was thorough, and he was one of the few who dared to publicly state, even after Johnson became President, that he had stolen elections, and even had people killed to achieve his political goals.

As a member of military intelligence, Bill Amos had personally witnessed Johnson's reaction to Haley's book. He watched as Haley's books were intercepted at the military base-exchange and burned before they could be sold to enlisted men. President Johnson's anger aroused the curiosity of Jan Amos. She asked her husband where she could get a copy of this intriguing book.

"Jan, if that book was found in this home, I would be court-martialed," he warned her. Bill Amos had seen Lyndon Johnson up close and personal. "That is the worst SOB I have ever been around," he told his wife. "He is so uncouth!"[220] What is more frightening about this particular glimpse of Lyndon Johnson is that on American soil he was controlling speech much as Hitler had controlled it in Nazi Germany. If the accusations in Haley's book had been untrue, surely Johnson would have simply sued the author. By burning *A Texan Looks at Lyndon: A Study in Illegitimate Power*, Johnson appears to have given credence to at least some of what Haley wrote.

Not only did people like Tommy Wright, who knew Johnson only by reputation, think he was capable of murder. So did those who were close to him. Even today, some agree, to a certain extent, with General Cappucci. They believe that Lyndon Johnson may have been involved in *some way* with Kennedy's death, even if it was only by covering up important information.

Johnson would certainly have had more control over a murder investigation if it had occurred in Texas. Stories vary as to whether Johnson and John Connally encouraged or discouraged the President to visit Texas before the end of 1963. However, several people close to Kennedy have recalled that shortly before the trip, he admitted that he regretted making the commitment. No one knows if the President would have survived a trip to anywhere but the Lone Star State. His vice-president did not always accompany him on campaign trips. But in Texas, Johnson shared the limelight with Kennedy. In Texas, Johnson had a personal friend who was a federal judge; consequently, in Texas, he would be able to take the presidential oath immediately after the death of his predecessor. And in Texas, he was able to manipulate Jackie Kennedy into posing with him and the new First Lady as he took that oath of office.

On the other hand, it is certainly possible that Kennedy was doomed no matter where he traveled. There is evidence that at least two assassination attempts were in the works before the Texas trip. One had been planned for Chicago for early in November, and if that failed, another was to have taken place in Tampa. Chances are, if Kennedy had been killed in Chicago, the Mafia would have been blamed. If he had been killed in Tampa, the anti-Castro Cubans might have taken the blame. If he had been killed in the Deep South, the Ku Klux Klan would have probably been blamed. There were potential scapegoats all over the United States.

Nevertheless, a question that continues to trouble those who believe Johnson was involved in the assassination is this: Did he *mastermind* the assassination? To some, the answer is "no." These individuals suspect that persons with much more power than Lyndon Johnson planned and executed President Kennedy's assassination. These same people may have also planned and executed the assassinations of Martin Luther King, Jr. and Robert F. Kennedy.

To others, the answer to the question is a resounding "yes." After all, a true *mastermind* does not leave fingerprints, footprints, or evidence of any kind that will lead directly back to him or her. Lyndon Johnson himself bragged that the press never discovered certain pieces of information about him. He bragged, "The damn press always accused me of things I didn't do. They never once found out about the things I *did* do."[221]

III
A RENDEZVOUS
WITH DEATH

Despite what the Warren Commission determined, there was foreknowledge of Kennedy's assassination. It was ignored by those who could and should have prevented John F. Kennedy's death. The very fact that some individuals knew beforehand that an assassination attempt would take place negates the possibility that a frustrated "lone nut" suddenly decided to kill the President.

CHAPTER 16

1960—AND SO IT BEGINS

"Don't you know that the number two spot is just a heartbeat away from the presidency?"—Lyndon Baines Johnson

Most of America was shocked by the murder of John F. Kennedy; some individuals, however, were *not* because they had already discussed the probability that the President would not live long enough to complete his first term.

There had been numerous threats on Kennedy's life even before his inauguration.

In December of 1960, Richard Paul Pavlick, a retired postmaster, plotted to kill the president-elect by ramming Kennedy's automobile with his dynamite-laden car. Pavlick was prepared to die himself to keep a Catholic out of the White House. Kennedy was saved because of a concerned postmaster who had received postcards from Pavlick which suggested his plans. He reported Pavlick to the police. Because of his actions, Pavlick was found to be mentally unstable and was institutionalized.[222]

Kennedy, like most of his predecessors, was aware that along with the power of the presidency also came vulnerability. If a president was to be approachable to the people, he had to risk the possibility of assassination. Kennedy knew that Adlai Stevenson, then Ambassador to the United Nations, and Vice-President Lyndon Johnson had both been treated disrespectfully on official trips to Dallas, Texas. He had even been warned by Stevenson himself that Dallas was a dangerous place to visit. But Kennedy knew that his life could be in danger anywhere in America.

Some have even suggested that Kennedy's days were numbered from the very day in November 1960 when he won the closest presidential election in U.S. history. Although Kennedy had won the Democratic nomination on the first ballot, he had been torn and undecided about the man to select as his running mate. According to Layte Bowden, a close friend of both U.S. Senator George Smathers (Florida) and President Kennedy, "Those close to Kennedy knew he had to offer the position to Lyndon Johnson whether he wanted to or not."[223] Johnson's name on the ticket would help the Democrats carry the southern states.

Johnson insider Iris Campbell stated in an interview in 2014 that Johnson had to be coaxed by Speaker of the House Sam Rayburn into accepting the vice-presidency. She remembered that Rayburn told Johnson, "When your party needs you and offers you the vice-presidency, you don't turn it down."[224] There is no question that Sam Rayburn wanted his protégé in the White House. It was common knowledge in the late 1950s and early 1960s that Lyndon Johnson was "Rayburn's boy." Sam Rayburn was determined to be a "king maker," having groomed Lyndon Johnson for the White House. At the 1960 Democratic Convention, he openly endorsed Johnson as the best Democratic candidate.[225]

Nonetheless, many Johnson supporters were shocked when Rayburn encouraged Johnson to accept the vice-presidential slot. Perhaps John Kennedy should have paid closer attention to the remarks the Speaker of the House made to Kennedy after Johnson accepted the vice-presidency. "Well," he drawled, "there is always the thought in a fellow's mind that he might get to be president."[226]

According to an unpublished memoir by Hyman Raskin, Kennedy had already offered the vice-presidential slot to another senator. However, after Kennedy met privately with Johnson and Rayburn, Kennedy was "made an offer he could not refuse." Raskin assumed Johnson had blackmailed his way onto the Kennedy ticket.[227]

Because Johnson's ally, John Connally, had already announced that Kennedy had Addison's disease, health issues were probably not what Johnson and Rayburn held over Kennedy's head. But it is certainly possible that the two men made sure the new Democratic candidate understood that they had evidence concerning his sexual affairs with numerous women, some of which might have compromised national security, and all of which would have appalled voters.

The question remains: Why would Rayburn, the powerful Speaker of the House, want Johnson in the less-than-desirable position of Vice-President of the United States? Phil Nelson's book *LBJ: The Mastermind of the JFK Assassination,* contains a great deal of circumstantial, anecdotal, and physical evidence that points to Johnson as the man who planned the Kennedy assassination. However, though Sam Rayburn died in 1961, he still had more influence on Johnson before and after the 1960 Convention and during his early days in the vice-presidency than anyone else. There is evidence that Rayburn may have orchestrated events so that Johnson would be the man standing in the shadows awaiting Kennedy's final heartbeat.

Many close to Johnson seemed to think that if the Democrats won the 1960 election, LBJ might somehow inherit the presidency. Bobby Baker, Johnson's "right-arm," told Don B. Reynolds, an insurance agent connected to Johnson, of an incident "during the swearing in of Kennedy in which Baker said words to the effect that the S.O.B. [meaning Kennedy] would never live out his term and that he would die a violent death."[228] Baker may have remembered an incident that took place in Lyndon Johnson's hotel room during the 1960 Democratic Convention. In his memoir *Wheeling and Dealing*, Baker recalled Senator Robert Kerr of Oklahoma, a close friend of Johnson, being "literally livid" because Johnson was seriously considering accepting the vice-presidential slot.

"There were angry red splotches on his face. He glared at me, at LBJ, and at Lady Bird," Baker wrote. "' Get me my .38!' he yelled. 'I'm gonna kill every damn one of you. I can't believe that my three best friends would betray me.' Senator Kerr did not seem to be joking. As I attempted to calm him, he kept shouting that we'd combined to ruin the Senate, ruin ourselves, and ruin him personally."

Johnson responded to this outburst by telling Baker to take Kerr into the bathroom and "explain things to him." Baker did this, and after hearing about the reasons for Johnson's decision to accept the offer, "Senator Kerr put a burly arm around me and said, "Son, you are right and I was wrong. I'm sorry I mistreated you."[229]

Lady Bird Johnson, however, had not been taken into the bathroom so that she also would understand what could happen in the future. She was still outraged at the idea of her powerful husband taking second place on the ticket. She protested vehemently until her husband, who towered over her, "tapped his wife's breast with his forefinger as he said emphatically, 'Don't you know that the number two spot is just a heartbeat away from the presidency?'"[230]

Because every vice-president in the history of the United States has been "a heartbeat away from the presidency,"this certainly could not have been news to Lady Bird Johnson." So, Johnson must have been making some other point to his wife. It is possible he was suggesting that as Senate Majority Leader, he would not "inherit" the Oval Office if something happened to John Kennedy, but as Vice-President, he would.

Regardless of why Johnson accepted the vice-presidential nomination, his decision was the root of numerous rumors and much speculation. Some Democratic insiders believed that Johnson had pushed his way onto the Democratic ticket, but what others described sounded more like blackmail. According to what Kennedy's personal secretary, Evelyn Lincoln, told author Anthony Summers, "LBJ had been using all the information that Hoover could find on Kennedy during the campaign and even before the convention. And Hoover was in on the pressure on Kennedy at the Convention."[231] Remarks attributed to Johnson during the convention indicate that he suspected or possibly *knew* that President Kennedy would not live to serve two terms.

Like all other presidents, Kennedy was not exempt from crank letters and random threats on his life. After the Bay of Pigs fiasco in 1961, the anti-Castro Cubans who felt betrayed by Kennedy and the United States made no secret of their bitter feelings. The closer Kennedy came to re-election time, the more serious the threats seemed to become. Almost half of America's voters had voted for Kennedy's opponent, Richard Nixon, in 1960. By the fall of 1963, Kennedy had made allies of some of those who had not supported him, but he had alienated more people than he had realized. Many of those people were Texans, who were still unhappy that Johnson was part of the Kennedy administration.

Regardless of the threats on his life, JFK supposedly insisted on making a trip to Texas—a trip that was planned in June 1963 after making a brief stop-over in El Paso, Texas.

Behind closed doors of the Cortez Hotel, Kennedy and his aides met with Vice-President Johnson and Texas Governor John Connally. It is uncertain what Johnson and Kennedy said to one another privately on that hot summer day, but, obviously, a heated exchange took place.

El Paso police officers were used as hotel security along with Secret Service agents. One member of the police force (who wishes to remain anonymous) overheard a memorable comment that Vice-President Johnson made as he exited the meeting with President Kennedy.

As Johnson stormed out of the Presidential suite, he growled, "No one talks to me like that! J. Edgar and I will take care of this!"[232] Naturally, the police officer had no way of knowing what problem Johnson and Hoover would "take care of," and he never learned whether the two men ever did so. But he never forgot the look on the Vice-President's face or the anger in his voice as he marched away from the President's room.

Connally and Johnson both claimed immediately after Kennedy's assassination that they had discouraged the Texas trip, especially the leg to Dallas. Kennedy, they agreed, had insisted on that phase of the trip. Connally, however, finally told a story years after Kennedy's assassination (and Johnson's death) that he would not have dared tell earlier. According to Doug Thompson, he sat next to the former Texas governor in 1982 on a TWA flight to Albuquerque. After discussing politics in New Mexico, Connally spoke about the plans that had led to President Kennedy's trip in Texas in November 1963.

"You know, I was one of the ones who advised Kennedy to stay away from

Texas," Connally said to Thompson. "Lyndon was being a real asshole about the whole thing and insisted."[233] If Connally had stated his concerns in June of 1963 at the Cortez Hotel in El Paso, could his words have triggered the verbal explosion from Johnson that the El Paso police officer overheard as the two men left the suite? Had President Kennedy taken Connally's warning seriously, at least at the time? Was Johnson livid because Kennedy might *avoid* the trip to Texas?

Officially, Johnson and his staff members claimed they were especially *unhappy* about the trip to Texas because a great deal of the money that would be raised would pay off Texas Senator Ralph Yarborough's campaign debts. Yarborough and Johnson were both Democrats, but they did not agree politically on numerous issues. Money that benefited Yarborough would not benefit Johnson at all.

Kennedy, however, realized that there would also be money left over for the 1964 Democratic campaign and that the trip would give him an opportunity to influence Texas voters. His popularity with Texas Democrats had dropped since the election. There had also been much speculation that during the three-day trip, Kennedy would attempt to force Connally, Johnson, and Yarborough to work as a team publicly, even if they feuded privately. Infighting between the three men had made news all over the state of Texas because the unity of the Democratic Party was being threatened.

A man by the name of Richard Case Nagell realized that more than the unity of the Democratic Party was being threatened. He warned J. Edgar Hoover that the President's life had been threatened. It seemed that Kennedy was losing support from some of his military advisers, from some members of the CIA, from members of organized crime who had supported him in the 1960 election, and, as Nagell discovered, from some in the FBI.

CHAPTER 17

THE VOICE OF JIM BUNDREN

"Glad you caught me… Things are going to get bad in Dallas.
I don't want to be in Dallas in November."—Richard Case Nagell

Afterafter Richard Case Nagell gained foreknowledge that President Kennedy would be killed, he revealed it in September 1963, first to J. Edgar Hoover and then to officials in El Paso, Texas. El Paso police officer Jim Bundren inadvertently was drawn into a bizarre story involving a military intelligence officer and the President of the United States.

With hindsight, Bundren realized that he had already stumbled on a fascinating character who might have had information about President Kennedy's death even before the fall of 1963. A few months before Kennedy's assassination, he received a call to check out a female vagrant being detained for erratic behavior in downtown El Paso.

Bundren could only remember her first name, "Jessie May," but her appearance was unforgettable. Dressed in filthy clothes that were not much more than rags, she also wore a headband which held her hair in a haphazard bun. The plastic headband had not been removed in so long that the woman's hair had grown through the teeth.

According to Bundren, "Jessie May" was clutching two grimy paper sacks and rambling about President Kennedy. A fellow officer took the sacks away from her and was about to have them burned when Bundren decided to examine the contents.

"I'm sure glad I did," he mused. "She had thousands of dollars mixed in among scraps of paper and trash." If that was not shocking enough, Bundren also found notebooks full of telephone numbers—numbers unaccompanied by names. Just out of curiosity, he contacted a friend who was the head of the El Paso office of the Secret Service.

"George," Bundren asked without explaining, "would you just check on a telephone number for me?" He randomly selected a number from one of "Jessie May's" notebooks. George promptly returned his call.

"Jim," he asked seriously, "where did you get that number?" Before Bundren answered, he asked that George check one more number. George called back even more quickly.

"I want to know how you got those numbers!" he demanded, and this time there would be no more stalling. Because of his association with George, Bundren learned more about the telephone numbers in her grimy notebooks than most police officers would have.

After "Jessie May" had been arrested and jailed, Bundren was told that her notebooks contained the private numbers of heads of state, chief executives, and high government officials from all over the world.

Bundren checked on the disposition of "Jessie May's" case a few days later, only to find that she had been released—and for the first and only time in his career, the arrest report, which he had personally completed, disappeared. "That was one of the strangest arrests I had ever made," Bundren grinned, but then he grew serious as he moved on to another strange arrest, one that concerned the death of John F. Kennedy.

Richard Case Nagell was nothing like "Jessie May," and he was not suddenly released from custody. His story gained national attention in El Paso, a city 635 miles west of Dallas, two months before Kennedy was assassinated.

Nagell and Officer Jim Bundren had never seen or heard of one another, but on September 20, 1963 their lives became entwined. Bundren was spending his day off from the police department earning extra money guarding a display of Gold Certificates. The display was in an area off the lobby of El Paso's State National Bank. Bundren was familiar with this bank because his beat included Oregon Street, where the bank was located. At 4:20 p.m, the sound of gun shots rang though the building. Bundren's plans for a peaceful weekend ended immediately.

Richard Case Nagell had walked calmly into the State National Bank from the Oregon Street entrance and fired into the upper edge of the wall behind the tellers' cages. The details concerning his motives, his actions, and his personal history vary depending upon who is telling the story.

The first witness to the incident, Patsy C. Gordon, was the teller Nagell encountered in the bank. Mrs. Gordon recalled to El Paso newspaper reporters that Nagell, neatly dressed in a blue suit with a white dress shirt and a red tie, approached her and asked for travelers' checks. Before she could accommodate him, Nagell pulled out a pistol and said, "Lady, this is a real gun."[234] Gordon later told Officer Bundren that Nagell added, "I want your money."[235] If she shared that last statement with anyone else besides Bundren, no one ever reported it.

No one seems to know exactly why Nagell deliberately startled the young woman by displaying a gun. It's also odd that he asked for travelers' checks instead of cash. The search following his arrest revealed that he had only twenty-seven cents in his pocket, so he obviously did need money. And yet, according to *official* reports, he did not demand cash. If he had truly wanted travelers' checks, he would have been required to sign a form and produce an identification card, both of which he surely would not have wanted to share.

Gordon admitted she had panicked at the sight of the pistol and ran away from her window. As she cowered under the counter, she heard shots fired into the wall above her. At that time, she did not know that Nagell was deliberately firing up and away from the employees and customers.

Gordon's unexpected reaction prompted Nagell to run out of the bank, pistol still drawn. Apparently, he was unaware that Bundren was nearby in a different area of the bank. Reacting to the sound of gun shots, Bundren raced to the lobby of the bank just as someone shouted, "He ran out the door." As Bundren loped across the lobby, he heard a bank officer yelling, "Jim! Blue suit, white shirt, red tie, white male!"

Nagell ran west on Oregon Street and was no longer in sight. The terrified bystanders gathered outside the bank told Bundren which way the suspect went. Pedestrians plastered themselves against the walls of downtown businesses and against the sides of cars parked along the street. It was obvious that none of the locals attempted to interfere with Nagell's daring escape.

Descriptions of what happened next can be found in various newspapers and books. Authors Dick Russell and Bob Ybarra both interviewed Nagell for their respective books years after the event. At the time of the so-called robbery, Nagell refused to speak to reporters. There are only two people who actually know what transpired after Nagell left the State National Bank that afternoon— Nagell himself, who is dead, and Jim Bundren, the officer who apprehended him, who is very much alive.

Nagell had no reason to expect a security guard to be in the bank that Friday. "It wasn't common practice in those days to have security guards in banks," explained Bundren. "Bank robberies were fairly rare." Therefore, Nagell could not have known that a police officer would chase him on foot. However, he must have realized that someone in the bank would have called the police or sounded the silent alarm. So, he did not waste any time as he escaped.

Bundren reached the corner of Oregon Street and Overland Street. "I was looking right and left," Bundren recalled, when he spotted a car attempting to exit the alley behind the bank. "A 1957 yellow and white Ford tried to pull out of the alley onto Overland Street." Nagell was attempting to ease the car into traffic. However, his timing was not good.

Two things prevented Richard Nagell's escape on September 20, 1963: the bumper to bumper traffic in downtown El Paso, and the fact that Bundren was determined to apprehend the suspect. Bundren recalled the event vividly even after 53 years.

He explained that he could see the driver through the car windshield. The man's face was so flushed that it nearly matched the red tie he was wearing. Every fiber in Bundren's body told him that this man was the bank robber. As he approached the driver's side of the car with his pistol drawn, he demanded that the suspect turn off the ignition.

"When I had him cornered, you could see in his eyes he wanted a shootout," Bundren remembered. "I said to him, 'Sir, don't try it.'" The retired police officer recalled that Nagell blinked a couple of times, but before Nagell could respond, Bundren quickly added, "I won't miss from this distance."

"Where did you put the gun?" Bundren then demanded.

"What gun?" Nagell answered.

Bundren continued, "I want to see both of your hands. Put them on the steering wheel." As Nagell raised his hands, his suit coat opened and Bundren saw a pistol hidden in the right front pocket of Nagell's pants.

As soon as the suspect complied, Bundren ordered, "Keep your hands where I can see them. Take your right hand and reach over and open the door." This directive kept Nagell from reaching into his pocket for the pistol.

Bundren removed the pistol from Nagell's pocket, handcuffed him quickly, and marched him back to the bank. Bundren felt a shootout would have occurred if Nagell had not jammed the pistol into his pocket. If he had laid the pistol on the car seat next to him, he could have grabbed it and tried to shoot his way out of the situation.

"I could have killed you anytime I wanted to," Nagell sneered as he was led back to the bank.

Bundren replied, "You would have lost." The police officer had no way of knowing that he had just apprehended an American who may have served the intelligence community as an international double agent. Suddenly, as the two men climbed the stairs that led to the bank lobby, the suspect kicked Bundren.

"You capitalistic SOB!" Nagell shouted. "I could have killed you!"

Bundren responded calmly, "You wouldn't have."

Bank employees had already contacted the FBI, but the police chief insisted that Bundren be the one to arrest and book Nagell.

"*You* are going to book him into the county jail," he emphasized to Bundren. "*Then* the FBI can take over."

During his interrogation by the FBI, Nagell claimed to have information about an assassination plot against President John Kennedy. He supposedly even knew that the assassination would take place during the President's trip to Texas.

Nagell had filed reports concerning this information with a variety of agencies; all but two of these reports can now be confirmed with documentation. During the El Paso interrogation, he again requested that the FBI agents contact the Secret Service immediately with his information about a planned assassination. As the arresting officer, Bundren had examined the suspect's wallet. "It contained a California driver's license and some kind of U.S. military certificate. There was a mimeographed newsletter. It was addressed to "Richard Case Nagell" from something called the "Fair Play for Cuba Committee."[236]

This was approximately six weeks after Lee Harvey Oswald had been photographed distributing pamphlets about the "Fair Play for Cuba Committee" in New Orleans. Of course, the El Paso police did not know this. So, neither the police nor the local FBI agents saw any significance to this newsletter. The organization "Fair Play for Cuba" would not become infamous until after November 22, 1963.

Other interesting items were found inside the trunk of the suspect's car—things that most people would not carry. "Nagell had photos of top secret military installations in Korea and Japan and even photos of dead Koreans." [237]

Inside the trunk were two suitcases/briefcases filled with documents, including several notebooks. Among those documents were certificates from the Army Military Intelligence School in Monterey, California, and records that Nagell had served in the Counter Intelligence Corps (CIC), which meant he had had top- secret security clearance in 1950. Also found were a set of police handcuffs, an extra pair of license plates, and a large amount of .45 ammunition and reloads. The key to the handcuffs was later found hidden in Nagell's clothing.[238]

"A box that would normally hold 45 rpm records was filled with photos, "Fair Play for Cuba" leaflets, and a tiny Minolta 16-millimeter camera."[239] A complete film-developing laboratory was also found. Years after the assassination, researchers realized that Nagell's small camera was similar to one originally found after the Kennedy assassination in Lee Harvey Oswald's sea-bag. Dallas police detective Gus Rose was pressured to change his description of that camera to a "light meter," but he refused to do so. However, the creators of the Warren Report had no problem altering the word "camera" to a less interesting term— "light meter."

Nagell appeared lucid as he was interrogated, but at times he would refuse to answer questions, and his various attorneys felt sure he was insane. From what author Dick Russell learned from Nagell in late October 1975, Nagell did not wish to be connected in any way to Lee Harvey Oswald, even if that meant he had to sit in a jail cell in El Paso while the Kennedy assassination took place.

According to Russell, Nagel claimed that he had told the FBI, "I would rather be arrested than commit murder and treason." In a Memorandum in Support of Petition for Writ of Habeas Corpus dated June 6, 1967, Nagell corrected this statement so that it read, "I would rather be arrested than commit treason."[240]

It is unclear what Nagell meant by "treason," or why he felt he might be drawn into the Kennedy assassination plot, but history shows that his foreknowledge was accurate. Numerous newspaper articles relate that while incarcerated in El Paso, Nagell was uncooperative and that he usually refused to make statements. That is why the comment he made to Bundren during his hearing eighteen days before the assassination was so memorable. As the two men sat waiting for the judge to arrive, Nagell glanced sideways at the man who had arrested him and blurted out, "Glad you caught me. Things are going to get bad in Dallas. I don't want to be in Dallas in November."[241]

To Bundren, this comment explained why Nagell had deliberately fired *above* the heads of the bank employees. He believed that "with Nagell's military experience, he knew how to create a diversion. This is why I think he fired shots into the top of the bank wall. It gave him time to escape in all of the confusion." Nagell did not share with Bundren his reason for not wanting to be in Dallas in November.

Bundren recalled that just to make conversation, he mentioned to Nagell that he had studied Nagell's military service. "You had a pretty good military record," Bundren conceded. He and the other police officers learned that Nagell had been a decorated Korean War veteran, been discharged in 1959 as a captain, and been awarded three Purple Hearts and a Bronze Medal. Instead of being pleased by Bundren's comments, Nagell retorted, "I don't talk about that." Then Nagell startled Bundren by adding, "I could have taken you."

Bundren ignored this and instead asked, "Why did you tell the newspaper I was just directing traffic that day?" Bundren had been offended by an erroneous news report that suggested he had apprehended Nagell just because he happened to be directing traffic near Nagell's escape route. Instead of answering Bundren directly, Nagell complimented the police officer.

"You're pretty sharp," he admitted.

Nagell was of very little help to his defense lawyers or to the doctors who tried to examine him for mental competency. He waffled back and forth between wanting a court-appointed lawyer and refusing any legal help at all. He seemed dissatisfied with every lawyer who was appointed. Though an insanity plea would have been the most logical defense, Nagell adamantly refused to plead insanity in December 1963.

"I will not tell him [any psychiatrist] my motive for going into the bank. I have always acted in principle of love for my country, and the same principle actuated my conduct on September 20, 1963, however inappropriate or incomprehensible it may appear. God and I, and also the FBI, know that I am not guilty."[242]

One of the things that troubled Nagell the most was that his notebooks, which the FBI confiscated, were never returned to him. At his insistence, the judge ordered the FBI to return the notebooks to the prisoner. In what became a legal circus of trials, incarcerations, and medical examinations that continued into 1964, Nagell was finally found guilty of attempted robbery.

During one trial, "He filed a motion to have the courts subpoena all of the FBI records relating to him, including materials seized from him."[243] Oddly enough, Judge Homer Thornberry denied the motion because he felt the FBI material would be irrelevant. It seems odd that Thornberry was not more interested in Nagell's prediction of Kennedy's assassination. Thornberry had been in the presidential motorcade the day Kennedy was killed and was a close friend of Lyndon Johnson..

Nagell's final lawyer was El Paso attorney Joseph Calamia, who was known and respected for his successful appeals. In 1966, he managed to have the original verdict reversed, and Nagell received a new trial. Questions lingered about Nagell's mental competency. Having been moved from El Paso to Springfield, Missouri and back to El Paso, he spent time in a variety of jails and prisons. One competency examination after another was ordered and conducted.

It's not surprising that Nagell, depressed and uncertain about his future and his family, attempted suicide several times. Nevertheless, he would not admit to being insane. He insisted he "wanted the truth to come out."[244] Calamia felt that Richard Case Nagell was a war hero with mental problems who should never have been incarcerated in the first place. Despite Calamia's passionate plea, a second jury found Nagell guilty.

Nagell's story did not attract as much attention as it should have. No one but New Orleans District Attorney Jim Garrison wanted to hear the ramblings of a war hero who claimed to have foreknowledge of JFK's assassination. Even Bundren admitted that, at first, he did not make the connection between Nagell's comments about "Dallas" and "November" and the Kennedy assassination. An article appeared in the *El Paso Times* on September 27, 1963, with the headline, "JFK PLANS TEXAS VISIT NOV. 21-22," but no one seemed to realize there might be a connection between the planned trip to Texas and Nagell's wild predictions that Kennedy was going to be killed in Dallas. The "Fair Play for

Cuba" pamphlets found in his car were evidence that Nagell had connections to Lee Harvey Oswald. He later admitted to Dick Russell that he was supposed to have eliminated Oswald.

After Kennedy was assassinated, Bundren began to wonder about the statements Nagell had made. "Nagell had to have had previous knowledge about the assassination," Bundren stated firmly to the authors in 2016. "He just got cold feet."[245] A former CIA contract agent's feelings about Nagell were not as compassionate as Bundren's. Lt. J. Goode, who must have known Nagell because of Goode's connection to U. S. marshals, bristled when Nagell's name was mentioned by the authors.

"When you are given a job, you do it," he said between clenched teeth. "He did not do his job."[246] Goode would not explain how he knew that Nagell had not completed his "job." It seems obvious that Nagell's "job" must have been to kill Oswald before November 22. Nagell never explained *why* he refused to eliminate Oswald. Strangely enough, Nagell's name does not even appear in the Warren Report, and yet, he and his actions were being discussed among intelligence agents like Goode years after the assassination.

Nagell seemed to realize that the arguments concerning whether he was a sane man who should be incarcerated or an insane man who should be institutionalized achieved the same purpose. Regardless of the verdict, Richard Case Nagell's credibility would be eradicated: He would be either a felon or a mental patient, and no one would believe either. Nagell seemed to view himself as a patriot who refused to carry out treasonous orders.

He wrote in a letter to author Dick Russell years after the "bank robbery": "What it all boils down to (the impetus behind the government's diligent prosecution of me in the 1960s, the true reason for my lengthy imprisonment, all of this injustice) can be explained in one sentence: I informed the Director of the Federal Bureau of Investigation, and others, as early as September 17, 1963, that Lee Harvey Oswald and two of his Cuban associates were planning to assassinate The President of the United States…and nothing was done about it."[247]

The date on Nagell's letter is important. Obviously impatient, he had waited only *three days* after sending his warning letter to draw national attention to himself by discharging a fire arm inside a federal building. This could have been his way of alerting government agencies to his location. Perhaps he had expected El Paso FBI agents to contact J. Edgar Hoover. He may have assumed Hoover would support his story about a letter to the FBI concerning Oswald and the death of Kennedy.

Years later, Dick Russell heard a story from Nagell that did not correlate with Jim Bundren's story of Nagell's arrest. Nagell told Russell that he had walked calmly out of the El Paso bank, went to his car, which he had parked in an alley, and waited for someone to arrest him. In Russell's book *The Man Who Knew Too Much*, Nagell is described as sitting patiently until Bundren finally approached him; Nagell then announced, "I guess you've got me. I surrender," and raised his hands.[248]

Whether Nagell was inadvertently captured that day in El Paso by a quick-witted police officer, later named Southwest Officer of the Year, or whether he deliberately caused a scene so he would have to be arrested, the result was the same. He definitely had an unbreakable alibi on November 22, 1963, when President Kennedy was assassinated; he was behind bars in an El Paso jail. He later told Dick Russell that he was not trying to establish an alibi for the assassination. Perhaps he was merely attempting, however dramatically, to catch J. Edgar Hoover's attention.

After hearing radio reports of the President's death, Nagell immediately asked to speak to an El Paso Secret Service agent. He did not want to speak to the FBI because he planned to reveal to the Secret Service that he had warned J. Edgar Hoover about the assassination before it had occurred. Instead of a Secret Service agent, an FBI agent appeared.

Nagell obviously did not feel comfortable sharing his frustrations with the FBI to an FBI agent. Once again, he asked to speak to a Secret Service agent. A few days later, a man claiming to be a Secret Service agent visited Nagell, but he was accompanied by two FBI agents. So Nagell refused to speak to him in front of the FBI. The three government agents left Nagell sitting in his jail cell, his story still untold.

On April 3, 1968, Nagell's conviction was finally reversed and he was acquitted. Fortunately, he did not have to serve his full sentence. However, by then, he had either been sitting in jails, prisons, or mental hospitals since September 20, 1963—more than four years.

Nagell shared a great deal of information with author Dick Russell, but he also withheld important details. He might have eventually shared everything he claimed to know about President Kennedy's murder, but he died right before he was scheduled to give a deposition to the Assassination Records Review Board (ARRB) in October 1995.

His death was ruled a heart attack, though his family stated he had had no previous heart problems. A trunk that, according to Nagell, contained "what everybody is trying to get ahold of" was missing from his house. Despite numerous efforts by family members to locate it, it is still missing.

Though the coroner ruled that Nagell died of natural causes, his family suspected foul play. But like so much of Nagell's life, his death is cloaked in secrecy. What is no longer secret is the fact that information he tried to share with authorities about plans for the President's assassination was ignored. If no one in authority had wanted to listen to Richard Case Nagell *before* the assassination, it makes sense that no one would want to listen to him afterwards.

What is still unclear is whether Nagell had been assigned to eliminate Oswald before the assassination date. If that is the case, it is important to know who ordered Nagell to kill Oswald—a detail Nagell never shared. For whatever reason, Richard Case Nagell claimed that he refused the order to kill Lee Harvey Oswald, and the FBI refused to act on his warnings about the President's assassination. The result were the deaths of John F. Kennedy *and* Lee Harvey Oswald.

CHAPTER 18

FORESHADOWING AN ASSASSINATION

"...from an office building with a high-powered rifle."—Joseph Milteer

Richard Case Nagell was not the only person to warn officials that President Kennedy might be killed. Army PFC Eugene B. Dinkin, a cryptographic operator, was stationed in France in 1963. As a cryptographer, he had received the highest clearance given by the military.[249]

Several weeks before the assassination, Dinkin apparently decoded messages which led him to believe "that a conspiracy was in the making by the 'military of the United States, perhaps combined with an 'ultra-right economic group.'"[250] He was so concerned about the information that he sent a registered letter to Attorney General Robert Kennedy on October 16, 1963. He warned the Attorney General that the President would be assassinated in November. When he received no response, Dinkin travelled to the U. S. Embassy in Luxenberg on October 25, 1963, to try to share his information with a Mr. Cunningham, the Charge d' Affaires. Cunningham refused to see him.

Frustrated by the fact that no one was willing to listen to him, Dinkin went AWOL just weeks before the assassination. He heard rumors that he was to be imprisoned because of mental illness and travelled to Switzerland, where he finally found an audience. On November 6, 1963, he told reporters in the Press Room of the United Nations in Geneva that someone was plotting against President Kennedy and that something would happen on the President's trip to Texas. The CIA confirmed this incident in 1964 to the Warren Commission, but the information was not publicly released until 1976 and Dinkin's name was not published until 1992.

Like Richard Case Nagell, Dinkin would soon find himself undergoing one psychiatric evaluation after another. One week after telling reporters that the President would be killed, Dinkin was arrested for being absent without leave and placed in a psychiatric hospital. Later, he was taken to Walter Reed Hospital for psychological testing.

Hiding controversial informants in mental hospitals is a common way for some government agencies to discredit those with inconvenient information.

What eventually happened to Eugene B. Dinkin is unknown. What *is* known is that the information he tried desperately to share with authorities was accurate, but it failed to initiate enough security precautions to prevent Kennedy's assassination. Like Nagell's story, Dinkin's name and experiences never appeared in the Warren Report. Unlike Nagell, Dinkin did not have ties to intelligence organizations. He had simply stumbled upon classified information that indicated President Kennedy's death was *planned*, and not by a "lone nut" assassin.

Not everyone who learned about the upcoming assassination tried to prevent it. Joseph Milteer was not in the military and certainly no a cryptographer, as Dinkin had been. In fact, he was a right-wing segregationist who was tape-recorded on November 9, 1963, by a Miami police informant. On the recording, Milteer was heard saying that the murder of President Kennedy was "in the working." Unaware he was being recorded, he elaborated that the best way to kill Kennedy was "from an office building with a high-powered rifle."[251]

He then made an uncanny prediction. "They will pick up somebody within hours afterwards...just to throw the public off. "[252] None of these predictions applied to President Kennedy's Miami trip because he was scheduled to arrive by helicopter. The only motorcade there involved a short route which would not provide much of an opportunity for an assassin. If Milteer knew there would be only a short motorcade, then he must have also known that the President's assassination would occur in a city in which a lengthy motorcade was planned.

Statements made by Milteer after Kennedy's assassination in Dallas indicate that the plans he had described to the FBI informant worked beautifully in Dallas. Milteer verbally celebrated to the same police informant: "Everything ran true to form. I guess you thought I was kidding when I said he would be killed from a window by a high-powered rifle." When the FBI informant quizzed him about whether his prediction might have been a lucky guess, Milteer replied smugly, "I don't do any guessing."[253]

However, Milteer's prediction about Kennedy's death and how it would take place could very well have been a guess. After all, motorcades were, and are, the most worrisome part of a Secret Service agent's responsibility. However, it seems odd that Milteer knew that the Dallas police would be able to apprehend a suspect as quickly as they did. History shows that this is exactly what happened in Dallas. As Milteer claimed, the speedy arrest of Lee Harvey Oswald and his subsequent murder did "throw the public off" for years and years.

FBI agent Don Adams realized that the so-called "investigation" of Milteer was odd, too. Though a first-year agent, Adams, who lived in Georgia, was assigned to find Milteer. He searched Milteer's small town of Quitman and everywhere near there. He was not able to locate Milteer until *five days after* the assassination.

Even then, he was only allowed to ask five specific questions: 1) With whom had he made contact recently? 2) Had he been to the Constitution Party's National Convention? 3) What were the organizations with which he was affiliated? 4) Had he any knowledge of the bombing of the 16th Street Baptist Church in Birmingham, Alabama on Sept. 15, 1963? and 5) Had he ever made any threats to assassinate the President, or had he participated in a plot to kill President Kennedy?[254]

Adams was dying to ask even more questions, but he had been ordered to ask only these five. What Adams had not been told by his superiors or his partner was that Milteer had been taped making a direct threat on Kennedy's life. He had referred to Kennedy as a "marked man" and also discussed how to get a rifle up into a building in pieces.[255]

Adams later found that an official FBI memo stated that Milteer had been in Quitman, Georgia on November 22, 1963; Adams knew this was untrue. An informant also knew this was not true. He reported in 1963 that Milteer called him on November 22 saying that he was in Dallas! In the early 1990s, Adams spotted a photograph that proved he had been correct. In a crowd of people standing on the east side of Houston Street and watching the presidential motorcade, he spotted a figure he recognized as Joseph Milteer.[256] What Adams never understood was why people in his own organization had covered up the fact that Milteer had not been in Georgia on November 22, 1963.

Nagell, Dinkin, and Milteer were only three of several individuals to claim to have prior knowledge of President Kennedy's death. Only weeks before the President flew to Texas, there were two other serious threats to his life. On November 2, 1963, President Kennedy was scheduled to attend the annual Army-Navy football game in Chicago. Various reasons have been given as to why this trip was cancelled. One reason may have been that the President of South Vietnam and his brother had just been assassinated. Another reason offered to the press was that the President had a head cold.

The Chicago assassination plot involved more than one person, but the background of one of the individuals was much like that of Lee Harvey Oswald's. Thomas Arthur Valle was an ex-Marine—"a disaffiliated member of the John Birch Society, a loner, a paranoid schizophrenic, and a gun collector… the perfect 'lone nut.'" He had been wounded in the Korean War, had suffered a concussion that plagued him for the remainder of his days, and had a history of mental instability."[257]

Chicago Secret Service agents received a tip that Valle had threatened President Kennedy. Two Chicago police officers pulled him over for a so-called traffic violation on November 2, 1963. Within his car they found a hunting knife, 3,000 rounds of ammunition, and an M-1 rifle.

Secret Service agents were also aware of a four-man sniper team which was in Chicago prepared to kill President Kennedy. Two of the men were arrested, but two were not.

Thomas Arthur Valle was not a part of the four-man sniper team, but he would have made a perfect patsy for an assassination attempt. However, Valle's arrest and the fact that the "registration for the license plate on the car that he was driving when he was arrested was classified—restricted to U.S. intelligence agencies," did not become known until after the President's assassination in Dallas."[258]

The story of the four-man hit team and Thomas Arthur Valle was not publicized. In fact, if an investigative reporter had not discovered this information after President Kennedy's death, no one would have known there had ever been plans to assassinate Kennedy in Chicago. Whether Valle was even involved in the Chicago plot to kill Kennedy is questionable. However, there is no question that the Secret Service and the FBI knew that assassins were waiting along Kennedy's motorcade route in Chicago. This information should have prepared government agencies for future assassination attempts, and Texas law enforcement should have known about the Chicago assassination attempt.

Another intriguing individual with prior information about the Kennedy assassination was Ivan (Igor) Vaganov, a Russian immigrant. Vaganov and his wife Anne lived in Pennsylvania but moved to Dallas approximately two weeks before President Kennedy was assassinated. Vaganov chose an apartment in Oak Cliff not far from Oswald's boarding house and Jack Ruby's apartment.

FBI agents interviewed him three hours after the assassination and found in his possession a high-powered rifle with a scope, and a Colt revolver. How the FBI even knew of Vaganov, much less where he lived, is unknown. Their brief interrogation seemed to satisfy them that Vaganov was harmless. However, as soon as the FBI left, Vaganov announced he was going back to Pennsylvania and would return on November 25 to get his wife. He also told her he was taking his rifle with him and planning on disposing of it. He supposedly left for Pennsylvania and was never seen again.

This was particularly disturbing to his wife because she had married him only two weeks before. Their honeymoon had been spent travelling from Pennsylvania through South Carolina, Georgia, Mississippi, Louisiana,

Oklahoma, and finally to Dallas. Vaganov had no job and no job prospects. His new bride told authorities that her husband was never home during the day even though he had no job. Igor Vaganov had so much in common with Lee Harvey Oswald that he, rarther thn Oswald, could easily have been apprehended after the assassination. "Vaganov was twenty-five years old, Russian born, spoke Russian, was new to the area, allegedly in possession of a rifle and a .38 caliber revolver, was in contact with the FBI, and on the day of the assassination, shortly after the murder, returned home, only to leave soon afterwards."[259]

What is not known about Vaganov is his location during the assassination. Oswald could at least prove he was at work. If FBI agents learned where Vaganov was that day, they did not publicize this information. It seems odd, to say the least, that Vaganov abandoned his new wife, left Dallas, and never returned. What is even stranger is that there is no record that the FBI ever searched for him.

It appears that the FBI ignored information that might have saved the President's life. Agents might have assumed that Milteer was nothing more than a braggart. They must have also assumed that Dinkin, a young enlisted man with a security clearance, and Nagell, a military officer who had worked for the intelligence community, were unreliable informants. Perhaps presidential threats were normally so harmless that the FBI could afford to ignore ones they considered trivial. On the other hand, should *any* threat to the President of the United States *ever* be considered "trivial"?

CHAPTER 19
CASTRO KNEW

"'Castro knew,' he said. 'They knew Kennedy would be killed.'"
—Tiny Aspillaga

The more assassination researchers delved into Kennedy's murder, the more they learned about witnesses who were never questioned—witnesses who had information and pieces to the assassination puzzle that would have been valuable to the Warren Commission.

Hank Gordon (a pseudonym), for example, was a retired airplane mechanic who returned to Red Bird Airfield in Oak Cliff, located just outside Dallas, for a few days during the month of November 1963. He had been called to service a Douglas DC-3 before the transfer to its new owner. The pilot of the Douglas DC-3 told Gordon he had been a pilot in Fidel Castro's Cuban air force. It was this pilot who monitored the servicing of the airplane, not the owner. The owner, an Air Force colonel, apparently trusted his pilot implicitly because he never appeared at the airfield after the first day. The owner had wanted the plane ready by Thursday, November 21. But the servicing was so involved that it was not completed until Friday, November 22.

Gordon enjoyed talking with the plane's pilot because the two men once worked together, but he noticed that the pilot never accepted Gordon's invitations to eat lunch at the airport restaurant. Instead, he consistently paid Gordon to bring sack lunches for the two of them from the restaurant. On Thursday, November 21, the pilot made a comment that Gordon never forgot.

The two men were eating lunch when the pilot said simply: "Hank, they are going to kill your President." When Gordon asked him what he meant, the pilot simply repeated himself.

Gordon insisted that the man elaborate, and for whatever reason, he did so. "Hank, I tell you, I was a mercenary pilot hired by the CIA. I was involved in the Bay of Pigs, which was operated by the CIA. I was there with many of my friends when they died, when Robert Kennedy talked John Kennedy out of sending in the air cover which he'd agreed to send. He cancelled the air cover after the invasion was launched. Many, many died. Far more than was told. I don't know all that was going on, but I do know that there was an indescribable amount of hurt, anger, and embarrassment on the part of those who were involved in the operation."

Gordon was unsure whether to believe the pilot. Was the man insane? The pilot's next words were even more chilling. "They are not only going to kill the President, they are going to kill Robert Kennedy and any other Kennedy who gets in that position."

All of this seemed truly unbelievable to Gordon. He knew that if he shared this story with anyone, his credibility as a businessman would be compromised. He might never be allowed to fly a plane again. Gordon explained his reservations to the pilot. "The pilot listened patiently [to Gordon's doubts], then simply murmured, in a matter-of-fact way, 'You will see.'"260

Because the owner was in such a hurry, the two men continued to work frantically as they checked every nut and bolt on the plane. Shortly after noon on November 22, 1963, as Gordon proceeded to refuel the plane, the pilot loaded baggage and cases of oil. It was not long before they heard the news that the President had been shot. Like certain others, this pilot had foreknowledge of the assassination. However, the pilot had not said "he" (referring to a single assassin) was going to kill the President; he had used the word "they."

It is possible that the owner of the Douglas DC-3 wanted the work on the plane completed by Thursday, November 21 so Gordon would not be at Redbird Airport on November 22. Gordon seemed to believe that the pilot knew about the assassination because his plane was used to bring to Dallas people or weapons used to kill the President.

Researcher Matthew Smith discovered that this particular DC-3 had been purchased by Houston Air Center, which was a front for the CIA. This would explain why there is no record of the plane departing from Redbird Airport on November 22, 1963; CIA planes are not logged in or out of airports. This also explains why "Hank Gordon" refused to use his real name, and why it was not revealed until Smith did so after Gordon's death.

"Hank Gordon" was a pseudonym for Wayne January, owner of American Aviation Company, which was located at Red Bird Airport in Dallas. January had also reported a strange encounter with three individuals who inquired about renting a small plane for the afternoon of November 22, 1963. One of those individuals had looked like Lee Harvey Oswald, according to January. Considering how many people with information about Oswald and/or the Kennedy assassination died not long after that event, January was probably wise to keep his foreknowledge to himself.

It has long been speculated that Fidel Castro might have had prior knowledge of President Kennedy's death. There is no doubt that he knew members of the Kennedy administration were trying to kill him. He may have suspected that he would be blamed for Kennedy's death, and a world war would result. It was not until 2012, when Brian Latell published *Castro's Secrets—The CIA and Cuba's Intelligence Machine,* that the world learned that Castro had, indeed, known something would happen to Kennedy in Texas in November of 1963.

Author Latell discovered that on November 22, 1963, Tiny Aspillaga, a Cuban who lived in a small hut in Jaimanitas, was proceeding with his usual assignment of tracking CIA radio chatter when he received a coded message from his headquarters at about 9:00 that morning. "The message instructed him to go over to a second structure that he used, a hundred yards away, and use the secure phone there to call back for instructions."

His orders were to stop all CIA tracking. Instead of focusing on the CIA spies who were both on and near the island of Cuba, or on Miami or CIA headquarters in Virginia, he was to direct his antennas on Texas.

"'I was told to listen to all conversations and to call the leadership if I heard anything important occur. I put all of my equipment to listen to any small detail from Texas. They told me Texas. It wasn't until 2-3 hours later that I began hearing broadcasts on amateur radio bands about the shooting of President Kennedy in Dallas.'" Aspillaga told this directly to researcher Brian Latell. He then added what was obvious from his own experience: "'Castro knew,' he said. 'They knew Kennedy would be killed.'"[261]

The Warren Commission was not told about any of the foreknowledge that researchers later discovered. It would appear that Commission members did not look for any evidence of foreknowledge. It seems unlikely that Richard Nagell, Joseph Milteer, and Eugene Dinkin, to name a few, knew that a person or persons were planning on killing Kennedy, but government agencies did not know. It is more likely that certain people in the government had also heard rumors about the President's upcoming murder. This may be why Nagell and Dinkin were "hospitalized" for mental problems. Instead of being grateful for their warnings, certain government agencies must have panicked because, once again, a plan to assassinate the President might be aborted.

One newspaper in Texas inadvertently published a small article hinting that President John Kennedy might not live long enough to attend a banquet planned for the evening of November 22 in Austin, Texas. Many Austinites were eagerly awaiting the arrival of President Kennedy and the First Lady on the afternoon of the assassination. The couple's itinerary indicated that they were to arrive at Bergstrom Air Force Base in Austin at 3:15.

The public did not find out until 10:25 that morning that they would be able to enter the Air Force base to observe the President and his entourage as they arrived. After a last-minute meeting with Secret Service agents, base officials agreed to accommodate all visitors to the base. This welcome announcement was published on page 27 of the *Austin Statesman,* which was sent to the printers shortly before the world learned that Kennedy had been shot.

This section of the newspaper was covered with large photos and news reports of the presidential party's visits to San Antonio and Houston. One article mentioned President Kennedy's tribute to Rep. Albert Thomas in Houston. However, the large headline read, *"BAFB OPENING GATES TO PUBLIC."*

CHAPTER 20

THE VOICE OF MICHAEL MARCADES

"I have only one memory of seeing my mother…"

A teacher in West Texas learned as an adult that the mother he barely knew was one of numerous people to accurately predict President Kennedy's assassination. Decades after his mother's death, Michael Marcades shared his story with the authors. The small table in his breakfast nook was covered with old documents, faded photographs, and handwritten letters. This ephemera was all that Marcades had left of his mother, Melba Christine Youngblood. The man had spent a large part of his adult life trying to discover more details about his mother. It was a long, frustrating search for this only son; his mother was an enigma. He knew she had loved him, but also that her emotional problems began long before Marcades was born, and they affected both of their lives.

Marcades invited the authors to visit him and his wife in his Odessa home in February 2015. Part of what he wanted to share was another side of a woman whom many know only as "Rose Cherami." Displayed throughout his home were pieces of his mother's artwork and several lovely photographs of her. Marcades seemed to enjoy discussing his mother's early life. In fact, he shared a manuscript he had been working on for years. Entitled *Rose Cherami: Gathering Fallen Petals*, it was a tribute to his mother's life. He asked the authors if they would be willing to read it and make suggestions about its form and content.

Part of the manuscript contained stories he had heard from his grandparents. There were few personal memories. "After all," Marcades says sadly, "I have only one memory of seeing my mother, and that's when I was ten years old."[262] Melba had given her son to her parents before his fifth birthday, and that was because she realized she was unable to care for him herself. The kindest thing Melba Christine Youngblood Marcades ever did was to allow her parents to rear her child.

Marcades' mother, born in 1923 in Houston, Texas, grew up on a farm. But farm life was not for Melba Christine, and she ran away to the "big city." Her story sounds like an overused Hollywood plot. Unfortunately, there was no happy ending.

Family photographs show her lovingly holding her beautiful baby son. Melba had been pretty enough to have been a Hollywood star. And yet, this woman with the angelic face and bubbly personality ended up like so many others during the Great Depression—hungry, addicted to drugs and alcohol, and estranged from her child and family.

A woman with many aliases, she is known to many as "Rose Cherami," the woman thrown from a car in the opening scenes of the Oliver Stone movie, *JFK*. Her life ended mysteriously (like so many others connected to the JFK assassination), on September 4, 1965 on a lonely backwoods Texas road. But there was an important difference between Rose Cherami and other women who craved an exciting city life. This young woman, who had left her child and husband for the glamorous life of the French Quarter in New Orleans, had met dangerous individuals, and then attempted to tell others that on November 20, 21, and 22, 1963, President Kennedy would be killed in Dallas, Texas. She revealed her story to Louisiana State Police trooper Lt. Francis Fruge while he was transferring her from Moosa Memorial Hospital in Eunice, Louisiana, to East Louisiana State Hospital in Jackson, Louisiana.

At the time, Youngblood was using the alias "Rose Cherami." In the past, she had also used the names "Patsy Rodman," "Christine Allen," "Patsy Allen," "Zada Rodman," and who knows how many others. She had been arrested, jailed, and treated in mental facilities. Life in the "big city" had not been kind to her. Her life as a stripper, entertainer, and prostitute brought her into contact with a wide variety of men. These included police officers, sailors, doctors, psychiatrists, and pimps. She was a "Jill of all trades." In fact, Jack Ruby employed her in his Dallas Carousel Club, she claimed.

Law enforcement records show that Youngblood had a long list of arrests for criminal mischief and even for assisting soldiers in their AWOL attempts. Her first arrest occurred in 1941, when she was only seventeen. Her trail of "adventures" took her through Oklahoma, Texas, Louisiana, and down into various parts of Florida, with an occasional trip to the Houston area to visit her son and family. Records indicate that she was arrested so often for vagrancy (an offense so minor that it was often ignored by authorities) that both the authors and Marcades wondered if his mother might have been used as an informant by various police departments. Perhaps the arrests were a means of obtaining information on various illegal activities she witnessed or knew about.

The story she told Lt. Francis Paul Fruge on November 20, 1963, was an intriguing one. She claimed she had been traveling from Florida with two men on their way to Dallas, Texas. She and the two men stopped at a bar in

Eunice, Louisiana, and an argument ensued. The manager of the bar kicked her out, forcing her to hitchhike. Later, the manager identified Cherami's two companions that evening as Sergio Arcacha Smith and Emilio Santana. The two men were anti-Castro Cuban exiles with CIA credentials.[263] These might have been the same two Cubans Nagell had mentioned in his letter to J. Edgar Hoover.

Stories vary concerning what happened to Cherami (the name she gave authorities) after she left the bar. According to witness Frank Odom of Eunice, Louisiana, he accidentally sideswiped her as he was driving on Highway 190. (Other versions are that her two companions in the bar pushed her out of the car). Regardless of how she ended up on the side of Highway 190, she was sideswiped by Odom, who then drove her to the nearby Moosa Memorial Hospital in Eunice.

The hospital administrator, Louise Guillory, called Lieutenent Fruge to take Cherami into custody because she had no insurance, seemed to be intoxicated, and appeared to be a drug addict. Fruge picked up Cherami and delivered her to the Eunice jail. It wasn't long before she began displaying withdrawal symptoms. Dr. F. J. DeRouen was called to the jail and, after examining her, committed her to East Louisiana State Hospital in Jackson. Fruge agreed to accompany Cherami in the ambulance. During the 100-mile trip, the officer learned things that may eventually have cost Cherami her life.

She admitted that her two male traveling compamions were on their way to Dallas to kill the President. Assuming she was disoriented because of her drug-induced state, Fruge simply let her talk. He ignored her comment about someone killing Kennedy because it seemed ludicrous at the time. Cherami spoke repeatedly about her "baby Michael" and about "picking up some money."

Cherami also shared with Fruge that a heroin deal was to take place in Houston, Texas, after the assassination. She mentioned the name of a ship that would arrive with the drugs; however, she mispronounced the name *SS Maturata* as "Mary Etta," but a U.S. Customs agent later realized she had meant *Maturata,* and he informed Louisiana authorities that Cherami was correct; this ship *was scheduled* to arrive soon in Port Arthur, Texas, which is near Houston.

At East Louisiana State Hospital on November 21, Rose Cherami repeated to the hospital staff the same "ludicrous" story she had told Fruge. She insisted that Kennedy was going to be killed in Dallas by her two male companions. She also admitted to Dr. Victor Weiss that she had worked as a stripper for a man named Jack Ruby in Dallas and also as a drug courier. Cherami mentioned she had seen Jack Ruby with a man by the name of "Lee Harvey Oswald" several times in Ruby's Carousel Club in Dallas. What caused her to mention Oswald in connection with Ruby is unknown unless she connected both men to Kennedy's upcoming death.

The Carousel Club wasn't the only club owned by Ruby with which Rose Cherami was familiar. Coincidentally, he also owned the Silver Slipper Lounge in Louisiana, where Smith and Santana had stopped the night before.[264] Cherami knew significant details, such as the fact that Jack Ruby's real name was "Rubenstein" and that he was sometimes known as "Pinky." She told Dr. Wayne Owen, another physician at the hospital, that "Ruby-Rubenstein" had been involved in planning the assassination of John Kennedy.[265]

Despite the drugs or alcohol Cherami had been using before her hospitalization, she was sober by November 22, 1963 and still a patient at the hospital. On the day of the assassination, she and a group of nurses were watching various television clips of Kennedy's tour of Texas and his arrival at Love Field in Dallas.

Suddenly, Cherami became agitated, exclaiming loudly, "This is when it's going to happen."[266] She was the only viewer in the hospital *not* shocked when the announcements about the shooting of the President and his subsequent death were made. After all, she had been warning people for more than three days that this event was going to occur. Perhaps she should have kept the information to herself.

When he heard about the President's death, Fruge remembered Cherami's stories and contacted his supervisor, Capt. Ben Morgan, who immediately travelled to the hospital to hear her story personally. Morgan was so convinced of her sincerity that he contacted *his* supervisor, Col. Thomas D. Burbank; Burbank insisted Cherami be taken into police custody.

During the weekend, Fruge contacted the FBI in Lafayette, Louisiana, explaining to the agent that a woman had accurately predicted the assassination. The agent stated, "They've already got their man. Case closed."[267] Morgan then personally contacted an old friend, Dallas Chief of Homicide Will Fritz about Cherami's story, assuming *he* would listen to him. He was wrong. When he hung up the telephone, Morgan told the others, "They don't want her. They're not interested."[268]

However, because of her statements about an upcoming drug deal in Houston, Cherami was flown Tuesday, November 26, on a small private jet from Baton Rouge, Louisiana, to Houston, Texas. The FBI was contacted by the chief customs agent in Houston about Cherami's claim. He was told that the FBI agents did not want to talk to her.[269] Cherami seemed almost relieved that she did not have to speak to the FBI. This could be because she had arrest sheets from Houston under numerous aliases. Maybe she saw no reason to draw any more attention to herself than she already had.

Rose Cherami survived longer than some of the other witnesses who spoke out about the assassination, but not by much. Because the record of her autopsy has been lost, all that researchers and her family know is that on September 4, 1965, her half-dead body was found in Big Sandy, Texas. Apparently, she had been run over by a vehicle; however, a doctor who examinered her shortly after she was found noted that above her temple was a "punctuate stellate laceration."[270] In layman's terms, this meant a gunshot wound to the head. Some of her wounds could have been made by a car accidentally hitting her, but a gunshot wound indicates a deliberate act. The young man who almost hit Cherami in the early morning hours described her body as having been placed strategically on the road.

Some records show Cheramie was dead on arrival at the hospital in Gladewater, Texas. Others show she had been injured, treated by hospital staff, and was alive for several hours. Regardless, by 10:00 a.m. on September 5, 1965, the young man who had found her on the side of the road was told by hospital staff that she was dead. He was also told that a doctor from Dallas had driven 80 miles in the early hours of the morning to Gladewater to treat Cherami, but his efforts had been futile.[271]

What died with Rose Cherami were the answers to mysterious questions about her knowledge and passive role in the Kennedy assassination. Was she an innocent eavesdropper who had simply heard too much? Was she a government informant who had talked too much? Perhaps Rose Cherami had outlived her usefulness, and thus ended up discarded on a dark, lonely road.

CHAPTER 21

THE VOICES OF LT. J. GOODE AND ROBERT "TOSH" PLUMLEE

**"...They had already found what they wanted
and weren't interested in it..."—J. Goode**

Over a span of several months, J. Goode regaled the authors with interesting stories about his military and intelligence career (*see chapter 6*). Finally, he admitted using numerous aliases in his line of work. This caused the authors to wonder if his real name was really "J. Goode." At one time, he slipped up and mentioned that he had sometimes used the alias "Randy Ely." (This was years before a "Randy P. Ely" had become the head of the U.S. Marshalls for the Northern District of Texas). At another time, Goode boasted about the nickname his fellow agents had bestowed upon him. Because of his excellent eyesight, he was known to close associates as "old Eagle Eye."

As Goode became more comfortable with the authors, he began to share more experiences about his time in the military, about his experiences after his discharge, and about what he witnessed the day of President Kennedy's assassination.

The authors asked Goode the same question they asked all interviewees: "Where were you on November 22, 1963?" His first answer was that he was attending a "special" meeting in San Diego. When asked why, he looked away and finally answered, "It was a meeting to determine what went wrong."[272]

The next question for Goode concerned the exact time of the special meeting in San Diego. He hemmed and hawed and finally responded, "In the late afternoon." His hesitancy indicated that there was even more to the story. The important question hung in the air: Was he in Dallas that day in November?

"Yes," he answered quietly as he again looked away. He and his boss, U.S. Marshal Robert I. Nash, were at the assassination site that day, having been informed that there was going to be a hit on Kennedy. Three abort teams were sent to Dallas to prevent the hit. One team went to Dealey Plaza, one team was assigned to the Trade Mart, where a luncheon was scheduled, and the third on the route back to Love Field Airport.

"The President was going to be taken out in one of these three locations,"

Goode explained. One of Marshal Nash's abort teams, consisting of Goode and two other men, had arrived the day before the assassination and spent the night in Dallas.

"Yes," Goode grinned, "we did go to the Carousel Club that night." He seemed almost embarrassed as he added, "It wasn't that big a deal." At the time of the assassination, Marshal Nash himself was standing at the top of the triple underpass. Goode was stationed below the triple underpass near the entrance to Stemmons Freeway. Two other marshals were stationed elsewhere in the Plaza. The sound of the first shots convinced both Goode and his superior that at least one of the shots had originated from the *southeast* side of Dealey Plaza.

Goode noticed two figures; one was crouched on the top of the County Records Building on the eastside of Houston Street, and one appeared to be aiming a rifle from a window on the top floor of the County Records Building. A rifle shot and a puff of smoke indicated someone had fired from the top floor. Goode and Nash recalled hearing four shots. The two men had seen the presidential limousine speed by them with the wounded President and Governor inside.

"There was so much blood visible that we thought Jackie Kennedy had been shot also," Goode stated. One of the details that Goode noticed that day was a man he knew as Roscoe White standing on the north side of the grassy knoll. When he mentioned that name, the authors immediately interjected, "Oh, you mean the Dallas cop." Goode shook his head and responded, "Not that day he wasn't. That day he was Secret Service!" This could explain the fact that witnesses who ran to the north side of the grassy knoll encountered a man who identified himself as a secret service agent even though no agents were assigned to that area.

Goode and Nash ran directly to the southeast corner of the Plaza from where they thought one shot had come; they discovered a rifle casing. They then continued searching the area while they proceeded to the County Records Building and then to the School Book Depository Building. There they helped the Dallas Police Department and the FBI search the building; they were present when the other casings were found.

Marshal Nash transferred the original casing he and Goode found to the FBI that afternoon. Nash shared with the FBI what Goode had witnessed at the County Records Building. The officials' skepticism prompted him to "drag Goode over to the Dallas Police Department to give a first-hand account of what he had seen."

The FBI soon dusted the ledge of the window in the County Records Building that Goode had pointed out. They found that a gun had been recently fired in the vicinity. Goode added, "They told us they would look into it further. We thought they would." Neither of the men ever heard this information mentioned again. After Oswald was arrested and charged with the assassination, said Goode, "There were more things I should have said but didn't. I would tell them what I saw and they would tell me that they would look into it. My commander finally said to me, 'You *know* the drill.' Goode realized the smartest thing he could do—the only thing he could do—was to keep what he knew to himself.

Because Goode had not mentioned an assassin firing from the Depository, the authors immediately asked if he believed Oswald had even shot at the President. His response stunned them.

"Which Oswald?" he asked casually. Before the authors could demand an explanation for this startling question, Goode continued. "I knew both Oswalds and didn't like either one of them. They were military intelligence. They were both in Dealey Plaza that day. I knew them, so I recognized them. I just didn't know why they were there." It was months later that he would discuss the two Oswalds again. When he did, he added that he had later seen the Oswald who survived the weekend of November 22, 1963 in Houston driving a taxi.

When asked why the casing he and Nash had found was never mentioned in any reports or by any officials, Goode stated bluntly, "They had already found what they wanted and weren't interested in it." That also applied to the fact that the two men heard *four* shots instead of three, and that Goode witnessed a figure shooting from the County Records Building, *not* from the Texas School Book Depository Building.

Goode was debriefed at the naval facility in San Diego, where he gave a deposition conducted by the Office of Naval Intelligence. He recalled that Nash created a report describing his and Goode's experiences on November 22, 1963. But according to David Turk, archivist for the U.S. Marshal Service, no such report can be found.

Nash was allowed to help question Lee Harvey Oswald. However, researchers know this only because Nash was mentioned in a deposition taken of FBI agent James W. Bookhout on April 8, 1964.

In his deposition, Bookhout listed the witnesses to Oswald's interrogation, and Nash's name was among them. Despite witnessing the questioning of Oswald, Nash was not asked to submit a report of what he had observed, unlike some of the other witnesses. Goode's deposition, though taken at the naval facility in San Diego, is not included in any way in the Warren Report. Goode heard that Nash had been given a "hard time" after the assassination. This may be why, in his obituary, the Nash family included information about his service in the military but did not even mention his service with the U.S. Marshals.

According to Goode, Nash was given a "hard time" by other government agencies because his and Goode's assassination accounts did not match that of the official Warren Report. That explains why Nash's written recollections of what he and Goode had witnessed on November 22, 1963, no longer exist.

Regardless, the fact that Nash's team was there to abort the assassination attempt is key evidence of an organized planned hit that was known about beforehand. The fact that his report was eliminated from the official record is evidence that what he knew was dangerous to the Warren Report because it contradicted the official story.

Robert "Tosh" Plumlee had no idea J. Goode and U.S. Marshal Nash were in Dealey Plaza on November 22, 1963, though his mission complemented theirs. Plumlee was involved in military intelligence and, because of this, became connected with the CIA in 1956. Like Goode, Plumlee also knew that there was a "Lee Harvey Oswald" involved in military intelligence.

He shared this information in a conversation with the authors on November 21, 2014. The authors met Plumlee at a small bookstore-coffee shop not far from Dealey Plaza, near where John F. Kennedy and his motorcade made the fateful turn onto Elm Street. Directly west of the coffee shop stands the Sixth Floor Museum, formerly the Texas School Book Depository.

"I was a pilot," Plumlee stated, "and they needed my skills in a gun-running operation to Havana, Cuba. The operation was called M-267 and it was an operation to supply guns and ammunition to students at the University of Havana."[273] Over the years, Plumlee continued to work for "military intelligence" by flying missions for the CIA.

Plumlee began to share personal stories about some of his intelligence assignments. In 1954, he entered the military's specialized operations at Fort Bliss, Texas, and worked with various military intelligence units of the Fourth Army. In the early 1960s, he was assigned to a Task Force that operated from the JM/WAVE station in Miami, which was also the CIA's "Cuba Desk."

Plumlee's memories included first-hand knowledge about the events of November 22, 1963. On November 20, 1963 Plumlee's assignment was to serve as a co-pilot on a top-secret mission to Dallas, Texas. Because of the warning Private Eugene Dinkin gave to military authorities, an abort team had been organized and ordered to Dallas. Those involved were members of military intelligence supported by certain CIA individuals. The purpose of the mission, as Plumlee understood it, was to abort the assassination of President John F. Kennedy in Dallas. Plumlee did not specify how many abort teams were in his group.

Plumlee was serving as co-pilot to Emmanuel Rojas, with whom he had worked before. Also, Plumlee's friend Sergio, whose last name he refused to provide, was the field operative for this operation. Plumlee admitted in 2018 that another person on the airplane that day was CIA agent Howard Hunt. Hunt denied this fact until shortly before his death, when he finally confessed to his son, St. John.

Team members departed from Lantana, Florida, on November 21, 1963, landing in Tampa, Florida. In Tampa, Johnny Roselli, a member of organized crime associated with mob bosses Santos Trafficante and Sam Giancana, both of whom were on Attorney General Robert Kennedy's "Most Wanted List," joined the team, along with a few other men. Plumlee knew Roselli from other missions. November 22, 1963 was not the first time the CIA had collaborated with organized crime members.

The team's next stop was New Orleans. Here, without comment, a few men departed the plane while others boarded. The flight then continued to Houston International Airport, where the group spent the night. On the next day, November 22, Plumlee remembered, they all rose early and flew into Garland Airport near Dallas. This is where Roselli left the group. Rojas, Sergio, Plumlee, and a few others then flew on to Redbird Airport in Oak Cliff, not far from Oswald's boarding house and Jack Ruby's apartment. At this point, Plumlee recalled, he and the other team members were taken to a safe house close to the Oak Cliff Country Club.

Some people have questioned whether Roselli was actually in Dallas the day Kennedy was killed. According to Bernie Sindler, who describes himself as "a protégé of mobster Meyer Lansky, who he considered his surrogate father," Roselli admitted that mobster Sam Giancana was involved in the Kennedy assassination. Roselli claimed that Oswald had been deliberately set up as a patsy, and that Jack Ruby "was chosen to eliminate Oswald because Ruby was dying of cancer and had nothing to lose." The most startling comment Roselli made to Sindler was that "Bobby Kennedy was to be next because of his continued harassment of the Mob." [274] Sindler realized how accurate Roselli had been when, in 1968, Robert Kennedy was assassinated. He did not know that Hank Gordon had heard a similar comment at Redbird Airport from a Cuban with inside information.

He also did not know that a man in Dallas that day in November 1963 knew *exactly* where Johnny Roselli was when Kennedy was shot.[275] Roderick MacKenzie, a former mobster (if there is such a thing) was also a surgical nurse. (Even members of the Mafia need back-up careers, it would seem, and nursing was preferable to the carnival life that MacKenzie was also familiar with!) Thanks to Dr. Robert Sparkman, the respected head of surgery at Baylor

Hospital in 1963, MacKenzie gained experience as a surgical nurse at Baylor. He also continued to associate with a wide variety of individuals, from mobsters Johnny Roselli and Jack Ruby to Jake Miranda, a member of the Defense Intelligence Security Command.

On November 22, 1963, MacKenzie was ordered to come to the basement cafeteria of Baylor Hospital at noon. When he arrived, he saw Roselli and Miranda, both dressed in suits, waiting for him at a table. Roselli left the table briefly to use a pay phone outside of the cafeteria. The three men made small talk; neither Roselli nor Miranda explained why they had insisted that MacKenzie meet them at Baylor on his day off. At about 12:40, Roselli went back to the pay phone, returning shortly but "visibly shaken."

"We won't be needing your services today after all," he told MacKenzie.[276] When questioned by the House Select Committee on Assassinations (not long before he was found dead), Roselli claimed that on the day of the assassination, he was in his apartment in Las Vegas. Of course, Tosh Plumlee contradicted this statement, and now, Roderick MacKenzie has, too.

A story a then twenty-six-year-old laboratory technician shared with the authors in 2015 now looms more important than it did at the time. Monzel Bailey recalled that her husband Jessell had worked at Baylor Hospital in November, 1963.[277] A day or so before the assassination, he told his wife that staff members at Baylor had been informed about the President's upcoming visit and that Baylor was to be prepared in case of a medical emergency affecting the President or his entourage. So, the officials who helped plan Kennedy's visit had selected *Baylor Hospital*, not Parkland Hospital, if the President needed medical assistance. Bailey also remembered that she called her husband at Baylor the minute she heard the radio announcer say that shots had been fired at the motorcade.

"I called my husband when I heard it on the radio and he said, 'They'll take him to Parkland because that's where they're headed." This explains why the medical personnel at Parkland Hospital had been caught off-guard that day. The staff there had not been warned that their hospital might have to receive the President or anyone else in the motorcade.

Could it also explain why Johnny Roselli and Jake Miranda were sitting aimlessly in the Baylor Hospital cafeteria not long before the assassination? Could the assassination explain why they wanted MacKenzie, a surgical nurse who worked often with the chief of surgery *at Baylor* Hospital, present there on his day off? Roselli's comment to MacKenzie after the last phone call indicated that MacKenzie was to be used that day in some capacity. Perhaps he would have assisted Dr. Sparkman and therefore would have been privy to details about the President's wounds.

Bailey continued with one last memory. "I talked to my husband until they could get a radio up there. I kept them informed about what the radio was reporting." Like so many other little stories that seemed unimportant at first, Monzel Bailey's anecdote about her husband's location on November 22, 1963 may be a very important piece to the assassination puzzle. It explains why Johnny Roselli disappeared after Tosh Plumlee's flight to Dallas, and it provides an alibi for him as far as being an active participant in the assassination. But it does not explain the mysterious phone calls right before Kennedy was shot and why he told MacKenzie that he would not be "needed after all!"

It also does not explain why MacKenzie was transferred to Parkland Hospital just two weeks after the assassination. His explanation is that he was supposed to ask questions of anyone and everyone who might have information about what occurred in Trauma Room 1 and during the aftermath of the assassination. Apparently, MacKenzie asked one too many questions because he was soon discharged from Parkland. This made it easy for him to leave Dallas, which he soon did.

Unaware that Bernie Sindler and Roderick MacKenzie had provided support for his story, Plumlee stared thoughtfully through the window of the coffee shop. Suddenly, he suggested that the authors join him as he retraced the path he had walked fifty-one years before. He guided them to an elevated area of the plaza, covered with trees and shrubbery which provided cover in 1963 for Plumlee and Sergio. Tourists to Dealey Plaza seldom venture to this area because it is opposite from where all the shots that killed Kennedy *supposedly* came.

Plumlee elaborated on his previous comments as he and the authors climbed to the elevated area linked to the Triple Underpass. This is where he and Sergio had concealed themselves among the trees that day in November.

Plumlee remembered that he was only in Dealey Plaza because Sergio had asked him if he wanted to accompany him to the Plaza to act as a spotter for the abort team. This request had caught Plumlee by surprise because he was supposed to have remained on the plane with the pilot.

The team was under extreme pressure because of flight delays. Normally, a team would have arrived several hours (or days) earlier so that it had ample time to survey the area. Only after his arrival in Dealey Plaza did Tosh Plumlee learn what plans were in place for Sergio's abort team.

The third member of this abort team, a man known to Plumlee simply as "Gator," was assigned a position near the Texas School Book Depository. Photos of Dealey Plaza taken during the assassination show two men sitting on the curb of Elm Street waiting for the motorcade. One of the men was holding a black umbrella. Photographs show that the other man was carrying a walkie-talkie. Apparently, Gator found a "suspicious" character and planted himself right next to him. If the "umbrella man" had plans to harm or insult the President, Gator was to make sure that those plans did not materialize. This explains why photos show a walkie-talkie in the back pocket of the man as he walked away after the assassination.

During our time with him, Plumlee stood quietly in the shadows of a tree much taller than it had been fifty years ago. He explained what "surveillance" meant in relation to an abort team.

"The abort team was not there to shoot snipers," he said. "You can imagine what chaos would have erupted if those on the abort team were trying to shoot back at the assassins. Innocent bystanders would have been killed." Therefore, the abort team's assignment was to interfere in a non-violent manner with anyone attempting to harm the President.

This interference could be something as simple as bumping into someone who appeared to be carrying a concealed weapon. Another type of interference could be standing casually next to someone acting suspiciously. A suspicious individual might be dressed differently, might keep his hands in his pockets, or might even be carrying something like an umbrella. (Goode explained that his role had been to prevent any cars traveling on Stemmons Freeway towards Dealey Plaza from interfering with the presidential motorcade.)

"This is where Sergio and I were standing," Plumlee stated. As part of their surveillance, he and Sergio checked various angles to determine the best location for an assassin. They decided that a sniper would use lampposts as markers. So, they positioned themselves so that a shot from that location would be impossible. "We aligned ourselves with the light posts in the Plaza. The ones we used that day have been moved since 1963," Plumlee added.

"Teams of assassins are made up of three people," he explained, "the shooter, the spotter, and the breakdown man. When shooting a moving target, you don't move your weapon along with the target, but you station your weapon in alignment with objects in the kill zone. That is why we used the lamp posts."

Plumlee and Sergio were frustrated that November day because nothing seemed to be going as planned. The teams were not all in position, and the radios they were using to communicate with did not work. Another problem, Plumlee remembered, was a diversion in the Plaza. An ambulance was called to Dealey Plaza to transport a man to the hospital.

Plumlee believed that this was not a coincidence. "This is a way for the shooting team to get into place while the chaos from the emergency situation is going on. We felt this was a diversion, so we went back up to check the Post Office parking lot. We figured the shooters would be getting into place."

Finding nothing suspicious, the two men returned to their original location just in time to hear the sound of gunfire. A look of sadness crossed Plumlee's face as he recalled the shock of that moment. He shook his head slowly and pointed. "One was fired behind me, to my left on the southwest knoll." He showed the authors the area where he thought that shot had originated.

Plumlee and the authors climbed back along the fence line between the Post Office parking lot and the south side of the triple underpass. It became apparent why Plumlee and Sergio had not seen the sniper. The end sections of the wall of the triple underpass were built at such an angle that they could hide any activity by someone standing on the triple underpass or from anyone on the Plaza.

Plumlee believed this shooter escaped through the Post Office parking lot immediately south of the triple underpass. All the assassin had to do was hand the rifle to his breakdown man, walk casually to the parking lot, and climb into his escape vehicle. The breakdown man would quickly dismantle the rifle and walk calmly away from the scene of the crime. No one would notice any activity in the Post Office parking lot because it was so far away from the motorcade route. After all, most of the attention was focused on the School Book Depository Building or the "grassy knoll" on the *north* side of Dealey Plaza.

Plumlee did not indicate whether he thought the sniper's bullet hit the President or not. However, the location he pointed out would have been perfect for a cross fire. Because the first shot or two occurred while the President's limousine was approaching the Stemmons Freeway sign (based on the Zapruder film), it's possible that Kennedy turned towards Nellie Connally, who sat on the left side of the Lincoln. She had just commented, "You sure can't say Dallas doesn't love you, Mr. President," and Kennedy's last words, according to author William Manchester were, "No, you can't."[278] Nellie Connally, who should know, recalled that Kennedy just smiled and nodded.[279] It's possible that President Kennedy did not have time to reply before the shooting began. Connally wrote in a magazine article that "in that instant, the first shot rang out."[280]

Her recollection indicates that Kennedy had been looking in her direction (southwest) right before the first shot. Because the limousine was behind the Stemmons Freeway sign, the Zapruder film shows only the President's reaction to what Parkland Hospital surgeons referred to as a "throat shot." A sniper on the top of the southwest side of the triple underpass could have fired the bullet that hit Kennedy in the throat, or in the left side of the head, a wound observed by two of the Parkland doctors. Nellie Connally's comment indicates that Kennedy obviously turned away from the right side of the car and directed his attention to her.

After the last shot rang out, the abort team found it necessary to disappear as quickly as possible. Because the abort team had been in Dallas on a secret mission, Plumlee admitted, "We had to high-tail it out of there." He and Sergio realized their efforts had been futile. Even from where they were standing on the south side of the Plaza, they had seen the result of the assassins' work. So, the two men scrambled back along the fence line between the Post Office parking lot and the knoll and slid down the muddy hill on the other side of the triple underpass. Plumlee managed to stay on his feet, but Sergio slipped and ended up covered with mud and dirt. A car was waiting for them on the other side of the underpass. They quickly merged into the Dallas traffic and escaped the nightmare at Dealey Plaza.

"We stopped and Sergio changed clothes in the parking lot of a Sportatorium," Plumlee recalled. "Then we headed to a safe house. We eventually arrived back at Redbird Airport and took off around 2 p.m." When asked who besides himself was on the plane departing that afternoon, he replied, "Rojas, and I was his co-pilot, Sergio, Gator, who was in the Plaza on the opposite side of the street sitting by the man with the umbrella, and two other guys." Johnny Roselli was *not* on the plane; no one seems to know where he was before, during, or after the assassination. The necessity of leaving immediately without drawing attention to himself explained why Gator simply turned and casually walked away after the assassination.

Looking back, Plumlee is still saddened that he, Sergio, and Gator were unable to prevent the President's death. However, he cannot help but question the true purpose of the abort team he had been asked to join. A worried look crossed his face as he wondered aloud, "I thought it was an abort team, but it could also have been a combination of abort and shooter." Obviously, Plumlee carries a heavy burden of doubt about the abort team's role in the assassination, because he can only verify the actions of the threesome he was a part of.

According to Plumleee, an assassin was placed on the south side of Dealey Plaza, and he probably escaped through the parking lot of the Post Office. He remembered smelling gun powder as he and Sergio made their escape. Strangely enough, two doctors (Dr. Marion Jenkins and Dr. Robert McClelland) who examined Kennedy at Parkland Hospital recalled a small wound in the President's left temple. The President's thick hair partially covered the entry wound, but Robert Kennedy's representative at the official autopsy claimed that he, too, noticed this wound. In fact, he said he inserted a small glass pipette through the wound. Other doctors seem to have thought the "wound" was nothing more than clotted blood. If Jenkins and McClelland were correct, the assassin's bullet could have struck Kennedy in the left temporal area at the same time that another bullet struck him on the right side of his head.

Like Tosh Plumlee, J. Goode and Marshal Robert Nash did everything they could to prevent the President's death and to expose the truth about it. They cannot be held responsible for the fact that the FBI and the Dallas police showed no interest in the information they tried to share with them. Hank Gordon (Wayne January), like so many other witnesses, kept his information to himself. Considering that Goode and Nash were ignored and Rose Cherami was killed, perhaps this was the wisest thing he could have done.

However, each of these witnesses' stories contains important pieces of information that should have been investigated. Authorities should have discovered whether the plane that Gordon serviced at Redbird Airport on November 20, 1963 was used to spirit at least one of the assassination teams out of Dallas. They should have also determined whether any of the abort teams in Dallas participated in the assassination. Of course, the problem is, any of this information would have shown that the President had been killed by more than one assassin, and certain members of the military-government had foreknowledge of his death.

(For several years after the assassination, Plumlee searched for his teammate Gator. He tracked him to Florida but was unable to make contact with him. By knitting together the pieces of the puzzle that Plumlee shared, together with information from other witnesses, the authors were finally able to find evidence to prove that Plumlee's friend "Gator" was actually Jim Bolden, who spent a great deal of his life hiding secret documents for various government organizations. His story appears in Chapter 68.)

IV
IN THE SHADOWS OF
DEALEY PLAZA

The moment Lee Harvey Oswald was arrested on November 22, 1963, his life and the lives of those who had ever come into contact with him changed forever.

CHAPTER 22

THE ACCUSED ASSASSIN

"I'm waiting for someone to come forward and give me legal assistance."
—Lee Harvey Oswald

It's been over fifty years since the name "Lee Harvey Oswald" became as well-known (and infamous) as the name "John Wilkes Booth." When the world first learned Oswald had been accused of murdering a Dallas police officer and the President of the United States, the public was also told that the two separate killings were nothing more than two simple acts of murder.

Officially, Oswald was described as an ex-Marine malcontent who had defected to Russia, married a local Russian girl, seen the error of his ways, and returned to America, where he was still discontented with politics and his lack of personal success. An argument with his wife one night supposedly triggered an emotional outburst which led to the assassination of President John F. Kennedy.

This "lone nut," according to journalists, law enforcement officials, and eventually, an elite group of government representatives, assassinated Kennedy, not because he disliked him, but because he desperately wanted attention. He supposedly killed the President all by himself with very little planning or forethought.

The American people were fed just enough information to support these assertions. This was partly because most of the facts about Oswald were either unknown or deliberately not disclosed. For several years, crucial pieces of information remained hidden because Oswald was himself murdered before he could be tried. The many questions about who this young man really was could not be answered, at least by him, because he had been silenced.

Oswald had no opportunity to confide in a lawyer of his choice. After his death, his wife, children, and mother were held in seclusion so that they were unable to talk publicly. So, the world learned about Oswald, his background, his personality, and his motives from the same people who had interrogated him. News reporters depended upon Dallas District Attorney Henry Wade, Dallas Homicide Chief Will Fritz, and Dallas Police Chief Jesse Curry for pertinent information. Those who wanted more than the official story had to look for it themselves.

Most Americans had no reason to doubt what they learned from the media. The government, with the help of law enforcement, including the FBI, convinced most people that there was enough evidence to convict Oswald of killing both Dallas police officer J. D. Tippit and President Kennedy. Though Oswald maintained his innocence from the moment he was arrested, few Americans questioned his guilt or the official story about him until a local Dallas night club owner, Jack Ruby, slipped into the basement of the heavily guarded Dallas Police Department and killed the accused assassin. The only fact the American people knew for sure was that Ruby had murdered a man identified as Lee Harvey Oswald on live television in front of millions of people. Perhaps Ruby was the one who really wanted attention. If so, he got it.

Suddenly, Oswald's protestations of being "a patsy" did not sound so ridiculous. Some people began to believe that Oswald was exactly what he had tried to tell people he was—that he had been set up to take the fall for the President's death. Maybe he was merely a young man in the wrong place at the wrong time. (What the public did not know was that there were other young men also in the wrong place at the wrong time that weekend! They were fortunate enough to live to survive that infamous weekend.) More importantly, the world did not know that for the previous twenty-four years, the lives of two young men, both named "Lee Harvey Oswald" had intersected repeatedly.

It took numerous researchers years to find evidence that a powerful organization had secretly merged the identities of two young boys. The boys seemed to share a name, a birth date, addresses and, from time to time, schools and military backgrounds. They even resembled one another. Their mothers were both identified as "Marguerite Oswald," though there was little physical similarity between the two women.

Is it any wonder that Warren Commission members were confused by what appeared to be contradictory facts concerning the President's accused assassin? When witnesses described Oswald driving a car, the Commission knew this was not possible (or unlikely) because the man they knew as "Oswald" had no driver's license. When one witness saw Oswald purchasing candy in an Oak Cliff store at the same time the "real" Oswald was at work in the School Book Depository, the Commission assumed that witness was mistaken. This happened too many times to be coincidental.

Nevertheless, the Dallas Police Department and eventually the Warren Commission had the unenviable responsibility of forcing puzzle pieces together that would not interlock. The "Oswald" who was arrested never claimed credit for Tippet's or Kennedy's deaths; he refused to admit that he had killed either of them. In this way, he was unlike America's three previous presidential assassins.

John Wilkes Booth had proudly proclaimed that he and his co-conspirators had murdered Abraham Lincoln. Charles Julius Guiteau had announced loudly that he had killed President James Garfield. Leon Czolgosz had openly admitted that he had killed President William McKinley, "because I done my duty."[281]

Oswald, on the other hand, adamantly proclaimed that he was "a patsy." As he was moved through the corridors of the Dallas Police Department, he readily answered media questions. Obviously, journalists and the public wanted to know anything and everything about Oswald and the assassination. They found themselves stymied by government roadblocks, conflicting testimonies, and the fact that the story of Oswald's life became a puzzle with missing pieces. A *complete* biography of Lee Harvey Oswald contains as much contradictory evidence as the assassination itself. Because there are no official records of what Oswald told his interrogators while incarcerated, even his last two days on earth are cloaked in secrecy.

One of the few facts that historians know is that a man identified as Oswald occupied cell F-2 on the third floor of the Dallas Police Department. Oswald was originally charged *only* with the murder of a Dallas police officer. Considering the bonds that tie law enforcement together and the public support that Dallas law enforcement had in 1963, it is almost miraculous that Oswald was not killed during his arrest. In fact, a lynch mob gathered outside the front of the Texas Theatre anticipating the arrested suspect's appearance through the front doors. Whether the angry citizens thought Oswald had killed a police officer or the President is unclear. There were other suspects (most of whom are unknown to the American public) that were held and/or arrested on November 22, 1963 on suspicion of murdering the President, not just Oswald. Apparently, the mob did not know about these individuals.

In an original Ft. Worth newscast, the announcer carefully stated that there did *not* appear to be a connection between the killing of Dallas police officer J. D. Tippit and the President's murder. Perhaps he reported this because he knew that one suspect had already been arrested in Dallas but released for lack of evidence—someone identified as Donald Wayne House. The mob of people waiting for Oswald outside of the theatre was focused only on a young man inside, not on House or any other suspects.

It's likely that Oswald realized he might be killed inside the theatre by Dallas police. Why else would he have repeatedly yelled, "I am not resisting arrest, I am not resisting arrest!" He offered little information about himself to the arresting officers; if he were keeping information from the police, the police were also keeping information from him. The Dallas news media appeared to know more about the charges that would be filed against him than Oswald did.

During a press conference on the evening of the President's assassination, a reporter asked Oswald if he was guilty of shooting the President. The man who had already been declared by the media as the prime assassination candidate did not know he would be charged with this crime. He answered the reporter with this statement: "I really don't know what the situation is other than I am accused of killing a policeman. I know nothing more than that. I'm waiting for someone to come forward to give me legal assistance."[282]

From the moment Oswald was arrested, he protested what he referred to as "police brutality." A bruise on his face could attest to that, and a police officer would admit years later that he had, indeed, slammed the butt of his rifle into Oswald's face. This fact was hidden for decades.[283] Oddly enough, Oswald's bruised appearance may explain why Chief Jesse Curry wanted the press to repeatedly see that the prisoner had not been harmed. Consequently, Oswald was paraded through crowded hallways, full of angry police officers who believed he had killed one of their own, and news reporters who had already been led to believe he had assassinated the President. The Dallas police should have anticipated that someone might impulsively shoot the accused assassin. Numerous individuals certainly had the opportunity.

If Oswald ever thought he would receive a fair trial in Dallas, Texas, he should have realized differently the night before he was killed. As Captain Fritz escorted the handcuffed prisoner from one floor to another, the doors to the elevator opened and Oswald and Fritz found themselves facing John Curington, a Dallas attorney who worked for millionaire H. L. Hunt. Recognizing Curington, Fritz boomed, "Meet the son-of-a-bitch who killed the president!"[284] Oswald must have begun to understand the seriousness of his predicament, but, if so, he did not allow anyone else to know.

At first, he reacted to his arrest the way most innocent people would. He demanded to know why he was being arrested, and he repeatedly denied doing anything wrong. Despite certain officials claiming that he was calm and collected, Special Agents James Hosty and James Bookhout, both of whom witnessed his interrogation by Captain Will Fritz, reported that Oswald frantically denied shooting Dallas Police Officer Tippit or shooting President John F. Kennedy.[285] Perhaps Oswald's military background and his time in a foreign country eventually helped him regain his composure, and he began insisting on his constitutional rights. When his mother visited him in jail, he reassured her that he would be fine.

"Everything is fine. I know my rights, and I will have an attorney. Don't worry about a thing." To his wife, Marina, he said, "It's a mistake. I'm not guilty. Don't cry. Try not to think about it. You mustn't worry about me." He then added a comment that any father in the world could relate to when he mentioned his two daughters. "Kiss Junie and Rachel for me. I love you. Be sure to buy shoes for June."[286]

The longer Oswald stayed in custody, the less confident he became. His denials continued but his demeanor changed. He began to worry more about what he perceived to be unfair treatment. For example, his appearance was noticeably different from the other men in the police line-ups. He pointed this out to the Dallas police. Nevertheless, they did not allow him to wear a jacket like the other men in the line-ups.

Because of press releases and press reports, the majority of Americans quickly swallowed the story that Oswald was the lone assassin. At first, the media and certain government officials referred to him as the "alleged" assassin, but their comments left little doubt that Oswald was, in fact, *the* assassin—indeed, the one and only assassin. Though he was not the only suspect arrested in the Dallas/Ft. Worth area on November 22 in connection with the President's assassination, his name and photograph were splashed all over local, national, and international media. Oswald was not the only employee in the Texas School Book Depository who had left the building after the assassination, but that is the story everyone now heard. They also heard almost immediately that all the shots had been fired from the Texas School Book Depository, though Marshal Nash and J. Goode had told authorities this was untrue.

Original newspaper and television accounts are invaluable sources of information for historians. However, on November 22, 1963, reporters were so unprepared for the horrific news that the President of the United States and the Governor of Texas had been shot that they reported almost anything they saw and heard. Some of these reports are especially valuable because they contain immediate reactions from eyewitnesses. Naturally, reports vary from witness to witness, which is to be expected.

Bill and Gayle Newman, for example, told what they had seen from the north side of Dealey Plaza. Jean Hill and Mary Ann Moorman testified as to what they had seen from the south side of the Plaza. Ruby Henderson and Carolyn Walther saw two men on the sixth floor of the Depository. Howard Brennan told a news reporter he had seen a young man on the sixth floor holding a rifle. Mr. and Mrs. Arnold Rowland thought they saw two figures in windows on the sixth floor, one with a rifle and telescopic sight. If the testimony of all these witnesses was accepted as true, why were the observations of former Navy Officer J. Goode and U. S. Marshall Robert Nash ignored?

What was *consistently* reported by newspapers all over the world was that Lee Harvey Oswald was an unhappy young man—unhappy with his country and with his wife. He was supposedly a man with few friends who preferred communism to democracy. Although some did know a Lee Harvey Oswald so described, others remember a very different Lee Harvey Oswald.

CHAPTER 23

THE VOICES OF HENRY J. ROUSSEL, JR., JAMES A. BOTELO, AND BILL J. LORD

"I know Lee did not kill Kennedy; he didn't kill anyone."
—James J. Botelo

One of those who disagreed with the Warren Report's description of Lee Harvey Oswald was a fellow Marine, Henry J. Roussel, Jr. In a telephone interview with the authors in 2019, Roussel recalled serving with Oswald for three or four months while the two were stationed in Santa Ana, California.[287]

"We [Roussel and his fellow Marines] were watching television when he [Oswald] announced he was going to Russia," Roussel recalled. "We were surprised! We knew he had studied Russian. He was self-taught." However, this was not as surprising to Roussel as it might have been to others. Roussel explained that he had an aunt who was also studying Russian.

"She was a stewardess for Pan Am; that airline was planning on adding flights to Russia, so they needed flight attendants who could speak Russian. Pan Am gave her a year off to learn the language." Roussel paused before adding a piece of information that most Americans still do not know.

"I fixed Lee Oswald up with a date with my aunt," Roussel admitted, but he then amended that statement. "It wasn't really a date," he added hurriedly. "I think they met at a café at lunch time a couple of times. You see, she wanted to improve her Russian, and he was the only person I knew who spoke it. She didn't think he had much of a personality," he chuckled.

In some ways, his aunt's appraisal matched Roussel's. He remembered that Oswald did not seem to go out of his way to talk to his fellow enlistees. "But he did call us all 'Comrade.' I thought that was strange."

When asked about Oswald's shooting skills, Roussel explained that he had never shot with him, but other barrack Marines on the firing range with Oswald joked that he was a "bad shot." Roussel's bunkmate was Nelson Delgado, a Marine who had shot with Oswald.

"Yes, Oswald scored as a 'marksman'," Roussel explained, "but that is the lowest ranking you can make and still qualify. It is nothing to be proud of." In fact, the typical Marine pride that the Corps is so well-known for is something that Roussel did not observe in Oswald. Years later, Roussel read that Oswald had been sent to the brig for an infraction while in Japan, "but he never talked about that!" In fact, Roussel remembered that Oswald seldom engaged others in conversation, and did not even talk about his home. However, Roussel knew that Oswald had been born in New Orleans; the two men were close in age and at one time had lived about six blocks apart from each other in New Orleans. This might have drawn some enlisted men closer together, but it did not seem important to Oswald.

Oswald's arrest for the murder of a police officer in Dallas, and then for the assassination of President Kennedy, surprised Roussel more than his defection to Russia. However, unlike the day when he had seen Oswald on television bragging about his imminent defection, Roussel in November of 1963 did not recognize his former fellow Marine as he was brought before the cameras in Dallas, Texas. In fact, the name Oswald "did not ring a bell, either," he admitted until the FBI showed up with questions.

"My uncle, who was the head of the New Orleans' branch of the IRS, told the FBI that I had known Oswald. So then they wanted to talk to me and my aunt. They questioned my aunt more than they did me because it seems that some Pan Am stewardesses were actually working for the CIA back then." Roussel remembered that his aunt had been shocked by the assassination.

"She just couldn't believe it had happened. I don't know if she believed Oswald had done it or not."

Not only can Henry Roussel, Jr. say that he is one of the few men who ever "fixed Lee Harvey Oswald up with a date with a relative," he can also say that his uncle, following the orders of Attorney General Robert Kennedy, helped "put Mafia don Carlos Marcello on the plane to South America"! Later, his uncle retired from the IRS and was hired by Marcello (who had managed to find his way back to the United States) as his personal tax accountant. Because he had grown up in New Orleans surrounded by the Mafia, Roussel did not think this odd. After all, he knew that the New Orleans condo he lived in was owned by Marcello. He did not know, however, that Oswald's uncle had worked for Marcello, and apparently, at one time, Oswald had, too.

Roussel had never heard of W.R. Morris, R.B. Cutler, or John Armstrong—researchers who found evidence that more than one man was using the name and identity of "Lee Harvey Oswald." Would Roussel have wondered why he did not recognize Oswald on television in 1963 if he had known there were *two* men known as "Lee Harvey Oswald"?

Jim Botelo knew his fellow Marine Lee Harvey Oswald better than Henry Roussel (although he did not set him up with any of his female relatives)! He was Oswald's bunkmate in Santa Ana, California.

"We roomed together," he recalled to the authors.[288] "Lee had the top bunk and I had the bottom." Botelo's voice was soft but firm. "Lee was a good man," he said quietly. Because of their close night-time proximity, Oswald seemed to talk to Botelo more than to other Marines. Although they did not really socialize together, they did spend much of their free time together.

"We bought a small stereo together. We bought records together. While the guys in some of the other barracks were listening to country music, we listened to classical music. Lee liked Tchaikovsky." Botelo laughed softly as he recalled, "We had a contest between a group next to us that liked country music. Both groups tried to drown out the other group's music." When asked why Oswald would have appreciated Russian classical music, Botelo replied, "I think the classical music helped him with his Communist front. You see, he wasn't a Communist or a Marxist. I asked him once why he did all this talking about Russia and Marxism. He kept talking about the Russian philosophy, and I finally said, 'You *can't* believe this philosophy!' That's when he told me: 'I really don't feel this way, but I have a job to do." Botelo paused before adding, "I don't think he was supposed to have told me that."

Comments like this caused Botelo to surmise that Oswald was working with (or for) the CIA. "What convinced me of this was his going to Russia. He didn't have enough money to go to Russia! I knew how much money he made a month—$120! And he would send some home to his mother." Botelo continued, "He got out of the military a couple of months early. He didn't tell me he was leaving. To me, going to Russia indicates he was a spy."

Botelo knew that Oswald was a good radar operator because he had been one, too. The two Marines had taken their radar classes in Biloxi, Mississippi. Botelo had not known that Oswald was from New Orleans. Oswald had only said then that he lived in Ft. Worth, Texas.

"That makes sense," Botelo said when the authors told him about Oswald's connection to Louisiana. "He used to go to New Orleans on weekends while we were at radar school." Both men had above top-secret (crypto) security clearances. (Oswald had been given this type of clearance even though records showed he had been placed in the brig in Japan.) Botelo explained that radar operators had to take all sorts of tests, and they had to score higher than Marines in other areas. That was one way he knew Oswald was intelligent. Intelligence, however, did not help his marksmanship ability.

"I never saw him shoot, but some of the guys who did said he sometimes hit other guys' targets!" Botelo suspected Oswald would do this deliberately. From time to time, he would be punished for misbehavior by having his clearance pulled.

"He would do things like salute a lieutenant when we met him and then turn around and shoot him the finger. Sometimes, he would talk back to the officers or senior staff members."

Botelo knew that when Oswald lost his security clearance, his punishment was a bit unorthodox. "The commander of our company was a colonel. Most companies just had captains. When Lee would do something to show disrespect, they would pull his security clearance, but he would be punished by being ordered to work in the commander's office. This office was full of top-secret information!"

As he thought back to his days with Oswald, Botelo remembered other oddities. He recalled that his bunkmate did not receive regular promotions like the other Marines did. He also remembered him studying the Russian language.

"I remember him receiving a Russian newspaper from Oakland. He would also go to the library to check out Russian books and he would study them. Lee was very intelligent, but he had difficulty pronouncing the Russian words. He could translate them, but it was hard for him to pronounce them correctly." Once or twice, Botelo took Oswald home to his family's farm in San Juan Batista, but Oswald did not seem to appreciate the rural lifestyle. Of course, this would not be surprising for a young man who had lived in New Orleans, New York, and Ft. Worth, none of which could be described as "rural."

Botelo was quick to say how surprised he was when he heard that Oswald had been accused of the murders in Dallas in 1963. After all these years since, he feels that more strongly than ever.

"Absolutely, Lee Harvey Oswald was a patsy! They used his trouble in the Marines to make him look like a malcontent so he would seem to defect." The former Marine, who seemed to have been as close to Oswald as he would allow anyone to be, paused for several moments before stating bluntly: "Oswald didn't have the fighter instinct. I know Lee did not kill Kennedy. He didn't kill anyone!"

James Botelo is not the only man who can honestly say he shared living quarters with President Kennedy's accused assassin. In a telephone interview, Bill J. Lord (no relation to the ABC news correspondent who covered Kennedy's assassination) recalled travelling on the cargo ship S.S. Marion Lykes with the man who would eventually be accused of killing President Kennedy.

"This was on September 20, 1959," Lord explained. "There were four passengers and I didn't know any of them."[289] The four passengers were Lord, retired U.S. Army Lt. Col. George B. Church Jr., Church's wife, and Lee Harvey Oswald. The ship sailed from New Orleans, headed first to France. It was logical for Lord and Oswald to share a cabin.

At the time, Lord had just graduated from Midland High School, in Midland, Texas, and was planning on studying in France. After the Kennedy assassination, Lord was asked to provide an affidavit concerning the time he spent as Oswald's cabin mate. The two young men shared a cabin for fourteen days. If Oswald had been excited about the idea of defecting to the Soviet Union, he did not tell Lord. In fact, Oswald told him he would probably return to the United States to work. He certainly did not tell Lord that he was going to the Soviet Union, a Communist country.[290] However, he did share with him that he was an atheist.

"Well, Oswald and I did not get along well," Lord admitted. "It was a personality clash, I guess," he added as he cleared his throat.[291] Other than sharing meals with his three travelling companions, Oswald spent very little time with them or with the crew. In Lord's opinion, "he apparently did not want to have any face-to-face contact with people." Lord elaborated, "He avoided me. I never saw him go off with other people, and I didn't see him reading anything." (In Lord's affidavit, he did mention that Oswald and Lt. Col. Church would listen to radio programs from Europe broadcast in a foreign language— German, he thought. There is no evidence that Oswald had ever studied German, but the language is similar to Russian, which he had studied).

The ship reached LaPallice, France, on October 5, 1959, at which time Mrs. Church asked Lord for his home address, which he gladly provided. Lord wrote his mother about his voyage and his roommate, but he never heard from Oswald or saw him again until November 22, 1963, when his face appeared on national television and on the front pages of most American newspapers.

Oswald and the Churches continued their journey onto Le Havre, France, where all three disembarked. As she had done previously with Lord, Mrs. Church asked Oswald for his address. He begrudgingly provided his mother's address in Fort Worth, *but* he spelled his name "*O-s-w-a-l-t*."

Four years later, when President Kennedy was killed, Lord was serving in the Air Force in North Dakota. He recalled awaking after lunch and hearing Oswald's name on the radio. When he realized that his former cabin mate was being linked to the assassination, he "just left the barracks and got coffee in a café." When asked why he had not immediately told anyone he had once known Oswald, he replied, "I don't know. I was in a bit of a shock."

It was not until a day or two later that Lord realized that he should make Air Force Intelligence aware of the fact that he had once shared a cabin with the President's accused assassin. After hearing his story, intelligence officers directed him to write a statement describing the time he spent with the accused assassin. Apparently, the military intelligence officers were satisfied with his statement because they did not question him further. Lord's mother sent him copies of the *Fort Worth Star-Telegram* so he could read about the assassination and its aftermath. "My parents had remembered Oswald's name from my letters," Lord explained.

"It was months and months before the Warren Commission asked me to write a statement for them," he added. Like Air Force Intelligence, the Warren Commission seemed satisfied with Lord's recollections. They found no reason to ask him about Oswald's religious beliefs or why the ex-Marine had been so interested in foreign radio programs from Europe. There is also no explanation given for why *Mrs. Church* was asked to write an affidavit for the Warren Commission, but her husband was not. It was Lt. Colonel Church who had spent time with Oswald as the two men listened to various radio programs from foreign countries. It was the Lieutenant Colonel who had a military background, not his wife. Surely, his observations would have been more valuable than his wife's. He was the individual who could have described the types of radio programs that caught Oswald's interest.

Apparently, no one was interested in why a retired Lieutenant Colonel and his wife would travel to Europe on a cargo ship, either. The couple may have simply been using an economical way to reach France, *or* the Lt. Colonel could have been placed on the cargo ship to monitor Oswald. Perhaps Mrs. Church requested the address of Bill J. Lord so that Oswald would not be suspicious when she also asked for his. Obviously, Oswald *was* a bit suspicious because he insisted on knowing why she wanted his address before giving it to her. Like so many others, Church and his wife were witnesses who were either ignored by the Warren Commission or inadvertently overlooked.

Fourteen years after the assassination, Bill J. Lord wrote a telling letter to President Jimmy Carter concerning Lee Harvey Oswald and his connection to the CIA and/or FBI. In the letter, Lord confessed that he and his family no longer felt safe in Midland, Texas, because they had been harassed. He suggested that this harassment was caused by the fact that he now knew that the CIA "did not conduct a real investigation of Kennedy's assassination because Mr. Oswald was a bogus defector...The CIA is concerned lest the knowledge that Oswald was a fake defector in 1959, linking him to CIA, also link him with CIA on November 22, 1963."[292]

Lord did not indicate how he had acquired the information he referred to, but there is no question that he suspected the CIA/FBI had not been truthful concerning President Kennedy's death. After the assassination of President Kennedy, the FBI indicated it knew very little beforehand about Lee Harvey Oswald. That statement was untrue.

As early as June 3, 1960, J. Edgar Hoover, the director of the FBI, sent an inter-bureau memo suggesting that someone might be impersonating Oswald by using his birth certificate. Hoover stated, "Since there is a possibility that there is an imposter using Oswald's birth certificate, any current information the Department of State might have concerning this subject would be appreciated."[293]

It is unclear what Hoover discovered about an Oswald imposter, but his memo serves as evidence that someone *was posing as Lee Harvey Oswald* while another Oswald was living in Russia, and the *FBI and the State Department knew* this. The upper echelon of the FBI was very familiar with the name "Lee Harvey Oswald," despite what was later told to the American public.

Even after the assassination, when agents from the CIA, the FBI, and the Secret Service, were scrambling all over the world to uncover everything there was to know about Oswald, along with the Dallas Police Department and thousands of news reporters, inconvenient information about the accused assassin did not reach the ears of most Americans. In 2013, a BBC reporter discovered that people in Russia who had known Oswald "remember him fondly—and refuse to believe he is guilty."[294]

Ernst Titovets was a medical student in Minsk in 1959. He met Oswald and enjoyed Oswald's company. "I just liked the guy," he told the BBC. He recalled that he and Oswald went to dances and concerts, pursued girls, and enjoyed practical jokes. Titovets even helped Oswald connect with his future wife Marina. He knew at the time that the KGB was spying on Oswald. He recalled helping the young American search for listening devices in his Minsk apartment, but they did not find the bug in the ceiling or the peephole in the wall.

Titovets was adamant about his friend's non-role in Kennedy's assassination. He remembered reacting strongly to the news that Oswald had killed the President.

"I couldn't believe my ears," he said. "I deeply believe he was innocent. He was incapable of killing anybody." In fact, the BBC was unable to find anyone in Minsk who knew Oswald and thought him capable of assassinating Kennedy.

One of his former workmates, Vladimir Zhidovich, referred to Oswald as a "good guy." He simply could not picture him as a killer. He had such fond memories of the accused assassin that he asked the British reporter if he would lay some flowers on Oswald's grave if he ever travelled to Texas. He explained that they would be from him and other co-workers who knew Oswald at the Minsk radio factory. Did the Russians know the same Lee Harvey Oswald that certain Americans knew? Or was the rude, disgruntled Oswald another man deliberately making his presence felt in America while the likeable, fun-loving Oswald was in Russia?

The British reporter was as surprised by the attitudes of Oswald's Russian friends as most Americans would have been. Of course, no one would expect Russians to be as upset by an American president's death as Americans would be. Though there were reports that Russian Premier Nikita Khrushchev and other Russians shed tears at the news of Kennedy's death, it still seems ironic that the man blamed for the president's death would be blamed by his fellow Americans but defended by those he met in a foreign country.

However, research shows that there were also Americans who saw a different side to Oswald than the one that was depicted by the Warren Report. It just took years for their opinions to be heard.

CHAPTER 24

THE VOICE OF PAT HALL

"My mother called and said, 'One of your boarders is being arrested for something.'"

P at Hall and her brothers were unfamiliar with the name "Lee Harvey Oswald." They knew him as "Mr. Lee." Unlike some of Oswald's associates, they have happy memories of Mr. Lee, one of the many boarders who rented a room in October 1963 from Pat Hall's grandparents, Gladys and Arthur Carl Johnson.

The Johnsons owned a café as well as a boarding house, so they hired Earlene Roberts to manage the boarding house on Beckley Avenue in Oak Cliff, a suburb of Dallas. The boarding house was such a safe place that Gladys Johnson's daughter, Stella Puckett, leaving Hall and her brothers after school.

Pat Hall was eleven years old when "Mr. Lee" became a tenant at her grandmother's boarding house. Her brothers were ten and six, and the new boarder was nice enough to play catch with them while they waited for their mother to pick them up after her photography studio closed for the day.

"I wasn't excluded," Hall explained, "but in those days, it was more appropriate for a young man to play with boys rather than girls."[295]

She remembered Mr. Lee as being a good-natured, polite man who got along well with children, as well as with the other boarders. She also remembered hi being treated differently than the other boarders. His room was a glorified closet, barely large enough for a narrow bed and a dresser. According to the Johnsons, this small area was added on to the original house as a small library. The four large windows provided plenty of sunlight, so the room appeared larger than it was. In their depositions to the Warren Commission on April 1, 1964, Gladys and A. C. Johnson both stated that the large windows were covered with curtains hung on curtain rods. Behind the curtains were Venetian blinds. Arthur Johnson was asked whether the curtains which had hung in Oswald's room were still there on April 1, 1964.

Mr. Belin: "Would those curtains still be on there today? Or might you have different ones now?"

Mr. Johnson: "No, we'd have different curtains now."[296] He offered no explanation for replacing the curtains, and there were no follow-up questions concerning why these curtains had been changed. Questions about curtains in

Oswald's small living area were crucial because, according to Buel Wesley Frazier, who drove Oswald to work on November 22, Oswald said he was going to Irving the night before the assassination to get some curtain rods for his room. The interviews of the Johnsons do not appear in the indexed Warren Report; instead, they are found in the *non-indexed* Volume X of the 26-volume addendum, making them difficult to find.

The Warren Commission attorneys interviewed both the Johnsons and their housekeeper, Earlene Roberts. Pat Hall remembered tension between her grandmother and Roberts, apparently due to Roberts overstepping her boundaries, she recalled. However, the couple depended on Roberts to rent rooms, to collect and record rent fees, and to clean the boarding house.

"I remember she sometimes made decisions without asking my grandparents," Hall commented. But in Oswald's case, Gladys Johnson herself approved him as a boarder, not Roberts; Johnson discussed the possibility of him renting from her about three weeks before he actually did so. However, Johnson left the paperwork to Earlene Roberts, so she was the person who *officially* rented the small room to Lee Harvey Oswald. (Ironically, Stella Puckett's mother, Gladys Johnson, was the woman who will always be remembered for renting a room to a man soon to be accused of killing President Kennedy.)

Though the Johnsons did not own a true "boarding house"—boarders were expected to provide their own food—Oswald was allowed to use the family refrigerator. "I remember him putting sandwich meat in the ice box," Hall recalled. She also remembered Mr. Lee being an avid reader, though she now suspects he might have been dyslexic. She remembered Oswald, when he wasn't reading, joining the other boarders in the living room to watch television, and he often walked to a nearby library to check out books. Coincidentally, this same library is where Dallas police were first sent to arrest the killer of Officer J. D. Tippit.

"Stella Fay Puckett" is a name unknown to many Kennedy assassination researchers; she was Gladys Johnson's daughter, and she happened to witness Oswald's arrest on the afternoon of November 22. As the owner of Puckett Photography, which was located directly across the street from the Texas Theatre, Puckett had a front-row seat to Oswald's arrest.

That afternoon, she glanced out her studio's front window and saw police officers forcefully dragging a man to a waiting police car. She did not know the man's name, but she did recognize his face. Many afternoons that fall, she had seen him playing football with her young sons in the front yard of 1026 North Beckley

After observing the police push Oswald into a police car, Puckett immediately phoned her mother at the family's business, Johnson's Café. No one answered. She later learned that the Johnsons, upset at the news of the President's shooting, had closed their restaurant as soon as the announcement of his death had been made and returned to Beckley Avenue.

Puckett's second call was to her mother's boarding house. When her mother answered, Puckett calmly informed her, "One of your boarders is being arrested for something." The response Puckett received surprised her as much as the scene still unfolding in front of her eyes.

"Well, that explains why the FBI is here searching his room," her mother replied.[297] This is how the Johnsons learned that the quiet, unassuming boarder paying $8.00 a week for a small, semi-private room in their boarding house was really named "Lee Harvey Oswald" and possibly was connected to the shooting of a Dallas police officer and the assassination of John F. Kennedy. What they never learned was how Dallas police officers and the FBI knew to come to their Oak Cliff boarding house.

After all, as far the Johnsons or anyone else in the boarding house knew, the man being arrested was "O. H. Lee," and not "Lee Oswald." Also, the address Oswald had given his employer at the Depository was the address of Ruth Paine's house in Irving. Even local FBI agent James Hosty, who was keeping tabs on Oswald, thought Oswald was living in Irving and had only recently learned he was living in some boarding house in Oak Cliff. He did not know exactly where. It is still unclear how the Dallas police and the Dallas FBI agents knew to descend on 1026 North Beckley Street in Oak Cliff. Pat Hall smiled and said to the authors, "Another anomaly!"[298]

Although the Johnsons and Earlene Roberts may have been thrust into history simply because they rented a room to a young man later accused of killing the President and a Dallas police officer, there are some questions concerning facts the Warren Commissioners chose to ignore. For example, Gladys Johnson admitted she had not brought her rent registers with her to her deposition in April of 1964. These registers should have contained the names and signatures of every person who had boarded at 1026 North Beckley for the last five to ten years. These documents would have been required by the IRS in case of an audit. They should have recorded every boarder; police could have checked these names to see if any of them were associated with Oswald, or if any might have been anti-Castro Cubans or anti-Kennedy right-wingers.

It is hard to imagine why the Commissioners did not *insist* on examining these important records. Earlene Roberts showed the most recent records to the Dallas FBI agents on the afternoon of November 22, 1963. The agents were surprised to find no entry for a "Lee Harvey Oswald." At the time, they apparently did not associate "O. H. Lee" with "Lee Harvey Oswald." Of course, neither did the Johnsons or Earlene Roberts; none of them made the connection until an image of Lee Harvey Oswald appeared on their television set. That was when all three identified the man at the Dallas Police Department as their "O. H. Lee."

By April of 1964, the Warren Commissioners knew how vital it was to know everything about Oswald's associates. However, they seemed uninterested in boarders who shared living quarters with the accused assassin. They did not analyze the signature "O. H. Lee" on the scrap of paper Roberts used to record a rental receipt; they did not bother to compare it to the signature of the man they had arrested. They allowed Gladys Johnson to bring nothing to her deposition hearing except a scrap of paper with the name "O. H. Lee" written on it. The Commissioners took her word that Oswald had written this name on a piece of paper on paying his first week's rent. They did not ask if there were other "records" kept on scraps of paper like this one. Perhaps there were other names on the rental records the Commissioners wanted hidden.

Some Warren Commission critics have even questioned whether this boarding house at 1026 North Beckley might have been used as a "safe house" for some organization. In that case, the names of informants or their aliases might have appeared on the official registers, and therefore the reason why no one in authority demanded to see them.

Another fact either overlooked or ignored by the Warren Commission was a statement made by the Johnsons concerning housekeeper Earlene Roberts. Approximately three weeks before the Johnsons' deposition, Roberts mysteriously left their boarding house in the middle of the night and never returned. Both Gladys and A.C. Johnson seemed confused by her actions. They told the Commissioners they had no idea why she left so abruptly and so secretively. Roberts apparently waited until all the boarders had gone to bed; she then disappeared silently into the night.

According to the Johnsons, a phone call to Roberts' sister, Bertha Cheek, provided very little information. Roberts apparently made a single phone call to her sister, but did not explain why she left her job. Cheek admitted to scolding Roberts for leaving such nice people as the Johnsons. However, she claimed she did not know her sister's whereabouts.

Obviously, someone in authority quickly located Earlene Roberts, because one week after the Johnsons mentioned her disappearance in their depositions, Roberts was providing a deposition herself. In it, she simply stated that the Johnsons were requiring too much hard work from her, so she left. There was no explanation for why she chose to leave in the middle of the night without leaving a resignation note or speaking to the Johnsons.

Another piece of information that Roberts did not mention in her deposition was that her sister, Bertha Cheek, was acquainted with a now infamous man—Jack Ruby. Cheek owned a boarding house on Swiss Avenue in Dallas. Supposedly, Jack Ruby had approached her in the fall of 1963 about a business proposition. It is possible that Earlene Roberts chose not to disclose this because she felt too closely connected to important figures in the Kennedy assassination. By now, the public knew she had rented Oswald a room and had interacted with him, to a certain extent. She had been the last person in the boarding house to see him alive. Her testimony about his actions and behavior, as well as about a Dallas police car she had seen stop in front of the boarding house while Oswald was changing clothes, brought her to the attention of numerous officials. The last straw may have been that her sister knew Jack Ruby. Perhaps Earlene Roberts' midnight escape was a desperate attempt to flee from the attention some accused her of seeking.

Questions linger about the 1963 tenants in the boarding house at 1026 North Beckley that may never be answered unless the tenant registers are finally located. When asked about these records, Pat Hall indicated that they were destroyed years ago. It is difficult to believe that the registers for 1963 would have been casually thrown away. After all, these were historical records. Oswald's signature alone would have been worth quite a bit of money. However, if his alias of "O. H. Lee" did *not* appear in the register, the Johnsons surely would have been asked why, and some sort of explanation would have been expected.

CHAPTER 25

THE VOICE OF BUELL WESLEY FRAZIER

"I know you have police out in the hall there, but I can get two or three good licks on you before they get in here!"

W hile Lee Harvey Oswald was being interrogated by the Dallas Police, the man who had mentored him when he first began working at the Texas School Book Depository and who had occasionally driven him to and from work from the Dallas suburb of Irving was undergoing a police interrogation himself. Buell Wesley Frazier lived half a block away from where Oswald's wife and children were staying in Irving. This tall, lanky nineteen-year-old from Huntsville, Texas, had been employed at the Depository only since September of 1963. However, he was a quick learner and a patient teacher who enjoyed helping others. Frazier was asked by his supervisor, William Shelley, to mentor Oswald when he began working at the Depository in October 1963.

On the morning of November 22, he drove himself and Oswald to work at the Depository. As far as Frazier knew, it was mere coincidence that Ruth Paine, a neighbor who had befriended Oswald's wife Marina, lived only a few houses from Frazier's older sister, Linnie Randle. Paine even offered to let Oswald's Russian wife and their children stay with her in Irving because, she said, she wanted to improve her Russian language skills. Randle was allowing her younger brother Buell to live with her and her family until he could save enough money to live on his own.

Paine had explained to Randle that Marina Oswald's husband was looking for work and asked Randle if her brother Buell knew of any openings at the Texas School Book Depository. Through what appears to be an innocent encounter between two neighbors, Oswald was able to obtain work in the same building as Buell Wesley Frazier. Oddly enough, it was Ruth Paine, not Oswald, who directly contacted the Depository and arranged for Oswald's employment interview. Who knows where Oswald might have been working on November 22, 1963, if Good Samaritan Ruth Paine had not assisted with his employment difficulties.

Though Frazier and Oswald never became close, Frazier was important to

Oswald. Unlike Oswald, Frazier had a driver's license and access to a car, so occasionally he drove Oswald from work to Irving on Friday afternoons so he could spend the weekend with his family. Oswald also rode back to work on Monday mornings with Frazier.

Frazier shared memories of Oswald with the authors on three different occasions. In 2019, we asked a question we had neglected to ask before. We inquired as to whether he had ever driven to Ruth Paine's house to pick up Oswald, or if Oswald had walked to Frazier's nearby house.

"November 22, 1963 is the only day that Lee walked all the way to my sister's house," Frazier replied. "Every other time, he either waited for me in Mrs. Paine's front yard or he walked towards my sister's house and I picked him up halfway."

When asked why Oswald had appeared at his sister's house on November 22 when he had never done so before, Frazier was quick to explain. "Well, that was my fault. I was running late that morning and I guess Lee got tired of waiting for me and just walked on down to my house. There wasn't anything mysterious about it. It was because I was late picking him up."[299]

Oswald had not needed to ride with his neighbor every day because he had rented a room in a boarding house in a Dallas suburb and could ride the city bus to work during the week. His absence lessened some of the tension in the Paine household. Three adults and four children in the tiny Irving house made living conditions difficult, especially when the husband and wife were having disagreements, as the Oswalds sometimes did.

Frazier remembered how lovingly Oswald always spoke of his older daughter, June, and how excited he was about the new baby daughter who arrived on October 20. He also remembered seeing Oswald playing with Ruth Paine's children out in the front yard of the Paine house. In the yard stood a large oak tree, under which Oswald and the children played. The children referred to him as "Mr. Lee," and they looked forward to his weekend visits.

The nickname the Paine children used for Oswald could explain why he used that particular alias when renting his room at the Beckley boarding house, though Oswald himself claimed that Earlene Roberts misunderstood his name and he had not bothered to correct her. (A simple handwriting test of the signature "O. H. Lee," which was written on a scrap of paper saved by the landlords of Oswald's boarding house, would have quickly determined whether Oswald deliberately signed an alias on a receipt, or whether Roberts simply wrote down the name she thought she heard. Unfortunately, no test was made.)

When Marina Oswald called the boarding house and asked for "Lee Oswald" one evening, she was told there was no boarder by that name. This is because, according to the landlords, Oswald had rented his room under the name "O. H. Lee." As suspicious as this sounds, this may well have occurred because Oswald was paying his rent in cash. It might have been more convenient if the name of a "cash-paying boarder" did not appear on IRS records. So, Oswald's "alias" may not have been suspicious at all.

Frazier recalled an Oswald similar to the one Pat Hall and Oswald's Russian friends remembered. "He tried to fit in with the other employees, was polite, and did what he was told to do. He was nice and kind to me," Frazier said." As a twenty-four-year-old ex-Marine, Oswald could have resented being paired with a younger man when he first began work at the Depository, but he did not. Frazier was told to show Oswald the procedures necessary to fill book orders, and it did not take the new employee long to catch on.

"I decided on the second day to give him a test," Frazier recalled. "I placed orders on a clip board for various textbooks which he had to find and fill. He and I were the only two employees that had access to all seven floors because we had to move the books around and also talk to publisher representatives that were on the second, third, and fourth floors. Sometimes, a school administrator would show up wanting a teacher's edition of some textbook, and we would have to go find it. I was really surprised that day. He filled every order correctly with no problem at all. After that, he worked on his own."

The two men spent a minimal amount of time together at work. Frazier usually ate his lunch in the basement of the Depository with another employee, Jack Dougherty. Oswald usually ate in the second-floor lunch room.

"We did not socialize after work or on weekends," Frazier explained. On Thursday, November 21, 1963, Oswald asked Frazier if he could catch a ride home with him that evening. "Sure," Frazier answered, "but this is only Thursday." This was the only time Oswald had ever asked Frazier for a ride on a weekday.

"I know, but I need to pick up some curtain rods. Marina made some curtains for me and I need to get the rods," Oswald explained.

On the way home, neither man discussed the President's planned visit the following day. Their conversation was similar to previous ones. They talked about the weather and Oswald's daughters. On Friday morning, November 22, Oswald walked down the street to Frazier's house and waited for him in the front yard. Frazier and his sister both noticed that Oswald was holding a package wrapped in brown paper that was about two feet long. As the two men climbed into the car, Oswald tossed the package into the back seat.

"What's in the package, Lee?" Frazier asked.

"Curtain rods," he answered.

"Oh, that's right," said Frazier. "You told me that yesterday."

That morning, the two men speculated on the possibility of rain as they drove into downtown Dallas. Frazier parked his 1954 Chevy Bel Air in the employee parking lot, a few blocks behind the Depository. Oswald picked up the paper package as he disembarked from the automobile and cupped it under his arm as he walked towards the Depository. He entered the building through the back doors; that is the last time Frazier saw the brown package that the FBI would soon use to connect Oswald to the assassination of President Kennedy.

As Frazier entered the Depository a minute or two after Oswald, he was approached by Junior Jarman. Jarman was one of the few Depository employees who consistently read the Dallas newspaper every morning. This morning he waved it at Frazier.

"Wesley, the President's motorcade is going to pass right in front of our building today." Frazier had not even been aware that the President was coming to Dallas. "Do you think Mr. Shelley would let us go out during our lunch time and watch it?" Jarman asked.

"I don't know," Frazier replied, "but I'll go ask." When Frazier approached William Shelley with the suggestion, Shelley indicated that he had to get permission from Jack Cason, the president of the Depository. He returned shortly afterward saying that Mr. Cason did not mind and that Frazier was to share this with all the Depository employees. So, Frazier made sure that all Depository employees, including Oswald, knew they were allowed to spend their lunch time in front of the Depository witnessing the motorcade of President Kennedy and his wife.

Some of the employees took advantage of this opportunity. Others watched from open windows. Some simply ate their lunches as they always did. Jack Cason simply left the Depository at 11:50.

Victoria Adams and Sandra Styles, Scott-Foresman employees, chose to stay in their fourth-floor office and watch the procession from their windows. On the fifth floor, Junior Jarman, Harold Norman and, eventually, Bonnie Ray Williams opened the windows that faced Elm Street so they could get a better view of the presidential motorcade. Williams spent part of his lunch hour on the sixth floor of the Depository near the window from which witnesses later claimed to have seen individuals. He stayed until about 12:20 p.m. According to the Dallas Police, he made the mistake of leaving his chicken remains and an empty Dr. Pepper bottle near the area which would soon become known as the "sniper's nest."

Frazier had no way of knowing who was on the upper floors, but he did know who was standing near him on the steps of the Depository. Controversy continues to swirl around the witnesses who waited on those steps. However, as Fraizer said at a conference in Dallas recently, "I am the only one in this room that was there that day."

Like many of the other employees, he wanted to take full advantage of the opportunity to see the President and the First Lady. The Depository was the perfect location for a close look at the presidential motorcade. Not long before the President's motorcade turned onto Elm Street, Frazier took his place behind his supervisor, William Shelley. Next to him stood a fellow employee, Sarah Stanton. Neither Frazier nor Stanton can be seen in photos taken that day because they stood on the top step, in the shadows of the Depository building.

Next to William Shelley stood Frazier's close friend and co-worker, Billy Lovelady. Because he was shorter than Frazier, Frazier suggested that Lovelady step down in front of him so he could get a better view. Consequently, a famous photo taken by news photographer James Altgens shows Lovelady staring intently at the President's limousine. (Like Frazier, Lovelady soon realized that his life would never be the same after November 22, 1963.) Though Lovelady and Frazier were friends, Lovelady was unaware that Frazier lived near Oswald's family and that Oswald sometimes rode with him to and from work. There had really been no reason for the two men to discuss Oswald.

According to Lovelady's Warren Commission deposition, right before noon he and some other employees on the sixth floor used elevators to head downstairs for lunch. Lovelady heard Oswald, then filling orders on the sixth floor, yell for them to hold the elevator, but his co-workers were in a hurry and went ahead without him. Lovelady took his lunch and stood on the steps of the Depository next to William Shelley. The photo by Altgens shows him standing right where he says he was. However, the photographer was so far away that enlargements of the area somewhat distort Lovelady's image. Frazier has looked at this photo numerous times. Each time he pointed to the shadows behind Lovelady.

"That is where I was standing," he said emphatically. "That is Billy. *Not* Oswald," he emphasized. Lovelady resembled Oswald so much he was mistaken for the accused assassin.

As Frazier watched the motorcade pass, he heard three shots and saw spectators begin running west towards the triple underpass. Shelley and Lovelady immediately ran in that direction, too, simply because that's where all the activity seemed to be. From their position on the steps, the men were unable to see whether anyone in the motorcade was hit by the shots.

"I think the only reason Billy and Mr. Shelley ran to the underpass area is because that's where so many other bystanders were running," commented

Frazier. Importantly, the witnesses on the Depository steps did not look up to the upper floors.

On the way to the underpass, Lovelady and Shelley encountered Gloria Calvary running from the area later known as "the grassy knoll" or the "grassy area."

"The President's been shot!" she cried, so Shelley and Lovelady changed directions and followed the crowds towards the railroad tracks, which were north of the grassy area. Frazier and Sarah Stanton moved down to the sidewalk in front of the Depository and talked with other bystanders about the sounds they had heard, still uncertain as to whether there had been shots or not.

Recently, Frazier shared a detail he had forgotten for decades. As he stood at the corner of Elm and Houston, he glanced up and saw Oswald walk from behind the Depository, cross Houston Street, and proceed south. He did not appear to be in a hurry, and Frazier did not think anything of the fact that he was leaving. Frazier looked embarrassed as he recalled his next actions.

"I know this sounds terrible, but remember, I was only nineteen, and it was my lunch hour, and I was hungry. I only had so much time to eat, so I went down to the basement of the building like I did every day and ate my lunch. I was sitting there reading a book and eating when a policeman came down the stairs and asked me my name. I told him, and he asked if anyone else had come down to the basement. I told him 'no,' so he went back upstairs."

The officer did not bother to search the basement to make sure the young man was telling the truth. After Frazier finished his lunch, he went upstairs and was told Shelley was conducting a roll call of employees. He remembered that Oswald did not answer roll call, but he wasn't the only one. Shelley then dismissed all employees and told them to plan on returning Monday at their regular time.

With Depository employees dismissed for the remainder of the day, Frazier decided to visit his stepfather, who was in an Irving hospital recovering from a heart attack. A radio broadcast indicated that the President had died and that a suspect had been arrested at the Texas Theatre in Oak Cliff. Little did Frazier know that the suspect was one of his co-workers, and that he himself would soon become a suspect also.

He was at the hospital only a short time when two Dallas detectives, Gus Rose and Bill Stovall, approached him and immediately arrested him. They had tracked Frazier to the hospital even though he had told no one at the Depository where he was going. When he demanded to know why he was being arrested, they announced that it was in connection with the President's assassination.

"That's ridiculous," Frazier responded, but they drove him directly to the

Dallas Police Department, where he was ushered into a third-floor office and subjected to hours and hours of intense questioning by detectives.

"It was like a military tribunal. I couldn't look right or left, up or down. When I asked for a glass of water, they told me they would check to see if I could have some." This nineteen-year-old finally found himself totally alone with Captain Will Fritz, a legendary interrogator, . who immediately slammed a typed piece of paper on top of the weathered desk separating the two.

"Sign this!" Fritz demanded. Frazier was a small-town boy from Huntsville, Texas, but he had been taught to never sign anything before reading it. As he read the words typed on the paper, his eyes widened with shock. The statement said he had helped plan the assassination of the President. The only thing the "confession" lacked was his signature.

"Sign it!" the head of the Homicide Bureau insisted again. When Frazier protested that the words on the statement were untrue, Fritz raised his hand to strike him. Will Fritz had chosen the wrong boy to intimidate. This young man, who still proudly wore his FFA jacket, grew up with a stepfather who was tougher than Fritz ever hoped to be.

In Frazier's opinion, his childhood had ended at age ten, when his stepfather put him to work doing whatever it took to pay his room and board—twenty dollars a week. Occasionally, Frazier's mother managed to persuade her husband to give her son a quarter from what he had earned. The boy knew that if he did not have the twenty dollars at the end of the week, he would have no place to sleep. At such a young age, he was limited in the types of jobs he could do. So, Frazier performed odd jobs around town and mowed lawns from dawn to dusk, no matter how hot it was.

"I remember a nice lady offering me a Mason jar of sweet tea one hot afternoon," he said quietly, "but my stepfather happened to walk around the corner of her house as she was handing it to me." He berated the boy for stopping long enough to drink a glass of tea, and when the woman told him of her insistence, the stepfather made it clear that his stepson was to do only what his stepfather told him to do.

This wasn't the first time neighbors objected to the way the stepfather treated Frazier; another man gave the stepfather a piece of his mind on finding out that the boy kept only fifty cents from what he was paid for mowing the large lawn. Once again, the stepfather was adamant that he controlled his household. Frazier finally convinced the people trying to help him that it would be worse for him at home if they said anything in his defense.

School was not a priority to Frazier's stepfather, but it was to his stepson. As soon as Buell Wesley Frazier left school each day, he was expected to work at a diner near Sam Houston State University. The grill did not close until midnight, so that is when the boy headed home each evening, knowing he had homework that needed to be completed. He also knew that he dare not turn on a single light in the house because it would awaken his stepfather. He did as much homework as he could by moonlight.

"I might be able to stay awake thirty minutes or so, but then I would just fall asleep and I had to get up at 6:00 in the morning to feed the animals and help with chores around the house." Frazier lived in fear of his stepfather's temper and what would happen to him if he crossed him. Sleeping late was never an option.

Frazier's stepfather was not the only frightening individual in the young man's life. He also knew "Pete" Kay, who was, along with his father, an important figure in the Dixie Mafia. According to Frazier, they offered him the chance to become a member of the "family." By then, Frazier had already met one group member, a man so heartless that locking eyes with him made his blood run cold. Frazier identified this man as Charles Harrelson; others who knew Harrelson also commented on how coldly he could stare down someone. Frazier decided to take his sister's advice and not take up the offer. They both thought he would be much safer in Dallas!

Of course, Capt. Will Fritz knew none of this. He also did not know that with his short, stocky build, he resembled Frazier's German stepfather. Consequently, Fritz's intimidating behavior did not catch Frazier off-guard. Even when the Captain rose from his chair and raised his arm as if to strike the young man, Frazier instinctively raised his own arm to block the blow. He then confronted Fritz with a threat of his own.

"I know you have police out in the hall there, but I can get two or three good licks on you before they get in here!" Frazier warned his adversary.

Fritz stared at him in disbelief. Frazier wondered if anyone had ever dared to speak to the Captain that way. His threat must have sounded sincere because Fritz grabbed the typed "confession" and stormed out of the room. Frazier never saw him see again.

However, the interrogation by other Dallas police officers lasted until the early hours of Saturday morning. They focused on the brown package Oswald had tossed into the back seat of Frazier's 1954 Chevy Bel Air. It did not matter how many times Frazier told them that the package was only two feet long, wrapped in the kind of paper that grocery sacks were made from, and that it did look like prepackaged curtain rods. It did not matter that Frazier knew this because he once worked at a five and dime store where he inventoried packages of curtain rods. That was not what the police officers wanted to hear.

Despite proclaiming his innocence, Frazier was arrested, fingerprinted, photographed, and given a lie detector test. Both his rifle and his pistol were confiscated by the police and not returned to him for quite some time. He was never offered an attorney, nor allowed to call his family.

Finally, after giving the same answers to the same questions for hours, Frazier was released about two o'clock in the morning. The police drove him back to the hospital in Irving where his car was parked. To his surprise, it was not in the same condition as when he had left it. It had been thoroughly searched; in fact, the back seat had been totally pulled out and was left lying on its frame. No one had ever shown him any type of search warrant. But at this point, the nineteen-year-old was just grateful to be out of jail and headed for his own bed.

On Monday, November 25, as the country observed a national day of mourning, employees of the Texas School Book Depository worked as usual, even though President Kennedy was being buried that day, as was one of their co-workers. Frazier remembered that for several days after the assassination, Depository employees worked silently, still stunned by the President's death and by the fact that someone they had known and worked with had been arrested for killing President Kennedy, then been murdered himself. Apparently, none of them questioned why the Depository was not closed on Monday, November 25, 1963, for the President's funeral, and no one dared ask for permission to attend Lee Harvey Oswald's funeral.

Frazier kept his own experiences with the Dallas police department to himself. He later discovered that his arrest record was completely erased, so there was no official record that the Dallas police had ever even considered him a suspect.

However, Captain Fritz may not have had the opportunity to do the same thing (typing up a confession and threatening him if he did not sign it) to Oswald that he had done to Frazier. Oswald's interrogation room was too crowded for that. Fritz once said that if he had ever had the chance to "question" Oswald alone, he could have gotten a confession from him. Now there is evidence of the methods he might have used.

The "Oswald" Frazier knew never discussed guns, shooting, or the President. The man described in the newspapers as the President's "accused assassin" was not the "Oswald" Frazier had known. Frazier was especially concerned about the police saying Oswald had carried a rifle to the Depository in Frazier's car on November 22.

For his own peace of mind, Frazier located a rifle with a serial number only a few digits off from the serial number on the rifle Oswald was accused of using to kill the President. He dismantled it and wrapped it in brown paper so he and his sister could compare the size with the way they remembered Oswald's package looking on that Friday.

"It was obviously still too long," he said. "Lee could not have carried even a dismantled rifle like that one under his arm." Frazier's sister agreed.

If Oswald had really been carrying curtain rods that day, they should have been found somewhere in the Depository. Supposedly, they were never found. However, a few years after the assassination, Frazier received an intriguing phone call. Once the caller established that she was speaking to the man who had driven Oswald to work on November 22, 1963, she quietly confided to Frazier that some curtain rods had indeed been found in the Depository after the assassination.

She then hung up without revealing her identity. Apparently, this woman wanted Frazier to know that someone knew his story was true. If this woman knew the truth, other people did, too.

What no one has ever mentioned is that Oswald could have easily blamed the brown package and everything else on Frazier. It would have been so simple for Oswald to say the brown package was lying on the back seat of Frazier's car when he entered it and that *Frazier, not him,* carried it into the Depository. Frazier, like Oswald, had access to the sixth floor. If Oswald were as deceitful and guilty as critics have portrayed him, he would have placed the blame on someone else. Who else would have been a better patsy than Buell Wesley Frazier? Perhaps Frazier was more fortunate than he realized.

He has often thought about what would have happened to him if he had foolishly signed the "confession" that Captain Will Fritz prepared for him.

"I would probably still be in federal prison," he commented. There is also a good chance that, like the man who rode with him to the Depository on that fateful November Friday, he would be dead.

In the end, it can be definitively said that Lee Harvey Oswald, guilty or innocent, did not try to do what Will Fritz did—attempt to place the blame on an innocent man!

CHAPTER 26

THE VOICE OF MARILYN JOHNSON

"He actually brought the shirt he was wearing that day in Dallas with him... He hid it in my dryer."

After the President was assassinated, Buell Wesley Frazier probably regretted ever working for the Texas School Book Depository. If so, he was not the only one. His co-worker Billy Lovelady had worked at the Depository since 1961. He began as a truck driver for the Depository and then was hired as a stocker. On November 22, 1963, he was helping lay a new floor on the sixth floor of the Depository. Boxes of textbooks were normally scattered throughout the sixth floor; on that day, Lovelady helped push them all to the east end of the room.

Lovelady grew up in Myrtle Springs, Texas, a community so small that the school-aged children were bussed to nearby Wills Point, which was quite small itself.

Fifty years after the assassination, Marilyn Johnson realized that she had heard important information from an assassination witness the day after the President's death. The information came directly from eyewitness Billy Lovelady.

Marilyn Johnson was only 18 years old and working in downtown Dallas on the day the President was killed. She and her husband Russell had moved to Dallas with their first baby just a year or so before the assassination. They lived in a modest apartment complex and, like most young couples, knew some of the neighbors who were about their age. On November 22, the Johnsons planned to drive to Terrell, a small town east of Dallas, right after work, having assured his parents they would be there that night to celebrate a family birthday.

"Dallas was crazy that day," Marilyn Johnson recalled. On the afternoon of November 22, businesses all over Dallas were closing because of the assassination. Johnson added, "Dallas felt so strange that day. People seemed scared. They walked faster down the street. Drivers drove faster than usual. It was like people wanted to get out of Dallas as fast as they could. The whole atmosphere of the city was one of fear. None of us knew what was going to happen next!"[300]

Because of the chaos which followed the assassination, both Johnsons were allowed to leave work early, so they did not have the opportunity to talk with anyone in Dallas. They stayed longer at the family party that evening than they had expected. "We came back late that Friday night," Johnson recalled.

On Saturday, November 23, Billy Lovelady, who lived in the apartment next to theirs, shared some information that even he did not realize would become so important. He and his wife sat down that morning with the Johnsons while their three children played with the Johnsons' baby. For the first time, the Johnsons learned that Lovelady worked at the Texas School Book Depository.

"That's when he told us he had been at the Depository when the President had been shot," Johnson explained. "Billy had even shown a cop how to get to the sixth floor, but he didn't know why [the cop wanted to go there]. This was the first time we even knew he worked at the Depository. Of course, until that day, it wasn't important," Johnson added. "We had never asked him where he worked, so we were really surprised with the stories he later shared with us."

Marilyn and Russell were more than intrigued that Lovelady had witnessed the President's motorcade. Russell, in particular, was a history buff who would have loved to have seen the President himself. And then they realized that Lovelady had actually *worked* with the accused assassin and *witnessed* the President's assassination.

Much of what Lovelady observed on November 22 was similar to what most other spectators saw. It wasn't long before he was being questioned by officials. He remembered the large, dark blue limousine the presidential party rode in, Jackie Kennedy in her pink suit, and then the sound of what he thought were firecrackers after the limousine passed the front of the Depository. It wasn't until a woman he knew ran up to the crowd still standing on the steps that he learned the President had been shot. Lovelady heard popping sounds himself, which he thought had come from "a little concrete deal on the knoll, between the underpass and the building on the knoll."

He asked the woman if she was sure the President had been shot, and she told him she knew because she saw blood. Lovelady noticed a group of people running towards the railroad tracks, so he and his supervisor, Bill Shelley, joined them. Lovelady remembered turning and seeing Depository superintendent Roy Truly and a police officer heading into the building.

Lovelady described spectators as "running and crying," and then police officers joining the bystanders, so he decided he better return to the Depository. Shortly afterwards, a police officer asked Lovelady to show him the sixth floor, so he guided the officer up to where he and the others had been working that morning. He had no idea why police were focusing on the sixth floor or on the Depository.

The Johnsons were amazed that they knew someone who stood on the steps of the Depository and saw the President in person. He also heard what must have been the shots that killed him, after which he helped a police officer find the infamous sixth floor. Neither the Johnsons nor Lovelady knew that the shirt Lovelady wore that Friday would embroil him in a decades-long controversy. It certainly did not seem important that Saturday, when he was recalling the events of November 22. However, a photographer had snapped a photo of the President's limousine during the shooting. Through the front windshield could be seen bystanders on the front steps of the Depository. One of those bystanders caught the attention of several individuals. Mike Shapiro of the WFAA television station in Dallas was one of those individuals.

An enlargement of the photograph, which would soon become famous, showed a young man wearing clothing that resembled what Lee Harvey Oswald wore on the day of the assassination. On November 25, 1963, Shapiro brought this to the attention of the Dallas FBI. The photograph was then shown to Roy Truly, the superintendent of the Depository, who knew the individual in the photo well. He had hired him about two years before. William Shelley also was shown the photograph. Both men identified the individual as Billy Nolan Lovelady. FBI agents were soon standing on Billy Lovelady's doorstep. Lovelady later shared with the Johnsons details of that surprise visit.

"Oh, yeah, he told us about the FBI agents coming to their apartment," Marilyn Johnson remembered. When Lovelady was also shown the photograph by the FBI, he recognized himself. There was no reason for him to deny standing innocently on the steps of the Depository. And, yet, Lovelady later felt tremendous pressure from the FBI. According to Johnson, Lovelady felt that the FBI was trying to connect *him* to the assassination, even after they had officially declared Oswald as the lone gunman. Like Buell Wesley Frazier, he didn't understand why he was being dragged into the situation.

Lovelady's resemblance to Oswald and the type of shirt he was wearing that day convinced some that the accused assassin had stood in plain sight while the President's motorcade drove by the Depository. Lovelady did not realize how much he and Oswald resembled each other until his own stepchildren saw Oswald being interviewed on television on Saturday, November 23. At first, the children thought the accused assassin was their stepfather. So, it is reasonable that many people questioned whether Oswald had also been standing on the front steps of the Depository while the assassination took place.

But Lovelady consistently insisted that *he* was standing in front of Buell

Wesley Frazier when the motorcade passed the Depository. Frazier supported his story, William Shelley supported his story, and if the Johnsons had been asked, they also would have said they knew from Lovelady himself on the *day after the assassination* where their neighbor had been standing on November 22, at 12:30 p.m.

Nevertheless, in February 1964, the FBI took numerous photographs of Lovelady wearing the same shirt he wore on the day of the assassination. Many throughout the world saw the AP photograph and were determined to prove that the man in the doorway had been Lee Harvey Oswald. Discrepancies arose when Lovelady was summoned to the Dallas Police Department and he inadvertently wore a different shirt than the one he had worn to work on November 22, 1963. Photographs of him in this shirt confused researchers for quite some time.

"Not long after the assassination," Marilyn Johnson continued, "Billy and his family moved to Irving, I think, and we moved into a house. But he and his family would come visit us. One time he actually brought the shirt he was wearing that day in Dallas with him. We couldn't figure out why, but we got the idea that he might have thought someone would give him a lot of money for it. When we all went to get something to eat that night, he hid it in my dryer. And when he and his family left for Irving later, he forgot it. Halfway home, he remembered, and even though it was really late, turned around and drove back to our house to get it."

The shirt simply proved that Billy Lovelady was standing exactly where he said he was standing that day in Dallas. It did not prove anything about Oswald. Apparently, some researchers suggested that Lovelady lied to the Warren Commission about his location during the assassination—that he was not standing where he said he was. When the pressure became too great, Lovelady shared with the Johnsons that he and his family were moving to "get away from the Kennedy assassination."

Marilyn Johnson said she and her husband stayed in contact with Billy Lovelady and his family for a while. They learned that the Loveladys had moved to Colorado. But questions lingered as to the "true" identity of the man captured on film standing on the steps of the Depository. Doubters must have thought Roy Truly was mistaken when identifying Lovelady in the photo. This also meant they were accusing William Shelley of lying about standing right next to Lovelady on the steps. Some have even gone so far as to question how Lovelady managed to have enough money to later start his own trucking business in Colorado.

However, Billy Lovelady never changed his story about where he was standing on that fateful day. Like his close friend, Buell Wesley Frazier, he also insisted that his only connection to Oswald was that they had worked together. If Billy Lovelady had created the story that he was standing on the top step of the Texas School Book Depository on November 22, 1963, as some people have claimed, then he created that story the day after the assassination, *before* the famous photograph showing him on the steps had even been published. He had already told his neighbors, the Johnsons, all about where he was, and what he had observed two days before people decided it might be Lee Harvey Oswald who was standing in the doorway of the Depository.

Ironically, someone who told the truth from the very beginning was still harassed by people determined to prove that Oswald was standing in that doorway. Leaving the state of Texas didn't guarantee a long life for Lovelady; he died in his sleep (presumably of a heart attack) at the age of forty-one. Even in his obituary, his wife Patricia did not attempt to hide how bitter she was about the way her husband had been treated just because he stepped out of the shadows to get a glimpse of John F. Kennedy that day in November.

Years after the death of Billy Lovelady, some still insist that he lied about his location that day in November. Like Oswald and many others, Lovelady is not able to defend himself. Perhaps Marilyn Johnson's recollections will reinforce what Lovelady and those near him repeatedly told the FBI and the Warren Commission.

CHAPTER 27

THE VOICE OF SANDRA STYLES

"Neither of us heard anyone walking down the staircase from the floors above, and, yes, those stairs were extremely squeaky."

While Buell Frazier and Billy Lovelady watched the presidential motorcade from the front steps of the Depository, Sandra Styles and Victoria Adams watched from the fourth floor. One of the most troublesome aspects of the story told by Victoria Adams is that someone altered her testimony in the Warren Report. This alteration changed the timeline Adams described so Oswald had time to escape from the sixth floor of the Depository without being seen or heard. This change would not have been necessary if everything had been as simple and truthful as the story presented in the Warren Report.

Victoria Adams signed a deposition stating that she and co-worker Sandra Styles descended the stairs from the fourth floor of the Depository at about the same time that Oswald or anyone else who might have been on the sixth floor should have been exiting. Neither she nor Styles observed Billy Lovelady or William Shelley, Lovelady's supervisor, on reaching the first floor. And, yet, Adams' deposition, printed in Volume VI of the Warren Report, states that the women saw *both men* in the hallway at the bottom of the stairs.

This error might not seem important, but it is, because it changes the timeline, placing Styles and Adams on the first floor several minutes later than they actually arrived.[301] All of this is crucial when determining whether any assassin could have shot the President from the sixth floor and run down the stairs as quickly as the FBI claimed Oswald had.

Victoria Adams retold her story to author Barry Ernest. Included in his book *The Girl on the Stairs* is an interview with Adams' co-worker, Sandra Styles. In 2016, Styles also spoke with the authors about November 22, 1963.[302] Like Adams, she was single in 1963 and working for the Scott-Foresman Textbook Company. After attending Baylor University in Waco, Texas, Styles moved to Dallas in May 1963. She was living in an apartment in Irving and commuting to downtown Dallas at the time of the assassination.

She recalled that she and the other women who worked on the fourth floor of the Depository were excited that the President's motorcade was scheduled to pass beneath their windows. Styles had no idea how important her and Adams' memories of the minutes following the assassination would become.

Styles explained that student textbooks were delivered to the warehouse section of the Depository. Storage for these books was on the first floor of the building. In the less automated day and age of the 1960s, Texas schools would order textbooks directly from the Depository. Additional educational materials had to be physically attached to the various book orders. It was part of Styles' job to place the teachers' materials next to the book orders so they could all be delivered to the schools together.

The fourth floor of the Depository was a combination of Scott-Foresman offices and storage area for these extra educational materials. Styles and Adams interacted briefly with workers like Lee Harvey Oswald as they added the extra materials to various orders.

Styles recalled years later: "The workers [like Oswald] all wore jeans and work shirts with their shirt sleeves rolled up. Some would wear khakis or other kinds of work pants." Other Depository employees like Styles and Adams, who worked for professional companies, dressed in office attire—dresses or skirts, blouses, sweaters, nylons, and heels. "There was no air-conditioning in the building except in the offices," Styles added.

When asked about Lee Harvey Oswald, Styles explained, "I did not know until later that he lived in Irving. It was mostly apartment houses in my area of Irving." When it came to a social life, Styles added, "We didn't venture out into Irving for entertainment. We went to Dallas. It was so close, you see." Styles paused for a moment as she thought back to those post-college days.

"We went to the clubs," she began, but she quickly added, "*dance clubs*! Yes, I had *heard* of the Carousel Club." Styles made it clear that she and her friends did not frequent clubs like the Carousel.

"Our favorite place was the Levee. People played banjos and sang songs from the 1930s and '40s. It was on Cedar Springs Street." Styles chuckled as she recalled, "They had four guys who played in a group there. The youngest had lots of hair and the oldest was bald." But Styles remembered that in the early 1960s, most people her age "gathered in each other's apartments and played games." In 1963, she happened to have four roommates with whom she shared her apartment. To make ends meet, Styles worked more than one job. "I worked three nights a week and on Saturdays at Sanger-Harris, a department store."

On that infamous Friday in November, Styles' day began like most other days, except that the employees knew they might get a chance to see the President of the United States and the First Lady during their lunch hour. The employees on the fourth floor would have a good view of the presidential motorcade from their windows. Like each floor of the Depository, the fourth floor had seven large double windows. Styles and Adams positioned themselves in front of an open window, waiting eagerly for the presidential motorcade.

"The limousine turned onto Elm Street and passed in front of us. The shots were fired. The limo slowed down. There were trees obstructing our view, but I could see movement of Mrs. Kennedy because of her hot-pink suit." Styles then added a statement that Victoria Adams may not have been aware of. Adams told author Barry Ernest that *immediately* after the shots were fired, she said to Styles, "I want to see what is going on."[303]

Adams may not have realized that her co-worker decided to check out the other windows for a better view of the street below her. According to Styles, "That was when I went to other windows to get a better view. I did not go to the manager's corner office, but I did try to see out of Mrs. Garner's [her supervisor's] office. I don't know what Vickie was doing while I was moving around."

Styles continued by describing how the Scott-Foresman area of the fourth floor looked that day. Besides the two administrative offices, there was a large open room. "There was a partial wall between us and the stacks where teachers' aids and other free materials were kept. Just to the west of the stacks was the break room, which was really just a table for eating and assembling packets to send out. The door to the stairs was in the back of the break room."

Styles was uncertain how long it took her to check out the five windows she had access to on her floor. However, based on an experiment the authors made using the windows on the sixth floor of the Depository, this probably did not take more than thirty seconds. While Styles was peering through various windows, any assassin on the sixth floor would have been frantically hiding his rifle and carefully tiptoeing down a creaking staircase, hoping that the employees on every other floor did not see or hear him.

Styles' story continued: "At some point she [Adams] suggested we go down to see what was going on, and we went to the public elevator. When it did not come right away, Vickie proposed going down the back stairs. We went across the full width of the office and down the back stairs. I am thinking all that took at least a minute, maybe closer to two." Styles then addressed what she felt was a discrepancy between her memories and Victoria Adams'. This is something she admitted not mentioning to author Barry Ernest.

"The discrepancy is in Vicky's insistence that we went down immediately upon hearing the shots and mine that we did not. My theory is that Oswald was ahead of us on the stairs, and others are trying to prove that he would have been behind us; therein lies the rub."

Styles admitted, "Neither of us heard anyone walking down the staircase from the floors above, and yes, those stairs were extremely squeaky." No one else on the fourth or fifth floors ever reported hearing anyone descending the staircase before or after the assassination, either, and there were people on both floors.

What Styles did not know at the time is that her supervisor, Dorothy Garner, followed her and Adams to the office doorway leading to the staircase. Garner told Ernest she could hear the women's heels clicking on the staircase as they descended. She was still standing at the doorway when Officer Marion Baker of the Dallas Police Department and Depository administrator Roy Truly ran up the stairs to inspect the upper floors. No one passed her doorway before Baker and Truly. Sandra Styles apparently misjudged how quickly she joined Victoria Adams on the staircase.

Like Adams, Styles contradicted a statement that someone on the Warren Commission attributed to Victoria Adams. The report quoted Adams as saying that she and Styles saw fellow employee Billy Lovelady and his supervisor, William Shelley, standing on the first floor just as they finished descending the staircase. Both Adams and Styles agreed separately that this was untrue.

However, there may have been a strategic reason for someone to add this erroneous statement to Adams' testimony. Both Shelley and Lovelady testified that they had run towards the grassy knoll area after the motorcade disappeared from sight. If Adams and Styles had, indeed, entered the first floor in time to see these two men, it would have lengthened the amount of time the two women spent exiting the fourth floor. There seems to be no other credible reason for why this information was *added* to Adams' testimony without her knowledge.

Another problem affecting the timeline for an assassin's escape was the testimony of Bonnie Ray Williams. Williams was also employed by the Depository, and on November 22 he was helping lay new flooring on the sixth floor. Williams' lunch that day became linked to Lee Harvey Oswald. After the assassination, a Dallas police officer was photographed proudly displaying a brown lunch sack and an empty Dr. Pepper bottle. In various books, including *Four Days*, the caption under this photograph read: "A lunch bag and a pop bottle, held here by a Dallas Police technician, and three spent shell casings were found by the sixth-floor window. The sniper had dined on fried chicken and pop while waiting patiently to shoot the President."[304]

It was not long before the investigators discovered that the lunch in question actually belonged to one of Oswald's co-workers, Bonnie Ray Williams, *not* to Oswald. Williams had no reason to hide the fact that sat and waited patiently for the President's motorcade. When questioned, he said he planned on watching the motorcade from the sixth floor. Williams and other co-workers who had been working all morning on that particular floor took the elevator down at about 11:50 a.m. Williams retrieved his sack lunch and returned to the sixth floor. He thought his co-workers would meet him there to watch the motorcade. He admitted sitting near what eventually became known as the "sniper's nest" until about 12:20 p.m. At no time did he see or speak to Oswald or to anyone else.

A fact that is not commonly known is that Williams did *not* leave the remnants of his lunch on the sixth floor. The chicken and Dr. Pepper were originally found on the *fifth floor*; they were brought upstairs and *placed* near the sniper's nest. This detail was finally revealed by news photographer Tom Alyea. Alyea followed the first group of officers from floor to floor in the Depository. He filmed the various floors and the officers as they searched for an assassin and evidence.

Alyea told fellow reporter Connie Kritzberg: "There were no chicken bones on the sixth floor. We covered every inch of it and I filmed everything that could possibly be suspected as evidence. There definitely were no chicken bones on or near the barricade or boxes at the window."[305]

Alyea also saw Capt. Will Fritz pick up the three casings found on the sixth floor before being photographed in their original location or processed for fingerprints. His film footage of the boxes scattered around the west side of the sixth floor is the only photographic evidence of how the area originally looked because the search team began *moving boxes* before any other photographer could take still photos.[306] This explains the numerous fingerprints of law enforcement found on boxes that should not have been touched so quickly. Alyea's footage is also proof that evidence like the food items were manipulated, and that several "official" photographs of the crime scene were staged. Now that this fact has been established, the question that comes to mind is: Could the rifle have been placed on the sixth floor by someone other than the accused assassin?

Other questions about how Oswald could have managed to shoot from the sixth floor must also be considered. How did investigators think Oswald managed to retrieve the rifle he supposedly brought to work that morning from wherever he hid it, reassemble it, and hide himself and the rifle on the same floor where Bonnie Ray Williams sat enjoying his lunch?

If Oswald planned on shooting the President from the sixth floor, he could not have guaranteed that no other employees would return to the sixth floor to watch the motorcade, just as Bonnie Ray Williams had. Surely he did not huddle between stacks of books with the rifle next to him. If he decided to hide on the seventh floor, he probably could have heard Williams riding the elevator down to the fifth floor at about 12:20 p.m.

Williams was repeatedly asked by officials about the exact time he finished his lunch and left the sixth floor to go down to the fifth floor. He never appeared positive about the specific time. Without a watch, Williams was unsure of when he took the elevator back to the sixth floor, how long he sat eating his lunch, and exactly when he gave up on any of his co-workers joining him on the sixth floor.

There was no way Williams could have known exactly what time he took the elevator down to the fifth floor to see if his co-workers were waiting there. He did say he thought he was on the sixth floor 10 to 12 minutes. He told the Commission members that he believed he went down to the fifth floor around 12:20 p.m. Williams also mentioned his assumption that he was alone on the sixth floor because it had been so quiet.

If Oswald were hiding on the seventh floor, it is highly unlikely he would have enough time to walk *carefully* down the stairs, work his way to the front window of the sixth floor, and arrange the so-called "sniper's nest," which apparently did not exist when Williams was on the sixth floor. Photographs of the sixth floor, taken thirty minutes or so after the assassination, show the east side of the sixth floor stacked with cardboard boxes, some full of heavy textbooks. Because of Tom Alyea, researchers now know that these photos show boxes which were not in their original positions. Neither Williams nor his two co-workers on the fifth floor heard anyone above them moving boxes. Perhaps the "sniper's nest" was nothing more than a corner with boxes of books shoved into it.

Hundreds of man hours were spent reenacting how an assassin could easily kill the President from the east corner of the Depository's sixth floor. Some experts claim even the best marksman would have had problems with accuracy because an Italian-Carcano rifle was such an inadequate weapon. Other experts are quite sure that any decent marksman could have made the shot easily. What is interesting is that the testimonies of Victoria Adams, Sandra Styles, Dorothy Garner, and Bonnie Williams create such problems with the official timeline that the real question is: Did *anyone* have enough time to set-up a "sniper's nest" on the sixth floor from which to shoot the President?

There is also the question: How much "evidence" was tainted and/or altered by Dallas law enforcement? If Capt. Will Fritz could make the mistake of handling evidence before it had been processed, obviously, other officers could have, too.

The strongest eyewitness to place anyone on the sixth floor during the President's assassination was Howard Brennan. He was seated about 93 feet away from the Depository, directly in front of it. When asked to identify the person he saw standing with a rifle pointed at Elm Street, Brennan said that only Oswald, whose photo he had already seen on television that afternoon, *most closely resembled* the man he spotted standing at the sixth- floor window.[307]

Later, after Oswald was safely dead and buried, Brennan claimed he could have *positively* identified Oswald on the evening of November 22, 1963, if he had not been afraid to do so. Once he felt free to talk, Brennan conveniently provided numerous details about the "man in the window." He described him as being in his early thirties with a fair complexion, slender and neat, possibly 5-feet, 10 inches, and about 160 to 170 pounds. He had no memory at all of hair color.

The Oswald arrested at the Texas Theatre on November 22, 1963, was 5-feet, 9 inches, and weighed about 135 pounds. That morning at the Depository, he was wearing a brown, button-down, long-sleeved shirt with a white t-shirt underneath. If Brennan could actually see as well as he claimed, then the man he saw standing in the window of the sixth floor was heavier than Lee Harvey Oswald and not wearing the same type of clothes.

If Oswald was firing a rifle, then he was most certainly not standing. The window sills on the sixth floor were approximately twelve inches from the floor and the window itself, based on photographs, opened only about twelve inches that day. Anyone firing a rifle from that spot would have had to lie on his stomach or crouch on his knees. Photographs of reenactments show the window fully opened and the rifle attached to a tripod. One reenactment took place from a platform placed outside of the window rather than from the sixth floor itself.

No matter how many experts have duplicated the assassin's shots, none of them have experienced the same emotions, the same adrenaline rush, or the same fear of being captured that an assassin would have felt. A professional assassin might have been so calm and well-prepared that he could handle a narrow window of opportunity, the realization that Bonnie Ray Williams might return to the sixth floor, and/or the possibility that any other employee might return from lunch ten minutes early. Lee Harvey Oswald was certainly not a professional assassin. There is no record he had ever killed anyone in his life. His military service had *not* included any type of combat.

If Howard Brennan did see a man dressed in khaki who "resembled" Oswald standing with a rifle on the sixth floor, perhaps that person remained hidden on the sixth floor until Dallas officials began their search. He might have blended in with various law enforcement officials, who would have simply assumed he was one of them. One thing is certain: Lee Harvey Oswald could not have blended in with police personnel, and the testimony of Victoria Adams and Sandra Styles indicates that he probably did not descend from an upper level of the Depository in time to meet Officer Baker and Roy Truly face-to-face only minutes after the assassination.

CHAPTER 28

THE VOICES OF
DRS. KARL DOCKRAY AND
JAMES HUDDLESTON

"Oswald just died. No one seemed to know why exactly."—Karl Dockray

Dr. Karl Dockray was not on duty at Parkland Hospital on Sunday, November 24, 1963, but fate seemed to push him there anyway. Dallas Chief of Police Jesse Curry had announced that Lee Harvey Oswald would be transferred from the Dallas Police Department to the Sheriff's Department on Sunday, November 24, 1963. What Curry did not announce was that there had been death threats against the prisoner made by telephone to the Dallas Police Department.

To guarantee the accused assassin's safety, the police announced they would escort him in an armored car to the Sheriff's Department. Newsmen and reporters were allowed to gather in the basement of the police department to witness Oswald's transfer. One FBI agent who did not accompany Oswald to the basement, according to homicide detective L. D. Montgomery, was Special Agent James W. Bookhout.

Bookhout later questioned Montgomery about the procedure he followed as Oswald was led to the basement. Indignant, Montgomery replied, "You were there, Bookhout. We handcuffed Oswald. We walked around to the elevator, got on the elevator to go down. Where'd you go? You were right there with us."

According to Montgomery, Bookhout responded, "I walked back to the squad room and turned up the squawk box." When Montgomery demanded to know why Bookhout had done this, he received a startling response: "...to hear the shooting. Didn't you know that the chief had received a call during the night that Oswald was going to be shot?"[308]

It is difficult to believe that an FBI agent would admit such a thing, but Montgomery's revelation was made in a taped interview. It is possible that Iris Campbell, who served as the eyes and ears of Lyndon Johnson in Dallas after the assassination, was also listening to the squawk box. She admitted to being on the third floor of the Dallas Police Department shortly before Oswald was killed, and she was the first to communicate the news to Lyndon Johnson.

In 2016, Richard Jones shared a personal story about the moment Lee Harvey Oswald was shot. A California tenager, he gathered around the television set with his family waiting for Kennedy's accused assassin to be transferred to the Dallas Sheriff's Department. Just as Oswald entered the basement of the Dallas Police Department, Jones' stepfather pointed to the television screen and said, "This is where it's going to happen." In a split-second, Jack Ruby stepped out of a crowd of news reporters and gunned down Lee Harvey Oswald.

When Jones and the rest of his family demanded to know how his stepfather had known what was going to happen, his stepfather replied, "That is how it's done." Jones later admitted his stepfather was once a member of the O.S.S. [forerunner to the CIA.] Apparently, experiences with this intelligence organization had provided Jones' stepfather with insights into how "patsies" are silenced when not killed during their arrests.[309]

Bookhout's comments indicate that FBI agents were familiar with this routine, too. For some reason, the agent was waiting upstairs in anticipation that Oswald would be shot instead of protecting the prisoner in the basement. Ordinary Dallas citizens could not enter the basement, but they gathered outside the police department to catch a personal glimpse of the man most people had already decided was Kennedy's assassin. Among those citizens was Dr. Karl Dockray. Today, Dockray is a well-known medical specialist in Texas. But on November 24, 1963, he was a radiology resident at Parkland Hospital in Dallas, Texas.

That Sunday was Dr. Dockray's day off, and he took his camera to the police department building, hoping to get close enough to the accused assassin to capture him on film.[310] Appreciating how historic the occasion was, he simply wanted photos to prove he had seen the accused assassin. Security was tight enough to keep Dockray away from Oswald, but not tight enough to block Jack Ruby. Dockray was armed with nothing more harmful than a German-made Voigtlander camera; Jack Ruby, on the other hand, was armed with a .38-caliber pistol. The local night club owner blended in with the newsmen, cameramen, and local police. He carried a press pass that someone had given him years before which he often used if he wanted to join a news event.

Ruby used it to enter the Dallas Police Department on the evening of November 22 when Dallas District Attorney Henry Wade was feeding information to eager members of the press.

It was not difficult for Jack Ruby to blend in with the police because his face was well-known to many of those in the department. Like many other Dallasites, numerous law enforcement officers frequented Ruby's strip club, the Carousel, or his other nightclub, the Vegas Club. At both, Dallas police sometimes received free liquor. On Sunday November 24, many Dallas police officers and most of the world had front-row seats to a show more memorable than any Jack Ruby had ever produced at his Carousel Club. And because of Ruby's actions, Dockray never got to see Oswald before the shooting. But, ironically, in only a matter of minutes, he would be photographing the accused assassin as he lay on a surgical table in Parkland Hospital.

The shots that killed John F. Kennedy were not heard around the world, but thanks to live television coverage, the shot that killed Oswald was seen around the world. Jack Ruby stole the spotlight from the accused assassin by lunging towards him and shooting him pointblank in the torso. Oswald's death erased any chance he had to prove his innocence or to confess his guilt. Rather than being transferred to the Sheriff's Department, Oswald was placed in an ambulance and rushed to the same hospital that had received President Kennedy and Governor Connally just forty-eight hours before.

As soon as word spread through the crowd that the alleged assassin had been shot, Dockray sprinted for his car. He knew the closest hospital was Parkland, so he followed the exact route that President Kennedy's motorcade had taken two days before. Entering via the same emergency room doors through which the late President had been taken, Dockray could tell that the news about Oswald had just reached the hospital staff. He realized he was still holding his camera and that this was the chance of a lifetime. He grabbed a white physician's coat from a nearby coat rack and prepared to take photos of some of the Parkland doctors who had recently attempted to save the President. Today, they would be trying to save the man accused of killing John F. Kennedy.

Out of respect for the late President, Oswald was not placed in Trauma Room 1; he was examined in Trauma Room 2 and then moved upstairs to surgery. Dockray recalled anesthesiologist Dr. "Pepper" Jenkins being at the head of the surgical table along with Dr. Robert McClelland, head surgeon. He knew that McClellend's expertise was in liver damage, so he was the perfect surgeon to deal with this specific emergency. Just as he was about to begin shooting photos, Dockray's camera broke. Dr. Jenkins must have realized how important this was to Dockray because he wrote out a pass so he could leave the operating room, find another camera, and return.

Dockray was familiar with the hospital, so it did not take him long to locate some of the newsmen mingling in the hallways. He explained his situation to a photographer from the magazine *Paris Match*, who allowed Dockray to borrow his camera. The young resident rushed towards the operating room but was suddenly stopped at the door by a man wearing a dark suit. Dockray had to show him Dr. Jenkins' pass before allowed to enter the operating room. Though a hospital should have been a sanctuary for the wounded, this operating room was now under armed guard. Officials were guarding a seriously wounded Oswald more closely *after* he was shot than *before* he was shot.

Dockray recalled residents pumping blood into Oswald while surgeons worked frantically to repair his damaged internal organs. As he snapped photo after photo, he darted around the operating table, weaving in and out. He knew he had to stay out of the way but still record this historic event. At one point, he ended up at the head of the operating table next to Dr. Jenkins.

"Hey, Karl," Jenkins said, motioning for the young resident to look at Oswald's wrist. "Look at this." He was pointing at a thin scar on the inside of Oswald's wrist. It was the kind of scar that typically remains after a suicide attempt. Dockray pointed out to Jenkins, however, that he had a similar scar on his own wrist caused by a Venetian blind falling on him. (It wasn't until years later that he and Jenkins learned that while Oswald was in Russia, he *had* attempted to take his own life by slitting his wrist).

The surgeons finished repairing the damage caused by Ruby's single gunshot had caused, stitched up Oswald's open torso, and deemed the surgery a success. More than fifty years later, Dr. Karl Dockray recalled: "Oswald survived until he was turned on his stomach so that a bullet, palpable beneath the skin of his back, could be recovered for forensics. I think that the alteration in position put him over the edge." A member of the medical team surprised the others when he announced, "Hey, I can feel the slug under the skin of his back!" The doctors had rolled Oswald partly over to try to remove the slug which, despite doing so much internal damage, had not exited Oswald's body.[311]

Suddenly, according to Dockray, "Oswald just died. No one seemed to know why exactly. Everyone just stood there for a moment, stunned. I don't remember anyone saying anything." Then the team sprang into action again, and Dockray remembered Dr. Robert McClelland using the electric paddles on Oswald's chest. Though Dr. Charles Crenshaw described Dr. Malcolm Perry as re-opening Oswald's chest and massaging his heart, Dr. Dockray does not remember it quite this way. In fact, he seemed confused when he heard that Crenshaw had written this. "But he was already sewn up," Dockray said and left it at that.

After Oswald was pronounced dead, Dockray returned the camera he had borrowed to the photographer from *Paris Match,* who offered him a hundred dollars for just one photo of Oswald's body.

"There was no way in hell I was going to do that," Dockray said emotionally. "It would have meant the end of my career!" Dr. Karl Dockray transferred his historic film to Jack Price, head administrator of Parkland Hospital. He never saw it again.

"I assumed Jack Price flushed the film down the toilet," he said years later. He had no idea that Price found the film canisters forty years after Oswald's death. They were lying in a desk drawer in Parkland Hospital—still undeveloped. When asked about the origin of the film, Price remembered that a doctor named Karl Dockray had given him the rolls of film on the afternoon of November 24, a short time after Oswald's death, the resident having explained that the film contained photos of Oswald and the doctors who tried in vain to save his life.

It was not until 2004 that others became aware of these film canisters. In January of that year, Price contacted researcher J. Gary Shaw. Knowing of Shaw's interest in the assassination, he personally delivered a small airborne express box containing three 4 ½" by 10" yellow envelopes marked "valuables envelope." What caught Shaw's eye immediately was that each envelope was dated "November 24, 1963."[312]

Shaw deliberately did not open the envelopes until Bob Force, a photographer from Cleburne, Texas, was with him. When the two of them unsealed the envelopes, they found nine canisters of unprocessed film. Shaw and Force both knew that forty-year-old film had to be handled carefully if any of the photographs were to be salvaged. It took quite some time to locate a film laboratory that could process film that old. When the two men finally discovered such a laboratory, they had to make a trip to Colorado. The trip proved worthwhile.

The black and white Kodak Tri-X Pan film was so old that most of the images were unrecognizable, but others showed just what Dr. Karl Dockray had seen through his view finder that day. There are images of the doctors in their scrubs and masks gathered around an operating table. Lying in the middle of the table is the body of Lee Harvey Oswald. Strangely enough, the man who actually took these photos never saw them, but the authors were able to view them in 2015 thanks to a private collector.

In 1964, Dockray was approached by FBI Special Agent Arthur Carter, who wanted Dockray's film. On file with the FBI is a record of Dockray being questioned by Carter. Dockray had never read this FBI report until the authors shared it with him. The report quotes Dr. Dockray as telling the FBI "that he would have to produce a 'subpoena duces tecum'" if he wanted to leave with the film. It seems that the young doctor had been astute enough to tell the agent he would need to be legally required to relinquish the film, though years later Dockray commented, "I do not recall using the legal term 'duces tecum.'" He added that the FBI report of his so-called "interview" contained many errors, "and it sounds made-up to me."[313]

Special Agent Carter seemed particularly interested in whether Dockray had observed any scars on Oswald's inner wrists. Dockray had no idea why the agent was questioning him about scars. He had not volunteered any information about this, and he does not remember telling the agent "he was unable to recall any scars on the inner wrist of Lee Harvey Oswald," as the FBI report reads. For whatever reason, Dockray did not mention to the FBI agent the conversation that he and Dr. Jenkins had about the scar on Oswald's wrist. But in 2014, he still remembered the conversation vividly when interviewed by the authors. Either the agent learned what he wanted to know from Dockray, or he never bothered to get the subpoena. In any event, the film canisters were still lying in a drawer in the hospital forty years after Oswald's death. Once again, an "official report" contained "errors" that went unnoticed for decades.

The FBI agent did not explain why he questioned Dockray about a scar he might have observed on Oswald's body. The agency knew that Oswald had attempted suicide by cutting his wrist while living in Russia. There were already questions and doubts that the man arrested for the President's murder might not be the same man who had defected to Russia in 1959.

Fifty years after he took those historic photos, Dr. Karl Dockray had no interest in seeing them. When asked if he had ever requested copies of the photos, he replied slowly, "No, there was so much going on and the place was just fraught with fear that I never asked for copies." He also added that he didn't care to have any now, either. "Years later," he went on, "Charlie Crenshaw called me looking for the film or prints, but I told him I didn't know anything about what had happened to the film after I gave it to Jack Price."

Because a young resident had the presence of mind to realize how historic the events of November 24, 1963 were, there is now visual evidence of how strenuously the Parkland doctors fought to save the life of a man most of the world then thought had assassinated John F. Kennedy. If Dockray had been allowed to take photos while doctors fought to save the President *or* at his Bethesda autopsy, historians might have more accurate information than they do.

Dr. James Huddleston was also in Oswald's operating room, but unlike Dockray, he did not have permission from Dr. Jenkins or any other medical personnel.[314] He and a few other senior medical students were making rounds when Oswald was shot. Though there were televisions in the patients' rooms, they happened to be walking between rooms at the time. As soon as they heard that Oswald was being sent to surgery, they donned surgical gowns and masks and mingled their way into the operating room.

Huddleston recalled, "He had IVs and blood going in all four extremities. At least two surgeons had their arms elbow-deep in Oswald's belly trying to stop the bleeding." Huddleston also remembered that the operating room was extremely crowded, with perhaps fifteen to twenty medical personnel present. In fact, it was so crowded that one of the surgeons finally looked up at Huddleston and the medical students and asked who the extra persons were. The medical students were immediately asked to leave, but they were able to witness about thirty minutes of one of the most memorable surgeries in the history of medicine.

Perhaps Huddleston and his colleages were so determined to observe Oswald's operation because they had also been at Parkland on November 22 when President Kennedy was admitted. The group of medical students were waiting patiently for Dr. Charles Baxter on the second floor lecture room. Suddenly, a nurse ran in demanding to know where Baxter was. She then told the students that the President had been shot and was being brought to Parkland.

When asked what he and the other students did at that point, the 84-year-old retired psychiatrist retorted, "What would you have done? Naturally, we ran downstairs to the emergency area, but by the time we got there, the President had been taken into Trauma Room 1 and the doors were locked so no one could get in." They did not see Mrs. Kennedy sitting in the hallway, so she must have been inside with the President at the time.

Huddleston had recently rotated through chest surgery service, and the chief of chest surgery had taken a liking to him. This skilled surgeon is one of the doctors who helped save Governor John Connally's life. He and Huddleston encountered one another in the doctors' dressing room after Connally's surgery concluded. Consequently, Huddleston knew a great deal about the Governor's wounds, the surgical procedures performed, and the progress made after his surgery. Huddleston pointed out that Connally could have easily died, too. His wounds were quite severe.

"He had a very large hole in his chest," he said in a telephone interview with the authors. Huddleston added that there some speculation as to who the assassin's intended victim had been—Kennedy or Connally? Because of this concern, the Governor was not moved to a regular recovery room.

"He was put in the deepest part of the recovery area," Huddleston explained. "No one had access to him except for a few people." But thanks to the relationship established with one of Connally's surgeons, Huddleton received frequent reports on the Governor's progress.

Huddleston also recalled that there was some skepticism among the medical staff as to whether a single bullet could cause as much damage as it supposedly had. There were also questions about the bullet's trajectory. Huddleston was not surprised to hear that certain medical personnel connected to Parkland on the day Kennedy was killed were forced to sign confidentiality agreements. He said he also heard rumors that doctors changed their original statements about the President's wounds, but had not heard that himself. However, the fact that he and other medical students were unable to observe the life-saving attempts made on President Kennedy is what motivated them to push their way into the surgery suite where some of those same doctors attempted to save the life of the man accused of killing him.

CHAPTER 29

THE VOICE OF ELYSSE GOLDSTRICH

"We just don't know the whole story and it was far worse than we could imagine."

D r. Karl Dockray is not the only lesser-known doctor who has recollections of that weekend in Dallas, Texas. It was with author Bill Sloan that Dr. Joe D. Goldstrich first shared his remembrances of being at Parkland Hospital when President Kennedy was rushed into Trauma Room One. Sloan included Goldstrich's memories and experiences in his book *Breaking the Silence*.

Goldstrich, assigned to Parkland's neurosurgical medical team, was on duty on November 22, 1963. He was a fourth-year medical student at the University of Texas Southwestern Medical School. Dr. William Kemp Clark was Parkland's chief of neurosurgery; that morning, Goldstrich had assisted Dr. Clark with a fairly new neck surgery procedure. After the procedure was completed, Clark asked him if he was comfortable performing a tracheotomy just in case their patient needed one. Goldstrich stated he was, so Clark felt confident in leaving the premises.[315]

That same day, Goldstrich's sister Elysse and her oldest daughter were running errands in Waco, Texas. Suddenly, an announcer on their regular radio station interrupted with the news that President Kennedy had been shot in Dallas, Texas. Elysse immediately rushed home to tell her husband Leonard, who was having lunch with Elysse's brother and a family friend.[316]

Dr. Goldstrich's lunch at Parkland Hospital was also interrupted by an announcement from a loud speaker. "Dr. Clark— STAT!" Goldstrich assumed the announcement concerned a problem with the patient on which Clark had recently operated. He knew Dr. Clark had left Parkland, so he raced to the nearest nurse's station to call the receptionist. Then, over the loud speaker, he heard an all-call for every major surgeon at Parkland. "Dr. Clark—STAT. Dr. Perry—STAT. Dr. McClelland—STAT. Dr. Baxter—STAT." Goldstrich knew something horrific had happened to someone. The receptionist informed Goldstrich that President Kennedy was being brought to the emergency room. He flew down the flight of stairs and was greeted by images so vivid that they would haunt him for years.

It was decades before he shared any of these memories with his family or friends. This was partly because many of the medical personnel in Trauma Room One understood that it would be best if they did not speak about the President's death. Goldstritch was never told *not* to talk about what he observed that day, but he was also never questioned by anyone. Chances are, officials did not even realize that the fourth-year medical student was even in the emergency room that day.

However, there was another, more important reason why Dr. Goldstrich told only a few close friends about that extraordinary day. According to his sister Elysse's recollection, her brother was too frightened to speak about that day because those who did talk "met a terrible demise. My brother was so scared," she added.[317] In 1965, memories of the President's throat wound would return to him as he observed battle wounds in the Dominican Republic. Goldstrich was serving as a physician in the U.S. Army at the time. Entry wounds on injured soldiers showed the same characteristics as the throat wound he observed on President Kennedy.

Goldstrich doubted that the President's throat wound was an exit wound, as official reports later declared, and his doubts increased after his wartime experiences. He saw too many entry and exit wounds to not know the difference. At Parkland Hospital in 1963, Goldstrich observed "a small, almost perfectly round hole right in the middle of the front of Kennedy's neck, just below the Adam's apple."[318] Goldstrich was standing very close to the left side of the emergency room table. He was particularly aware of the throat wound because he had recently been preparing to perform tracheotomies. Goldstrich was still in Trauma Room One as the President's body was transferred to a casket.

Years later, when he saw the "official" photos of Kennedy's autopsy, he knew without a doubt that the large, ragged wound depicted in the photos had not existed when Kennedy's body left the hospital. Not until then did his doubts lead him to think there might have been a conspiracy and, later on, a cover-up.

"The more I realized how impossible it would have been for the neck wound I saw to have been an exit wound, the more I changed my mind."[319] If the throat wound was an entry wound, as so many of the Parkland doctors *first* said it was, then at least one shot must have originated from the front of the presidential limousine. Obviously, someone needed to alter the President's throat wound so that an entrance wound would look like an exit wound. This alteration was necessary because if the throat wound was really an entrance wound, then a single assassin located behind the limousine could not have killed the President.

In 1992, Dr. Goldstrich decided he could no longer stand by and listen to the false statements made by the autopsy doctors, government agents, and Warren Commission members concerning the President's wounds. Only then did he finally share his experiences with author Bill Sloan. Before his interview with Sloan, the only statement he would make to his family was the simple comment, "I was there." No matter how many questions his family asked at the time, Goldstrich would not elaborate.

But as the years passed, for whatever reason, he gradually began to share pieces of information with his sister. He still did not know why Dr. Malcolm Perry had cut a diagonal hole over the small, round bullet hole already in Kennedy's throat. The small bullet hole seemed perfect for a tracheotomy, at least to Goldstrich.

Over the years, he also shared graphic details about the "blood and gore" surrounding the President as he lay on the operating table at Parkland Hospital. His memories made his sister realize that "we just don't know the whole story, and it was far worse than we could imagine."

Dr. Goldstrich did not speak to the authors because, at that time, he was assisting with a documentary about the assassination. However, he was part of a panel of Parkland doctors who spoke at a 2015 JFK Lancer symposium. The story he shared there had not changed since the day he first spoke to Bill Sloan.

Goldstrich's sister believes her brother has tried to forget the tragedy of November 22, but like many other witnesses, had been unable to do so. Memories of the assassination were especially hard for him for two reasons. First of all, while growing up, his best friend was Henry Zapruder, the son of Abraham Zapruder, the man whose film of the assassination is known throughout the world as "the Zapruder film." Secondly, during his time in the Army, Goldstrich was often reminded of what he had seen in Trauma Room One. In the Army, he was assigned to the ballistics and forensic pathology unit; part of his job was to observe gunshot wounds and determine if they were entry or exit wounds. Seemingly, he could not escape the memories of that historic day, nor the erroneous descriptions, both spoken and written, by other professionals. Like Dr. Charles Crenshaw, who refused to change his memories about what happened during Oswald's surgery, Goldstrich is determined to set the record straight about President Kennedy's throat wound.

His testimony about the original appearance of the wound in the President's throat gives credence to the theory that some person(s) hurriedly autopsied the body of President Kennedy before an official autopsy began. Bullets and fragments may have been removed. If so, the "official autopsy" cannot be considered actual evidence because it as full of errors as the Warren Report appears to be.

CHAPTER 30

THE VOICE OF TOMMY WRIGHT— PART II

"That's how I saw the dead body of the man who killed the President."

Tommy Wright was just one of many individuals whose lives were touched by the tragic events in Dallas in November 1963. He and another member of Ft. Worth's K-9 unit were assigned to guard the borrowed limousine in which President Kennedy's entourage rode on the evening of November 21 and the morning of November 22, 1963. After flying from Houston, the presidential party would be driven from the Carswell Air Force Base to the Texas Hotel in downtown Ft. Worth.

Though the presidential entourage was not expected to arrive in Fort Worth until late on November 21, Wright, his fellow officer, and their canines went on duty at 8:00 p.m. that day. As soon as the party reached the hotel, the two officers spent the remainder of the night repeatedly circling the limousine in which the President would ride the next morning.[320]

Wright and a fellow officer were well aware of the stringent security measures being taken in Ft. Worth. They knew the limousine was to be continuously guarded by two officers and two canines. Wright told the authors he had approved of Kennedy as president. "The only thing I didn't agree with him on was that he didn't like the canine units. This was because of how the canine units had been used by the police in Birmingham, Alabama, during the Civil Rights riots. I guess it's just as well he didn't know the K-9 unit was protecting his car that evening," Wright chuckled.[321]

Wright also recalled that the white limousine was searched thoroughly on the afternoon of November 21 to make sure no one had planted a bomb. As a police officer, he felt pride guarding this particular vehicle. Wright was one of the persons responsible for ascertaining that the car had not been tampered with after Kennedy, the First Lady, and Governor John Connally rode in it through the streets of Ft. Worth. He and his fellow officer spent a long sleepless night making sure the President would be safe the next morning as he returned to Carswell Air Force Base.

Though a Secret Service agent indicated that his agency was not overly concerned about the President's safety in Ft. Worth, Tommy Wright breathed a sigh of relief as his duty ended the morning of November 22, 1963. He watched the presidential limousine drive away; Wright assumed that his duty from the night before would be his only brush with history. He had no idea that he would soon be assigned to guard the corpse of the man accused of killing the President. In a matter of hours, Wright's duties suddenly included protecting something more important than a limousine.

Wright could not forget the evening of November 24, 1963. In a soft voice, he recalled, "It was a dreary, misty, and bitter cold night." Once again it was his association with the K-9 unit that caused the police to request his services. He and another officer, along with their canines, were driven to a part of Ft. Worth with which he was unfamiliar. Neither man was initially told what his assignment would be.

After they arrived at a mortuary, they were told they would be guarding the corpse of Lee Harvey Oswald. Wright remembered the building as small and located in what seemed to be the "middle of nowhere." He and the other officer took turns circling the building, in order to prevent anyone from entering and stealing the body of Lee Harvey Oswald.

There were concerns that an angry, grief-stricken person might attack the morticians as they performed their duties. After all, the citizens of Dallas had been embarrassed by the assassination and then by the murder of the accused assassin—all within forty-eight hours. Some felt that Oswald, though his guilt had not been proven, did not even deserve a burial.

The Ft. Worth police were determined to prevent any more violent acts, at least on their turf. The leaden skies spitting bitterly cold rain that Sunday night seemed much more appropriate for an embalming than Friday's sunny weather had been for the President's murder. As the night wore on and the temperatures dropped, the mortician took pity on the officers and told them to take turns coming inside to warm up from the cold. Upon entering the small room for the first time, Wright noticed that two men were working on the body of Lee Harvey Oswald.

"It was so cold and wet that night that they let my partner and me take turns stepping inside the embalming room to warm up. That's how I saw the dead body of the man who had killed the President." Wright recalled the room in which the embalming was taking place "as being very small and the body laid on what looked like an old wooden table. Only two other men were in the room. I thought they would be wearing surgical gowns and masks, but they weren't." Wright assumed that the men were performing an autopsy when they were actually doing an embalming.

He vividly recalled one of the men pouring what looked like a sack of sawdust into Oswald's body cavity. He shook his head as his wife prompted him to relate this detail. Apparently, this seemed unbelievable to him, even years later, but it is what he saw. According to a mortician questioned about Wright's recollection, Wright probably saw the part of the embalming process in which paraformaldehyde—a powdery preservative that resembles sawdust—is poured into the body cavity to keep the internal organs from decomposing as quickly as they otherwise would.

Wright seemed almost embarrassed to admit that he had seen a man holding a large sack and simply pouring its contents into Oswald's stomach cavity. However, his memory was confirmed by the mortician, Paul Groody, in an interview with researcher Jack White years later. Groody explained that he "over-embalmed" the body with several times the usual amount of formaldehyde so that the body would be well-preserved for all time."[322]

Wright also remembered that from time to time, the mortician and his assistant were asked by men dressed in dark suits to step out of the embalming room. This correlates with mortician Paul Groody's recollection that he and his assistant, Allen Baumgardner, were ordered to leave the embalming room by men he thought to be FBI agents.

Wright was unable to prevent either Kennedy's or Oswald's death, but he had the satisfaction of knowing that no one stole Oswald's body, at least not during his watch. He never learned why FBI agents would temporarily halt Oswald's embalming process and insist the morticians leave the room. Wright was not close enough to the corpse to notice ink remnants on the hands of the accused assassin, but Paul Groody was, and it is thanks to him that this curious fact was made public. It isn't uncommon for prints to be taken from a corpse if authorities never had the chance to fingerprint the person alive. In Oswald's case, the police had had him in custody since the afternoon of November 22. He had already been fingerprinted. It seems strange that more fingerprints (or palm prints) would be required after his death. If they were required, why did the printing take place in secret?

CHAPTER 31

VOICES FOR PAUL GROODY

"It was my father and Allen Baumgardner who lifted Oswald's body out
of the old casket and moved it into the new one. They had plenty of time to
look at that body."—Donald Groody

The death of Lee Harvey Oswald was almost as shocking to the American
public as the death of John F. Kennedy. Both men were being protected by
Dallas police officers when they were shot down. The lives of both men
had been threatened not long before their deaths. Perhaps Americans should not
have been surprised when Jack Ruby killed Oswald, but most of them were. The
public and the Dallas police assumed Oswald was safe as long as he was in custody. The basement of the Dallas Police Department should have been one of the
most secure places in the city. However, in an attempt to accommodate the media,
Chief of Police Jesse Curry and City Manager Elgin E. Crull allowed a carnival-
like atmosphere to endanger the accused assassin. Oswald became as much of a
"sitting duck" as President Kennedy had been.

The people of Dallas were already being shamed because of the President's
death. To the world, the city must have seemed wild and unruly if the Dallas
police could not even guarantee the safety of the accused assassin. The President
had been trapped in his own vehicle, and Oswald was trapped by a crowd of
police officers and newsmen. Instead of taking a short ride in an armored car
to the Dallas Sheriff's Department, Oswald was rushed to Parkland Hospital's
emergency room, where he soon died.

His body was autopsied immediately because government officials seemed
to want him buried as soon as possible. This time the Dallas County coroner
was allowed to follow the law. No officials were demanding that Oswald's body
be flown out of Dallas. However, it became necessary to move it to Ft. Worth
because not a single funeral home in Dallas would accept it, a fact that brought
his brother Robert to tears.

Secret Service Agent Charles Kunkle helped Oswald's family by contacting
Fort Worth mortician Paul Groody. Secret Service Agent Mike Howard stated,
"If it hadn't been for the Secret Service, Oswald probably would have been
put in the county dump or something 'cause nobody wanted to touch him."[323]
According to Virginia Groody, her late husband Paul was told by the Secret

Service that they "wanted Oswald buried right away because of safety's sake."[324] The Secret Service and the FBI were concerned that someone might attempt to steal Oswald's corpse.

With the help of Allen Baumgardner, Paul Groody embalmed Oswald on the evening of November 24, 1963, only hours after his autopsy. It was one of the most unusual embalmings in which Groody was ever involved. The mortician mentioned several times to numerous people how different Oswald's embalming process was from others he had performed. He assumed this would be a quick, routine procedure. But that was not to be the case. Years later, in an interview, mortician Allen Baumgardner recalled that he and Groody were interrupted numerous times by officials, who told them to leave the embalming room, and then told when they could return. Each time the men (government agents, according to Groody) entered the embalming room, Groody and Baumgardner were ordered to leave.

Groody revealed that he found ink on Oswald's palms. In fact, he had to remove the ink before he could dress Oswald's corpse. Through the process of elimination, Groody could determine who had inked Oswald's hands; he just did not know why. He also did not know why government officials and news reporters waited in a room next to the embalming room. That was the first and only time that had ever happened at Miller's Funeral Home.[325]

Most researchers are familiar with Groody's story about Oswald's embalming and burial, and they also know Groody was involved in the controversial 1981 exhumation of Oswald's body. What most people don't know is that Paul Groody and his wife left Fort Worth and moved to Abilene, Texas, in the early 1970s. Groody apparently abandoned the lucrative mortuary business.

Instead, he bought an amusement park connected to Nelson Park Zoo and hired high school students to run the rides during the summer. This is how Gene Williams came to know former mortician Paul Groody, a man he described as a "character."

"He was a big, tall guy with a great sense of humor. He could tell the best jokes!" Williams laughed as he remembered the summers he worked for Groody.[326] After Williams came to know Groody better, the older man shared some interesting stories with him. "He finally started talking about what he had done for a living in Ft. Worth and mentioned his most infamous client. Paul still owned a house in Ft. Worth even while he lived in Abilene," Williams continued.

"I remember him saying Oswald's embalming was the most unusual one he ever did. He said that he and an assistant had other men in the embalming room with him—FBI, he guessed—and that they would make the two of them leave the room at certain times, and then call them back in. They'd say, 'Okay, now you can go on,' but then for some reason, they would stop them again and send them out of the room again."

Groody also told Williams that Oswald's body was moved to two or three different places, but he did not know why. Williams was unsure whether Groody meant before or after the embalming. It is possible Groody was referring to the fact that the driver of the hearse carrying Oswald's coffin led news reporters on a wild goose chase. He was attempting to keep Oswald's burial site a secret.

As an adult, Williams looked back on those summers with Groody as enjoyable times "even though Paul only paid us a dollar an hour and we worked long hours. But, hey, I was a teenager and it was enough money to buy gas back then and we had a good time while we worked at the park. Paul was nice to work for, except for the dollar an hour!" Groody and his wife Virginia lived in a trailer at Nelson Park Zoo. While almost everyone in America had a private telephone, the Groodys did not. They were not even listed in the Abilene telephone directory. The only way they could be reached by telephone was through the Nelson Park Zoo.

In an interview with Groody's son Donald, the authors discovered that he and his sister at first were not told that their father had changed professions. Both of the Groody children were in college at the time, and Gene Williams remembered the sister visiting the parents once or twice. Donald Groody also said that his father had heart surgery sometime after 1963; he suggested this might be why his father left the mortuary business. He also reiterated that his parents did not sell their house in Ft. Worth and often returned to Ft. Worth on weekends.

What Williams and Donald Groody never knew was that Paul Groody became a close friend of one of Abilene's most infamous characters, Billie Sol Estes. In fact, he and his wife Virginia, lived at one time with Estes in his lake-front house. There is no evidence one way or the other whether Groody knew Billie Sol Estes before he moved to Abilene, but it is possible. Estes owned a funeral home in Pecos, Texas at one time, so the two men may have known each other because of this. Undoubtedly, Groody knew of Estes' reputation as a con man, but he also knew that he could be generous and soft-hearted.

Donald Groody remembered his father discussing the October 4, 1981 exhumation of Oswald's body.[327] After opening the original casket and identifying the clothing as original, Paul Groody and his wife sat in the hallway with Marina Oswald Porter while Dr. Linda Norton, a forensic specialist, oversaw the second autopsy. They remembered Marina Oswald Porter as a pleasant, middle-aged woman who maintained her composure during this difficult situation. Her primary concern was that her former husband's body might not even be in the casket.

Paul Groody caused quite a controversy when he questioned the condition of Oswald's skull. Though neither he nor Allen Baumgardner remained in the examining room while Oswald's skull was examined, they did have the opportunity to observe the body closely when they later removed it from the examining table and placed it in a new casket. Critics have argued that Groody and Baumgardner did not spend enough time with the body to examine it. They have also criticized Groody for not immediately questioning the discrepancy he noticed concerning the skull cap.

As Donald Groody said in an interview, "It was my father and Baumgardner who lifted that body out of the old casket and moved it to the new one. They had plenty of time to look at that body."

Baumgardner, who eventually purchased Miller's Funeral Home, explained that he and Groody had not focused on the skull at the time. But it was not long afterwards that Groody suddenly remembered that Oswald's skull had not shown evidence of a brain autopsy.

"He asked me, 'Did you see the skull cap on Oswald's skull?' Baumgardner recalled. "I remember telling him that I could not remember seeing one."[328] The two men were referring to the fact that during a complete autopsy, the top of the skull is sawed off so that the brain can be removed. When the skull cap is replaced, it is simply placed on top of the skull. No adhesive is used because skin holds the skull cap in place for quite some time. No evidence of separation between the two parts of the skull means that the top part of the skull was never removed. Groody was particularly concerned about this because the whole purpose of the exhumation was to prove that the body in the casket was the same body buried on November 24, 1963. Groody suddenly had doubts.

Some of this fascinating story Groody shared with Gene Williams. He told him, for example, about the way Dallas and Ft. Worth officials had tried to keep Oswald's funeral as secret as the embalming had been. Despite efforts to bury Oswald privately, those in charge of the funeral were not able to keep reporters away from the cemetery. Paul Groody became an eyewitness to history, just as the reporters did.

After the unusually short funeral service on November 25, reporters described how few people attended Oswald's burial in Ft. Worth's Rose Hill Cemetery. The only mourners for Lee Harvey Oswald were his widow, his two children, his mother, and his brother, Robert. Reporters were asked to serve as pallbearers, since no one else was available—it had been difficult enough to find a minister to preside over the graveside services. However, because Oswald's death and burial occurred within one day of each other, and because the police deliberately kept the site of the burial secret, it would have been unusual if people *had* attended the funeral. The eyes of most of the world were on the state funeral of President Kennedy. Very few cared about Oswald's funeral. Photos taken that day at the cemetery show a typical family in mourning. Oswald's widow held her older child on her lap, and she and his brother Robert sat with bowed heads while her mother-in-law, Marguerite Oswald, clutched Oswald's one-month-old baby daughter.

Reporter Mike Cochran, who acted as a spur-of-the-moment pallbearer, recalled that Oswald's casket was first taken into a small chapel in the Ft. Worth cemetery. Law enforcement officers opened the casket to prove that an empty casket was not being buried. Later, before the casket was lowered into the grave, Marina Oswald asked that it be opened once more.[329]

Of course, the scene was quite different from the funeral being held simultaneously in Washington, D. C., for the man Oswald was accused of killing. Both President Kennedy and Lee Oswald left behind widows and two small children. But there were no muffled drums or caissons or parades of dignitaries in Ft. Worth. No eternal torch was lit after Oswald's coffin was covered with dirt. However, his mother later recorded the thoughts that ran through her head as her family walked solemnly away from the gravesite.

"I shall never forget. The cemetery flag was at half-staff. Of course, I knew it was flying low because our President had died. But to me, you see, it meant also that my son was being buried under a flag that was at half-staff, too. Sometimes there is joy even in sorrow."[330] Marguerite Oswald's sorrow seemed genuine, though some of her behaviors seemed quite bizarre.

At times, she seemed angry that her daughter-in-law was receiving so much attention and sympathy. As Oswald's mother, she felt she should be the beneficiary as well.

However, some saw a different side to this woman. Only days after her son's death, she paid a call on Buell Wesley Frazier and his sister Linnie Randle. Very quietly, she asked Randle to thank her brother Buell for saying such kind words to reporters about her son. Even after Randle invited her into his home, Oswald's mother simply shook her head and walked away.[331]

Marguerite Oswald also visited the boarding house where her son lived in Oak Cliff. There, she thanked Mrs. Gladys Johnson for "taking care of my son and for the way you treated him after his death. You did not trash his memory or drag it through the mud."[332] These stories were not printed in the newspapers, but they were just as much a part of Marguerite Oswald's life as the negative ones were.

Paul Groody's son shared one more fascinating story with the authors concerning his father. His father told him that the superintendent of Rose Hill Cemetery was murdered one night sometime after the Kennedy assassination. Though he was shot numerous times in the back, his death was ruled a suicide. Groody was never sure whether the man's death was tied to the Kennedy assassination or whether it was just an unlucky coincidence.[333]

His son Donald is not sure to this day why his parents decided to move to West Texas. Perhaps it was simply to get away from the Dallas/Ft. Worth area. Perhaps he was reconnecting with a friend, Billie Sol Estes. As late as the 1980s, Paul Groody admitted to a reporter that he had been scared in 1963 because both the President and Oswald had been killed.

"I did not know if some other nut was going to shoot the dumb undertaker," he confessed.

CHAPTER 32

VOICES OF NEIGHBORS OF DONALD WAYNE HOUSE

"Lawrence, that's the best suspect I ever saw, except for one thing: He didn't do it."—Det. A. C. Howerto

Donald Wayne House, a twenty-two year-old from Ranger, Texas, may have simply found himself in the wrong place at the wrong time on the morning of November 22, 1963. He arrived in Mesquite, a Dallas suburb, having driven 116 miles from Ranger to visit an Army buddy, Randall Hunsucker, who lived there. For whatever reason, House had not called Hunsaker beforehand to make sure he would be home. Consequently, the visit never took place.

Instead, House spent some time in downtown Dallas, but his activities and his exact whereabouts seem to be unknown, even after all these years. What *is* known is that he was arrested on the afternoon of November 22, 1963, by Ft. Worth police, though there are two official versions as to how and why this arrest occurred.

In 1983, Elston Brooks of the *Fort Worth Star-Telegram* reported in a newspaper supplement called *Turning Point* that House had been seen and heard on the grassy knoll in the Dealey Plaza area shouting, "I shot the President." A female witness saw him jump into his car and speed off towards Ft. Worth. The witness remembered the car's license plate number, and she provided it to the Dallas police. Dallas police reported it to the Fort Worth police, who were, consequently, waiting for House on the Ft. Worth end of the turnpike. Ten years after Brooks reported this story, M. Duke Lane investigated some of the interesting details about it. The story he discovered was *similar* to the one published in 1983 but not exactly the same.

Brooks reported that House was arrested immediately by Ft. Worth police officers, and that they had found several boxes of dynamite in the back seat of the man's car. Capt. Lawrence Wood recalled that "the man [House] was hysterical."[334] The car was confiscated by Secret Service agents so they could examine the dynamite. Captain Wood remembered that "the guy stuttered, and that he was so scared he couldn't get a single word out, no matter how long he tried."[335] This does not correlate with what Lane later discovered.

According to Lane, House was brought to the attention of Dallas County Deputy Sheriff J.C. Watson by two women from Grand Prairie. They had encountered House at a gas station and, having heard about the assassination, asked him if he had any more current information. House related to them the description of the alleged assassin broadcast over the radio. The description matched House himself so closely that the women called the Grand Prairie police; Grand Prairie police then called the Dallas police with House's license number. The Dallas police made a general broadcast which described the green and white Ford the young man was driving as well as the license plate number. House did not mention anything to the women about having been in Dallas during the assassination, much less having supposedly shouted, "I shot the President."

Ft. Worth police officer W. D. Roberts spotted House's car, reported it to police dispatch, and requested backup. Officer B. G. Whistler responded, as did Officer B. L. Harbour. Officer Roberts forced House to pull over to the curb and Officer Whistler approached the car with a shotgun trained on the occupant. They demanded that he exit the car and keep his hands where they could be seen. House was frisked and handcuffed before being put into the back of the police car.

Nowhere in their report do the officers mention that House was "hysterical." In fact, "All of the officers involved described the arrest 'as odd' because during all of this time House never said a word."[336] Officer Roberts was particularly surprised by House's behavior. He recalled later that he "couldn't imagine how you could pull a man out of his car, frisk him, handcuff him, and pour him into the back of a patrol car in a matter of just seconds, all the time with a shotgun aimed at him, and he never even asked why he was being arrested."[337]

Whistler confirmed Roberts' description of the arrest. House's arrest report supports Roberts' and Whistler's accounts, also. It reads, "The subject never once appeared nervous and in fact he was unusually calm."[338] House never questioned why he was being arrested and taken to jail.

The article in the *Turning Point* does not mention the condition of House's car. However, Roberts described it as "absolutely spotless. There wasn't even a slip of paper in the glove box."[339] This meant that there was no registration information or ownership papers in the car, but a quick check revealed that it had been registered to Donald House. Officers discovered the dynamite box to be empty, and House later claimed he had just used it as a tool chest. He did not explain why there were no tools in the "tool chest."

According to Ft. Worth Police Capt. Lawrence Wood, who provided the information to staff writer Elston Brooks in 1983, House explained that he worked for a dynamite company in West Texas and that he had stopped in Dallas to watch the presidential motorcade. His original plans that morning had been to visit an Army buddy in Mesquite, Texas, who, apparently, had not been home. House gave no explanation for why he had not contacted his friend before making the long trip to the Dallas area.

One of the many strange facts concerning Donald Wayne House was that after the President was shot but *before* House was arrested, the Dallas police were *already* calling his mother in Ranger to determine his location. They had to call her three different times before they could make her understand the gravity of the situation. There is no record of what the Dallas police told her, but it seems odd that a mother would not be more concerned about such an urgent call from the police concerning her son.

According to a Ranger neighbor who knew House's older sister, Wilma, there was tension and conflict between Mrs. House and her son, Donald. According to Wilma, the son was often borrowing money from the mother. Perhaps this is why Mrs. House initially refused to talk to the police.

The authors learned from this neighbor that the House family lived in the older part of Ranger and did not socialize with many of the townspeople. Donald's older sister Wilma did not have a driver's license. But only in the coldest weather would she accept a ride from neighbors; most of the time, she walked from her home to the nursing facility where she worked. Her classmates remembered her as a shy, sweet girl who kept to herself. She lived with her elderly mother and spent her non-working hours taking care of her. According to a Ranger acquaintance who sometimes offered Wilma rides to work, Wilma and her brother Donald were not close at that time. Wilma had said her brother returned home only because he needed money from his mother.

However, Wilma's brother was no deadbeat. He graduated from high school and enlisted in the Army. Wilma shared with a classmate the fact that her brother's return to Ranger, after military service, did not please her mother. This may be why on November 22, 1963, Mrs. House seemed unconcerned about the phone calls from the police. However, after the third attempt, she decided to call her niece in Haltom City, a suburb of Ft. Worth. Her son usually stayed with Mrs. House's niece and nephew when he visited Ft. Worth, so she assumed he went there on November 22. Donald's mother and sister known no more about his whereabouts or travel plans than his Army buddy did.

House's cousin in Haltom City heard House's description broadcast over the radio, so she called her husband Kenneth and asked him to find out how House could have had anything to do with the assassination of the President of the United States. This is how Kenneth Wilson happened to encounter the Fort Worth police on the afternoon of November 22. As they were examining Donald House's car, Wilson explained to the police that House was his wife's cousin and that the car they were examining actually belonged to Wilson himself even though it was registered to Donald House. The police immediately took Wilson to the police station as an investigatory witness. Photos show Wilson being escorted by the police into City Hall, but he is not in handcuffs.

Television coverage of Donald House, however, painted a different picture. He *was* handcuffed, but he appeared calm, much as Lee Harvey Oswald had appeared in Dallas when being moved down the halls of the police station. House, unlike Oswald, did not shout out to the news reporters. One reporter, hoping to startle the twenty-two-year-old, demanded roughly, "Why did you do it?"

"I didn't," House responded calmly, not even asking what "it" referred to.

Capt. Lawrence Wood asked Detective A. C. Howerton to question the suspect because Howerton was famous for getting the truth from suspects. It is unclear how long Howerton spoke to House, but he claimed to have obtained the following information from him: "House worked for a dynamite company in West Texas and was using the empty dynamite boxes as tool chests. He had stopped in Dallas to watch the Presidential motorcade, and after the shots were fired, he excitedly shouted, 'They shot the President.'"[340]

At the conclusion of the interview, Howerton announced to Wood, "Lawrence, that's the best suspect I ever saw, except for one thing: He didn't do it."[341] It is possible that Howerton's comment ["the best suspect he ever saw"] wasn't related to the President's death. The Ft. Worth police had been told by Dallas police that they already had the President's killer in custody.

There is no way of knowing how much more information the police could have obtained from House if they had not released him after the call from the Dallas police. That call indicated that "Oswald had been apprehended and House was to be released."[342] House himself remembered that he was interrogated for about three hours and left in his cell for another hour before being released. He may not have even known why he was eventually freed.

Officer W. D. Roberts, however, knew exactly why House was let go. He recalled going to the police station to dictate his arrest report. He was about halfway through when the Ft. Worth police chief entered and told him "not to bother completing the report" because the suspect had been cleared by federal agents. The Dallas police had an even better suspect in custody, so House was allowed to return to his car. This was only a matter of hours after the assassination. How much investigatory work could have taken place that soon?

It is only because Donald House's sister Wilma confided in neighbors, however, that the authors know that the FBI did not drop its investigation of House. Agents showed up in Ranger to interrogate House's mother—a development that Wilma shared with her friends at the time. But House seemed to be close-mouthed about his arrest. A former House classmate remembered: "Donald didn't really talk about that day. I don't know anything about where he was in Dallas that day. I didn't know the FBI came to Ranger to talk to his mother about that day."[343]

It is not surprising that House had bitter memories of his experiences in Dallas, but it does seem strange that he barely mentioned what had happened to him, especially because he was cleared of all charges. Apparently, the FBI was satisfied that House was simply in the wrong place at the wrong time. Perhaps the story of him shouting "I shot the President" was nothing more than a misunderstanding that House himself corrected during his interrogation.

There are two more intriguing facts about Donald Wayne House. While he was being interrogated by Ft. Worth police, Dallas police received a call reporting a person removing a rifle from a light-green two-toned vehicle. This car was registered to a "George T. Hunsaker" of Dallas. The police apparently did not make the connection between the names "Randall Hunsaker," House's Army buddy, and "George Hunsaker" because there is no evidence that they investigated this coincidence.

The second intriguing fact is that, for whatever reason, four months after his arrest, House sold the immaculate six-year-old Ford that Kenneth Wilson had told police *he* owned.[344]

Because House was never questioned by Dallas police as a witness to the assassination, which he should have been, having admitted to the Ft. Worth police that he had seen the killing, the authors contacted him by phone in 2013 to ask exactly what he had witnessed in Dealey Plaza on November 22, 1963. The moment his wife realized that the authors were interested in the Kennedy assassination, she slammed down the telephone . Perhaps she knew her husband was tired of recalling his experiences on the day the President was killed. Consequently, the authors could not include his memories of what he saw and heard that day in Dealey Plaza or of what must have been a horrendous experience at the hands of the Ft. Worth police department.

V
LEE AND
HIS SHADOWS

One cannot know whether Lee Harvey Oswald was guilty or innocent unless one knows how many individuals used his name, his birth date, photos, and official records to convince the public that a single disgruntled American murdered the President of the United States.

CHAPTER 33

SHADOWS OF DOPPELGANGERS

"Well, sir, the Lee Harvey Oswald I met in November 1962 was not the
Lee Harvey Oswald I had known ten years previous."
—John Pic, Oswald's half-brother

Until the afternoon of November 22, 1963, very few Americans had ever heard of Lee Harvey Oswald. A few Texans had read the name in their local newspapers in 1959 when a man by that name defected to Russia. But, for the most part, a name that would soon become synonymous with "assassin" was unfamiliar to the world. The public would not learn until decades later that there were at least two men designated "Lee Harvey Oswald" whose lives intertwined with each other's. One seems to have served as a doppelganger for the other. The German word "doppelganger" refers to someone who resembles a non-relative so closely that he or she could be his or her twin. Lee Harvey Oswald may or may not have known he had at least one "doppelganger," but evidence shows he did have one. His doppelganger impersonated him for nefarious reasons.

Thanks to New Orleans District Attorney Jim Garrison and to researchers like John Armstrong, there is documentation that more than one individual using the name "Lee Harvey Oswald" became involved with the Kennedy assassination. In his 893-page book *Harvey and Lee*, Armstrong described over 40 sightings of at least two men impersonating the "official" Oswald just in the month of November 1963. There is evidence that the CIA or some other agency created two Oswald families in the 1940s whose lives became interwoven. There is more evidence of two men named "Lee Harvey Oswald" who also shared mothers named "Marguerite Claverie Oswald." What is still unknown is the real identity of the other "Lee Oswalds" who interjected themselves into New Orleans, Dallas, Austin, Houston, Russia, and Mexico when another Oswald was somewhere else.

This is why it was possible for legitimate, uninvolved witnesses to describe a man who identified himself as "Lee Harvey Oswald" as being in Mexico City at the same time as "lee Harvey Oswald" was placed in Dallas. Some saw him in New Orleans and in Dallas at the same time. Others saw him in Austin and in Dallas at the same time.

There is evidence that there were two different Marines, both named "Lee

Harvey Oswald," one stationed in El Toro, California and one stationed in San Diego. At one time, one was sent to Atsugi, Japan, while the other remained in California. Eventually, one "Oswald" defected to Russia while the other remained in New Orleans. Obviously, one person could *not* be in all those places at one time. But that does not mean that all the witnesses were mistaken or intentionally lying. In fact, there were simply too many instances where someone identified as "Oswald" seemed to be in more than one place at the same time.

(As far-fetched as the idea of an American defecting to Russia seems, former CIA officer Victor L. Marchetti admitted that the Office of Military Intelliegence did run a program in the 1960s which included about 36-40 young men who were *trained* to *appear* disenchanted with America. This training program was run out of Nags Head, North Carolina. Its purpose was to create double agents.[345] Lee Harvey Oswald may well have been one of these agents.)

There is documentary evidence that one Oswald belonged to Platoon 2060, while the other was a member of either Platoon 1069 or 1070. One was trained in radar and the other in aviation electronics. One was assigned to shipping and receiving while the other served in the 1st Armored Amphibian Company.

At least two of the different "Oswalds" bore a striking resemblance to one another. The main difference was in height, which was not obvious in photographs. One had straight, thinning hair and the other had thicker, curly hair that was a shade darker. So, it is not surprising that on November 22, 1963, witnesses heard the name "Lee Harvey Oswald" on radio, saw a familiar face in the newspaper and on television, and assumed that person was the same "Oswald" they had known.

When Oswald's older brother Robert and his mother Marguerite first met Lee Harvey Oswald on his return from Russia in 1962, they both thought he seemed different, but they could not quite put their fingers on the change. According to their testimonies to the Warren Commission, they accepted the differences though they did not understand them.

Other individuals also noticed a difference. Some realized that the woman whom Americans knew from newscasts as Oswald's mother, Marguerite Claverie, was as different in appearance from the other Marguerite Claverie as the two Oswalds were alike.

The "Marguerite" the American public came to know lived with her son Lee Harvey in 1947 Benbrook, a small suburb of Ft. Worth, Texas, at 101 San Saba. Thanks to researcher John Armstrong, the following information was obtained from the Oswalds' neighbors. Georgia and Walter Bell purchased property across from 101 San Saba and built their own residence. They both recalled that their female neighbor, Marguerite Claverie Oswald, was short, fat, and not overly friendly. At the time, she worked as a practical nurse for John Long in his home, and rather than calling herself "Marguerite," she referred to herself as "Marge."[346]

According to Armstrong, who spent ten years researching *Harvey and Lee*, the "Marguerite Claverie" who lived in Benbrook, Texas, differed in appearance as well as in personality from another "Marguerite Claverie Oswald," who had also once lived in New Orleans and later in Fort Worth; in fact, both women lived in the same cities at the same time.

Myrtle and Julian Evans of New Orleans knew this Marguerite Claverie Oswald to be a tall, strikingly beautiful lady with black hair who dressed impeccably. Having married a man named Edwin Ekdahl in Rockwall County, Texas, on May 4, 1945, she had her new husband move in with her at her residence on Victor Street in Dallas. Two months later, they moved to Benbrook and rented a house on Granbury Road. Marguerite's son, "Lee Harvey," entered the first grade at Benbrook Common School. This Lee Harvey's birth date was listed as July 19, 1939. The birth date may have been deliberately changed by Marguerite Claverie so that Lee Harvey would be eligible to enter public school. *Possibly,* July 19, 1939 was the actual birth date of this Oswald.

One of the Lee Harveys had his tonsils removed at age five in 1945; in the spring of 1946, during first grade, his mother was admitted to Harris County Hospital for a mastoidectomy. The tall, attractive Marguerite Claverie left her husband in Texas during the summer of 1946, and she and her son Lee moved to Covington, Louisiana. Lee enrolled in Mrs. Hester Burns' first grade class at Covington Elementary School in September of 1946.

During January 1947, this Marguerite Claverie and Lee moved back to Fort Worth to live again with Mr. Ekdahl, this time at 1501 Eighth Street in Fort Worth. This Marguerite Claverie worked as a clerk for Burt's Shoe Store in Fort Worth.[347]

No wonder the members of the Warren Commission could not make heads or tails out of these confusing scenarios. Yet, it is unlikely that what thoroughly confused the Warren Commission was coincidental. It is vitally important to know when this subterfuge began and what organization orchestrated it. Evidence that Armstrong uncovered shows that two different boys grew up as "Lee Harvey Oswald" and their mothers were two women named "Marguerite." As outlandish as this seems, Armstrong's evidence documents the two paths the "Oswalds" travelled and how often they intersected. Armstrong's research also explains many of the anomalies that have puzzled researchers for decades.

It seems that the tall, attractive Marguerite Claverie Oswald gave birth to three sons, "John Pic," "Robert Edward Lee Oswald," and "Lee Harvey Oswald." The short, dumpy Marguerite Claverie Oswald may or may not have given birth to a son named "Lee Harvey Oswald."

If the man accused of killing President Kennedy was named "Joe Smith," "Thomas Jones," "Billy White," or any other common name, no one would have been surprised by the confusion that surrounded the multiple school records, addresses, photos, and physical appearances attached to an individual named "Lee Harvey Oswald." But the name *Oswald* as a surname was not that common in America.

It is certainly possible that a young boy could begin his life in New York City at about the same time that another young boy began his in New Orleans, and that both were named "Lee Harvey Oswald." However, it seems more than coincidental that both mothers' names were "Marguerite Claverie Oswald."

The members of the Warren Commission were puzzled by some of the conflicting stories and data that surrounded the accused assassin. They could not understand why the woman who claimed to be his mother did not know the exact date of her third son's birth. She also mentioned having more husbands than Oswald's mother supposedly had. She mentioned working at various businesses even though the Commission members had evidence she had been working elsewhere at the time.

For example, there is evidence that a woman named Marguerite Claverie Oswald and her son called "Harvey" lived at 126 Exchange Place in New Orleans in February of 1955. They moved during the spring of 1955 to Ft. Worth, Texas. Another Marguerite Claverie Oswald and her son "Lee Harvey" moved from their apartment at 1452 St. Mary's in New Orleans to the same address (126 Exchange) a few weeks later. *Coincidence?* More likely, someone or some organization was controlling these individuals. The question is w*hy*.

It is understandable why the Warren Commission ignored information that simply did not make sense or did not fit with its predetermined conclusion. Fortunately, Armstrong and other researchers have not ignored these diverging details because they are vitally important. They cast doubt on whether the man arrested in the Texas Theatre in Oak Cliff, Texas, for the murder of a Dallas police officer and later for the assassination of the President was *really* the man responsible for the deaths of either of these men.

A preponderance of evidence shows that the "official" Lee Harvey Oswald, who still appears in history books as the assassin of John F. Kennedy, was a composite of at least two different men who used the same name.

It may be impossible to ever know for certain whether the "Lee Harvey Oswald" who defected to Russia in 1959 was the same "Oswald" seen in

Houston on September 25, 1963, by Marietta Gerhart and her husband Elmer. This Oswald had two unusual companions, Charles Harrelson and Charles Rogers. Harrelson was found guilty years later of murdering Federal Texas Judge John Wood and has been identified by numerous people, including police artist Lois Gibson, as one of the infamous three tramps arrested in Dealey Plaza after the Kennedy assassination. Charles Rogers, also seen with Oswald on the evening of September 25, 1963, was the only suspect in the gruesome murders of his parents years later, and may have also been one of the tramps in Dealey Plaza on November 22, 1963.

It is interesting to speculate on whether the Oswald who defected to Russia was the same "Oswald" who took a bus trip to Mexico City in the fall of 1963. It is difficult to determine whether the defector was the same man hired by the Texas School Book Depository. And the question that still haunts the world is: Was the Oswald hired to work in the Texas School Book Depository the person who shot John F. Kennedy? On that fateful day in November 1963, there may have been two men using the name "Lee Harvey Oswald" in Dallas, and, possibly, in the Depository. If so, this would explain many contradictory statements that witnesses provided to the Dallas police, the FBI, and the Warren Commission. The answers to these questions could make all the difference in determining whether the "Oswald" with whom Americans are familiar was a patsy, an assassin, or an accomplice in the most infamous crime of the twentieth century.

The Lee Harvey Oswald depicted in the Warren Report was honorably discharged from the Marines in September of 1959. He "officially" came to the attention of the CIA and FBI when he publicly defected to Russia later that year. He considered himself a Lenin Marxist, rather than a Communist. Oswald seemed pleased with the publicity he received as a defector. At the time of his defection, he indicated he would not be returning to the United States.

After Oswald's arrest on November 22, the FBI and other government agencies claimed to know very little about him. It seems impossible that the FBI, CIA, and the State Department had no information about Oswald, the defector. After all, the townspeople of Vernon, Texas, knew about him in 1962. According to Armstrong, the Oswald who defected to Russia in 1959 was not the youngest son of the tall, attractive Marguerite Claverie Oswald; he was the "son" of the short, dumpy Marguerite Claverie who lived in Vernon at the time and was employed by Vernon residents Byron Phillips and Bob Leonard, and later at the Leslie McAdams ranch. This "Marguerite" reached out to local Vernon community members for money to help her son and his Russian wife and child afford their return to America.

One person in Vernon who rejected her solicitation was Warren D. Pruitt Jr., an attorney for the W. T. Waggoner estate. Pruitt felt no sympathy for Marguerite Oswald or her son. In fact, he told Marguerite Oswald bluntly, "I would not give a plug nickel to anyone who renounced his citizenship."[348]

Some of Vernon's other townspeople felt differently and were kind enough to give money to an openly begging woman, and to sponsor Marguerite's Russian daughter-in-law's entrance into the United States. Rancher Byron W. Phillips signed an affidavit in 1962 guaranteeing that Marina Oswald would not become a ward of any political subdivision of the United States of America.[349] Why he risked his good name for a woman he had never met, who had married a defector, is unknown. Somehow or another, Marguerite Oswald must have persuaded him to sponsor a Russian daughter-in-law she herself had never met.

Genevieve Smith, another resident of Vernon, was not asked to sponsor Marina Oswald; she only knew Marguerite Oswald through her connections with the Fargo Baptist Church. Marguerite was working for Byron Phillips, a deacon in the Baptist church at the time. Smith told the authors that some members of the Fargo Baptist Church attempted to help the older woman by giving her money. They assumed she would send it to her son Lee to help him return to the United States.

"The church wanted to help a mother get her son, his wife, and baby home," recalled Smith. Smith also recalled a fact many people did not know. She remembered that Lee Harvey Oswald had made a trip to the small community of Fargo (near Vernon) to visit his mother not long after returning to the United States from Russia. After fifty years, Smith still sounded surprised that Marguerite Oswald never repaid any of the money so generously given to her, though she knew church members found out that the Red Cross had paid for Lee Harvey Oswald's return to America.[350] In fact, Marguerite Oswald never mentioned the money again. Perhaps she simply forgot, just as she forgot her son's birth date when she testified in front of the Warren Commission.

It is clear that numerous people in Texas could have shared all sorts of information about Lee Harvey Oswald and his family with the FBI if they had been asked. It does not seem logical that the FBI knew less about an American defector than the members of the Vernon, Texas community. If there is any doubt about the FBI being familiar with Lee Harvey Oswald before the Kennedy assassination, the following information proves otherwise.

On October 24, 1963, Oswald's birth certificate once again became important to the FBI. Less than one month before Kennedy's assassination, FBI agent Milton Kaack reviewed Oswald's birth certificate in New Orleans. FBI records do not indicate the reason for this sudden interest. However, years later,

Armstrong was unable to locate the original birth certificate. One cannot help but wonder if the sudden interest in Oswald's birth record in October of 1963 also explains the missing birth certificate. This makes one also wonder what information on his original birth certificate needed to remain a secret and what *other* documents may have been hidden to "blend" two different lives.

If the lives of two young boys really were controlled by some government entity, then this procedure seems to have begun in the late 1940s. There is evidence of two different Lee Harvey Oswalds paralleling each other in New York, New Orleans, and Ft. Worth. Through school records, childhood friends, and property records, researchers have discovered that the two Oswalds were seldom far apart.

That changed when one Lee Harvey Oswald was stationed in Japan from 1957-1958. While he was in Japan, another Lee Harvey Oswald was busy working at the Pfisterer Dental Lab in New Orleans. Palmer McBride remembered working with Lee Harvey Oswald at that lab.[351]

Researchers are still confused about these two different Oswalds. While one Lee Harvey Oswald defected to Russia from October 1959 until June 1962, the other Lee Harvey Oswald was living in plain sight in the United States. On January 20, 1961, Oscar W. Delatte, assistant manager of the Bolton Ford dealership in New Orleans, met with two men who wanted to purchase ten Ford Econoline Trucks for the Friends of Democratic Cuba. Delatte had a purchase order form from a Lee Harvey Oswald made out in the name of "Friends of Democratic Cuba." After the assassination, Delatte gave the purchase order form to the FBI.[352] This purchase order may have made the FBI realize that there were at least two men connected to the Cuban revolution, both of them using the name "Lee Harvey Oswald."

Early in 1961, James Spencer, a salesman for Dumas Milner Chevrolet in New Orleans, encountered a Lee Harvey Oswald at the car dealership; Oswald was inquiring about a 1958 Chevrolet.[353] Obviously, Palmer was encountering a man using the name "Lee Harvey Oswald" who differed from the "official" Oswald living in Russia at the time.

In May of 1961, Ray Carnay, news director for the Balaban Radio Stations in Dallas, Texas, met a Lee Harvey Oswald who had contacted him at the Dallas/Garland airport in connection with anti-Castro activities. After the assassination, Carnay shared this information with a friend, Dallas Police Officer Arthur Hammett. This could not have been the Lee Harvey Oswald who had defected to Russia because *that* Oswald was still living in the Soviet Union at the time.[354]

In October 1961, a Lee Harvey Oswald and Celso Hernandez were taken to the New Orleans Levee Board headquarters for suspicious behavior. After the Kennedy assassination, Officer David Lousteau remembered the two men being questioned. Neither man was charged with any illegal activity. But the name "Lee Harvey Oswald" stuck in Lousteau's memory.[355] This incident occurred when the other Lee Harvey Oswald was living in Russia.

In April 1962, the Texas Employment Commission (TEC) made a notation that a Lee Harvey Oswald applied for work with its office in Ft. Worth, having taken the General Aptitude Test Batteries.[356] At about the same time, the wife of the Lee Harvey Oswald living in Russia gave birth to a daughter, June Lee Oswald.

In June 1962, "defector" Oswald arrived back in the United States with his wife and baby daughter. They landed in New Jersey and then travelled to Ft. Worth, arriving there on June 14, 1962. The former defector also applied for work with the TEC in June, but he was not given the usual battery of tests because staff members assumed the two men using the same name were the same person. The staff members had no idea that this second Oswald had been in Russia when the first Oswald applied for work in April and taken the battery of tests. This second Oswald began work on July 17, 1962, at Leslie Welding in Ft. Worth. He received his first pay check on July 21, 1962.

During the summer of 1962, the Oswald who had defected to Russia was living with his wife and baby in Ft. Worth while another Lee Harvey Oswald was living in New Orleans. This latter Oswald was known to frequent the famous Court of Two Sisters restaurant and was often seen there by the doorman, Leander D'Avy. After the assassination, several waiters remembered that this Oswald resided in a little apartment above the restaurant.[357]

The Oswald living in Fort Worth with his Russian wife Marina and baby June quit his job at Leslie Welding. When he visited the TEC office in Dallas this time, a staff member requested his file from the Fort Worth office. The counselor, Helen Cunningham, reviewed it and made note of the fact that he had taken the general aptitude tests in April 1962. What the TEC did not know was that this Lee Harvey Oswald had been in Russia in April 1962. Nevertheless, this Oswald began his new job at Jaggars-Chiles-Stovall in Dallas on October 12, 1962.[358] The *other* Oswald was still living in New Orleans.

In November 1962, a Lee Harvey Oswald was identified by Lynn Davis Curry in Augusta, Georgia. Curry drove for the Dixie Cab Company and remembered picking up a "Lee Harvey Oswald." After the assassination, Curry shared important information with the FBI about this individual. First of all, he did "resemble" the Lee Harvey Oswald arrested for killing the President. More importantly, she remembered him introducing himself as "Lee Oswald" and shared with her a great deal of information about being in the Marines, travelling to Russia, marrying a Russian girl, and supporting Fidel Castro. "Before leaving the cab, the young man insisted that Curry write down his name, 'Lee Oswald,' and said that Curry would be hearing his name again in the future."[359]

There is no evidence that the FBI checked out Curry's story. But it is proof that a year before the assassination, someone was setting up the Lee Harvey Oswald living in the Dallas area with his Russian family. It would be interesting to know whether the Lee Harvey Oswald living in Dallas was totally unaware of being impersonated, along with his family.

On Thanksgiving Day of 1962, Robert Oswald invited his brother Lee and his family to his home in Ft. Worth. He also invited his half-brother, John Pic. Pic had not seen Lee Harvey Oswald since his younger brother was thirteen years old. Lee Harvey had apparently changed so much that Pic did not even recognize him that Thanksgiving.

"I would have never recognized him… he was thinner, he didn't have much hair, his face features were somewhat different, his eyes were set back, he did not have the bull neck that he had had when he went into the Marines," Pic told the Warren Commission. He then stated to a Commissioner, "Well, sir, the Lee Harvey Oswald I met in November 1962 was not the Lee Harvey Oswald I had known ten years previous."[360]

John Pic also noticed that weekend an odd thing about the name his half-brother used. Pic invited Lee and Marina to visit him in San Antonio, Texas. When his half-brother wrote down his name in Pic's address book, he did not write down "Lee," as he was known to both of his brothers; instead, he wrote down "Harvey."[361] Was this an overt clue that he was *not* the brother he was pretending to be, or did he now think of himself as "Harvey"? If so, what could explain the change?

The multiple appearances of men named "Lee Harvey Oswald" did not end in 1962. By 1963, men identifying themselves as "Lee Harvey Oswald" seemed to be all over Texas and Louisiana. At the same time, Lee Harvey, his wife, and his daughter were living on Neely Street in Dallas. Someone named "Lee Harvey Oswald" was receiving mail at 1106 Diceman Avenue. This fact was discovered by an architect, Daniel Thomas McGown, in late March. He noticed some mail, one envelope of which was addressed to Ruby and bore the return address of "Lee Oswald, 1106 Diceman Avenue, Dallas, Texas," lying in the entry to Jack Ruby's Carousel Club., Thinking "Lee Oswald" might be a female friend of his, he drove to 1106 Diceman Avenue, only to find that the name on the mail box was "Lee Harvey Oswald." Once again, too many Lee

Harvey Oswalds seemed to be living in the same vicinity—and one of them had written to Jack Ruby.[362] Whoever wrote this letter could not have guaranteed that the mail would be seen by anyone but Ruby. This indicates that Ruby *was* in contact with someone using the name "Lee Oswald."

In August of 1963, Lee, Marina, and June Oswald were living in New Orleans. At the same time, another man using the name "Lee Harvey Oswald" was living in the Irving, Texas area.

According to Cliff Shasteen, a barber in Irving, this Oswald frequented his barbershop, which was less than a mile from the home of Ruth Paine. This Oswald made a point of mentioning that he travelled to Mexico often. The barber described him as having a widow's peak and very dark hair. He also remembered that this Oswald drove a station wagon he had seen parked at Ruth Paine's house. It was a 1955 Chevrolet, and Shasteen's description matches the station wagon belonging to Ruth and Michael Paine.[363]

This suggests that Ruth and Michael Paine may have known the two different men using the name "Lee Harvey Oswald." If not, then it was simply coincidence that Ruth Paine soon met the Oswald family and impulsively invited Marina to live with her.

There are other indications that the Paines knew more about the Oswalds than they later told the FBI. For example, information from their babysitter raises questions. During the months of July and August 1963, Loretta Cline, a babysitter for the Paines who lived around the corner, was watching Paine's children. Cline and her mother noticed a pregnant woman in the Paines' backyard. After the assassination, Cline and her mother assumed they had seen Marina Oswald in Ruth Paine's backyard. However, this woman could not have been Marina Oswald because she was in New Orleans from May 10 until September 21, 1963. *This* pregnant woman spoke English; Marina spoke very little English. The woman seen in the backyard gave birth in late August or early September of 1963.[364]

Marina Oswald's language difficulties are verified by a man who met her afer the assassination. A year or so after the deaths of Kennedy and Oswald, according to Bruce Spielbauer, Marina moved to the Dallas suburb of Richardson and into a house directly across the street from his family. She deliberately did not remove the previous owner's name on the mailbox to insure her privacy. Spielbaurer remembers that his mother had warned him, "Don't you ever bother that woman—she has been through enough." He eventually babysat Marina's two children. He recalls, "At that time, she really did not speak English. Very broken, mostly one or two words at a time."[365]

Ruth Paine herself could have testified to the fact that at least one other man was impersonating Marina's husband. On September 23, 1963, Olin Benjamin interviewed a "Lee Harvey Oswald" for a job at Al Semtner Drug Depot in New Orleans. But on this day, the Lee Harvey Oswald accused of killing Kennedy two months later was at home all day, having spent the weekend with his family. Paine had driven to New Orleans and also spent that entire weekend with the Oswalds. Paine could have testified that Lee Harvey Oswald had *not* interviewed for any job that day. She could have also explained the other pregnant woman who was mistaken for Marina, but she was never asked.

On Monday, September 23, Paine drove Marina Oswald and her daughter June back to Irving to await the arrival of her second child. Marina's husband watched as Paine and his family disappeared into the New Orleans traffic. Mystery still surrounds what Oswald *and* his doppelganger did while Marina accompanied Paine to Texas.

CHAPTER 34

THE VOICE OF DOROTHY COX

**"John's stories were just too colorful—too much like
something out of a James Bond book."**

For years, Dorothy Cox and her family had personal reasons for questioning the Warren Report. A family member (a brother) had privately investigated Kennedy's murder and reached some startling conclusions. Cox
reminisced with the authors about the funeral of her brother, author-investigator
John R. Craig.

The family stood quietly in the cemetery as they visited with friends and
guests. It was a cool day in September 2007 in Houston, Texas. The grass at
the Veterans National Cemetery was still green and damp. Several men in tan
suits that none of the family recognized mingled with the mourners. Some of
the family members noticed that the men were carrying concealed weapons.
Finally, two of the strangers approached the family and asked if they were
related to John Craig. Dorothy and her relatives nodded.

"Did John ever tell you about the time he went to Arizona and posed as a
mobster?" one of the men asked. The family members nodded. John had shared
numerous outlandish stories with the entire family, and, yes, they did remember
this particular one.[366]

"Did you believe him?" the man asked, smiling.

"No" came the choral response.

"What we didn't say," Dorothy Cox laughed, "was that none of us had
believed *most* of the stories John told us. John's stories were just too colorful—
too much like something out of a James Bond book." The two strangers shocked
Craig's family by murmuring softly, "You should have believed him. We were
there with him when it happened." Apparently, the two men were with the CIA,
and they knew John R. Craig had been used numerous times by the Company
for various assignments.

Craig's family could hardly believe that people were actually verifying
what they had considered unbelievable stories. They knew Craig had worked
for the Houston Parks Department and, yes, they had known he had been a
private investigator and had worked for the Texas Veterans' association. But
none of them dreamed that the stories they had rolled their eyes at were true,
and that his ordinary jobs had simply been covers so he could complete top-

secret assignments.

However, Craig's second wife Ellen admitted to the authors that she knew her husband had worked for numerous intelligence agencies, including the CIA and the FBI. Craig had also been well-known as the author of several books, but one of the most fascinating was *The Man on The Grassy Knoll*. This was the story of what was known in Houston as "The Icebox Murders."

What John Craig and his co-author Phil D. Rogers did not allow the public to know was that Craig was asked to write this book, and for a very specific reason. Of course, much of the information in the book came from research and from Craig's police and CIA contacts. However, what no one else knew was that Craig also had access to personal information from his aunt, Marietta Gerhart, the confidant of Edwina Rogers, one of the two victims in the "The Icebox Murders." Gerhart had waited years after the murders to share information with the only person she trusted at the time—her nephew, John Craig.

She not only provided inside information about Edwina Rogers and her husband Fred, both of whom had been brutally murdered in 1965, but she had also been privy to information about the prime suspect— the Rogers' son Charles, who disappeared right before the victims' bodies were discovered by the Houston police. One piece of information that Craig might have doubted if Marietta Gerhart had not been his trusted aunt was that there was a strange connection between Charles Rogers and Lee Harvey Oswald, the accused killer of President Kennedy.

Marietta Gerhart's husband Elmer served as the pastor of Lord's Church in Houston. He and Marietta were in a unique position to discuss the victims of the shocking murder and their son, Charles. Edwina Rogers had been a devoted member of the congregation of Lord's Church for several years. Fred rarely attended, but members of the congregation and the Gerharts recalled their son Charles from when he was a youth. From his mother, Marietta knew stories about Charles that others did not.

She knew that Charles had lived in a separate section of his parents' house and that he paid the mortgage for his parents. Edwina and Fred were grateful that they were able to maintain their home because of their son, but the relationship between Charles and his parents was tenuous at best. He insisted that no one enter his living area. He was so secretive that his parents did not always know when he was in the house and when he wasn't. Neighbors reported seeing him searching through dumpsters in the middle of the night. Local teenagers noticed even more than the adults. They saw him scuttling through the alleys at night and quickly dubbed him "Creeper."

Edwina Rogers may not have known about her son's nocturnal wanderings, but she did know about other odd behaviors and activities. She shared these stories with Marietta Gerhart, who eventually shared them with her nephew, John Craig. The stories were horrifying but intriguing. Craig and his co-author were determined to discover everything possible about Charles Rogers and his parents and why Charles might have murdered them.

What was unknown by Houston police at the time of the murders was that there might be a connection between Charles Rogers and the assassination of John F. Kennedy. But Marietta Gerhart knew of this possible link, and she knew it the day she saw a man identified as "Lee Harvey Oswald" on the front page of the Houston newspaper. This man's name and face were familiar to her because he had visited her and her husband only two months before the President's assassination.

Marietta's intriguing tale began with an odd visit by two individuals on the evening of September 25, 1963. It was a Wednesday evening; prayer services and choir practice had just concluded. Marietta and Elmer were relaxing and about to tune into one of their favorite television programs. The sound of the doorbell interrupted their routine around nine-thirty. Interruptions were not unusual occurrences because Pastor Gerhart was often sought out by parishioners at all hours of the day and night. Both he and his wife were trusting individuals who were well-liked by their church members and neighbors. Nevertheless, it was late and dark, so Marietta cautiously glanced out of the window and turned on the front porch light before opening the door.

On the doorstep stood two men, each holding a small suitcase. They appeared to be "unkempt, sweaty, and tired."[367] One of the men was dark-haired, slender, and of average height. The other was over six feet tall with blonde hair and handsome features. Neither of them was familiar to Marietta, but they seemed to know her.

The shorter man politely asked if she was Mrs. Gerhart and consistently addressed her as "ma'am." He held up some sort of identification and introduced himself as "Lee" and his companion as "Charles." Marietta remembered that he gave their last names, but she could not recall them later.

"Lee" went on to say he and his companion were traveling from New Orleans to Mexico and that they were supposed to meet a friend named Carlos at the bus station. However, Carlos had not shown up, so the two men walked from the bus station to Lord's Church, a distance of about two miles. Marietta noticed that the men had a hand-drawn map showing the route from the bus station to the church. Lee then asked if he could use the Gerharts' telephone.

Elmer Gerhart overheard his wife's conversation with the two strangers. Realizing the men were unfamiliar to her, he quickly crossed the room to stand at her elbow. Gerhart then directed the two visitors to the fellowship hall, which was next to the Gerhart home. Both he and his wife could not imagine why someone named "Carlos," whom they had never heard of, would have given these two men directions to their church. Nevertheless, being the charitable individuals they were, they allowed the strangers to use the telephone in the office of the fellowship hall. For whatever reason, the Gerharts felt more comfortable with the two visitors in the Fellowship Hall than in their home.

There was no question that the two men were tired and hungry. Elmer Gerhart quickly provided them with sodas, and Marietta brought bowls of leftover stew and cornbread from her kitchen. Neither man mentioned who Lee had called or why, but both seemed appreciative that the Gerharts were sharing their dinner with them. The two sat down with the pastor and his wife, their heads bent over their bowls of stew. They apologized profusely for eating so hungrily but also asked for seconds, which the Gerharts promptly provided.

When questioned by the pastor, Charles volunteered that his friend Lee was a Lutheran and that he was a Baptist. The Gerharts maintained a polite demeanor, but they both continued to worry that these two unassuming men with directions to their home might be there to rob them.

When Lee and Charles finally finished eating, they thanked the Gerharts and explained that Carlos would be meeting them "down the street" in about ten minutes. Pastor Gerhart offered them some cash, but they refused, adding that Carlos would be "taking care of them." Thanking the Gerharts again, Lee and Charles departed the fellowship hall and headed quickly towards the opposite side of the street.

Curious about the two men's destination, the Gerharts moved immediately to the darkened sanctuary,where they peeked through the windows of the front door of the church. What they saw stunned them. Standing under a street light, waiting for "Lee and Charles," was a man they both recognized. The man waiting for the two strangers—the man they had referred to as "Carlos"—was none other than their former parishioner, Charles Rogers.

Lee and Charles began conversing with Rogers. Gradually the three men moved deeper into the shadows and proceeded down the street. Neither of the Gerharts had any doubts about who the third man was. What they could not understand is why Charles Rogers was using the name "Carlos," and why he had not met the two strangers at the Gerharts' home instead of on the sidewalk.

Elmer Gerhart had reason to suspect Charles Rogers' clandestine meeting with their two visitors might be connected to CIA activities. Gerhart was certain that Rogers had been hired by the CIA seven years before because Rogers had used him as a reference. Rogers had been a good candidate for the CIA; the

Navy had already taught him cryptography and provided him with short-wave radio experience. In fact, he had even been assigned to the Office of Naval Intelligence. Charles Rogers' later employment with Shell Oil Company allowed him to also perform covert activities in other countries.

Elmer Gerhart, too, had a strong link to a CIA agent. In 1943, Gerhart met a man in Acapulco, Mexico, "Carl," who had been so overwhelmed by guilt that he later confided confidential information to Gerhart. "Carl" had been a double agent in the X-2 counter espionage section of the OSS and been ordered to take a man's life. He followed his superiors' orders, but the murder weighed heavily on his conscience. Elmer Gerhart became the OSS agent's counselor, and the two remained close for the rest of their lives. Throughout the years, "Carl" visited the Gerharts' home often; Marietta's family members were aware of these visits, but they understood them to be secret. The former OSS agent trusted the Gerharts, but no one else was allowed to see his face or know his real name!

At the time of his CIA application, Charles Rogers could not have known that Gerhart already had a CIA connection, but Gerhart's approval may have been one of the deciding factors in Rogers' being accepted into the Company. As he watched Rogers speak with the two men under the street lamp that night in September, Gerhart wondered out loud why Rogers had not met the men at Rogers' own house. More importantly, it bothered the pastor and his wife that Rogers felt free to provide two strangers with directions to their house. After all, Charles Rogers and his parents lived only six blocks away from the Gerharts. Why hadn't he directed them there? Was it possible that Rogers learned of Gerhart's close friendship with "Carl," the former OSS agent? Had he assumed Gerhart was also part of the CIA? If so, why had he tried to make sure the Gerharts did not associate him with the two strangers? As odd as the events of the evening had been, none of them seemed particularly important until two months later.

On November 23, 1963, still as shocked as most Americans by the President's death, Marietta Gerhart nearly fainted when she opened the morning paper and saw the front-page photo of the man accused of killing the President. She was sure he was the same man who, two months before, had introduced himself to her as "Lee"[368]—the same man who had eaten her stew and cornbread and then rendezvoused with their former parishioner, Charles Rogers. Her husband agreed.

The Gerharts immediately reported everything they knew to the Houston FBI. The agent they spoke with said he would pass the information on to his superiors and that someone would call them if their information was deemed relevant. No one ever called.

However, there *was* an unexpected call that same day from Charles Rogers' mother, Edwina. Distraught, she soon began sobbing—about the President's death and "personal circumstances." Gerhart took the call and assured her he would pray for her; he also encouraged her to attend church the next day. She did, and Marietta, knowing how upset she had been the day before, sat next to her.

Marietta realized that Edwina Rogers needed to unburden herself. The Gerharts became shoulders for Edwina to cry on. Craig family members admitted to the authors that Marietta had a way of eliciting information from others; during the eighteen months after the assassination, Edwina apparently shared frightening stories about her son. So, it would not be surprising if Edwina Rogers admitted to her pastor and his wife that she, too, had recognized the name "Oswald."

Regardless, at the conclusion of the church services on November 24, Edwina Rogers asked the pastor to pray for her. Only minutes after the services ended, televisions all over the nation broadcast the shocking video showing the President's accused assassin being shot himself. As the Gerharts watched the televised replay of the murder, they knew beyond any doubt that the man they watched grimacing in pain was the same man who had visited with them that night in September.

Gerhart was so sure that he contacted the Houston FBI again. But the agent seemed less interested this time than he had before. Disturbed by this, Gerhart reached out to his former OSS friend. The agent also knew Charles Rogers. Unlike Houston's FBI, the agent returned Elmer's phone call quickly, but his response only deepened the mystery around Charles Rogers and Lee Harvey Oswald.

"'Elmer,'" he said. "'I concur with your version of the facts. I believe that the man you and Marietta saw was who you believe him to be.'" Gerhart was flooded with relief until the agent added "...'Elmer, you and Marietta have done your duty. There is nothing more you can do. I am asking you, as a friend, to drop it—*now*. Let the government handle it. Leave it alone, please. They are aware of the situation. That is all I can tell you.'"[369]

The Gerharts understood the warning. Based on what they had observed that evening at their church, they were not sure Oswald was the "lone nut" officials and the press had already made him out to be. The FBI might not want to hear what the Gerharts had to say, but the Gerharts "had seen Oswald meet a man they both knew to be a covert agent of the CIA, who had preferred to use an alias in the encounter, and who evidently had not wanted them or his parents to know of this meeting."[370] They had to wonder if they were now in danger because of what they had seen.

This question became more and more important as the months after the assassination unfolded. Stories about assassination witnesses dying mysterious deaths began to spread. Perhaps these people should have kept their stories to themselves. The Gerharts intended to do just that. They had no idea that Charles Rogers would enter their lives once more.

A year and a half after the assassination, on Father's Day, June 20, 1965, as Marietta rolled the trash container to the curb at dusk, she was startled by a figure stepping out of the shadows.

"'Don't be afraid. It's only me—Charles Rogers,'" a man said to her. She recognized him immediately and despite his soft tone, her heart jumped.

Rogers assured Marietta that he just wanted to thank her for being such a good friend to his mother, and he added that he would be leaving town for a while. Still unnerved, Marietta tried to smile as she told Rogers she would pray for him. She watched him stride down the street to meet another man, who appeared to be waiting for him. She couldn't be sure, but she had a strong feeling that the other man was the same "Charles" who had accompanied "Lee" to her house in 1963. She hadn't thought to ask Rogers why his mother had not been at church that morning or if his father had had a pleasant Father's Day.

Marietta had no way of knowing that Edwina and Fred Rogers had both been murdered that day in their own home. But Charles Rogers *must* have known. Surely, if he had been innocent of their deaths, he would have called the police as soon as he returned home that evening. Or, if he had left town immediately after seeing Marietta Gerhart, he would have returned to Houston as soon as his parents' deaths became the lead story of every newscast in the area. He did neither.

The investigation of the murders by John Craig and Phil Rogers led them to believe that Charles Rogers had murdered his parents earlier in the day and returned home that evening and methodically dismembered his parents' dead bodies, chopped up their organs, and placed their larger body parts, including their severed heads, in their own refrigerator. Perhaps the man Marietta had seen Rogers meeting that evening assisted him in this gruesome task.

Some of the scenes in Craig's and Rogers' book *The Man on the Grassy Knoll* have been criticized because the authors included dialogue in scenes they could not have witnessed. But what the critics do not know is that Craig received information that Edwina Rogers shared with his aunt, Marietta Gerhart. Apparently, Edwina Rogers had become suspicious of her son's strange activities. Chances are, much of the dialogue in the book between Edwina and her son Charles came from statements Edwina shared privately with Marietta. But John Craig promised to keep his relationship with Marietta Gerhart a secret. So he could not reveal in the book how he knew about some of the personal conversations between Edwina and her son.

Edwina Rogers knew that her son left her home during the week of the President's assassination. Because there was only one telephone in the Rogers' household, she answered strange calls for her son and even took messages for him. Intrigued by what she was being told, she sorted the names and telephone numbers, copied them, and hid them in her home.

Edwina Rogers realized that her son must have returned these strange phone calls at a nearby pay phone because he did not use the only telephone in their home. She was frightened for her son's life, and the only people she felt she could share her fears with were the Gerharts. She indicated to them that she would have to confront her son at some point in time. He might move out of the house if he knew his mother was aware of his strange activities. Edwina Rogers obviously never suspected how far her only son would go to protect those activities.

After the murders of the Rogers, the Gerharts began to fear for their own lives. It seemed odd that Charles Rogers showed up for no particular reason on the very day his parents were killed. About two months after the Rogers' deaths, Marietta heard what she assumed was an intruder in the church. She knew she had locked the church the evening before, and yet, it sounded as if someone had entered it. Her husband, who had been ill for quite some time, was asleep upstairs. Not wanting to upset him, she simply called the police.

An officer responded and heard the intruder himself. In fact, he spotted a tall, blonde-haired man running towards an exterior door. The officer got close enough to the intruder to grab and rip off a piece of his shirt, but the man escaped.

Though nothing like this happened again, Marietta Gerhart decided to keep everything she and her husband knew about Charles Rogers, Oswald, and the tall, blonde man whom she knew simply as "Charles" to herself, at least until her husband passed away. Not long before she herself died in 1990, she decided that if the FBI wasn't going to investigate these events, someone else should. That is when she contacted her nephew, John Craig, and even gave him money to help with any expenses he would incur in an investigation. She was determined that someone find out everything about Charles Rogers and his connection to Oswald.

All of Craig's family was deeply interested in this particular investigation because they had felt close to Edwina Rogers. They remembered when she helped with a family member's wedding; John and his siblings recalled her from church services. Her death had troubled all of them.

Though the family members knew that John and fellow investigator Phil Rogers were looking into what became one of Houston's most famous "cold cases," they did not know that Craig had been more than an average private investigator. Ellen Craig, his second wife, recalled an incident that showed just how many covert contacts her husband had.

"A young man who was new to the FBI was telling John about an exciting case he was working on," Ellen recalled to the authors. "He told him it was so top-secret that he and his partner did not even know how to reach their supervisor. They had to go through an intermediary to contact him. John asked the name of the supervisor and walked over to the telephone and dialed a number. The supervisor answered. You should have seen the shocked look on that young man's face. He realized then that John Craig had more contacts than he did!"

Ellen Craig also recalled that CIA agents often visited her husband via helicopter in the small town where they lived north of Houston. So, she has strong suspicions about how her husband learned certain facts about Charles Rogers' activities and about his CIA connections.

The investigation led Craig and his co-writer to conclude that Charles Rogers was one of several "tramps" noticed in Dealey Plaza on November 22, 1963. According to internationally recognized forensic artist Lois Gibson, the three men referred to as "tramps" photographed being casually escorted by Dallas police officers the day Kennedy was killed were named Chauncey Holt, Charles Harrelson, and Charles Rogers. Gibson used her scientific training and expertise to compare facial and hair features with numerous photos of the three "tramps." She even met Chauncey Holt in person and was able to compare his physical features with the tramp photos. Holt admitted to her that he had been one of the "tramps." He went on to confess that he had been hired to produce false identification badges for various individuals to use in Dealey Plaza on November 22, 1963.

Craig felt sure that Charles Rogers was one of two assassins standing behind the picket fence on the grassy knoll that Friday in Dallas. He discovered that the man Lee introduced to the Gerharts as "Charles" on September 25, 1963 was Charles Harrelson, a man eventually convicted of killing a Texas judge in 1979. Harrelson was recognized by several people who knew him as one of the tramps taken to the Sheriff's Department on the afternoon Kennedy was killed. Perhaps it was because of Chauncey Holt's badges that the three men were not photographed or fingerprinted by the Dallas police. In fact, they were not even held for questioning.

Lois Gibson also examined photographs of other men who claimed to be the three men in the famous "tramp" photos. None of these men's physical characteristics matched those of the "tramps' in the photographs. As Gibson stated, "No one has been able to argue about what I physically described. Some are sure that the tramps are not Holt, Harrelson, or Rogers, but their arguments are not based on physical evidence. They simply believe the "tramps" were someone else."[371]

For years before and after her husband's death, Marietta Gerhart feared for her life. After all, she did not know for sure what Edwina Rogers had told her son Charles on the day she may have confronted him about his activities. Nevertheless, Marietta knew that Edwina Rogers had been sick with worry herself and been determined to find out about her son's part in the President's assassination. Because there was no evidence of robbery in the Rogers house, it was evident to the police and to the Gerharts that the Rogerses had been killed for personal reasons. The knowledge Marietta carried with her concerning Edwina Rogers' fears led her to seek her nephew's promise not to share Marietta's story until after her death.

One of the things John Craig and Phil Rogers wanted to know was whether Charles Rogers was still alive and how he escaped prosecution for his parents' murders. Craig spoke to numerous people who seemed to know Rogers and his aliases, so even though Rogers had been declared officially dead in 1975, Craig suspected he was still active in covert activities in South America.

Based on what the authors learned, Craig was correct. Lt. J. Goode admitted to working with Charles Rogers. In his words, Rogers was a "whacko!" Goode provided a few more details about Rogers—details that correlate with information John Craig learned.

"He was a gambler just like his father, he had a pilot's license, and he worked for the CIA in South America," Goode declared. When asked why he called Rogers a "whacko," he paused before elaborating.

"Well, you know when two people are talking about the different things they have done, and they are trying to top each other?" he began. "It's hard to top the question he finally asked me: 'Well, have you ever killed your parents?'"

Goode assumed that Rogers was probably dead, but he did not know for sure. When shown the famous photos of the "tramps" in Dealey Plaza on November 22, 1963, he stated adamantly that the shorter one was definitely Charles Rogers.

If Charles Rogers is not dead, he has a grave in Houston's Hollywood Cemetery waiting for him. Fred and Edwina Rogers originally purchased three plots, one for their young daughter who died in 1929, and one for each of them.

Like most parents, they assumed their son would marry and want to be buried next to his wife. The bodies of Rogers' parents had been so dismembered after their murders that there was no point in placing them in two different caskets. So, they shared a single coffin, and the cemetery now has a vacant plot waiting just for Charles Rogers.

The book *The Man on the Grassy Knoll* contains important information about a strange encounter between a pastor and his wife and Lee Harvey Oswald, Charles Harrelson, and Charles "Carlos" Rogers, a man who may have murdered his own parents to protect himself and his associates. Because of this chance encounter, Marietta and Elmer Gerhart spent years in fear, afraid that what had happened to the Rogers couple might also happen to them.

Unlike those who were harassed for sharing information about Oswald, the Gerharts were ignored, at least by the police and the FBI. Like so many other witnesses, Marietta Gerhart insisted on keeping her silence and telling her story from the grave. She died still not knowing why Kennedy's accused assassin Lee Harvey Oswald (or someone who looked just like him) appeared on her doorstep two months before the assassination, and why he was obviously connected to a CIA agent named "Carlos" whom she knew with certainty as Charles Rogers.

The strong possibility that Charles Rogers murdered his own parents to protect himself and his associates suggests that he might have been connected to another organization, not just the CIA. The Mafia expects its members to swear total allegiance to the Family; one of the questions a "made man" must answer is: "Would you kill a family member if you were told to?" Perhaps Charles Rogers answered "yes" and then had to prove his loyalty.

CHAPTER 35

SHADOWING
LEE HARVEY OSWALD

"The man I remember as Oswald was a trim, energetic, compact,
well-dressed person. The other 'Oswald' was a "trifling, shiftless,
good-for-nothing lout."—Laurel Kittrell

One of the facts that "Lee and "Charles" shared with the Gerharts on the evening of September 25, 1963, was that the two men were planning on travelling to Mexico. The next day someone named "Lee Harvey Oswald" bought a bus ticket to Mexico City. The "Lee" who visited the Gerharts supposedly left New Orleans and travelled to Houston on September 25. He, or someone impersonating him, then bought a bus ticket to Mexico City via Laredo, Texas, and arrived in Mexico City on the morning of Friday, September 27, just as Oswald told the Gerharts he was planning to do. John Craig's research convinced him that the passenger on the bus to Mexico was really Charles Rogers impersonating Lee Harvey Oswald.

Another "Lee Harvey Oswald" left New Orleans and travelled to Austin and then Dallas on September 25. He visited the State Selective Service Headquarters in Austin and was interviewed by Mrs. Lee Dannelly. Oswald claimed that he was in Austin to protest his "undesirable discharge" from the Marines. From Austin, he travelled to Dallas, arriving in the evening. According to Sylvia Odio and her younger sister, Oswald and two other men visited them in Mexico City on the evening of September 25. Oswald was introduced by the two men as "Leon."[372]

The confusion caused by the various sightings of "Lee Harvey Oswald" continued. According to FBI records, a "Lee Harvey Oswald" left Mexico City by bus and arrived at Nuevo Laredo on the morning of October 3, 1963, though Laurel Kittrell of the Texas Employment Commission in Dallas encountered a "Lee Harvey Oswald" around this time in Dallas, Texas. This "Oswald" wore a black motorcycle jacket and was interviewed by another employment counselor. He overheard the woman Kittrell was interviewing mention the fact that she had been employed in California by Murray Chotiner. The woman referred to Chotiner "as a big gangster."[373] This comment caught "Oswald's" attention, and he addressed Kittrell:

"'Excuse me,'" he said, 'I don't mean to be butting in, or anything like that, but didn't I hear that colored woman tell you she had worked in California for Murray Chotiner?'" When Kittrell refused to answer his question because all interviews are confidential, Oswald responded, "'Well, I'll be damned.'" He then grew angry and slapped his hand on her desk. He then repeated, "'I'll just be damned,'" and his look of anger changed to one of fright.[374]

Kittrell had no idea that she would ever see this man again. However, a few days later, she received a phone call from a supervisor informing her that a "Mr. Oswald" was being sent to her for a re-interview. It was not long before a young man wearing a black motorcycle jacket appeared in front of her. He was so similar in appearance to the other young man in the motorcycle jacket that she quizzed him about that.

"The other day, a young man like you, in a motorcycle jacket, stopped by my desk to ask me about a colored woman who had worked in California for a man named Murray Chotiner. Aren't you that same man in a motorcycle jacket I remember?" She added, "Did you work in California for Murry Chotiner?" The young man simply shook his head no.

"'He's a crook,'" he said, and when Kittrell protested this negative comment, he insisted,"Well, he is.'" Kittrell decided that the young man probably had worked for Chotiner, and she indicated this on his application form.[375]

As the interview continued, Kittrell learned from this young man that he spoke three languages, one of them Russian. He also informed her he had married a Russian girl and worked in a factory in Minsk, Russia. "Oswald" provided her with an address in Irving, Texas. She also discovered he had been given an undesirable discharge from the Marines, and that he had dropped out of high school but earned his GED. She completed the interview and reassured the young man that he would now be considered for future employment.

Three or four days later, she recognized a young man who resembled the other Oswald, though he was not wearing a motorcycle jacket. Surprisingly, she found herself interviewing *another* man who identified himself as "Lee Harvey Oswald."

At first, she assumed he was the same man she had interviewed previously. Even though the two men shared a strong resemblance, Kittrell realized they were *two different people*. The test given to this "Oswald" this day showed that his spelling was below average, but he did have an unusual kind of intelligence. His conversation with Kittrell indicated that he was highly interested in guns and politics. Kittrell was not aware that someone using the name "Lee Harvey Oswald" had applied at the Fort Worth branch of the TEC in April of 1962 and taken the same test. This "Lee Harvey Oswald" gave an address in Oak Cliff and a new telephone number.[376]

"In contrast to the man I remember as Oswald, who kept a military neatness, complete with shined shoes, this fellow was definitely a shaggy type—clean but shaggy." He identified himself as a member of the Teamsters Union but admitted he did not have a driver's license. What he also did not have was a union card.

"I don't have one. They haven't got it to me yet," he told her. Kittrell recalled that the two "Oswalds" looked very much alike in "size, shape, and outline. Generally, there was a marked difference between them in bearing and manner. The man I remember as Oswald was a trim, energetic, compact, well-dressed person." The other "Oswald" she described as a "trifling, shiftless, good-for-nothing lout who sprawled oafishly over his chair, and whose movements seemed curiously uncoordinated, like those of a person who had been drinking."[377]

On two different occasions after the Kennedy assassination, Kittrell attempted to contact authorities with information she felt indicated the existence of two men using the name "Lee Harvey Oswald." It was not until 1965 that the FBI bothered to interview her. In a 90-page FBI report, Kittrell connected Oswald to Jack Ruby. As Kittrell read through the Warren Report, she noticed a photograph of a man with an appearance strikingly similar to the "Teamster" she had interviewed. It was not until she "turned to the Report's index that she found that the picture was that of Jack Ruby's assistant, Curtis Laverne "Larry" Crafard." This is a detail that would have connected Oswald to someone close to Jack Ruby. If Crafard had been using Oswald's name in the Dallas area, it would explain why so many people saw and spoke to a man they thought was "Lee Harvey Oswald" when evidence shows that Oswald was counting textbooks in the Depository.

It is also possible that the FBI/Warren Commission did not want the name "Murray Chotiner" to be mentioned in the same report as Lee Harvey Oswald. After all, though Chotiner was an attorney who had supported Richard Nixon since 1946, he was also connected to Teamster Jimmy Hoffa and mobsters Carlos Marcello and Mickey Cohen. Perhaps someone was more concerned with Oswald's name being linked to the Mafia than with the fact that someone was impersonating him.

Kittrell's story was not the only convoluted tale that officials heard. To make matters more confusing, Dallas attorney Carroll Jarnagin stated in a Warren Commission deposition that he saw Lee Harvey Oswald in the Carousel Club in downtown Dallas on the evening of October 4, 1963. But according to FBI report # 124-10178-10458, Agency File Number 89-67-173, dated November 27, 1963, Oswald spent that night in a motel in Alice, Texas, 404 miles away with a pregnant wife and a young daughter. However, according to Ruth Paine's Warren Commission statement, Oswald was at her house in Irving that day.[378]

The Oswald saga becomes even more confusing. On October 4, another Oswald impersonator was photographed in Mexico City outside of the Soviet Embassy. He identified himself as "Lee Harvey Oswald."[379] Even the FBI assumed this man was an impersonator, not the real Oswald.

The confusion increased as mysterious appearances of different "Oswalds" occurred more frequently. On October 25, 1963, five days after the birth of Oswald's second child, Aldene Magee of Baton Rouge, Louisiana, was approached by a man who wanted to rent an apartment. He identified himself as "Lee Oswald."[380] The "official" Oswald was in Dallas at the time.

During the workdays of October 31, November 1, and November 2, men in the Dallas area resembling Oswald applied for a job at the Statler Hilton, purchased ammunition at Morgan's Gun Shop, and visited Dial Ryder's gun shop to have a scope mounted on a rifle. [381] These sightings occurred while the Lee Harvey Oswald who would soon be arrested for killing two people was at work at the Depository.

During the first week of November 1963, Edith Whitworth observed Oswald driving a woman and a child outside her furniture store in Irving, Texas. He parked and the family entered her store. Oswald asked for directions to the nearest gun shop.[382] This was a Wednesday, and employee records show the "official" Oswald working at the time at the Depository. Four days later, on November 10, one Oswald was at the Sports Drome Rifle Range and another was at Ruth Paine's home with Marina and the children.

On November 12, the "official" Oswald rode to work with Buell Wesley Frazier from the Paines' house to the Depository. According to Robert Kermit Patterson, a man identifying himself as Lee Harvey Oswald visited his business, Contract Electronics, that day, not far from Jack Ruby's Carousel Club. The "official" Lee Harvey Oswald was at work at the Depository.[383]

The next day—November 13—while the "official" Oswald was working at the Depository, another "Oswald" and a woman were visiting Hutchison's Market during the middle of the day.[384] When Marina Oswald was questioned after the assassination about this visit, she denied that her husband could have been at the grocery market.

"Lee was at work," she said. "He couldn't have been there."[385]

She did not mention whether *she* had been at the market. Technically, there should have been no way that Marina Oswald could have known for sure that her husband was *not* at Hutchison's Market. But *she* would have known positively whether *she* was there or not. She did not address this fact, and apparently no one thought to ask her about it. Is it possible that Marina Oswald was associated with two different men, both using the name Lee Harvey Oswald?

On November 15, someone impersonating the "official" Oswald applied for employment at an Allright Parking garage. Presumably, an employee of a parking garage would be required to have a driver's license, but the "official" Oswald did not. This Oswald drew attention to himself by asking the manager, Hubert Morrow, how tall the parking garage was and how much of downtown Dallas could be seen from it.[386]

On November 17, Vern Davis saw and spoke to a Lee Oswald in a bar on Expedition Street in Dallas. He remembered that Oswald was discussing Kennedy's and Johnson's upcoming trip to Dallas. Davis also saw Jack Ruby enter the bar as he was leaving. He had known Jack Ruby for ten years, but met Oswald for the first time that day. Days later, he recognized him on television.[387]

On that same day, a commercial photographer named Harold Reynolds in Abilene, Texas, a city 262 miles west of Dallas, found a handwritten note left in his apartment mailbox; it was signed "Lee Harvey Oswald." Reynolds recalled that the note said something like, "Call me immediately—urgent," and that two Dallas telephone numbers were also written on it. The note was addressed to "Pedro Valeriano Gonzalez," a Cuban exile leader. Gonzalez was president of the Cuban Liberation Committee in Abilene and lived next door to Reynolds. So, the note may have been left at Reynolds' apartment by mistake, or Oswald or someone he knew may have deliberately left the note at the Reynolds' apartment, knowing that Reynolds and Gonzalez were friends.[388]

Reynolds had attended a few anti-Castro meetings with Gonzalez; at one meeting, he saw a man who resembled Lee Harvey Oswald. When Reynolds gave the note to Gonzalez that evening, he noticed that his neighbor became extremely agitated as he read it. Reynolds casually asked him who Oswald was, and Gonzalez's reply was "some attorney from Dallas."[389] Shortly afterwards, he saw Gonzalez a few blocks from his apartment talking on a pay phone. This struck Reynolds as odd because he knew Gonzalez had a telephone in his apartment.

But this was not as odd as the fact that almost immediately after Jack Ruby shot Oswald, Gonzalez left Abilene and reportedly moved first to Los Angeles and then to Venezuela. If Oswald had really traveled to Abilene five days before the assassination to contact Pedro Valeriano Gonzalez, this would explain where he was on that Sunday November 17, 1963. Of course, it is also possible that someone in Abilene left this note to deliberately connect Lee Harvey Oswald with anti-Castro Cubans.

Another Abilene connection to Oswald, the future accused assassin, involved a sighting of someone claiming to be Lee Harvey Oswald. Clyde Fletcher recalled that about a month before the assassination, a young man brought his early 1950's Ford station wagon into an Abilene body shop. The automobile needed a new universal rear joint. The young man lacked the twenty-two dollars necessary for the part, so he asked to use the telephone to make a long-distance call. Whoever he spoke to agreed to wire him the money. Leaving a young woman in the car, the man hiked about eleven blocks to the Western Union office.

Even after fifty-four years, Fletcher remembered that when the man returned with the money, he emphasized that his name was "Lee Harvey Oswald."

"The guy insisted that I write down his name on the work order and then repeated, 'Lee Harvey Oswald.' I didn't think anything about it until after the assassination when I heard his name on the television."[390]

Fletcher described the man as being extremely tall, which does not match with the "official" Oswald. Fletcher realized that when he saw Oswald on television after the assassination. However, he cannot explain why the man who obviously was not the "official" Oswald made a point of mentioning that he *was* Lee Harvey Oswald.

A few years later, the owner of the body shop sold the business to Fletcher, but the original owner insisted on burning all of his previous work orders.

"I sure wish he had not burned those work orders," Fletcher told the authors, "because Oswald's name and the date were written in my handwriting right there on the top line." Fletcher also commented that he had seen the man and woman as they drove up to the station, so he knew they had been driving on Highway 80 and been coming from the west.

"They must have come from Midland—Odessa—maybe El Paso," he explained. "Somewhere from West Texas, and they were headed east." It is also possible that the Oswald impersonator might have been returning from Mexico.

Evidence shows that on November 18, one Oswald was in Juarez, Mexico, while another Oswald was at work at the Depository. Then on November 20, 1963, Ralph Yates picked up a man who *identified* himself as Lee Harvey Oswald hitchhiking on the Thornton Freeway in Dallas at 10:30 a.m. This Oswald was carrying a long package, which he described to Yates as "curtain rods." The man then showed Yates a picture of himself holding a rifle.[391]

Oswald asked Yates if he thought the President could be assassinated with such a rifle. He then asked him if he thought it was possible for the President to be shot with a rifle from a tall building. Yates dropped this "Oswald" off at the corner of Houston and Elm right across the street from the Depository. At that time, the "official" Oswald was already in the Depository checking textbooks. It seems that this imposter deliberately connected himself to the Depository. He also made deliberate comments about curtain rods and shooting the President.

Unfortunately for Ralph Leon Yates, after he recognized the accused assassin on television, he reported his November 20th experience to the FBI. He felt obligated to tell authorities what he knew; after all, he told a co-worker on the day he picked up the stranger. So, Yates talked to FBI agents on November 26, December 10, and then on January 3 and 4, 1964. His story did not vary, no matter how many times agents questioned him. He insisted he did not want publicity because he was married and had five children. He simply felt that, as a good citizen, he should report what had happened to him.

J. Edgar Hoover instructed SAIC Gordon Shanklin to give Yates a polygraph test. The tests were inconclusive, but Yates' story still seemed to be a problem for authorities. If Yates was telling the truth, then his story was more evidence of someone closely resembling the Oswald who worked in the Depository, setting him up as a "patsy." Despite (or because of) the inconclusive polygraph test, Yates and his wife were told by the FBI that he should immediately enter himself as a patient at Woodlawn Mental Hospital. Yates took their advice and lived to regret it.[392]

Yates was transferred to other mental hospitals, including the Terrell State Hospital, the Veterans Hospital in Waco, and eventually the Rusk State Hospital. His wife never knew everything that happened to him in these institutions, but she did learn that he was given strong tranquilizers and been subjected to over forty electric shock treatments. The shock treatments affected his short-term memory, but not his long-term memory. He never forgot his experience with the man who looked just like Lee Harvey Oswald.[393] Sadly, Ralph Yates died in 1975 at Rusk State Hospital at the age of 39. Years of institutionalization would certainly discredit any stories he ever told about a man looking like Oswald who mentioned curtain rods and asked about shooting the President with a rifle.

To add to this puzzle of too many Oswald pieces, on November 20, 1963, two people contacted Wayne January of America Aviation and inquired about chartering a small plane. They told him their itinerary was Mexico and that they would leave the afternoon of November 22. A third person was in the car, and January claimed he looked like Oswald.[394] This is the same Wayne January who used the pseudonym "Hank Gordon" when he told about a Cuban pilot warning that Kennedy would be killed.

Some of these multi-Oswald appearances might be explained if the Oswald who had worked for the Depository missed work often. But his supervisor reported that he was always on time and never missed work. So, who were the men using Lee Harvey Oswald's identity while he was at work in Dallas? One of them might well have been Charles Rogers, as John Craig believed.

If any of these men were the real "Lee Harvey Oswald," then who was the man also using this name and filling textbook orders at the Depository? If John Armstrong's theory about two men using the identity "Lee Harvey Oswald" is correct, then one of the Oswalds must have been "Lee" Harvey Oswald, while the other Oswald was "Harvey" Oswald. Apparently, the lives of these two men had been controlled and interwoven since they were children.

As November 22 approached, more and more sightings of men resembling and identifying themselves as "Lee Oswald" occurred. A day or two before the assassination, while the "official" Oswald counted textbooks in the School Book Depository, five employees of the Dobbs House restaurant in Oak Cliff saw a man they thought was Oswald at 10:00 a.m. This restaurant was located right across the street from "Oswald's" boarding house on North Beckley. The men noticed him because he was complaining loudly about his order. Another customer in the restaurant that morning also noticed "Oswald." This was Police Officer J. D. Tippitt. Of course, at 10:00 in the morning, the "official" Oswald was busy at the Depository.[395]

Ten hours before the assassination, Mary Lawrence saw Jack Ruby and a man who looked like Lee Harvey Oswald together at a restaurant. This could not possibly have been the man who was spending the night at Ruth Paine's house with his family.

On the day of the assassination, while the "official" Oswald was riding with Buell Wesley Frazier to the Book Depository, another man resembling him was seen at the same time at the Top Ten Record Store in Oak Cliff. Store owner J. W. (Dub) Stark and employee Louis Cortinas both saw him. Stark sold this "Oswald" a ticket to the Dick Clark Caravan of Stars show which was to take place that night. The man resembling Oswald arrived at the store at 7:30 a.m. to make sure he could purchase a ticket. Later that afternoon, Stark thought he recognized the customer when Oswald's photo was televised all over the country; Stark still had the ticket stub to prove he sold this man a ticket early on the morning of the assassination. The customer who seemed to resemble Oswald had no reason to show any identification that morning, so there is no way of knowing who this man really was.[396]

But at 10:00 a.m. another man resembling Oswald made sure he was remembered. He stopped at the Jiffy Store on Industrial Boulevard, a half-mile from the Depository, to purchase two beers from Fred Moore. This "Oswald" showed his license to prove he was old enough to purchase the alcohol. Moore remembered that the name on the license was "Lee Harvey Oswald." This man returned thirty minutes later to buy another beer and two pieces of Peco Brittle. He seemed to be deliberately imprinting his image and name on the memory of this store owner. But this could not have been the "Oswald" at work in the Depository.[397]

As strange as these occurrences are, they don't compare to the odd situation that occurred *after* the assassination. Several witnesses, including a deputy sheriff, saw a man wearing a white t-shirt who resembled Oswald run out of the front of the Depository into Elm Street and get into a station wagon, which then headed west.

Deputy Sheriff Roger Craig insisted to the day he died that he saw a man whom he swore was Lee Harvey Oswald escape from the Depository not long after the assassination. That afternoon, Craig had the opportunity to observe Oswald at the Dallas police station; he always maintained that he saw this same man leave the Depository in a Rambler station wagon. Of course, this does not correlate with the evidence that showed Oswald rode on a bus and then a taxi. But Craig could have been correct if *two* men who resembled each other were in the Depository that day.

Craig refused to change his story though pressured to by his own sheriff's department. He later lost job after job, and his life became a nightmare. After several unsuccessful attempts on his life, Craig supposedly killed himself on May 15, 1975.

This tragedy is compounded by the fact that there were *two more* witnesses who saw what Craig saw. During all the years that Craig refused to change his story, buried deep in the National Archives were two depositions by Marvin Robinson and his employee, Roy Cooper, which verified Craig's story.

The two men were driving west on Elm Street when they, too, saw a man resembling Oswald run from the side of the Depository and jump into a Rambler station wagon. Documentation verifying their statements has been "lost" in the National Archives for decades.[398] Helen Forrest and James Pennington also confirm what Craig saw. Forrest said, "If it wasn't Oswald, it was his identical twin."[399] Helen Forrest's comment about an identical twin may have been a slight exaggeration, but, obviously, there were men who resembled Oswald so closely that witnesses could not tell the difference.

Like Buel Wesley Fraizer, who saw an Oswald depart from the back side of the Depository, other witnesses saw a man they thought was Oswald walk out of the front side of the Depository and head east on Elm Street. He was wearing a long-sleeved *brown* shirt. A bus driver who sold this Oswald a ticket later identified him as the suspect pictured on television that afternoon. This Oswald became impatient with the traffic around the downtown area and left the bus to catch a taxi.

For some reason, he asked to be dropped off six blocks past his boarding house on Beckley Street. This in itself seems suspicious. Did he suspect he was being followed? Was he supposed to meet someone at that corner, and that person did not show up? Or, was he trying to avoid being seen by anyone? If so, he mistimed his arrival.

The housekeeper of the boarding house, Earlene Roberts, was sitting in the living room watching television when a man whom she recognized as "O. H. Lee" entered the boarding house. Without acknowledging her, he moved quickly towards his room. Within minutes, he reappeared wearing a different long-sleeved brown shirt over a white t-shirt, gray trousers, and a light-weight jacket. He hurried out the front door. Roberts watched him stop on the corner of Beckley and Zang before she returned her attention to the television.

While in the boarding house, Oswald supposedly retrieved a loaded pistol that he then carried to the Texas Theatre. This seems to indicate that he was concerned about his safety. He may have realized that the plot to kill the President had actually materialized. He might have even suspected that he would become the accused assassin and that he would need to protect himself.

The most incriminating evidence against Oswald was not that he left the Depository; it was that he then went directly to his boarding house and supposedly armed himself with a pistol. This indicates that Oswald did not go to the Texas Theatre just to enjoy an afternoon matinee. His behavior at the theatre also negates the idea that he might simply have been hiding from authorities. Other patrons' observations indicate that Oswald was looking for someone at the same time that a large number of police officers were looking for him.

CHAPTER 36

THEATRICS IN OAK CLIFF

"I saw a second man that looked almost like Oswald being led out through the back door of the theatre."—Butch Burroughs

B etween 1:00 and 1:07 pm, the Oswald wearing the brown shirt (hereafter referred to as Oswald 1) bought a theatre ticket from Julia Postal at the Texas Theatre on Jefferson Boulevard in Oak Cliff. Butch Burroughs, who ran the theatre's concession stand, claimed that Oswald 1 entered the theatre minutes after the movie feature started. Burroughs told the police that the film started exactly at 1 p.m. and that Oswald had been in the theatre since the opening credits. At 1:15, Burroughs sold this man a bag of popcorn.

A patron in the main section of the theatre, Jack Davis, remembered Oswald 1 sitting next to him during the movie's opening credits. Then he noticed him changing seats in the theatre. It appeared Oswald 1 was meeting someone at the theatre who may have known about the assassination plot. Oswald 1 may not have been given a description of his contact, which would explain why he moved from seat to seat throughout the theatre. He may not have trusted this individual, and that is why he carried a pistol with him.

Jack Davis stated that only minutes after the opening credits, Oswald 1 squeezed past him and took a seat right next to him. Oswald 1 immediately got up and moved across the aisle to sit by another person. Burroughs remembered Oswald 1 sat next to a pregnant woman. Several minutes after Oswald 1 took his seat next to her, the woman got up, went to the back of the theatre, and up the stairs to the women's restroom. Burroughs never saw her again.[400]

That is when Oswald 1 walked to the back of the theatre to the concession stand and bought popcorn. Jack Davis then saw Oswald 1 re-enter the theatre and sit in the middle section. This is where he remained until the police arrived.

At the same time as Oswald 1, dressed in a brown shirt, was sitting in the theatre, Oswald 2 (who strongly resembled the first Oswald), wearing a white shirt and a light-colored Eisenhower jacket, was walking down Patton Avenue, six blocks from the theatre. Dallas police officer J. D. Tippit was patrolling the area. He noticed the young man, pulled his patrol car over to the curb, and spoke to him through the passenger window.

Jack Tatum saw the men converse for a moment. Tippet then got out of his car and began walking to the sidewalk. He barely reached his front tire when Oswald 2 pulled out a pistol and fired three times. Even after the officer fell to the street, Oswald 2 walked over to his body and put one more bullet into his head. He then hurried away.

At 1:17, a citizen used the police radio in Officer Tippet's car to report that a police officer had been shot. The citizen gave the dispatcher the address. There was no discussion at this time of a suspect. At 1:19, the dispatcher was still reporting the location of the shooting. At 1:20, the dispatcher reported that a suspect was running west on Jefferson Street. He added that there was still no physical description.

Two minutes later, at 1:22, however, the police dispatcher suddenly reported that "a white male, 30, 5'8,"very slender build, black hair, a white jacket, white shirt, and dark slacks" was a suspect in the killing of a Dallas police officer. Official logs from the dispatcher show that this description was not called in from the witnesses at the scene. It is unclear how the dispatcher learned this information. Regardless, the description did not fit that of Lee Harvey Oswald as he was dressed that morning at the Depository, nor does it match the description of him when arrested in the theatre shortly afterward.

About 1:35, Oswald 2, wearing a white t-shirt, sneaked into the Texas Theatre without buying a ticket. He was observed acting suspiciously by Johnny Brewer, who worked at Hardy's Shoe Store nearby. Brewer informed Julia Postal that a man sneaked into the theatre, and she promptly called the police. Apparently, there were two men in the Texas Theatre at the same time who resembled each other. Oswald 1 (the one in the long-sleeved brown shirt) could not possibly have shot Officer Tippet because he was already in the theatre at the time the shooting occurred. Though the original police dispatch described a dark-haired man wearing a white shirt with dark trousers, the Dallas police soon arrested a man wearing a long-sleeved brown shirt who had been in the theatre since a few minutes after 1:00.

Burroughs claimed Oswald 2 slipped into the movie theatre without paying at 1:35 and headed upstairs to the balcony. The police swarmed the first floor and arrested Oswald 1 on the ground floor. Oswald 1 was the man with the pistol; he was led out the front door of the theatre and driven to police headquarters shortly before 2 p.m. Stella Puckett observed this arrest from her photography studio across the street.

The scene of this arrest was almost as chaotic as any in a Keystone Kops movie. Dallas police officers and even the Dallas Assistant District Attorney, William Alexander, swarmed the Texas Theatre because the owner of a neighboring store reported that a white male acting suspiciously "had slipped into the theatre without buying a ticket." Some officers entered through the front door and headed to the balcony of the theatre, while others entered through a back door. Among those who entered through the backdoor was Dallas Police Officer C. T. Walker.

In his deposition to the Warren Commission, he was one of the first to mention that two men sitting in the theatre were searched before Oswald was. Whether this was a common practice or whether it was due to extreme caution on the part of the police officers is unknown. It does indicate that the police officers were either unsure of their suspect or stalling to see how Oswald would react.

According to the police report, when Dallas police approached Oswald 1, he tried to shoot the arresting officer. There was a scuffle and all the officers involved were fortunate they were not shot. Oswald 1 was smart enough to shout loudly so that the police, and more importantly, other patrons could hear: "I am not resisting arrest! I am not resisting arrest!" His behavior while being arrested indicates he was afraid he would be killed before he was taken into custody.

Meantime, a large crowd gathered in front of the theatre, having heard that either a "cop killer" or the President's assassin, depending on the story, was inside. Forty-five minutes after entering the theatre, Oswald 1, who had been found sitting on the main floor of the theatre wearing a brown shirt, was handcuffed and hustled out of the theatre through the front doors. Butch Burroughs and Pat Hall's mother, Stella Puckett, were among the numerous witnesses who saw this happen.

The citizens in front of the theatre could easily have turned into a lynch mob, though they could not possibly have known anything about the man being arrested; the police could not have known much, either. Oswald was not on the "people to watch" list dispersed before President Kennedy's visit to Texas, though his defection to Russia three years earlier had been widespread news, especially throughout Texas.

A much-publicized photo showed Oswald being practically dragged out of the front of the Texas Theatre, then surrounded by Dallas police vehicles. If police truly thought the suspect had killed a fellow officer and then attempted to shoot the arresting officer, it is easy to see why they were so upset. However, it is difficult to understand why one of the arresting officers still had a large cigar clenched in his teeth.

In 2017, Officer C. T. Walker's sister-in-law Carolyn Crowder shared with the authors what Walker told her years earlier. She recalled that her brother-in-law was shocked by the actions of the crowd gathered outside the theatre. He referred to them as a" potential lynch mob."

"He told me he thought they might try to tear Oswald's clothes off," she said.[401] In his deposition, Walker quoted some of the members of the crowd as shouting, "Kill the S.O.B.", "Let us have him. We want him."[402]

Butch Burroughs described another scene that most of the other witnesses did not see. He noticed that after Oswald 1 was led out the front door of the theatre, other policemen led Oswald 2 out of the theatre through the back door. Burroughs later swore that this took place "three or four minutes later."

"I saw a second man that looked almost like Oswald being led out through the back door of the theatre." Burroughs apparently was a witness to what appeared to be two different arrests.[403]

Burroughs was not the only person to see this odd event. Bernard Haire, the owner of a nearby hobby shop, was another witness to two different arrests, just minutes apart. Before Oswald 2 was escorted from the balcony by Dallas police officers and led out the back door of the theatre, Haire was captured in a photo standing in front of the theatre at the time of Oswald's 1 arrest.

At that time, Haire did not realize the accused assassin was being arrested. He just knew some kind of commotion was occurring in front of the theatre. When Haire walked to the alleyway behind his hobby store, he saw what he thought was the "official arrest" of Oswald.

What Haire actually witnessed was the arrest of Oswald 2. He saw the police put Oswald 2 in a police car and drive off. For years, Bernard Haire told people he watched as Lee Harvey Oswald was arrested, taken out the *back* door of the theatre, and placed in a police car. It was not until 1988 that he realized the official arrest of Oswald actually occurred in the *front* of the theatre.

Some people might question the memories of Burroughs and Haire. However, an official homicide report on Officer J. D. Tippet verifies their memories. It states that "the suspect [Oswald] was later arrested in the *balcony* [italics added] of the Texas Theatre."[404] Apparently, *someone* was arrested in the balcony *after* Oswald 1 was arrested on the floor of the theatre.

But the two suspects were bound for two different destinations. Shortly after 2:00, Oswald 1 was driven to City Hall, and Oswald 2 was escorted somewhere else. Shortly after the arrest of Oswald 1, T. F. White noticed a man resembling Oswald wearing a short-sleeved white shirt sitting in a car in El Chico's parking lot five blocks north of the Texas Theatre. Because White did not know that Oswald 1 was already in custody, he thought the man in the car might be the suspect the police were searching for. Rather than confront a possible assassin, he copied down the car's license plate number.

White later was told that the license number (but not the vehicle) was registered to a friend of Officer J. D. Tippet. The friend was Carl Mather, who worked for Collins Radio in Dallas.[405] Mather finally testified before the HSCA, but not before he was granted immunity by the Justice Department. His testimony, like others, remains classified in the National Archives. Obviously, Mather knew important information that is *still* secret.

It makes sense that certain officials would not want two Oswalds to be seen in the theatre at the same time. Someone might wonder if the wrong Oswald was arrested. Dallas police seemed to be assisting Oswald 2 as they escorted him out of the rear exit of the theatre. He certainly was not being man-handled the way Oswald 1 was. He also did not end up at the Dallas police station.

When Oswald 1 was asked about a bruise on his forehead, he replied on camera only that a police officer had hit him. Oswald kept to himself the details of what really happened in the Texas Theatre.

What Oswald 1 experienced outside of the public eye and behind closed doors at the Dallas Police Department is a mystery—at least to the public. Somehow or another, two different wallets were found by Dallas police officers, and both were identified as Oswald's. One wallet with Oswald's identification was found lying near the body of Officer J. D. Tippett. This wallet was used as evidence to connect Oswald 1 with the killing of the officer. However, while Oswald 1 was being transported to police headquarters, another wallet was removed from his person. This was just the beginning of the mistakes that were to follow.

The Dallas Police explained that on November 22, 1963, there were no recording devices available, and Capt. Will Fritz claimed that he kept no notes during the many hours of Oswald's interrogation. Apparently, he did not keep notes on his interrogation of Buell Wesley Frasier, either, unless a typed "confession" would be considered "notes." The public saw Oswald 1 on television as he was moved from his jail cell to Captain Fritz's office. He was heard to claim that he was "only a patsy" and to say that he had not spoken with an attorney, though he wished to do so. His interrogators described him as "cool" as he was being questioned, and that he "smirked" at times.

The police reported that his Russian-born wife, Marina, and his daughters visited him at the jail, along with his mother Marguerite and his brother Robert, both of whom he had not seen in a year. When Marguerite and Robert visited with Oswald 1, his wife, mother, and brother felt like he was trying to reassure them that this was all a big mistake.

Oswald 1 did not seem desperate, even after he was accused of assassinating the President. Dallas police were befuddled by his demeanor. Unlike his co-worker Buell Wesley Frazier, who was protesting loudly to Capt. Fritz, Oswald did not even point out the officer who had hit him during the arrest. Dallas police officer C.F. Bentley admitted in an interview to Bill Drenas, Stan Clark, and Ken Holmes, Jr. that he was the one who had caused the bruise on the suspect's face.[406]

As officers like C. T. Walker tried to subdue Oswald, Bentley stated that he hit Lee Oswald in the face with "a vertical butt stroke of his shotgun." Bentley's uncle, Dallas detective Paul Bentley, "then punched Lee, tearing some of the skin off Lee's forehead with the Masonic ring he wore."[407] This was at the same time that other officers were attempting to remove a pistol that they said Oswald was reaching for.

Despite what occurred at the theatre, the Dallas police were determined to prove that Oswald had not been brutalized while in captivity, so he was paraded in front of cameras from time to time. This allowed Jack Ruby to murder the accused assassin in front of the entire world. Because Dallas Police Chief Jesse Curry and City Manager Elgin Crull were more concerned about the reputation of the police department than the prisoner's safety, they allowed the basement of the police department to be filled with members of the media. One of those pretending to belong there was Carousel Club owner, Jack Ruby.

During the short time he was incarcerated, Oswald was subjected to hour after hour of interrogation, though he had no attorney present to protect his constitutional rights. But Capt. Will Fritz had no chance to interview Oswald privately, as he had with Buell Wesley Frazier. Too many people wanted to be part of the questioning. While Oswald 1 was downtown in the police station, an Oswald lookalike was leaving Dallas as quickly as possible. No one would have ever known this if an Air Force sergeant hadn't climbed aboard the wrong airplane. Sgt. Robert G. Vinson's future changed the moment "Oswald" boarded the same plane he happened to be on.

CHAPTER 37

THE "VOICE" OF
SGT. ROBERT VINSON

"That guy … that guy looks just like…"

A s an Air Force Sergeant, Robert G. Vinson became involved in an event that haunted him and his wife for the rest of their lives. For years, he was compelled to remain silent due to a secrecy agreement he and his wife had been pressured to sign. On November 22, 1963, he was thirty-four years old and trying to catch a flight from Andrews Air Force Base, located in Prince George County, Maryland, back home to his wife in Colorado Springs, Colorado.

It was not uncommon for airmen in uniform with appropriate papers to catch free rides to their home bases if military aircraft were flying that way. At Andrews Air Force Base, Vinson signed his name onto the check-in sheet. At first, he was told no flights at all were leaving from Andrews that day. But soon a helpful airman pointed out a C-54 on the tarmac and told him he could fly on it because it was headed to Lowry Air Force Base in Denver.

The plane was familiar to Vinson except for one important detail. "It carried no markings…except for an emblem on its tail that appeared to be a graphic of the earth, rust brown with white grid marks on it separating latitude and longitude."[408] Most planes had "USAF" and serial numbers on their tails. This one had neither. However, it was headed to Denver, and that's all that mattered to Vinson.

Oddly enough, Vinson was the only passenger. The pilot and copilot were two men dressed in coveralls instead of uniforms. Neither spoke to him or asked him to sign the manifest, a procedure which is required by the Air Force. The flight was uneventful until about 12:30, when a voice came over the loud speaker announcing the President had been shot at 12:29. If this time is accurate, someone in the United States Air Force knew about the assassination and reported it one minute before some of the President's Secret Service agents knew.

The plane immediately made a 90-degree turn and flew southward. A little more than three hours later, Vinson realized the plane was over Dallas, Texas. "The plane made a very rough landing, and Vinson saw that they were on what looked like a big sand bar…Two men jumped from a jeep and ran to the airplane. They wore off-white, beige coveralls such as those worn by repairmen who work on streets, highways, or sewers."[409] The two silently boarded the airplane and sat up front, away from Vinson. At the time, Vinson made no connection between the way the pilot and the co-pilot were dressed and the type of clothing the two new passengers were wearing. He did notice that one man looked like a Cuban; he appeared to be over six feet tall. The other man was a Caucasian about 5-foot-7 to 5-foot-9.

Approximately two hours later, the plane landed, but not in Denver. Vinson watched as the pilot, co-pilot, and the other two passengers departed quickly, leaving him sitting alone on the airplane. It was dark outside, but Vinson knew this was not his destination. Nevertheless, he grabbed his bag, exited the plane, and walked towards the only building that was lit. Inside was an Air Policeman. When Vinson inquired as to where he was, the airman replied, "You're at Roswell [Walker] Air Force Base in Roswell, New Mexico."[410]

Vinson explained that he needed to get to Colorado Springs, but the airman stated firmly that the base was under full alert and that no one could enter or leave. Both the airman and Vinson knew that a plane had just landed, but neither commented on that. The base alert was not lifted until almost 9:00; that's when Vinson managed to catch a bus to Colorado Springs. There, his wife Bobbie broke the news that the President had died. Vinson shared the strange and incredible story of his trip home from Andrews Air Force Base, including the odd behavior of the pilots and his fellow passengers. His story became stranger the next day.

On Sunday, November 24, while watching the transfer of Lee Harvey Oswald, Vinson startled his wife by announcing, "That guy … that guy looks just like the little guy on the airplane. I swear that is the little guy that got on the plane."[411] The "little guy" he pointed to was Lee Harvey Oswald, and in a matter of moments, he lay on the floor, fatally wounded.

Both Vinson's wife and his brother advised him to keep quiet about what he had experienced, and he did so for forty years. Not until 2003, in his book *Flight from Dallas,* did Vinson publicly speculate on the Oswald look-alike and how he and the two crewmen may have been involved in Kennedy's assassination.

As a "reward" for his silence, the CIA insisted he work for it, despite the fact that Vinson did not have the abilities nor the skills typically needed by the "Company." "Perhaps, as far as the CIA was concerned, Robert Vinson had been bought and paid for."[412] If he had known how many other people witnessed Oswald look-alikes, he might have stepped out of the shadows and told his story sooner.

But on that day in November, the idea that an Oswald doppelganger might have escaped while a "patsy" took the fall for two murders was not even being considered. Robert Vinson was one of the few who knew of that possibility. Once he became an employee of the CIA, he learned that airplanes like the one he had inadvertently flown on the day Kennedy died were owned and used by the CIA. Robert Vinson suddenly realized that the same organization that had quickly recruited him in 1965 had assisted an Oswald look-alike leave Dallas shortly after the assassination. Considering how dangerous knowledge like this could be, Vinson was fortunate to have been temporarily sworn to secrecy instead of being permanently silenced.

CHAPTER 38

A BACKGROUND OF SHADOWS

"If George's death was engineered, it is because you focused such attention on my husband that the real conspirators decided to eliminate him."
—Mrs. George de Mohrenschildt

S gt. Vinson knew nothing about the background of the young man who resembled Lee Harvey Oswald. As someone unfortunate enough to realize there was more to the assassination than the Warren Commission reported, he deliberately did not seek further knowledge about either Oswald.

The same cannot be said for a great number of researchers. Despite the FBI's assurances that Oswald was guilty of killing President Kennedy and that the case was closed, certain individuals continued to research Oswald's background. Some of the information they uncovered caused consternation for certain members of the FBI, for the Dallas Police Department, for some members of the intelligence community, and for the Secret Service. It may have caused life-threatening problems for people like George De Mohrenschildt.

Some of the discrepancies about Oswald's background did not fit into the official propaganda being fed to the American public. There is official evidence that a "Lee Harvey Oswald" defected to Russia in 1959. There is also evidence that a "Lee Harvey Oswald" resided in Minsk, Russia, and that he married a Russian girl and fathered a daughter. The FBI, the CIA, and hundreds of historical researchers discovered a great deal of information about the man accused of killing President Kennedy, but not all of it was made available to the public.

Family records indicate that an "Oswald" was connected by family to Carlos Marcello, head of the New Orleans crime family. Oswald's paternal uncle, Dutz Murret, was a runner for Carlos Marcello and his crime family.

Newspaper articles show that in 1963, an "Oswald" pretended to be a Cuban sympathizer, which connected him to Castro expatriates. This is the Oswald photographed in New Orleans handing out "Fair Play for Cuba" pamphlets. This was the same "Oswald" who debated Carlos Bringuier and Edward Scannell Butler on a radio program titled *Conversation Carte Blanche* on August 21, 1963 in New Orleans.[413]

There is evidence that an "Oswald" may have been connected to the Secret Service when he worked at the Reily Coffee Company in New Orleans during this time. This evidence comes from Adrian Alba. Alba's garage was located next door to the Reily Coffee Company. He had a contract with the Secret Service to garage three of its cars. Alba saw Oswald walk to his garage almost every day.

Alba recalled that on one particular day, a man driving a Secret Service car identified himself as an FBI agent. Alba remembers this because it would have been quite unusual for an FBI agent to drive a Secret Service car because the FBI had its own garage where it housed its cars.

Alba saw the man who identified himself as FBI pull over to the curb. He then noticed Lee Harvey Oswald walk over to the Secret Service car and receive an envelope from the driver. Oswald bent over and, Alba assumed, hid the envelope under his shirt, because when he turned around, Oswald had nothing in his hand.[414]

Alba's observation suggests that Oswald walked daily to Alba's garage to do more than just drink Cokes and read magazines. The garage was the perfect place for him to meet Secret Service contacts. Undoubtedly, he never intended for Alba to notice this brief meeting between himself and a Secret Service agent who had *pretended* to be an FBI agent.

Documents show that an Oswald also had connections to the FBI. It is known that Oswald asked to speak to FBI Special Agent John Quigley in New Orleans after his arrest on August 10, 1963. Texas Attorney General Waggoner Carr believed that Lee Harvey Oswald was a FBI informant. He stated this to the Warren Commission. Carr was told that Oswald had been recruited as an FBI informant in September of 1962 and been given informant number S-179.[415] Carr and the Secret Service informed the Warren Commission about this detail. Journalist Alonzo Hudkins refused to name his source for this information, but he felt confident enough to raise the question in an article in the Houston *Post*.[416]

Little did Hudkins know that in 2005 a memorandum from James J. Rowley, the chief of the Secret Service, to John McCone, Director of the CIA, would surface. Dated March 3, 1964, and stamped CONFIDENTIAL, it stated: "Oswald subject was trained by this agency, under cover of the office of Naval Intelligence...During preliminary training during 1957, subject was active in aerial reconnaissance...Subject received additional indoctrination at our own Camp Peary Site from September 8-October 17, 1958...While in the Soviet Union, he was on special assignment in the area of Minsk...It would not be advantageous at this time to divulge the specifics of that assignment...*At the time of the Dallas action, the Oswald subject was only seldom in our employ* [italics added by the authors]"[417]

This memo has caused quite a controversy in the research community.

Some researchers still maintain that it is a hoax. Others are unsurprised that the original cannot be found. After all, neither the Secret Service nor the CIA would ever admit, even today, that any government agency used Lee Harvey Oswald as an agent or informant.

There is evidence that at least one Oswald was obviously connected to government intelligence. CIA contract employee Gerry Patrick Hemming reported that the owner of Reily Coffee worked for the CIA for years.[418] Oswald obtained employment at Reily on May 9, 1963. This does not mean that every Reily Coffee Company employee was connected to the CIA, but it is likely that some CIA informants probably found employment there.

An "Oswald" applied for a job at Mason Marble and Granite at the end of July. One of the references he listed was a "Charles Harrison," whom he claimed worked at Tulane University.[419] "Charles Harrison" might be the same "Charles *Harrelson*" who would soon accompany Oswald to the home of Elmer and Marietta Gerhart in Houston.

In Marina Oswald's testimony to the Warren Commission, she claimed that her husband had only one friend in Dallas from August 1962 until April 1963. That friend was George de Mohrenschildt. He was a 52-year-old Russian geologist and petroleum engineer. This man belonged to many distinguished circles—from Dallas' White Russian community to Texas oil magnates. He was associated with the Bush family and even knew the family of Jacqueline Kennedy.

De Mohrenschildt arrived in the United States in 1938 and, by 1941, the FBI had information about him in their open "Internal Security" files. He was under surveillance as a suspected spy from 1941 until the day he died.

Gary Taylor, de Mohrenschildt's son-in-law, admitted in his testimony to the Warren Commission that he believed his father-in-law was a spy. Taylor felt that his father-in-law was the controller for Oswald and that he had told Oswald where to live and where to work.[420]

This could explain how Oswald became an employee of the Jagger-Chiles-Stovall firm. It specialized in commercial photography, as well as top-secret work for the Department of Defense. Dennis Hyman Ofstein, a fellow employee at this firm, stated in his Warren Commission testimony dated March 30, 1964 that he thought Oswald went to Russia as an agent for the United States government.[421] Ofstein and Oswald had more in common than their positions at Jagger-Chiles-Stovall. Ofstein admitted to attending the Military Language School in Monterey, California. A comment made by Warren Commissioner Lee Rankin during a Warren Commission executive session on January 27, 1964, indicates that the Commissioners knew Oswald *also* had attended the Monterey

Language School. "...We are trying to run that down to find out what he studied at the Monterey School of the Army in the way of languages," Rankin stated to fellow Commissioners.[422]

There is some question as to what language or languages Oswald studied at the language school; Ofstein specialized in Russian. It could be mere coincidence that these two men later met in Dallas at Jagger-Chiles-Stovall. An important questions is: Did Oswald have access to the highly classified material this company was working on for the Department of Defense? Regardless of the answer to that question, it seems almost unbelievable that he was able to obtain a job at a top-secret firm after defecting to Russia.

Some researchers have suggested that George de Mohrenschildt helped Oswald obtain his job at Jaggers-Chiles-Stovall. He may have also been the man who introduced Ruth and Michael Paine to the Oswalds, before the Oswalds moved to New Orleans in the summer of 1963.The Oswalds and the de Mohrenschildts saw each other often. If de Mohrenschildt was one of Oswald's handlers, as de Mohrenschildt's son-in-law claimed he was, then de Mohrenschildt must have turned this responsibility over to someone else in New Orleans. Instead of following the Oswalds to Louisiana, he and his wife moved to Haiti—six months before the assassination.

George de Mohrenschildt was conveniently out of the country when the man he had taken under his wing was accused of killing two men, one of whom was the President of the United States. According to Joan Mellen, in her book *Our Man in Haiti*, when de Mohrenschildt heard about the assassination of Kennedy, the assassin's name was said to be "Lee."

"Could it be *Lee* Oswald?" he immediately asked.[423] There is no reason why de Mohrenschildt should connect the common name "Lee" to Lee Harvey Oswald unless he knew much more about him than he ever admitted to the Warren Commission. After the assassination, de Mohrenschildt's comments about Oswald varied from time to time. Some of his comments about Oswald were derogatory. In fact, he wrote an unpublished manuscript titled "I Am a Patsy, I Am a Patsy." In it, he described Oswald as a man focused on assassinations. At other times, he indicated that Oswald was not capable of killing President Kennedy.[424]

What de Mohrenschildt really knew about Oswald and about the Kennedy assassination may have weighed heavily on him. By 1977, he seemed ready to share information with investigators. Oddly enough, on the day of his sudden death, he was interviewed by journalist Edward Jay Epstein. He admitted to Epstein that he had been ordered by the CIA to monitor Oswald.

Before Epstein was able to continue the interview, which was interrupted by lunch, de Mohrenschildt was dead. According to the coroner, he killed himself with a single shot to his head. His wife argued that, despite some mental problems, her husband had not been suicidal.

"...If George's death was engineered, it is because you focused such attention on my husband that the real conspirators decided to eliminate him just in case George actually knew something, just like so many others involved in the assassination," she told the Dutch journalist Willems Oltmans after her husband's death.[425]

Numerous characters like de Mohrenschildt attempted to leave the shadows that surrounded the Kennedy assassination by sharing their secrets. One of the characters in the assassination drama who can never step out of the shadows is Kennedy's accused assassin, Lee Harvey Oswald. The world may never know if he was truly guilty, as the Warren Report claimed.

If the President was actually shot by someone from the Depository, then Oswald, like every other employee in the building, had a narrow window of opportunity to kill him. Because of his job description, he had access to all seven floors, which was not true for all employees. However, of all the groups named as possible suspects in the assassination— the CIA, J. Edgar Hoover, anti-Castro Cubans, the military complex, the Mafia, Texas oilmen, Kennedy's successor, Lyndon Johnson, and possibly a Greek billionaire—Oswald had less motive than any of them.

At first, the world assumed he was desperate for attention and wanted his time in the spotlight. However, Oswald never admitted he had anything to do with the killing of a Dallas police officer or the President of the United States. If what he wanted was attention, then all he had to do was confess to both these murders.

Despite what was described as an "open and shut case" by Dallas District Attorney Henry Wade, the Dallas Chief of Police Jesse Curry admitted after Oswald's death that there was no evidence that actually placed Lee Harvey Oswald on the sixth floor of the Depository during the killing of the President.

On the other hand, was Lee Harvey Oswald the ordinary boy-next-door who just happened to be in the wrong place at the wrong time? Some believe that the young man who made the mistake of defecting to the Soviet Union because he was disenchanted with his homeland was nothing more than the "patsy" he claimed to be. However, his actions before, during, and after the assassination leave questions that are difficult to answer.

For example, Oswald supposedly wrote a letter to the Soviet Embassy while staying in Irving. Ruth Paine claimed that Oswald even used her typewriter, which offended her. In the letter, the writer referred to a recent visit to Mexico

City and made the comment that he had wanted to extend his Mexican visa, but in order to do so, he would have had "to use his real name."[426] If this letter, which was never dusted for fingerprints, had been written by Oswald, then it certainly raises numerous questions.

Why would an ordinary American citizen ever use an alias? If Oswald was as disgusted with the Soviet Union, as he claimed to be when he returned to the United States in 1962, why was he reaching out to the Soviet Embassy on November 9, 1963? Perhaps the most important question is: Did Oswald actually write this letter, or did someone else create it to link him to a trip to Mexico City and to subversive activities? It seems obvious that Lee Harvey Oswald, whether an assassin or a patsy, was not just an *ordinary* American citizen. *Ordinary* American citizens do not need "handlers" like the Paines and de Mohrenschildt. *Ordinary* American citizens do not use aliases instead of their "real names." Intelligence agents and spies often do.

Although it was widely reported that Oswald was the only employee to leave the Depository after the assassination, this is not true. He was, however, the only one who went home, retrieved his pistol, and went to a movie theatre near his boarding house. Though he bought popcorn, he did not sit down and enjoy the movie. Instead, as other patrons reported, he moved from seat to seat, always sitting next to someone. This would make one think he planned on meeting someone in the theatre.

For a twenty-four-year-old arrested for killing a police officer, a crime of the utmost seriousness anywhere in the United States, Oswald appeared calmer than one would expect. Capt. Will Fritz of the Dallas Police Department commented after Oswald's death that Oswald seemed to be familiar with interrogation methods and strategies. Perhaps this is why he did not seem frightened when interviewed by reporters. Perhaps he also had convinced himself that there was not enough evidence to convict him.

Some people suspect that Oswald played *some* role in the assassination of the President, even if it was an inadvertent one. There is circumstantial evidence that he became involved in a dangerous game with the CIA, FBI, and the Mafia from which he was unable to completely extricate himself. Perhaps he was deliberately standing where his supervisor, Roy Truly, and Dallas Police Officer Marion Baker saw him in the Depository. After all, if a person wanted to make it clear he was nowhere near any upper floors during an assassination attempt, he might very well deliberately stand in the open drinking a Coke so others would notice him.

If Oswald realized ahead of time that authorities could quickly determine a man's ability to fire three shots, hide a rifle among boxes of books, run down

THE LONE STAR SPEAKS

four flights of stairs without anyone seeing or hearing him, purchase a Coke, open it, and begin drinking it, he might have pushed his way through the front doors and into the crowd of people standing on the steps of the Depository. Then his photo would have been among those observing the motorcade. At least he would have had witnesses to prove his whereabouts.

Realistically, no assassin would bring his weapon wrapped in a paper sack and let the person driving him to work see it. Oswald must have known that others might see the package as he walked from the parking lot to the Depository and into the building that morning. As a former Marine, he knew that even a dismantled rifle is longer than curtain rods.

Once Oswald was in jail, he must have felt relatively safe. As he was being walked to the basement of the Dallas Police Department to be transferred to the Sheriff's Department, Detective Jim Leavelle commented to him, "If someone tries to shoot you, I hope he's as good a shot as you are."[427]

"No one's gonna try to shoot me," Oswald replied calmly. He may have realized there was insufficient evidence to convict him in a court of law, as Chief Curry later indicated, or perhaps he knew he was innocent of both shootings, and eventually a lawyer would be able to prove it. This may explain why he coolly faced a basement packed with reporters, photographers, and law enforcement—plus an armed night-club owner.

None of the individuals pushing and shoving each other to capture a prize-winning comment or photograph had been searched for weapons. Oswald could have been gunned down by any of those waiting in the basement. The surprised expression on the accused assassin's face indicated he had certainly not anticipated his own assassination. Like most other Americans, he assumed he would be allowed to defend himself in a court of law. Sadly, the lack of security in the Dallas Police Department sealed his fate. Years later, George de Mohrenschildt, a man who had "befriended" Oswald, may have had his fate sealed by the fact that he began to talk to a reporter.

VI
DALLAS IN
BLUNDERLAND

The mistakes made in Dallas before, during, and after the assassination allowed President John F. Kennedy and Lee Harvey Oswald to be murdered; they then contributed to the inaccuracies found in Secret Service reports, police reports, FBI reports, and eventually, even in the Warren Report.

CHAPTER 39

THE VOICE OF JACK HARDY

**"Oh, he sorta resembled that guy that they later
arrested for the assassination..."**

Blunders involving the President's security began well before he reached Dallas. Throughout his administration, President Kennedy struggled with the idea that security was a necessary evil. He understood that Secret Service agents were required to follow certain procedures even if it meant trading their lives for his. However, everyone on his security detail knew that he also insisted on a certain amount of privacy. This sometimes caused problems for the agents. Shortly before Kennedy's trip to Texas, San Antonio police detective Jack Hardy witnessed Secret Service agents discussing how the President wanted security handled despite known threats against his life.

Both FBI and Secret Service agents were accustomed to threats being made against the President. They had been dealing with them for almost three years. Early in November 1963, the FBI in Chicago received a telephone tip from a man who identified himself only as "Lee." He warned that a group of conspirators was planning to kill the President. The FBI took this warning so seriously that on November 2, they, the Chicago police, and the Secret Service acted to circumvent a possible assassination.

In Tampa, Florida, on November 18, the route of the presidential motorcade was altered because of plausible threats to the President's life. Were extra precautions not taken in Texas because the President did not want them, or because security became lackadaisical once Kennedy arrived in Dallas? The FBI and the Secret Service listened to the threats in Chicago and Tampa, took them seriously, and made sure the President was kept safe. Their behavior seemd to be different in Dallas.

Detective Hardy knew that security protocols were followed in San Antonio, and apparently, in Houston and Ft. Worth as well. However, in Dallas, local law enforcement, Dallas FBI, and local and White House Secret Service agents either violated various security measures before the assassination or ignored evidentiary protocols afterwards.

Though there were no documented threats against the President in San Antonio, there were some in Houston. The November 23, 1963, issue of the *The*

Dallas Times Herald carried a small story reporting that threats had been made against President Kennedy while he was in Houston. Houston's Police Chief, H. Buddy McGill, told a reporter that the Houston police had received four telephone calls threatening the President's life while he was visiting that city. McGill and his officers followed procedures and turned this information over to the Secret Service. The Houston police were unable to trace the calls, but they knew the Secret Service should be aware of these threats. McGill confided some specific information that was hauntingly accurate.

"The President should wear his bullet-proof vest," one caller warned.[428] Whether this was a warning or a threat, the Secret Service did not use this information effectively in Dallas, because, as it turned out, the President did, indeed, need a bullet-proof vest, or at least a bubble-top on his convertible. If the FBI and the Secret Service had taken this warning as seriously as they should have, they would have surrounded the President with motorcycle officers and Secret Service agents, whether Kennedy liked it or not.

This did not happen, even in San Antonio. Detective Hardy remembered vividly that the San Antonio police were told by the Secret Service that the "President did not want agents on the back of his limousine."[429] Later, in Dallas, a similar comment was heard by Capt. Perdue Lawrence of the Dallas Police: "I heard one of the Secret Service men say that President Kennedy did not desire any motorcycle officer directly on any side of him, between him and the crowd."[430] Hardy also recalled a discussion among security personnel about a possible bomb threat.

According to Hardy, the San Antonio police believed that the President himself was taking unnecessary risks. After all, the official limousine was equipped with a special bubble-top cover. Though it was not bullet-proof, it might deflect a bullet and would would make an assassin's view more difficult. However, Hardy remembered a Secret Service agent "quoting" President Kennedy as saying he "did not want the bubble-top on; he wanted that God-damned bubble-top sent back to D.C."[431]

The only unusual occurrence that Hardy recalled in San Antonio on November 21, 1963 was minor but, nonetheless, intriguing. Hardy was positioned on the corner of Broadway and Jones streets in the industrial part of San Antonio. He was dressed in his uniform. Before the motorcade arrived in his area, a young man approached him and asked if the President would be coming down this street. Hardy assured him that he would.

Years later, Hardy said that he noticed that the young man was wearing the type of coveralls that mechanics often wear. What had caught Hardy's attention was a Volkswagen emblem on the front of the coveralls. This had seemed odd

THE LONE STAR SPEAKS

to him because he knew there was no Volkswagen dealership in the San Antonio area at that time. When asked if he remembered what the young man looked like, the authors were surprised when he casually answered, "Oh, he sort of resembled that guy they later arrested for the assassination, but it couldn't have been because he was in Dallas then."[432]

Whoever this young man was, he walked away from Hardy and, obviously, did not cause the President any problem that day. Nevertheless, with no prompting whatsoever, Hardy recalled that a young man in San Antonio inquired about the President's route, and this young man resembled Lee Harvey Oswald. The man might have travelled to San Antonio from an area that *did* have a Volkswagen dealership, or the coveralls could have been part of a disguise. After all, coveralls were worn by the four individuals who had flown with Sgt. Robert Vinson from Dallas to Roswell in the aftermath of November 22, 1963. It is possible that the man's inquiry was a harmless one. It is also possible that, just as in Chicago and Miami, an assassination attempt was also planned for San Antonio, or that someone was "testing the waters" to see how tight security for the President actually was.

THE LONE STAR SPEAKS
THROUGH PHOTOS

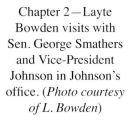

Chapter 1—The
Kennedy children
minus Joseph Jr.
(*From jfklibrary.org/
public domain*)

Chapter 2—Layte
Bowden visits with
Sen. George Smathers
and Vice-President
Johnson in Johnson's
office. (*Photo courtesy
of L. Bowden*)

Chapter 2—President Kennedy's trip to Las Vegas.
(Photo courtesy of L. Bowden)

Chapter 2—President and Mrs. Kennedy on November 22, 1963.
(Photo courtesy of L. Bowden)

Chapter 3—Kennedy and Marilyn
Monroe make eye contact the
morning after her infamous
Happy Birthday tribute.
(*Public Domain Photo*)

Chapter 7—Lyndon B. Johnson plays Santa Claus on his ranch, December 1971.
(*Photo courtesy of Kellye Conger Green*)

Chapter 7—Kellye Conger Green and Lady Bird Johnson at the Johnson Ranch.
(*Photo courtesy of Kellye Conger*)

Chapter 9—James Jenkins witnessed an autopsy but believes there were two.
(*Authors' Photo*)

Chapter 9—Gawler's Funeral Home document shows President's body was removed from shipping casket.
(*Public Domain Photo*)

Chapter 11—Robert T. (Sonny) Davis worked with the Warren Commission but did not agree with its findings. (*Authors' Photo*)

Chapter 12—Candy Barr

Chapter 12—Cabin at Lake Brownwood where Candy Barr lived. (*Authors' Photos*)

Chapter 13—
Campbell was a
top aide to Lyndon
Johnson's
"Man in Texas,"
Cliff Carter. (*Photo
courtesy of Iris
Campbell*)

Chapter—13 Iris
Campbell (center)
or Iris (Cassevettes)
with Jack Ruby.
(*Photo by unknown
photographer*)

Chapter 13 The Johnson White House in Johnson City, Texas. According to a
tour guide, Johnson added on to this house in 1960 planning on it becoming his
"executive office" when he became President. (*Authors' Photo*)

Chapter 13—Cliff Carter and President Johnson.
(*Public Domain Photo*)

Chapter 13— Speaker of the House
Sam Rayburn with protégé Lyndon
Johnson.

Chapter 13—David Ferrie's apartment
in New Orleans where he performed
cancer experiments on mice in the
early 1960s. (*Authors' Photo*)

Chapter 14—Malcolm Wallace (center) was known by some as Johnson's "hit man." (*University of Texas Yearbook*)

Chapter 16—An unexpected partnership. (*Authors' Photo*)

Chapter 16— Democratic Convention— John Kennedy, Adlai Stevenson, and Lyndon Johnson all wanted the Democratic presidential nomination in 1960. (*Public Domain Photo*)

Chapter 17—Officer Jim Bundren arrested Richard Case Nagell in El Paso on
September 20, 1963 and was honored as "Officer of the Year."
(*Photo courtesy of Jim Bundren*)

Gets Football

Pres. Kennedy was to be presented a football autographed by team members of the No. 1 ranked University of Texas from Athletic Director Darrell Royal when the President landed in Austin.

Royal was one of the Austin greeting party, along with other officials.

Had Gone To Press

Page 27 of The Austin Statesman Friday had gone to press just minutes before the tragic news came from Dallas Friday afternoon. The page is still being carried in this issue in order for the entire edition to reach our readers as soon as possible.

Chapter 19—(newspaper)
Austin newspaper had already mentioned the President in the past tense the morning of November 22, 1963, before his death.

Chapter 21—U.S. Marshall Robert Nash(R) led an Abort Team in Dealey Plaza on November 22, 1963. *(Public Domain Photo)*

Chapter 21—Robert (Tosh) Plumlee was a member of an abort team in Dealey Plaza on November 22, 1963. *(Authors' Photo)*

Chapter 21—Plumlee is standing on the triple underpass where he believes at least one shot originated. *(Authors' Photo)*

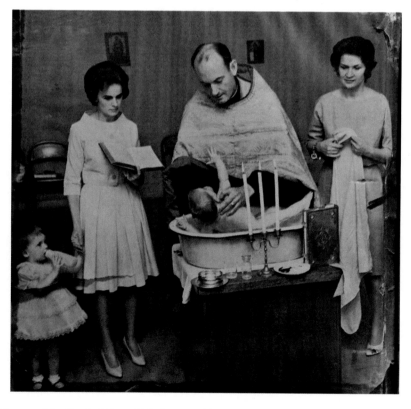

Chapter 22—Lee Harvey Oswald's Baptism Certificate.
(*Photo courtesy of Texas Christian University, the Marguerite Oswald Collection.*)

Chapter 22—Rachel Oswald being baptized. (*Photo courtesy of Texas Christian University, the Marguerite Oswald Collection*)

Chapter 23—Bill J. Lord roomed with Oswald on the cargo ship *S.S. Marion Lykes* in September 1959. (*Public Domain Photo*)

Chapter 25—Buell Wesley Frazier drove Oswald to work on November 22, 1963. (*Authors' Photo*)

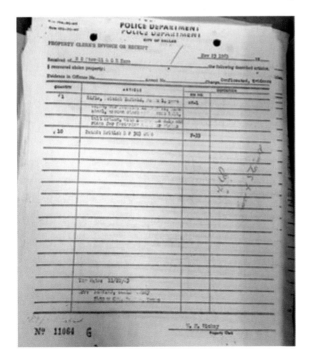

Chapter 25—Police document indicating that a British Enfield rifle was removed from the home of Buell Wesley Frazier. (*Public Domain Photo*)

Chapter 26—The Lovelady family lived next door to Marilyn Johnson, who heard Lovelady's story on November 23, 1963. (*Authors' Photo*)

Chapter 27—Sandra Styles worked on the fourth floor of the Depository. (*Photo courtesy of S. Butler*)

Chapter 28—Cannisters of film from Dr. Karl Dockray. He took photos on November 24, 1963 of the Parkland Hospital doctors trying to save Lee Harvey Oswald's life. (*Photo courtesy of the J. Gary Shaw Collections from the Baylor Poage Library*)

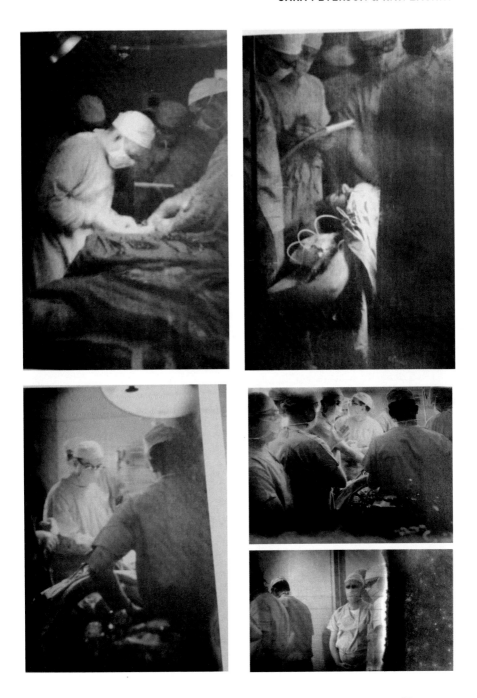

Chapter 28—Dr. Karl Dockray's photos of surgeons working on Lee Harvey Oswald on November 24, 1963. (*Photos courtesy of the J. Gary Shaw Collection from the Baylor Poage Library*)

Copy of original

Miller's Funeral Home

BUREAU OF VITAL STATISTICS

No. 129-1745 ~~Sunday~~

Date of Death November 24, 1963 Hour 1:07 PM

Name of Papers Lee Harvey Oswald

Full Name " " "

Residence 1026 N. Beckley, Dallas, Texas

Place of Death DOA Parkland Hospital, Dallas, Texas

In County _____ years, 13 months _____ days

Cause of Death Gunshot Wount Left Side

Doctor J.P. Pierce McBride

Insurance ?

Social Security No. 433-54-3937

Male   White   Married

Sex   Color or Race   Single, Married, Widowed or Divorced   *

~~Black~~ Brown

Color of Hair   Color of Eyes   Height   Weight

Husband or Wife of Marina

Date of Birth October 19, 1939

Month 18 Day Year

Age 24 Years, _____ Months _____ days

Occupation Laborer - Printing-Book - Sheet Metal Work

(a) Trade, Profession or particular kind of work

Birthplace New Orleans, La.

State or County

Name of Father Robert Edward Lee Oswald

Birthplace of Father _____

State or County

Maiden Name of Mother Margeruite Claverie

Birthplace of Mother _____

State or County

Informant Robert L. Oswald   Brother

Relation

Address 1009 Sierra Drive, Denton, Texas

Phone

Business _____   Phone _____

Remains now at _____

To be moved _____

Day _____ Date _____ Hour _____ M.

Chapter 28—Miller's Funeral Home Vital Statistics sheet
contains errors about Lee Harvey Oswald.

Chapter 31—Marguerite Oswald at her son's grave. (*Photo courtesy of Texas Christian University, Marguerite Oswald Collection*)

Chapter 31—Marguerite Oswald tells her side of the story. (*Pamphlet courtesy of Lora Meyer*)

Chapter 32—Man arrested in Ft. Worth on November 22, 1963 identified as Lee Harvey Oswald.

Chapter 33—Photo of Marguerite Oswald personalized for and sent to Lora Meyer. (*Courtesy of Lora Meyer*)

Chapter 33—Ruth Paine House in Irving, Texas. (*Authors' photo*)

Chapter 34—Elmer and Marietta Gerhart had a strange encounter with Lee Harvey Oswald on September 25, 1963. (*Photo courtesy of Dorothy Cox*)

Chapter 34—John R. Craig, author of *The Man On the Grassy Knoll*. (*Photo courtesy of Dorothy Cox*)

Chapter 34—Internationally recognized forensic artist Lois Gibson works on her model of Charles Rogers. (*Photo courtesy of Dorothy Cox*)

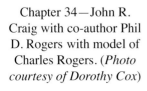

Chapter 34—John R. Craig with co-author Phil D. Rogers with model of Charles Rogers. (*Photo courtesy of Dorothy Cox*)

Chapter 36—Tippit's last mysterious call came from the Top Ten Record store across the street from the Texas Theatre. (*Authors' photo*)

Chapter 36—The Texas Theatre where Oswald was arrested. (*Authors' Photo*)

Dear Sirs.

This is to inform you of events since my interview with comrade Kostine in the Embassy of the Soviet Union Mexico city, Mexico.

I was unable to remain in Mexico city indefinitly because of my Mexican visa restrictions which was for 15 days only. I could not take a chance on applying for an extension unless I used my real name, so I returned to the US.

I and Marina Nicholyeva are now living in Dallas, Texas.

The FBI is not now interested in my activities in the progressive organization FPCC of which I was secretary in New Orleans, Louisiana since I no longer live in that State.

The FBI has visited us here in Texas. on Nov. 1st agent of the FBI James P. Hosty warned me that, if I attempted to engage in FPCC activities in Texas the FBI will again take an "interest" in me. This agent also "suggested" that my wife could "remain" in the US under FBI "protection". That is, she could defect from the Soviet union. Of course I and my wife strongly protested these tactics by the notorious FBI.

I had not planned to contact the Mexican city Embassy at all so of couse they were unprepared for me, Had I been able to reach Havana as planned the Soviet Embassy there would have had time to assist me. but of couse the stupid cuban consule was at fault here, I'm glad he has been replaced by another.

Copy of original in hands of James P Hosty

Chapter 38—Oswald's Letter to the Soviet Embassy in Mexico City.
(Copy purchased by authors from Swarthmore College)

Chapter 40—Motorcade from Ft. Worth to Carswell Airfield on November 22, 1963. (*Photo courtesy of Bill Poston*)

Chapter 40—President Kennedy greeted warmly in Ft. Worth on November 21, 1963. (*Photo taken by unknown guest*)

Chapter 40—John F. Kennedy prepares to speak to a crowd in the parking lot of the Hotel Texas on November 22, 1963. (*Public Domain Photo*)

Chapter 40—JFK at Hotel Texas breakfast on November 22, 1963. (*Photo taken by unknown guest*)

Chapter 40—Breakfast at Hotel Texas on November 22, 1963. (*Photo taken by unknown guest*)

Chapter 44—John Tower was the "mystery man" who accompanied Bill Decker to Ruidosa, New Mexico. (*Photo courtesy of authors*)

Chapter 44— Sheriff Bill Decker. (*Photos hanging in former Sheriff Bill Decker's office*)

Chapter 44—Sheriff Bill Decker's office looked right down Elm Street. Visible would have been the gazebo, part of the picket fence, and the motorcade. (*Authors' Photo*)

Chapter 44—A view of Dealey Plaza from the Post Office. (*Public Domain Photo*)

Chapter 46—Eugene Boone, Dallas Deputy Sheriff.

Chapter 47—"Vaccinator" designated as A. J. Hidell. (*Public Domain*)

Chapter 50—Tramps being led away from the Pullman car. (*Public Domain Photo*)

Chapter 51—Lee Harvey Oswald's
address book page with name of FBI agent
Hosty in it. (*Public Domain Photo*)

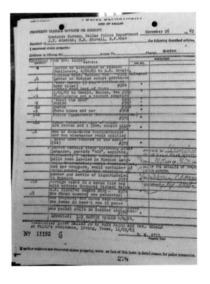

Chapter 51—Proof that Minox
Camera was among Lee Harvey
Oswald's items confiscated by
police. (*Public Domain Photo*)

Chapter 51—Special Agent Ural E. Horton,
Jr. with Special Agent in Charge Gordon
Shanklin. (*Photo courtesy of FBI*)

Chapter 52—Joyce Gordon danced in Jack Ruby's Carousel Club. Shown here are Dale and Ruby together. (*Photo courtesy of Joy Dale*)

This informal, learn as you show school was founded last June by Jack Ruby, manager of one of Dallas' most popular burlesque clubs, the *Carousel*. Located on busy Commerce Street, the *Carousel* is a strong rival to another well-known Dallas burlesque club, the *Theatre Lounge*, which parades its tantalizing Texas bare belles on Jackson Street. The *Carousel* has featured burlesque as its main attraction for about a year.

Chapter 52—Article on Jack Ruby's "learn as you show" school from the magazine *Adam*.

Chapter 52—Jack Ruby's "Cool School" featured in the magazine *Adam*.

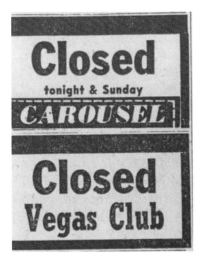

Chapter 54—Newspaper The Carousel and Vegas Club were closed the weekend after the assassination, but not on the day of the President's funeral.

Chapter 54—J. J. Singsong knew Jack Ruby socially. (*Photo courtesy of J. J. Singsong*)

Chapter 57—Joe Brown's Texas courtroom, where Ruby was found guilty and Lee Harvey Oswald might have been tried. (*Authors' Photo*)

Chapter 59—Despite his illegal activities, George McGann (*second from right*) was also a good friend to those he trusted. (*Photo courtesy of James Weaver*)

Chapter 59—Big Spring's George McGann loved automobiles, which he often used to transport illicit drugs. (*Photo courtesy of James Weaver*)

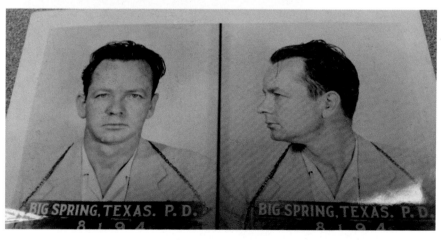

Chapter 60—Charles Harrelson, friend of George McGann.
(*Public Domain Photo*)

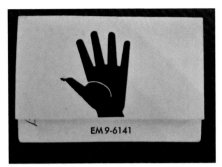

EM 9-6141

Buy your
PROTECTION
from
Joe Campisi & Associates
GENERAL INSURANCE

5526 Dyer   Suite 207

EM 9-6141

Chapter 61—This business card was found in George McGann's wallet after his death. (*Courtesy of J. Gary Shaw*)

Chapter 61—The Egyptian Lounge was frequently visited by Mafioso, including Jack Ruby, the night before the assassination.
(*Authors' Photo*)

Chapter 61—John "Huck" Huckabee admitted hiding McGann's car from FBI agents. (*Authors' Photo*)

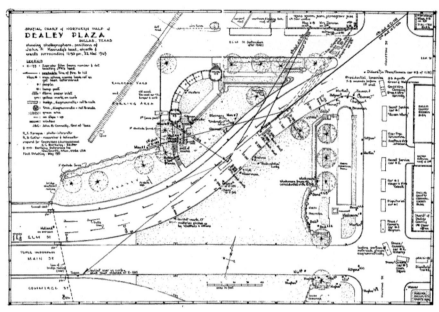

Chapter 64—Surveyor's map of Dealey Plaza's Sewer Drain System. (*Public Domain Photo*)

Chapter 65—Billie Sol Estes stands in his West Texas field of dreams. (*Public Domain Photo*)

Chapter 65—The gravesites of Billie Sol Estes and his wife were moved from Granbury, Texas in 2017. (*Authors' Photo*)

Chapter 67—Jim Bolden's business card. (*Authors' Photo*)

Chapter 67—Jim Bolden used his home as a repository for secret government records. (*Photo courtesy of Deb Lee*)

Chapter 67—Bolden's secret closet, located in a spare bedroom, where he hid documents behind a bookcase. (*Authors' Photo*)

Chapter 67— Jim "Gator" Bolden was in Dealey Plaza November 22, 1963 as a member of the same abort team as Plumlee.

Chapter 69—Midland attorney Jack Ladd saw the Roscoe White artifacts that Ricky White was safeguarding. (*Authors' Photo*)

Chapter 68—Roscoe and Geneva White. (*Photo courtesy of J. Gary Shaw*)

Diary purports to detail CIA plot to murder JFK

Chapter 68—Detective J. D. Luckie's note on Roscoe White's diary. (*Courtesy of J. Gary Shaw*)

Chapter 68—Roscoe White's controversial diary mysteriously disappeared from his son's Midland home.

CHAPTER 40

THE VOICE OF BILL POSTON

"Dallas was a 'colder city'...Fort Worth was much 'warmer.'"

Like law enforcement officials in Chicago and Tampa, those in Ft. Worth were on their toes for the upcoming presidential visit in November 1963. One of the Ft. Worth citizens who attended the breakfast for the President on the morning of November 22, Fred Weaver, noticed that rifle guards were posted on the rooftops of buildings surrounding the Hotel Texas. "He thought to himself, 'It's silly to think anyone could hurt the President with all of that protection around.'"[433]

The President's official limousine had been flown to Dallas. This meant that a car for the presidential party to use in Ft. Worth would have to be procured from a local dealership. Bill Poston of Ft. Worth recalled how a Lincoln Continental from the Golightly dealership came to be used by President and Mrs. Kennedy and Governor Connally on the evening of November 21 and the morning of November 22, 1963. A black and white photo of the presidential party seated in that Lincoln Continental still hangs proudly in the Circle Grille café in Dallas, Texas, even after all these years.

Poston remembered clearly that in November 1963, Secret Service agents approached him about borrowing a four-door convertible to use for the President's motorcade in Ft. Worth. The agents knew Poston as the owner of Golightly Auto Sales in Ft. Worth, and that he happened to have available a white, four-door Lincoln Continental convertible, the only one in Tarrant County. They contacted him to see if they could use it for the motorcade.

According to Poston, the agents told him that they were saving the dark blue official limousine with the bubble-top for Dallas "because there is going to be trouble."[434] They explained to Poston that they did not anticipate needing the official presidential limousine in Ft. Worth, however.

"Dallas was a 'colder city' during those days, and Ft. Worth was 'much warmer'," Poston added. By this, he meant that the citizens of Ft. Worth were friendlier towards the President, and the Secret Service agents knew this.

The agents checked the Lincoln Continental thoroughly and determined that it needed to be serviced; they decided to also replace the tires. It was detailed by the Trinity Lincoln-Mercury dealership in Ft. Worth, where brand new tires with white sidewalls were added. At this point, the Secret Service agents took the car into their custody.

Ft. Worth law enforcement took the responsibility of guarding the President's limousine seriously. Tommy Wright was a thirty-eight-year-old Ft. Worth police officer, one of the very first in that city to work with the K-9 unit. Wright and his partner, along with their two specially-trained canines, were assigned to protect the automobile in which the President would ride to and from Carswell Air Force Base. Wright was particularly concerned that someone would plant a bomb underneath the car. This car was not bullet-proof or armored. Neither was the official presidential limousine. However, the official limousine was equipped with special running boards and handholds, as well as a bubble-top that could be attached to the limousine.

Wright and his partner went on duty on November 21, 1963 at 8:00 p.m. and guarded the limousine until 11:00 a.m. th following day. Their protective routine included circling the limousine with their dogs in tow hour after hour, all night long. Both police officers could guarantee that, because of their strong sense of responsibility, no one had tampered with or even touched the Lincoln Continental that evening or morning.

Poston was correct that the Ft. Worth crowds were warm, large, and friendly. Wright's wife Evie remembered that the crowds in front of the Texas Hotel, where the President's party stayed on the evening of November 21, were large partly because the officials of Carswell Air Force Base had guaranteed that busloads of friendly faces would be waiting for the President. Evie worked for the Army depot at the time, so she was one of those "friendly faces."

"The Army bussed all of us workers down there to the parking lot of the Hotel Texas that morning," she recalled in 2014. "Anyone who worked for the government was bussed to Carswell and to the parking lot of the Texas Hotel to see the President. They wanted to make sure there were lots of people there."[435] Army officials had no concerns that any of its employees would be rude or disruptive.

Inside the Hotel Texas, a large group of Democrats and Republicans, both men and women, were gathered to see not only the President, but also his lovely and fashionable wife, Jackie. At the conclusion of the breakfast, the President and the First Lady were given Stetson hats, which he promised to model on Monday morning in the White House. The presidential party made the return trip to Carswell Air Force Base and boarded Air Force One for the short flight to Dallas. The Secret Service returned the white Lincoln Continental to Bill Poston minus the new white wall tires they had temporarily placed on it. Still a historic artifact, this automobile is now in a museum. It is not the last vehicle in which President Kennedy rode, but it is the last vehicle he rode in *safely.*

While Wright was making sure the President's automobile was safe, some of the President's Secret Service agents were eating and drinking at a Ft. Worth "coffee house" called The Cellar. This was not reported until December 2, 1963, when a well-known, syndicated newspaper columnist, Drew Pearson, discussed it in his column.[436] The agents had not eaten since early that morning, and several of them stayed at The Cellar drinking until the early hours of November 22, even though they were technically on duty at the time.

Despite the comment that the Secret Service agent made to Bill Poston about using the bubble-top on the presidential limousine in Dallas, it was removed as soon as the rain dissipated. This has caused more controversy than any other decision made about the presidential trip. Though the bubbletop was not bullet-proof, it would have acted as a deterrent to anyone attempting to shoot the President. It had been used many times before, and not just when it was raining or windy. But it was not used in Dallas, despite the fact that a full-page advertisement in a Dallas newspaper that day referred to Kennedy as a "traitor." The advertisement had a black border surrounding it similar to one that would be used for an obituary.

None of the newspapers in Houston, San Antonio, or Ft. Worth carried privately-sponsored editorials criticizing President Kennedy. But The *Dallas Morning News* did, and the President saw it that morning before he left Ft. Worth.

"We are headed into nut country today," he commented to his wife. Perhaps the black—bordered editorial prompted Kennedy to make a casual comment to his wife about how easy it would have been for someone to have killed him the night before.

"You know, last night would have been a hell of a night to assassinate a president. I mean it. There was the rain, and the night, and we were all getting jostled. Suppose a man had a pistol in a briefcase." The President had gestured as if he were shooting a pistol. "Then he could have dropped the gun and the briefcase, and melted away in the crowd."[437]

And yet, President Kennedy trusted the men who had already protected him for 1,037 days, so he shrugged off his concerns. He might have been more concerned if he had known that his Texas driver, William Greer, had never been provided with an emergency drill plan, and that he had never been officially taught to cut the wheel and stomp on the accelerator at the first hint of trouble. [438] Greer had not needed any particular training in San Antonio, Houston, or Ft. Worth, but Dallas was different.

The rivalry between the citizens of Ft. Worth and the citizens of Dallas was obvious based on comments heard by Secret Service agents. Right before the President's party left for Carswell Airforce Base, the agent driving the President's limousine visited a local Ft. Worth police officer. "Sgt. Dick Yaws had commented, 'If you have trouble, it'll be in Dallas.'"[439]

Did the Secret Service agent ignore this warning, or did he assume the Ft. Worth officer was exaggerating? Perhaps he took it for granted that the Dallas police and local FBI and Secret Service agents would make sure anyone with a suspicious background would be kept away from the airport, the motorcade route, and the Trade Mart, where the President was to speak to a large group of Dallas citizens.

History shows that the Secret Service agent who thought the bubble-top would be needed in Dallas was correct, but his foresight, much like the fateful dream Abraham Lincoln had the night before his assassination, was ignored.

CHAPTER 41

THE SECRET SERVICE AND ITS TRAGEDY OF ERRORS

"There was a chorus of warnings. And then there was a catastrophe."
—William Manchester

From the moment the President stepped into his official limousine at Love Field Airport in Dallas, security protocols seemed to change. Some Secret Service agents defended their actions that day; others admitted there was a breach of security. There is no question that the Secret Service failed to protect the President on November 22, 1963. After all, he arrived safely in Dallas, but was soon rushed to a nearby hospital with fatal wounds.

It did not take long for certain individuals to blame President Kennedy himself for his assassination. Such accusations came from some of the agents who had sworn to protect him. The stories about Kennedy being uncooperative with his Secret Service agents first surfaced in 1967 with the publication of William Manchester's book *Death of a President*, a book that Jackie and Robert Kennedy authorized and finally approved.

It was common knowledge among Secret Service agents that the President often took unnecessary risks. Manchester stated in his book "…The President was inclined to overrule the Service, which meant that good advice was apt to be tossed out with the bad."[440] (Though Jackie and Robert Kennedy had insisted that Manchester remove numerous passages from the original manuscript, they did not ask that the previous statement be omitted).

Several decades later, Vincent Palamara, author of *Survivor's Guilt: The Secret Service and the Failure to Protect President Kennedy*, extensively researched the statements made by Manchester and dispelled the myth that President Kennedy's demands concerning his security led to his own death.

As Secret Service Chief James J. Rowley commented to the Warren Commission, "No president will tell the Secret Service what they can and cannot do."[441] Fifteen years later, the House Select Committee on Assassinations found that, in 1963, the "Secret Service had possessed information that was not properly analyzed, investigated, or used in connection with the President's trip to Dallas."[442] Was Kennedy a difficult president to guard because he had insisted on personal contact with the public? Layte Bowden, who knew Kennedy well, stated in an email to the authors, "Kennedy was always challenging the Secret Service."[443] She was referring to his habit of pushing into crowds to shake hands, not to mention the times he evaded security to meet with various paramours.

Nevertheless, the challenging personal contact Kennedy insisted on did not affect the protective security measures taken in Chicago, Tampa, San Antonio, Houston, or Ft. Worth. Why were so many security issues ignored in Dallas? Col. Fletcher Prouty quoted William McKinney, who in 1963 was a member of the 112th Military Group at the 4th Army Headquarters, Ft. Sam Houston, Texas: "All the Secret Service had to do was nod and these units would have performed their normal function of protection for the President in Dallas... If our support had not been refused, we would have been in Dallas."[444] It is doubtful that the President even knew how many warnings his staff members and protectors received before the Texas trip. As William Manchester wrote, "There was a chorus of warnings. And then there was a catastrophe."[445]

★ PRESIDENTIAL MOTORCADE ★

The planning of the President's motorcade route in Dallas fell squarely on the shoulders of the White House Secret Service. Though local law enforcement officials were more familiar with the city, they did not make the final decisions. Dallas Chief of Police Jesse Curry emphasized this in his book *JFK: Assassination File.*

"The Secret Service was entirely in charge of arranging the route," he wrote.[446] Because of the route the Secret Service selected, the drivers of the various vehicles in the motorcade had to slow their vehicles to a dangerously low speed. Numerous occupants of the vehicles, as well as spectators, commented on how slowly the cars moved that day.

The film taken by bystander Abraham Zapruder shows that William Greer, who was not the President's regular limousine driver, paused momentarily during the gunfire. Kennedy's regular Secret Service driver, Thomas Shipman, had died unexpectedly of a heart attack at Camp David exactly six weeks before the assassination. Because of Greer's seniority and because of Shipman's death, Greer drove the President's limousine that day in Dallas. Instead of accelerating when shots were fired, Greer looked back at the President, then appeared flustered. Precious seconds were lost that might have saved the President's life.

However, one of the most important elements of the President's motorcade was the particular route it followed.

Secret Service agent John Norris later described Dealey Plaza perfectly when he stated, "That plaza's the Bermuda Triangle of Dallas…Anyone trained in security could take one look at it and know it was an ideal place to get Kennedy."[447]

A route that required a 90-degree turn should never have been chosen. Kennedy became an easy target when the motorcade slowed to make its turn from Main Street to Houston Street, and then again as it slowed to turn from Houston Street to Elm Street. The turns onto these two streets could have been avoided. There were very few spectators waiting in Dealey Plaza anyway, and a route that continued straight on Main Street would have been the safest.

The official explanation as to why this particular route was chosen was that the limousine would later have to jump a small curb to reach Stemmons Freeway. How important was this maneuver compared to the President's safety? Surely, because the Secret Service agents had test-driven the route a few days beforehand, they must have realized that the most logical place for the staging of a crossfire would be in Dealey Plaza.

If the Secret Service agents ordered that all windows in buildings along the route be closed, and that one officer be placed on the rooftop of each building, a sniper would have thought twice before firing. Law enforcement would have either seen him or recognized his location at the first shot. In 1961, Secret Service Chief Inspector Michael Torina specified that "whenever a Presidential motorcade must slow down for a turn, the entire intersection must be checked in advance."[448]

Nothing of the sort was done before the President's limousine traveled down Houston Street or Elm Street. According to Walter S. Bowen and Harry Edward Neal, authors of *The United States Secret Service*, "If the President is to lead a parade, agents and policemen patrol the roofs of buildings along the parade route."[449] No security measures like these were taken to protect the President from anyone behind windows of high buildings or on fire escapes. Manhole covers and sewers were also to be checked and sealed. This did not happen, either.

According to Police Capt. Perdue Lawrence, no instructions were given to the Dallas police to watch windows, "although it was Lawrence's usual practice to do so."[450] On November 18, 1963, Dallas Police Chief Jesse Curry and Forrest Sorrels, the Dallas Secret Service Agent in Charge, rode the proposed motorcade route. "Sorrels glanced up at the Dallas skyline, saw his own dentist's office, and said aloud, 'Hell, we'd be sitting ducks.' …There were over 20,000 windows overlooking the route; obviously, they couldn't have a man in everyone."[451]

The fallacy in this statement is that every window would not have required an agent. Anyone in law enforcement could have stood on top of a building, and by glancing downward, seen a protruding rifle; he could have also observed a shooter in any other buildings aiming at the motorcade. The twenty deputy sheriffs who stood aimlessly in front of the Criminal Courts Building could have been utilized on tops of buildings. However, Dallas Sheriff Bill Decker was following orders when he assigned them to stand and do nothing more than observe the Presidential motorcade.

★ BUBBLETOP ★

Another decision made that day at Love Field Airport involved the bubble-top for the Presidential limousine. The Secret Service agent in Fort Worth assumed it would be used. Once the rain cleared, the bubble-top was removed and stored in the limousine's trunk. Various individuals have been blamed for this decision. Some researchers claim that Vice-President Johnson's aide, Bill Moyers, made this decision. Others say Kennedy's aide, Kenneth O'Donnell, decided the bubble-top should be removed. Still others blame the decision on the President himself.

So who did make the decision to remove the bubbletop? According to Jackie Kennedy's press secretary, Pamela Turnure, the President himself telephoned her twice on the day before his departure for Texas. The subject of the conversation was the First Lady's concerns about her hair being windblown during the motorcades. Perhaps at the urging of Mrs. Kennedy, Turnure suggested that the bubble-top be used so that the First Lady's hair would stay in place. The President informed her that was out of the question unless there was rain.[452]

So, according to Turnure, President Kennedy himself resisted the idea of using the bubble-top even when he knew his wife would have preferred it. The same way he suppressed fears about his own death, he must have convinced himself there would be no unusual occurrences—that no one in the Presidential limousine would be harmed.

The President knew how his wife felt about motorcades—that she did not want to look windblown. Nevertheless, he supposedly insisted that both he and the First Lady be visible to the crowds. However, like every other president, Kennedy also knew that the final decision for the security surrounding his Presidential party and motorcade was solely up to the Secret Service. Several people have "taken the responsibility" for ordering the removal of the bubble-top. The truth of the matter is that several people may have *helped* make the decision to remove the bubble-top.

★ MOTORCYCLES ★

The same agents who were apparently unconcerned about 90-degree turns for the limousine also altered the motorcycle escort pattern that Dallas Police Capt. Perdue Lawrence planned. "During a November 19th security meeting in Dallas with no Secret Servicemen present, it was agreed that 18 motorcycles would be used, some positioned alongside the limousine, similar to the plan used in the prior stops of San Antonio, Houston and Ft. Worth. However, at another meeting on November 21, those plans were changed."[453]

Typical motorcade security around the Presidential limousine in Miami, Houston, San Antonio, and Ft. Worth included two Secret Service agents on the rear of the limousine. Six motorcycles were normally positioned on each side of Kennedy's limousine. Dallas police officer Marion Baker testified to the Warren Commission that there was a last-minute change made at Love Field Airport, shortly before the motorcade began. Captain Lawrence told the HSCA in 1978 that he planned for four motorcycles to be on each side of the President's limousine in Dallas, but Secret Service agent Winston Lawson reduced that number to two on each side.[454] Dallas motorcycle officers B.J. Martin and Marion Baker supported Lawrence's claim, adding that the motorcycles' positioning was also changed. According to them, this change was also made at Love Field Airport. "The motorcycle escorts were told to stay to the rear of the limousine."[455]

★ AGENTS ON RUNNING BOARDS ★

Even more changes occurred at Love Field Airport less than one hour before the President was killed. Secret Service shift leader Emory Roberts told two agents to stand-down and remove themselves from their positions on the limousine. Film of the presidential party shows Agent Henry Rybka jogging up to the President's limousine to position himself on the running board next to the President. Agent Roberts can be seen motioning Rybka away. He and agent Donald J. Lawton, who also thought he would be accompanying the motorcade, were left behind at the airport. Their confusion is obvious: The film shows them throwing their arms up in a questioning pose. By eliminating these two agents, Agent Roberts removed the two men who might have acted as shields for the President.

It has been reported in numerous books and articles, and stated by various law enforcement officials, that Kennedy did not want Secret Service agents riding on the bumper of his car. The truth is that this appeared to be nothing more than a rumor circulating among Secret Service agents. Palamara interviewed numerous agents attached to the Presidential Detail who dismissed this rumor. Secret Service agent Robert I. Bouck admitted, "I never heard the President say that personally. I heard it from other agents."[456] According to several other Secret Service agents, Kennedy had not intervened over the security of the motorcade. Secret Service agent Rufus Youngblood, who was part of the vice-presidential detail, stated, "The agents had assigned 'posts and positions' on the back of the car."[457]

Advance man Martin Underwood had no knowledge of Kennedy ordering agents off of the presidential limousine. Secret Service agent Winston Lawson wrote in a letter to Palamara that he did not know of any standing orders for agents to stay off the back of the car. Arthur L. Godfrey, Special Agent with the White House detail, stated bluntly, "That's a bunch of baloney; that's not true. He never ordered us to do anything."[458]

White House photographer Cecil Stoughton sometimes rode on the rear step of the President's car. (For whatever reason, Stoughton was assigned on November 22 to ride in a car further back from the President's. This prevented him from taking what would have been historic and valuable photographs of the assassination). Palamara names a great many more Secret Service agents who could not verify that President Kennedy insisted that no agents ride on his car.

★ AGENTS' REACTION TIME ★

Still another blunder noticed by spectators and Congressman Ralph Yarborough, who rode with Vice-President Johnson in the motorcade, was that the Secret Service agents attached to President Kennedy reacted more slowly than normal. Yarborough later stated that he was "amazed at the lack of instantaneous response by the Secret Service when the rifle fire began."[459]

Agent John Norris told author Bill Sloan, "Except for George Hickey and Clint Hill, everybody else just basically sat there with their thumbs up their butts while the President was gunned down in front of them."[460]

This slow reaction time of four of the President's Secret Service agents could be the result of the fact that they had spent several hours drinking alcoholic beverages in a lounge in Ft. Worth the night before the assassination. Although this was a violation of the Secret Service manual, no agents were punished for this breach of protocol.[461] Nevertheless, a lack of sleep and an abundance of alcohol might explain the seconds lost between the first shot, which did not kill the President, and the last shot, which did. Could the fact that the President's personal security guards were tired from a lack of sleep and affected by alcohol drunk the night before explain some of their atypical behaviors on November 22, 1963?

After the sound of gunfire echoed through Dealey Plaza, only one of the agents assigned to the President ran towards the presidential limousine, and he was not even assigned to the President; he was assigned to protect First Lady Jacqueline Kennedy. Secret Service agent Clint Hill managed to reach the President's limousine, but not before the fatal shot ripped through Kennedy's skull.

In all fairness, Secret Service Agent John D. Ready did start to run from the back-up car to Kennedy's limousine, but he was called back by Secret Service Agent Emory Roberts—the same Emory Roberts who, at Love Field, removed the two Secret Service agents who should have been positioned next to President Kennedy. Roberts later explained that the speed of the vehicles and the distance between them was too great for "effective protective measures."[462] If Secret Service agent Clint Hill had reacted the way Roberts did, Jacqueline Kennedy, who had crawled out of the car, would have probably fallen from the presidential limousine and been crushed by the follow-up car.

Apparently, despite the fact that Secret Service agents were expected to lay down their lives to protect the President, the safety of Secret Service Agent Jack Ready apparently took precedence over the safety of the President on this particular day. Ready did not rush to the President's limousine as shots rang out. Ironically, earlier during the motorcade, he *had* jumped off the running board of the follow-up car to prevent a youngster from taking a photo of the President.

Had Kennedy's Secret Service agents become lax because he himself took so many risks in and out of the White House? Had he and they convinced themselves that he was invincible from assassins? If so, they were all tragically wrong.

CHAPTER 42

THE VOICES OF MOTORCADE BYSTANDERS

"I was so close to Jackie Kennedy that I could have touched her."
—Shirley Peters

Both before and after the President's assassination, error after error occurred which might have been understandable if Kennedy's trip had been planned by volunteers. But these mistakes were made by professionals, and they affected the ease with which Kennedy was killed. Even some Dallas locals were surprised at the lack of security procedures taken on that day in November.

Years after the assassination, Kathy Reid remembered her mother describing her experiences on the day Kennedy was killed. In 1963, Marjorie Ross worked in downtown Dallas on an upper floor of an office building that faced Main Street. She and her co-workers were thrilled to learn they would be able to look directly down on the President's motorcade from their office windows. Fortunately, her supervisor allowed her and her friends to get an even better view of the presidential couple.

The women were allowed to leave work and join the crowds on the sidewalks of Main Street. Reid vividly recalled that no officials searched their offices, and her supervisor had definitely not been told to close all windows. Photographs in numerous books about the assassination show large numbers of people leaning out of windows and huddling on fire escapes. Because no officials checked any of these spectators, any one of them could have been a professional sniper or an irate citizen. Managers and supervisors of the various companies housed in the buildings overlooking the motorcade should have been ordered to keep all windows closed until after the motorcade passed. And spectators should not have been allowed to stand on the fire escapes.

Another former Dallas citizen, Jill Swartz, remembered having to fight her way through the crowds to get to Titches Department Store. "There were so many people on the sidewalks that some of them had been pushed into the street. The women, in particular, were there to see Jackie Kennedy."

Shirley Peters certainly was. She recalled years later: "I was so close to

Jackie Kennedy that I could have touched her."[463] Peters waved at the President and his wife and then worked her way back through the crowds to her office building. She could not wait to tell her co-workers how close she got to the presidential limousine.

"By the time I got upstairs to my office, everyone had heard on the radio that the President had been shot," recalled Peters, who saw many of her co-workers crying. At first, she had no idea what was wrong. Then she did not believe the words she heard coming from their mouths.

"The President's been shot," they clamored.

"He can't have been!" Peters answered. "I just waved to him." In the length of time it took for Peters to return to her office, the presidential limousine had turned onto Houston Street and then onto Elm Street. The motorcade then entered the kill zone.

Any one of the hundreds of bystanders greeting the President could have used a small weapon to harm him or any member of his party. Just as the President had described the night before, an assassin could have pocketed his weapon and blended in with the crowds. Perhaps it was a miracle that Kennedy wasn't shot long before he reached Dealey Plaza.

If spectators like Ross, Swartz, and Peters questioned security that day in Dallas, why did FBI agents, Secret Service agents, and local law enforcement not realize how unsafe Kennedy's motorcade was? Perhaps it was because Kennedy had survived so many other motorcades. Nevertheless, deputy sheriffs should have been placed on top of buildings along the motorcade route. A single officer on top of the Texas School Book Depository would have been a deterrent to anyone shooting from an upper floor or from another building. An order from the Dallas Police to the owners of various buildings to keep all windows closed during the motorcade would have prevented anyone from openly shooting at the President. One open window would have drawn attention to itself. And if the Dallas police did not demand these precautions, the Dallas FBI certainly could have and should have.

CHAPTER 43

THE VOICE OF GARY LOUCKS

**"Well, you always look at who would benefit most in any murder.
And Johnson did benefit."—Sam Kinney**

Mistakes multiplied as the President lay dying in Parkland Hospital. Traffic continued to rush past the Texas School Book Depository even though Elm Street was now a crime scene. Spectators trampled over the grassy knoll and entered the parking lot behind it. All of these areas may have contained evidence that should have been protected.

Strangely enough, a Secret Service agent contaminated a crucial part of the crime scene while cleaning up the President's blood and brain tissue covering a large portion of the presidential limousine. Agent Samuel Kinney, who had been driving the Secret Service car that followed the President's car in the motorcade, was one of the first agents to see the interior of the presidential limousine after Kennedy and Connally were removed and taken into Parkland Hospital. Years after the President's death, he finally shared some of his most horrific memories about that nightmarish day in November. He also explained why he felt it necessary to deliberately contaminate the scene of the President's murder.

Retired Secret Service agent Sam Kinney looked straight into Gary Loucks' eyes and told him, "You can't kill a president unless it is a conspiracy. One man couldn't do it."[464] This was the first time Kinney had ever discussed that tragic day in 1963—the day he drove the follow-up car in President Kennedy's Dallas motorcade. Loucks shared memories about Sam Kinney and his connection to the Kennedy assassination in a telephone interview. He later added comments via emails.

Kinney and Loucks had been neighbors in Florida for several years before the subject of the Kennedy assassination ever arose. On one particular night, Kinney was apparently in a reminiscing mood. Through the years, Loucks had become more than a neighbor to him. He had become his confidante. Kinney must have trusted Loucks completely because he shared with him stories he had not shared with many others. He also made him promise that he would not tell anyone about these stories until after Kinney's death.[465]

In 1986, on a warm evening in Florida, Kinney suggested the two men have a drink together. When Loucks agreed, Kinney then suggested, "Let's go in the Florida room" (an enclosed patio). As Kinney sipped his drink, he began to muse about his early years, his time in the military, his first marriage, and November 22, 1963.

Kinney reminded Loucks that he served as a Secret Service agent for Presidents Truman, Eisenhower, and Kennedy. But he felt particularly close to Kennedy. Both he and Kennedy served in the Navy during World War II and were about the same age. Kinney elaborated that Kennedy was different with his Secret Service agents than Truman or Eisenhower. Kennedy was friendlier, even to the point of having a beer with them occasionally.

Eventually, the conversation turned to a topic Loucks will never forget. Kinney spoke as if he needed to get something off his chest. His eyes focused on a spot on the wall, Loucks remembered, and he spoke so softly his neighbor had to strain to hear him. When Loucks realized that Kinney was discussing President Kennedy's assassination, his only thought was: "Holy crap! This is historic!" Loucks already knew that Kinney was Secret Service agent on duty in Dallas on November 22, 1963, and that he drove the vehicle directly behind the President's limousine starting at Love Field Airport. Sam Kinney had a front row seat to the murder of his beloved President.

He explained that evening that officially he agreed with the conclusions of the Warren Report. Privately, he knew better. He told Loucks he *knew* one shot originated from the grassy knoll area.

"I saw the smoke and heard the shot," he said softly. Kinney's car contained other Secret Service agents and two of Kennedy's staff members, David Powers and Kenneth O'Donnell. Two Secret Service agents stood on the running boards of Kinney's vehicle. The car followed the presidential limousine all the way to Parkland Hospital.

After the first shots, Mrs. Kennedy's Secret Service agent, Clint Hill, rushed from his position on the running board of the follow-up car towards the President's limousine and managed to climb onto the trunk of the massive vehicle. Hill turned his head back toward Kinney and gave a thumbs down signal to him and to the other agents in the car. Even so, Kinney was unprepared for the gruesome sight that awaited him in the hospital parking lot.

He watched the President and Governor Connally as they were lifted out of the limousine. It was then that he fully realized how much damage must have been done to the President. The car's leather seats were covered by a blanket of red mixed with gray brain matter. The blood spatter, along with red rose petals, seemed to stretch from one end of the limousine to the other.

Kinney's primary responsibility as a Secret Service agent was to maintain the various White House vehicles. So, he immediately had the President's limousine moved closer to the hospital and assigned two Dallas police officers to keep onlookers away. Despite the fact that he was contaminating a crime scene, he recalled to Loucks, he asked for a bucket of water and a rag, and an orderly from the hospital complied. As quickly as possible, Kinney attempted to clean up the blood and gore, hoping to hide the visible proof of the President's wounds.

"He did this," explained Loucks, "not to hide evidence but as a sign of respect for the President. He didn't want anyone to see what he had seen." Perhaps Kinney hurriedly wiped down the interior of the car for the same reason that Secret Service agent Clint Hill removed his own jacket to cover the President's head wounds before Kennedy's body was removed from the limousine. These two agents did not want the world's last memory of John F. Kennedy to be gruesome images they would never forget.

"He did not want people to remember him like that," Loucks added. "He didn't want people to see all of that. It wasn't because he was trying to destroy evidence. They didn't even have forensic evidence back then." It would appear that Kinney, overcome by the emotions of the moment, forgot his formal training. Kinney also admitted another important assassination detail to Loucks, a detail still being hotly debated by historians.

"He said that he was the one who placed the bullet on the gurney in Parkland Hospital."

Kinney found the "pristine bullet" lying in the President's limousine as he cleaned the interior.

"I don't know why," Kinney said to Loucks. "I just tossed it on the gurney." Theories abound concerning how an undamaged bullet ended up on a gurney first identified as Governor Connally's. Some suspected that Jack Ruby, who had been seen by two different people at the hospital, was sent there to plant an extra bullet. Others assumed it fell out of Connally's body. Sam Kinney could have corrected these misconceptions, but it must have seemed pointless to hdo so. After all, the President was dead. Minutes after his murder, it didn't seem all that important to Kinney how that bullet landed in the presidential limousine, and even less important how it showed up on a gurney in the hospital.

As that summer evening in Florida progressed, Kinney continued to share memories that were his alone. He commented: "Thank God, Clint Hill did not fall off of that car [the President's limousine] because [if he had], I wouldn't have been able to stop. I would have run over him." Kinney finally stopped talking; he simply looked at Loucks and said, "Okay, I guess you'd better not tell anybody about this…at least not until I'm dead…"

Gary Loucks kept his promise to Sam Kinney and did not share his memories until after both Kinney and his wife died. Looking back, Loucks realized that the assassination had a terrible impact on Kinney. "I doubt if everyone realized it," Loucks said, "but I did. On the anniversary of the assassination, Kinney would make comments like 'On this day so many years ago...'"

"We didn't discuss the assassination too much after that," Loucks added. "I guess he had gotten it off his chest. I don't know if Sam was dissatisfied with the government after the assassination, but he was never the same afterwards." He said softly, "It was almost like PSTD."

Loucks had no doubt that Kinney truly cared about John Kennedy. "He was *his* President." Kinney also mentioned to Loucks that he, of course, knew about Kennedy's philandering. Nevertheless, it was an agent's job to protect the President, and that included hiding information the President did not want the public to know. So Kinney kept behind-the-scenes activities to himself. He resigned from the Secret Service not long after the assassination.

"He did not like Johnson," Loucks said firmly. "He did not like some of his Secret Service agents or the way Johnson acted."

When Loucks asked about the rumors about Johnson being involved in the assassination, Kinney would just say, "Well, you always look at who would benefit most in any murder. And Johnson did benefit."

Loucks remembered that Kinney talked a great deal about two particular Secret Service agents—Rufus Youngblood, who was Johnson's agent, and Clint Hill, who was assigned to protect Mrs. Kennedy from 1960-1963. "One day," said Loucks, "I walked over to Sam's and saw Youngblood and Hill there visiting with him. So, I just backed out and went home. I did not want to interrupt when his friends were there."

Surprisingly, even after sharing all these secret details with Loucks, Kinney, when asked about possible shots from the grassy knoll, offered the same reply, even in front of Loucks: "Never happened."

Loucks admitted, "I would look at him like 'That's not what you told me!' but Kinney never told anyone else what he told me. He didn't want it told until after he died." Of course, Sam Kinney was not the only person in the follow-up car to lie about what he saw and heard that day in Dealey Plaza. Five years after Kennedy's death, aides Kenneth O'Donnell and David Powers admitted to the future Speaker of the House, Thomas "Tip" O'Neill, that they, too, believed at least two shots came from behind the fence on the grassy knoll. O'Neill reminded O'Donnell, a fellow Bostonian, that he had not said this to the Warren Commission.

"You're right," O'Donnell replied. "I told the FBI what I had heard, but they said it couldn't have happened that way and that I must have been imagining things. So, I testified the way they wanted me to. I just didn't want to stir up any more pain and trouble for the family."[466]

Like Powers and O'Donnell, Sam Kinney did not want to cause more pain and anguish for the family or for the American people, either. However, he must have realized that his actions that day in November would compromise the official investigation. If he had simply pointed out the bullet he had spotted in the limousine and had it immediately placed into evidence, there would have been no question that another bullet was indeed fired into the limousine. Its location in the limousine could have provided evidence concerning the direction from which it came. Its clean condition might have also indicated it was a missed shot.

Kinney may never have admitted that he found the bullet and placed it on the gurney for another reason: he did not want to be accused of tampering with evidence. One bullet hit the President in his upper shoulder, but it penetrated about an inch. It could have eased out between Kennedy's shirt and jacket as the President was lifted out of the car. This could have been the bullet Kinney found. His handling could have removed what small amount of blood stains were on it. A bullet which only slightly penetrated the President's back would have been a "dud." This bullet wound is the one Gerald Ford admitted he "relocated" so it would align with Kennedy's throat wound.

Photos of the presidential limousine at Parkland show a bucket, a rag, and the back of a man leaning into the President's car. These photos were the only evidence that the car was cleaned even before it was flown back to Washington, D.C. Some critics of the official investigation have suggested that this is further proof that a cover-up began immediately.

However, if Secret Service Agent Sam Kinney is to be believed, when he deliberately attempted to conceal the interior of the President's limousine, which stood as a silent witness to Kennedy's death, he did so *not* to hide a conspiracy but to simply help the American people remember John F. Kennedy walking down the steps of Air Force One at Love Field instead of lying mortally wounded in his blood-splattered limousine. Like most people, Kinney had no idea that Abraham Zapruder had filmed the assassination, and that one day the entire world would witness the President's gruesome death.

Kinney's story also raises the question: How many other witnesses said what the government wanted them to say? How many others led the world to think they agreed with the Warren Commission when, in reality, they knew better?

Because Governor John Connally was also wounded during the assassination, he and his clothes were considered evidence, just as Kennedy's were. An examination of his jacket and shirt could have provided valuable evidence about the number of bullet holes and the direction from which the bullets came. Before forensic experts could examine it, though, the clothing was removed from Parkland Hospital by Vice-President Lyndon Johnson's top aide, Cliff Carter. Photos show him carrying two brown-paper bags. In one of them, a nurse placed Connally's bullet-ridden clothes. However, Carter directed Texas Congressman Henry B. Gonzalez to sign for the clothing rather than sign for it himself. Gonzalez took the bags of clothing to Washington, D. C., and stored them, unopened, in a closet in his office. He explained later he knew the bags contained Connally's personal effects, but he did not realize that the jacket the Governor was wearing that day was among them.

Gonzalez remembered that after the assassination, Cliff Carter sent two Secret Service agents to Gonzalez's D. C. office to retrieve the bags. Neither agent signed for the clothing, so there is no way to know their identities. Gonzalez was in Texas and did not discover the clothing removed until returning to Washington, D. C. According to Governor Connally's wife Nellie, the clothes were mailed to her, "unpressed and uncleaned, in exactly the same condition as when they had been cut from him at Parkland."[467]

Assuming the garments had already been examined for forensic evidence, Nellie Connally admitted in her book *From Love Field* that she directed a cleaner "to remove the stains on the jacket as best he could butto do nothing to alter the holes or other damage."[468]

By the time the Warren Commission asked to examine Connally's clothing, his suit coat was already cleaned and pressed. This destroyed any evidence that could have been found. To clean it, Connally's wife dipped his blood-stained shirt into cold water. She admitted this to a *Life* magazine writer, but she insisted she was not trying to destroy evidence. She was only trying to preserve the shirt. She had waited almost two months to do anything to the shirt, assuming some official would want it as evidence. When no one requested it, she decided to take matters into her own hands. Without meaning to, she made sure two of her husband's garments that sday were no longer evidence.

Nellie Connally's mistake was, undoubtedly, an honest one; the "mistake" made by the those who did not keep the Governor's clothing as evidence was inexcusable. Once the Governor's clothing had been laundered, the chain of evidence was broken, and the evidence could no longer be used in court. This might have occurred because the media and officials like Dallas District Attorney Henry Wade already announced to the world that Lee Harvey Oswald killed the President and seriously injured Governor Connally. Of course, it might have occurred so that incriminating evidence of more than three shots could never be proven. Why President Johnson's close aide hid Connally's clothing for two months after the assassination is still a mystery.

Besides the fact that important pieces of evidence were lost almost immediately after the President's death, what is also disconcerting is that witnesses did not reveal everything they knew to investigators. Certain individuals in various government agencies found a way to keep witnesses from telling the world what they really saw and heard. They also made sure pieces of evidence like the Governor's clothing did not fall into "the wrong hands." Not all of these decisions were made to protect the American people. Undoubtedly, the Kennedy family did not want publicized gruesome photographs from the President's murder. But it is doubtful if that was the reason Governor Connally's clothes were hidden. Evidence that either disappeared or never surfaced at all became a common occurrence during the Kennedy investigation.

CHAPTER 44

THE VOICE OF DOROTHY WEAN

"He's scared to death to go to the Dallas PD or the FBI."
—Sheriff Bill Decker

T he story of John F. Kennedy's death and the search for whoever was behind it involved even the American hero Audie Murphy. Information about him came from conversations the authors had with Texas Congressman Ralph Hall. The sister of movie actor/war hero Audie Murphy (Dorothey Wean) told the authors in a telephone interview that Rep. Hall was close to her brother. Dorothy Wean also told us her late husband Gareth discovered a fascinating connection between Murphy, Sheriff Bill Decker of Dallas, a Texas Senator, and Lee Harvey Oswald.

According to Mrs. Wean (who later typed the manuscript for a book that included this story), Gareth shared the following story with her: Two weeks after the assassination of President Kennedy, Sheriff Decker and his close friend Audie Murphy met Wean and his law enforcement partner in Los Angeles, California, for lunch. Wean and his partner (whom he refused to name) were both part of the Los Angeles Police Department at the time. Decker shared startling information about the Kennedy assassination with them. He began by insisting that Oswald had not shot Kennedy.

"'There's a man in Dallas,' he began, 'I've known for a long time. He knows the *entire truth* about Oswald's involvement. He's scared to death to go to the Dallas PD or the FBI…This man feels that it's his duty to tell someone what he knows in case something happens to him.' Decker explained that, according to his friend in Dallas, there had been 'a terrible *double-cross*.' The sheriff then insisted to the other three men that there had been no conspiracy involving his department or the Dallas Police Department.

'I've known all these people too long…I would have known it…Believe me, something as crazy as this … I'd feel it in my bones.' Decker went on to say that he could try to convince his Dallas friend to talk to Wean, his partner, and Murphy."[469]

A week later, a Decker call arranged a meeting in Ruidoso, New Mexico, with the three men and Decker. Wean, his partner, and Audie Murphy flew from Burbank Airport on a small, two-engine plane and landed on a dirt airstrip outside of Ruidoso. Decker was waiting for them in his Sheriff's car. In town, the three met Decker's mysterious friend "John."

"John" quickly told the other three what he had already shared with Decker. Oswald had been an agent of the U. S. government who had been acting under orders of CIA agent E. Howard Hunt. He described Hunt as a "super patriot" who had been involved with the Cuban invasion in 1962. When numerous plots to kill Fidel Castro failed, Hunt devised a plan to "attempt" to kill Kennedy so that the American public would demand a counterattack on Cuba. The "attempted" assassination would look so genuine that no one would suspect it was false. A "patsy" with connections to Cuba would be arrested; that "patsy," of course, was Lee Harvey Oswald.[470]

"John" went on to explain that Oswald was convinced to just fire three shots into the air to draw attention to the Texas School Book Depository. He was then supposed to leave immediately and rendezvous with agents who would help him escape to Mexico while a retaliatory invasion of Cuba was complete. Oswald was also told by Hunt that President Kennedy did not know anything about the "fake assassination," but high-ranking members of his cabinet did.

Only a few members of Hunt's closest men knew all of the details of the plot. "John" could hardly believe that any one of these men would commit treason by killing the President. However, some group of individuals infiltrated the plot and turned a "fake assassination" into a real one.

"John" then slid a thick, business-size manila envelope across the table to Wean. It was sealed and "further secured by red sealing wax about the size of a quarter with a thumbprint impression, a procedure police used to protect vital evidence from being tainted before it reached the court."[471]

According to John, the envelope contained "irrefutable documents" which verified his story. Wean passed the envelope to his partner, who later gave it to Murphy to secure in a safe in his California home.

In a matter of days, Murphy received several telephone calls from Sheriff Decker. Decker said Hunt was desperate to hide his connections to Oswald, and the FBI, military intelligence, and the CIA were also terrified of being connected. "John" had second thoughts about giving the envelope to the three men; he now wanted it back immediately.[472]

For whatever reason, Audie Murphy told Decker that he and Wean tore up the envelope and scattered the pieces over the desert as they returned to California. Decker passed this on to "John," who warned the three men that if they were lying, they would be destroyed. The men took this warning seriously; Wean did not repeat the story until both his partner, Sheriff Bill Decker, and Audie Murphy were dead. In 1987, he included the details in a memoir, but it was not until 1996 when he revealed that the mysterious "John" had been Republican Senator John Tower; by then, Tower had died in a plane crash in 1991, just as Audie Murphy had in 1971.

After Murphy's death, Wean tried to contact Murphy's two sons to explain that important papers were secreted in his father's safe. However, a woman whom Wean did not identify would not allow him to speak to the sons, so Wean died in 2005 without ever knowing exactly what papers were in the sealed envelope Senator Tower gave to him or what happened to them after Murphy's death.[473]

This story is another example of numerous officials "supporting" the Warren Report because they were afraid not to, or because they truly believed another world war would occur if they revealed everything they knew about the assassination. It shows that even the highest government officials, or other important people, might lie to protect national security—a fact that is not as surprising today as it was in 1963.

However, people like Iris Campbell knew this even before the assassination. As she told the authors, "If (Lyndon) Johnson told someone to lie on a deposition, he would do it."[474] Gary Loucks discovered this fact when he overheard retired Secret Service Agent Samuel Kinney lie about his memories of that day in Dallas. Speaker of the House Tip O'Neill learned that Kennedy's closest associates lied about what they saw on November 22 because they were told to. Gov. John Connally only allowed a few people to know that he disagreed with the Warren Report, so officially he is considered to be a Warren Report supporter. Sheriff Bill Decker and Senator John Tower publicly supported the Warren Commission, but if Gareth Wean's story is true, both knew that Oswald was set up to take the fall.

When J. Edgar Hoover announced that Oswald was the only suspect, FBI and Secret Service agents, as well as other law enforcement officials, must have realized they were not supposed to discover, and certainly not publicize, "inconvenient facts." However, many investigators continued to seek the truth, even if their reports would be hidden in the National Archives and not released for years. Therefore, it is unfair to blame every investigator for an incomplete investigation just because their superiors may have tied their hands.

Those who continue to believe that all of the facts lie within the Warren Report should consider how many of the statements in that report are untrue. Victoria Adams wasn't the only witness to discover that her testimony was changed. If witnesses are willing (or forced) to lie even on official documents and under oath, then the truth becomes the core of an onion, with layer upon layer of lies and misleading information covering it. Therefore, researchers and historians must verify and re-verify what is reported even in "official documents" because so many individuals either refused to tell, or did not feel free to tell, what they really knew. They must also consider whether the lies these individuals told are as repugnant as the fact that American citizens felt too threatened to tell the truth.

CHAPTER 45

THE VOICE OF BARRY WALTERS

"Well, I'm not going or talking to them.
They didn't believe me the first time."—Ralph Walters

D eputy Sheriff Ralph Walters was one of those citizens who tried to tell what he saw that day in Dallas. He learned that certain types of information were better left unshared.

Almost immediately after the assassination, fingers of blame were pointed in every direction. Texas, as well as the rest of the world, was blaming Dallas. Even the Texas Attorney General, Waggoner Carr, admitted, "The first thing I thought was, 'Those crazy people in Dallas— what have they done now?'"[475] The FBI pointed fingers at the Dallas police. The CIA pointed fingers at the FBI and vice versa. The Secret Service blamed the FBI, and then even blamed President Kennedy himself.

No one received more blame than Dallas law enforcement personnel, even though some decisions were totally out of their control. For example, both Dallas Police Chief Jesse Curry and Homicide Capt. Will Fritz wanted to have a police car containing Dallas police officers in the presidential motorcade. The Secret Service determined that this would not be necessary.

According to local Dallas law enforcement, the Secret Service made it plain that security for the presidential visit would be handled by the White House detail. So, Dallas deputy sheriffs simply stood on the steps of the Sheriff's department as the motorcade passed.

Dallas Sheriff Bill Decker told the head of Dallas Secret Service, Forrest Sorrels, on November 21 that he could provide an additional fifteen deputies to beef up security.[476] However, on the morning of November 22, 1963, Decker announced to his deputies that no personnel from the sheriff's department would be needed. So, the Sheriff told his men to stand on the steps of the sheriff's department and simply observe the motorcade as it passed by. At least these "unnecessary" law officers were standing outside, rather than inside the building, as some law enforcement officers were. Photographs show the deputies standing quietly on the steps of the sheriff's department on Main Street.

Deputy Sheriff Luke Mooney knew that the deputies were not asked to provide any security measures. Mooney stated, "I was merely a spectator with a number of other plain clothes officers on Main Street. We in the sheriff's department had nothing to do with security."[477] Because of this, several of the deputies were among the first to hear and recognize gunshots as they were fired at the motorcade. Many of them immediately ran across Dealey Plaza looking for the source.

One of those deputies was Ralph Walters. In 1963, Walters worked in the Civil Division of the sheriff's department in Dallas. A few years ago, his son shared a story about the Kennedy assassination with fellow teachers during a lunchroom conversation. He startled the group by telling them that on November 22, 1963, his father and another deputy sheriff were standing on the corner of Main Street and Houston watching the President's motorcade when they heard the first shots. The two deputies immediately ran towards what became known as the grassy knoll area.

According to a teacher who heard Walters' story that day, behind the wooden fence that separated the knoll from the Depository parking lot, the two deputies found a rifle. Following protocol, they turned it over to FBI officials but never saw or heard about it again. The son remembered his father telling him that he and his partner testified to government officials and to the Warren Commission about what they found that day in November. But their testimony never appeared in the Warren Report or anywhere else!

Ralph Walters swore until the day he died that there was a cover-up concerning President Kennedy's death. His son said his father was afraid to talk about everything because "other people had seemed to be targeted when they talked."[478]

A phone call to Ralph Walters' son Barry elicited more information. Only nineteen years old when Kennedy was assassinated, the young man was mature enough to remember November 22 well and also to recall important information his father shared with him. Like most deputies, Ralph Walters thought highly of Sheriff Bill Decker. In fact, in August 1970, he was one of the Dallas deputies who gathered outside his hospital room when Sheriff Bill Decker died.

Walters told his family that he and his partner ran straight to the grassy knoll area and searched behind the fence "because he saw movement up there."[479] Later, during the afternoon of November 22, Sheriff Decker summoned all of his deputies to his office and told them the Dallas Police Department was handling things "and we are going to stay out of it." However, Walters and his partner were called to testify "twice before the Warren Commission."[480] None of Walters' "official" testimony reflects what he told his son about finding a rifle.

Deputy Ralph Walters probably thought that his part of the assassination story died until the 1970s, when two men whom Walters assumed were Secret

Service agents came to his home with the information that "certain people wanted to re-open the Warren Commission investigation."[481]

"Well, I'm not going or talking to them," Walters told them flatly. "They didn't believe me the first time."[482] In his official report to Sheriff Decker, Walters mentioned that several other officers ran into the freight yards, and that he and some other officers began searching the grassy knoll area for about five to six minutes after the assassination. He then stated that he and other officers were among the first ones to enter the Depository through the front doors and that he was on the 6th floor when Deputy Eugene Boone discovered a rifle.[483]

In Walters' official deposition, there is no mention at all of anything being seen or discovered behind the picket fence. Walters' words may have been changed, or he may have been told to forget what he saw behind the fence. If so, this is probably why Ralph Walters refused to cooperate with the HSCA investigation in 1977. As he told the investigators, he told the truth once and no one wanted to hear it. Why would he trust investigators a few years later?

In a telephone interview, Barry Walters said he can't be sure what important information his father shared with Dallas law enforcement in 1963 and with the Warren Commission in 1964. However, he did not deny that he once told fellow teachers about his father finding a rifle behind the grassy knoll, though now, for whatever reason, he does not remember exactly what he told his fellow teachers.

In fact, during the conversation with the authors, he suddenly recalled that his father and his partner never reached the fence area behind the grassy knoll. "They only ran part way up the knoll and then turned and ran to the School Book Depository Building," he said over the telephone.[484] Even Ralph Walters' official deposition contradicts this comment. However, like his father, perhaps Barry Walters is exhibiting the same attitude his father did in the 1970s. Government officials did not believe his father's story in 1963; perhaps Walters assumed they would not believe it now, either. Or like so many others, perhaps he doesn't want his name attached to the word "conspiracy."

Two important details stand out in the story Walters told his family: 1) a rifle was found behind the picket fence and given to FBI agents, but it was never processed into evidence and 2) this information was shared with the Warren Commission, but it was not included in the Warren Report. It's difficult to imagine that a shooter behind the picket fence would leave his weapon unless there was no way to exit the area without being seen with it. Such behavior seems quite amateurish. Of course, that is exactly what the Warren Commission decided ex-Marine Lee Harvey Oswald did; he supposedly left *his* weapon on the sixth floor of the Depository building.

CHAPTER 46

THE VOICE OF EUGENE BOONE

**"There's more we'll never know about how
Oswald managed to do this."**

"We were pretty naïve as a nation back then," Eugene Boone admitted to the authors in December 2013.[485] As the youngest deputy Sheriff Bill Decker had ever hired in Dallas, Boone was only twenty-five years old when John F. Kennedy was killed. He had joined the sheriff's department the year before, with military experience on his resumé. He joined the Army at age sixteen by claiming to be seventeen. This was not unusual at the time.

After being honorably discharged from the Army, he began working for the *Dallas Times-Herald* in the advertising department. Boone was in charge of selling advertising for the newspaper's entertainment section. This brought him into contact with Jack Ruby, the owner of the Carousel Club.

While the authors interviewed Boone in the dining area of his charming house, his wife Charmaine served iced tea and homemade chocolate chip cookies while Boone recalled his somber story. Though 80 years old, he still could not forget the events of that fateful day in Dallas some fifty years before.

Boone had been thrilled to be hired by the legendary sheriff, Bill Decker. "I had been involved with the Young Democrats in Dallas," Boone explained, "and since Decker was a Democrat, this might have influenced his decision to hire me." For some reason, Boone was not assigned a partner like most of the other deputies.

He explained that there were 600 deputies in the Dallas area in 1963, but there were twenty-three municipalities, and sixteen had no police force at all. He admitted, "There was some friction between the sheriff's office and the Dallas Police Department on high profile cases." The case Boone was about to become involved in would definitely be classified as "high profile."

Sheriff Bill Decker was a legend among Texas lawmen. As the chief deputy of Sheriff Smoot Smith, he helped capture Raymond Hamilton, a member of the notorious Depression-era Barrow gang. Hamilton was in an hours-long standoff with the Dallas Police Department when Decker offered to help. Boone grinned, "Decker yelled out, 'Raymond, this is Bill Decker. Come on out,' and

Hamilton did.'" Apparently, Decker's no-nonsense reputation carried weight even with Hamilton!

"His office was always open. He was a 'sheriff's sheriff'...a great man," Boone beamed. He recalled Decker not getting along well with Dallas Police Capt. Will Fritz, however. The attitude of the sheriff's department back then was that "Dallas County starts at 505 Main Street, which is the headquarters of the sheriff's department, and goes out to the county line," Boone stated. He explained that deputies didn't have time to stop and decide whether an incident fell into their territory or not. They simply acted when action was needed.

On November 22, 1963, Boone and his wife were living in Oak Cliff, a Dallas suburb. "It was such a nice little community," his wife recalled. At the time, the couple had an eleven-month-old toddler and an eleven-day-old infant. Boone remembered that members of the sheriff's department were given no instructions about what to do or where to be during President Kennedy's visit to Dallas. But he said this was "not unusual because the Secret Service tells you what they need from you in situations like this. Sometimes they need you for traffic control." He then added, "A week to ten days before the President arrived, the Secret Service came to check out Dallas."

At the time, Boone knew, as did most of the citizens of Texas, that there was "a riff" between the state's liberal Democrats and the conservative Democrats. Lyndon Johnson leaned on Governor Connally and Senator Yarborough to help smooth over the problems between the two groups," according to Boone.

"As a department, we didn't have any responsibilities that day [November 22]. There was talk about Adlai Stevenson's recent reception in Dallas, and talk about the President's safety." Even in 1963, Boone had been aware that the John Birch Society and individuals like H. L. Hunt influenced Dallas politics.

Boone explained, "If anything was to happen, I thought it would be [from] the right wing." Speaking for her husband and herself, Charmaine Boone chimed in, "*We* were just excited that the President was coming." Boone remembered the large crowds who turned out to see Kennedy that day.

"The crowds were unbelievable. Six to eight to ten people deep. They overflowed into the streets." A faraway look came into his eyes and he said softly, "We were pretty naïve as a nation back then."

Fifty years after that November, Boone recalled how he had been thrown into history because of what happened one block from where he was standing.

"I was on the steps of the sheriff's department at 505 Main Street and watched the Presidential motorcade pass by. The motorcade turned on to Houston Street and then on to Elm Street. I heard the first shot and recognized it immediately as gunfire. I started running towards Houston Street. As I came around the concrete abutment [in Dealey Plaza], I heard two more shots. By then, the President's car was going under the underpass. People were indicating shots were coming from the grassy knoll area."

Boone and a Dallas police officer both ran in that direction. He helped the police officer climb over the white fence that bordered the knoll so he could drop into a parking lot behind the area. He then clambered over the fence himself. The other officer ran towards the underpass; Boone went north towards the freight cars. Neither man searched any of the cars in the parking lot. (There is no documentation that the owners of the cars parked behind the picket fence were ever found, and no evidence that the trunks of the cars were ever searched. This is true also for the cars parked in the southwest parking lot of the Post Office on the other side of Dealey Plaza.)

At the two-story railroad switching tower that sat at the end of the parking area, Boone encountered employee Lee Bowers. Bowers had a view of the parking lot behind the white picket fence and of part of the grassy knoll in front of it.

"He told me he had not heard or seen anything back there. So I searched along the fence area and the hedge area. If someone had been back there shooting, they would have had to be standing in the flower beds. But there were no footprints." Boone said he is aware that the story Lee Bowers told later to others differed from what Bowers told him immediately after the assassination. "But when I asked him about what he saw or heard, he said he hadn't heard or seen anything. That's all I can say about that," he said with a shrug.

A controversy concerning what Bowers did or did not see or hear arose almost immediately after the assassination. In Bowers' testimony to the Warren Commission, he mentioned that he had seen three different cars drive into the parking lot that was previously sealed from traffic. Police had been guarding the parking lot since 10 a.m. on November 22. That was not all he saw.

"At the time of the shooting, there seemed to be some commotion [on the grassy knoll], Bowers stated." When his interrogator questioned him further about what he had referred to as a "commotion," Bowers seemed to stumble over his words: "I just am unable to describe it. Rather it was something out of the ordinary, a sort of milling around, but something occurred in this particular spot which was out of the ordinary, which attracted my eye for some reason which I could not identify."[486]

Bowers seemed to be attempting to share information that might indicate shooters on the grassy knoll. In testimony given on April 2, 1964, he appeared to be torn between trying to describe what he had observed and still please his interrogators.

On March 31, 1966, he was interviewed again by attorney Mark Lane. This time he included the fact that what had possibly caught his attention moments before the assassination was either a flash of light or a puff of smoke. When asked by Lane why this statement was not in his original testimony, he explained, "I was there only to tell them what they asked."[487] This may be why he did not mention it to Deputy Boone on November 22, 1963. Boone remembered asking if he had seen anyone firing, or if he himself heard shots. Bowers later testified that he heard three shots, but he may not have realized that they were shots when Boone first encountered him. He may have thought they were firecrackers, like so many other people assumed. It's also possible he did not realize that the three cars moving through the parking lot might be important.

Sadly, Lee Bowers was killed in a car accident near Midlothian, Texas, four months after his interview with Mark Lane. Even his death is controversial. Some claim he was forced off the road by another car; some suggested at the time that he had attempted suicide; his brother suggested he might have had a sneezing attack and accidently struck a concrete abutment. A local Justice of the Peace determined that no autopsy was necessary and his body was cremated.

Bowers' minister, Wilfred Bailey, later admitted that Bowers had come to him and discussed the Kennedy assassination. "Lee did discuss that day with me. He said he saw movement behind the fence. He believed something was going on, but he was never more specific than that."[488] Obviously, what Lee Bowers saw died with him four hours after his car plowed into a concrete abutment and four months after sharing his story on film with Mark Lane.

Eugene Boone seemed to be completely honest in recalling what Lee Bowers told him immediately after the assassination. Both men were functioning under the most extraordinary circumstances. Boone was frantically searching for an assassin, and Bowers was being confronted by an armed deputy. This might explain the discrepancy between the testimonies of the two men.

In his dining area that day, Boone paused as he sipped his iced tea and thought back to that day in 1963. He continued to reminisce as the authors scribbled frantically on yellow legal pads. Boone recalled assuring himself that Bowers had nothing to do with the assassination, so he began to question witnesses who took pictures of the assassination and escorted them to the sheriff's department. He then walked back towards the Depository building, where bystanders and law enforcement were gathered. There, the officers and deputies were split into groups of five to six each and directed to search each of the seven floors of the Depository.

Boone remembered carrying his flashlight as his group was led to the sixth floor. He played a critical role that day in the aftermath of the assassination, though history has not shined as bright a spotlight on him as it has on others.

Boone modestly stated, "I just happened to be on the sixth floor of the Texas School Book Depository Building, and the room looked like a mess. The boxes were stacked four to five cases high. The floor was one large room with a support post. The elevator in the center of the building was shut down. As I approached the north corner of the building, I spotted the rifle hidden between two stacks of books. I looked at my watch and it was 1:22 p.m. Central Standard Time."[489] Boone leaned his elbows on the kitchen table as he described the actual moment when he spotted the rifle later linked to Oswald.

"A box of books had been placed over the two stacks. This hid the rifle from plain sight. I spotted the rifle by using a flashlight. I said, 'Here's a rifle,' but I never touched it. It looked like it was diagonal from the sniper's nest. The two stacks of books formed a crevice, and a top box had been pushed across the top to create this crevice. It had to have been set up before the event," he speculated.

Boone followed protocol that day by not touching the rifle until it was photographed. Lt. J. C. Day, however, lifted the rifle from the crevice and showed it to fellow officers. As a result, it's Lieutenant Day who is usually credited with finding the rifle, but Boone's name does appear on at least two official reports made by the Sheriff's Department and the Dallas Police Department. However, he was never given the opportunity to scratch his initials into this vital piece of evidence. He simply left the Depository and returned to the sheriff's department to write the official report required by Sheriff Bill Decker.

Boone described the atmosphere at the sheriff's office as one of "chaos," and that atmosphere continued for the remainder of that day and for weeks that followed.

"The world press wanted to talk to anyone. I didn't talk to any of them. I referred them to the sheriff." He remembered arriving home late the night of November 22.

"We had two boys, you know," he said softly, apparently lost in thought. His wife finished his thought, "Eugene gathered his family in his arms and thanked God we could be together."

Silence filled the room before Boone began speaking again. Somehow, the warm, cheerful kitchen and the smell of fresh-baked chocolate chip cookies seemed incongruous with the solemn topic at hand. Boone did not speak about the emotions that flooded him on that dreadful evening in November; instead, he moved on to what he experienced the next day.

On November 23, the night before Lee Harvey Oswald's murder, the accused assassin was to be transferred to the Sheriff's department. That day,

Sheriff Decker received information about a possible attempt on Oswald's life. He telephoned the head of the Dallas Police Department, Jesse Curry, to relay this information. Boone stated that Curry told Decker, "I'm under pressure to move him so the press has access." Because of that pressure, Chief Jesse Curry allowed the most important prisoner his department would ever "protect" to be murdered right in front of the media, numerous police officers, and the world. The man who murdered the accused assassin was familiar to Eugene Boone. Like many other members of Dallas law enforcement, he saw him often.

"People don't understand Jack Ruby," Boone said thoughtfully. "He could never be a police officer, but he hung around police officers." Because of his background with the *Dallas Times Herald*, Boone knew that Ruby was known as a "cash with copy" customer. This meant that his finances were so unstable that he was required to pay "up front" for his advertising. Even Boone's wife Charmaine heard about the colorful character who owned the Carousel Club, and even seen him once or twice. On Sunday morning, November 24, 1963, Charmaine was at home with two babies, but her husband was on duty at the sheriff's department.

"Someone reported: 'There's a fight at City Hall,'" Boone said. "Then the report was: 'There's been a shooting.'" Boone was not watching television, but his wife was. Like most of the world, she was interested in seeing the accused assassin as he was transferred from a cell at the police department to a cell in the sheriff's department. Normally, this transfer would have taken place sooner, and it certainly could have taken place in the middle of the night with no witnesses.

However, the media would not have been happy about this. Plus, homicide detective Will Fritz wanted every possible moment to question his recalcitrant prisoner. Consequently, Oswald was transferred in front of a large group of reporters, police officers, and one night-club owner who had no business being there at all.

Charmaine watched in horror as a man she recognized lunged at Oswald with a pistol. She immediately called her husband to tell him what she had witnessed.

"No, it couldn't be Jack," Boone's voice boomed over the telephone, but he would soon discover that his wife had been correct. After years of consideration, Boone has decided that Ruby truly thought he would return to the Carousel Club after killing Oswald and be the main attraction of his own night-club.

"Stanley Kaufman was Ruby's lawyer and he agreed with me about that. But I never talked to Ruby after he was arrested," Boone recalled.

Boone smiled as he revealed Sheriff Decker's personal motto: "Nobody dies in *my* jail. We'll take them to Parkland to be pronounced dead." Therefore, after Ruby's arrest, four deputies sat with him twenty-four hours a day to make sure no one hurt him and that he did not kill himself. Strangely enough, Decker's motto was almost prophetic. Ruby did die—at Parkland Hospital.

Eugene Boone was called to testify before the Warren Commission, but no one asked him whether he knew Jack Ruby. Boone's feelings about Kennedy's assassin can be summed up in one sentence: "I believe Lee Harvey Oswald acted alone when he shot the President," he stated quietly. He added that he does not have much use for conspiracy theorists. However, he weakened his own statement by adding, "If there *was* a conspiracy, it was to get Oswald into the right place at the right time. But I believe he acted alone as far as the shooting goes."

After a pause, he continued, "There's more that we'll never know about how Oswald managed to do this. I've never understood how a man can defect to Russia, give up his citizenship, and then be allowed back into the country." Boone also thought it quite odd that in 1963, just a few years after Joseph McCarthy's anti-Communist rampage and in the middle of the Cold War, Ruth Paine wanted to "learn Russian." Paine was willing to let a Russian woman, Marina Oswald, and her two babies live cost-free with her just so she could improve her Russian speaking skills, even though Paine was adept enough to be a part-time teacher of Russian at St. Mark's School in Dallas. This struck Eugene Boone as peculiar.

His doubts about whether someone assisted Lee Harvey Oswald with the assassination of John F. Kennedy place Boone on the side of conspiracy theorists, even as he proclaimed his dislike for such individuals. And yet, the questions he asked were valid ones. And the very act of asking them made him one of those who have questioned Warren Report conclusions that Eugene Boone supported. If Oswald had help finding a job in a building overlooking the President's motorcade, then Oswald was not the only person to plan Kennedy's shooting. If even *one* person assisted (or controlled) Oswald, then a conspiracy existed, and that would have made Eugene Boone quite uncomfortable.

CHAPTER 47

VOICES FROM THE SIXTH FLOOR

"...It's a Mauser..."—Deputy Constable Weitzman
"...It's a Mauser..."—Deputy Eugene Boone
"...It's a Mauser..."—Captain Will Fritz
"...I believe it is a Mauser..."—Dallas District Attorney Henry Wade
"...It's a Carcano..."—Warren Commission Report

After the assassination, Deputy Roger Craig was up on the sixth floor of the Depository with Deputy Eugene Boone. Craig and Deputy Luke Mooney saw the three spent 6.5-millimeter cartridges before the rifle was even found. Captain Fritz of the Dallas Police Department and Deputy Constable Seymour Weitzman then joined the other officers on the sixth floor. Weitzman was an expert on guns and ammunition. His testimony shows that he and Boone discovered the rifle hidden between cartons of boxes on the sixth floor. Captain Fritz and Lt. J. C. Day of the Police Department examined the rifle but were unsure of the type. Deputy Weitzman, who owned a sporting goods store, determined at the time that it was a 7.65 Mauser. In his testimony to the Warren Commission, he repeated what he first thought on initially laying his eyes on the rifle—it was a Mauser.

He was so sure at the time that the next day he wrote in his deputy's report that the rifle found on the sixth floor was a 7.65 German-made Mauser. In his testimony to the Warren Commission, Weitzman said he told the FBI he had found a 7.65 Mauser.[490] Apparently, the other officers who saw the rifle that day took their cue from Weitzman, who was more of a gun expert than they were.

It is possible that Weitzman and the other officers were incorrect, and that the rifle they were examining was actually an Italian Carcano. The two rifles are similar in appearance, and only under strong light could the words "MADE IN ITALY" be seen on the barrel. According to his Warren Commission testimony, Weitzman misidentified the type of scope on the rifle that day. He had described it as a Weaver scope. Later, he was told that the scope had been made in Japan.

For the record, Weitzman and Craig, under oath and in sworn testimonies, both stated that the rifle they saw on the sixth floor had been a 7.65 German-made Mauser. Capt. Fritz took charge of the rifle, which meant he must have observed it closely and handled it; he agreed with Weitzman that it was a

German-made Mauser. He even ejected one live round from the chamber. This bullet was tested for fingerprints, and *none* were found.

In the early morning hours of November 23, Dallas District Attorney Henry Wade held a press conference at which he identified the rifle used in the assassination as a Mauser.[491] He also stated that a paraffin test on Oswald's cheek was negative for any particles of nitrate, which would normally indicate that Oswald had not recently fired a rifle—any rifle. However, law enforcement officials continued to look for evidence to tie Oswald to the assassination and to the killing of Dallas police officer J. D. Tippit.

That same day, information in reports about the "assassin's weapon" suddenly changed. In news stories, the 7.65 German-made Mauser rifle became a 6.5 Italian-made Mannlicher-Carcano. Some have speculated this was because the FBI had just released information that Oswald supposedly purchased an Italian Carcano rifle in March of 1963 through the mail; he ordered it under the name of "A. J. Hidell."

Of course, all these law enforcement officers, including a deputy who owned a sporting goods store, may have simply confused the two types of rifles. What is clear is that the Dallas Police Archives have *no signed affidavits* by any police officer stating that he found a *Mannlicher-Carcano* in the Depository on November 22, 1963. Does this mean that these law enforcement officers *refused* to acknowledge *in writing* a mistake concerning the type of rifle found on the sixth floor of the Depository?

According to authorities, Oswald denied even owning a rifle. The Dallas police quickly decided that the name "A. J. Hidell" was an Oswald alias because the name was found in his address book and on an identification card. It is hard to believe that Oswald had such a faulty memory that it was necessary for him to write down his own alias. Is it possible "A. J. Hidell" was someone he knew, like the other people listed in his address book? In fact, evidence shows that while Oswald was in the Marines, he knew a fellow Marine by the name of John Rene Heindel, who was nicknamed "Hidell." This same man was from Louisiana and lived in New Orleans at the same time Oswald did.[492] Also, listed among Oswald's belongings is a card showing he had been vaccinated by someone named "A. Hidell."

A receipt with Oswald's handwriting on it was also found among his possessions. It indicated that he "purchased the Carcano through mail order from Klein's Sporting Goods of Chicago."[493] The rifle was sent to a Post Office box rented in Oswald's name. The Post Office receipt for the rifle should have been signed by the person who received it. Oswald's signature would have proven that he had the rifle in his possession at one time. However, the receipt which should have been retained by the Post Office was reported lost by Postal Inspector H. D. Holmes. So, there is no proof as to who actually took possession of the rifle when it arrived at the Dallas Post Office. Any competent attorney would have used this evidence to weaken the case against Oswald.

New information about a Carcano linked to Oswald suddenly changed the stories about what type of rifle was found on the sixth floor. Dallas District Attorney Henry Wade changed his story so that the Italian-made 6.5 Mannlicher-Carcano rifle became the alleged murder weapon. Both Deputy Boone and Deputy Weitzman admitted they had been mistaken in identifying the rifle on the sixth floor as a German-made Mauser.

Deputy Roger Craig was the only witness who refused to change his testimony about the type of rifle he saw that day. In an unpublished manuscript titled *When They Kill A President,* Craig recalled: "After a *close* examination, much longer than Fritz or Day's examination, Weitzman declared that it [the rifle found on the sixth floor] was a 7.65 German Mauser."[494] Obviously, Deputy Craig believed that Deputy Weitzman examined the rifle closely enough to properly identify it.

Though it caused Craig personal and career problems, he told the same story until the day he died. Craig also reported seeing a man matching Oswald's description leave by the front door of the Depository. The man jumped into a green and white Rambler station wagon. Craig also refused to alter this testimony, even though Dallas officials assured him he was mistaken.

Deputy Eugene Boone knew Craig well. When asked by the authors his opinion of Craig's testimony, Boone thoughtfully replied, "I think he truly *believed* he saw what he said he saw."[495]

The Italian-made Carcano now officially called the murder weapon bore a stamp on its barrel: *Made Italy* and *Cal 6.5.*[496] Though the shape and form of a Carcano is similar to a German Mauser, in good light the wording on a Carcano would have immediately indicated that the rifle was not a Mauser. It seems that any mistake concerning the two rifles could have been corrected within an hour or so. It is hard to explain why it took so long for the words *Made Italy* and *Cal 6.5* to catch the attention of law enforcement.

There were other reports of rifles besides the German Mauser and the Italian Carcano being found on November 22, 1963, in Dealey Plaza. ATF Agent Frank Ellsworth, in an interview with researchers Mary and Ray LaFontaine, reported that as one of the law enforcement officials in the Depository after the assassination, he searched the floors after the German Mauser was found and removed. He confirmed that a Mannlicher-Carcano was also found by a Dallas police detective, but on either the *fourth or fifth floor* of the Depository, "not on the same floor as the cartridges."[497]

According to the Warren Commission, an announcer on Dallas television station, KBOX, broadcast that a rifle was found in the Depository's fifth floor staircase.[498] There is no evidence that this rifle was ever on the sixth floor, and there is no evidence that Oswald or any other shooter was ever on the fourth or fifth floors.

These were not the only extraneous weapons found around the Depository that day. A film taken by Charles Mentesana showed Dallas police officers removing a rifle from the roof of the Depository. They carried it carefully down the steps of the fire escape, an officer holding it above his head. There was no scope attached to this rifle.[499] WBAP-TV reported that another rifle was found on the Depository's roof—a British Enfield 303. In addition, a Johnson 30.06 rifle was reportedly found somewhere in Dealey Plaza.[500] How many rifles were scattered throughout the Depository Building and Dealey Plaza, and why? If there were other rifles found, why were they not processed into evidence by law enforcement, and why were the guns' owners not considered suspects? These rifles were ignored, just like the rifle Ralph Walters found behind the picket fence.

Buell Wesley Frazier shed a little light on this confusing situation when he told the authors in May 2015 that he recalled seeing a Mauser in the School Book Depository on November 20, 1963, two days *before* the assassination.[501] It belonged to Warren Caster, an employee with Southwestern Publishing Company. Southwestern Publishing Company was then located on the second floor of the Depository. Caster was proud of his rifles and brought in both a Mauser and a .22- caliber rifle to show to Frazier's supervisors, William Shelley and Roy Truly, as well as to some of his fellow workers two days before the assassination. Other workers verified seeing Caster displaying these two rifles on November 20, 1963.[502] As freely as individuals carried guns and rifles in the state of Texas, there is no way to know how many weapons were actually transported into the Depository.

There is also no way to truly know what items were in the garage belonging to the woman who allowed the Oswalds to live with her in Irving. Ruth Paine, who brought the Oswalds' belongings from New Orleans to Texas in September 1963, admitted she never saw a rifle in her garage. Marina Oswald vacillated on whether her husband even owned a rifle. So, it would have been simple for someone to plant a rifle on the sixth floor and blame it on Oswald. If a rifle *was* planted on the sixth floor, whoever staged the "sniper's nest" may have blundered once again and hidden the wrong rifle. After all, the casings found on the sixth floor did not match the Mauser found and identified by all law enforcement officers on the sixth floor. They did, however, match an Italian Carcano that quickly became connected to Lee Harvey Oswald.

Lt. Carl Day of the Dallas Police said he lifted Oswald's palm print from the Mannlicher-Carcano that was then sent to Washington, D. C. for forensic examination. However, the FBI agents in Washington were unable to find Oswald's print on the rifle. In 1993, Day explained this inconsistency by admitting that the print he lifted was put on the rifle weeks and maybe months before November 22, 1963. This information should have been made public thirty years earlier. There is no way of knowing whether Day was ordered to keep this information private or whether he made this decision himself. Regardless, by not stating that the print was old, Day let others assume the palm print was recent.

Coincidentally, Buel Wesley Frazier owned a British Enfield 303 rifle which was similar to the one found on the roof of the Depository. But it wasn't Frazier's; his had been confiscated by the Dallas police that afternoon from his sister's home. It was processed into evidence, unlike the other miscellaneous rifles found around Dealey Plaza. This is probably because Frazier was a suspect at the time.

If all the rifles found on November 22 had been processed into evidence, and if all their owners had been questioned, there might not still be suspicions concerning the blunders made by various law enforcement officials in Dallas in 1963. And, if those assigned to interrogate Warren Commission witnesses had asked all the pertinent questions that should have been asked, witnesses might have been allowed to tell everything they knew. Of course, if these individuals were only allowed to tell what officials *wanted* them to tell, the stories of what they *really* saw and heard could not surface for years, if they ever surfaced at all.

There may not have been proof that any of the owners of the various rifles were involved in the assassination. But in Dallas in 1963, proof was sought only from certain individuals and only if it verified a story that seemed to already be in place. After all, according to what Chief Jesse Curry told Dallas reporterTom Johnson on July 16, 1964, "We don't have any proof that Oswald fired the rifle, and never did. Nobody's yet been able to put him in that building with a gun in his hand."[503] And yet, the Warren Commission ignored this and named Lee Harvey Oswald as the one and only assassin of John F. Kennedy. The Warren Report still sits on library shelves all over the world, even though it is full of errors.

CHAPTER 48

THE VOICE OF PAUL GOWER

"It was an *exceptionally* dirty bore."—Agent X

Deep in the heart of West Texas is the small city of San Angelo. It is known for authentic Mexican food, fabulous steakhouses, Fort Concho, and boutiques that make it a shopping mecca for West Texans. Rowena, Texas, a hamlet near San Angelo, is touted as the birthplace of the infamous Bonnie Parker, Clyde Barrow's partner in crime.

San Angelo is also home to Goodfellow Air Force Base. What is not commonly known is that Goodfellow has been used for years as an intelligence base for all branches of the military. It is the final training point for military intelligence officers who have graduated from the prestigious U.S. Department of Defense Language Institute in Monterey, California. Military intelligence students arrive at this base for their last exams before receiving their orders for Virginia or Georgia.

San Angelo is also home to Angelo State University. Like many retired teachers, Paul Gower called San Angelo "home." He taught in the San Angelo public school system. In December 1993, a group of his fellow history teachers escorted their student teachers to a restaurant to celebrate. The soon-to-be-teachers had just finished their student teaching and would soon be graduating with teaching certificates in December.

A man who will be identified only as Agent X was one of those student teachers. He was quite a bit older than the other student teachers, who are usually in their early twenties. In January of 1960, he decided to join the 90th Special Rifle Company of the U.S. Marine Corps Reserves. After being sent to boot camp in San Diego, California, he served in the Reserves until mid-1967. It is while Agent X was in the Marine Corps Reserves that he attended college, after which he obtained a job in Dallas as a clerk for the FBI.

He later became director of the Marine Corps in the Intelligence Center at Quantico while the center was being established. Agent X was eventually stationed at Goodfellow Air Force Base in San Angelo, where he retired. It was then that he decided to add a teaching certificate to his degree, so he enrolled at Angelo State University.

On that afternoon in 1993, he and a group of teachers sat in a San Angelo restaurant eating dinner and having a few beers. Because November marked the thirtieth anniversary of President Kennedy's death, the topic of the assassination arose. Two teachers in Gower's group heatedly debated the "lone assassin" theory. Gower was one of the experienced teachers in the group; he listened carefully to the discussion and later shared with the authors a story few people have ever heard.

Gower and the authors sat in a quiet area of the San Angelo Public Library, and Gower seemed to pay unusual attention to anyone who walked through the area. He kept his voice low as he recounted an experience from more than twenty years earlier.

"Another teacher and I moved down to the end of the table," he began, "to discuss our opinions of what had happened that day in Dallas."[504] Gower paused and looked through the large windows of the library, watching people saunter down the sidewalk. "I told the other teacher that the Warren Commission was wrong with their findings about the lone assassin and the rifle used," Gower recalled. While the two men were exchanging comments, Agent X moved over and joined them. The story he recalled halted their conversation and left them with their mouths hanging open.

"I know more about the rifle found in the Depository than most people," Agent X said. Taking a swig of beer, he continued. "I *handled* the rifle that night after Oswald used it." Taking another sip, he added, "I built the shipping box for it."

Stunned, the two teachers stared at him silently. Agent X seemed to enjoy their rapt attention. Slowly, he raised his mug to his lips before describing how carefully the accused assassin's rifle was placed in the box he himself had built. Agent X explained that the box was given to Agent Vincent Drain of the Dallas FBI at 11:45 p.m. on November 22, 1963, and flown to Washington, D.C. for testing. His statement was verified by Agent Drain. In his testimony before the Warren Commission, Drain stated that at 8:00 p.m., the division chief of the FBI telephoned to inform him that the FBI in Washington was demanding that the rifle be taken to D. C. To keep the chain of evidence intact, an FBI agent insisted that Drain hand-deliver the rifle to the nation's capital.[505]

According to Agent X, Drain had two clerks pack the rifle. Drain's job was to deliver the evidence to Washington, wait until it was examined by FBI specialists, and return the rifle to Dallas. Drain and the rifle arrived in Washington on November 23. The rifle was examined by ballistics expert Special Agent Robert Fraizer. It was returned to Dallas early on Sunday, November 24. After Oswald was killed that day, the rifle was then taken *back* to Washington on November 27.[506]

Agent X then made a startling statement about the rifle supposedly used to kill

President Kennedy and wound Governor John Connally. It has never appeared in any assassination documents. Looking directly at his two questioners (us), he said pointedly, "The rifle had a dirty bore... an *exceptionally* dirty bore."[507] Gower's eyes met Agent X's. Gower remembered that he looked questioningly at the former FBI clerk. Gower, a weapons expert in the military, had hunted most of his life. He interpreted Agent X's comment to mean that the dirty bore was evidence that the rifle had not been fired in quite a while—and certainly not two days before Oswald's death on November 24.

"Chances are it had been stored and collected dust particles in the barrel," Gower explained to the authors. "After he said that," Gower remarked, "he looked me square in the eyes, downed his beer, and left."

Another weapons expert who was asked about the term "dirty bore" elaborated on Gower's explanation. He said that any materials left in a rifle barrel could certainly affect the accuracy of the rifle. He also added that a rifle that had just been fired three times would not have had an *exceptionally* dirty bore because the three bullets would have partially cleaned out the barrel as they exited. Like Oswald's palm print that Lieutenant Day described as "old," apparently the rifle Oswald was accused of using that day had not been fired in quite some time.

Is there any way to verify Agent X's story? What *can* be proven by the Warren Report is that on the afternoon of the assassination, Agent X *was* on the sixth floor of the Depository with a Dallas police officer. At the time, he was a clerk for the FBI. No explanation has ever been given for why an ordinary FBI clerk was on the sixth floor of the Depository during one of the most important criminal investigations in the history of the United States. It is hard to imagine why the FBI would trust a mere clerk to package up the most important piece of evidence linking Lee Harvey Oswald to the assassination. A crucial question is: Why were his and a Dallas police officer's fingerprints and palm-prints all over the boxes around the "sniper's nest?"

Agent X's name is listed in the Warren Report. In fact, the report states, "All the remaining prints on Box A were the palm-prints of Robert Studebaker, a Dallas police officer, and an FBI clerk."[508] Agent X's fingerprints were found on several of the boxes tested in the FBI Laboratory in Washington. It is obvious why Oswald's prints might have been on numerous boxes; he moved boxes throughout the Depository, including on the sixth floor. It is questionable as to why fingerprints of FBI agents and Dallas police officers are on various boxes. The crime scene should have been protected and left exactly as it was found. Fingerprints were proof that Agent X and Studebaker handled, and possibly moved, boxes on the sixth floor.

Few people even know that Agent X handled "Oswald's rifle" or that he examined the barrel. Agent X may or may not have learned how many others involved in the testing of that same rifle, or of the evidence on the sixth floor of the Depository, died not long before they were scheduled to testify before the HSCA in 1977. As it turns out, they all died between June of 1977 and November of 1977, and all *before* they could share what they knew about the rifle Oswald supposedly used in the assassination, or about the fingerprints found on the sixth floor.

Louis Nichols, the former #3 man in the FBI who worked on the JFK investigation, died in June of 1977 from a heart attack. Alan Belmont, special assistant to J. Edgar Hoover, died in August of 1977 from a *long illness*. James Cadigan, a document expert with access to classified documents, died in August of 1977 from a fall in his home. J.M. English, who headed the FBI forensic laboratory where the "Oswald" rifle was tested, died in October of 1977 from a heart attack. Donald Kaylor, the fingerprint expert who examined the prints found on the sixth floor of the Depository, died in October of 1977 from a heart attack. William Sullivan, the head of Division 5, the counter-espionage/intelligence division of the FBI, was shot and killed by someone using a high-powered rifle near his home in November of 1977. That seems like an unusually large number of people from such a small group, and all of its members were scheduled to testify under oath, and soon, before the HSCA, which was re-examining Kennedy's death.

While Agent X was busy packing a Carcano, numerous Dallas police officers were still identifying the assassin's rifle as a German Mauser. Did Agent X wonder why an *Italian Carcano* was being sent to Washington to be examined by forensic experts? Did he wonder why it was returned to Dallas the day before Oswald was buried and then sent *back* to Washington again for further testing? If so, he won't discuss any of this. He also will not explain why he was chosen to handle the rifle, or why he once told Paul Gower that the rifle had an "exceptionally dirty bore," a description that never appeared in any official documents. This description, however, could have raised doubts about whether the rifle officials linked to Oswald had even been fired on November 22, 1963.

According to Agent X, he had been curious enough to examine the interior of the Carcano rifle barrel. That is more than Robert Frazier did. The FBI firearms expert examined the rifle on November 23, 1963, and then again on November 27. His deposition shows that he was questioned by Warren Commission member John McCloy specifically about whether he found metal foulings in the barrel of the rifle. Astonishingly, his reply was: "I did not examine it for that."[509]

The metal foulings should have been examined to determine if they matched the bullets found in President Kennedy and the Governor Connally. Why on earth would a weapons expert not thoroughly examine the weapon that supposedly was used to kill the President of the United States? It is vital that questions like these continue to be asked because the answers the public has been given so far are so incomplete and questionable.

Agent X may have never realized that the story he shared with a small group of West Texas teachers might have proven Lee Harvey Oswald's innocence. He may be refusing to talk because of a confidentiality agreement he signed or because of what happened to the other men who examined the rifle.

The authors contacted Agent X by telephone, hoping he would answer these questions. When asked about that day in November, he immediately snapped, "I will *not* talk about that."[510] Nevertheless, his cryptic comment, "It was an *exceptionally* dirty bore" indicates that he knows more than he's telling. Perhaps he has forgotten that he once admitted to a group of teachers, "I know more about the rifle found in the Depository than most people."

CHAPTER 49
THE VOICE OF DANNY PETERS

"One of my friends smarted off something, and one of the 'officials' pushed his face into the brick wall!"—Danny Peters

Numerous students in Dallas were released from school on November 22, 1963 to view President Kennedy's motorcade. One of the many students allowed to skip school that day was high school senior Danny Peters. Because of this, he and five friends ended up being in the wrong place at the wrong time. Fifty years after that dramatic day, he recalled the fear he felt when the "men in suits" accosted him and his friends shortly after the President's assassination.

The teenagers were allowed to leave Woodrow Wilson High School so they could watch the President's motorcade pass through downtown Dallas. One of Peters' friends looked older than the others; he bought the group a six-pack of beer, which he casually placed on the floor board of his car. Peters admitted that he and his friends had been much more focused on an upcoming football game between their school and its arch rival South Oak Cliff than they were on the President's visit. The play-off game was scheduled to take place on Saturday, November 23.

Consequently, the four students drove to South Oak Cliff to taunt their rivals. School was in session, so no one was visible on the campus; none of the rivals were even aware of the group of boys yelling insults as they sped by the campus. Nevertheless, Peters and his friends felt a sense of pride because they supported their school with their sophomoric actions.

Finally, the teenagers decided they should at least get a glimpse of the President's motorcade because that was their excuse for missing school. So, they headed towards downtown Dallas. None of them ever dreamed that what they saw soon appeared in newspapers and magazines all over the world.

As they exited Stemmons Freeway, they observed a large, dark-blue Lincoln Continental fly past with a man in a dark suit hanging onto the back of the car. Peters' perception was of a classic car enveloped in vivid red. The dramatic hues caught his attention, but Peters and his friends did not realize what a historic sight this was; they had no idea they were seeing the President's limousine on its way to Parkland Hospital, and they certainly did not understand the significance of the red images.

"After the car went by," Peters explained, "we parked and walked across the railroad trestle, where I heard later they thought Oswald went afterwards. There were a few people around but no one in particular. The railroad trestle came out behind the Texas School Book Depository building, so we crossed behind there."[511] When asked if he noticed anyone coming out of the building, running or acting oddly, Peters shook his head and said they did not see anything unusual at all.

"We walked around the building," he continued, "and up to the corner, across Elm Street to the corner of the County Records Building. We did not notice people acting strange or anything, but suddenly five or six guys in black suits, or at least dark suits, surrounded us." Peters took a deep breath before continuing.

"They had us pretty much spread-eagled against the Elm Street side of the Record's building wall. One of my friends smarted off something, and one of the 'officials' pushed his face into the brick wall! All this time they were asking us questions like, 'Who are you? What are you doing here? Let's see your I.D!'"

Totally unaware of what had happened just minutes before, Peters and his friends complied quickly and showed their school identification cards to the officials, who never offered to show them any identification at all. Still unaware that the President had been shot, the teenagers explained that they were high school students. The main thing on their minds, Peters admitted, was the fact that there was a six-pack of beer sitting on the floorboard of their car. The students did not know if the officials questioning them were plainclothes detectives, Secret Service agents, or FBI officials, but they did know that they would be in a great deal of trouble if their six-pack of beer was discovered.

Peters smiled as he thought about the irony of the teenagers' situation that day. He added, "Once they realized we were probably who we said we were, they walked us back to the railroad switching yard. There was a tower there, and they took us up inside so they could call our school to find out if we really went there." Their principal verified that Peters and his friends were who they said they were. They were then turned over to two Dallas police officers.

The interrogators never explained to Peters and his friends why they questioned and searched them. Peters remembered that none of them dared ask the officials any questions. Like typical teenagers with guilty consciences, all they could think of was the alcohol they had bought illegally. The teenagers were relieved at being released, but they still had to worry about whether the police officers would notice the six-pack sitting in plain sight in their car.

Fortunately, the two Dallas police officers seemed to think the incident was humorous. They walked the group part-way back to the car and did not get close enough to notice the beer on the floorboard. Peters and his friends still had no idea that something horrific had occurred on Elm Street. It wasn't until they returned to the silent halls of their high school that they realized something was terribly wrong.

As Peters explained, "The halls were always noisy and full of life." On the afternoon of November 22, 1963, they were as quiet as a tomb except for muffled sobs coming from classrooms. Peters recalled peering inside a classroom and asking, "Why's everybody crying?" That is when he and his friends were finally told that the President and the Governor had been shot.

Once the investigation into the assassination began, Peters expected officials to contact him and his friends about what they might have observed (or did not observe) behind the Depository but, to his amazement, no one did.

"After all, they knew our names, they knew where we went to school, and they didn't know whether we had seen anything important or not. They never asked." The fact that he and his friends did not observe anything unusual behind the building from which the assassin supposedly fired should have been important to the investigators. If nothing else, the officials could have learned that, at this time, there was no activity behind the Depository—no one running from the building, with or without a rifle.

Peters still wonders if the officials' lack of interest in him and his classmates was because they looked so young. Yet, the accused assassin was not much older than they were. Buell Wesley Frazier, whom the Dallas police accused of assisting Oswald, was only a year older than Peters and his classmates, and while these agents were frisking six harmless teenagers, assassins might have been escaping from the area. The Dallas police officers did not even check the trunk of the teenager's car. Is it any wonder Lee Harvey Oswald was able to casually walk away from the Depository without being questioned? Was he the only person in the Depository who left without being noticed?

CHAPTER 50

THE VOICE OF DOYLE BRUNSON

**"I knew Charles Harrelson for about five years.
I would say the tall 'tramp' was Charles Harrelson."**

According to Capt. Glen D. King of the Dallas Police Department, the primary responsibility for President Kennedy's safety fell on the shoulders of the Secret Service. Nevertheless, even after the assassination, the Dallas Police Department did not believe it had shirked its responsibilities. Fifty-four officers were stationed at Love Field Airport for the President's arrival; 178 officers were sent out to the motorcade route, with one placed on each signalized intersection; and two to four at each intersection where a turn was required. In addition, officers was placed anywhere the motorcade would pass under a railroad trestle. Even plainclothes detectives and uniformed officers were scattered throughout the crowds.[512]

And yet, windows were open in buildings, people were hanging from fire escapes, and no law enforcement were assigned to the tops of buildings.

The same group of individuals unable to protect the President sprang into action the moment shots were heard. Dallas police officers, deputies, local FBI agents, along with a Dallas U.S. Marshal and an ATF agent began combing Dealey Plaza for assassins, witnesses, bullets and shells, fingerprints, weapons, and any other types of evidence. Naturally, their major responsibility was to find the assassin or assassins. It took officials 74 minutes to locate and arrest a man who quickly became known as the "lone assassin."

Some of the blunders made immediately after the assassination were, undoubtedly, caused by the shock and emotion permeating the city. However, researchers have questioned for years whether the mistakes made by law enforcement that day were all as innocent as they appeared, and more and more Americans wonder what really happened in Dallas that day in 1963. Many have suggested that numerous individuals already knew that a patsy was in place to take the blame for the President's death.

While officials were searching the Depository and questioning witnesses and possible suspects, numerous sites around the assassination scene may have harbored assassins. In the Dal-Tex building, for example, a man using the name "James Braden" was detained, but allowed to walk away and disappear into the crowd. Later, it was discovered he was actually Eugene Brading, a courier for the Mafia.

At least six men were found hiding in railroad cars behind the grassy knoll area. Based on photographs of the scene, three of them were casually escorted to the police station by Dallas police officers. Some were detained for a matter of days, but three were released almost immediately. These have become known to researchers as the "three tramps;" they have been "identified" various ways. Many researchers believe strongly that the tallest of the three men was Charles Harrelson, who was found guilty in 1979 of assassinating a Texas judge. Even Lois Gibson, a world-famous Houston police forensic artist, concluded after thoroughly examining photos of Harrelson that, in her professional opinion, the "tall tramp" was indeed Charles Harrelson.[513]

A man who knew Harrelson personally agrees with Gibson. Doyle Brunson told the authors he has looked at that famous photo many times. Brunson knew Harrelson because he sat across poker tables from him for years, watching many expressions cross his face.

"I knew Charles Harrelson for about five years," Brunson commented. "I would say the tall 'tramp' was Charles Harrelson." [514] Brunson added some information about Harrelson that has become common knowledge, mainly because Harrelson's son Woody became a well-known actor.

"You know, Harrelson was found guilty of killing a judge," added Brunson, who knew of Harrelson's reputation for being cold-blooded. When it came to murder, Harrelson seemed to have no conscience. Brunson's voice was soft but serious when he commented, "I heard he said that a man's head was just like a watermelon with hair to him." A man with this attitude could certainly have been paid to kill a president.

However, not everyone agrees with Lois Gibson and Doyle Brunson. Billy Bankston, the son of well-known Dallas businessman W. O. Bankston, insisted in his Oral History at the Sixth Floor Museum that the tall "tramp" was *not* Charles Harrelson. His reasoning was that Charles Harrelson was so well-known to the Dallas police at that time that if he had been arrested that day, police officers would have recognized him immediately, and this recognition would have been obvious to others. Others have argued that photographs of the Dallas police escorting the three men from the railroad cars to the sheriff's department indicate that they were *not* treated like serious suspects. The three men were not handcuffed, and one deputy even walked with his back to them.

Dallas law enforcement may not have known that Harrelson was an associate of Edward "Pete" Kay and George McGann, members of the Dixie Mafia. And yet, Bankston was recorded as saying it wasn't unusual for Harrelson to visiting the DPD on occasion. If Bankston was correct when he stated that Dallas law enforcement *knew* Harrelson, perhaps that is *why* they escorted the three men so casually. Perhaps that is why the men were released so quickly. We know the three were not placed under arrest; there are no Dallas arrest records for them. One Dallas police officer, Marvin Wise, did write the names of two of the "tramps" on a slip of paper, place it in his hat, and eventually toss it into his police locker.[515] More than a year later, he found the note and threw it away. By then, the whole world knew the assassin was Lee Harvey Oswald, so why would the names of three men found near the assassination site be important? Wise did not explain why he neglected to write down the name of the third man. Unlike FBI agent Jim Hosty, who destroyed a note Oswald left for him, Wise was not reassigned or sent to another state as a result of his actions.

No explanation was ever given for why the two officers who accompanied the tramps to the sheriff's department acted so nonchalantly. On this day of all days, everyone should have been considered a serious suspect. The police officers seemed unconcerned, despite the fact that they were escorting "tramps" seen boarding a railroad boxcar who could possibly be the assassins. Authorities certainly did not treat Danny Peters and his high school friends in this cavalier manner. Did high school teenagers look more suspicious than "tramps" hiding in a boxcar?

The best record of the Dallas Police Department chaos moments after shots were fired at the President is the Dallas Police transcript of their radio log. The first indication that Dallas police realized something serious occurred was at 12:30 p.m. A dispatcher relayed Sheriff Decker's orders to police officers: "Go to hospital. Get men on top of the underpass. See what happened up there. Go up to overpass. Notify Station Five to move all men available out of my department back into the railroad yards and try to determine what happened and hold everything secure until Homicide and other investigators can get there."[516] This is the *first* piece of evidence that the shots may have come from in front of the President's limousine—from the overpass or the railroad yards.

So, when did law enforcement decide that the assassin shot from the Texas School Book Depository? What caused Dallas motorcycle officer Marion Baker to rush immediately into the Depository? The only answer appears to be found in the next radio dispatch.

"At **12:35**: *Witness states shots came from Book Depository."* We know this anonymous witness was not any of the employees standing on the steps of the

Depository. Many of them, like Bill Shelley and Billy Lovelady, ran towards the grassy knoll area. Photos do not show bystanders on the steps looking upwards towards the sixth floor.

At **12:37**: Another order was received: *"Get men to cover the Texas School Book Depository. One guy possibly hit by ricochet off of concrete."* This referred to bystander James Tague.

At **12:40**: Another report was received by police officers: *"...happened at the triple underpass, between the triple underpass and Stemmons. Possibly six or seven more people may have been shot."* Immediately after this dispatch came one that makes the Dallas police seem well-prepared to arrest *someone* from the Depository, rather than a suspect from the overpass.

At **12:40**: *"Send me a squad for a prisoner at Elm and Houston."*

"Do you have a suspect?

"No." Though no suspect was found, Dallas police were prepared to arrest *someone*.

Three minutes later, at **12:43**, thirteen minutes after the first shots were heard, a description was sent out to all squads.

"Attention all squads. The subject in the shooting at Elm and Houston is reported to be an unknown white male approximately thirty, slender build, height five feet six, weight one hundred sixty-five pounds, reported to be armed with what is thought to be a thirty-caliber rifle—no further description or information at this time." At this point, no roll call of Depository employees had taken place. Officers were not finished searching it or nearby buildings. How could such a precise description of any suspect be available this soon, and how could anyone know what type of rifle was used?

12:45: Another broadcast of the suspect's description was sent. The dispatcher now reported: *"We have the building saturated by now and we should have something before long."* It is unclear who provided the dispatcher with this information.

12:49: *"No clothing description."*— Physical description of suspect is rebroadcast.

12:55: *"Any clothing description?"* \

"No, not yet."

At **12:43**, it would have been impossible for anyone to have had a clothing description of the assassin, much less a physical description, because no Depository employees suspected the assassin might be anywhere in the building, much less among them. This begs the question: Where did the dispatcher get a description of an assassin, and how did he know there was only *one*?

The first police officer to enter the Depository was Marion Baker, and as he testified to the Warren Commission, people were already returning to the Depository when he entered the front doors. In fact, the Depository supervisor, Roy Truly, who had watched the motorcade from the front steps, was already back in the building. Surely employees would not have re-entered a building if they even suspected an assassin might be hiding there. Baker focused on the Depository simply because he noticed pigeons flying off the roof after the gun shots. The odds are that gun shots from *any* of the neighboring buildings would have startled the pigeons.

Witness statements from individuals who watched the motorcade during their lunch hour from the steps of the Depository indicate that they stood discussing the President, the First Lady, and then the shocking information that the President had been shot. So, it is unclear how many minutes passed before Baker was able to park his motorcycle, enter the building, speak with Roy Truly, and confront Oswald.

While Baker and Truly attempted to use the elevator and then decided to use the stairs instead, Lee Harvey Oswald was in the second-floor lunch room drinking a Coke. After Baker spotted Oswald, Truly reassured him that Oswald was an employee, and the two men proceeded to climb the stairs to the upper floors. Though the exact time Baker entered the Depository is debatable, there is no question he was the first officer to see Oswald in the Depository after the assassination.

Even then, Baker did not consider Oswald a suspect, so he did not report his appearance or anyone else's to the dispatcher. How could *anyone* know what the assassin looked like at 12:43 p.m. on November 22? Just as important, why did authorities think that twenty-four-year-old Oswald, who was 5-foot-9 and weighed 150 pounds, matched the description given by the dispatcher at 12:43 p.m.?

Those waiting at the Dallas Trade Mart for the President to speak were clueless about the seriousness of the situation. At **12:48,** a request came from an officer at the Trade Mart for someone to *"see if the President will be able to appear out here. Got all these people out here. Need to know whether to feed them or what to announce out here."*

Even after a dispatcher clarified that the President and the Governor were involved in a shooting, the officer asked again: *"Can you obtain information from someone if the President is going to appear at the Trade Mart?"* This officer was focused on how to handle the hundreds of people waiting for the President at the Trade Mart.

At Elm and Houston, a police officer was begging for the fire department to bring ropes. *"Send lots of rope to Elm and Houston. We are getting a tremendous crowd down here. Lots of rope."*

1:12: Information came in from an officer at the Depository which contradicts what was later reported in the Warren Report. *"We have found empty rifle hulls on the fifth floor and from all indication, the man had been there for some time."* The confusion only became worse. The tidal wave of chaos that slammed the Dallas law enforcement agencies was producing a tragic comedy of errors.

1:18: A citizen used Officer J.D. Tippit's police radio to call in that a police officer was shot. *"We've had a shooting here."* "Here" referred to *"Between Marsalis and Beckley,"* then *"404 Tenth Street,"* then *"501 East Jefferson,"* then *"501 East Tenth,"* and finally *"519 East Jefferson."* Then a dispatcher questioned the citizen about Chesapeake Street. The actual address was 404 Tenth Street. One wonders how the Dallas police ever located the dead police officer.

1:19:No description was given of the person who supposedly shot Officer Tippit. However, by 1:22, a very thorough description suddenly went out. *"White male, thirty, height five foot eight, very slender build, black hair, a white jacket, white shirt, dark slacks."*

1:33: The description of Officer Tippit's killer was rebroadcast. During this time, another officer reported that he and his men were *"shaking down houses in 400 block of Jefferson."* Another squad of officers was sent over to Tenth and Crawford to check out a church basement in the area. Suddenly, an excited voice came over the radio: *"He is in the library at Jefferson—east 500 block—Marsalis and Jefferson. In the library. I'm going around back. Get somebody in front. Get them here fast."*

Another police officer proclaimed, *"They've got him held up, it looks like, in this building over here on the corner."* An officer responded, *"We are all at the library. We're in front. We're all at the library."*

The dispatcher provided additional information to the men frantically searching for the person who killed one of their own.

"Suspect in this shooting, white male, 27, five feet, eleven, 165 pounds, black wavy hair, fair complexion, light gray Eisenhower jacket, white shirt, dark slacks. He is apparently armed with a .32 dark finish, automatic pistol, which he had in his right hand."

The dispatcher added, *"For your information, they have the suspect cornered in the library at Marsalis and Jefferson."* A moment later, officers received the first good news they heard all afternoon. *"They do have the suspect under arrest now."* But almost immediately, another comment contradicted this statement.

"It's the wrong man. Disregard all information on the suspect arrested. It was the wrong man." The only explanation for why the man was released and no longer considered a suspect came from one officer: *"It was just a boy running to tell them what happened; he works there."* Naturally, anyone running might look suspicious. Nevertheless, valuable time and effort was wasted on someone who appeared to be totally uninvolved. Apparently, this young man was released because library employees knew him, just as Oswald was released from the Depository because Roy Truly knew him and could vouch for him.

1:40: Dallas officers were informed: *"Shells at scene indicate that the suspect is armed with an automatic .38 rather than a pistol."* Five minutes later, a report came over the police radio that the suspect had just gone into the Texas Theatre on West Jefferson and was supposedly hiding in the balcony.

1:46: Officers in downtown Dallas reported: *"We have a man. We would like to have you pass this up on to the CID to see if we can pick this man up—Charles Douglas Givens. He's colored, six foot three, 165 pounds. He has a police record, and he left the building where he worked as a porter."*

In hundreds of reports concerning the assassination, it is always written that Lee Harvey Oswald was the *only* employee to leave the Depository after the assassination. Yet, here in the official record is evidence that he was not. There is no explanation for why Givens' name was used by the dispatcher but Oswald's name was not.

1:47: The dispatcher repeated: *"They think suspect is in Texas Theatre... In the* balcony..." Next, the dispatcher announced: *"En route to Texas Theatre. Have someone cover the rear and the theatre at the fire escapes... There's about five squads back here with me now."*

A few moments later, another dispatch is heard: *"Some squads are going to the Texas Theatre."* At this point, most of the police energy was focused on locating and apprehending a man who killed a fellow officer, rather than on locating whoever shot the President and Governor Connally.

1:51: Over the radio, Chief of Police Jesse Curry asked about patrolman J.D. Tippit. He was told that he was DOA at Methodist Hospital. Curry's first question was: *"Did they get the suspects?"* It is unclear why the police chief thought more than one person killed the patrolman.

1:52: The dispatcher proclaimed: *"We have apprehended a suspect in the shooting at the Texas Theatre... He is en route to the station... Caught him on the lower floor of the Texas Theatre after a fight."*

1:53: The dispatcher questioned, *"Suspect was arrested?"* and he received the answer, *"Yes."* In the short span of six minutes, the Dallas police located and apprehended a man suspected of killing a Dallas police officer. Among the arresting officers was Dallas Assistant District Attorney Dallas William Alexander.[517]

What most of the world did not know was that another man who resembled Oswald was escorted out of the Texas Theatre through the *back* entrance. Researchers only know this because a witness, Bernard Haire, observed the young man being placed into a Dallas police car. It was not until Haire saw the famous photo of cigar-chomping Detective Bennett grappling with the man the world knew as Lee Harvey Oswald *in front* of the theatre that he realized he saw someone else.[518]

Unfortunately, Bernard Haire is the only person who has admitted to seeing someone besides Oswald arrested near the Texas Theatre on November 22, 1963. Could this man be the person mentioned by the dispatcher as being in the *balcony* of the theatre? If he was truly arrested that day, why is there no arrest record? If he was an innocent bystander, why is there no mention of his apprehension in any official documents? Where did the Dallas police take him? All of these questions remain unanswered. What *is* known is that, unlike Buell Wesley Frazier, this individual never stepped forward and described what must have been a terrifying experience.

Despite the quick apprehension of the man suspected of killing a Dallas police officer, certain members of the DPD continued to make mistakes while Oswald was in their custody. It is unclear if the police already connected Oswald to Tippit's murder *and* the President's assassination. From televised news reports, the American public heard reporters ask Oswald if he killed the President.

"No, sir," he replied politely. "I didn't kill anybody." The public also heard Oswald say that he had not been charged with killing the President. In fact, Oswald was not officially charged with killing *Officer Tippit* until 7:10 p.m. on November 22, and he was not charged with the murder of President Kennedy until 1:30 a.m. on November 23.

At the time Oswald was first charged with Tippit's murder, the few hand-written notes attributed to Capt. Will Fritz and the Oswald interrogation make *no mention* of Officer J. D. Tippit. "Whilst Oswald was accused of the murder of Officer Tippit, there is nowhere any reference to it [in Fritz's notes]."[519] Though Oswald officially was arrested for shooting a Dallas police officer, the Dallas chief homicide investigator already decided he was the President's assassin also, just as he decided that Buell Wesley Fraizer was his accomplice. The few notes that were eventually found concerning Oswald's interrogation were ones which Captain Fritz repeatedly denied making.

It is common knowledge that Fritz did not ask for a stenographer as he interrogated Oswald and did not use recording devices. This may have been a common practice in Dallas at the time, but even Oswald knew that notes were being taken as he was being questioned because he once commented to the police, "You took notes. Just read for yourself if you want to refresh your memory."[520]

The handful of notes that are available make it obvious that Fritz and numerous others were crowded into a small interrogation room. In the room at various times were: James Hosty, FBI Special Agent, the man who had visited Oswald's wife, ignored a note Oswald left for him, and then destroyed it; Harry D. Holmes, U.S. Postal Inspector repsponsible for maintaining the receipt indicating who picked up the mail-order rifle Oswald ordered; Robert I. Nash, U. S. Marshal who tried to tell other law enforcement that his associate had seen someone shooting from the County Records Building; James W. Bookhout, FBI Special Agent; Roger Craig, Dallas Deputy Sheriff, who reported seeing someone who looked like Oswald run out of the front of the TSBD; T. J. Kelley and David B. Grant, Secret Service agents; and Detectives Billy L. Senkel and Fay M. Turner, Dallas Homicide and Robbery Bureau, among others. It seems that the only person absent from Oswald's interrogation was an attorney.

CHAPTER 51

FROM THE VAULTS OF THE FBI

"The public must be satisfied that Oswald was the assassin..."
—Deputy U.S. Attorney General Nicholas Katzenbach

Within hours of the assassination, some considered it extremely important to prove that President Kennedy had not been the victim of a conspiracy. J. Edgar Hoover and the new president, Lyndon B. Johnson, were soon evaluating information and evidence provided by the FBI. Even before his death, Lee Harvey Oswald was labeled the "lone assassin." After his death, it was much easier to convince the world that no one else was involved in the assassination.

The only Dallas FBI agent familiar with the name "Lee Harvey Oswald" was Special Agent James Hosty. He had been attempting to contact Oswald at his Irving residence for weeks. Instead of speaking to Oswald, who was not at home, Hosty spoke to Ruth Paine and to Oswald's wife, Marina.

Hosty was assigned Oswald's case because Oswald had been a defector, not because officials thought he was dangerous. Therefore, Hosty did not make the Secret Service aware that a former Soviet defector disgruntled about his undesirable discharge from the Marines was living in the Dallas area. Oswald's name was not on the FBI list of persons to be put under surveillance during the President's trip. No doubt Hosty's inaction was a blunder, even if it was an understandable one. The question is: Were other individuals on the FBI watch list monitored as casually as Oswald was?

Another major blunder Agent Hosty made was destroying a note left by Oswald at the Dallas FBI office. The note was delivered about ten days before the assassination. Oswald handed it to Nan Lee Fenner, a receptionist. Supposedly, she just glanced at the note, but later recalled what it said—something about Oswald demanding that Hosty stop bothering his wife, and if he did not, Oswald would blow up either the FBI office in Dallas or the police department. According to Fenner, the note was signed "Lee Harvey Oswald." Not taking the note seriously, Hosty tossed it into his file drawer at the FBI office.[521]

It was not until after Oswald's arrest that the note suddenly became extremely important. After the assassination, Hosty claimed to his superior, J. Gordon Shanklin, that Oswald's note only mentioned that Hosty should stop bothering Oswald's wife *and* that it was not even signed. According to Hosty, Shanklin ordered him to destroy the note, which he did by tearing it up and flushing it down the toilet. Shanklin later *denied* telling Hosty to destroy the note.

It is important to know for certain whether the note bore Oswald's signature or not. If there had been no signature, Hosty would have had every right to shrug off the note and later exhibit it as evidence he had had no way of knowing who wrote it. Surely, Special Agent in Charge Shanklin would not have panicked over an *unsigned* note. However, a threatening note *signed* by Oswald (or anyone else) should have been kept on file, not destroyed. The most incriminating piece of evidence indicating the note bore Oswald's signature comes from the fact that a Hosty supervisor, Ken Howe, found the note in Hosty's desk drawer and immediately took it to Special Agent Shanklin.[522] How would Howe have connected this note to Oswald if it had not been signed?

If the note said what Fenner remembered, then Oswald should have been arrested for threatening a federal agency. Is it possible Oswald deliberately wrote a threatening note so he *would be* arrested, much as Richard Case Nagel got himself arrested in El Paso two months before the assassination? If this was Oswald's plan, then his arrest would have prevented him from being in the Depository the day the President arrived in Dallas and would have prevented him from being accused of killing anyone.

Another possibility is that Oswald may have wanted to be arrested so he could warn the FBI there was a plot to kill the President in Dallas. If so, that would explain why Hosty later destroyed a note that would have embarrassed the agency. Lee Harvey Oswald could have been the same "Lee" who telephoned a Chicago FBI agent to warn him of a possible presidential assassination attempt in Chicago two weeks before Kennedy's trip to Dallas. Perhaps the words "blow up" had been a warning that Oswald's role as an informer was in jeopardy—that his cover had been "blown." If so, why would agents ignore this information? Was he already the patsy he later claimed to be? If *any* of these scenarios are accurate, this would explain why Agent James Hosty deliberately destroyed a note from Oswald that should have been taken seriously. And there must be some reason why Shanklin ordered an FBI agent to destroy evidence connected to the President's accused assassin. Perhaps he was attempting to prevent Director J. Edgar Hoover from learning about the note!

It is obvious that both Shanklin and Hosty wanted any information concerning the controversial note kept secret. Unfortunately for both of them, word about the note became a topic of conversation throughout the Dallas FBI. Special Agent Ural Horton and fellow agent Bill Mabray were assigned to Abilene,

Texas, but they happened to fly into Dallas Love Field from training at Quantico on the afternoon of November 22, 1963. Both men were immediately put to work interviewing witnesses, and it was quite some time before they made it home to Abilene. During this time, they heard stories about a note the accused assassin left with Nan Fenner. Apparently, neither man realized that *no one* was supposed to know about this note or how it arrived at the Dallas FBI building!

Nine years after the assassination, Horton drove Special Agent Gordon Shanklin to Abilene to attend a retirement party for Agent Coleman Mabray. According to an official statement that Horton signed on July 23, 1975, Shanklin asked him his opinion of Agent James Hosty. Not knowing that the story about Oswald's note was "top-secret," Horton responded that Hosty was a "damned fool" if in fact he received a note from Oswald and did not open a case on him, or at least check out the situation.[523] Horton explained to Shanklin that during the weeks following the assassination, he heard about the note. He realized that Shanklin was astonished by his comments. What he did not know was whether Shanklin was surprised about the note or surprised that Horton *knew* about the note. Nevertheless, Horton, much like U. S. Marshal Robert I. Nash, was "given a hard time" because he discussed a subject the FBI wanted kept private.

Also unknown to the American public, and even to the Warren Commission, was a memo United States Deputy Attorney General Nicholas Katzenbach sent three days after Kennedy's death to President Johnson's press aide Bill Moyers: "The public must be satisfied that Oswald was the assassin; that he did not have confederates who were still at large; and that the evidence was such that he would have been convicted at trial."[524]

How could Katzenbach have known all of this so soon? Surely, it is not coincidental that he waited until the accused assassin was permanently silenced to send this memo to President Johnson. There is no indication whether J. Edgar Hoover or Attorney General Robert F. Kennedy approved this memo. If Robert Kennedy *had* approved this memo, was it because he feared that a thorough investigation of his brother's death would reveal secrets about Kennedy's administration that would affect the late President's legacy? Obviously, Katzenbach knew that this memo would halt a *thorough* investigation, and that the results of any "so-called investigation" had already been determined.

For whatever reasons, certain high-placed individuals in the United States government desperately wanted all Americans to believe that President John F. Kennedy was killed by a single individual, Lee Harvey Oswald. Will Fritz, chief of the Dallas Homicide Division, was told to cease and desist his investigation of any leads that did not point towards Oswald. Fritz and his department were actively investigating the President's murder until November 23, 1963. In

March 1975, Fritz told a friend that on November 23, 1963, he "received a telephone call from the new president. As Fritz put it to this friend, 'But when the President of the United States called me and *ordered* the investigation stopped, what could I do?'"[525]

As far as President Lyndon Johnson knew, Capt. Will Fritz and numerous other investigators complied with his directive. However, official documents show that Dallas law enforcement did not cease to investigate the President's murder. Many Dallas police officers, FBI agents, and other law enforcement personnel continued to question witnesses and gather evidence. They had no idea that their findings would never be seen by the commission President Johnson appointed to determine the "truth" about President Kennedy's death. Some of their findings are "hidden" in the twenty-six volumes that accompanied the Warren Report. Others may have been destroyed altogether, just like the note Hosty destroyed.

One of the most important blunders made by those in charge of uncovering the truth about Kennedy's death was printed in black and white in a memo from J. Edgar Hoover to President Lyndon Johnson. It was dated November 29, 1963. In the memo, Hoover addressed questions that President Johnson had asked him via a telephone call. As the head of the FBI, it can be assumed that Hoover had access to the most accurate information available. So, it is mind-boggling to read what he told Lyndon Johnson.

He informed the President that only "three shots had been fired at the President...The President was hit by the first and the third bullet, and the second one hit the Governor...One complete bullet rolled out of the President's head...We have also tested the fact that you could fire those three shots in three seconds... On the *fifth floor* [emphasis added] of the building where we found the gun, and the wrapping paper, we found three empty shells that had been fired and one that had not been fired."[526]

This statement is either full of factual errors, *or* the assassin's rifle and shells were *planted* on the wrong floor. This memo could have been used in court to demonstrate how many errors were made by the various law enforcement groups investigating the President's death. Of course, it is possible that the weapon and the shells were actually *found* on the *fifth* floor. If so, three Depository employees watching the President's motorcade from that location would have seen and heard a would-be assassin. Maybe the empty shells were lying on the floor of the fifth floor for days. If that were true, it would prove that no shots were ever fired from the Depository, at least not from a Mannlicher-Carcano—or perhaps a German Mauser—or a British Enfield.

VII
THE SHADOWY
WORLD OF
JACK RUBY

Though the Warren Commission claimed that Lee Harvey Oswald and Jack Ruby never met, the lives of the two men became entangled on November 24, 1963. There is evidence that Oswald and Ruby did know each other before that day; regardless, their names are locked together in history, even if they were never before connected in life.

CHAPTER 52

THE VOICE OF "JOY DALE"

**"They [the FBI] wanted me to say he was connected to the mob,
but as far as I know, he wasn't."**

Not everyone who patronized the Carousel Club reacted the way the anonymous West Texas woman did. Jack Ruby's ex-strippers were often the first to defend the dancing that took place in the club. They considered it an art; after all, they did have to belong to the American Guild of Variety Artists in order to be employed there, and some had attended Ruby's "stripper school."

Joyce McDonald Gordon felt she knew Jack Ruby better than most. She saw a side of him that most people did not know. Under the stage name of "Joy Dale," she danced and stripped in the Carousel Club but, thanks to Ruby's generosity, she continued to work there as a club hostess while she was pregnant.

Over fifty years later, she fondly recalled to the authors that the Jack Ruby she knew and loved was a "swell person." When the Warren Commission questioned her, she stated that she worked for Ruby approximately two-to-three months, and that she had known him personally as well as professionally. In her testimony, she stated that Ruby gave several people she knew "a helping hand" when they needed it. For instance, he helped out one unemployed man by giving him a job until he found permanent work. A young girl wanted to return to Texas from a different state, so Ruby helped her get back on her feet.[527]

Gordon admitted Ruby would sometimes lose his temper, but she believed it was because he was simply an "emotional" man. She felt that when Ruby" went off" on someone, it was for a good reason. She also referred to him as a "busybody." He wanted to know everything going on around him. "He reminded me of a little old lady in a small town who wanted to know everything going on," Gordon said with a chuckle."[528]

Another performer from the same time period, Beverly Oliver, sang and performed a ventriloquism act at the Colony Club, right down the street from the Carousel Club. She wrote in her book *Nightmare in Dallas* that she, too, knew Jack Ruby well. Some researchers have questioned whether Oliver really knew Ruby at all, because she has no photos of the two of them together. However, without meaning to, Joyce Gordon verified some of Oliver's memories.

Gordon remembered Beverly Oliver, but her memories were not fond ones. She did not believe that she and Oliver were the "same type of people."

Gordon also contradicted some of the statements Oliver made in her book. "She [Oliver] was out to make the buck and didn't give a damn who she hurt, and, no, she was not close to Jack Ruby. She was the type of woman who hung all over men. She hung all over Jack [Ruby] and Abe" ["Abe" refers to Abe Weinstein, the owner of the Colony Club, where Oliver performed.][529] Oliver might very well dismiss Gordon's comments as professional jealousy. Regardless, both she and Gordon spoke from their own experiences, even if they disagreed on certain details.

Abe Weinstein and Jack Ruby both allowed performers to visit each other's clubs. Oliver claimed she was at the Carousel Club some of the time, but not as a performer. Despite the fact that Gordon had no use for Oliver, Gordon's memories of Oliver and Ruby verified some of what Oliver recalled about the club owner.

As far as Gordon could remember, "Jack kept the women he dated away from the Carousel Club." So, perhaps Jack Ruby did not date Beverly Oliver, as she claimed in her book, but he did, indeed, know her. Gordon added that she had fond memories of Tammi True, another dancer at the Carousel Club, who also described Jack Ruby as a "kind man."

Though it had been more than fifty years since Joyce Gordon performed at the Carousel Club, she still recalled some of her co-workers. For instance, she remembered a man with strange hair and eyebrows who performed in a ventriloquist act at the club. She referred to him as a "wannabe friend of Jack's. Lots of people wanted to be friends with Jack, and he wanted to be friends with lots of important people."

Gordon's comment about the ventriloquist with the "strange hair and eyebrows" was an important one. The only person connected to the Kennedy assassination who fits this description is a man named David Ferrie. He often wore inexpensive toupees and fake eyebrows and was known for his ventriloquism skills. New Orleans District Attorney Jim Garrison attempted to tie him and his associates to Kennedy's assassination. Gordon's memories of this strange-looking ventriloquist who performed at Jack Ruby's Carousel Club would have strengthened Garrison's case if the district attorney had known to ask her.

Joyce Gordon did not recall Lee Harvey Oswald ever being in the Carousel Club, however. But she did remember that a woman from New Orleans who stripped under the stage name of "Jada" was one of Beverly Oliver's only friends. "The other girls didn't like Beverly much, or Jada, either. Jada acted like what she really wanted was to dance nude. I remember a time when Jack, who sometimes helped run the lighting system, pulled her off stage because she was about to strip off all her clothes. The club would have been closed down if she had done that!" Gordon explained indignantly.

The ex-dancer continued, "Jada was one of the strangest people I've ever known. She would do things like jump around on the stage screaming and yelling, but it got the audience's attention! In his magazine article "Who Was Jack Ruby?" Gary Cartwright described Jada's routine thusly: "Her act consisted mainly of clutching a tiger-skinned rug and making wild orgasmic sounds with her throat."[530]

Cartwright admitted that Ruby and some of his employees, including Jada, visited his apartment. He remembered an interesting comment Jada once made to him, in front of his roommate Bud Shrake, concerning Ruby and Oswald. Cartwright forgot to include this in his article about Jack Ruby for *Texas Monthly* in 1975. "After the assassination, Jada told us Ruby once introduced her to Lee Oswald at the Carousel. Beverly Oliver was also introduced." Cartwright verified Jada's comment with Oliver, who recalled the incident clearly.[531]

This single comment which, for whatever reason, was not included in the *Texas Monthly* article, would undoubtedly have caused a storm of controversy—something Cartwright and/or the magazine would not have wanted. Nevertheless, it is anecdotal evidence that Jack Ruby and Lee Harvey Oswald (or someone impersonating Oswald) visited the Carousel Club in Dallas, Texas, at least according to Ruby's most infamous stripper.

Gordon recalled that Jada was paid more money than the other strippers. "Jack paid her $400 a week, and that was a lot of money. I heard that she was killed in a motorcycle accident in Louisiana. That's where she was from—Jack found her in New Orleans."[532]

From what Gordon remembered, the Carousel Club remained open only three or four months after the assassination. "I stayed there for a month after Jack was put in jail." Gordon was pregnant with her second child at the time. She shared the news about her pregnancy with Ruby, who, instead of firing her, as most club owners would have done, offered to reduce her salary but let her work as a ticket-taker/hostess. "He even said he would get me some pretty maternity clothes," Gordon remembered, a smile in her voice. Experiences like these are why Gordon recalled Jack Ruby as a generous and kind-hearted man. She tried to visit him a few hours after his arrest for killing Oswald, but the police would not allow her.

"Channels 4 and 8 interviewed me that day about him," she added, obviously proud of this memory. The publicity from the television coverage may be why Gordon was also interviewed numerous times by the FBI—"more times than they say they did," she insisted. "There are things I could have told them about

THE LONE STAR SPEAKS

Jack, like when my oldest daughter, Cindy, had her eye put out. She was only four years old and had emergency surgery. She had to have someone stay with her, so Jack would go to the hospital and sit with her while I worked, so I could continue to earn my salary."

Gordon's voice trembled as she recalled the following: "One night after I got off work, I went back to the hospital and Cindy wasn't in her bed. I went looking for her. I found her at the nurses' station. She and Jack and the nurses were all eating ice cream! That's the Jack Ruby I knew, but that's not what the FBI wanted to hear. They wanted me to say he was connected to the mob, but as far as I know, he wasn't."

Like most Americans alive at the time, Gordon can still remember exactly where she was the day of the Kennedy assassination. She was in Dallas, close to the assassination site, on a bus with her young daughter. Coincidentally, she and her daughter were on their way to Parkland Hospital, where they had an appointment with an eye doctor.

"I heard the shots," Gordon said. "Four of them. People on the bus kind of joked about that. We didn't realize what the sounds were. Someone said, 'Sounds like someone's shooting at Kennedy.' Of course, we didn't know that's what was really happening. We had to get off that bus at the Adolphus Hotel and get another one for Parkland. So I was at Parkland Hospital when they announced the President had died. That's when *I* found out he had been shot. Everyone there was hysterical. People were just stopping their cars and crying. It almost caused a traffic jam. My daughter became hysterical because of how emotional everyone around us was."

Gordon added, "After the eye appointment, I went back to the club. Jack was hysterical, too, which upset my daughter even more. She had never seen her 'Uncle Jack' like that. He kept saying, 'I'll kill the SOB who did it if I get a chance.' Not 'I'll kill a particular person,' just 'the SOB who did this.' He was so concerned about Jackie because she had just lost her baby and now her husband." Gordon's memories of Ruby's behavior correlate with the explanation he later gave for shooting Oswald.

She continued, "Jack told Andrew [Armstrong], the bartender, 'Put a wreath on the door and [a sign saying] we'll be closed till further notice.' He put his felt hat on, and down the stairs of the club he went." Gordon then added a detail that only those close to Ruby would have known.

"Jack got his shoes shined every day by this black shoeshine man. He was so upset that afternoon that he left his little dog Sheba upstairs in the club, so I picked her up and went down the stairs after him. Jack was at the shoeshine stand getting his shoes shined. Just sitting there, saying nothing."

344

"'Jack, what are you going to do with Sheba this weekend?' I asked him. He looked up at me, surprised."

"'What are you doing here?' he asked me, as if he hadn't seen me upstairs."

"'Jack, I've been here trying to talk to you. Cindy's [Gordon's daughter] upset you wouldn't talk to her.' He just took Sheba from me and said, 'See you later' and walked away."

Thinking back about how emotional people were in Dallas that day, Gordon elaborated, "You know, there was a lynch mob in front of the Texas Theatre. Not everybody knows that." Gordon then returned to the subject of her former boss. "Jack knew everybody downtown. He had his opportunity to kill Kennedy's assassin, and he took it. He was also the kind of guy who, if he liked you and you got arrested, he'd have you out of jail in thirty minutes!"

Gordon did not believe the claims that Jack Ruby was running guns to Cuba. "But," she interjected, "my fingerprints *were* on the gun he used to kill Oswald. I told the FBI that." She explained that Ruby would ask her to retrieve the gun from his office if they left the Carousel Club late at night. "Sometimes Jack would give me a lift to Oak Cliff ,where I lived." Gordon's apartment was approximately a mile and a half from Ruby's apartment.

Gordon paused for a moment. "The FBI talked to me many times, always wanting me to say Jack was part of the mob, trying to put words in my mouth, that Jack was a 'wanna-be mobster.' He would have liked to have been the top club owner, but he wasn't. My father met Jack, and when he heard he had killed Oswald, he was just hysterical because I stuck by Jack."

"'Are you going to stick by him after what he did?' he demanded."

"'Hell, yes,' I said to him. 'If a person's good to me, you taught me to stick by them.'"

When asked if she knew why Ruby told Earl Warren and Gerald Ford that he talk more freely if they took him to Washington, D.C., Gordon replied quietly, "I don't know why Jack said that." She then added, "But I don't think Oswald was trying to kill the President. I think he was shooting at Connally because Connally [as Secretary of the Navy] gave him his dishonorable discharge." Gordon was not the only one who so speculated. That Connally was the real target began floating around Dallas not long after the assassination.

Gordon paused and then continued with more memories of Jack Ruby. Apparently, he had tried to stay in shape, even though Gordon described him as "stocky." He even had a treadmill at work.

"One time he took my boyfriend and me to Ports O' Call, a nice restaurant, for my birthday," she recalled. "Jack got tickled at me because I was a little on the naïve side. I hadn't ever been to nice restaurants." Gordon's thoughts then returned to the subject of Kennedy's accused assassin.

"I was with my boyfriend in his new apartment when Jack shot Oswald. We were listening to music and the announcer broke in and said a nightclub owner, Jack Ruby, had shot Oswald."

"'My God, he did it,' I said and went into hysterics until my boyfriend slapped me to calm me down. My whole world dropped out from under me. There was no future that I could see."

After a moment or two, Gordon seemed to gather her thoughts and continued. "You know, Jack was never actually convicted of killing Oswald," she explained. "The FBI told my mother that I would have to testify at his second trial, but Jack died before it began." Joyce Gordon, for whatever reason, did not testify in Ruby's original trial. When asked about claims Ruby made that he was being injected with cancer cells, she admitted she did not really know what to make of this strange assertion. "Well, he was always healthy, always working out. I just don't know," she said thoughtfully.

Joyce Gordon was one of many people who knew one side of Jack Ruby. There is no reason to think that her memories were fabricated. However, like so many others, she did not know everything about the man who could be generous and kind to her and her daughter and also kill a man in front of millions of witnesses.

CHAPTER 53

THE MULTI-FACETED RUBY

"Son, you don't want to find Jack Ruby. He's involved with the mafia."
—A Dallas bartender

The Warren Commission led Americans to believe that Jack Ruby's life, like Oswald's, was placed under a microscope and every detail examined. History shows otherwise. Who was the real Jack Ruby? He is remembered simply as the man who killed Lee Harvey Oswald in "cold blood" before Oswald had a chance to be tried by a jury of his peers.

Some who actually knew Ruby, however, described him as a "cuddly teddy bear," a man who would give someone the shirt off his back if he knew he needed it. To them, he was a man who would share his apartment when a friend needed a place to live. To most people, he was just a businessman who was part-owner and manager of the Vegas Club and the Carousel Club in Dallas, Texas. To a select group, including the Dallas police, he was a man who offered "favors."

According to journalist Gary Cartwright, Ruby's Carousel Club was a place where Dallas Police officers drank regularly without paying, and where"Ruby leaned on his girls to provide sexual pleasures for favored clients."[533] A story with the headline "Ruby Often Wined, Dined Dallas Cops" even appeared in the *New York World-Telegram* on Sunday, December 4, 1963."[534] Ten days after Oswald's murder, a reporter uncovered facts that proved embarrassing to the Dallas Police Department.

Jack Ruby was also known by some as a short-fused, quick-tempered egomaniac and a gun- running mobster. "Ruby used to boast that he could hit harder than Joe Louis," a famous American boxer.[535] There were numerous police records chronicling "his violence, using fists, knees, blackjacks, revolver, and knuckle dusters. New and used knuckle dusters were found in his trunk after he was arrested for killing Oswald."[536] The truth of the matter is, he was probably a combination of all of the above, and very few people saw every side of his multi-faceted nature.

The question on the lips of most Americans on the afternoon of November 24, 1963, was: Why did Jack Ruby kill Lee Harvey Oswald? Answers varied. There was world-wide speculation that Ruby "silenced" the accused assassin before he could talk. But the official answer was that the emotional club owner wanted to spare Mrs. Kennedy the traumatic journey back to Dallas to testify at Oswald's trial. Some of his employees and girlfriends felt he had simply let his emotions dictate his actions. Others, who also knew Ruby well, laughed about his "grief" over the death of the President and refused to believe the official story.

What the public did not immediately know about Jack Ruby was that he had life-long connections to the Chicago mob and more immediate connections to the Mafia run by Louisiana's Carlos Marcello.

Jerry Cline, whose father Durward owned a music store in Dallas, found out from Jack Ruby's bartender that Ruby had shady associates. Jerry's older brother Jack played in a six-piece band at Ruby's nightclub, the Silver Spur, but he did not like his boss. "Jack Ruby scared Jack Cline, and he never forgot him." Jerry never forgot the comment Ruby's bartender made to him the day he was looking for a customer who owed money to the music store. Following a lead to the Silver Spur, he asked politely for Jack Ruby.

"'Son,' the bartender said softly, leaning forward, "'you don't want to find Jack Ruby. He's involved with the Mafia.'"[537]

It was not commonly known that Ruby sold guns to anti-Castro Cubans. However, two of the Warren Commission attorneys, Burt Griffin and Leon Hubert, discovered Ruby's connections to underworld figures, anti-Castro Cubans, and extreme right-wing Americans. The two men assumed that Ruby's smuggling of guns to Cuba was a result of his Mafia connections. This is because they did not know that Ruby also had ties to agencies just as dangerous as the Mafia. It took other researchers to discover Ruby's close connection to the CIA.

Ruby's role as an FBI informant was known by only a handful of people. Only Dallasites were aware that Ruby was unusually close with members of the Dallas Police Department and with certain politicians. One detail that did not surface until 2011 was the fact that Jack Ruby—small-time strip-club owner and wannabe national hero—at one time had a security clearance from the CIA and been allowed to fly on a top-secret experimental aircraft.[538] But Ruby must have been concerned about the FBI, the Dallas Police, and newspaper reporters discovering that he was more than a local strip-club owner.

Perhaps this is why, while incarcerated in Dallas, he panicked and told a friend: "They are going to find out about Cuba. They are going to find out about the guns. Find out about everything." Jack Ruby had reason to be frightened. Eventually, an FBI report surfaced suggesting that Ruby had been a "bagman" for a group of individuals who stole weapons from the U.S. military and then sold them to anti-Castro Cubans.[539]

Ruby's CIA and gun-running connections were ignored by the Warren

Commission, despite the fact that Oswald was eventually linked to both. Consequently, the final report of the Warren Commission stated that there was *no* connection between Jack Ruby and Lee Harvey Oswald and *no* connection between Jack Ruby and the Mafia or any other organization.

Regardless of who Jack Ruby associated with, most people who knew him agreed that his moods were mercurial. Depending on the day and on his mood, Jack Ruby could be quite personable. He made a point of knowing everyone he thought was important, especially policemen, judges, restaurant owners, politicians, and businessmen. He solicited patrons for his clubs by pushing his business cards on everyone he met.

Jack Ruby was especially eager to pass out business cards to the Dallas Police, whether he did so at the police station or on the street. His Vegas Club was more of a dance club than a nightclub; it most definitely was not the strip club that the Carousel Club was. According to a woman who often patronized the Vegas Club, it was "a big room, packed like sardines, dark, with spotlights, drinks, music, laughter, dancing, but with about as much décor as Jack's apartment. This is where policemen and firemen came to play, *not* to hire whores! Some brought their wives. My hubby was welcome anytime, but it was not his cup of tea."[540]

Even Candy Barr, the most famous strip dancer in Texas, jitterbugged in the Vegas Club before and after she became a famous stripper. However, the dancing at the Vegas Club did not include the removal of clothes. Ruby's sister, Eva Grant, made sure that it was an "oasis of safety" for girls like Juanita Slusher, better known as "Candy Barr." Barr fondly remembered that Ruby's sister had strict policies about customer behavior lest they be thrown out. "The first rule was that everyone who entered the club had to be treated with respect," she added.[541] Men weren't afraid to bring along their "sheltered life-style" wives.

Barr added that the Vegas Club atmosphere resembled Prohibition parties in the 1920s. Both couples and singles patronized it because it was a safe place to let their hair down and dance. "The place was a joint, but a straight one, and it had the approval of the Citizens Council, which periodically arranged for visits by people from out of state and guests of Chamber of Commerce officials," reminisced Barr.[542]

The Carousel Club, which was managed by Eva's brother, Jack Ruby, was a different animal. Today, many people recall being in Jack Ruby's Carousel Club at one time or another, but after Ruby killed Oswald, they were reluctant to admit it. Some shared their memories of the club only if their names were not used. When they were watching the floor show, they never dreamed that someday Jack Ruby's actions would make his sleazy club world-famous.

Not long before November 22, 1963, one such young woman and her husband traveled from their small West Texas town to Ft. Worth. Both were students at Texas Christian University. Chances are the young man never wanted his girlfriend or his girlfriend's parents to know that he and a great many other TCU students enjoyed a different type of entertainment at the Carousel Club. The entertainment offered there was not often seen in West Texas. Normally, the couple patronized Pat Kirkwood's "Cellar" in Ft. Worth. The "Cellar" became almost as infamous after the assassination as Ruby's Carousel Club because several of President Kennedy's Secret Service agents partied there until the wee hours of November 22, 1963.

The West Texas woman, who after all these years still does not want her name used, recalled that in November 1963, she and her husband drove to Dallas for a convention, and stayed at the Statler-Hilton. She remembered a group of fellow convention attendees walking down Commerce Street one evening after dinner; the group wandered into Jack Ruby's Carousel Club. She does not remember seeing Ruby that evening, but then again, her eyes were glued to the floor of the club. The woman recalled being so embarrassed by the scantily-clad strippers that for most of the night she kept her eyes on her hands in her lap.

Though it was dark inside the club, she did not like its ambiance. All she wanted to do was leave and go home. Occasionally, she would glance up and just as quickly glance back down. Finally, she asked her husband if they could please leave. He realized she had never been in a place like the Carousel, and that it was not the place for her. So, they started towards the exit, but not before she heard a man's voice cry out, "Take it off!"

The young women who performed in Ruby's notorious Carousel Club had been instructed on how to "take it off," at least according to an article that appeared in the winter 1962 issue of *Adam* magazine. Billed as "the man's home companion," the magazine spotlighted Ruby's Dallas strip club in a story entitled "Cool School."

Ruby openly bragged to the writer of the article that he had founded a "learn as you show" school for "wanna-be" strippers. The Carousel Club was described as one of Dallas' "most popular burlesque clubs."[543] Written like a paid advertisement by Jack Ruby, the article told readers that the cover charge was only $2.00, and beer and set-ups were served. The club catered to "large stag groups, especially college students and oil or cattle conventions."[544]

Ruby explained that he launched an "Amateur Night" for young women who enjoyed stripping in front of an audience (even if they had not graduated from Ruby's "Cool School" for strippers.) Though most of the article and all of the photos naturally focused on the women who became "stars" via the

Carousel Club, Ruby managed to be quoted himself. "…Many of the girls perform at Amateur Night under the urging of their boyfriends," he told the magazine writer.[545]

The photographer of Ruby's curvaceous "coeds" is unnamed in the article, but it was none other than Jack Beers. Beers is the photographer who took the photo of Ruby with his gun pointed at Oswald; he snapped his photo six-tenths of a second before photographer Bob Jackson took the Pulitzer Prize-winning photo of Ruby actually murdering Oswald. Won 1962, when he was shooting photos of Jack Ruby's strippers, Beers could hardly have imagined that a year later he would capture Ruby himself on film shooting a man in cold blood!

CHAPTER 54

THE VOICE OF DUKE STEPHENSON

"The only thing Jack Ruby liked was money...
He never did anything for nothing."

Not all of Jack Ruby's employees remember him the way Joyce Gordon did. Duke Stephenson, for example, saw a different side to his employer. The musicians who played in Ruby's two clubs came and went. Some were professionals who had been playing for years. Others, like Stephenson, were college students majoring in music at nearby North Texas State University. Stephenson explained to the authors that he was completing his master's degree in music in 1959. Like most students, he needed extra money. He was a talented drummer, and his services were needed at Jack Ruby's Carousel Club. Considering that Ruby's musicians were basically playing strip music, Stephenson's talents were most likely wasted, but the job helped pay his tuition bills. So, from 1959-1960, the young musician provided the beat for the "bump and grind" movements associated with Ruby's strippers.

Ruby was impressed with Stephenson's abilities and his sense of responsibility. As he thought back, Stephenson explained, "I don't remember how I got the job. People usually came looking for me instead of me having to look for a job. I was also in a road band."[546] He described Ruby as a "professional businessman who treated me very well." The young drummer never saw anything unusual going on at the club. He commented, "I never saw anything that bothered me. Ruby treated me fine. He paid me well. I demanded it, and there was never a problem."

However, Stephenson did realize that he was treated differently by his employer than the other musicians. He remarked, "I knew I was the only one of the band members who got to go to Ruby's back room behind the stage of the Carousel Club." The back room contained a safe, into which he would put cash sales, and this is where Ruby was also known for hosting illegal poker parties. Stephenson stated that Ruby always paid him and the other band members in cash. He believed Ruby appreciated his professionalism. "He treated me professionally, maybe because I demanded respect."

SARA PETERSON & K.W. ZACHRY

Stephenson admitted that the Carousel Club could have hosted Mafia visitors from time to time. He added, "There were a couple of gentlemen that came in once or twice. They seemed out of place. Jack sat down at a table and talked to them. I was never invited to sit with them. They had on professional-looking dark suits. The club was dimly lighted, so they would not have needed the sunglasses they wore." Stephenson reiterated, "These men were definitely out of place in the club. But no names were *ever* mentioned. Jack was very private."

According to Stephenson, he never saw the side of Ruby that some people later described. "I never saw him lose his temper. He trusted me to pay the other musicians, and always in cash." At that time, Stephenson was more concerned with his studies at North Texas State University than with any drama at the Carousel Club.

In 1963, Stephenson was employed in Jal, New Mexico, as a band director. A former student of his, Milton Thorpe, was surprised by a story Stephenson shared with some of his students two days after Jack Ruby murdered Lee Harvey Oswald. The students had no idea that their quiet band director had any connections to the now infamous Jack Ruby. Apparently, Stephenson was as shocked by what his former boss did to Lee Harvey Oswald as Ruby's other employees were. Maybe this is why he shared some of his past night club experiences with his students.

He explained to the band class on November 26, 1963 that, as a graduate student, he once worked for Jack Ruby at his Carousel Club as a drummer. The students asked Stephenson about Ruby and why Stephenson thought he shot Oswald. The band director answered them cryptically: "Ruby never did anything for nothing."

Thorpe remembered Stephenson telling him, as he was putting away band instruments that day: "The only thing Jack Ruby liked was money, but I have no idea if he killed Oswald out of emotion."[547]

To the authors, Stephenson recalled his reaction to Ruby's murder of Oswald: "I was shocked. It was out of character. He wasn't a violent man. He demanded the best from people, but so do I."[548]

Throughout the years, some people have suggested that Jack Ruby had multiple personalities. Stephenson's response to this was, "I don't think it's possible he had more than one personality." Other than the two men Stephenson saw in the club who seemed out of place, he did not remember much about any other individuals who patronized the Carousel Club. He was quick to add, however, that he was too busy being a musician to worry about the comings and goings of different individuals.

Milton Thorpe recalled Stephenson telling him that he called someone he knew in Dallas after Ruby shot Oswald. He wanted more information about the situation. The person he spoke to told Stephenson something that only became known a few years later. Stephenson told Thorpe that the person he spoken to on the telephone mentioned that there was a rumor that Ruby might have cancer.[549] "People did speculate at the time as to whether Ruby might have some sort of brain disease or tumor which had caused him to impulsively shoot Lee Harvey Oswald, but there was no mention of cancer."

In a telephone interview, Stephenson seemed quite surprised that anyone remembered him working for Jack Ruby. At first, he did not recall telling this story to any of his students. But he thought for a minute and said, "Oh, I think I did mention it to my band students."[550] He remembered Milton Thorpe, and when he heard what Thorpe had recalled, his only comment was, "I don't remember all of that. I'm not saying I didn't say what he told you, but I don't remember."

But no wonder a high school student would vividly recall the interesting details his band director shared with him in November 1963. It is the band director himself who is now a bit vague about what he told his students. However, his memories of Jack Ruby are clear. In the interview, Stephenson did not mention that the FBI questioned him after the assassination. FBI case number 44-1639-4064 shows that Stephenson had, indeed, worked for Jack Ruby as a drummer, but by 1961 he was living and teaching in Puerto Rico. Of course, Stephenson may not have known the FBI was looking for him because the agents received their information from his ex-wife who lived in Houston at the time. Stephenson did not mention why he left his job at the Carousel Club and moved to Puerto Rico, 2,123 miles from Dallas.

CHAPTER 55

THE VOICE OF J.J. SINGSONG

**"Jack Ruby called me from Parkland Hospital
not long after the assassination."**

J. J. Singsong managed to avoid discussing her association with Jack Ruby after his arrest, though she knew him quite well. On the other hand, Candy Barr (Juanita Slusher) was one of the people connected to Jack Ruby who found the FBI on her doorstep after Ruby killed Lee Harvey Oswald. She claimed she knew him only as a friend, but that did not keep the FBI from thinking otherwise.

It was only her love for dancing that led Barr, after her waitressing job, to spend hours at different clubs. She didn't care about the alcohol or the men; she just loved to dance. Her evenings would begin at Dallas' Round-Up Club with its western theme. This club would close at 2 a.m., but this was too early for Barr to call it a night. So, she would head to the Silver Spur, which was managed by Eva Grant, Jack Ruby's sister. Ruby also worked at the Silver Spur.

It was here that Barr met Ruby, who was one the few men who had ever treated her gently and respectfully. Barr was lonely, and Ruby filled a void. He treated her like his little sister, but she thought of him as a kindly uncle. Barr never danced for Ruby as "Candy Barr," but she loved going to his Vegas Club to just relax and dance the night away.

When asked about Jack Ruby years later, Barr was forthcoming about the man who treated her with respect. She, like Joyce Gordon, remembered him as a kind-hearted man. "He may have been a cut-throat competitor, but he genuinely cared about the people who worked for him," she said. She then added a comment about the man who employed her as a dancer: "Abe Weinstein *pretended* to care."

One of the persons who supported her during her incarceration in the Huntsville prison was Jack Ruby. Only Jack Ruby genuinely tried to help her, seemingly without strings attached.[551]

The FBI must have wondered about the connection between Texas' famous stripper and Jack Ruby because "not more than ten hours after Ruby shot Oswald, the FBI came to interrogate her in Edna, Texas, grilling her hour after hour concerning her part in the plot to kill the President."[552] Of course, the FBI knew that Barr was once the girlfriend of mob boss Mickey Cohen. According to Barr, Jack Ruby used her as a conduit to Mickey Cohen.

Ruby's girlfriend, who laughingly identified herself to the authors as "J. J. Singsong," verified that Cohen visited Dallas from time to time. She herself met Cohen at the Dallas Athletic Club in the 1960s. Dallas authorities may or may not have known Cohen was in Dallas. But women like Barr and Singsong certainly did. She and Singsong were so naïve at the time that she did not even know that Cohen was a part of the Mafia

After Jack Ruby murdered Lee Harvey Oswald, Joyce Gordon and other women known as Jack's "girls" willingly provided information to the FBI about their now infamous employer. However, J. J. Singsong, who admitted to a brief affair with Jack Ruby, shared her personal experiences with only one official— her father. He was a Dallas police officer, and he forcibly placed her into a mental institution as soon as he learned of her involvement with Ruby.

Years later, she admitted to the authors that, at the time, she did not know why her father had been so concerned about her. He finally explained to her that he was "hiding" her, not only because she needed treatment for alcoholism, but also because he already realized certain things. As a police officer, he knew that people tied to the assassination were apt to be hurt or to disappear. After all, if Oswald, one of the most important characters in the assassination drama, could be killed as he stood surrounded by Dallas police officers, so could anyone else who might know important but inconvenient information.

The police officer's daughter was one of those Ruby girlfriends whom Ruby kept away from the Carousel Club. However, she received an unusual phone call from Jack Ruby while the President's body was still in Trauma Room 1. Ruby had somehow worked his way into the crowds at Parkland Hospital right after the shooting of the President on November 22. Nearly hysterical, he called Singsong from the hospital.

"That poor woman, that poor woman," he sobbed. "And those poor little kids! She's lost her husband. They've lost their father!"[553]

"Where are you, Jack?" J.J. Singsong asked.

"I'm at the hospital," he answered. "I need you to meet me!"

"Jack, I can't meet you. You know that," she replied. She didn't need to remind Ruby that 1) she was married and 2) her father was on the Dallas police force and he was unaware that she and the nightclub owner had been seeing each other for quite some time. Her father would not have approved for several reasons. To begin with, Ruby was considerably older than her, and more importantly, she was married and had three children.

"But I was not a stripper or a showgirl," Singsong said in an interview in 2015. "I was only in the Carousel once or twice, and that was in the afternoon, when it was closed. I didn't even know the strippers. I went to Jack's Vegas Club to dance. And Jack was very protective of me. He would sit me at a table with Dallas cops and remind them that my father wouldn't want anything to happen to me. So, I could dance and dance and then go out with Jack to get something to eat after the clubs closed."

As the woman recalled that memorable day in November of 1963, she mentioned that Ruby did not appear to be crying over the dead President. "It was Jackie and the kids that he was thinking of," she said softly. "Jack was a very emotional and tender-hearted man. Or, at least, the Jack Ruby *I* knew was. He was either up or down emotionally. Looking back, I see now that he might have been bi-polar, and, of course, there wasn't any medication for that even if it had been diagnosed."

That day, Ruby continued to beg Singsong to meet him somewhere. He needed to be with her and talk about his feelings, she assumed. But there might have been another reason he was so desperate to talk to her.

Singsong dragged herself to work in downtown Dallas on the morning of the assassination. Employed at the time as the secretary to the president of an oil company, she felt exhausted, having been out at the "Vegas Club" the night before, dancing until midnight, then dining with Ruby at the Cotton Bowling Palace. Singsong had no idea that Ruby spent the earlier part of the evening with Lawrence Meyers and Joe Campisi, both of whom were connected to the Dallas mob, and with Beverly Oliver.

It was common knowledge that Jack Ruby could often be found at Campisi's Egyptian Lounge, the Cabana Motel, the Lucas B&B Restaurant, and at Dallas newspaper offices, as well as around the Dallas Police Department. What only Dallas insiders knew was that he often met "associates" at the Cotton Bowling Palace. According to George Taylor, "My brother Alfie was a crack pool player who hung out at the Cotton Bowling Palace in Dallas. It was a hub of night life and frequented by Jack Ruby. Alfie figured the Feds would swoop down on the Cotton Bowling Palace and investigate all known Ruby associates. No Fed ever showed."[554] Taylor's memory supports Singsong's story that Jack Ruby used the Cotton Bowling Palace when he wanted to meet quietly with "business associates."

Jack Ruby, it appears, arranged to meet with a particular business associate in the early morning hours of November 22, 1963. He allowed Singsong to accompany him because he trusted her, at least up to a point. Ruby and Singsong were sitting at a table at the Cotton Bowling Palace when an attractive, dark-haired man approached Ruby and sat down. Ruby introduced him to Singsong as "Tony DiMaggio."[555]

"I'm Joe's brother," the man said, smiling.

"I don't believe you!" Singsong exclaimed. The man pulled out his wallet. "I remember it was so old and beat-up—just about falling apart!" she recalled. He showed her his driver's license. It was an Illinois license with a Chicago address and the name was, indeed, "Tony DiMaggio."

"This is a picture of my wife," he said as he flipped to a small photo of a young blonde posed provocatively on her knees. "It was one of those model, glamour-type shots," Singsong remembered, "and the woman favored Monroe."

"Did you know Marilyn Monroe?" Singsong asked in amazement.

"Of course," he replied. "She was my sister-in-law." It was at this point that Ruby handed Singsong some cash and told her to go amuse herself with the games because he and Tony "needed to talk business."

Singsong felt insulted. This was the first time Jack had ever treated her "like one of his 'girls.' I felt like he was treating me like some bimbo. He had never made me leave a conversation before. I had always sat with him when he discussed things with people. This was very unusual."

Ruby did not mention the conversation later, when he and Singsong headed to his Oak Cliff apartment. They arrived about 4:00 a.m., and the place had looked like it usually did, she recalled.

"It was a typical bachelor's apartment. Papers all over the counter. Never a bedspread—always just tangled sheets. He shared it sometimes with a roommate, George Senator. I couldn't stand him [Senator] and his curly gray hair. So, if he was at the apartment when we arrived, Jack would tell him to go somewhere else." That night, Senator was already elsewhere.

Singsong remembered that she and Ruby did not talk of the President's visit later that day. "I didn't even know he was coming to town," she explained. "I didn't keep up with things like that. I hadn't spoken with my father in a while, so I hadn't heard anything from him."

This is why Singsong was so surprised on November 22 to see crowds of people lining the streets as she made her way to Titche's Department Store in downtown Dallas. "I only had one pair of stockings," she laughed, "and I had danced the toes out of them the night before!" Hurrying into Titche's during her lunch break, she asked someone in the crowd why so many people were standing on the sidewalks.

"We're waiting to see the President and Jackie!" someone told her. Almost at that moment, the motorcade arrived, and there on Main Street, the President was within an arm's length.

"I could have touched his arm if I had wanted to," Singsong said, unable to quite keep the excitement out of her voice even today. "He was suntanned and waving at the crowds. There's a photo of him with his arm raised, and that's exactly how he looked." When Singsong finished her shopping at Titche's and returned to work, she was greeted with the shocking news that the president had just been shot.

"He can't have been," she exclaimed in disbelief. "I just saw him. That can't be right." But the radio reports contradicted her. Employees at the oil company were sent home that day, and that is why Singsong was home lying down when Jack Ruby called her that afternoon.

"He never called me at home because of my husband, you know," she explained, "and that's one reason I was so surprised."

It was thirty years later that Singsong, now divorced from her husband, shared this story with a researcher. The researcher showed her a photo of New York Yankee, Joe DiMaggio, standing with three other men.

"This is the man I saw that night," she said, pointing to a specific figure. She then drew a circle around the figure of the man who had shown her his wallet less than twenty-four hours before the assassination. Years later, the authors showed Singsong that same photo. She drew an arrow to a figure identified in the caption as "Vincent DiMaggio," the oldest brother of the famous Joe and Dom DiMaggio. Whether the man she met during the early morning hours of November 22 was really related to the baseball legend is debatable. The man who introduced himself as "Tony DiMaggio" might have just strongly resembled Vincent DiMaggio. None of Joe DiMaggio's brothers carried the name "Tony," not even as a middle name. However, other family members did, and one of them might have met with Ruby the night before the assassination.

Joe DiMaggio had never hidden his hate for John and Robert Kennedy. He blamed them for the death of his former wife Marilyn Monroe, whether she had committed suicide or not. He had even banned Kennedy's brother-in-law Peter Lawford from Monroe's funeral. According to author Morris Engelberg in his book *DiMaggio - Setting the Record Straight*, DiMaggio was asked if the Mafia might have killed one or both of the Kennedys.

DiMaggio replied, "When you mess with the big boys…"

DiMaggio also made a telling comment about all of the Kennedys, past and present, when he said, "It's in their blood, and what they did to me will never be forgotten. They murdered the one person I loved…I can never forget what their father and uncle did to Marilyn, especially their uncle."[556]

Joe DiMaggio's bitter feelings towards the Kennedys make Singsong's story even more intriguing, about a meeting between a man identified as Tony

DiMaggio and Jack Ruby hours before the assassination. Regardless of who this man was, he obviously had important business with Jack Ruby not long before the President arrived in Dallas.

After more than fifty years, Singsong has not forgotten that memorable evening. "I still don't understand why Jack sent me away from that table," she said. "But knowing how gentle and kind Jack could be, I still think he impulsively killed Oswald because of his feelings for Jackie and the kids. I'm not saying he didn't have a temper. He could blow up in a minute, but with me he was kind and loveable."

This man who could be tender-hearted and decent often carried a pistol with him, and on Sunday, November 24, 1963, he worked his way into the basement of the Dallas Police Department and shot the man accused of making Jackie Kennedy a widow.

As questions arose about if and why Oswald killed the President, more questions were immediately asked about why Jack Ruby silenced the accused killer before he could be brought to trial. Was it to save Jackie Kennedy from having to return to Dallas for Oswald's trial? Was it to keep Oswald from sharing information he shouldn't have shared? Was it to keep Oswald from being tried and, possibly exonerated?

A question that has never been asked until now is: Did Ruby's actions have anything to do with his meeting with a man who identified himself as "Tony DiMaggio"? Evidence has shown that Ruby "ran guns" to Cuba in the years before the assassination. Had he sold guns to someone using the name "DiMaggio" that were later used to kill the President? If so, this may be why Ruby was so desperate to talk to J.J. Singsong, who witnessed the meeting of the two men. Perhaps he needed to warn her to keep quiet about his early-morning meeting with a man calling himself "DiMaggio."

After the day of the assassination, Singsong never talked to Jack Ruby again. When he was in jail, she did send him a letter via his first lawyer, Tom Howard, but she never received a response. It wasn't long after Ruby's arrest that Singsong confessed to her father that she knew the night club owner well, and considered him a friend. Naively, she threw herself on her father's mercy and begged him to do something to help Ruby. Her father, who was close to homicide detective Capt. Will Fritz, instead found a place to "lock her" away for several months. Perhaps he had inside information about Ruby and the assassination that he knew would endanger his daughter. This information might have come from Will Fritz. Singsong recalled that Fritz often visited her family's house, both before and after the assassination.

Besides making sure that Singsong was never questioned by the FBI, her father made sure she would not be called to testify at Ruby's trial. Though the couple "dated," the Dallas police kept her relationship with Ruby secret from her father and her husband, and these men were now keeping it secret from the Warren Commission.

Questions about Oswald's activities before, during, and after the assassination were expected. After all, he was formally accused of killing police officer J. D. Tippit and President John F. Kennedy. But questions about Jack Ruby's actions before, during, and after the assassination are just as important, though they did not appear to be at the time. Only J.J. Singsong and the mysterious "Tony DiMaggio" knew about Jack Ruby's activities in those early morning hours of November 22. Neither of them volunteered this information to the Warren Commission. However, they weren't the only ones who neglected to mention interesting details about Jack Ruby. Ruby's tax attorney, Graham R. E. Koch, failed to mention to the Warren Commission that five days before Ruby killed Oswald, he changed his power of attorney.[557] Even the Warren Commission could not be blamed for information never shared with them.

CHAPTER 56

THE VOICE OF CONGRESSMAN RALPH HALL

**"...Not long after Ruby killed Oswald,
four FBI agents showed up at my office in California ..."**

J.J. Singsong was not the only person hesitant to admit knowing Jack Ruby and having contact with him prior to the assassination. A Texas state senator and future United States Congressman discovered how quickly the FBI could track down anyone who might have important information. When Jack Ruby told people he "knew everyone," he was not exaggerating. Because he sometimes had legal issues involving his employee contracts and his liquor licenses, Ruby knew various attorneys, not to mention a whole lot of people in law enforcement.

After Ruby shot Oswald, his apartment, his clubs, and his car were searched by Dallas police. One of the items found in his apartment was a card with the name of a Texas state senator written on it and the Senator's telephone number. The Senator's name was Ralph M. Hall. According to an FBI interview conducted on December 19, 1963 (File #DL 44-1639), Hall's name was found in Ruby's car. In a telephone interview with the authors, Hall confirmed this. The now elderly politician shared his memories of the Kennedy assassination and the days that followed it in a telephone interview.

"I was scheduled to meet with Kennedy that evening in Austin," he said quietly, "but he didn't make it. Governor Connally had invited my wife and me to the dinner he was giving that night at the Governor's Mansion. I was driving out of Dallas to pick up my wife and children to head to Austin when I heard about the assassination."[558]

Hall was not only a Texas state senator in 1963, he was also president and CEO of Texas Aluminum. He maintained an administrative office for Texas Aluminum in California. After the assassination, he flew to California to take care of some business.

"Not long after Ruby killed Oswald, four FBI agents showed up at my office in California. They were very serious and told me anything I said could be held against me and all that. When I asked what they wanted with me, they demanded to know how well I knew Jack Ruby. I asked them how they knew

I *knew* Jack Ruby, and they said my name was written on something found on his nightstand."

Hall paused a moment."I explained that my name was there because he had tried to borrow money from me and I had turned him down. In fact, he tried to borrow $25 from me once and I turned him down. Ruby also wanted me to talk to one of the city judges, Lou Sterrick, to help him get back his liquor license, but I refused to do that, too." In the FBI's interview with Hall on December 19, Hall advised the agents that he interviewed a man named Jack Walsh several days before Kennedy's assassination. During the interview, Walsh told Hall that he knew Jack Ruby.

Texas Senator Ralph Hall was eventually elected to the U.S. House of Representatives. He was a very close friend of war hero/actor Audie Murphy. "I knew Audie very well," Hall explained. "I helped get the statue of him erected in Greenville." Hall did not know any of Murphy's wives, but he did know his sisters, whom he referred to as "the girls." "They were all nice girls and Audie loved them very much. They were poor growing up, but they were nice people." Hall's recollections then returned to Jack Ruby.

"Ruby had a dive near the Adolphus," Hall recalled. His tone of voice indicated he had not cared much for Ruby. "I had some conversations with him," he admitted. Ruby's Carousel Club was popular with celebrities and businessmen who stayed across the street at the Adolphus Hotel. According to Hall, country-western singer Marty Robbins, for instance, wanted to go to the Carousel every time he was in town, and he would ask Hall to get him "tickets" (complimentary passes).

Hall did so, but one time he had to pick them up at the club in the company of his own wife, who "had studied to be a Baptist missionary." The couple were starting up the stairs that led to the Carousel Club "when a scantily-dressed woman passed us going into the club. My wife said firmly, 'We're not going another step.'"

The name "Ralph Hall" could easily have become as well-known as Joe Tonahill and Melvin Belli. This is because Ruby at first wanted Hall to defend him in court against charges of killing Oswald. Hall chuckled. "I told him to send me a $350 retainer, but I never heard any more from him." Hall did not express any regret that Ruby chose another attorney.

As a U. S. Congressman, Ralph Hall served in the House of Representatives from 1981 to 2015. Nowhere in the Warren Report is it mentioned that the name of a Texas state senator (who eventually became a United States Congressman) was found in the apartment of Jack Ruby. Chances are, this was because the explanation was so innocent that it was unnecessary to include it in the official report. But it does raise the question: What other names and information did the FBI file as "unimportant" and keep from Warren Commission members?

CHAPTER 57

TWO OSWALDS, ONE RUBY

"As I remember it, there was myself, Jack Ruby, Lee Harvey Oswald,
Sam Giancana, John Roselli, and an FBI man."—Paul Buccilli

The fact that FBI agents contacted former Congressman Ralph Hall shortly
after Jack Ruby's murder of Oswald shows that officials suspected a link
between the two men. This was true of other individuals as well. However, much of what witnesses shared with Commission investigators was later scattered amongst the twenty-six volumes of the Warren Report that most Americans never read or, as in the case of Hall's information, went unrecorded.

The two big questions never completely answered were: If there really were two Oswalds, as several researchers have speculated, did either of them know Jack Ruby? If either did, was one or both of them involved in a conspiracy to kill the President? Despite all the investigative resources available to the FBI and the CIA, it was independent researchers who found the most important evidence linking Oswald and Ruby. Some of this evidence came from individuals who stepped forward voluntarily, but some surfaced only because researchers, insistent on knowing more than the Warren Report provided. dug for it.

While New Orleans District Attorney Jim Garrison was conducting his own investigation of the Kennedy assassination in the late 1960s, he was contacted by a former Dallas taxi driver, Raymond Cummings. Cummings had seen a newspaper article which included a photograph of a New Orleans man with a distinctive physical appearance. The man was identified as "David Ferrie," and Ferrie was quoted as saying he had never been to Dallas, Texas. Cummings knew better, and he had the courage to explain to Jim Garrison how he knew Ferrie was lying. He told Garrison that he had driven Ferrie and Lee Harvey Oswald to Jack Ruby's Carousel Club sometime in 1963.[559]

According to an FBI investigation conducted by Special Agent Paul L. Scott Jr. on November 27, 1963, Dorothy Marcum [also spelled "Markham" in FBI documents] was overheard by Hubert B. Braden and his attorney Warwick Jenkins on November 26 discussing Jack Ruby and Lee Harvey Oswald.

"Dorothy Markham related that her Aunt *Billie* [last name was unknown at that date was later found to be "Hadley"] was employed by Jack Ruby at the Carousel Club, in Dallas, Texas. Dorothy's Aunt Billie reportedly told

Dorothy on Sunday, November 24, 1963, that Lee Harvey Oswald had worked for Jack Ruby at the Carousel Club in June or July 1963. Dorothy Markham also indicated during this conversation that she had once dated Jack Ruby sometime during the past year."[560]

In FBI interviews later that same day with both Markham and her aunt, Billie Hadley, agents were told that Hadley *had worked* at the Carousel Club, but she never saw Lee Harvey Oswald in the company of Ruby or at the Carousel Club. In addition, Markham stated that she had never dated Jack Ruby and that she knew him only casually.[561] The agents may have suspected that the two women were too frightened to admit the truth, but there was no proof that Warwick and Braden had heard Dorothy Markham's comments on November 26, 1963.

During the summer of 1963, as Francis Irene Hise was being interviewed for a job by Jack Ruby, she saw a young man enter the Carousel Club whom Ruby referred to as "Ozzie." Lee Harvey Oswald's Marine nickname had been "Ozzie." Sometime after Hise was hired as a waitress at Ruby's club, she encountered "Ozzie" again, and he even offered to buy her a drink. The "official" Oswald was at this time living and working in New Orleans. However, the man whom Hise had seen at the Carousel Club resembled the "official" Oswald so much that Hise identified him as the man she saw in the Carousel Club, even though the man must have been a look-alike.[562]

Jack Ruby's auto mechanic, Leon Woods, recalled that Oswald and Ruby knew each other. He knew this because Oswald drove Ruby's car to Roy's Auto Shop for repairs. Roy was unaware that the "official" Oswald had no driver's license. The mechanic also recalled that he drove Oswald back to Ruby's Carousel Club. Woods could have been a valuable source of information about individuals connected to Jack Ruby. As the manager of Gibb's Auto, where Ruby parked his 1960 Oldsmobile, Woods maintained records of those who brought in cars for repairs, and who drove them out after they were ready.

The FBI believed these records were valuable enough to examine. The records certainly would have shown if Lee Harvey Oswald had ever brought Ruby's car to this parking lot. Unfortunately, the record book was never returned to Leon Woods, and it was *never* shared with the Warren Commission. Dallas reporter Earl Golz attempted to locate the record book; strangely enough, he was told by the FBI that they knew nothing about it.[563]

Dallas detective H. M. Hart discovered another connection between Lee Harvey Oswald and Jack Ruby. A confidential informant told him that, in September 1963, Ruby rented an apartment in Oak Cliff for a man named "Lee Oswald." The apartment was in a building next to the apartment complex where Jack Ruby lived. The informant also related that the building manager asked

Oswald to move simply because he disliked him.[564]

One of Ruby's dancers, Kathy Kay, remembered seeing Oswald in the Carousel Club. In fact, she danced with him there. Bill Demar, an entertainer at Ruby's club, stated that Oswald was at Ruby's Carousel Club a week before the assassination. He remembered this because Oswald participated in Demars' memory act. Even Dallas attorney Carroll Jarnagin saw Ruby and Oswald conversing in the Carousel Club. He overheard Oswald make a comment that seemed unimportant at the time; he said to Ruby, "Don't use my real name. I'm going by the name of O. H. Lee."[565]

"O. H. Lee" is the name by which Lee Harvey Oswald was known by his landlady at the Beckley rooming house. How could Jarnagin have known this detail at that time unless "Oswald" or someone impersonating him actually made that comment?

The more the Dallas police investigated Ruby's connections, the more witnesses they found who had seen Ruby with someone known as "Oswald." Walter ("Wally") Weston, for example, the master of ceremonies for the Carousel Club, recalled noticing Oswald at the club with Ruby at least a couple times before the assassination.[566] Weston also remembered that five days before the assassination, Ruby had a meeting with six to eight "friends" from Chicago. Weston said Ruby introduced them to him by saying, "These are friends of mine from Chicago."[567]

Myron Thomas Billet, better known as Paul Buccilli, was one of those men. Buccilli was a convicted murderer. He admitted to being at Ruby's club the night Weston said. He also admitted: "As I remember it, there was myself, Jack Ruby, Lee Harvey Oswald, Sam Giancana, John Roselli, and an FBI man."[568] The conversation centered on "a hit" on President John Kennedy.

Buccilli claimed that he and Giancana left because they did not want to be a part of the assassination. But he realized that the meeting most likely led to the death of the President.

"Three weeks later, JFK was hit, and we all knew it was not done by one man. Sam [Giancana] told me then that he figured this would get us all killed before it was over."[569] Giancana was either psychic or astute. Oswald was executed in front of millions of television viewers. Roselli was murdered and his body found in pieces stuffed into an oil drum. And Giancana was shot execution-style in his own kitchen by someone he trusted enough to allow him access.

Supporting Weston's and Billet's stories was a waitress and champagne hostess named Ester Ann Mash. She recalled to researcher Jim Marrs that she saw Lee Harvey Oswald in the Carousel Club with Ruby and men she referred to as "gangsters" from Chicago in 1963. It was not until November 24, 1963, when Mash, like millions of others, watched Ruby gun down Oswald that she realized Oswald was one of the men taking part in that meeting. She remembered screaming, "Oh my god! That's the weird little man who was at that secret meeting with Jack and those Mafia types."[570]

Still another employee of Ruby, Clyde Malcolm Limbough, remembered Oswald visiting the Carousel and going to the back room on three separate occasions.[571] The "back room" was where illegal poker parties often took place; it was also where Ruby conducted "private" business. This is the same "back room" where musician Duke Stephenson was given money by Ruby to pay the other band members.

Not long after the assassination, Bill Cherry, who worked for the Petroleum Engineers Publishing Company in Dallas, discovered that at least one individual inadvertently observed things at the Carousel Club that he later thought he would regret.[572] Cherry was friendly with a young intern at the publishing company named James Womack. Womack was an unusually outgoing and congenial person to work with, until Kennedy's assassination. He then became noticeably quiet and withdrawn—so withdrawn that Cherry finally insisted on knowing if something had happened.

"Something wrong?" he recalled asking Womack. "Are you sick?" Womack denied that there was any problem, but his attitude did not improve. Cherry continued to press him to explain his change in behavior.

"I guess I'd better talk to someone," Womack finally admitted, so the two young men moved into the company mail room, where no one could hear their conversation. Cherry learned that for a few weeks before the assassination, Womack had been working, with a friend, at Jack Ruby's Carousel Club during after-hours.

"He told me that his friend was putting in new door jambs in the back part of the club," Cherry recalled to the authors. He and his friend worked late at night and off-the-clock.

"He also told me that Ruby would show up with one to four other guys, and they would go up to Ruby's office. One of those guys was Lee Harvey Oswald!"

Womack recognized Oswald when his image was shown on television for killing a Dallas police officer. That was surprising enough to Womack, but to hear that Oswald was also accused of killing the President was shocking. But it wasn't as shocking as seeing Jack Ruby murder a man Womack had seen him talking to just a few nights before the President's assassination!

Cherry now realized why James Womack was no longer the carefree eighteen-year-old he had been before November 24, 1963. Now he carried the almost unbearable burden of knowing that Jack Ruby was somehow connected to the man accused of killing Kennedy. If Ruby would gun down someone he entertained in his own club, would the people who ordered Ruby to kill Oswald also kill James Womack because he saw Oswald with Ruby?

Just sharing his story with someone he trusted seemed to make Womack feel better, but he still feared for his life, and Cherry assumed this is why he soon quit his job and left Dallas. Cherry did not know if Womack's unidentified friend, who had also seen Ruby and Oswald together, was as lucky.

If only a handful of these witnesses can be believed, then it appears that Jack Ruby and a "Lee Harvey Oswald" did, indeed, know, and associate with, each other. That is not surprising considering that one of the Oswalds was connected to Carlos Marcello. Oswald's uncle Charles "Dutz" Murret was not only associated with illegal gambling, but with the Marcello organized crime family. Because Ruby was also connected to organized crime and to New Orleans, the two men probably crossed paths. Oswald died without admitting to any organized crime connections. The strongest link to Marcello was his uncle. However, Murret died "after a brief illness" at the age of 63, two weeks after the Warren Report was issued. His death is seldom mentioned as "convenient," but it certainly guaranteed that "Dutz" Murret never again discussed his nephew or the Marcello family!

However, it is difficult to determine whether Ruby knew *both* of the men using the name "Lee Harvey Oswald," or just one.

On November 14, 1963, while the "official" Oswald was counting textbooks at the Depository, a man resembling him and using his name was seen at the New Port Motel in Morgan City, Louisiana. Corrine Villard had known Jack Ruby for years. She did not know the young man who sat nearby in the lobby of the New Port Motel, but Ruby obviously did.

As he visited Villard, Ruby repeatedly turned towards the young man and winked at him. Then the waitress saw the two men meet at Ruby's car in the parking lot. On November 22, 1963, Villard recognized the younger man as he was paraded in front of the media in Dallas, Texas, and accused of killing a Dallas police officer. Besides Villard's memory, there is also hard evidence that Jack Ruby and a man identified as "Oswald" did meet at the New Port Motel. Two Dallas constables, Mike Callahan and Ben Cash, saw a receipt from the New Port Motel dated November 14, 1963, with both Oswald's and Ruby's names on it.[573]

The Area Commercial Manager of Southwestern Bell telephone company, Raymond A. Acker, provided proof to the Dallas police that phone calls took place between Oswald and Ruby—the actual phone records. Ruby was infamous for insisting that a phone call was an emergency call if the line was busy. At the time, the telephone company kept records of all local calls if they were deemed "emergency calls." Acker assumed that the Dallas Police Department would be eager to acquire proof of a connection between Oswald and the man who killed him. He found out that this was not the case. In fact, after he gave the records to the police department, an officer strongly suggested that he return home and keep his story to himself.[574] According to newspaper editor Penn Jones, Acker was transferred not long afterwards to Kansas City, Missouri. Obviously, the Dallas Police Department was already determining which information should be recorded and which information should be ignored.

Rose Cherami, who claimed she worked for Jack Ruby (known to her as "Pinky") at one time, said she knew that Lee Harvey Oswald and Jack Ruby were more than just acquaintances. Cherami revealed the following to Lt. Francis Fruge of the Louisana State Police about Ruby and Oswald: "Them two queer sons-of-bitches. They've been shacking up for years."[575]

She was not the only person to refer to Ruby as a homosexual, though this information would have shocked Ruby's numerous girlfriends. In a Criminal Intelligence report dated December 2, 1963, written by Detective H. M. Hart of the Dallas Police Department, a confidential informant stated, "Ruby is a homosexual and has attended homosexual parties in Dallas recently with Lee Harvey Oswald." The informant also stated that Oswald was considered to be a "trade" by other homosexuals, meaning that he took only a passive part in homosexual acts. The informant added that a stripper using the name "Dixie Lynn" attended some of these parties in Dallas and told him she had seen Ruby with Oswald. At the end of the statement, Detective Hart noted that his informant was a homosexual and considered reliable by the Dallas Police Department.[576]

More and more people came forward after the assassination to tell of encounters with a man they thought was Lee Harvey Oswald. For instance, Helen McIntosh explained that on November 21, 1963, she was visiting a Southern Methodist University professor friend who lived at 223 South Ewing. She remembered that, on that evening, a young man knocked on the door of the professor's apartment. When she answered the door, the young man asked for Jack Ruby. The professor spoke up and said that Jack Ruby lived next door in Apartment 207. After the assassination, McIntosh recognized the man who had knocked on the door and asked for Jack Ruby—none other than Lee Harvey Oswald.[577]

Still another occurrence involved a sighting of a man who resembled Oswald. According to Mary Lawrence, the head waitress at the Lucas B&B Restaurant, Oswald was sitting in the restaurant at 2:15 a.m. on November

22, 1963, when Jack Ruby entered. Oswald joined Ruby at his table and the two talked for more than half an hour. Her statement was ignored by the FBI because agents knew that the "official" Oswald was at Ruth Paine's house in Irving, Texas that evening. But what most of the FBI did not know was that there were two men using the name "Oswald" that resembled each other so closely that dozens of people mistook one for the other.[578]

Ruby's girlfriend J. J. Singsong was with Ruby about that time at the Cotton Bowling Palace. When asked if he could have left while she played various games in the Palace, she told the authors that he certainly could have. Lucas B&B Restaurant was near the Cotton Bowling Palace. This means that Ruby had not wanted Singsong to hear his conversation with the mysterious "Tony DiMaggio," and he also did not want her to see him with Oswald, even if this particular "Oswald" was a look-alike!

CHAPTER 58

FRIENDS IN SHADOWY PLACES

"Ruby was one of our boys."—Johnny Roselli

The Dallas police, the FBI, the CIA, and the Secret Service were not the only people investigating Jack Ruby's possible connection to the murder of President Kennedy. Industrious news reporters realized there was more to the story than the various agencies were telling them. This was especially true if the reporter represented a newspaper outside of Dallas, Texas.

Peter Worthington of the *Toronto Star Telegram*, for instance, discovered a great deal about Jack Ruby by questioning Ruby's employees, his roommates, his friends in the Dallas Police Department, strippers who had worked for him, "and even ladies who had been beaten up by him."[579] Some of these individuals had escaped the notice of the FBI. Others told more to friendly reporters than they had to intimidating government agents. Víctor Reisel of the *Port Arthur News,* for example, uncovered information about Ruby that was not part of the nightclub owner's "official" biography. Worthington, Reisel, and other researchers recognized the connection between Jack Ruby and Chicago gangsters.

Before Ruby moved to Dallas in 1947, other more important mobsters had already infiltrated the city. According to David Scheim, in his book *Contract in America*, a large group of Chicago gangsters moved into the Dallas area around 1946. One of the most infamous was Paul Roland Jones, a man with whom Jack Ruby was associated. In fact, Ruby became connected to the Mafia at a very young age. Though he became involved with the Dave Miller Gang in the 1940s, he was, before that, an errand boy for Al Capone in Chicago. One of his responsibilities was to deliver sealed envelopes for Capone. During tese early years, he was exposed to gambling, and learned that certain unions were controlled by the Mafia.

Los Angeles police detective Gary Wean told author Anthony Summers that he knew Ruby was connected to California mobster Mickey Cohen, boyfriend of stripper "Candy Barr," because, as a Los Angeles policeman in 1946 and in 1947, he saw the two men together in Cohen's limousine.[580]

By the 1950s, Jack Ruby had graduated from errand boy to nightclub manager. He soon realized that illegal money could be made from businesses which leased jukeboxes and pin-ball machines. Gambling and prostitution were also a lucrative means of income. Because Carlos Marcello controlled a large part of the slot machine industry in Texas, Jack Ruby surely crossed paths with him. By ingratiating himself to both the Chicago mob and the New Orleans mob, Jack Ruby had friends in shadowy places.

In the 1950s, the mob in Dallas became an extension of the Carlos Marcello organization. Marcello had been set up by, and answered to, a more powerful mobster, Meyer Lansky.[581] In Dallas, Jack Ruby was connected to the Silver Spur Club, the Vegas Club, and the Sovereign Club, which he later renamed the Carousel Club. Neither of these clubs was the "classy" venue Ruby always dreamt of. However, he did begin to associate with important underworld figures. In Dallas, he was close to the Campisi brothers. Joseph and Sam Campisi owned the well-known Egyptian Lounge, which was famous for its steaks and its mob-associated customers. Many of these same figures also patronized Ruby's clubs.

A former Dallas sheriff told news reporter Peter Worthington: "I used to visit Ruby's Silver Spur whenever I wanted to find someone from the Syndicate."[582] Some of the notorious characters that the sheriff probably encountered in the Silver Spur were Murray "The Camel" Humphreys, Paul "Needle Nose" Labriola, Romeo Jack Knapp, and Frank "The Enforcer" Nitti. Such men obviously felt comfortable in Jack Ruby's club and did not worry about being harassed by the Dallas authorities. After all, Jack Ruby made a point of being the friend of local policemen.

Though Joseph Campisi presented himself as a respectable Dallas businessman, behind the scenes he was so connected to the mob that, in 1957, he represented the Mafia at the Apalachin Mafia convention in New York. Campisi was considered the number two mob-connected man in Dallas; another associate of Jack Ruby, Joe Civello, was the number one man.[583] Campisi assured the Warren Commission that Ruby had no connection to organized crime. Ironically, the Commission accepted this statement as true!

An employee of Ruby, Bobby Gene Moore, was so surprised when a Dallas television reporter stated that Ruby had no gangster connections that he contacted the FBI immediately to assure them this was false.[584] Ruby's connections to Civello are some of the most interesting. According to John Curington, H. L. Hunt's right-hand man, Civello was also connected to Hunt.

Hunt instructed Curington to go to the Dallas Police Department on Saturday, November 23, 1963 because he wanted to know how much security was in place for Oswald. He ordered Curington to report back to him as soon as he returned, no matter how late it was. Consequently, Curington telephoned Hunt around midnight to report that no one challenged him when he entered the police department. "He was neither stopped not questioned, and no one checked his briefcase.

Hunt then asked Curington to contact Joe Civello, the head of the Dallas organized crime family and ask him to stop by the Hunt home because Hunt wanted to talk to him. Civello did so at 6:00 a.m. on Sunday."[585] Less than five hours later, Jack Ruby, a man known to be connected to organized crime himself, managed to avoid the so-called security at the Dallas police station and impulsively shot the President's accused assassin. It could have been a coincidence that Ruby had two transcripts of Hunt's *Life Line* radio program in his pocket at the time of his arrest.

Curington knew the Sunday morning visit between Hunt and Civello was not been the first such time the two men met. He explained in his book *H. L. Hunt: Motive & Opportunity* that Hunt "made sure that he had at least a casual relationship with Civello."[586] Curington accompanied Hunt while visiting Civello's liquor store near Love Field Airport. The three men also met at the Admiral's Club at Love Field.

Hunt and Civello knew each other well enough to discuss how someone could protect against being linked to a serious crime. Civello offered four suggestions: 1) Make sure the person hired to commit the "serious crime" was unknown to the public, 2) Kill him as soon as the crime was successfully committed, 3) If that is not possible, convince him to not turn against you, and 4) Never let him go to court. Always make him plead guilty so there will be no trial.[587] These suggestions did seem to fit the Kennedy-Oswald-Ruby triangle.

Before he was arrested, Oswald was unknown to most of the world. If he had not shouted "I am not resisting arrest," he could easily have been killed in the Texas Theatre. If Capt. Will Fritz treated him the way he treated Buell Frazier when arresting him, then Oswald would have signed a confession, even if he was not guilty. When Oswald refused to admit guilt, Jack Ruby made sure he never went to trial. Perhaps Civello's suggestions *were* followed that weekend.

Though Curington knew Hunt and many of his employees well, he was surprised to hear in January 1970 that John Brown, a sales manager in Hunt's company, HLH Products, was listed as a pallbearer at Joe Civello's funeral. Brown was "a key employee who reported only to Hunt or to Curington."[588] He somehow managed to hide his association with Joe Civello.

The Warren Commission never discovered Jack Ruby's Mafia connections, but the House Select Committee on Assassinations did. Its investigators found that Civello was a personal acquaintance of Jack Ruby, and that he was tied to Carlos Marcello. By then, of course, Civello was dead and so was Jack Ruby. Neither one could admit or deny anything.

Curington was also a witness to a strange incident that occurred not long after Kennedy's death. Hunt called him early on a Saturday morning and told him to come down to Hunt's office. Hunt's business was housed in two large downtown Dallas buildings—the Mercantile National Bank building and the Mercantile Securities Building, which were located next door to one another. A large steel door connected the two buildings. It usually stood open so employees could move from one building to another.

On this particular morning, Curington was ordered to close and lock the door and to make sure no employees were working in the buildings. He was also told to stand in the lobby of the building where Hunt's office was located because a woman would soon enter the lobby. Curington was told to ignore her but to make sure no Hunt employees entered the building before or after the woman entered.

Curington admitted to being curious about all of this, but as a loyal Hunt employee, he took orders without asking questions. When the woman entered the lobby, Curington recognized her immediately. Her image had been in newspapers around the world and on television recently. The woman whom he pretended not to see was Marina Oswald, and she walked directly to the elevator. Curington did not look to see what floor the elevator stopped on, but the woman returned in about twenty minutes. Once again, he and she ignored one another, but this time she left through a back door in the building, and Curington could see her enter a black automobile with U.S. government license plates.[589]

Hunt never discussed the incident with Curington. It's difficult to imagine what the "richest man in the world" could have wanted to say to Marina Oswald. Because he had banks in Dallas, New York, Chicago and, more importantly, in Switzerland, he could have easily arranged for private "donations" to be made to the widow of a man who might have been killed because someone knew ahead of time about the lack of security in the Dallas Police Department. Those "donations" might have also guaranteed that the widow said whatever government officials needed her to say.

Ruby was also connected to another member of the Mafia, Russell D. Matthews, who was an associate of mob boss Santos Trafficante. Matthews, like Joseph Campisi, became involved with the Dallas-based mob. Matthews was generous enough to allow his Turtle Creek apartment to be used by out-of-town "guests" like Big Spring gambler George McGann. Matthews and numerous associates were described by informants and local officers as "paid killers," which probably explains why George McGann idolized him.[590] Matthews was a handsome man who was never seen without sunglasses; one of his "associates" had shot out his eye. The man did not live to brag about it, however.

Another associate of Ruby was Lewis McWillie. McWillie was a gambler, gun runner, drug smuggler, and mob hitman. He was heavily involved in illegal gambling in the 1940s and operated several gambling joints in the Dallas area. McWillie once was business partners with W. C. "Pappy" Kirkwood. Kirkwood operated the 2222 Club, which was known for its illegal gambling casino.

The customers who patronized this establishment were like a Who's Who of the rich and famous of Texas. Joe Patoski wrote that Sam Rayburn, the Speaker of the U.S. House, and Nenetta Burton Carter, the wife of Ft. Worth mogul Amon Carter, were known to visit the club. W. C. Kirkwood was the father of Pat Kirkwood, who later owned the Cellar in Fort Worth, where some of Kennedy's Secret Service agents spent the evening and early morning hours before the assassination.[591]

McWillie and associates Meyer and Jake Lansky were managers of the mob-owned Tropicana Hotel in Havana before Castro closed the casinos.[592] There is no question that McWillie and Ruby were friends. They visited each other when both were in Havana in 1959. Telephone records show that Ruby contacted McWillie many times in 1963.

It was convenient for Jack Ruby to contact New Orleans mob associates because he often visited the Louisiana city in search of "talent." On one of these trips, he may have met Rose Cherami, just as she claimed. He definitely found the stripper billed as "Jada" in New Orleans at the Sho-Bar. He was so impressed with her unusual, provocative act that he convinced her to come to Dallas to perform at his Carousel Club.

It would have been impossible for any mob-connected individual to do business in New Orleans without knowing Carlos Marcello. Nothing mob-related took place without Marcello's knowledge. Ruby kept in contact with the Marcello organization by travelling to New Orleans and by making telephone calls to Carlos Marcello's brother Pete, owner of the Sho-Bar on Bourbon Street in New Orleans. He also kept in contact with Vincent Marcello, who had the jukebox and slot machine business, thanks to his father Carlos.

Although Teamster leader Jimmy Hoffa did not publicize his relationship with Ruby after the Oswald slaying, there definitely had been one. After the assassination, the Justice Department documented a link between Jack Ruby, Frank Chavez, and Tony Provenzano, who was a captain in the Genovese Mafia family.[593] It is hard to imagine how the FBI and the CIA overlooked connections like these.

Perhaps this oversight resulted from the fact that men like Sam Giancana and Johnny Roselli later admitted their close connection to two powerful organizations—the Mafia and the CIA. If there is any doubt that Ruby was connected to the Mafia, it can be dispelled by a comment made by Roselli to columnist Jack Anderson: "Ruby was one of our boys."[594]

"Jack knew *everybody!*" was a typical comment from Ruby's employees after the assassination. By "everybody," they meant strippers, politicians, prostitutes, law enforcement officers, businessmen, club owners, judges, and doormen. Texas Senator Ralph Hall was not the only politician to come into contact with Jack Ruby. For years, the Mob was influential in different political campaigns and with different candidates.

Richard Nixon was just one politician with a strong connection to the Mafia community. Mobster Sam Giancana and Nixon met in the 1940s when Nixon was a congressman from California. Giancana and Nixon exchanged favors periodically. Giancana admitted to his brother Chuck that he financially supported both Nixon and Kennedy in the 1960 election.

In 1947, Giancana called in a favor from Nixon. He requested help when one of his mob associates was called as a potential witness for the House Committee on Un-American Activities. This mob associate was none other than Jack Ruby. In a memo addressed to a congressional committee investigating organized crime, but not discovered until 1975, an FBI assistant stated: "It is my sworn testimony that one Jack Rubenstein of Chicago ... is performing information functions for the staff of Congressman Richard Nixon, Republican of California. It is requested Rubenstein not be called for open testimony in the aforementioned hearings." Though the FBI subsequently called the memo a "fake," the reference service Facts on File considers it authentic.[595] President Richard Nixon admitted to an aide, Roger Stone, that the facts in the memo were true. "'It's a hell of a thing. I actually knew this Jack Ruby fella. Murray Chotiner brought him back in '47. Went by the name Rubenstein. Our informant. Murray said he was one of Lyndon Johnson's boys…We put him on the payroll!"[596]

Sam Giancana verified Nixon's memory. He explained why he owed Richard Nixon his support. "Shit, he even helped my guy in Texas, (Jack) Ruby, get out of testifying in front of Congress back in '47 …sayin' Ruby worked for him."[597] Whether Ruby actually worked for Richard Nixon, or whether Nixon was so indebted to Giancana that he pretended this was the case, the two names are now linked. In fact, a photograph has surfaced showing a young Richard Nixon. Standing behind him is a man who certainly looks like a young Jack Ruby.

It is possible that Ruby was also tied to the FBI as an informant. Author Gary Cartwright discovered that the FBI approached Ruby several times and tried to use him in that capacity. Rather than refuse to help the FBI, Ruby inundated them with useless information about his competitors. Ruby may have needed money from time to time, and he always wanted to be "in the know." However, he also must have known what would happen to those who shared too much information with the FBI.

Ruby reinforced the image that he was a pathetic, wannabe "somebody" who pretended to know more than he did. Is this why the Dallas newspapers described him as a misguided patriot so overcome with grief for Mrs. Kennedy and her children that he impulsively killed President Kennedy's accused assassin? Perhaps the Dallas reporters should have spoken to the same people Toronto reporter Peter Worthington spoke to—the ones who laughed at the idea of Jack Ruby being interested in politics or caring about Dallas' reputation.

Ruby may not have cared about Dallas, but he cared about money. As Ruby employee Duke Stephenson told the authors, "The only thing Jack Ruby liked was money."[598] Dallas Police Lt. George Butler observed, "Ruby would do anything for a buck."[599] That included running guns to Cuba and pimping women. As early as 1956, an Intelligence Report to Capt. R. H. Lunday from Detective H.M. Hart indicated that, besides operating a night club, there was evidence Jack Ruby was acting as a pimp. He was observed making dates for two particular women at the Royal Grill in Dallas and renting rooms for them and their clients at the Adolphus Hotel.[600]

Does this mean Jack Ruby would silence Oswald for money? Someone may have convinced him that Dallas and the world would appreciate his impulsive gesture, and a jury of his peers would either find him "not guilty by reason of insanity" or sentence him to a short prison term. Most of the telegrams sent to Ruby during his incarceration praised him for killing Oswald. Perhaps Ruby was led to believe that a great deal of money was waiting for him upon his release. This explanation for his "impulsive" actions is much more logical than the one he offered to the world. If there is any truth to this scenario, then Jack Ruby learned the hard lesson that his "associates" were not as loyal as he thought they would be.

The only people who might have been surprised by Ruby's vicious side would probably have been his girl friends who knew him as kind, compassionate, and generous. And, indeed, Ruby could exhibit all of these traits. What would surprise almost everyone is that there is irrefutable evidence that the same man known for pushing unruly customers down the stairs—the same man who "impulsively" shot Lee Harvey Oswald—is also the same man who had a security clearance from the CIA in 1961.

CHAPTER 59

THE VOICE OF MEL BARNEY

"Only those with 'secret clearance' and a 'need to know' were allowed on the airplane. Jack Ruby flew on it two times."

Dallasite Mel Barney discovered an unknown detail about Jack Ruby that raises more questions about his connections to important people. Barney was a Texas Instruments engineer in the Airport Surveillance Radar Department from 1958 to 1989. He worked on top-secret experiments involving radar and an automatic pilot system for airplanes. He was issued three patents that improved the Automatic Terrain Following Radar Program [ATFR], a system allowing airplanes to fly on automatic pilot at a low 200-foot altitude. This allows airplanes to fly below radar and not be detected in enemy territory.

Working on the original test flights using the ATFR did not require more security clearance than Barney already had at Texas Instruments. But in 1961, he was summoned to Washington, D. C., by a person he soon realized worked for the CIA. When he returned to Dallas, Barney's security clearance was elevated because he was now working with the Company. During Barney's career, he was issued five different levels of security clearance: "Strictly Private, Confidential, Secret, Top-Secret, and Black."[601] Barney explained to the authors that "Black programs were only known about by a few Congressmen, the CIA, the President, and the company responsible for the program."

Barney was also assigned to a new CIA agent. The relationship lasted twenty years. As part of a "Black" program, Barney and his fellow pilot, Joe Truhill, flew experimental flights demonstrating how low an airplane could fly on autopilot. They even flew the airplanes over the Appalachian Mountains. Security was arranged by Grant Dove, the manager of Texas Instruments in Washington, D. C. The military was greatly interested in this new autopilot capability. Barney remembered flying admirals, generals, and various pilots from allied nations. Every individual who flew on the airplane had to be cleared by the CIA or the FBI.

It was not until 2011 that Mel Barney recognized a familiar name on one of his old manifest lists. He wrote a book titled *Four Wars* which included a copy of two of these manifest lists. According to the September 1, 1961 manifest, a guest named "Jack Ruby" flew on two different experimental flights. Seeing this infamous name brought back vivid memories to Barney. He suddenly remembered recognizing Jack Ruby, who climbed aboard the airplane. Barney briefly wondered why he was there but, as co-pilot, he had more important duties than asking about Jack Ruby's interests.

Barney knew that the passenger he remembered was the same Jack Ruby eventually connected to Lee Harvey Oswald. He knew this because years earlier, Barney entertained visiting engineers and managers at Jack Ruby's Carousel Club. The Carousel was a favorite social spot, particularly for visiting pilots. Barney was quick to assure the authors that he did not know Ruby well; however, Ruby would acknowledge him when he and his clients entered the Carousel Club because Ruby knew how many customers Barney usually brought with him.

Consequently, Barney was stunned when he realized that the nightclub owner somehow received clearance from either the CIA or the FBI to fly on a top-secret aircraft. The manifest showing Ruby's name and Barney's memory of him are proof that Jack Ruby was more than the *nobody* and the *wannabe* that the Warren Commission made him out to be.

Of course, Ruby tried to tell the Warren Commission this himself when he begged Chief Justice Earl Warren to bring him to Washington, D. C., to testify. Because Warren and the other Commissioners did not understand Ruby's past, he shared information with the few he trusted. One of these was Deputy Sheriff Al Maddox. In a taped interview, Maddox explained how he came into possession of a handwritten note from Jack Ruby.

Ruby was on his way to Parkland Hospital in 1967; perhaps he realized he would not be returning to his jail cell. As he passed Maddox, he pressed a handwritten note into his palm. "…I'm going to tell you … that I'm being framed for the assassination, period—that I shot Oswald to silence him."[602] This note is now in the possession of a private collector, but Maddox had shown it to researcher Mark Oakes. Oakes assured the authors he saw and read the note before it was sold.

Surely the Warren Commission would have taken Jack Ruby's role in the assassination more seriously had they known he had been used by the CIA and/ or FBI, or some other entity, to silence Lee Harvey Oswald. Of course, someone made sure the Warren Commission did *not* know this.

This fact could also explain why certain FBI and CIA agents ignored evidence that those "out of the loop" were uncovering. Even if Barney's manifest was revealed to officials in 1963, chances are it would have been "lost," "misplaced," or hidden. Ruby's name on a manifest list that demanded high security clearance could never be totally ignored! After Ruby's death, speculation began immediately that his demise shortly before he would have been moved out of Dallas to Wichita Falls for a new trial was a bit too convenient. Perhaps too many hidden details like the one Mel Barney discovered explain why Ruby died so suddenly.

Regardless, consider the statement Mel Barney made to the authors:"Only those with 'secret clearance' and a need-to-know security level were allowed on the airplane." Surely this proves that Jack Ruby was more than a sleazy night club owner. Obviously, he had connections to powerful individuals or he could not have flown on that top-secret airplane. Could these powerful men have used him to 1) run guns to Cuba, 2) share information with his Mafia associates, and 3) silence a "patsy?"

VIII
THE DIXIE MAFIA:
DEEP IN THE HEART
OF TEXAS

Jack Ruby's connections to the Chicago Mafia also extended to the Dixie Mafia. This means the fingers of the assassination plot spread from Dallas to West Texas.

CHAPTER 60
VOICES FOR GEORGE MCGANN

"Whatever they told you George did, it was probably ten times worse"...
—Marcelas Weaver

Before Jack Ruby murdered Lee Harvey Oswald, most of the world had never heard of him. But he was connected to so many illegal activities and underworld characters that people like young George McGann of Big Spring, Texas, were sure to meet him eventually.

Ruby seemed to make a point of surrounding himself with pretty young females. Beverly Oliver was a seventeen-year-old singer/ventriloquist who would eventually marry McGann. In the 1960s, she performed at Abe Weinstein's Colony Club, near Ruby's Carousel Club. It was not long before she met Jack Ruby. She began stopping by the Carousel Club on her way home from work late at night.

Oliver detailed her experiences with Ruby in her book *"Nightmare in Dallas."* She also briefly mentioned her husband at the time, George McGann, a man she described as a professional poker player with connections to the Mafia. What she didn't mention, perhaps because she didn't even know, was that he may have had some connection to the Kennedy assassination.

When people think of the Mafia, they usually associate it with places like New York, Chicago, Florida, New Orleans, Las Vegas, and even California. They might be surprised to know that the Dixie Mafia, which seems to have originated in the Louisiana area, spread to Houston, Dallas, and eventually to West Texas. It was sometimes affiliated with the Texas Mafia. The residents of Big Spring, Texas, are still surprised by how active one of their own community members was in the Dixie Mafia.

George McGann's parents moved him to Big Spring when he was only a year old. As an only child, he grew up both spoiled and neglected. His parents lived in one of the nicer homes in the community. It sat on a tree-lined street that was the envy of many of his classmates. Jim Hayworth, who knew McGann because they were both interested in motorcycles, recalled, "The McGanns lived in a very nice house in Edwards Heights. It was pretty, with red brick, and had red bricks for the driveway and sidewalks. The driveway was much nicer than other driveways in Big Spring."[603]

Ayra and "Ike" McGann sent their young son to a private Catholic school.

Residents of Big Spring still recalled George McGann as a young boy at St. Thomas' Catholic Church, where he completed the required Catechism classes. Local newspaper articles chronicled his early birthday parties, and George once won a baby pageant.

However, his classmates also recalled that his mother was too busy playing bridge at the Big Spring Country Club to attend many of George's school functions. Because of this, some of his classmates felt sorry for him, especially because he tried to make excuses for his mother's absences. His father was known as a workaholic who didn't have time for his son, but he was unusually strict. This might be because McGann needed more structure than some children. Perhaps he needed more structure because he was starved for attention.

By the time McGann entered his teens, he was attending classes at Big Spring High School. According to those who knew him there, he dressed like a typical teenager of the 1950s. The tall, dark-haired young man wore rolled-up blue jeans and t-shirts. His poor vision forced him to wear thick, Buddy Holly-type glasses. In some ways, he was like most of the other students. However, there were also major differences.

"I remember him as a loner, almost like James Dean in *Rebel Without a Cause,* one of his former classmates said. "George was always cocky, and he walked on the balls of his feet. Unlike most of the teenage boys in Big Spring, he was not interested in athletics."[604] He was also indifferent to school work, but this was probably because he was unusually smart. The typical high school classes did not challenge him. Perhaps it was boredom and the need for excitement that drew him to motorcycles. Regardless, even though the high school girls thought him charming, suave, and well-groomed, their athletic boyfriends did not care for McGann.

It was during his junior year of high school that his parents bought him his first motorcycle. He was the only boy in high school at the time to own one. Most of his classmates did not even own used cars, much less motorcycles. It seems that McGann's parents provided their only child with money and objects; what they did not seem to provide was attention and affection.

In an attempt to win friends, McGann hung out in front of neighbors' houses and offered free motorcycle rides to his classmates. The motorcycle may be what earned him his "bad-boy" image. Ironically, despite the James Dean motorcycle look, the thick glasses and the black frames did not enhance his "wild one" reputation. For whatever reason, the other high school boys did not include him in their activities, and his circle of friends was quite small.

Over fifty years later, a former male classmate recalled, "I don't remember George ever getting suspended or even getting sent to the principal's office. But my friends and I didn't run with him. *We* were athletes."[605] The jocks may have alienated McGann, but the teenaged girls were drawn to the quiet, bespectacled, good-looking young man even if their admiration for him irritated their boyfriends. Girls liked his dark hair and his almost immaculate appearance. Chances are they also felt sorry for the young man who never seemed to want to go home. Boosie Weaver, a former acquaintance of McGann, shared a story that defined the relationship between McGann and his father.

"When George was a teenager, he and I drove up to his house one night. I had wrecked his motorcycle earlier in the evening and we had come to explain the accident to his father. As soon as George's father realized that the motorcycle had been wrecked, he began hitting George with his fists. George did not even lift a hand to defend himself. He just stood there and took it. I never knew whether George ever told his father I was the one who wrecked the motorcycle."[606]

It is unclear whether this was an isolated incident or whether such beatings occurred often. This much is certain: McGann's father did not have a good relationship with his only child. The idea of solving problems with violence is a lesson McGann learned at an early age and one that he carried with him into adulthood.

Another former classmate recalled the time McGann convinced her to take a spin on his motorcycle. She was terrified—of the motorcycle and what her parents would do to her if they caught her.

"I prayed to God all the way that I would do whatever, if He would just get me home safely!" she laughed.[607] But she remembered McGann fondly as a "nice boy." There was no romantic relationship between the two, but they were close friends.

"The bond between me and George was one of unconditional friendship. He seemed to always hold me in high esteem."[608] McGann later asked this friend to serve as Matron of Honor at his first wedding.

As far as anyone knows, McGann the teenager was uninvolved with drugs. In the fifties in Big Spring, most of the students knew nothing about drugs. "Most of the boys drank beer sometimes," according to a current Big Spring resident, "but that's all. The worst thing you could do was smoke a cigarette. I don't remember George even smoking."[609]

McGann's circle of friends and acquaintances consisted mainly of young men who enjoyed racing and motorcycles. Many of them are still residents of Big Spring and have no illusions about some of McGann's escapades. James and Marcelas ("Boosie") Weaver knew McGann well. In an interview, Boosie's first words about his old friend were honest ones: "Everyone you have talked to in Big Spring" he said, "probably sugar-coated their stories about McGann. Whatever they told you he did, it was probably ten times worse."[610]

Boosie was twenty-one when he returned to Big Spring from the Air Force to enroll at Big Spring's Howard College, where he met Ike McGann, McGann's father, who offered the returning airman a job at his oil supply company. Only sixteen at the time, his son George interrupted the interview between Boosie and the elder McGann when he rode up on his motorcycle.

Perhaps Ike McGann thought the young ex-airman would have a calming influence on his teenaged son; he hired Boosie on the spot. But he explained that Boosie's job was primarily to keep his son out of trouble. McGann Sr. must have realized that he had lost control of George. Apparently, he could see the handwriting on the wall, but rather than handle his son himself, he delegated the responsibility to a twenty-one-year-old he barely knew.

Boosie was living in his parents' basement at the time. He recalled that McGann frequently arrived at Boosie's house with his pockets full of money. There was never any explanation for the origin of the money. McGann and Boosie played Rummy together, and even back then, McGann was known to cheat at cards. However, he would bring Boosie cigars, and the two became great friends. This was not the relationship Ike McGann had anticipated.

One of the stories still told in Big Spring is that during McGann's high school years, motel chains would pay him and some of his friends to lie around the motel pools to drum up business. However, even at that time, McGann was beginning to gain a reputation for being a "tough guy." This reputation had already spread to Midland, a city located forty miles west of Big Spring.

McGann attended dances in Midland at one particular dance hall. People there learned not to "mess around with him," according to a friend. One time, McGann and Boosie both had dates in Midland. They decided to take separate cars.

Boosie laughed as he recalled, "Well, George hopped into his shiny new Lincoln" and took off for Midland. He decided to race me. He was driving his Lincoln at 110 miles-an-hour plus. A Martin County deputy stopped George and gave him a big fat ticket. They were going to throw him into jail, but George told them his good friend, R.H. Weaver, my brother, was a county judge, so they let him go."[611] This wasn't the first or last time McGann used his friends to avoid legal problems.

Today, the Settles Hotel in Big Spring is a historical landmark and one of the most elegant hotels in West Texas. There is still an "Elvis Room' because Elvis Presley once stayed at the hotel while performing nearby. Big Spring was also the stomping grounds of the notorious Billie Sol Estes, whose favorite eating establishment was Carlos' Restaurant.

However, the Settles Hotel was not always as regal as it is today. At one time, it was a favorite gathering place for McGann and his friends. Lonnie Smith, former Big Spring Chief of Police, remembered hearing stories about McGann. Smith's brother was the District Attorney's chief investigator back in the 1960s. Smith knew that McGann and his friends were involved in "high dollar poker games at the Settles Hotel, and prostitutes ran freely through there."[612]

The Chief of Police in Big Spring at that time was a former Texas Ranger named Jay Banks. Smith stated that Banks "ignored gambling and prostitution if it wasn't causing any problems or public outcry."[613] According to Smith, McGann, Boosie, and a friend named Sonny Tucker loitered at the Settles Hotel and stole bottles of whiskey from the hotel's liquor closet. They hid the bottles under their coats and absconded with quite a few on each trip. For safekeeping, the three stashed the stolen whiskey bottles in a janitorial closet and returned to pick them up later.

There was very little loyalty among these thieves. Sometimes, McGann would leave Boosie at his home and return to the hotel to steal Tucker's stash of whiskey before Tucker could return. One has to wonder what Ike McGann would have thought had he known that the young man he hired to "watch over" his son was laughingly nicknamed "Baron Moonshinen" by George McGann.

Boosie and McGann continued their carefree lifestyles until George married in 1956. Boosie was McGann's best man when he wed Mary Beth White of Stanton, Texas. (Stanton is smaller than Big Spring and a mere twenty miles southwest.) Still popular with the girls, McGann had a reputation for being a gentleman around women. In fact, he was quiet and reserved, according to some. If McGann's parents thought marriage would have a stabilizing effect on their son, as they probably did, they were soon disappointed.

The young couple moved into a nice home in Big Spring not far from McGann's parents. In 1958, their only child, a boy, was born. Apparently, McGann continued to participate in illegal poker games even after he married; unfortunately, he lost much more money than he ever won.

His first *reported* brush with the law occurred in 1959. Newspaper articles tell the story of a husband and wife from Midland, Texas, who publicly accused McGann of "savagely and brutally attacking them at the Crawford Hotel in Big Spring." The couple stated that the attack was "intentional and deliberate and caused severe damage and injury." Even the wife was beaten by McGann and his associate, E. T. ("Sonny") Tucker.

"She suffered a severe beating about her head, both legs, chest, stomach, and ribs; her legs were severely swollen and her neck was severely injured." Her husband was "severely beaten about the head and face, the shoulders and chest; his right hand was broken, and at least three of his ribs were broken."[614] The couple sued McGann and Tucker for assault and battery; they also sued the Crawford Hotel for negligence.

The injured couple provided no explanation for why McGann attacked them, but it was common knowledge in Big Spring that McGann hosted illegal poker parties in the hotel. It is unknown whether the couple from Midland were trying to leave without paying their debts or whether they won and McGann was unhappy.

It seems logical that McGann and Tucker would be found guilty due to the severe injuries of the victims and the fact that they were able to identify their attackers. However, before the case was tried, the husband and wife decided to drop their action against the hotel and the attackers.[615] It is still a mystery how a quiet young man who was so respectful to his girlfriends evolved into someone who would savagely beat even a woman.

This was only the beginning of the violent life of George Albert McGann, and one that inevitably led to his murder. By late 1961, newspaper articles reported that McGann and his wife were accused of arson and insurance fraud. The complaint filed on March 24, 1962, against the couple said that they deliberately destroyed their house and personal property by fire.

Big Spring residents still recall that the talk around town then was that McGann needed money and set his own house on fire. Insurance investigators found enough evidence of arson to charge McGann and his wife with insurance fraud. The McGann family was not home at the time, and very few of their personal items were even in the house when the fire began. Rumors throughout Big Spring were rampant.

McGann, community members claimed, told his wife to pack up anything she valued, and to go somewhere with their son for the weekend. McGann claimed he was, at the time of the fire, in Andrews, Texas, 65 miles west of Big Spring, playing poker. According to Boosie Weaver, this story was true, but McGann had arranged for his friend Sonny Tucker to torch his home while McGann played poker in Andrews.

One of the main problems with McGann's alibi was that too many personal items had been removed from the house. The insurance company refused to pay, and the McGanns were put on trial in Big Spring. Unlike the assault case in 1961, this case wasn't dismissed, but both of the McGanns were found "not guilty" and the insurance company forced to pay them $18,000. However, in May 1963, the couple divorced. McGann's ex-wife was given custody of their five-year-old boy.

Though McGann did not grow up in Chicago, New York, or New Orleans, some of the people he began to associate with would have felt comfortable in the company of Al Capone and his associates. More than forty years after McGann's death, some authors are still ignoring his connections to cold-blooded, hired killers like his friend, Charles Harrelson. Harrelson was convicted of killing a Texas judge, John Wood, on May 29, 1979. He was also connected with George Edward (Pete) Kay and Kelsey Nix, both of whom were deeply involved with the Dixie Mafia. FBI records indicate that George McGann was involved with *all* of these men—and not just at poker parties.

CHAPTER 61

THE VOICE OF TEXAS RANGER AL MITCHELL

**"If McGann's plans came from higher individuals,
those orders came from the Dixie Mafia."**

The few authors who have even mentioned McGann or his acquaintances have trivialized McGann's activities. However, retired Texas Ranger Al Mitchell, who is familiar with the name "George McGann" and with some of his former friends, shared some compelling information with the authors.

"When McGann and his group of West Texas boys planned robberies, murders, and poker stealing parties in Big Spring, Midland, Odessa, Lubbock, that part was not being controlled by the Dallas/New Orleans chain. Around Big Spring, McGann and his gang were called the 'Crossroaders.' But if their plans came from the higher individuals [in Dallas or New Orleans], those orders came from the Dixie Mafia," Mitchell explained.[616] (Even if McGann considered himself a "Crossroader," he undoubtedly knew that the term had dangerous connotations to those in the know. Frenchy Brouillette, known as "Mr. New Orleans," described crossroaders as "elite gambling cheats and affiliated boosters, safecrackers, jewel thieves, burglars, and con men who worked in traveling crews.")[617]

Some locals in Big Spring still maintain that McGann was *never* part of the Dixie Mafia. Some *insist* that the Dixie Mafia did not even exist. But after McGann's death in 1970, Dallas Police Capt. Paul McCaghren set the record straight.

"McGann was known to have connections in several southern states," McCaghren stated emphatically to a newspaper reporter. McCaghren had met with other law enforcement officers from the southern states the year before in Atlanta, Georgia. "We determined that there was a large gang with connections in the South. McGann topped our list of known Dixie Mafia members."[618]

The gang members themselves might not have called themselves the "Dixie Mafia," but law enforcement certainly did. An article appearing in The *Dallas Morning News* on November 6, 1969, indicated that law enforcement was concerned about outsiders entering Dallas for nefarious purposes.

"The announcement that pressure on outsiders is to be accelerated underscores the concern of intelligence officers who have been reporting on the activities here of a gang dubbed the Dixie Mafia." This gang was described as "no run-of-the-mill criminal element but a well-financed and highly mobile gang with connections in a number of major cities across the southern United States."[619]

Another term was used across the state in conjunction with organized crime, and McGann may well have been connected to it, also. This term was "Texas Mafia." A former friend of McGann commented on McGann's feelings about the term "Dixie Mafia."

"George made fun of the name 'Dixie Mafia.' He told me personally, 'There's no such thing as the Dixie Mafia. The closest thing to the Mafia in Dallas is the Campisis, who owned restaurants in Dallas.'"[620] But ask former Big Spring Chief of Police Lonnie Smith, and retired Texas Ranger Al Mitchell, and they will tell you that the Dixie Mafia is real, and George McGann was a part of it. Perhaps McGann had ulterior reasons for denying the existence of the Dixie Mafia.

"People didn't mess with McGann. He got crossways with the Dixie Mafia, which led to his murder," Mitchell stated.[621] He also confirmed that there *is* a Dixie Mafia, and that McGann had been playing with the "bad boys."[622] Why did McGann deny any association with the Dixie Mafia? One possible answer is that he was known for being tight-lipped. His friends and enemies would discuss McGann's escapades, but McGann seldom revealed anything. Another reason could be that he knew that people like Carlos Marcello, head of the Dixie Mafia, would not appreciate any comments about his organization. To Captain McCaghren, the name of this particular group of criminals was unimportant.

"I don't care what you call it—Dixie Mafia or something else—McGann had connections in Texas, Mississippi, Florida, Alabama, and Georgia," McCaghren stated.[623] Regardless of the name of the group McGann led, it was because of McGann's various illegal activities that his name and photo ended up on the FBI's Most Wanted List. How did a nice boy from a middle-class neighborhood in West Texas end up wanted by the FBI?

Perhaps it was because McGann moved to Dallas in 1963 after his divorce. His circle of friends grew to include people well known to the FBI. He and R.D. Matthews, for example, became close friends. In fact, Matthews allowed McGann to stay in his high-rise apartment in the exclusive Turtle Creek district of Dallas. Some of McGann's Big Spring friends such as John Currie recalled visiting him there. To McGann, it seemed as if he was moving out of a dull, slow-paced West Texas community and into the exciting, neon world of Dallas.

In reality, he was moving into the enticing but shady world of organized crime, a large sea of criminals in which he would be a small fish, rather than the big fish he had been in a small West Texas pond. It is unclear how McGann met Matthews, who introduced him to this member of organized crime, and what Matthews saw in McGann that drew the two men together.

R. D. Matthews became close enough to McGann to be his best man at his second wedding; he was also close enough to Joseph Civello to be considered his right-hand man. Civello was closely associated with New Orleans mob boss Carlos Marcello. Some of McGann's friends remember that George idolized the lifestyle of the Dallas mobsters.

John Currie of Big Spring, however, did not remember McGann the same way McGann's other friends do. "George wasn't exactly connected to the mob," he explained to the authors as he sat quietly in his living room. "But R.D. Matthews paid his bills and called me and told me that if George ever needed money, to call him." Currie went on to say: "George didn't ever act as if he was afraid of these people." He then added that he visited McGann while McGann was living in Dallas.

"I traveled to Dallas quite a bit back then, and so a few times I would stop by and see George at the Matthews apartment. I had met Jack Ruby a couple of times when I was a student at Texas Christian University."[624]

Currie paused as he thought back to those days in Ft. Worth. He explained that back then, Ruby's Carousel Club was a popular destination for young men in college.

"One time, some of the men I worked for when I was in college invited me to go with them to a boxing match in Dallas. We met Jack Ruby and R.D. Matthews there. In fact, they sat with us. The other times I met Ruby was at his club in Dallas." Currie did not mention whether he introduced George to Ruby.

McGann made other friends besides Jack Ruby who eventually became well-known to law enforcement. Besides Charles V. Harrelson and Pete Kay, he also associated with Jerry Ray James, Stanley "The Creeper" Cook, Johnny Ross Patrona, and Kirksey Nix McCord. After his murder, the names and phone numbers of these people were found in McGann's black address book. Many of the names handwritten in the book were of people with arrest records. Some, like Stanley "The Creeper" Cook, were already notorious. Also found on McGann's body was an unusual business card advertising "Campisis' Egyptian Lounge." Joe Campisi and his wife were the first people to visit Jack Ruby in 1963 after his arrest for killing John F. Kennedy's accused assassin, Lee Harvey Oswald.

The McGann address book is undeniable evidence that he was closely connected to criminals and, most likely, organized crime. Some of the other names discovered in it include Sam Campisi and his telephone number at his Egyptian Lounge, and R.D. Matthews. Matthews and Campisi were closely connected to Jack Ruby, who must have known them before McGann did. Obviously, some of Ruby's associates became McGann's associates, too.

With friends like these, it wasn't long before McGann developed a reputation that far exceeded the one he earned while in Big Spring. When his second wife, Beverly Oliver, first mentioned him to her boss, Abe Weinstein, the owner of the Colony Club, Weinstein did not mince words in describing her new boyfriend.

"Beverly, George is trouble. That entire bunch he runs with are Trouble with a capital 'T.' Please take my advice: Steer clear of him. He's a mean man."[625] Oliver ignored Weinstein's advice and eventually married McGann on July 31, 1966. It wasn't long before the new Mrs. McGann realized that Weinstein's advice was right on the money.

McGann bought a Dallas "restaurant/ bar/nightclub," where he hosted gambling parties in the backroom."[626] He renamed it "George's Lounge." Even before arriving in Dallas, McGann knew the famous professional poker player, Doyle Brunson. Brunson remembered McGann well and even mentioned him in his autobiography, *The Godfather of Poker*. Brunson knew, even then, that McGann was not much of a poker player, though McGann loved the excitement of the game, and like most players, the idea of making money quickly and effortlessly. One of McGann's biggest problems, according to Brunson, was that "he tried to play poker with the best."[627]

Brunson became reacquainted with McGann when McGann moved to Dallas. By then, McGann had become acquainted with R. D. Matthews, "a big member of the mob." Brunson described Matthews to the authors as "the King of the Texas Bad Guys," and added: "George idolized him, and he wanted to follow in his footsteps. R. D. was a nice enough guy until he lost at poker. Then he would terrorize everybody!"

Brunson remembered that McGann did not talk about the Dixie Mafia. Brunson was not personally afraid of McGann, and did not know that many people in Big Spring were, although he admitted, "I heard he killed about nineteen people. But I wouldn't be afraid to reach across the table and slap him. And he wouldn't have reciprocated if he knew he was wrong."[628]

Both in Big Spring and in Dallas, according to Clifford Hart, another McGann friend, McGann was known as an "Outlaw."

"Everyone knew that George knew Jack Ruby," he told the authors.[629] The word in Big Spring was that McGann was involved in poker games where literally millions of dollars would pass across the table. Regarding it as a more dependable source of income, McGann also dealt in "stolen stuff." Some of his Big Spring friends laughed about years later.

"He would hijack trucks full of TVs, freezers, refrigerators, washers, dryers, and other large appliances. He would turn around and sell them or give them to his friends," continued Hart. Speculation was that he was stockpiling various types of merchandise in a warehouse. He acquired the merchandise by illegally by hijacking truckers' shipments. He did this so often that he fell under the scrutiny of the FBI. Clifford Hart was right when he stated, "George hung out with the 'real bad guys' in Dallas." In his high school yearbook, McGann had not been voted "most likely to succeed;" neither had his classmates voted him "most likely to become infamous." However, he quickly earned this latter distinction.

The escalation in McGann's behavior was becoming more obvious, as were changes in the way he dressed. Friends from Big Spring were still wearing blue jeans and work shirts, but after moving to Dallas, McGann "was dressing in dark slacks, dark turtlenecks, and dark sports coats."[630] Obviously, McGann was imitating the dress and behavior of his new friends and business acquaintances in Dallas. As far as he was concerned, he had left his West Texas small hometown in the dust. To some of his former Big Spring friends, McGann was living an enviable life in the big city.

Jimmy Whitefield, for example, was so impressed with George McGann's new lifestyle that he told his cousin, Robert Mesker, all about McGann. Mesker already knew McGann by reputation, and McGann heard about Mesker's fighting abilities and his skills at pool. McGann arranged for Mesker to travel to Dallas so he could stage bare knuckle fist fights between Mesker and anyone who dared to oppose him.

"George was a real gambler," Mesker told the authors.[631] "He paid me $100 to fight, and I always won." He repeated, "I *always* won my fights. I was too mean to lose. That's why George liked me." McGann also took Mesker to the Carousel Club in Dallas, where Mesker met the owner, Jack Ruby.

Mesker's impression of Jack Ruby was that he was "a good guy," and he thought McGann and Ruby seemed to know each other. McGann also took Mesker to bars in Huntsville, Texas. It was here that Mesker met Charles Harrelson. As tough as Mesker was, he admitted that he actually was scared of Harrelson.

"He had cold-blooded eyes, and when he looked at you, he looked right through you." While in Huntsville, Mesker learned that Pete Kay was also a townie. Mesker speculated, "Pete Kay was the head of the Dixie Mafia in Houston. I believe Pete Kay framed Charles Harrelson for the hit on Judge

Wood. George and his buddies lived by the 'Old Code: Keep your mouth shut...Do the time...And your family will be taken care of.'"[632] Harrelson was eventually sentenced to prison for the murder of Judge Wood. Mesker is not the only person to speculate that Harrelson took the rap for a crime he did not actually commit.

Beverly Oliver admitted that her book did not discuss certain parts of her life with George McGann. But she did distinctly recall visiting Campisi's Egyptian Lounge one night with her husband and some of his friends. Among those in the group were Charles Harrelson, Kirksey Nix, Stanley Cook, R. D. Matthews, and Billy T. Dyer. Oliver walked into the room and overheard her husband and his friends discussing the Kennedy assassination.

According to Oliver, she spent part of the evening of November 21, 1963, with Jack Ruby. He surprised her with a green and white polka-dotted dress which she wore to dinner and then to an all-night party in Ft. Worth. She was still wearing her new dress the next day when President Kennedy arrived in Dallas.

Oddly enough, an FBI interview with Warren T. Gammon of Clockwise Fashions in Dallas verified that Jack Ruby did, indeed, purchase three party dresses. At "approximately 5:00 p.m., Ruby and a girl entered Clockwise Fashions and advised they were interested in buying some party dresses. Gammon could recall that he sold Ruby three party dresses and that two of the dresses were taken with him that evening, the remaining one to be picked up the following Wednesday."

It is unclear who the young woman was, but there is now proof that Jack Ruby purchased three party dresses the evening before the assassination. One of them could have been Oliver's polka-dotted number.[633]

The next day, still wearing her new dress, Oliver was in Dealey Plaza in Dallas with her movie camera just as Kennedy's motorcade traveled down Elm Street. She unintentionally filmed the murder of the President. Oliver says she never shared this story with her husband because her film was confiscated by FBI agents three days after the assassination.

As Beverly listened to the conversation between her husband and his friends, "she proceeded to reveal to everyone that she had met Lee Harvey Oswald in Jack Ruby's club. In fact, Ruby introduced them. Then she revealed her shocking experience at Dealey Plaza and the fact that she knew the assassin's fatal shot came from a gunman in front of the President—from behind the fence on the grassy knoll. 'Anyone thinking Oswald was the lone assassin is out of their ever-loving mind,' Beverly commented. McGann's friends seemed engrossed by Beverly's commentary and startled by her statement: 'Jack [Ruby] introduced me to Oswald at his club shortly before the...."' McGann grabbed Beverly from her chair and forced her out of the room. He held her firmly and shook her. "Don't you dare talk about the assassination again! Do you understand...Never, ever, ever, again can you do what you did. The assassination cannot—under any circumstances—be discussed again, ever! You don't know what kind of trouble you could bring. So help me, if you do, I'll kill you myself. I swear."[634]

Apparently, Oliver took her husband's threat seriously because she claims she did not mention the Kennedy assassination again until after her husband's death in 1970. Today, she still says she never discovered why her husband was so adamant about not discussing the Kennedy assassination with anyone.

CHAPTER 62

GEORGE MCGANN'S "HOMECOMING"

"George was one of the best thieves, whether it was appliances, jewelry, or safe-cracking."—Jimmy Johnson

Two hunded and eighty-nine long miles separate Dallas from Big Spring, Texas. Nevertheless, stories about McGann's activities in the Metroplex area reached the ears of the citizens of his hometown. According to former Big Spring resident Jim Hayworth, "George was always flamboyant. One story was that he and two friends went to a private lounge on the outskirts of Dallas. His friend was a pool shark, and that night they all won a lot of money from the guys there on pool games." Hayworth grinned as he recalled the details of this colorful story:

"McGann wanted to get back to Dallas and told the other two it was time to leave. A pool player who had lost a lot of money to them said, 'Leave? What makes you think you're leaving?' McGann looked at him and asked innocently, 'Are you saying you would rob us?'

"The other man answered, 'Whatever it takes to get the money back.' McGann responded casually, 'Well, speaking of robbery,' and he pulled out a pistol, pointed it at the man, and directed his two friends to rob him and everyone else in the room."[635]

During the robbery, McGann supposedly considered stealing someone's ring, which was set with a small diamond. He examined it closely and laughed as he tossed it aside. Small and inexpensive items were not worth his time. If McGann was simply a thief, he might not have been forced to leave Dallas. But he wasn't just a thief. One evening during a poker game in the joint he owned ("George's Lounge"), McGann picked up his pistol and, without blinking an eye, shot a "friend," according to his wife, Beverly Oliver. Bystanders were shocked by this outrageous act, but no one dared to object.

McGann then forced his wife to help him dispose of the dead body. However, word of the shooting reached the Dallas Sheriff's Department. An all-points bulletin was issued for McGann and his wife. McGann found out from his attorney that Sheriff Bill Decker was looking for him. The couple were on the run in Oklahoma when they were stopped by a state trooper, who forced them to turn themselves in. What neither of the McGanns knew at the time was that George's Lounge had been "wired" by local law enforcement.[636]

In Texas, it was common knowledge that if Sheriff Decker wanted a suspect for questioning, the suspect better appear. So McGann returned to Dallas and turned himself in to Dallas authorities. His wife was not charged, but McGann was; he claimed he killed the man in self-defense, but he was found guilty and initially sentenced to ten years in prison. Amazingly, even that light sentence was suspended, and he was placed on probation. This might have been because none of the witnesses contradicted his story of self-defense. Apparently, they were more frightened of McGann than they were of law enforcement.

Though McGann was released and did not serve any jail time, he was banned from Dallas and sent back home to Big Spring. To him, though, this was nothing more than a slap on the wrist. However, two groups benefited from his absence in Dallas—law enforcement and his fellow "business associates." McGann apparently drew too much attention to himself and to the Dixie Mafia.

Two of his probation requirements were that he be employed, and that he stay within 50 miles of Big Spring. Becoming employed might be a problem for a man on probation for murder, unless he had close friends in his hometown. And a little thing like staying within 50 miles of Big Spring? To McGann, merely a minor inconvenience. As he saw it, what the authorities did not know would not hurt them.

Big Spring Chief of Police Jay Banks lived in Dallas at a time when he served as a Texas Ranger. Like McGann, he arrived in Big Spring under a cloud. His penchant for gambling had cost him his position with the Texas Rangers. However, Banks' contacts with the Dallas/Ft. Worth area provided him with inside information about George McGann and his activities.

According to John Currie, a Big Spring banker who had known McGann since he was a child, as soon as McGann returned to his hometown, Banks summoned him to his office. He told McGann in no uncertain terms that he was no longer welcome in his home town. Odds are, Banks knew that McGann's activities in Dallas included much more than gambling. Currie admitted to the authors that he ran interference between Banks and McGann. After all, he had known George McGann since McGann was ten years old.

The banker stated, "Jay Banks asked me to keep an eye on George."[637] Currie was aware of McGann's poker games which, despite the 50-mile limit, took place all over West Texas—from Big Spring to Midland/Odessa, from Andrews to Lubbock. Currie explained that he "kept George's gambling money for him." He recalled that a man from Dallas called not long after McGann returned to Big Spring, assuring Currie that "he would guarantee money for George anytime he needed it."

Currie thought back for a moment and then remembered, "That guy's name was Matthews—R.D. Matthews." This was the same R.D. Matthews who had worked for Joseph Civello and Carlos Marcello, the same R. D. Matthews who had served as McGann's best man at his wedding to Beverly Oliver. Obviously, McGann's connections to the underworld followed him to Big Spring.

"George didn't trust banks, but he would trust me with his gambling money," Currie said. "I just kept it in an envelope in my office for him." (McGann's distrust of banks might have been the result of his distrust of the IRS.)

Not long after returning to Big Spring with his new wife in tow, McGann began socializing with Boosie Weaver's older brother, James. McGann left West Texas in 1963 dressed like most of the other young men in Big Spring, but he returned dressed like R. D. Matthews, Joe Campisi, and Jack Ruby. Each of his outfits consisted of a sports coat, slacks, and matching tie. Often he wore a matching turtleneck with a sports coat and slacks. Business professionals in Big Spring wore suits and ties, but they did not wear turtlenecks and sports coats.

McGann's appearance caused him to stand out, and it wasn't long before some of his friends began imitating his style. Jim Hayworth, who also knew one of McGann's best friends, Jimmy Whitefield, recalled that Whitefield soon began emulating McGann's dress; he, too, sported turtlenecks and sport coats.

"I hadn't ever thought about it, but he must have been imitating George," Hayworth commented years later.[638] Other friends of McGann remember that McGann even had his nails manicured once a week, which was unheard of for most men in West Texas.[639]

One of McGann's followers was Gary McDaniel of Garden City, a tiny community 20 miles southwest of Big Spring. Like McGann, he did not really fit in with the other students in his local school. One thing his classmates remember is that McDaniel absolutely hated farming, which is how his adopted father and almost everyone else in the community made their living.

For entertainment, Garden City teenagers had nowhere to go except to Big Spring. So it's not surprising that McDaniel, bored with small-town life, latched on to someone like McGann. It was not long after McDaniel began associating with McGann that his appearance changed as much as Jimmy Whitefield's had. He began to dress differently.

After graduation, McDaniel attended one or two Garden City homecoming reunions. Most of his fellow classmates were surprised at his appearance. "He wore a professional-looking suit and drove a nice, new car. We wondered what he was doing to make that kind of money," Taylor Etchison told the authors.[640]

However, that was one topic that McDaniel avoided at the reunion.

George McGann did not discuss his finances with others, either. As part of his so-called "probation," McGann had to show proof of employment, so he and some Big Spring friends purchased Holiday Motors. One of the friends providing financial assistance to McGann was Billy Jo Kilpatrick.

McGann's interests in cars and motorcycles had not waned while living in Dallas. According to Jim Hayworth, "I heard about McGann from a friend, and I met him when he moved back to Big Spring from Dallas. The word was that he had been kicked out of Dallas by the mob. I had a motorcycle, and he had a business that sold motorcycle parts. He came across as a nice guy, but I did hear he was connected to the mob."

Hayworth paused before continuing thoughtfully: "The story around town was that he was on the mob's hit list and told to get out of Dallas. The reason? He was attracting too much attention to them." Hayworth chuckled, "He was supposed to lay low in Big Spring, but, instead, he ran a booking business there and hosted parties with lots of money at stake. I also heard he *owed* people money."[641]

Another friend, Jimmy Johnson, stated matter-of-factly, "George would slip out of town in the middle of the night to do a 'job' and be back the next morning."[642] Johnson also heard that McGann gambled often and that he was in the Mafia. "He was one of the best thieves—whether it was appliances, jewelry, or safe cracking," Johnson added, shaking his head.

An unusual business card found in McGann's wallet after his death in 1970 might also offer a clue about other ways McGann earned money. It also linked him to a group of individuals that most people have never heard of. The card advertised general insurance from a name familiar to everyone in Dallas—Joe Campisi. This was the same Joe Campisi who owned the Egyptian Restaurant where Jack Ruby had eaten the night before the assassination, the same Joe Campisi who admitted being the first person to visit Ruby after he was arrested for shooting Lee Harvey Oswald.

The card read "Buy your PROTECTION from Joe Campisi & Associates"; this was followed by an address and telephone number. What was unusual about the card (besides the fact that the Campisi family was known for being restauranteurs, not insurance agents) was that it included a photo of a black handprint. This symbol is connected to a group of Sicilian extortionists who immigrated to America in the early 1900s.

The members terrorized local business owners and forced them to pay for "protection." Some of the members even began a more duplicitous venture. They first frightened the locals by sending letters with the imprint of a black hand and mentioning a monetary figure that would assure them protection. Then another group of members, pretending to be honest businessmen, approached the threatened locals and offered to accept less money to protect them from the so-called Black Hand Society. Of course, the men all belonged to the same criminal organization, so the Society made money one way or the other.

If a business owner had the audacity to refuse to be threatened or "protected," society members harassed, beat, or even murdered the brave soul. Eventually, the Society evolved into the modern-day Mafia.

Joe Campisi's family emigrated from Sicily to America in 1901, so it is quite possible that his ancestors were early members of the Society of the Black Hand. Why else would this insignia appear on a business card that offered insurance referred to as "protection"? In 1978, eight years after the business card was found on George McGann's dead body, Joe Campisi was questioned by the HSCA about his connections to Jack Ruby.

When asked his occupation, he answered that he was in the restaurant business. He made no mention of the insurance business, general or otherwise. He also claimed to have nothing to do with organized crime, and that his friendships with people like the Carlos Marcello family and Benny Binion came about simply because he knew almost everyone through his popular restaurant. He was also close to Dallas Sheriff Bill Decker and former District Attorney Henry Wade.

The fact that George McGann carried an intriguing business card from Joe Campisi with black handprint image may have meant nothing. Or it could be proof that he was an extortionist, and that the Society of the Black Hand, which had once flourished all over the United States, still existed in 1970. None of McGann's friends referred to the Society, but they all knew that McGann kept many secrets about his activities.

Robert Mesker remembers that McGann made money by selling some motorcycles and motorcycle parts from the Holiday Motors dealership, "but George never sold any cars off the lot. Holiday Motors was just a front for another business. George would take cars down to El Paso and sell them, then load up his own car with drugs in the trunk and wheel-wells and drive back to Big Spring to sell the stuff."[643] This was not what his probation officer had in mind as a means of employment, but it did keep McGann's pockets lined with cash money.

Though friends like Carl Hart stated that McGann might have lived in Big Spring, but didn't do his "business" there, it seems obvious that McGann was involved in some sort of illegal "business" in Big Spring. In fact, many of his acquaintances knew that McGann's Dallas activities continued in West Texas.

To many in Big Spring, he was known as "someone you didn't mess with," and others just referred to him as an "outlaw." The latter term may sound harsh, but McGann had been wanted by the FBI.

His probationary status did not deter him from robbing several establishments in his own hometown. He also continued to hijack commercial vehicles so he could steal the appliances they were transporting. Generous in his own way, he offered "free" appliances and televisions to friends. He did not mention that they had been stolen. Some friends turned him down; some did not.

For example, a woman who had always thought highly of McGann recalled an interesting encounter with him not long after he returned from Dallas. The 7-11 convenience store on Gregg Street in Big Spring had recently extended its hours to eleven at night. All other stores in Big Spring closed at eight.

One Saturday night, the woman realized about 9:00 p.m. that she did not have milk for her children's breakfast the next morning. Fortunately, the 7-11 was still open, so she made a quick trip to the store. Approaching the store, she noticed a long, sleek sedan parked at an odd angle in the parking lot.

"I guess it was a Lincoln; I didn't know much about cars. I drove a 1953 Ford back then," she explained.[644] Not only did the size and the appearance of the car catch her attention, but she was also struck by the fact that it was locked, with the interior lights on and the engine running.

The woman rushed into the store and headed for the dairy section. Suddenly, a male voice behind her startled her. "Well, what are you doing out this late?" The voice belonged to George McGann, whom the woman had not seen in years. He gave her a quick hug and began asking about her family.

"What surprised me," she commented years later, "is that he knew the name of each of my four children. A flag went up because I did not know he kept up with me and my family." McGann then admonished her, "You shouldn't be out alone this late at night." He then surprised her by adding, "If there is anything you or your family ever need, just let me know." The woman had no idea what he was referring to. At the time, she was just pleased with the offer.

As they left the store together, the woman asked McGann who owned the expensive car in the parking lot. "That's mine," he answered simply. The woman left for home still wondering why the interior lights had been left on with the engine running. It never occurred to her that McGann might have been worried that someone might be waiting for him in his dark vehicle, or that he might have been preparing for a quick get-away.

The woman's husband was asleep when she returned home that night, but the next morning she related excitedly, "Guess what? Guess who I ran into last night? George McGann!" Her husband's eyes widened.

"Where?" he demanded.

"At the 7-11," she answered. "And he offered to get us anything we needed at a real good price." Her husband, normally calm and unruffled, reacted in a most unusual way.

"We can't take any of that stuff he is offering!" he proclaimed adamantly.

"Why not?" she asked innocently.

"Because it probably is all stolen. No one is able to give away stuff free or even at a good price unless it is stolen." Her husband than looked at her seriously. "I want you to remember something: It you run into McGann again, you smile, you nod, but you don't have anything to do with him. He's trouble!"[645]

McGann's friends did not refer to him as "trouble," but they thought long and hard before discussing his activities with the authors. James Weaver thoughtfully stared off into space before he answered any questions about his old friend George McGann.

"Now, let me see," he said, thinking out loud. "What's the statute of limitations on that? Oh, yes, I can answer some of your questions about that."[646] He then proceeded to describe McGann as a "great thief" of large appliances. He even admitted that he personally accepted some of McGann's "gifts." George McGann had been dead for over forty-five years, and his parents and first wife were also dead. Yet McGann's friend still seemed hesitant about answering certain questions.

McGann stole for practical reasons, but he also seemed to get a rush from successfully stealing from others—whether he was stealing money from friends at a poker party or televisions from a delivery truck. He was especially fond of stealing jewelry, which he "fenced" as quickly as possible. Boosie Weaver laughed as he recalled, "He would get these wild ideas about getting enough money to go to Mexico. One evening, he robbed John Nutts' Grill and Drive-In on Gregg Street because he wanted enough money to go to Mexico. During the robbery, he realized he was hungry, so he decided to just go ahead and cook himself a steak."[647] It wasn't bad enough that McGann robbed the businessman of his hard-earned money. He also stole a steak, cooked it, and left a mess on the grill and counter for the owner to clean up the next morning. This simply rubbed salt into the wound, but McGann thought nothing about sharing this story with his friends.

His penchant for stealing jewelry became common knowledge among his friends. Clifford Hart, for example, knew that McGann had a partner in Midland forty miles away. The two of them worked together to sell stolen jewelry. McGann distributed some of his stolen merchandise in Big Spring, and used a horse trailer to "tote his wares. He loved jewelry. He stole it, he sold it, and he kept some for himself," Hart recalled.

"That was George," Boosie Weaver admitted. "George was a thief and did not have a conscience when it came to stealing things." He often shared some of the stolen merchandise, but he did not *always* share information about his exploits.

"One day, he came in with a shoe box filled with $100 bills and wanted my brother James to drive him to the Mardi Gras in New Orleans," explained Boosie Weaver. New Orleans is a bit beyond the 50-mile range set by his probation, but this did not seem to bother McGann. Boosie Weaver did not elaborate on whether his brother complied with McGann's request.

Big Spring resident Roe Fulgham explained to the authors he knew McGann only slightly. He stressed that he was not a "friend" of McGann. "Holiday Motors just happened to be across the street from another of McGann's friends, John Huckabee. Huckabee was a mechanic who owned a garage."[648] Fulgham remembered that McGann rode up one day on a motorcycle, and a friend of Fulgham introduced them.

"McGann seemed like a real con man to me," Fulgham declared. "He talked about himself a great deal, and everything he did, according to him, was great. He talked about how much money he made at a poker game and, without batting an eye, pulled out a wad of bills." However, other people remembered McGann as a quiet man who did not brag much about anything. Perhaps he kept his most serious activities to himself.

Despite the fact that McGann was an outlaw, he could be likeable and, consequently, had quite a few friends. They included Clifford Hart, Gary McDaniel, James and Boosie Weaver, Jimmy Whitefield, Billy Joe Kilpatrick, Jack Hopper, Bill Moore, and Robert Mesker, to name a few. These young men often gathered at Huckabee's garage. Like many young men in the 1950s and 1960s, they were all interested in cars and motorcycles.

In fact, McGann and John Currie became part-owners in a race track on the edge of Big Spring. Jimmy Johnson remembers riding motorcycles with McGann, even racing their bikes at the track. According to Currie, it was at this track that he once met a man who identified himself as "Chuckie from San Antonio." Currie saw this same man several other times at the track; "Chuckie" was obviously there to meet with McGann. "Chuckie" was a tall, thin man with piercing eyes. Later, he moved to Midland and stayed about a year.[649] During this time, his son "Woody" would be born in Midland. "Chuckie" was none other than Charles Harrelson!

On that particular day at the race track, Currie overheard McGann talking to Chuckie about Carlos Marcello, the infamous underworld boss from Louisiana. From the conversation, he gathered that McGann was familiar with Marcello.

In fact, McGann once mentioned going to Mardi Gras and meeting Marcello there. With acquaintances like Charles Harrelson and Carlos Marcello, it's no wonder the FBI showed up one day in Big Spring looking for George McGann.

McGann had previously caught the attention of the FBI in Dallas. His offenses were so serious that his name was placed on the FBI's Most Wanted List. In an interview with a former friend of McGann who wishes to remain anonymous, the authors learned that the friend still remembers driving by McGann's auto lot and seeing FBI cars surrounding it.

"I called George and told him, 'Hey, you've got company at your place. FBI cars are all over that place.'" McGann sped to Holiday Motors immediately. "I heard they found a 55-gallon oil drum full of marijuana," the friend continued.[650] But that is not the only thing he remembered about George McGann.

"He had me take a car with nine or ten bullet holes in it to a guy who repaired cars in Big Spring. He was a Hispanic named Junior Something or other, on East Second Street. It wasn't George's car. He said it belonged to some people from out of town, but they needed him to fix it for them."[651]

It is possible that this bullet-ridden car is the same one McGann purchased through John Currie's bank. Currie and his wife wanted the car returned because of a lien on it. The couple had to go all the way to the outskirts of Philadelphia to collect the car.

When they arrived in Philadelphia, they discovered that the car looked better than Bonnie and Clyde's death vehicle, but it had obviously survived a shootout of some sort. According to Currie, "It had bullet holes all in it, and the sheriff had kept the rearview mirror because it had finger prints on it. I got stopped twice by police as I was driving it home to Big Spring—police had noticed the bullet holes in the car. Finally, I called the Pennsylvania sheriff to ask him to give me a note explaining why I had the car."[652] Currie provided no explanation as to why George McGann's car was full of bullet holes. McGann must have kept that trivial detail to himself.

This wasn't the only time the FBI came to Big Spring looking for McGann. Another time it was Big Spring Police Chief Jay Banks himself who called to warn McGann that the FBI was in town looking for him and for the contents of his car.[653] "Huck" Huckabee, who owned a garage just west of McGann's Holiday Motors, recalled that memorable day not long before he died.

"George called me one day and said, 'Come over and get my car and put it in your shop and clean it out.' His trunk was full of small plastic sacks of pills. The FBI was looking for the car."[654] So Huckabee hurried across the street and did as McGann requested. It wasn't long before the FBI agents located the car at Huckabee's garage. They searched the car thoroughly and even tore out the seats. But thanks to Huckabee, they didn't find whatever they were looking for.

The description of the contents of McGann's car varies depending upon who is recalling the story. Huckabee said he found only baggies of drugs (amphetamines). Other McGann friends have hinted that a small gun and its case were also in McGann's car that day. Huckabee admitted to the authors that he knew what type of weapon the others were referring to. He referred to it as a Remington Fireball XP-100, and he said he saw it. But according to him, it was not in McGann's car that day. It is fairly obvious, however, that the FBI did not make a trip to Big Spring just because McGann stuffed some pills into little sacks in his car. Huckabee was unbothered by the FBI's visit. No matter how much trouble McGann caused for his friends, according to Huckabee, "you couldn't keep from liking him."

One story that numerous people in Big Spring related to the authors involved a group of McGann's "business associates" appearing in Big Spring with a dead body in the trunk of their car. According to those who remember this event, McGann was expected to dispose of the body. He had informed his friends at Holiday Motors that some "pretty important men were coming into town."

Glenn Wallace described what he saw that day to Roe Fulgham. "You won't believe what I saw today," he began. "A big black limo drove up to George's car lot. Four guys in suits and ties got out, went into George's office, and then came out with George. They opened the trunk of their limo. George looked into it, pulled out a wad of bills, and gave them some money." Glenn Wallace, unable to contain his curiosity, loped across the street and asked McGann, "Hey, what was in the trunk of the car?" McGann just looked at him and replied, "A body bag." Wallace didn't ask any more questions. It is possible McGann had ordered a hit on someone and was paying the killers for a successful job. Like any good businessman, he checked the "merchandise" to be sure the job was done properly.

When "Huck" Huckabee used the words "business associates" in connection with George McGann, he admitted he was referring to the "Mob." Clifford Hart was at Huckabee's garage that day when the "business associates" showed McGann a body bag. He also recalled that memorable day when some of McGann's "friends" showed up with a dead body in the trunk of a car. Billy Joe Kilpatrick was working at Holiday Motors that day, so was in the perfect spot to notice that the corpse was still wearing beautiful hand-made leather boots. McGann's "friends" asked Kilpatrick if he would like a pair like those, and he assured them he did.

According to Huckabee, McGann enlisted his help that day in disposing the body his "business associates" had brought to Big Spring. Huckabee loaded his truck with the corpse and a great deal of lye and headed out to the desert that surrounds Big Spring. Huckabee explained to the authors, "The desert around Big Spring is full of lots of dead bodies that were burned and buried." The authors didn't ask him how he knew this.

Once the body was disposed of, Kilpatrick became the recipient of one pair of slightly used but beautiful western boots. He realized immediately where they had come from, and the thought of wearing them scared him to death, according to friends who laugh about his reaction even now. McGann's friends seem vague as to who actually ended up with these beautiful western boots, but, obviously, someone did. After all, the man whose body ended up in the desert certainly didn't need them.

Another individual who verified that McGann sometimes discussed "bodies in the desert" was San Jose Dick McMorran. According to McMorran, McGann would sometimes make comments like, "Yeah, they found him dead in the desert shot full of holes—terrible case of 'suicide.'"[655]

A story still told in Big Spring revolves around McGann renting a posh apartment on the outskirts of Lubbock, Texas. Here, he set up high-stake poker games even though this violated his probation. Big-time gamblers like Doyle Brunson came from all over the southern part of the United States to take part in these parties. Some say McGann began the evening as one of the poker players, but during the game, he would sneak out and come back disguised as a robber and steal the other players' money. Supposedly, he also took a percentage for hosting the parties. The rumor was that he got away with these planned robberies twice, but the third time the other players were ready for him.

That might explain an incident that Roe Fulgham recalled. He and Glen Wallace were eating breakfast at the Sands Restaurant in Big Spring when McGann and three of his friends entered. Fulguhm immediately noticed that McGann was not his typical, immaculate self. In fact, he had scratches all over his face.

Fulgham stopped him as he walked past his table and asked, "What have you been into?" The other men with McGann stopped, but McGann walked right past Fulgham and Wallace without saying a word. His companions explained that someone had shown up at a poker game with a rifle and attempted to rob them. They looked embarrassed even as they explained, "George came out the winner. You should have seen the other guy!"

There was no explanation given for why McGann had not explained this himself—if events occurred the way his friends described them. Fulgham recalled that it looked more like someone tried to pull something, like a mask, from McGann's face and "scratched the heck out of him!"[656] Perhaps McGann's face was scratched when another poker player unmasked him. Perhaps he had an altercation with a female. Either way, McGann was not talking. However, an arrest photo does exist showing McGann with a bruised eye and puffy cheeks, proof that, at least on one occasion, George McGann did not walk away a winner.

However, most people seemed to fear Big Spring's version of Clyde Barrow. Gambler T. J. Cloutier wrote about the night McGann robbed a poker game in Dallas. He had the nerve to come back the next day, buy chips, and join the next game. "Everybody was too afraid of him to spoil the mood with the rude mention of yesterday's robbery," Cloutier recalled.[657] They were also afraid of some of his friends.

Whether McGann's "associations" were made through illegal gambling, robberies, or other nefarious activities, there is no doubt he involved himself with some dangerous people. Before he returned to Big Spring, McGann partnered with some of them as they plotted highway robberies. Besides owning George's Lounge, where he hosted illegal poker parties, McGann involved himself in interstate gambling, which is one reason he was wanted by the FBI. One of his cohorts was a man named Stanley "the Creeper" Cook.

Cook was known as a murderer who seemed to have nine lives. According to a Big Spring resident who knew McGann well, "George ran with a guy named Stanley the Creeper and they were both hit men."[658] This individual stated that "the Creeper" would hide outside the poker games and 'hit' the people when they left. His reputation for robbery and murder caused someone to eventually put a contract on Cook's life. According to Dallas newspaper reports, one or more individuals took Cook out into the country and shot him in the abdomen—seven times. Nevertheless, he managed to crawl back to town, having survived the attempt on his life.

According to Boosie and James Weaver, another "business associate" of McGann made the FBI's Ten Most Wanted list. Known as a pool shark, he came to Big Spring frequently to gamble on pool games. In fact, he robbed other outlaws all over the South, not unlike McGann. According to Johnny Hughes in an article on McGann titled "*George McGann: Gambler, Con Man, Hit Man, Kennedy Assassin?*" McGann told Hughes quite a bit about this "business associate." "When the word hit the gamblers' grapevine that this particular individual was in town, joints would close and folks stayed armed and indoors."[659]

Some of McGann's associates were frightening to his hometown friends. When Charles Harrelson visited McGann in Big Spring, he was introduced to nineteen-year-old Robert Mesker. Though Mesker was an impressive fighter, he was scared of Harrelson. Mesker quietly stated to the authors, "He had cold-blooded eyes. When he looked at you, he looked right through you."[660]

Despite what is known about the company McGann kept, some in Big Spring still claim that George McGann was nothing more than a small-time hood who liked to gamble and play poker. However, most unimportant gamblers did not make the FBI's Most Wanted List. The address books of "small-time hoods" did not usually contain the names of dangerous criminals like Pete Kay, Charles Harrelson, R. D. Matthews, and Stanley Cook.

Regardless of the men McGann associated with, he was known for his loyalty to his true friends. But one particular friend would, undoubtedly, disagree with this statement. He knew McGann well enough to serve as a pallbearer at McGann's funeral. In fact, he thought the two of them were good friends. However, when he and his wife divorced and he wanted custody of their son, he discovered that McGann could quickly become a friend's worst enemy.

This man discovered that his ex-wife moved to Lubbock and began associating with McGann. A private investigator informed him that his ex-wife was selling drugs for McGann, probably cocaine. The man knew George McGann well enough to state the following as fact.

"George would do anything that was unlawful. George owed money to the IRS, and several times they would track him down for it. Once, they found twenty or thirty thousand dollars on him and they took it as partial payment for what he owed."

As he thinks back, this former friend couldn't help but chuckle. "When he would fill out IRS forms, he would write 'Thief' in the space for "Occupation" just to goad them. He could be the most charming, well-mannered man you ever met. He'd hold the door open for you. He dressed nicely, looked immaculate …" His voice trailed off before he added softly, "But he would kill you in a minute if you crossed him."[661]

This particular former friend of George McGann learned just how heartless McGann could be. McGann actually ordered a hit on his former friend, possibly because of the friend's ex-wife. Rumors about the hit spread around Big Spring.

Howard County Sheriff Aubrey Standard told McGann's former friend, "You better start carrying a gun." The Sheriff went on, "I don't think anything will happen to you if your son is with you, but you better carry a gun."

He then gave the man a business card with his name and telephone number on it as well as three other numbers written on the back. The Sheriff explained that if the man was stopped by the police for carrying a gun, he was to show them that card and have law enforcement call him. That would keep the man from being arrested for carrying an unlicensed weapon.

"The only reason I wasn't killed, I know in my heart, was because someone powerful in Big Spring stopped the hit," McGann's former friend told the authors. When asked how a local businessman could halt a planned hit on someone, the answer the authors received from George McGann's former friend was a pointed one.

"Let's not go there," he said quietly.[662] As unbelievable as this man's story sounds, his son can verify some of his father's memories concerning George McGann.

"A business associate of George McGann who lived in Midland came to my dad, put a hand on his shoulder, and said, 'Where is your gun?' My father said it was in the glove compartment of the car, and the man responded, 'You put it on the front seat. You'll need it.'"

"He was warning my dad," the young man continued, "that there had been a hit put on him." When asked how this business associate would know, he replied, "He probably was in the meeting when they planned it. These men met in Odessa once a month or so to plan their activities." By "activities," he meant illegal poker parties, robberies, and murders.[663]

CHAPTER 63

GEORGE MCGANN'S LUCK RUNS OUT

"When the mob has a hit on you, there's nowhere you can hide."
—George McGann

Towards the end of his short life, George McGann found out what it was like to have a "hit" placed on him. He continued to carry lots of cash, possibly because he knew that if he was killed, it would not be for his money. Jim Hayworth remembers seeing McGann in a bar once with a briefcase full of $100 bills. Someone who seemed to realize McGann's life was in jeopardy noticed the money, which McGann wasn't attempting to hide, and asked him, "Why don't you take a couple of those briefcases and leave and hide out?"

"When the mob has a hit on you," McGann replied, "there's nowhere you can hide." With the word out that his days were numbered, McGann seemed resigned to the fact he was going to die young and violently, so he continued to break the law and associate with known criminals. It was all he knew how to do. For some reason, he preferred taking what was not his, including other people's lives.

On the last day of his life, McGann was not his usual cocky self. Perhaps the murder of his associate Gary McDaniel made him realize that his past was quickly catching up with him. He wasn't known for sharing confidential information, so it is still unclear even today why he suspected his life was going to be cut short.

What is known is that on the day he was killed, he stopped by to see his friend John Currie at the bank. "Never before in all the years that I had kept his money had George ever come in and asked for all of it at once," Currie remembered.[664]

"I've got a game in Lubbock and I've got to take it all," McGann explained. So, the banker counted out $14,000 and gave it to him. Jimmy Johnson, who was about twenty at the time and a student at Texas Tech University in Lubbock, recalls that McGann supposedly gave some of the $14,000 to McGann's wife Beverly before he left for a big poker game.

To pick up a friend, McGann stopped by James Weaver's house in Midland.

Weaver assumed the friend intended to go with McGann, but apparently he changed his mind. Still, McGann picked up the man's car, which was full of stolen jewelry, for the drive to Lubbock. The plan was for McGann to join a large poker game there. Whether the jewelry was to be fenced or used as money in the poker game is anybody's guess.

Before leaving Big Spring, McGann briefly visited a local joint known as "The Watering Hole." He knew he would find Robert Mesker and Jimmy Whitefield playing pool there—it was a favorite hangout for McGann and his friends. Located on West Highway 80, it was owned by another McGann friends, Bill Moore.

Assuming Mesker, Whitefield, and Moore would accompany him to Lubbock, McGann demanded that they leave that very minute so that he could get to Ronnie Weedan's house in Lubbock, where the poker game was to be held, on time. Normally, Mesker would have been happy to go with McGann. He had been up to Lubbock a few times before to play pool.

That day, though, he explained to McGann that he would go but not right then because he was in the middle of a pool game with "a guy from out of town. The games were going for $100 a pop, which was very unusual in Big Spring, but this guy was from out of town and I was winning. I didn't want to stop," Mesker told the authors.

McGann, too impatient to wait, left Big Spring alone. That September night in 1970 might have turned out differently had any or all of McGann's friends accompanied him to Lubbock. George McGann might not have died—at least not that night—if his usual entourage was with him.

To this day, his friends still refer to September 30, 1970 as "that night." One of those friends compared him to the main character James Dean played in the 1950s movie "Rebel Without a Cause." Dean's character, like George McGann, did not enjoy a happy 1950s home life. Nor did James Dean himself. Like McGann, Dean loved cars and motorcycles, and often drove them too fast. He was killed in a car wreck that could have been avoided on September 30, 1955, *exactly* fifteen years before George McGann would be killed at an illegal poker party he could have avoided.

Some people in Big Spring heard about McGann's death as early as midnight on September 30. Based on information that several people shared with the authors, some in Big Spring probably knew more about what happened that night than the officials in Lubbock who investigated.

However, the events preceding McGann's death are confusing and still controversial. Numerous acquaintances of McGann have admitted they were supposed to be at the poker party that night with McGann, but only one ever told anyone he was. Jim Hayworth remembers his friend Jimmy Whitefield admitting he was at Ronnie Weeden's house in Lubbock where McGann was killed. According to Whitefield, McGann received a phone call that night, interrupting the conversation by saying, "Hang on a minute. He's going to kill her if I don't do something." McGann apparently laid the phone down and left the room. The person on the other end of the line, who refuses to be identified even now, then heard gun shots. McGann never returned to the telephone.

Robert Mesker, however, recalled "that night" differently. He remembered that he and Jimmy Whitefield and Bill Moore were still at The Watering Hole in Big Spring playing pool when "someone" called about midnight. Moore answered the phone.

"They just gunned down George in Lubbock," the voice at the end of the line said. The caller did not identify himself. McGann's three friends immediately called the sheriff's department in Lubbock and were told that the department had not received any information that anyone had been shot at that address. The mysterious out-of-town pool player who had been betting "$100 a pop" against Robert Mesker suddenly decided he had lost enough money for the evening and disappeared into the cool West Texas night. It is possible that his role in McGann's death was to keep McGann's friends occupied so they would not accompany him to Lubbock. According to Mesker, the stranger never again returned to Big Spring to play pool.

One of the most intriguing stories that floated through Big Spring was that McGann was shot twice in the stomach but did not die immediately. Boosie Weaver heard that "George was in a bedroom with a woman. Heard the fight, heard gunfire, came down the hall, and got shot in the hallway. Laid in the hallway for two hours. He was then turned over and shot again." Though he moaned and pleaded for someone to call an ambulance, no one did.

Others in Big Spring began hearing all kinds of rumors about what had occurred that night in Lubbock. Nell Rogers heard that McGann had been in Lubbock the night he was killed with "people he did business with. The story was they were going to do away with someone else, not George. George went up to Lubbock to prevent this."[665]

James Weaver heard a very different story. "He was going to play poker. He drove to Lubbock to Ronnie Weedan's house," Weaver stated. "At the house, a friend of theirs made a pass at another guy's wife. Ronnie and McGann's friend got into a fight."[666]

According to the Big Spring man whom McGann planned to kill, "I was probably the second or third person to hear about George's death. My father-in-law had some kind of two-way radio or police radio and heard it that morning.

He called me about 6:00 or possibly 6:30, and I immediately called John Currie because I knew he would want to know. But as for *my* reaction to his death, I didn't give a shit."

He continued, "A woman that night supposedly got away from the apartment during the shooting. I wouldn't be surprised if it was my ex-wife."[667] Apparently, this man did not know that some of McGann's other friends heard the news of the shooting as early as midnight. *They* were probably the first to hear of McGann's death.

McGann's wife Beverly was at home when she got the call from John Currie that McGann had been killed. She immediately called Monalee Tonn, a woman who had befriended her at the Baptist Temple Church in Big Spring. Tonn, for Beverly's sake, was saddened but not terribly surprised.

She stated years later that the police were "always around George's business. To get to George, they would mess with Beverly. They would often raid the house and confiscate her clothes. The guys that hung around Holiday Motors were tough and rowdy, not people you would want to offend or get on their bad side."[668]

She recalled the morning Beverly called her about her husband's death. "Beverly was so upset when she got the news that she called me to come and pick her up. She asked me to drive her to George's dealership, where she could retrieve some papers." Tonn knew just by looking at Beverly that she was in shock.

"She never went anywhere without her makeup on or her hair all fixed up. She was always dolled up, but not this time." This time Beverly wore no make-up, and it was obvious her eye lashes were missing.

The same men Tonn referred to as 'rowdy" were already gathered around the outside of Holiday Motors when the women arrived. Beverly marched straight to McGann's desk to retrieve whatever it was she needed.

It took several days to determine the circumstances surrounding George McGann's death, and there are still questions about everything that happened that night. Apparently, no law enforcement officials took seriously the midnight telephone call from McGann's friends in Big Spring; they waited to investigate until Ronnie Weedan called them at 5:55 a.m. to report the shooting. According to the *Lubbock Avalanche*, "Two men died in a blaze of gunfire in a plush four-bedroom house at 90th and Ave. S—a residence previously raided as a gambling place. Found dead across from each other in a spacious den were Jerry Michael Meshell, 29, of Lufkin and George Albert McGann of Big Spring."[669]

The two men was officially declared dead at 6:00 a.m. by the justice of the peace. Weeden claimed to officials that the two men shot each other. That isn't what the investigation showed, however.

Information from the official inquest showed that Meshell died from two shots from a .38-caliber pistol, which may have belonged to McGann, and McGann may have killed Meshell. However, the autopsy showed that McGann was shot by two different pistols. He had two .45 bullets in his body, but he also had two .38 bullets which had originated from the same pistol that killed Meshell. This evidence is what convinced a jury that Meshell probably shot McGann, but that Weedan then used McGann's own gun to ultimately kill McGann.

A friend of McGann later explained, "A man in Houston named Carl [unknown last name] kept talking to me about a guy he met in prison named"'Ronnie.' He said he was about the meanest man alive. The guy said he was in prison for killing a guy from West Texas. Ronnie told Carl he shot McGann twice with his gun and then picked up George's gun and shot him with that one, too. That is why he was convicted. He couldn't claim self-defense if he used the dead man's gun."[670]

Reports of McGann's death in the *Big Spring Herald* were not particularly sympathetic even though he was a hometown boy and his mother still lived in Big Spring. The story of his death began with the following statement: "George Albert McGann, who avoided trouble at home but attracted it elsewhere, had told friends on more than one occasion that he would be eventually rubbed out. He proved an accurate prophet, being one of two killed in a south side Lubbock residential shootout last Tuesday."[671]

Years later, Beverly Oliver McGann Massegee stated that her then-husband George was actually "assassinated." In her book *Nightmare in Dallas*, she pointedly stated, "McGann was part of the Dixie Mafia."[672] In the October 1, 1970 issue of the *Big Spring Herald,* Paul McCaghren, who was the Dallas Assistant Chief of Police, alleged that "McGann was a possible leader of a criminal organization known as the Dixie Mafia, active in southern states."[673] At the time, the paper also reported, "McGann's widow denied that her husband was involved 'with any gang.'"[674]

Beverly Oliver McGann later admitted that she knew how connected her husband was to organized crime. Perhaps her denials after McGann's death occurred because she was simply trying to prevent the same people who had killed her husband from killing her! Some have described McGann's death as nothing more than a poker party fracas and suggested McGann was simply caught cheating. Others who knew McGann better than his poker-playing associates believed there was much more to the story than the newspaper reported.

CHAPTER 64

ORGANIZED CRIME PAYS ITS LAST RESPECTS TO GEORGE MCGANN

"At the funeral, there were a lot of people that weren't nice people. I could tell by looking at them."—Huck Huckabee

Because of the length and complexity of the murder investigation, George McGann's funeral was not held until October 4, 1970, at Nalley-Pickle Funeral Home in Big Spring. Oddly enough, it wasn't his widow who made the funeral arrangements. Because his father had already passed away, this task fell to the mother of the deceased, Ayra McGann. She called a young woman who had served as matron of honor at her son's first wedding and asked her to accompany her to Lubbock to bring back her son's body for burial. As much as the young woman wanted to help the grieving mother, she refused because her husband insisted that she have nothing to do with McGann's funeral.

"I agreed to help," she explained more than forty years later, "but my husband threw a fit when he found out and refused to let me. He wouldn't let me attend the funeral, much less *help* with it."[675]

"'You are not going to the funeral of that mobster!'" he screamed when she told him what Mrs. McGann asked of her. "I had to tell his mother I could not help her."

"Well, will you at least go with me when his body is ready?" his mother asked. I had to say, "My husband says 'no.'"

Later, she was so glad she listened to her husband. Apparently, word traveled around Big Spring that the FBI would be observing and photographing everyone who attended McGann's funeral. The funeral of a "small-time poker player" would not normally bring out FBI agents with cameras. In fact, this had never happened at any *other* Big Spring funeral.

No one in town was particularly comfortable being photographed by the FBI, and several people avoided it by going to the funeral home before the funeral.

Nell Rogers was one who chose to pay her respects beforehand.

"I went to the funeral home the night before the funeral, while no one else was there," she recalled. That same evening, a young mother and her four-year-old son also paid their respects to McGann. As an adult, the son recalled in a telephone interview that his mother took him with her to the funeral home.

"No one else was there but us. Holding my hand, my mother walked slowly up to the funeral home. I remember thinking it was creepy to be looking at a dead body. The casket was open with the body on view. My mother went up to it and reached out, touching McGann's face and saying, 'Oh, my, he looks swollen.' I didn't think much about this at the time, but as an adult, I wonder now how well she knew George McGann."[676]

The man also remembered that his mother, for some reason, became the next owner of McGann's white German shepherd, appropriately named "Bandit."

"I remember going with my mom to get the dog. My mother seemed familiar with the McGanns' house; she walked right in like she'd been there before, and the dog came right to her. He seemed familiar with her, too," he recalled. "He came right to her."

Today, people in Big Spring still refer to George McGann's funeral as one of the most unusual funerals ever held in this West Texas town. In rolled the men in their large, expensive, dark cars, wearing tailored black suits and dark sunglasses. These same men, it seems, handled most of the arrangements for the fallen mobster. If they knew that the FBI set up surveillance around the funeral home and was recording people entering and exiting the funeral, they did not seem to care.

McGann's out of town "business associates" ordered a floral arrangement for the ceremony. It was a large heart-shaped design created from white roses with a streak of red roses cascading from the top, dividing it into two pieces. Some of McGann's Big Spring friends suggested this was a Mafia symbol representing the fact that the deceased had fallen out of favor with his "associates." Another friend, however, thought it simply meant McGann's death had broken their hearts.

Regardless, the funeral home was packed with men who looked nothing like the local mourners. One McGann friends stated, "The men could have been characters out of the 'Godfather' movies." Another friend, Huck Huckabee, simply said, "At the funeral, there were a lot of people that weren't nice people. I could tell by looking at them."[677]

As the funeral service progressed, many of the locals craned their necks to get a glimpse of the well-dressed out-of-towners. Despite McGann's reputation, numerous mourners were there because they had actually cared about George McGann. Others were there to support his mother and wife.

Pallbearers for McGann were mainly Big Spring friends. But sprinkled

THE LONE STAR SPEAKS

among them were faces the FBI surely recognized. These included Stanley "the Creeper" Cook from Dallas and Pete Kay from Huntsville. A special floral arrangement sent from New Orleans was signed "Sandy and Kirksey Nix." Kirksey Nix was well-known in Louisiana for his Mafia connections. There was also an arrangement from Harold Pruett, a man who had been arrested with McGann several times.

One of the most intriguing signatures on the "Attendees" list was that of "John Quigley." Researchers familiar with Lee Harvey Oswald's history immediately connect this name to an FBI agent who interviewed Oswald after his arrest in New Orleans in August 1963. However, a well-known florist in town bore the same name and probably handled floral arrangements for McGann's funeral. If so, he would have attended McGann's funeral. Of course, it is possible that Special Agent John Quigley was sent to the funeral by the FBI. Forty-five years after McGann's murder, one of his close friends offered a possible explanation for why an FBI agent connected to the Kennedy assassination might attend George McGann's funeral. However, the explanation deepened the mystery surrounding George McGann's life and activities.[678]

A priest, the Reverend William F. Meagher of the Immaculate Heart of Mary Catholic Church, and the Reverend James Puckett, pastor of Baptist Temple, co-officiated at the service. The priest was there because McGann was raised a Catholic; the Baptist minister was there because McGann's wife attended the Baptist Temple Church in Big Spring.

Several of McGann's friends still remember remarks made by the Catholic priest. Instead of using words that were comforting and supportive to McGann's family and friends, he alluded to his illegal activities, though some of the people associated with those activities were sitting directly in front of him. He even used the words "burn in hell" during the homily. Years later, Beverly McGann Massagee recalled her husband's funeral as "very nice," but McGann's friends are still appalled at comments the priest made that day.

It may be coincidence that the life of this same priest ended a day later. He was killed in a one-car accident when his car rolled over on US Highway 80, two miles east of Midland on October 5, 1970. Meagher had served as a priest in Big Spring for approximately eighteen months. According to a news report in the *Odessa American*, an autopsy on the priest showed that he died of injuries received in the car crash. "Apparently a coronary attack was responsible for the accident. Justice of the Peace, John Biggs, said that Reverend Meagher was alive at the time of the crash, but the coronary caused him to lose control of the car."[679]

Because there were no witnesses, the investigators had to use evidence at the scene of the accident to determine how it occurred. The investigation showed that the car left the road, then swerved back on. The official report showed that the priest apparently lost control of the car, and it overturned four times, ending up in an upright position. The accident report does not disclose what caused the priest to lose control of the car. Is it possible he was *forced* off the road? At the time, no one would have thought to ask that question.

The police were unaware of visits that McGann's "business associates" made to some of his Big Spring friends not long after his funeral. Most of the visits were made to pay off poker debts McGann had owed. For example, according to a friend of McGann who still wishes to remain anonymous even now, men in dark suits and sunglasses drove up in a black limousine and parked in front of his house. They knocked politely on his front door. The man, having seen them through his front window, was already concerned about why they were there. He didn't recognize them, but he knew they were not from Big Spring.

As much as he dreaded opening the door, he was more afraid of *not* opening it, and cautiously cracking it open. One of the men asked politely, "May I speak with you?" Swallowing the lump in his throat, he just nodded "yes."

To his surprise, the strangers motioned for him to join them in the large black Cadillac from which they had exited. The Big Spring man was a poker player, but never played with any of these men. One of the men in the dark suits flipped open a small notebook and asked, "Did George McGann owe you $800?" Literally shaking, the Big Spring man once again could only nod "yes." The "business associate" whipped out a wad of bills and counted out $800. He said solemnly as he placed them in the man's hand, "From this day forth, you don't know any George McGann. Understand?" For the last time, the man nodded "yes."

However, the same "business associates" made a visit to share some pertinent information about the priest who made inappropriate comments at McGann's funeral. Men in sunglasses appeared at the home of another friend of McGann. When the subject of the funeral and the priest's comments arose, the men in the suits and glasses said simply, "We took care of that S.O.B." Did this comment indicate that the priest's death was *not* an accident? Perhaps the verdict of "accidental death" rendered by the Justice of the Peace concerning the Reverend William F. Meagher might have been different if the J. P. knew about this conversation.

Long after McGann's death, people in Big Spring and in Dallas still talk about some of his escapades. Sheriff Buford Pusser of "Walking Tall" fame accused Geoge McGann of participating in the murder of his wife in Tennessee. The murder occurred on August 12, 1967 as Pusser and his wife Pauline responded to a disturbance call. A car suddenly appeared alongside the sheriff's car. The occupants opened fire and killed Pauline Pusser. Sheriff Pusser suffered a shotgun wound to the face and was left for dead. After eighteen days in the hospital, Pusser managed to identify four assassins: George McGann, Gary McDaniel, Kirksey McCord Nix, and Carl Douglas White.[680]

Law enforcement in Dallas connected the so-called Dixie Mafia to nineteen murders. There is no way of knowing how many of these murders are connected to George McGann. There is also no proof concerning who actually "controlled" McGann. An acquaintance of McGann is unsure who McGann answered to, but he thought it might be Kelsey Nix, the right- hand man of mob boss Carlos Marcello.

Doyle Brunson claimed that McGann's bookie was Curt Gentry of Midland, but a "bookie" was not necessarily connected to the mob and did not usually give orders to men like McGann.

It was understood that McGann always took care of "his hits" personally and did not ask others to do the dirty work.

Rumor had it that Gary McDaniel and Stanley Cook were just two of McGann's acquaintances whom someone wanted dead. The "hit" on Stanley Cook was unsuccessful, and he managed to outlive McGann. Gary McDaniel was not so lucky.

Beverly Oliver discussed his death in her book but did not mention how he died. She simply wrote that a man appeared at the McGanns' house in Big Spring one evening in 1969. Stuffed inside the trunk of the man's car was the corpse of Gary McDaniel. It seems logical to assume that McGann ordered McDaniel's death, and this is why he helped transport the body 200 miles and dump it into a lake. After all, if McDaniel was killed by law enforcement or rival gang members, there would have been no need to hide his body. It seemed that the body had to be disposed of out of town so it would not be connected to the West Texas area.

So McGann and the driver of the car moved the corpse to a lake near Dallas. However, a law enforcement official familiar with the case said that evidence has shown that McDaniel, near Midland, Texas, was actually tied to a tree and shot to death. It was not long after McDaniel's death that the man who drove his body out of West Texas was himself found dead near the Texas-Oklahoma border. Apparently, it did not always pay to be friends with George McGann in Dallas or in Big Spring.

No judge's order was ever going to curtail George McGann's activities. He went where he wanted to go and did what he wanted to do. There is evidence

SARA PETERSON & K.W. ZACHRY

that he was involved in burglaries, bookmaking, illegal gambling, drug dealing, and murder, all while he was on probation!

CHAPTER 65

WHERE WAS GEORGE MCGANN ON NOVEMBER 22, 1963?

"George was a character—real quiet, didn't brag—so when he said something, you knew it was the truth. We believed him."—Robert Mesker

According to members of the Ft. Worth Police Department, they were able to close 29 open cases after George McGann was killed. This did not include one of the most famous murder cases of the century. Though McGann was known for being tight-lipped about his activities, he did finally share a fascinating story with three of his closest friends not long before he died.

One night in 1970, McGann and his three friends were playing pool at the Interlude Lounge in Big Spring. McGann admitted to Jimmy Whitefield, Bill Moore, and Robert Mesker that he was worried about being killed himself. His companions asked why he was so worried. Chances are they assumed it was because of retaliation for some of the various "hits" McGann was known to have made. They had no idea he was about to discuss one of the most infamous events in American history.

McGann told his three friends that he strongly suspected that the FBI, the CIA, and even the Dallas police chief were involved in the plot to kill John F. Kennedy. He then explained why he believed this.

With the sound of pool balls clicking in the background, McGann confessed that he had been in Dealey Plaza the day President Kennedy was killed. His reason for being there was to assassinate the President from a manhole on Elm Street. Supposedly, an "associate" was there also to take photos so McGann would have proof for those who had hired him. For this historic assignment, he had been promised $25,000, which was a great deal of money in 1963.

After a few moments of stunned silence, McGann's friends asked who had hired him for this "hit." His answer was a simple one: "People in the Dixie Mafia." McGann also shared with them that some other people they knew had also been in Dallas that day, too, namely Charles Harrelson and Pete Kay. Both of these names were familiar to his pool-playing companions. They had seen them with McGann on several occasions, and had even met them in Huntsville.

McGann elaborated that, on November 22, 1963, he was in a van with a false bottom and a trap door. The day before the assassination, one of his unnamed partners pulled the van over the entrance to an opening behind the white picket fence that separated the parking lot from what became known as the "grassy knoll." McGann slithered down into the drain undetected. His partner then drove the van away. The parking lot, which was owned by a deputy sheriff, was reserved for employees. Anyone entering or exiting needed a key.

McGann told his friends that he spent the entire night before the assassination and the next morning in the drain. This was to make sure he was not detected by any type of security that might check out the knoll and the parking lot area. Long before researcher Jack Brazil personally demonstrated in 1992 that an individual could have escaped from Dealey Plaza through Dallas' underground sewer system and arrived safely at the Trinity River, researchers Penn Jones, Jr., Jim Marrs, and John Judge did the same thing in the 1960s. According to Judge, "Penn Jones crawled through the pipes under Dealey Plaza and discovered that one direction leads down Elm Street and back to a vertical shaft that opens at the juncture of the picket fence on the Knoll and the railroad track abutment that crosses Elm Street as part of the Triple Underpass. If you pass that point, it eventually leads down to the Trinity River plain."[681]

Jim Garrison was also interested in the idea that the drain system beneath Dealey Plaza could have been used to either harbor a sniper and/or provide a means of escape for at least one of the assassins. This might explain why the CIA airplane that had flown Sgt. Robert Vinson to Dallas landed on the dry Trinity River bed not long after the assassination. The drain system could have served as an escape route for the two passengers who joined Vinson on the CIA airplane. So, the story that George McGann told his friends not long before he was murdered may not be as farfetched as it may have sounded at the time.

McGann's acquaintances were unsure about the details concerning the weapon he used that day. But several of his friends personally knew that he prized an unusual handgun that he kept concealed in a special silver case with a blue velvet lining. He showed it to Moore and Whitefield a few times, so they assumed that was the weapon he or his partner used. This may have been the same weapon that some people think was hidden in the trunk of McGann's car the day the FBI came to Big Spring looking for him.

When McGann completed his story to his friends, the three men just nodded and continued their pool game. All three were surprised he had shared something this important with them in the pool hall. McGann usually took his friends to his office at Holiday Motors if there was going to be a "serious" talk; this time he didn't. However, there were only the four of them in the lounge that evening, so no one else could have overheard the conversation. As shocking as the story was, none of his friends questioned its validity.

"George was a character—real quiet, didn't brag—so when he said something, you knew it was the truth. We believed him," Mesker concluded. [682] None of McGann's friends shared this story with anyone until recently. Two of the three men in whom McGann confided are now dead. Only one person remembers everything McGann said to his friends that evening. That person is Robert Mesker.

Is there evidence that McGann was even in the Dallas area in November 1963? There is no doubt that McGann moved to Dallas after his divorce from his first wife became final in May of 1963. Though he had been making trips back and forth to Dallas for years, he was now free to live there.

Johnny Hughes, a poker historian, recalled in his book *Texas Poker Wisdom* that George McGann once shared a curious story with him. According to McGann, at the time of the Kennedy assassination, he owned a brand new red and white Cadillac, which soon became familiar to law enforcement. After the assassination, the Texas Rangers pursued and arrested him in East Texas. McGann claimed this was because his new Cadallac resembled one owned by a man on the FBI's Most Wanted list. Rather than charge McGann, the Rangers moved him from one small town to another, keeping him in jail. When he was finally released, uncharged, he found his new Cadillac sitting in a bar ditch with dents not there when he left it. [683]

The story shows that McGann *was* in the Dallas area in late 1963 after the assassination. There are no known photographs of him in Dealey Plaza on November 22, though there are of a man who appears to be Charles Harrelson. But because he and Charles Harrelson were such close friends, McGann's story of being involved in the assassination sounds more plausible. He and Harrelson could have been working together. The fact that George McGann, Charles Harrelson, Charles Rogers, and Lee Harvey Oswald may have been in close proximity to one other at the time of Kennedy's murder seems more than coincidental.

Elmer and Marietta Gerhart could vouch for the fact that Harrelson, Rogers, and Oswald all knew one other. McGann's friends knew that he and Harrelson were well acquainted. It seems logical that McGann would have known "friends of friends." Three of the four left Dallas of their own free will; only Oswald was arrested, accused of killing two men, and then murdered himself.

McGann's story concerning Kennedy's death could very well have been nothing more than a figment of his imagination. After all, he is not the only person to claim participation in the assassination. His confession, however, does explain why he exploded when, three years after the assassination, his wife began discussing the President's death. Her comment that the shots came from the north side of Dealey Plaza may have been too close to the truth. McGann waited seven years to discuss how President Kennedy had been killed, and it was not long before he was killed himself. Perhaps his admission of guilt was almost a "death bed confession."

His story suggests that members of the Dixie/Texas Mafia paid him to kill or at least assist in killing President Kennedy. But he also mentioned that the FBI, CIA, and Dallas police were involved. He probably suspected that the Mafia had infiltrated all three of these groups. Certain individuals were probably proud members of more than one organization.

One thing that both George McGann's friends and enemies all agreed upon is that he would eventually meet a violent end. Whether he was killed as part of a "hit," as the Lubbock police suggested, because he had cheated the wrong poker opponent, or because he knew too much about the Kennedy assassination, for some reason George McGann was lured to a poker game in Lubbock, Texas, in 1970 from which he never emerged alive. Roe Fulgham voiced the opinion that so many agreed with: "We knew it was coming." George McGann had made dangerous enemies. At least his body was not stuffed into a trunk of a car, tossed into a lake, or buried in the West Texas desert like the victims of other "hits." Nevertheless, his death may have been a warning to certain other individuals.

IX
THE WEST TEXAS
CONNECTION

The secrets eventually uncovered in West Texas concerned money, guns, hidden documents, and a possible connection to the death of John F. Kennedy.

CHAPTER 66

VOICES FOR BILLIE SOL ESTES

**"The secret that everybody wanted to know was:
'Where was the money?'"—Sue Goolsby**

E ven today, the name "Billie Sol Estes" elicits either great sympathy or great animosity from those who knew him or knew of him. Growing up near Abilene, Estes was raised in the fundamentalist Church of Christ. Some of the church's teachings about the immorality of dancing, for example, he took seriously; other teachings, like the moral gravity of theft and dishonesty, he seemed to take less seriously.

West Texans still recall that Estes often invited teenagers from area Churches of Christ to his expensive home in Pecos for barbeques and swimming parties. The teenagers understood that Estes would not allow the boys and girls to swim together. Apparently, he thought the sight of someone of the opposite sex in a swimsuit would create lustful thoughts.

Perhaps Estes' idea of morality and ethics focused on the wrong fundamentals. As a lay minister, he preached one thing and seemed to do another. Obviously, he had a keen eye for business. After moving to Pecos in 1951, he began to sell irrigation pumps and to buy land suitable for growing cotton. He had an innate talent for working the system; in this case, he manipulated federal subsidies. Estes took advantage of a government loophole so he could lease acreage from farmers, and then get paid by the government to let the land sit fallow. In 1953, Estes was named one of the ten outstanding young men in America by the U.S. Junior Chamber of Commerce. The Chamber was unaware of how Estes was becoming so financially successful.

It was not long before Estes had his finger in almost every pie in Pecos, Texas. As Robert D. McFadden of the *New York Times* wrote, "He bought land and farmed cotton, eventually acquiring 26,000 acres. He acquired mineral rights, sold farm equipment, built grain elevators, and went into real estate, construction, trucking, a mortuary, and the newspaper business."[684] People still wonder today whether Billie Sol Estes accomplished all this by himself or if he had had support from those in high offices.

Estes made millions by leasing grain silos to the U. S. government, and then cornered the Texas market on the use of anhydrous ammonia as a fertilizer.

But his real money came from mortgaging storage tanks to local farmers and then leasing them back. The problem was that only one of these tanks really existed. Later, Estes was to argue that there was no fraud involved because those who leased the tanks knew at the time that they did not exist.

If it had not been for Henry Marshall, a Texas agent with the Department of Agriculture, who investigated Estes' business dealings, Estes might have continued to operate under the radar of the U.S. government. By then, he had made powerful friends in high places. Letters in the Lyndon B. Johnson Presidential library indicate that he was connected to both Johnson and Senator Ralph Yarborough, and was even invited to and attended the Kennedy Inauguration. What Estes learned too late was that friends in high places could disappear overnight.

When negative stories concerning Estes' business activities appeared, President Kennedy publicly stated that his administration would be monitoring Estes' activities to ascertain that they were legal, yet privately he was furious that a newspaper reporter would dare to connect Estes to his "New Frontier." The reporter, Earl Mazo of the *New York Herald-Tribune*, was personally chastised by the President's brother Robert. More importantly, the President himself banned Mazo's newspaper from the White House.[685]

If Henry Marshall had been willing to ignore Estes' underhanded dealings, he would have probably received a promotion and eventually died a natural death in his bed. However, Marshall had more integrity than Estes and his cohorts expected. Sadly, his integrity probably cost him his life. On June 3, 1961, he was found dead on his Texas ranch, and though shot five times in the stomach with his own rifle, his death was ruled a suicide.

As a result of Marshall's investigation, Estes was assessed a small fine, but Estes continued to operate as usual. In fact, he was appointed to the National Cotton Advisory Board. In 1962, John Dunn, the owner of the *Pecos Independent and Enterprise,* became interested in Estes' rise to fame and fortune. The editor of the newspaper, Oscar Griffin Jr., eventually won the Pulitzer Prize in 1963 for articles exposing Estes' shenanigans. Griffin discovered, however, that exposing someone with Estes' connections could be dangerous, especially when Estes owned a rival Pecos newspaper.

Estes had both supporters and detractors. Many could not help but admire the young man's success. Others were persuaded that anyone who had gone from rags to riches so quickly must have done so illegally. However, his business escapades might have become yesterday's news if certain people associated with Estes had not begun to die mysteriously. Henry Marshall was only the first.

One associate to suddenly die was George Krutilek, Estes' accountant.

Krutilek was questioned intensively on April 2, 1962 by the FBI concerning his business dealings with Billie Sol Estes. On April 4, 1962, his decomposing body was found in his car in the desert near Clint, Texas, a small town not far from El Paso. Despite the fact that a hose from his exhaust was stuck in the window of his car, a doctor determined he had not died from carbon monoxide poisoning. Like Marshall's death, Krutilek's death was ruled a suicide even though a bruise on his forehead indicated foul play. The circumstances were strange enough that a newspaper reporter from the *San Angelo Standard-Times* asked the question publicly that so many others were asking privately: "What did the accountant Krutilek know about Billie Sol's business that warranted murder?"[686]

Krutilek was not the last Estes connection to mysteriously die. Harold Eugene Orr, president of the Superior Manufacturing Company of Amarillo, was also involved in Estes' frauds. Arrested along with Estes, he was sentenced to ten years in federal prison in 1964. But before he could begin his sentence, or reduce it by sharing information with the authorities, he, too, was found dead of carbon monoxide poisoning. This death was ruled "accidental" because Orr supposedly decided that one of the last things he needed to do before entering prison was to change the exhaust pipe on his automobile. Unfortunately, Orr made two vital mistakes: he used inappropriate tools, and he forgot to raise the garage door. Perhaps the biggest mistake he made was to have become involved with Billie Sol Estes.

His was not the last mysteriousEstes-related death. Howard Pratt, the office manager for Commercial Solvents in Chicago, was also found dead in his car from carbon monoxide poisoning. Commercial Solvents was the supplier of the fertilizer Billie Sol Estes sold to farmers in Texas. Obviously, Pratt would have known a great deal about Estes' business dealings. He never had the opportunity to discuss them with authorities.

Coleman Wade was a building contractor from Altus, Oklahoma who became associated with Billie Sol Estes. Estes' fertilizer tanks were built by Wade's company. During one of Estes' many legal battles, Wade met with him in Pecos. As he was returning home in his small airplane, he was killed in a crash near Kermit, Texas. In West Texas, a light airplane crashing is not unusual. The high winds that control the desert skies can be treacherous even to large aircraft. However, immediately after the crash, federal investigators appeared and roped off the crash area for several days.

One of America's most trusted news commentators, Paul Harvey, revealed a shocking story in his column *Crossfire*. He described a secretary (Mary Jones) in the Department of Agriculture in Washington, D. C., being physically removed from her office. As if forcing her to leave her office was not humiliating enough, she was also locked up in a mental institution for twelve days. Her supervisor, Battle Hales, indicated that he had evidence that Billie Sol Estes received special treatment from the Department of Agriculture. His secretary knew where the documentation was filed. Apparently, she could not be allowed to support Hales' claims.

An Abilene associate of Billie Sol Estes knew even more about the way Estes managed to receive preferential treatment. Estes shared with an Abilene friend that he made frequent trips to Washington, D. C., and always with $50,000 in his pocket. His strategy was simple: He rented an entire hotel, ordered enough liquor to "float a battleship," arranged with Washington pimps to have the most beautiful prostitutes in the city sent to the hotel, and then began phoning specific politicians.

"I've got a little party going on, and oh yes, you might not want to bring your wife to this one. Know what I mean?" was his standard invitation. Inevitably, the politicians would repay Estes with various contracts. Estes was not the only individual employing these strategies; perhaps he kept a lower profile than people like Bobby Baker, but he did earn special treatment from the government for his efforts.[687]

Both Hales and his secretary also received a "special type of treatment." He was locked out of his office and denied access to his private files. Senator John Williams of Delaware described the treatment that Hales' secretary received: "She was railroaded to a mental institution because she knew too much."[688] Eventually declared sane, Mary Jones begged Agriculture Secretary Orville Freeman to at least compensate her for the expenses connected to her twelve-day institutionalization. After all, as a secretary in the Department of Agriculture, she was nothing more than a pawn on a political chessboard; Freeman ignored her.

Obviously, Battle Hales' records were so important that the Department of Agriculture did not dare release them. Purely by accident, the authors happened to meet Jim Mangham, a tourist in New Orleans in the fall of 2015. When he learned that we were writing a book on the Kennedy assassination and the various individuals connected to it, he shared with us an intriguing story that added to the mystery of Billie Sol Estes and his Washington associates.

According to Mangham, "The summer of 1962 was my freshman year in college. I was living in Shreveport, Louisiana, and spent the summer in Washington, D. C. I stayed with my uncle, who worked for the CIA. I was able to get a job as a mail boy in the Agriculture Building. The Agriculture Research Service had a mail room of its own. My job was to wheel a cart up and down the halls and drop off and pick up mail from what seemed like an endless string of offices.

"One day, someone in the Administrative Building across the street from the main Agriculture Building asked me to help them with a mission. I was the only summer college student in the mail room. I guess that is why they requested me." [Author's note: He may very well have been requested because his uncle was in the CIA.]

Mangham paused for a moment before continuing. "The mission I was summoned to help with was to wheel some agriculture records over to the Treasury Department, where they burn used money which is to be replaced.

"An electric furnace is a couple of floors below street level and the furnace is in a pit below that. There is an angled concrete chute that dumps stuff down into a fiery hell. One slip of a foot and a person would be a goner. I cannot say I had a chance to investigate the boxes of records I helped to burn. But I remember coming to the conclusion that I probably helped cover up some of the evidence in the Billie Sol Estes scandal. I believe Lyndon Johnson was linked to the scandal, but perhaps the records which I helped burn eliminated some of the convicting evidence."[689]

Mangham's recollections are evidence of two things: First, the Treasury Department burns more than just used money. Second, the problems of Billie Sol Estes were so extensive by 1962 that even a young college student was aware of them.

Thanks to a handful of individuals who suspected that Estes' business practices were probably illegal, the saga of Billie Sol Estes became front page news, and not just in Texas. Henry Marshall, Dr. John Dunn, Oscar Griffin Jr., and Marj Carpenter all deserve credit for exposing the illegal activities of a young man once deemed "outstanding."

Dunn, Griffin, and Carpenter all worked with and for the *Pecos Independent and Enterprise*. As an investigative reporter in Pecos, Carpenter was also a correspondent for the *San Angelo Standard-Times*. Her research showed that the serial numbers on the fertilizer tanks did not correlate with the number of tanks Estes leased. She also discovered that serial numbers on tanks had been changed. Suddenly, it appeared that Estes' illegal dealings stretched from Pecos, to Austin, to Washington, D.C.

Reporters discovered that there would be repercussions for outing Estes' activities. Estes' lawyers kept Dunn tied up in litigation to the point where his medical practice suffered. Carpenter, a wife and mother, found her own life threatened because of the information she revealed.[690] A great many suspected that people other than Billie Sol Estes were fearful that their names would be tarnished along with Estes'. After all, Estes had been a vocal supporter of Vice-President Johnson, Senator Ralph Yarborough, and President John F. Kennedy. It was hard for many to believe that those in the Kennedy administration also did not benefit from Estes' wheeling and dealing.

To make matters worse, the Kennedy administration was slow to react to the charges brought against Estes. According to Ralph de Toledano, "Nothing was done until private citizens nudged Texas authorities into breaking the case."[691] Mary Jones could certainly have testified that Kennedy's Secretary of Agriculture Orville Freeman did not intervene on her behalf!

Estes eventually was found guilty of defrauding the federal government; he served time in the penitentiary. He was smart enough to accept the consequences for his actions without naming others who might also have been involved. Considering how many of Estes' associates died unnatural deaths, accepting a prison sentence was probably the safest move Estes could make. Those close to Estes indicated for years that he took the "fall" for those in more powerful positions.

One of Estes' secretaries explained to the authors that the "secret that everybody wanted to know was: 'Where was the money?'"[692] She assured the authors that there was no money left. Estes once lived like a millionaire, but suddenly he was bankrupt. Some suspected that Estes hid funds in bank accounts outside of the United States. One of his daughters once came to class at Cooper High School in Abilene wearing a beautiful diamond pendant. When a classmate commented on it, she smiled and explained, "My dad brought it to me from Switzerland!"[693]

Whether or not Estes hid money outside of the U.S., he admitted to donating thousands and thousands of dollars to various politicians. All appreciated his generosity, but Lyndon Johnson seemed to expect it. Estes purchased a runway once part of a World War II air base near Pecos. This long private airstrip made it convenient for the Vice-President to fly into Pecos without the necessity of a flight manifest. A man close to Estes for most of his life recalled to the authors that Johnson used this airstrip as a way to meet privately with Estes. This man would speak about a meeting on Air Force 2 less than two weeks before Kennedy's death, only if his identity was kept secret.

"I was allowed to tag along when Billie met Lyndon one day at Billie's private airstrip. Lyndon was waiting for us inside his plane. I don't remember everything Billie and Lyndon talked about, but I have never forgotten one thing the Vice-President said to Billie. 'The next time you see me, I'll be on Air Force 1.'"There was a long silence before the man continued. "It took years for me to understand how important those words might be. Even when President

Kennedy died a week or two later, I didn't realize what they might have meant." As fate would have it, in a matter of days the entire world saw photos of Lyndon Johnson standing on Air Force 1 next to his predecessor's widow.

CHAPTER 67

THE "VOICE" OF FRED MICHAELIS

"Stay quiet and live!"

The name "Fred Michaelis" is not well-known to researchers, although he is remembered by one of Estes' former secretaries, Sue Goolsby, and he was also mentioned briefly in the book *Billie Sol: King of Texas Wheeler-Dealers* by Estes' daughter Pam. Both women remember Michaelis as either being "dumb and ignorant" or "sly as a fox." More people would be familiar with Michaelis if he had lived long enough to publish his own version of the Billie Sol Estes story, but like so many others, he died unexpectedly.

An unpublished manuscript describing Fred Michaelis' association with Billie Sol Estes contains pieces of information that only Michaelis knew. To some, Michaelis was Estes' "front man;" to others, he was nothing more than Estes' chauffeur. In reality, he was probably both.

One of the many questions about Billie Sol Estes concerns how he managed to live to the age of 88 when so many others connected to him died early deaths. According to Michaelis, the answer lies in the fact that Estes secretly taped conversations between himself and powerful political associates. Michaelis assisted the man he referred to as "Sol" in this tape-recording, even of government prosecutors. (This did not mean Michaelis used sophisticated wire-tapping equipment. A simple way of recording a telephone conversation at that time was to have a reel-to-reel tape recorder placed next to a telephone extension with someone quietly operating it.)

This move was one of the smartest Estes ever made. He learned through his first trial that even if Lyndon Johnson allowed his personal attorney to act as a defense lawyer, the defense might not be vigorous. In fact, Johnson's attorney prevented Estes from taking the stand in his own defense—a defense so effective that Estes was convicted and sentenced to prison. However, nothing about Lyndon Johnson surfaced!

Michaelis spent almost four years living with Estes at his home in Abilene. Federal investigators were well aware of this. As far as they were concerned, anyone associated with Billie Sol Estes was guilty of something. This "guilt by association" affected Estes' family members and even one of his secretaries, Sue Goolsby. Though federal agents spent thousands of dollars spying on Estes and his family, they apparently they did not know that Estes used Michaelis' home in another part of Abilene to receive mail and to meet with friends and business partners.

Estes also used a former hotel on the southeast side of Abilene as a meeting place. Previously a Ramada Inn, the hotel was converted to a half-way house for recovering alcoholics. An alcoholic himself, Estes empathized with those whose lives had been negatively affected by liquor. Oddly enough, Estes during this time became acquainted with Paul Groody, the mortician who embalmed and buried Lee Harvey Oswald, and the mortician's wife Virginia. It is logical that morticians and owners-directors of funeral homes would gravitate towards one another.

Michaelis and Billie Sol Estes were inseparable from 1975 to 1979. During those years, Michaelis learned that the government wanted basically one thing from Estes—the millions of dollars he supposedly earned through his wheeling and dealing. According to Michaelis, Estes admitted to him that these "missing funds" were personally given to Lyndon Johnson and other government officials as bribes. A former Estes secretary told friends of travelling to Amarillo with Estes to meet Vice-President Johnson at the airport. She saw Estes hand Johnson a briefcase; according to Estes, the briefcase was filled with cash. Fortunately for Estes and Johnson, this secretary was never questioned by authorities.

Another Estes secretary, Sue Goolsby of Abilene, was not as lucky. She was hounded by the FBI and the IRS and finally had to hire a lawyer to defend herself. Goolsby admitted that Estes kept her in the dark about most of his business dealings. Unlike other secretaries, she did not accompany Estes when he delivered briefcases to important individuals. In fact, she recalled that, inevitably, Estes would send her shopping or on errands anytime his business acquaintances met with him in his Abilene office. Goolsby may or may not have known about financial "donations" to Lyndon Johnson and other politicians, but according to Michaelis, these donations continued even after Johnson became President.

"Sol couldn't very well tell the IRS the money went to bribe the President," Michaelis wrote in his memoir. However, Estes' problems continued even after Johnson's death in 1973 because the LBJ empire was being protected long after Johnson himself was dead. For whatever reason, certain individuals felt safe only when Estes was in prison. Even after he served his first sentence, federal authorities pursued him and charged him with conspiracy to conceal assets as well as committing mail fraud.

Fred Michaelis was quite familiar with documents that could have proven Billie Sol Estes innocent of all charges. He claimed that Judge John Hill, who had been appointed by Lyndon Johnson, refused to allow the evidence to be admitted. In his memoir, Michaelis stated bluntly: "This evidence proved Sol's innocence and was not allowed to go before the jury. I feel that this was due to political influence. This influence came from the still powerful remnants of the LBJ political machine."[694]

Billie Sol Estes began his second incarceration in 1979; he was released in 1983. This time, rather than being imprisoned in the maximum security facility at Leavenworth, Kansas, he was incarcerated in Big Spring, Texas. This was a minimum-security prison referred to as "Club Fed." It was a prison for "white collar" crime as well as a witness protection facility, especially for convicted Mafisoso. One of the better-known Mafia members housed in Big Spring's facility was Stanley Buglionie. His nickname became "One-Eyed Bug" because he lost an eye. Originally from New York, he was sent to Big Spring as part of the witness protection program. He and other inmates enjoyed a three-par golf course, a swimming pool, and tennis courts. Estes and others even joined the prison choir.

One of the most interesting visitors to the prison during Estes' incarceration was the widow of Lyndon B. Johnson. According to a retired security guard at the prison, Lady Bird Johnson, on more than one occasion, flew to nearby Midland and then drove to Big Spring to visit someone she identified as a "cousin." This person was probably ex-banker Ruben Johnson. Eventually, Lady Bird helped him receive a pardon from President Clinton. Ruben Johnson had been close to LBJ, and like other Johnson associates, that closeness resulted in a prison sentence. Bobby Baker and Billie Sol Estes could sympathize with him! Oddy enough, Estes, during this time period, spent much of his time in the Big Spring prison working on a tell-all book. It is possible Mrs. Johnson also visited him. No doubt she would have been interested in the stories Estes might tell.

In late 1985, Billie Sol Estes found himself facing one of the most shocking charges to date. He was accused of raping his maid. Michaelis believed that this was just another ploy to separate Estes from his freedom. It is also possible that this was a way to punish Estes for a memoir his daughter published in 1983. Fortunately for Estes, the fact that he had documentation of a vasectomy proved his innocence. At this time, Estes discovered that some of his Mafia friends from Fort Leavenworth and Big Spring could be counted on when the chips were down. Michaelis described their reaction to the rape charge.

"They were mad about the whole thing. The only thing they wanted to know was where we wanted the lady's body. I urged that the lady be left alone." Obviously, the maid had been used by powerful individuals.

Once again, Michaelis blamed Estes' problems on the Lyndon Johnson political machine. "Lyndon had long been dead, but his machine was still trying to cover up his misdeeds." Michaelis felt that by ruining Estes' reputation, his enemies would also ruin his credibility.

In 1987, an Estes associate, Clyde Foust, dictated to Michaelis the details of a meeting he had tape recorded in 1961. During the meeting, Mac Wallace, Cliff Carter, and Estes discussed the murder of Henry Marshall. Wallace admitted to having murdered Marshall. He and Carter wanted money from Estes as payment for Marshall's death. According to Foust, he heard Estes protest that he never wanted Marshall killed and was not going to pay them for a murder he was not a part of.

Estes realized he had to convince Lyndon Johnson that he was not a part of any murders. If Cliff Carter would not approach Johnson for him, someone else would have to. Foust contacted Lady Bird Johnson's brother, Anthony Taylor, in Santa Fe, New Mexico. Taylor owned a retail shop which carried Mexican imports. Foust attempted to explain to Taylor that Estes wanted nothing more to do with Malcolm Wallace or Cliff Carter. Estes admittedly scammed and cheated numerous individuals, but he claimed that he never ordered anyone's murder.

Rather than sympathizing with Estes, Lady Bird Johnson's brother was outraged. Taylor interpreted Foust's words as an attempt at blackmail. It is not known whether Estes' plea to Johnson was ever received. What *is* known is that Anthony Taylor did, indeed, live and work in Santa Fe, New Mexico and that he was close enough to his presidential brother-in-law to be given an impressive appointment during Johnson's administration. This lends credence to the story Michaelis related concerning Clyde Foust's trip to New Mexico.

It was only after several years of hiding out in the woods of Austin, Texas, that Fred Michaelis was able to confront what appeared to be paranoia, but what might actually have been cold, hard reality. He personally saw how much damage could be done to Billie Sol Estes and anyone ever connected to him. Consequently, Michaelis displayed remarkable courage as he attempted to transfer his memories about Estes to paper. He did not gloss over his friend's faults, and he did shed new light on the way Estes was treated by those who benefitted greatly from his financial wheeling and dealing.

Michaelis worked with an editor in an attempt to publish a memoir concerning his relationship with Billie Sol Estes and his perceptions of the scandals surrounding his friend. The editor commented to the authors that she and Michaelis constantly worried about their own safety. They both realized that Michaelis' information supported Estes' story that Mac Wallace ordered the elimination of numerous individuals who might present problems for Lyndon

Johnson.

This editor shared with us Michaelis' unpublished manuscript and another unpublished manuscript titled *Texas Mafia* written by Stephen Pegues, now deceased. The editor received the latter manuscript from Billie Sol Estes himself, who had received it in 1998 from author Gaylon Ross.

Michaelis' editor was personally familiar with the assorted characters who populated his book. She had known Michaelis and Estes well, and she had also known Mac Wallace, Paul Groody, and Kyle Brown. From time to time, she cooked for the men and even accompanied Michaelis and Estes to the motel on East Highway 80 which served as a half-way house for alcoholics and as a meeting place for Estes and his friends. She personally saw the FBI agents who shadowed Estes and his friends. Several agents even attended the funeral of Michaelis' mother.

The editor had no idea that Michaelis would not live long enough to complete his manuscript. Because she knew the Estes family well, she contacted Pam Estes immediately after hearing that Michaelis, following a wreck in the late spring of 2009, died on June 16.

"Pam," she recalled saying, "it's so mysterious to me. Fred had a wreck—hit a deer. He was on a motorcycle—broke his hip. While he was in the hospital, strangers began bringing him food and medicine. He died soon afterwards in the Round Rock Hospital."[695] She then added as an afterthought, "His laptop had been wiped clean." Whoever deleted Michaelis' story did not know that his editor had a hard copy of Michaelis' unpublished manuscript. Later, the woman who served as editor for Michaelis' memoir began to fear for her own life. Perhaps Michaelis' motorcycle accident had been nothing more than a traffic mishap. Perhaps his death was as coincidental as the one-car wreck that killed Texas Ranger Clint Peoples in 1992, and a similar wreck that took the life of Mac Wallace in 1971. Nevertheless, doubts lingered, as did a gnawing fear that she might die next.

When Billie Sol Estes passed away on May 14, 2013, one of the first people contacted by the Estes family was Michaelis' editor, who visited Estes at his house in Granbury just the day before his death. He had seemed fine to her. In fact, she recalled him making notes for an article he was planning to write.

At his funeral, the editor shared her concerns about Estes' sudden death with two men who she thought to be Secret Service agents. The editor knew that someone sent Estes a batch of chocolate chip cookies, and his daughter even commented to reporters after his death that her father had died with cookie crumbs on his lips. The editor feared that Estes might have been poisoned. Of course, Estes was 88 years old, so it was assumed he simply died of a heart attack. There did not appear to be any reason for an autopsy.

Perhaps the editor's fears were brought on by the sudden appearance of a mysterious mourner. As she stood before Estes' coffin, she felt the presence of someone behind her. Turning quickly, she was confronted by a tall, elderly gentleman. She realized the two of them were alone in the chapel.

The man wore thick black glasses and a black hat tilted crookedly on his head. She was surprised he had not removed his hat out of respect for the dead. He spoke softly, but his words sent a chill down her spine.

"I know you," he said quietly. "You cooked fried chicken for me once." Her knees almost buckled as she felt the blood draining from her head. She realized she recognized the man's voice. His facial features were different, though the black-rimmed glasses seemed familiar, but it was his voice that reminded her of someone she had known years ago.

"I can't place your voice with your face," the woman said hesitantly.

"You're not supposed to," he replied, his eyes meeting hers. It was then that she realized the familiar voice belonged to a man who had supposedly died years before—the same man Billie Sol Estes and Fred Michaelis had named as the murderer of Henry Marshall and possibly other individuals.

Without thinking, she blurted out, "I know your voice. You're Wallace—Mac Wallace!" This time the mysterious mourner was the one whose face paled. The woman fled from the chapel, found the nearest restroom, and lost all of her lunch. Who could she tell about the mysterious mourner? Who would believe her? More importantly, did she dare tell *anyone* that a man whom she knew as Mac Wallace—a man supposedly dead—had attended Billie Sol Estes' funeral?

The next time she noticed Wallace, he was standing alone in the cemetery observing Estes' graveside service. She had the distinct impression he was watching her, just as she was watching him. The only conclusion the editor could draw was that Wallace entered the witness protection program after his death was staged. But this did not explain why he appeared at Estes' funeral. She was overwhelmed with questions. Did he suspect Estes might have staged his own death, which was unlikely at age 88, or was he simply paying his respects to an old friend? Was he there to observe the mourners? Why had he revealed himself to her? Was it a warning that she was still being watched?

The editor was concerned enough about Wallace's appearance to decide that Michaelis' manuscript should remain unpublished. She realized that, as far as she knew, the most incriminating evidence had already been revealed by Estes himself in a book titled *JFK: le Dernier Termoin*. However, the book had been published only in France. No English translation had ever been published. Obviously, this would limit its audience. Was it possible that Wallace heard that

Estes was writing another article, one that might tell more than he had already told?

The most crucial pieces of evidence Estes had were incriminating tapes of his private conversations with powerful individuals. When Pam Estes was questioned by the authors about the location of the recordings her father made throughout the years, her emailed reply was curt. "Not for publication." Now that Pam Estes herself has passed away, no one seems to know where these historical tapes are hidden. Some researchers suspect they never existed, but Fred Michaelis knew differently. However, in his memoir, he did not indicate where Estes secreted them.

The infamous tapes that seem to have guaranted Estes a long life, as long as he was willing to serve time and keep his mouth shut, would, undoubtedly, answer many questions about the individuals he dealt with, and the discussions he had with them. A little-known fact is that the graves of Estes and his first wife were exhumed in 2016 and the bodies moved to a family cemetery. A mortician who assisted with the transfer assured the authors that the caskets were not opened before they left the original burial site or during the transfer. Billie Sol and Patsy Estes now rest closer to home. Who knows where the reel-to-reel tapes (which by now may have been transferred to cassettes or compact disc) rest, or with whom?

Even today, there are those who still claim that no one would have been victimized if the government had allowed Billie Sol Estes to continue to operate his bogus activities. Apparently, these individuals have forgotten how far Estes, or at least his associates, would go to hide their illegal acts.

Not everyone knew that, in March of 1962, an arsonist attempted to destroy the *Pecos Independent and Enterprise* by setting the newspaper building on fire. Those who had the courage and integrity to investigate Estes and his associates received warnings and even threats. Obviously, the people who gained from Estes' manipulations also had the most to lose. Unlike Estes, who was wise enough to quietly accept his prison sentences, these individuals did not intend to lose their careers or their freedom, even if it meant others lost their lives.

If the wheeling and dealing of Billie Sol Estes had not been linked to Lyndon Johnson and his political machine, Estes' name would never have been connected to the Kennedy assassination..

Estes made the mistake of associating with individuals closely connected with Lyndon Johnson. This is why Billie Sol Estes demanded immunity before he would testify under oath about the numerous individuals he claimed were murdered on the orders of Lyndon Johnson. Without that immunity, he could have been charged as an accessory after the fact.

The most dangerous but important thing that Estes did was to publicly accuse Lyndon Johnson of using Mac Wallace and others to kill numerous individuals, including John F. Kennedy, who dared to stand in the way of Johnson's political career. Perhaps naming names eased his conscience.

CHAPTER 68
VOICES FOR JIM BOLDEN

"People from all over would showed up on Jim's doorstep with things he was supposed to 'store' for them."—Ben Bretz and Milton Thorpe

T he 1990s were a perfect time for the Roscoe White story to appear. The thirtieth anniversary of the President's death was approaching, and news media and historians/researchers/authors were making the public aware of new evidence discovered since 1963.

Part of this evidence in West Texas came from a gentleman named Jim Bolden. The authors stumbled on this man's name in the Presidential Archives/ Museum in Odessa, Texas. Among cartons and cartons of Kennedy memorabilia were two boxes filled with copies of telegrams sent to Jack Ruby after he killed Lee Harvey Oswald, plus copies of police dispatches from Dallas, Texas, from the weekend of November 22-24, 1963. There was also a video tape labeled "The West Texas Connection."

Stapled to a handwritten cover-sheet was a business card belonging to J. R. "Jim" Bolden of Texaco Exploration and Production, Inc. It seemed strange that a Texaco employee would possess confidential government documents. There was no way to determine how long Bolden had these in his possession, or why he donated them to the Presidential Museum. A quick phone call to the telephone number on the business card provided some information.

One of Bolden's relatives answered the authors' call and informed them that Jim Bolden had passed away on May 15, 2013. Questions about why he had these particular papers in his possession were partially answered. Bolden, having retired from Texaco, taught certified concealed handgun training until shortly before his death. This still did not explain why he had copies of confidential documents. All his family would share with the authors was that "all sorts of people would bring Jim papers to 'store' in his house. People from all over would show up on his doorstep with things he was supposed to 'store' for them."[696] Bolden's daughter did admit that not long after President Kennedy's assassination, some men left important assassination documents with her father.[697]

This response raised more questions than it answered. Information in Bolden's obituary led to personal friends and associates who confided details that Bolden had shared with them. Milton Thorpe and Ben Bretz were just two

SARA PETERSON & K.W. ZACHRY

of several men who, because of his concealed handgun /NRA program, had interesting conversations with Bolden.

Thorpe and Bretz served as assistants in Bolden's classes, and the men often met socially after class. They both knew that Bolden had a secret room in his house in Odessa where he stored the interesting "packages" that "men in suits and black limos" often left on his doorstep. Bolden seldom, if ever, knew who these strange individuals were or who they represented, but he knew they were from the government. The room that he and Thorpe created to hide the boxes, envelopes, and packages was hidden behind moveable built-in book cases. Bolden had also installed sophisticated surveillance equipment inside and outside his house.

Only once did one of his students observe these "strange delivery men" arrive at Bolden's house with packages that needed to be transferred to Bolden immediately. As soon as Bolden realized that the visitors required his attention, he excused himself from the class he was teaching and asked his students to wait outside the house. It was obvious that these men needed to speak to Bolden as quickly as possible. At the conclusion of the conversation, the men exited from a different door and drove away in their black vehicles. Bolden then resumed class as if nothing had happened.

Occasionally, Bolden would make his friends aware that he needed to leave town. Before he left, he made sure to call one particular friend and tell him he was on an assignment and how he could be reached. Later, his friend discovered that these trips were usually to New York, and that Bolden deliberately took a different route going and coming. Bolden shared as much information as he could with the friend just so someone would know if something went wrong and he did not return. For numerous reasons, this particular friend, who simply smiled when he was asked if he was part of the CIA, believed that Bolden definitely was a CIA asset until the day he died. According to all of Bolden's friends, "Jim left the military, but he never 'really left' military service, if you know what I mean."[698]

Though Bolden was very careful about what he told others about his military duties, he enjoyed recounting stories from his childhood. He grew up in the 1940s in the southern part of Louisiana, among the gator-filled swamps. This was a time when young boys were allowed to roam the countryside, much like real-life Tom Sawyers and Huck Finns. Jim and his family lived on a houseboat outside the floodgates.

Growing up on the bayous, Bolden learned survival and self-preservation skills, which meant he was extremely observant and appreciative of the beauty of the environment around him. Perhaps his love for his surroundings and his observational skills led to his interest in photography. Bolden read every book about photography he could lay his hands on. Then, with an inexpensive Brownie camera, he taught himself the basics of photography, including how to develop negatives.

He became so familiar with the bayous that he was able to spend days at a time away from home and always return safely. His parents learned not to worry about him because of his survival skills. Bolden spent so much time in the backwoods and swamps of Louisiana that he was able to blend in with the natural landscape around him—a skill that would serve him well later in the military.

Bolden's parents did not realize how observant their son was until one day in 1947 when he came home and described a man he saw in town at a small grocery store. The store was patronized by locals, so it seemed odd for a man wearing an unfamiliar military uniform and speaking in a foreign tongue to frequent it, especially two years after World War II had ended. Bolden observed this man several times in the store. Finally, consumed with curiosity, he asked the store clerk what language the stranger was speaking. She told him the man spoke German.

Apparently unconcerned about what she was saying, the clerk added that the man was a German soldier from a German submarine trolling outside of the floodgates in the bayou. When the men on the submarine ran out of food, they sent this particular soldier into town to buy more. Though World War II was over and the Germans defeated, this group of soldiers was still patrolling the coast of the United States.

Bolden's father worked offshore for Texaco at the time, and though assigned to a platform, he and the other Texaco employees had no idea a German submarine was surveying the coast of Louisiana. Bolden's parents did not believe their teenaged son, no matter how many times he regaled them with this story. They assured him that he was imagining a German soldier walking freely on American soil and shopping in an American grocery store two years after his country was defeated.

To convince his parents he was *not* imagining things, Bolden sneaked back to the store, hid among the trees, reeds, and shrubs near it, and photographed the individual as he entered and exited the store. The developed film clearly showed a German soldier purchasing supplies from an American store. Amazed, his parents immediately showed the photos to the Coast Guard, who investigated the situation.

The Coast Guard discovered that the the grocery store owner was a German sympathizer. Quite willingly, he supplied the crew of the nearby German submarine with food and supplies. The submarine had maneuvered into the Gulf and been spying from a few hundred yards off the Louisiana banks. Thanks to Bolden's keen observational skills, the Coast Guard put an end to this surveillance.

Bolden's photographic skills were brought to the attention of the American military, and he was recruited at age eighteen into the Army Air Corps. At least, that's what he told his family and friends. However, according to certain friends, Bolden admitted later he had not really been in the Army Air Corps; in fact, he had not even been required to attend boot camp. Bolden served in the United Nations' Air Force and registered as a Warrant Officer.

Ben Bretz and Milton Thorpe both surmised from comments Bolden made that during the Korean War, Bolden was used by the CIA to take aerial photographs of North Korea. It seems that Bolden was more than just a talented photographer. He also had the skills to create and develop a special camera with a lens so powerful that from 4,000-5,000 feet in the air, it could photograph a man and show the part in his hair. Bolden adapted the camera so it could be used in the belly of a plane. The negatives from this camera were four feet square, which meant the photographs were at least that size. The negatives enabled him to create extremely precise aerial maps of enemy territory.

Bolden also flew on classified missions in the top-secret U-2 spy plane. Though he was not a certified pilot, Bolden learned the skills necessary to fly a military plane. Therefore, at times, the actual pilot would be blindfolded as the craft approached the border of North Korea, for example, and Bolden would maneuver the plane over the target areas and photograph military installations. This accomplished two things. The United States military gained valuable photos of the enemy's military installations, and the official pilot had "plausible deniability" because, technically, he could swear *he* had never flown his plane over enemy territory.

Bolden's survival skills were frequently called upon when he was sent into enemy territory in North Korea. One of his missions was to find a way into North Korea, observe an enemy camp, and return without being noticed. To do this, Bolden used the camouflage skills he learned as a boy in the bayous. He attached mud, leaves, dirt, and branches to his body, scaled trees, and positioned himself so he could sit for hours, even days, if necessary, without being seen. This meant not moving a muscle, even when pelted with bird droppings or when small animals perched on his body. After dark, Bolden would slide down the trees and slither through the tall grass until he could reach a tree closer to the enemy's camp. Then the camouflage process would begin all over again until he infiltrated the camp.

Bolden thought he had already proven to his commanding officer that he could circumvent any security system. However, the commanding officer had one more challenge for him; he wanted to see if Bolden could evade the U.S. military's tightest security. Confident that Bolden would be stopped and "captured," he was startled out of a light sleep to discover Bolden standing over his bed and grinning down at him. The best security America had to offer was no match for Jim Bolden. And, according to Bretz and Thorpe, he could also pass any lie detector test because he was expert at controlling his breathing and heart rate.

There is no question that Bolden's photographic skills, camouflage skills, and patriotism made him a valuable asset to the American military and to the CIA. His friends referred to him as a "spook"—a term used to describe CIA spies. Perhaps this is why various organizations trusted Bolden to store different types of sensitive material connected to the Kennedy assassination.

Fascinated by President Kennedy's death, Bolden told friends that the elite military group which normally preceded visits by important dignitaries to cities had not been ordered to Dallas on November 22, 1963. The 112th Military Intelligence Group at 4th Army Headquarters at Fort Sam Houston usually arrived a week or so before a president's visit to make sure security measures were in place. Unlike local authorities or even the Secret Service, these individuals deliberately dressed like civilians and mingled with the crowds during a President's visit. Bystanders would never know that the short-sleeved man wearing Bermuda shorts next to him was there to protect the President.

But what Bolden discussed the most was the Zapruder film, a home movie of the assassination taken by Dallas businessman Abraham Zapruder. The film showed the motorcade as it traveled down Elm Street from the Texas School Book Depository until it disappeared under the triple overpass. It showed the final gun shot which struck the President's head. Bolden seemed certain that this movie was not accurate.

Bretz could not resist asking Bolden one day if he might have been over Dallas on November 22, 1963, taking aerial photographs of the President's motorcade. Bretz's eyes twinkled as he shared Bolden's response with the authors.

"Jim wouldn't answer, but he had an interesting grin on his face. He wouldn't lie to you if you got too close to the truth, but if you guessed something, he just wouldn't answer." Bretz could not help but wonder if Bolden had used his special camera to take photos of President Kennedy's murder and if the photos recorded much more than the Zapruder film.

Friends and relatives of Jim Bolden realized that he took many secrets with him to the grave. Even today, as they discuss the few things he shared with them, they shake their heads and suggest he knew many more things than he admitted to. Not until his last few years did Bolden allow even his closest friends a glimpse into his intriguing affairs.

Odessa, Texas, seems like an odd place for James Bond-like characters to appear. And, yet, Bolden's neighbors and friends describe activities worthy of any cloak and dagger novel. For example, the secret closet in the center of Bolden's home was not exactly commonplace. It was designed to hold "official" documents entrusted to him. He also had a fire-proof safe in another part of the house for even more important items.

Certain well-dressed individuals seemed to know exactly when Bolden was home and when he was prepared to receive their packages. His friends and family members knew only that he "stored" items for important individuals.

What they discovered after his death was that Bolden had secret depositories all over the state of Texas. It had been his responsibility to protect copies of important documents. This was before the age of computers, flash drives, etc.

Like many other intelligence-connected individuals, Bolden operated on a "need to know" basis. One thing he learned was that, after the Kennedy assassination, important documents either disappeared or were destroyed. This is why "the men in suits" sought out Jim Bolden. They expected him to hide and preserve copies of confidential documents. Bolden was told that documents relating to the Kennedy assassination, particularly items relating to Lee Harvey Oswald and Jack Ruby, were being "lost" in Dallas and in Washington, D. C.[699]

Government officials were particularly concerned about documents like Oswald's "historic diary," Ruby's telephone records, and telegrams that hundreds of individuals sent to Jack Ruby while he was incarcerated. Obviously, Bolden was not the only individual to hide copies of confidential records. There may very well be secret closets, attics, basements, garages, and storage units all over the United States full of hidden records!

What is most interesting about Jim Bolden's story is that individuals close to the investigation of President Kennedy's death either suspected that important documents *might* disappear or *knew* they had *already* disappeared. What is still unknown is whether these individuals were FBI agents who did not trust the CIA, CIA agents who did not trust the FBI, or individuals from *other* agencies who did not trust either agency! Jim Bolden eventually shared copies of some of these important documents with other people. What no one knows for sure is where all the originals are and what other secret documents are still hidden throughout the United States.

Bolden's story was so intriguing that the authors spent extra months investigating his background. When former CIA asset Robert "Tosh" Plumlee mentioned that an associate nicknamed "Gator" was part of an abort team in Dallas on November 22, 1963, he provided a clue that the authors used to eventually solve part of the mystery concerning Jim Bolden and the Kennedy assassination; the clue also answered the question concerning the identity of a mysterious figure pictured sitting on the curb in Dealey Plaza next to a man who became known as "the Umbrella Man." "Umbrella Man" was identified as Louie Steven Witt, and his reason for carrying and raising an umbrella may or may not have been completely innocent. However, any plans he had for harming the President were thwarted by the tall, thin man next to him with a walkie-talkie in his back pocket. We the authors suspected that that man might have been Jim Bolden, but it took more than two years of investigation to determine whether our suspicions were right.

A telephone call to a man who knew Bolden for twenty-five years verified Plumlee's memories.[700] Plumlee remembered that "Gator" had been reared in Louisiana (hence the nickname "Gator"), that he had been in the Air Force during the Korean War, and that he had invented a special camera. He also recalled that his friend was missing part of a finger, and had an unusually large Adam's apple.

By the time Milton Thorpe and Ben Bretz knew Bolden, he had gained weight and was sporting a beard. Both changed his appearance somewhat. However, the friend who knew Bolden for twenty-five years recalled that Bolden once told him he had injured a finger when he was younger. This man also verified that Bolden was both tall and thin during his younger years (this description matches photos of the man sitting in Dealey Plaza next to "Umbrella Man)," and that some friends had, indeed, called him "Gator."

Bolden confided to the man he had a box of materials concerning the Kennedy assassination. He then asked him who he thought had killed Kennedy. When the man blurted out "not Oswald!" Bolden agreed with him, and the two men began discussing theories about the assassination. Their discussions continued until shortly before Bolden's death. Bolden believed that shots were fired at the President from behind the fence bordering the north knoll area. He learned later that two individuals stood behind the fence; one was responsible for killing the President; the other was responsible for dismantling the rifle, hiding it in a secret compartment in a nearby car, and then driving casually out of the parking lot behind the Depository.

Bolden never admitted to this man or to Thorpe or Bretz he had actually *witnessed* the assassination from a curb on Elm Street, but this explains why he was so fascinated with the Zapruder film. Having witnessed the murder, he knew whether the scenes in the film were accurate or not, especially because he was a trained military observer. Bolden must have deliberately chosen to sit where he did that day because the man holding the umbrella was acting suspiciously. Regardless of whether the "Umbrella Man" was harmless or not, Jim Bolden's presence prevented him from doing anything more than raising his umbrella.

This means that no poison dart was shot from the umbrella (as some have speculated); it also means that the two men sitting on the curb were not acquaintances or cohorts. It explains why the man next to "Umbrella Man" had a walkie-talkie in his back pocket, and why he walked rather than ran away from the assassination site. Like Plumlee and Sergio, Gator needed to blend in with the other spectators and escape as quickly and unobtrusively as possible.

The fact that his abort team could not prevent John Kennedy's death must have haunted Jim Bolden, as it haunted so many other people. It may explain why he spent hour upon hour discussing the inaccuracies of the Warren Report with close friends, why he was willing to hide assassination-related documents for so many years, and why he finally donated some of those documents to the Presidential Museum and Archives. He wanted someone to find and use them.

His trail of breadcrumbs led the authors from Odessa to Louisiana to the deserts of West Texas and finally to Dealey Plaza itself. It wasn't until the Fall of 2018 that the authors were able to verify that their original suspicions about Gator were correct. The man sitting next to "Umbrella Man"—the man Plumlee knew as "Gator—was none other than Jim Bolden, another assassination eyewitness who deliberately stayed in the shadows until the day he died.

CHAPTER 69

VOICES FOR ROSCOE WHITE

"Tricia told the highway patrolman she could not think of anything she was involved in that would warrant someone from the government following her."—Nina McConnell

illie Sol Estes and Jim Bolden were not the only West Texas connections to the assassination of John F. Kennedy. In the early 1990s, Ricky White stunned Texas and most of the nation with suspicions that his father, Roscoe White, participated in the assassination of President Kennedy. White's saga is one of the most controversial of all the assassination stories. Many researchers found his claims intriguing, but others believed that too little evidence backed up his story. His suspicions were based on the following facts:

a) Roscoe White and Lee Harvey Oswald were on the same ship, the *USS Bexar*, from San Diego to Yokosuka, Japan, in August 1957.

b) Both men applied for hardship discharges from the Marines, and both men's applications were granted. White's discharge was in 1962 and Oswald's was in 1959.

c) Roscoe White moved his family to the Dallas area in early 1963, where Lee Harvey Oswald was already living. Beginning in October 1963, Oswald was employed by the Texas School Book Depository, which was two miles from the Dallas police headquarters, where Roscoe White became an apprentice policeman in October 1963.

d) In 1963, Roscoe White's wife Geneva worked for Jack Ruby, who eventually murdered Kennedy's accused assassin. Geneva denied this association until 1988, when a photo of her posing with Ruby in the Carousel Club surfaced. At that point, she was unable to deny the connection.

e) In March 1963, Roscoe White and his family travelled from Dallas to Van Horn, Texas. Ricky White remembers his father and three other men testing their rifles at a desert area outside the small town.

f) On November 22, 1963, President Kennedy was murdered.

g) Lee Harvey Oswald, Kennedy's accused assassin, was murdered by Jack Ruby two days later, during Ricky White's third birthday party. Ricky and his guests were playing while Roscoe and some of the other fathers were watching Oswald's transfer as braodacst live on television. The moment after Jack Ruby shot Oswald, Roscoe interrupted the celebration with the announcement, "Party's over!" With no other explanation, all the party guests were sent home. This would have made sense if White had rushed to the police department. Instead, he packed up his family and took them to his mother-in-law's house in Paris, Texas. His wife and children stayed there for three days. The only information Roscoe later shared with his wife was that he and two other men went to Dripping Springs, Texas during the time she was with her mother. After three days, he returned to Paris and brought his family back to Dallas.

h) In October 1965, two years to the day after Roscoe White joined the Dallas police force, he resigned.

i) In 1968, Roscoe White moved his family to Mountain Home, Arkansas, where he was supposedly employed by the Post Office. The Whites returned to Dallas later that year, moving to Richardson, a suburb of Dallas.

j) In 1971, Roscoe White took a job in Dallas with M & M Equipment. On September 23, 1971, he was severely burned on the job. He died approximately twenty-four hours later. Shortly before he succumbed to his injuries, he made a deathbed confession to his minister, Jack Shaw. During an interview with the authors, Ricky White recalled the shocked look on the face of the minister after hearing Roscoe's confession. Shaw could not share any details with White's children, of course. However, he later told them that not long after their father's death, he received a telephone call from a man who identified himself as a retired FBI agent. This agent wanted to buy whatever information Roscoe shared with the minister. Ricky wondered out loud to the authors, "If my father had been such an unimportant character, like lots of people say, why would anyone offer money for his deathbed confession?"[701] Another question is: How did a retired FBI agent know White even made a deathbed confession?

k) A case summary dated August 22, 1975, prepared by the Dallas District Attorney's office indicated that 34 photographs of Lee Harvey Oswald which possibly linked him to the CIA were taken from Geneva White under false pretenses. The three men involved in the theft made a verbal contract with Geneva to sell the photos for a million dollars. The men nullified the contract by not contacting Geneva, not returning the photos, and not delivering the money. They were arrested by FBI agents, and the photos were recovered.

l) After examining the photos, FBI agents considered them important enough to send to the HSCA, which was meeting in Washington, D.C. in 1976.

m) While the HSCA was still examining Geneva's photos, Phillip Jordan, a neighbor of the Whites in Paris, Texas, who had known Roscoe White well, warned Ricky that there was a plan in place to blame the assassination of John F. Kennedy on Roscoe White. Ricky could not believe it. The HSCA committee questioned Geneva about any possible connection she had to Jack Ruby; she denied any association with the Dallas night club owner. Despite its interest in Geneva's photos, the HSCA did not follow up on the leads concerning Roscoe White.

n) In 1982, Ricky White visited Paris, Texas, to sort through some items left to him after his grandfather's death. While going through the house, he found a footlocker in the back of a closet. Before leaving for Midland, where Ricky then lived, he stopped to visit Phillip Jordan, the man who had warned him about Roscoe's possible involvement in the assassination. Jordan reiterated his warning: "Let me tell you this: Your dad WAS involved in the JFK thing. He was on the grassy knoll. Because of your dad and his involvement and what I know, I have been shot three times."[702] Ricky hauled the foot locker back with him from Midland. It took a few years for Ricky and Tricia to look through all of the contents. When they did, they found that the foot locker contained, among other things, a diary belonging to Roscoe. In the diary, Roscoe described a plot to kill President Kenned and his own role in the assassination.

o) It took Ricky several years to read all of his father's diary because the first part contained routine information about Roscoe's time in the military, which was of little interest to his son at the time.

p) Other items in the footlocker included White's service record, an unmarked key to a safety deposit box, a receipt for $100,000 in bearer bonds, a photograph of Roscoe from his military days, as well as a photo of Lee Harvey Oswald that had never been seen before.

q) In January of 1988, Ricky and Tricia shared the contents of the footlocker with their close Midland friend, T.J. Boyd. She advised them to contact Midland District Attorney Al Schorre, which they did.

r) Al Schorre listened to Ricky's story and then contacted local FBI agents.

s) These agents contacted the Whites in January 1988 about the contents of the footlocker; FBI agents Ron Butler and Bob Farris asked Ricky to bring the items from the footlocker to the FBI's Midland office. Eager to please and hoping to know the truth about his father's past, Ricky boxed up the items and carried them to the FBI office.

t) He told the authors in 2014 that while the agents examined the items, Senator Arlen Specter of Pennsylvania, who had served as a lawyer for the Warren Commission, questioned Ricky via speaker phone. Specter also told the Midland FBI agents to make copies of everything in the box, which they did. No explanation was given for why a Senator from Pennsylvania would be telling the FBI what to do. However, the FBI agents themselves also questioned Ricky White for more than five hours. Despite this, none of the agents would even speculate on the authenticity or importance of the items White had shown them. In fact, Ricky felt as if they were questioning his honesty.

Frustrated, he gathered up the items his father had thought were so important and returned home with them, dumping them unceremoniously on the pool table in his den. Ricky White had finally gotten the nerve to tell law enforcement about his father's secrets, only to be scorned by those in authority.

Later that day, an FBI agent came to White's home. He explained to Tricia that he had accidentally left his note pad in Ricky's box of items. Tricia welcomed him in and directed him to the box of items scattered on the pool table.

Tricia recalled, "As the agent started across the room, I heard Ricky yell from the bedroom, 'Who's at the door?' I turned around to answer Ricky and to explain that it was an FBI agent, then wonder why he was there. As I turned back, the agent brushed past me saying, 'I found it, thanks.' It wasn't until two days later that the Whites realized that the most important item among Roscoe's artifacts was missing. The diary that had described the plot to kill the President was gone. Ricky, Tricia, and their daughters were the only individuals in the house except the FBI agent.

u) According to Ricky White, his father's diary was seen and read by him, his wife Tricia, his mother Geneva, Denise Carter, a friend of the family's, David Dakil, and an attorney in Lubbock, Texas, Jerry Smith. Others, like family friend T.J. Boyd, also knew the diary existed because the Whites had shown it to them.

v) Suddenly, the Whites and their friends began experiencing strange events. According to Boyd and McConnell, Tricia realized that cars were following her even when she was doing nothing more than shopping. One day, she and a neighbor managed to write down a license plate number; Tricia called a friend, who was a county investigator, and he agreed to run the plate for her. It wasn't long before he called her back and demanded to know "what she was involved in" because the car following her was "leased to someone associated with Quantico." (On April 5, 2018, in a Facebook message, Tricia did not recall using the word "Quantico." She does recall being followed only once, and that the car was registered to a rental agency the government uses. She also states she was not frightened). Her friend Nina McConnell remembered, "Tricia said that she could not think of anything she was involved in that would warrant someone from the government following her."[703] Again according to Boyd and McConnell, Tricia felt as if she was constantly being followed by men in vehicles. She began going out of her way to lose them, taking indirect routes, even to the grocery store. Her friends remembered that she and Ricky were terrified and felt harassed.

w) In November 1988, a photo appeared in *Time* magazine which showed Roscoe's wife Geneva modeling a showgirl outfit in front of Carousel Club owner Jack Ruby. Geneva was forced to admit that she had lied to the HSCA and to her family about having worked for infamous night club owner Jack Ruby.

x) In January 1989, Geneva and her two sons, Ricky and Tony, met with a group of Midland oilmen interested in the Whites' story. Midland attorney Jack Ladd incorporated the group under the name MATSU. At this time, Ladd and the members of the group examined the Roscoe White artifacts.[704]

y) In 1989, according to Suzahn Smith, the wife of a West Texas rancher, two researchers, J. Gary Shaw and Joe West, on a tip from a Mafia informant, drove all the way to Crane, Texas, to visit the woman's husband about guns stolen from his ranch in 1963. The two men believed there was a connection between the theft of the guns and the assassination of President Kennedy. Shaw and West sought the help of Crane County Sheriff Ray Weatherby; they and the sheriff were puzzled on discovering that the official theft report was missing from the sheriff's files.[705]

z) In early 1990, Ricky White contacted researcher Larry Harris in Dallas with the details of his father's story. Harris then contacted researcher and author J. Gary Shaw. Harris, Shaw, and Larry Howard owned the JFK Assassination Information Center in Dallas. (Shaw brought in private investigator, Joe West, who accompanied him to Crane in 1989).[706]

aa) In the summer of 1990, Ricky discovered a heavy aluminum canister hidden in the attic of his grandmother's house in Paris, Texas. In it were his father's Marine Corps dog tags, a green stenographer's book with newspaper pictures pasted inside, and three cables protected by plastic material. The cables contained Roscoe White's serial number, but were addressed to the code name "Mandarin."

One cable was dated October 1963 with the following assignment: "To eliminate a national security threat to worldwide peace." Another code name, "RE-rifle," also appeared on the cables. The stenographer's book contained numerical codes and hieroglyphic-like symbols. There is no doubt the steno book belonged to White because inside its front cover was his name and serial number. Handwritten were the words "players or witnesses."

Some of the newspaper photographs were of well-known individuals—people like President Kennedy, his brother Robert Kennedy, Jack Ruby, and Lee Harvey Oswald. Some of the photos were not as easily identified. Under one photograph of a handsome young man were the hand-written words, "Big mouth you talked after all." There was also a newspaper photograph of the President's head exploding as a bullet hit it during the assassination. In a photo that showed the stockade fence behind the grassy knoll area, the letter X was superimposed on the fence. Underneath this photograph, someone had written, "Mandarin kills K uses 7.65 Mauser in assassination." All of these artifacts were personally examined by the authors at the Baylor University Poage Library on October 25, 2013. Roscoe White had owned a 7.65 Mauser, according to his son, Ricky White.

In September 1990, Geneva White suddenly produced another diary she claimed to have found. Investigator Joe West, who had been working closely with Geneva, should have realized what Ricky and others noticed immediately. The diary was a fraud. Even her son was adamant that this "diary" had not been written by his father. "That's not my daddy's handwriting. And that's not the way he wrote."[707]

Ricky and Tricia both believed that his mother created the second "diary" herself because the genuine diary had been stolen. The most important piece of evidence Roscoe left in his footlocker was the diary, which had disappeared from the Whites' house in Midland, Texas. Over the years, the fact that the handwriting and wording in Geneva's "discovered" Diary do not correlate with the original diary has tainted all of the other evidence. Because of this, many researchers have "thrown the baby out with the bathwater."

An interview with Midland District Attorney Al Schorre's investigator J. D. Luckie shed light on the intitial Midland investigation concerning Roscoe White. He recalled that the very subject of the Kennedy assassination had made Schorre nervous. "Schorre was nervous about the whole thing," he said. "When you realize how many people connected to the assassination had died, you get nervous."[708] Schorre may have also known that the Kennedy assassination was still so controversial that elected officials often avoided it. Regardless of the reason, Luckie and the Midland District Attorney's office were unable to investigate the Roscoe White story at length.

THE LONE STAR SPEAKS

"The minute the FBI got involved, we were on the outer perimeter. The District Attorney's department was swarmed by FBI from outside of Midland," Luckie recalled. He also remembered one particular FBI agent, who had worked on the White case, and an interesting comment he made. "Agent Tom Farris said to me, 'J.D., you will never know the true story.'" Based on his own observations, Luckie does not believe, as some have suggested, that Ricky White fabricated the story about his father's role in the assassination. "I think there is something to his story," he concluded.

What Luckie and researchers did not know at the time is that a witness in the Dallas police station overheard a conversation supporting the idea that Roscoe White may have been involved in the Kennedy assassination. In the spring of 1993, Mike Robinson, a previously unknown witness, shared his experiences for the first time with John M. Nagel, who videotaped Robinson's story. In 1963, fourteen-year old Robinson was friends with the son of a Dallas police officer, Capt. Frank Martin. Consequently, he was allowed to view the presidential motorcade from the third floor of the Dallas police station.

"I looked out the window," he recalled, "and two blocks away, I saw the flashing red and blue lights of the motorcade, then the black limousine's flags on the hood, and a pink dress...Heading straight towards us down Harwood was the President of the United States and his wife...As the car made the turn, I could see him clearly. He was smiling, looking towards the crowds standing on the southeast side of Main and Harwood...The car passed by so quickly, and I was disappointed I could not watch him up close longer."[709]

Robinson and his friend had the afternoon free, so they walked to the Majestic Theatre to see a movie. There, they heard the news that the President had been shot. They immediately headed back to the Dallas police station, arriving in time to witness Lee Harvey Oswald being brought in.

There was suddenly an increase in security around the police station, so the two teenagers remained near Captain Martin's office. Robinson overheard numerous comments from the police that the man just brought in was suspected of killing a police officer, J.D. Tippit, and had also killed the President.

He looked down the hall and saw a police officer holding a rifle high in the air and trying to keep it above the crowd of reporters. "He stopped at the end of the hall about four feet from me, turned back toward the reporters, and said, 'This is the gun we found inside the Texas School Book Depository Building.'"[710] When the officer was asked if the gun was the weapon that had killed the President, Robinson heard him reply, "We believe this is the weapon."[711]

A few minutes later, Robinson heard Lee Harvey Oswald say he had not killed anyone, that he was just a patsy. At about three in the afternoon, Robinson needed to go to the bathroom. Captain Martin had one of the detectives escort him down to the "lowest level of the building where the officers had their lockers, and he was told that the restroom was just past the locker room."[712] Robinson was in a toilet stall when he suddenly became emotionally overwhelmed by the fact that the President he had waved to was really dead.

Suddenly, Robinson heard two men enter the bathroom and begin talking. Instinctively, he lifted his feet and simply listened to the conversation. They were whispering, but in the quiet restroom, Robinson was able to hear their conversation.

"You didn't get Oswald where you were supposed to, then you go and kill a cop…Now we are going to have to kill Oswald before he gets to Washington."[713] Through the crack, Robinson could see the blue trouser leg of a police officer with a gold stripe running down the side. Frozen with fear, the teenager waited a few minutes after the men's departure before exiting the restroom himself.

In the locker room, he encountered a police officer who glared at him. Robinson could not help but wonder if he was the officer whom he had overheard in the restroom. As an adult, Mike Robinson was shown photos of every officer who served on the Dallas police force in 1963. He identified a photograph of Roscoe White as the man who stared menacingly at him that day in 1963. The fact that he did not come forward with this story until thirty years later is an indication of how terrified Robinson had been. The information, however, would have been valuable to the Warren Commission and might have altered its findings. It would have also been valuable to a West Texas news team that included the Roscoe White story in a documentary in 1993.

The individuals on the documentary team interviewed numerous witnesses and visited locations pertinent to the assassination. The series was quite popular with West Texas viewers. The news reporters discovered so much new information that they intended to extend the series beyond the planned twelve segments. Somehow, word about a local West Texas news story spread far beyond Midland and Odessa. The team's research and discoveries were brought to the attention of Senator Arlen Specter—the same Arlen Specter who had interrogated Ricky White earlier. According to Suzahn Smith, who served as a researcher on the assassination story, Specter made a brief stop at the Midland airport (where the studios of the television were located) to tell reporter Becky Neighbors and her supervisor John Foster that they had not discovered any important information. Also, apparently, he insisted that the series end immediately.[714]

If all of the Roscoe White story was as manufactured as the second diary appears to have been, why did Senator Arlen Specter, a Warren Commission attorney, become so interested in the evidence as a senator? After all, if everything Ricky White shared with the public was irrelevant and even counterfeit, wouldn't Senator Specter have simply allowed the Whites and their associates to make complete fools of themselves? Instead, he urged the end of the news team's investigation. Was it because of what the team had already uncovered, or was it because he was afraid they would uncover more?

CHAPTER 70

MORE VOICES FOR ROSCOE WHITE

"I was hired by a group of businessmen to form a corporation ...
to publicize White's story."—Jack Ladd

The team of West Texas newscasters planning a 30th anniversary documentary on the Kennedy assassination learned that Jim Bolden had information relating to their investigation. He had questioned the official report himself, they discovered, and had copies of documents connected to the assassination.

These were the same newscasters who also stumbled on another intriguing story with ties to West Texas. In the fall of 1992, by chance, a local West Texas television personality-producer overheard Suzahn Smith discussing a theft of guns and rifles from her husband's ranch a few months before Kennedy's assassination.

The story fascinated the producer. She learned that almost thirty years after the assassination, two historical researchers, J. Gary Shaw and Joe West, approached Smith and her husband with the suggestion that the weapons stolen from her husband in March of 1963 might have been used later that year in the Kennedy assassination.

The news team originally planned to focus their documentary series on the controversial topic of Roscoe White—a story that spanned three decades. The team believed there was enough evidence to warrant more investigation of White's possible participation in the assassination. However, the information about the 1963 gun theft broadened the scope of their investigation.[715]

The news team followed clues and evidence all over West Texas—from Midland to Odessa, from Crane to Van Horn. Eventually, the team followed leads to Kennedy's accused assassin's widow, Marina Oswald Porter, and even to a dying ex-convict in Dripping Springs, Texas. The ex-convict confessed stealing the weapons from Smith's husband early in 1963 and selling them to a man with the now infamous name of "Jack Ruby." Any doubts the team had about this man's veracity faded when he drew a road map showing how to get from Dripping Springs, Texas, to the isolated West Texas ranch in Crane where he found the guns he eventually sold to Ruby.

The team wondered if there could be a connection between the stolen weapons and the story Roscoe White's son Ricky told the FBI about his father's possible involvement in the assassination. Roscoe admitted to his wife he had gone directly to Dripping Springs after Ruby killed Oswald. This seems to indicate *some* connection between Dripping Springs and Kennedy's assassination.

One of the most interesting parts of Ricky White's story concerned his memories of his family's trips to Van Horn, where Roscoe "wanted to hunt." In March 1963, Roscoe, his wife Geneva, and their two sons, Ricky and Tony, made the long 600-mile trip from Paris, Texas, to Van Horn, Texas.

From the desert town of Van Horn, Ricky and his father drove out to a ranch in the middle of the desert. A small ravine ran through the ranch, and the Sierra Blanca Mountains could be seen in the distance. There they met three men who also had young boys with them. While the men practiced shooting at targets with rifles in the ravine, the boys played around a cabin that stood nearby. The boys looked inside the cabin and saw some sort of equipment.

A postcard that Ricky's mother sent back to her in-laws that weekend is evidence that this trip did take place. In order to verify Ricky's story, the news team, with its cameraman, followed Ricky's directions to the general vicinity of the ranch in Van Horn. There, locals helped them find the exact location where Roscoe White had rendezvoused with the three other men. Without their help, the team would never have located the cabin, because it was camouflaged by a small grove of mesquite trees.

One of the members of the news team, Mike Gibson, asked a friend of his, Eddie Owen, who had served in the National Guard in the 1960s as a radio specialist, to accompany the team to Van Horn. Owen was there to identify any equipment the team might find. The news team was pleased to discover the cabin precisely where Ricky had said it was, but was disappointed that no equipment appeared to be inside. Behind the cabin, however, stood a small shed.

Curious, the team opened the shed door and discovered old radio equipment, including transmitters. Owen thought the equipment unusual enough to examine it more thoroughly. So, Gibson called in another expert, G.B. Brock of Odessa, to accompany them back to Van Horn. In the 1960s, Brock had been chief of communications for the National Security Agency. If anyone would recognize this type of equipment, he would.

Brock immediately described the equipment as "very high powered and sophisticated" and said the antenna was pointed towards Mexico City.

Brock commented, "This equipment was used for security reasons for illegal operations, I'm sure." He could think of no legal reason why it should have been on this ranch property. The team retrieved the equipment and brought it back to the news station.

The more the team discovered, the more excited they became. The newscasters realized how important it was to have documented evidence of each discovery, so they made sure to film every part of their investigation, from interviews to locations, so it could all be included in their news documentary. On May 12, 1993, part one of a twelve-part series, titled *The West Texas Connection,* was broadcast.

The series earned praise from viewers and generated numerous comments in the West Texas area—maybe too many comments. News of the documentary reached Senator Arlen Specter—the same Arlen Specter who injected himself into the Midland FBI's investigation in 1988, and the same Arlen Specter who devised the "single bullet theory" for the Warren Commission. He was not happy to hear that people in Midland, Texas, were once again discussing the Roscoe White story.

Suddenly, the news team began receiving anonymous threatening letters and telephone calls; however, most of the viewers were as fascinated as the news team. A group of Midland businessmen were greatly interested in White and his father's claims about the assassination. In an interview with the authors, Midland attorney Jack Ladd recalled the day Ricky White brought a cardboard box full of "artifacts" to his office. He showed the evidence to Ladd and a group of Midland businessmen who were particularly interested in White's evidence. Jack Ladd explained to the authors, "I was hired by a group of businessmen to form a corporation (which they named MATSU) to publicize White's story."[716]

The anonymous phone calls to the television studio and the news team indicated that someone felt threatened by the information being presented in the documentary. At first, the threats did not deter the team's investigation, but then someone broke into the news station itself and stole all of the raw footage from the investigation. Even this would not have completely deterred the news team. After all, most of the footage had already been shown to the public, and the team had announced it would follow up with more information as it became available, which it intended to do.

What the team did not anticipate was the personal appearance of Senator Arlen Specter of Pennsylvania. Though the team originally requested that Specter respond to the information in their documentary, it had not seen or heard from him until the day he made an unexpected trip to Midland and summoned two members of the news team to a brief meeting. The Senator ridiculed

Ricky's story overall, including the investigators and the information they had uncovered. His point was that this investigative story was of no importance whatsoever.[717]

The photocopies of Ricky's evidence, which the FBI made at Specter's insistence in 1988, were, according to Specter, of little significance. That would explain why the FBI never publicized them. However, five years later, a *news story* was important enough for Specter to stop in Midland to put a halt to it and to any further investigation of President Kennedy's murder.

Apparently, the team's discoveries were greatly at odds with the Warren Commission Report, which Specter had endorsed wholeheartedly. It is unclear whether this illustrious senator was also worried about the safety of Ricky White and the newscasters. Also unclear is how many other investigations were stalled or halted by Senator Arlen Specter's involvement.

Marina Oswald Porter, widow of Lee Harvey Oswald, called the producer of *The West Texas Connection* and asked her to please continue the investigation. She believed the investigators were on the right track. She, like Ricky White, simply wanted to know the facts and the truth, no matter what the conclusions would be. But after Specter's visit, the owner of the news station decided to stop the investigation. What else might the team have uncovered had it been allowed to continue?

EPILOGUE
SHADOWS FROM THE PAST

For many of the individuals closely connected to John Kennedy and his assassination, the sun has set for the final time and, for a great many more, the shadows deepen. The results of the first official investigation of the late President's death were published in 1964. Since then, people throughout the world have argued about whether Kennedy was actually killed by one disgruntled malcontent or by a group of individuals determined to end his administration.

Many supporters of the Warren Commission have claimed that Americans simply could not accept the fact that a single individual could eliminate someone as powerful as the President of the United States.

The authors maintain that the opposite of this statement is more likely the truth. It is easy for Americans to realize that in a free country, where citizens have the right to bear arms, any individual can take the life of a President or that of any other elected official. What is more frightening to consider is that a group of individuals from various organizations might decide to sidestep the democratic process and kill the person occupying the highest position in the land. This could easily happen today, tomorrow, or anytime in the future.

More and more people have reached the conclusion that this is exactly what happened in 1963. This is why the investigations by the House Select Committee on Assassinations, by the Church Committee, and even the trial conducted by New Orleans District Attorney Jim Garrison occurred. Those associated with these groups found too many unanswered questions in the Warren Report; they also knew enough about history to understand that the "unthinkable" idea of disparate groups working together for a common cause was not only possible, it had happened numerous times throughout history.

To insist that Kennedy could not have been killed by various groups of individuals means that other assassinations, like Julius Caesar's, must be ignored. History shows that this popular Roman leader was killed by a large group of politicians so sure of the righteousness of the deed that they openly claimed *credit* for his death. Part of their plan involved the pre-determined fact that each senator would stab Caesar at least once so that each would be equally guilty of his death. The plotters also attempted to justify the murder to their fellow citizens. They did not hide behind claims of "national security," nor allow a "patsy" to take all of the blame for their actions.

THE LONE STAR SPEAKS

The Warren Commission ignored numerous groups with strong motives for wanting John F. Kennedy dead. Segregationists hated him. Rightly or wrongly, the families of the men killed and imprisoned because of the Bay of Pigs disaster blamed America's president for the debacle. Some of Kennedy's military advisors had begun to distrust him and to question his patriotism. To be "soft on Communism" was still considered to be treasonous. Certain CIA members were also unhappy because of the Bay of Pigs. J. Edgar Hoover was personally furious with John and Robert Kennedy.

Only a handful of insiders knew how power-hungry the Kennedy family was. Robert Kennedy was so determined to know any information that might be politically detrimental to his family that he created his own private detective agencies. According to a former Senate investigator and to Sydney Goldberg, these agencies were known as either "the Three Eyes," which stood for International Investigators, Incorporated, or "the Five Eyes," when the location of Indianapolis, Indiana was added to the name.

These detective agencies, according to Otto Otepka, a security evaluator for the State Department, were used by the Kennedys to tap the telephones of numerous individuals. "There's no question that they carried out wiretaps," Otepka stated to author Jim Hougan, "not only against [Jimmy] Hoffa and organized crime, but here in Washington, against government employees."[718]

Certain details collected from the wiretaps were used to intimidate individuals, to control and manipulate information, and to destroy careers, if necessary. Those aware of these secret activities may have had reason to want the President and his brother out of the White House.

Other administration insiders learned about Kennedy's womanizing, both in and out of the White House. Though this did not seem to worry most of his associates, it did concern some of them—even some of his Secret Service agents. Some saw his lack of sexual morals as a serious character flaw. They wondered if a man who pretended to be an upright husband and father, but would cheat on his wife, and cheat in business dealings, would also risk matters of national security?

Some individuals were especially concerned that the Kennedy administration, despite its hard-nosed approach to crime, appeared to be secretly in bed with the Mafia. What they did not know is that, according to mobster Sam Giancana, Kennedy was just one of several powerful political figures connected to organized crime. Giancana told his brother Chuck that Franklin Roosevelt, Harry Truman, Richard Nixon, and Lyndon Johnson all had had dealings with the mob.

"'Chuck, what did I tell you before? Did you think I was bullshittin' you?

We always own the President. It doesn't matter what the guy's name is …we own him. We own the White House.'"[719]

The difference between Kennedy and his predecessors was that the other politicians paid their debts to the Mafia, one way or another. Kennedy seemed to be "repaying" those who helped him win the election by allowing his attorney general to harass them.

There is no question that the Attorney General's "war on crime" elicited angry reactions from several crime families. Not only was Chicago's Giancana unhappy, so was Louisiana's Carlos Marcello, Florida's Santos Trafficante, and even New York's most powerful mob family, the Magaddinos. A conversation recorded between Stefano Magaddino and his son Peter on October 31, 1963 is evidence of how enraged the Mafia family was because of the President's brother, Robert.

"He should drop dead," Magaddino said, "They should kill the whole family, the mother and father, too."[720]

This comment could explain a little-known event that occurred shortly after the President's assassination. Kennedy's parents made their annual winter move to Palm Beach, Florida. Because of the President's death, Secret Service agents were no longer assigned to the couple. Off-duty local police officers served as guards for the Kennedys' Florida estate. Rita Dallas, Joseph Kennedy, Sr.'s nurse, recalled an unusual situation never reported by any newspapers.

She spotted a complete stranger entering the Kennedys' large home. Realizing he was an intruder, she sought help from a policeman in front of the home. Meanwhile, the intruder brazenly climbed to the second floor and, when caught standing in front of the fuse box with the panel door open, refused to identify himself or to explain his behavior.

Though the stranger was promptly arrested, Dallas was unable to discover any information about the intruder or his activities. The local policeman told her nothing more than "he had connections in Dallas (Texas)." A few days later, she asked what had happened to the man and was told, "I don't know, Mrs. Dallas. One day they've got him in jail. The next day he's gone, just like that. Nobody's talking."[721]

Chances are, the intruder was a professional. He had been too calm to be a typical burglar. He also seemed determined to complete his assignment; he could have taken advantage of Dallas' departure and disappeared. He did not.

Someone may have taken Magaddino's suggestion seriously. Perhaps the intruder intended to kill one or both of the senior Kennedys. Perhaps he intended to flip the switch that controlled the electricity to Kennedy, Sr.'s bedroom, thereby cutting off his oxygen. Robert Kennedy would have certainly gotten the message if one or both of his parents had been murdered. Or, perhaps the intruder allowed himself to be arrested so that the Kennedy family would realize it was still vulnerable and under surveillance. The fact that the intrusion was kept secret was typical of so many of the events that shrouded the Kennedy family.

Two weeks before the assassination, Robert Kennedy obtained a voodoo doll made in the image of Lyndon Johnson. At a party, Kennedy supporters enjoyed themselves thoroughly as they poked needles into it.[722] Johnson's fear of losing his place on JFK's ticket and the emotional turmoil that personal affronts must have caused him could have been motivation enough for him to either plan and/or assist in Kennedy's death, as well as control any investigation of the President's murder. If Billie Sol Estes is to be believed, Kennedy's death would simply was a political necessity to Lyndon Johnson.

What was obvious to almost everyone was that Lyndon Johnson was miserably unhappy and, possibly, desperate. Rumors were rampant that he would be replaced on the 1964 ticket. He may have been powerful enough to keep himself out of prison, but associates like Bobby Baker and Billie Sol Estes could not, and their mistakes reflected on him. And there was always the chance that one or both would eventually write a tell-all memoir, as they both eventually did!

The Warren Commission could have spent years investigating, if an honest, thorough investigation of Kennedy's assassination was considered essential. A meticulous investigation would have revealed the names of those who had planned, orchestrated, and covered up the President's death. Obviously, an investigation of this magnitude would have taken much longer than the nine months President Lyndon Johnson allowed the Warren Commission. It would have also required the Kennedy family, the FBI, the CIA, the Office of Naval Intelligence, and all others with inside information to share it with law enforcement. Mafia members might have revealed even more by the questions they *refused* to answer.

A complete investigation would have even shown that there was at least one person who might have been so obsessed with Kennedy's young wife that he would have had the President killed for personal reasons. However, it might have taken at least five years for this piece of the puzzle to fall into place.

In his book *Nemesis,* Peter Evans revealed in 2004 that Greek tycoon Aristotle Onassis once admitted financing the murder of President Kennedy's younger brother Robert in 1968. Not long before his 1975 death, Onassis told New York photographer Helene Gaillet, "You know, Helene, I put up the money for Bobby Kennedy's murder."[723]

If Onassis was telling Gaillet the truth—and Gaillet had no reason to doubt him—his main reason for killing John F. Kennedy's brother was because Robert Kennedy strenuously objected to Jacqueline Kennedy's plans to marry Onassis, the man Robert Kennedy referred to as "the Greek."

If this strange story is true, then another possibility concerning Kennedy's assassination must be considered: Would Onassis have had *John F. Kennedy* killed so he could someday marry his widow? As absurd as most people might consider this idea, there is some circumstantial evidence to support it. There is no question that a man as wealthy as Aristotle Onassis could have paid any number of assassins to kill almost anyone. He had connections to the Greek Mafia and was accustomed to getting everything he wanted—and he had wanted Jackie Kennedy for quite some time. President Kennedy's personal secretary, Evelyn Lincoln, agreed with William Harvey's wife that the First Lady and Onassis became romantically involved when the First Lady vacationed on his fabulous yacht in October 1963.

In Lincoln's opinion, Jackie Kennedy began an affair with Onassis "before Dallas."[724]Of course, tell-all books have taught middle-class Americans that extra-marital affairs among the rich and famous always take place. It seems, however, that Onassis wanted more than an affair.

According to Onassis' friend Ellen Deiner, Onassis, in his huge, luxurious Paris apartment at 88 Avenue Foch, created a secret, locked room which could only be described as a "shrine" to Jacqueline Kennedy. It was covered with a combination of large framed posters of Jackie as well as smaller framed photos hung on the walls and placed decoratively around the room. Among these photos was one of her on her wedding day to John Kennedy, but the most shocking item in the room was a large framed photograph of Jackie "on that horrible day in 1963 when she stood next to Lyndon Johnson as he took the oath of office." This photograph showed the President's widow in her pink suit covered in her dead husband's blood. [725] It seems odd that Onassis would want to remember Jackie Kennedy covered in her dead husband's blood. Or does it?

What many people do not consider is that powerful *individuals* are always connected to powerful *organizations*, and that they often work hand-in-hand with one another. It isn't unusual for one group to use inside information to plan the murder of a person who is either a weak link or an impediment to forces larger than he is. The American people had no idea how many enemies President John F. Kennedy made, including enemies his father made before his son was even born. They also did not know how closely these enemies might work to remove an individual who was not cooperating with them.

Those who planned Kennedy's murder may have worried that witnesses would eventually come forward and share information contradicting the official findings of the Warren Commission. There seemed to be a contingency plan for inconvenient witnesses. The person who had to be silenced immediately was Lee Harvey Oswald. Whether Jack Ruby was ordered to murder him or not, he made sure the entire world watched as he guaranteed Oswald would never reveal more than he already had.

In his book *Mary's Mosaic,* Peter Janney related the story of Kennedy's paramour, Mary Pinchot Meyer, the ex-wife of senior CIA officer Cord Meyer. Washington insiders knew that Meyer and the President had been involved in a love affair. Apparently, someone also knew that she had kept a secret diary; what may have caused her murder was the fact that she commented to numerous friends that the Warren Report was a whitewash and that the truth about the assassination should be told.[726]

Two weeks after the release of the Warren Report, she was shot to death while taking her daily morning jog. An unknown assassin shot Meyer once through the back of the head and then once through the heart. One man was immediately arrested but found not guilty at trial. No one else has ever been arrested for Meyer's murder. It is uncertain what happened to her secret diary; it was never found. Peter Janney, whose father was a CIA agent during this time, believed that Meyer knew "that certain people within the agency had engineered the [Kennedy] assassination."[727] Like Oswald's, Meyer's voice was also silenced before she could tell everything she knew.

It might seem surprising to some that a woman connected to the CIA could be executed. However, seven FBI agents also died mysteriously not long before being scheduled to testify before the HSCA in 1977. All these agents were somehow connected to the rifle Lee Harvey Oswald supposedly fired. .

Numerous potential witnesses to the Kennedy assassination met with strange deaths. Some were ruled suicides; others were one-car accidents. Some were officially ruled natural deaths, usually because of a sudden heart attack, even if the witness was young with no health problems. And then there were those killed in "fluke" accidents.

One of the so-called suicides was that of well-known newspaper columnist Dorothy Kilgallen. Kilgallen's death might not have appeared suspicious had she not interviewed Jack Ruby during his trial in Dallas. What she learned during Ruby's trial, from him, from his lawyers, and from Dallas insiders, caused her to confide to her hairdresser, "…If the wrong people know what I know, it could cost me my life."[728]

Kilgallen claimed there was "something queer" about Jack Ruby's killing of Oswald. Apparently, there was something queer about Kilgallen's death, too.

If she did not commit suicide, perhaps she was killed because she called the Warren Report "laughable" and continued to tell her friends that what she had discovered about the assassination would be "the scoop of the century."

Kilgallen's death was ruled a suicide despite the fact that the death scene appeared to have been staged.

She was found dead in a room she never slept in and in a bed she never used. The bed was not rumpled the way it would have been if someone had actually slept in it. Kilgallen was not dressed in her typical night clothes. In fact, she was still wearing her make-up and false eyelashes, as well as a hair piece. A book she had already read was turned upside down on her lap. Finally, the toxicology report showed that she had ingested a powerful drug for which she had no prescription. The most incriminating detail was that her notes about the Kennedy assassination were missing and have never surfaced.[729]

If Mary Pinchot Meyer were killed by a typical Washington, D. C. assailant, her secret diary would have been found and given to her children. If Dorothy Kilgallen had accidentally or deliberately killed herself, her carefully guarded assassination notes would have been found in her townhouse. Of course, these are not the only pieces of important information that have gone missing.

Researchers and historians have been patiently awaiting the release of Kennedy assassination documents the government has been withholding from the public since 1963. As of October 2017, about 6,000 pages of "new" information were released. Unfortunately, this was only 12% of the total expected. Many of the released documents contained redacted information, which was expected, and much of the information released in 2017 was not new to researchers.

John M. Newman, a retired U. S. Army intelligence officer and assassination reasearcher, determined that some documents were released with *different* document numbers than originally assigned. One, in particular, proved that Oswald was a CIA source, even though the U.S. government has denied this since 1963. This is just one more example of a government agency intent on hiding important information about the Kennedy assassination—information it does not want its citizens to know.

During the last seven years, the authors interviewed more than 200 witnesses. Many had never before told their stories publicly. A common thread that runs through most of these stories is that these people were sharing information that others had not been privy to. Midland attorney Jack Ladd led the authors to the former assistant attorney general of Texas who had been present while certain Warren Commission members questioned assassination witnesses. Like Buell Wesley Frazier, who had stood on the steps of the Depository and watched the

President's motorcade, Assistant Attorney General Robert T. Davis could say about the Warren Commission investigation, "I was there. You weren't!" Davis learned personally that President Lyndon Johnson and FBI Director J. Edgar Hoover controlled all information that reached the eyes and ears of Warren Commission members.

The comment "I was there" applies to numerous other witnesses who spoke about their memories of the death of John F. Kennedy and its aftermath. James Jenkins and Dennis David were at Bethesda Medical Center on November 22, 1963; they described two different ornate *coffins* and one shipping casket arriving. Apparently, the ornate casket that left on Air Force One at Love Field did not contain the President's corpse. Dennis David shared a fact he had kept to himself for years. On the evening of the President's autopsy, David happened to walk by two Secret Service agents standing outside the autopsy theatre. He overheard one agent say to the other, "Well, at least we don't have to feel like pimps anymore." David realized that Kennedy's personal behavior had not been appreciated by some of the men who guarded him. Had this affected how ineptly they protected him on November 22, 1963?

Jenkins witnessed and assisted with Kennedy's autopsy. He and others were warned that they could not open the second ornate coffin, and told there would be sanctions if anyone lifted the lid of the second ornate casket sitting near the autopsy area. Jenkins was *there* at Bethesda Naval Hospital, so he saw and heard certain individuals interfere with the doctors trying to perform a complete autopsy. For example, he heard Admirals Burkeley and Galloway instruct Dr. Humes to remove the President's testicles.[730] Jenkins did not hint at why this might have been done, but, logically, this would remove evidence of sexually transmitted diseases. The most important thing that Jenkins observed was that the President's spinal cord had been surgically severed *before* this autopsy began, and that had not happened in Dallas!

Dennis David was shown photographs from the autopsy; the wounds in the photos differed from the way they were later described in the Warren Report. David knew this because he was there when the photographer displayed his photos.

For years, Dr. Joe Goldstrich would only say three words about that day at Parkland Hospital. "I was there." Only recently has he spoken about what he saw .

Iris Campbell was on the third floor of the Dallas Police Department when Jack Ruby shot Oswald. She had been placed there by the new president, Lyndon Johnson. Her comment fifty years later that "Oswald got himself killed" is a telling one. Obviously, those close to the Kennedy-Johnson administration knew more about the assassination than they allowed the public to ever know.

Some individuals did not immediately realize they had witnessed important events. Mel Barney, for example, found a manifest list for classified flights demonstrating a new, secret auto-pilot system. There in black and white was the name "Jack Ruby," a man Barney remembered as the owner of the Carousel Club. His name on that manifest list proved he had either CIA or FBI clearance at that time. When a woman who had spent part of the night before Kennedy's assassination with Ruby heard this, she casually told the authors, "I told you he knew *everybody*!"

Some of the witnesses interviewed for this book still insist on anonymity. A few had been forced to sign confidentiality oaths; some still do not want their families to know they ever associated with people like Jack Ruby or even been in his infamous Carousel Club. Some witnesses have recently gone to their graves with information they said they wished they could share but, for various reasons, could not.

Most witnesses have declared that it is time the whole truth was known about how and why John F. Kennedy was killed. If this means that America is forced to face the fact that Kennedy was not the knight in shining armor that his widow depicted after his death, then so be it. Historical truth is more important than myth. Information about Abraham Lincoln's assassination is still being uncovered, especially about the various conspirators and guard who disappeared that night at the theatre. Archaeologists have made discoveries centuries after historical events; these discoveries have changed how we see the world. Why couldn't there be more to the Kennedy assassination than the cut-and-dried story the Warren Commission produced?

Because few people ever get to be a part of any historical event, the rest of the world must depend on the stories that witnesses share with the public. Though these will sometimes contradict each other, the fact that certain people were *there*, and that they saw and heard what the rest of the world did *not* see and hear, makes them invaluable to researchers and to those who love history. None of the persons the authors interviewed even pretended to know or understand the entire story of John F. Kennedy's assassination. They do, however, know what they witnessed.

Tommy Wright was posted outside of Oswald's embalming room. He knew government agents repeatedly interrupted the embalming procedures and insisted the mortician and his assistant leave the room. He knew this because he observed this. Mortician Paul Groody observed the ink that suddenly appeared on Oswald's lifeless hand. Witnesses like Wright and Groody provided details that did not appear in official reports.

Kyle Brown could accurately repeat what Billie Sol Estes and Lyndon Johnson's aide said to one another because he was sitting next to them.

Layte Bowden could describe the startling interaction between her and President Kennedy because she was *there* when it happened.

Jim Bundren knew the details about the capture of Richard Case Nagell because he was the officer who apprehended him. He also heard the intriguing comment Nagell made about November, 1963 and Dallas, Texas because he was sitting next to him.

Tom Alyea knew that "certain types of evidence" later photographed on the sixth floor of the Depository were touched, moved, rearranged, and planted. He knew this because he was there; more importantly, he was there with a movie camera which provided a visual record of the mistakes made by professional law enforcement personnel.

The mistakes Alyea observed are inexcusable, and if they had become known, they could have guaranteed Oswald would have been found innocent by an impartial jury. However, Alyea did not share this information immediately. For whatever reason, he kept certain details secret. As Iris Campbell told the authors, "If Lyndon [Johnson] told someone to lie on a deposition, he would do it."[731]

Perhaps the same is true for Capt. Will Fritz. He did not seem to mind forcing Buel Wesley Fraizer to sign a pre-written confession even as Frazier was denying everything in it. Consequently, some of the most incriminating evidence against Oswald was tainted, but this would not be known if Tom Alyea had not talked.

Tosh Plumlee and J. Goode were in Dealey Plaza when the President was killed. As part of abort teams that had been sent to prevent the assassination, they knew their assignment was to stop a planned assassination attempt. To his amazement, Goode discovered that even his supervisor, U. S. Marshal Robert I. Nash, could be ignored by government officials if his information contradicted a foregone conclusion. If Nash's observations were ignored, then what Goode saw and heard that day was also ignored.

Other witnesses to various events tied to the assassination learned first-hand that what they told investigators was changed before the information was printed. Reporter Connie Kritzberg learned that the FBI inserted details into news stories that altered the words of doctors she interviewed. Dallas newscaster Sam Pate would not have been surprised by that, because he had a similar experience. His car was equipped with a police radio, so he could hear comments made by officials as he moved his own vehicle in and out of the presidential motorcade. He had just begun to report the location of the motorcade to his audience when he heard gunfire. Inadvertently leaving his recorder on, he strained to see what had happened. On the police radio, he heard Chief Curry announce that the President had apparently been hit and that Parkland Hospital should stand by. Pate immediately reported to his radio audience that gun shots had been fired at the President's motorcade. His exact words were: "There is trouble in the motorcade. I repeat, there is trouble in the motorcade. Parkland has been notified to stand by."[732]

That afternoon, Pate was told something that might explain the puff of smoke he saw. Pete Lucas, owner of Lucas B&B Restaurant, a place where Jack Ruby and Oswald or his double had been seen together, informed Pate that the man who killed Kennedy had gotten away. However, he was not referring to Oswald. He reported the man's name as "Bruno" and that he had been in the storm sewer.

Lucas knew even more, though he did not explain where he acquired his information. "He blew Kennedy away with a .45 automatic."[733]

Dallas news reporter Sam Pate would not have been surprised to hear about Kritzberg's altered story. Pate was in a mobile news unit moving in and out of the President's motorcade; he had just moved in front of limousines and was updating the radio audience on the location of the motorcade. The sound of gunshots interrupted his broadcast; without thinking, Pate left the radio recorder running while straining to see what happened. "He observed a puff of smoke come from the storm sewer and watched as the limo picked up speed and headed toward him."[734]

The restaurant owner also knew Bruno had escaped through the sewer and exited near the Post Office on the south side of Dealey Plaza. Someone in a car was waiting to drive him away. (Tosh Plumlee speculated that some of the assassins escaped using the Post Office parking lot. If Plumlee is correct about one sniper being on the south side of Dealey Plaza, then the driver of the car might have been that sniper. He would have had time to escape into the parking lot while the other shooter wound his way through the sewer.)

Pete Lucas added that Bruno was associated with the Chicago Mafia and that he knew Jack Ruby. A logical assumption is that Lucas, whose restaurant was often patronized by the night club owner, heard all of this from Ruby himself. If so, Ruby either forgot to swear Lucas to secrecy or he misjudged Lucas' ability to keep information to himself!

The next thing that happened to Sam Pate might have had nothing to do with the story Lucas told him or with his assignment on November 22. Despite having been praised for his on-the-spot reporting following the shooting of the President, Sam Pate was fired on the morning of November 23 "due to budget reasons."[735]

If this wasn't shocking enough, a few days later, Pate was asked to record a "reenactment tape" of the live recording he had made immediately after shots were fired at the motorcade. Pate agreed to re-record from memory what he had reported on November 22. Consequently, millions of people do not know that the words they assume were from a live broadcast were actually *re-recorded* and are not what Sam Pate originally said. Instead, most people recall hearing: "It appears as though something *has* happened in the motorcade route."

Unlike other witnesses who either did not know their words were changed, or who feared challenging authorities, Pate insisted on letting Special Agent Bob Gemberling know that the majority of what was released to the public was not original. J.Edgar Hoover was forced to bring this to the attention of the Warren Commission. Considering that Pate had the recorder operating when he first heard shots, it's possible he was forced to re-record the tape so that the shots were never heard by the public. The Warren Commission listened to *part* of Pate's tape and determined that no shots were audible. Pate continued to write about the assassination and the re-recorded tape. Two bombs were planted in his car, but he survived both attempts on his life. Pate was obviously revealing too much information!

In the case of Sandra Styles and a Depository co-worker, someone *added* *i*nformation to their story so they appeared to have reached the first floor of the Depository later than they really had. This changed the timeline, which affected how quickly Oswald could have descended from the sixth floor.

Then there were witnesses like Jerry Coley who were bluntly told by the FBI that their visit with him "never took place" even though several people witnessed who knew it. Of course, it is obvious that individual agents had no reason to silence or threaten witnesses to the assassination or anything associated with it. Their superiors must have ordered them to alter testimony, re-record historic tapes, add information to newspaper articles, etc.

Some of them, like the witnesses to the various rifles found in the Depository, may have circumvented these tactics by never *officially* changing their depositions even though they stood by the "party line" anytime they were questioned. Secret Service agent Sam Kinney and Governor John Connally are prime examples of men who saved their careers, and possibly their lives, by going along with the Warren Report.

However, badges of honor should be awarded to Jerry Coley, Sam Pate, and all the other patriots who insisted on telling the truth. Instead of disparaging them and others who have suggested that Kennedy was killed by conspirators, Americans should be asking the following questions: Why *wouldn't* certain CIA individuals use certain Mafia members to assassinate a political liability? Why *wouldn't* certain FBI agents follow orders from an autocratic director connected to an autocratic president? Why *wouldn't* a vice-president who wanted to be President cooperate with individuals who financed his previous campaigns?

There is no doubt that numerous individuals had reasons for wanting President Kennedy out of office. One question lingers, though: Why did the President have to be killed, especially in such a shocking manner? With hindsight, it seems reasonable that a truthful news story about Kennedys' flagrant affairs would have ended his political career. However, it would have also tarnished the Democratic Party.

So, why wasn't Kennedy killed with some drug to make his death appear to be natural? The Kennedy family could still have controlled his autopsy so that the public never knew about his Addison's disease or his long history of sexually-transmitted diseases. Why was he brutally murdered in broad daylight in front of citizens, political associates, and staff members? One possible answer: so that other politicians would realize that the same thing could happen to them.

The poet Dylan Thomas expressed his fear of autocratic kings and dictators in his poem *The Hand That Signed the Paper*. He described how five fingers connected to a single hand controlled the world when it "felled a city," "taxed the breath," "bred a fever," and "did a king to death."[736] What is more frightening today than a dictator who can control his dominion with a simple signature is a group of individuals who leave no "paper trail." These individuals do not have the courage to sign an edict. They make their decisions behind closed doors, refuse to allow the publication of anything that might incriminate them or their associates, surround themselves with "plausible deniability," and set up others to take the blame. The hands of these individuals are more deadly than those who openly sign death decrees.

Those brave enough to come forward over the years should be seen as well-intentioned, loyal citizens, not as attention-seeking "nut cases." Some have risked their careers; others have been ridiculed, and even placed in mental institutions. Still others, like Jerry Coley, have even risked their lives to share their personal experiences. Many, like Coley, have finally announced, "I really don't care whether people believe me or not. I know what I saw."[737]

However, as the world learned in October 2017, when only a handful of assassination-related documents were released by the Assassination Board (and some of those were heavily redacted), some individuals and organizations will still do everything in their power to hide the truth——the *whole* truth—about those responsible for the murder of John F. Kennedy.

AFTERWORD
"IF WE SHADOWS HAVE
OFFENDED..."

Many Americans admit to being disillusioned by and disappointed in President John F. Kennedy. The flaws so carefully hidden during his short life were larger than anyone ever suspected. He spent his entire life trying to meet his father's expectations and accomplish what his father failed to do—attain the presidency. Failure for John Kennedy was never an option. Without question, his sexual morals were lacking, but there was little difference between him and Lyndon Johnson and other powerful men Kennedy knew.

Americans have also been shocked that the Kennedys were associated with the Mafia. Once again, they were not the only politicians who used anyone and everyone to gain political office.

Lyndon Johnson and Richard Nixon allowed staff members and supporters to serve prison terms while they retreated to their comfortable homes. As far as anyone knows, Kennedy did not.

Character flaws were and are a part of all elected officials. Such office-holders are just as human as the people who vote them into office. Whether they set the tone for their countrymen's attitudes and behaviors or simply join the fray, they are no better and no worse than their constituents.

John F. Kennedy's legacy has, to a certain extent, been tainted by his personal weaknesses. But that does not mean his successes should be forgotten. The creation of the Peace Corps, which was an outreach program between the United States and foreign countries, was an indication that Kennedy understood that war is a nightmare to be avoided if at all possible.

For this reason, he was also willing to use back channels to communicate with a Russian premier who once pounded his shoe on a desk at the United Nations. Kennedy obviously realized that Nikita Kruschev needed to save face. The President probably sympathized with that; some of his actions show that he, too, dreaded public embarrassment.

The young President successfully negotiated a nuclear test ban because he realized that the future of the world depended more upon restraint than on weapons and strength. He pushed for realistic progress concerning civil rights because he understood that biases ingrained for centuries will not dissolve overnight. Despite criticism from civil rights leaders who thought he was "dragging his feet" for political reasons, Kennedy understood that no amount of power, presidential or otherwise, could force people to change their feelings overnight.

Perhaps the most important accomplishment of the Kennedy administration is one that the President did not live to see fulfilled. He challenged Americans to set a goal of reaching the moon within a decade, a goal that led to enormous technological and scientific advances that continue even now. Most of the technological "toys" that human beings enjoy today exist because of Kennedy's dream. His futuristic ideas changed the thinking of people of all ages. Children suddenly wanted to grow up to be astronauts rather than cowboys. A new interest in physical activity captured the imaginations of Americans throughout the country. Anyone old enough to have been in public school during Kennedy's administration remembers the "President's Physical Fitness" tests used to measure strength and stamina.

Kennedy's election showed the world that individuals did not have to wait until they were senior citizens to accomplish great deeds. If *he* could lead the the most powerful country in the world at the age of forty-three, then other young men and women could do likewise. The image of Kennedy as healthy and vigorous was a false one, but as a motivational technique, it was just what the country needed. Like President Franklin Roosevelt, John F. Kennedy hid the fact that he himself could not scale mountains; however, he convinced Americans that *they* could, and that changed the future for the better!

ENDNOTES

1 *JFK Assassination: The Reporters' Notes,* published
by Dallas Morning News, 2013, p. 86.

SECTION I: SECRETS FROM THE SHADOWS

Chapter 1 End Notes

2 Wills, Garry. *The Kennedy Imprisonment*, Boston, Massachusetts: Little, Brown & Company, 1982, p. 128.

3 Parmet, Herbert S. *Jack— The Struggles of John F. Kennedy.* New York: Dial Press, 1980, pp. 196-197.

4 Oppenheimer, Jerry. *The Other Mrs. Kennedy.* New York: St. Martin's Press, 1994, p. 293.

5 Reeves, Thomas C. *A Question of Character,* New York: The Free Press, 1991, p. 66.

6 Ibid. pp. 67-68.

7 Parmet, Herbert S. pp. 111-112.

8 Leaming, Barbara. *Jacqueline Bouvier Kennedy Onassis: The Untold Story,* New York: Thomas Dunne Book, 2014, p. 70.

9 Hersh. Seymour. The *Dark Side of Camelot,* New York: Little Brown, & Company, 1997, p. 17.

10 Dallas, Rita and Jeanira Ratcliffe. *The Kennedy Case.* New York: Popular Library, 1973, p. 154.

11 Collier, Peter and David Horowitz. *The Kennedys - An American Drama*, New York: Warner Books, 1984, p. 211.

12 Wolfe, Donald H. *Last Days of Marilyn Monroe,* New York: William Morrow and Company, Inc., 1998, p. 178.

13 Lawford, Patricia Seaton. *The Peter Lawford Story,* New York: Jove Books, 1990, pp. 147-149.

14 Duke, Alan. *Rare Photo Shows Marilyn Monroe with JFK, RFK*:http://www.cnn.com/2010showbiz/06/01/2010 marilyn.birthday. CNN, June 2, 2010.

15 Dallas. pp. 38-39.

16 Ibid. p. 145.

17 Hersh. p. 225.

18 Gallagher, Mary Barelli. *My Life with Jacqueline Kennedy,* New York: David McKay Company, Inc., 1969, p. 39.

19 Ibid. p. 132.

20 Shaw, Maud. *Caroline Kennedy at 16, Ladies Home Journal*, November 1973, Vol. XC, No. 11, p. 116.

21 Gallagher. p. 33.

22 Ibid. p. 44 and 86.

23 Ibid. p. 234.

24 Ibid. p. 49.

25 Ibid. p 222.

26 Manchester.p. 349.

27 Burke, Richard E. with William and Marilyn Hiffer. *The Senator: My Ten Years with Ted Kennedy*, New York, New York: St. Martin's Press, 1992, p. 42.

28 Ibid. p. 50.

29 Ibid. p. 108.

30 Heymann, C. David. *Bobby and Jackie*, New York, Atrid Paperback, 2009 p. 127.

Chapter 2 End Notes:

31 Bowden, Layte. Interviews with the authors via telephone and emails February 5, and 14, 2016. All information and quotes are attributed to these interviews.

32 Leaming. p. 49.

33 Reeves. p. 32.

34 Bowden, Layte. Interview with the authors via telephone and emails as well as her book *Under the Radar During Camelot*, Miami, Florida: Figleaf Ltd., 2013, p. 88

35 Margolis, Jay and Richard Buskin, *The Murder of Marilyn Monroe: Case Closed*, New York, New York: Skyhorse Publishing, 2014, p. 22.

36 Ibid. p. x.

37 Ibid. p. xi.

38 Bowden. Interviews.

39 Bowden. p. xii.

40 Bowden. Interviews.

Chapter 3 End Notes:

41 Farris, Scott. *Inga*, Guilford, Connecticut: Rowman & Littlefield, 2016, p. 13.

42 Ibid. p. 360.

43 Ibid. p. 106.

44 Ibid. p.

45 Ibid. p. 214.

46 Ibid. pp. 217-218.

47 Arvad, Inga. *Papers of John F. Kennedy. Personal Papers. Correspondence, 1933-1950: Friends. Arvad, Inga.* Presidential Library and Museum: Boston, Mass.

48 Ibid.

49 Ibid.

50 Farris. p. 221

51 Arvad letters.

52 Holm, Axel. Interview with the authors via telephone about Inga Arvad on January 28, 2017 and February 19, 2017. All of his information and quotes are attributed to these interviews.

53 Holm. Interview.

54 Holm, Axel. *Nogalas Woman had intimate Connection with Kennedy*. Nogales International. com. November 22, 2013.

55 Arvad Letters.

56 Holm, Axel. *Nogalas Woman Had Intimate Connection with Kennedy*. Nogales International. com. November 22, 2013.

57 Arvard Letters.

58 Holm.

59 Holm. Interviews.

60 Farris. p. 374.

61 Von Post, Gunilla, and Carl Johnas. *Love, Jack*, New York: Crown, 1997.

62 Both letters were auctioned and the purchasers are unknown.

63 Hersh.p. 388.

64 Ibid.

65 FBI Memo, March 20, 1962 RE: *Judith E. Campbell*. www.paperlessarchives.com.

Chapter 4 End Notes:

66 Giancana, Sam and Chuck. *Double Cross*, New York: Warner Books, Inc., 1992, p. 227.

67 Oppenheimer. p. 121.

68 Hersh. p. 140. and Roemer, William F. Jr. *Man Against the Mob*, New York: Ivy Books, *1989.*.

69 Giancana. p. 230.

70 Ibid.

71 Summers, Anthony. *Official and Confidential: The Secret Life of J. Edgar Hoover*, New York: G. P. Putnam's Sons, 1993, p. 269.

72 Giancana. p. 286.

73 Ibid.

74 Ibid. p. 279.

75 Summers. p. 269

76 Reid, Ed. *The Grim Reaper*, Chicago, Illinois: Bantam Books, 1969, pp. 162-163.

77 Davis, John H. *Mafia Kingfish.* p. 109.

78 Ibid. p. 112

79 Giancana. p. 309.

80 Willis. p. 252.

81 Giancana. p. 215.

82 Helppie, Chuck. Interview with authors via telephone on March 31, 2017. All of his information and quotes are attributed to this interview.

Chapter 5 End Notes:

83 Beschloss, Michael R. *Taking Charge— The Johnson White House Tapes*, New York: Simon & Schuster, 1997, pp. 31-35.

84 Warren, Earl. Interview by Alfred Goldberg, March 26, 1974, jfkassasinationfiles.com.

85 Russo. p. 362. Interview with the authors via telephone on June 5, 2016.

86 Bechloss, Michael. *Taking Charge*, New York, New York: Simon and Schuster, pp. 61 and 65.

87 Holland, Max. *The Kennedy Assassination Tapes*, New York: Knopf, 2004, pp. 121-122.

88 McNamara, Robert. *Testimony before Church Committee*, July 11, 1975. CCIR p. 158.

89 Russo. p. 428.

90 David, Lester and Irene David. *Bobby Kennedy, The Making of a Folk Hero*, New York: Dodd, Mead & Co., 1986, p.228.

91 Davis. p. 243.

92 Thomas. p. 338.

93 Ibid. p. 338.

94 Beschloss, Michael R., editor. *Taking Charge*, New York: Simon & Schuster, 1997. p. 14.

95 Ibid. p. 68.

96 Shenon. p. 543.

97 Shenon. p. 511.

98 "Jim" Interview in person with the authors on March 28, 2015. All of his information and quotes are attributed to this interview.

99 Hougan, Jim. *Spooks— The Haunting of America— The Private Use of Secret Agents*. New York: William Morrow and Company, Inc., 1978, blurb.

Chapter 6 End Notes:

100 Goode, J. Interviews in person with the authors on August 5, 2013, October 13, 2013, August 7, 2014, February 10, 2015, October 4, 2015. All of his information and quotes are attributed to these interviews.

101 Wills. p. 222.

102 Hinkle, Warren and William Turner, *Deadly Secrets: The CIA-Mafia War against Castro and the Assassination of J.F.K.*, New York: Thunder's Mouth Press, 1992, p.36.

103 Hersh. pp. 175-176.

104 Ibid. p. 220.

105 Russo, Gus. *Live By the Sword*, Baltimore, MD.: Bancoft Press, 1998, p. 84.

106 Willis. p. 269.

Chapter 7 End Notes:

107 Anderson, Christopher. *Jack and Jackie: Portrait of an American Marriage*, New York: William Morrow and Company, Inc., 1996, p. 41.

108 Campbell, Iris.Interviews in person with the authors, September 28, 2013, June 12, 2014, August 20, 2014. All of her information and quotes are attributed to these interviews.

109 Galbraith, John Kenneth. *Ambassador's Journal*. Boston, MS.: Houghton Mifflin Company, 1969, p. 384.

110 Anderson. p. 47.

111 Bradford, Sarah. *America's Queen*, New York: Penguin Books, 2000, p. 95.

112 Hersh. p. 5.

113 Mahoney, Richard D. *Sons & Brothers*. New York: Arcade Publishing, 1999, p. 159.

114 Mills, Tom. Interview in person with the authors on April 23, 2016. All of his information and quotes are attributed to this interview.

115 Wood, Randall B., *Architech of Amerocan Ambition*, Cambridge, Massachusetts: Harvard University Press, 2007, p. 880.

116 Admiral Burkley's interview on October 17, 1967. JFK Library p. 8.

Chapter 8 End Notes:

117 Admiral Burkley's interview on October 17, 1967. JFK Library p.8.

118 Shenon, Philip. *A Cruel and Shocking Act,* New York: Henry Holt and Company, 2013, p. 20.

119 Russo. pp. 304-305.

120 Manchester. p. 298.

121 Ibid. p. 299.

122 Ibid. p. 298.

123 Ibid. p. 301

124 Ibid. p. 302.

125 Rike, Aubrey. *At the Door of Memory*, Southlake, Texas: JFK Lancer Publications & Publishers, 2008, p.63.

126 Calloway, Sharon. *Oral History Interview with Sixth Floor Museum*, 2002.

Chapter 9 End Notes:

127 Jenkins, James. Small group discussion and Interview with the authors on November 22, 2013. All of his information and quotes are attributed to this small group discussion and interview.

128 Custer, Jerrold. *Deposition for Assassination Records Review Board*, October 28, 1997.

129 Clark, Hugh. Interview in person with the authors on November 22, 2015. All of his information and quotes are attributed to this interview.

130 Boswell, J. Thornton. AARB deposition on February 26, 1996, p. 11.

131 David, Dennis. Interview in person with the authors on November 17, 2016. All of his information and quotes are attributed to this interview.

132 Wade, Henry. *Oral History Interview with Sixth Floor Museum*. July 20, 1992.

133 *New York Times*, July 3, 1997, http://nytimes. com/l997/07/03/us.ford-made-key-change-in-kennedy-death-report).

Chapter 10 End Notes:

134 Kritzberg, Connie. Interview with the authors via telephone on July 26, 2016. All of her information and quotes are attributed to this interview.

135 Coley, Jerry. Interview with the authors via telephone on April 26, 2017. All of his information and quotes are attributed to this interview.

136 Trask, Richard. *Pictures of the Pain,* Danvers, Mass.: Yeoman Press, 1994, p. 235.

137 *JFK Assassination: The Reporters' Notes,* as reported by Wick Fowler, published by Dallas Morning News, 2013, p. 135.

138 FBI Memorandum, October 1, 1975 to Office of U.S. Attorney General

139 Fulton, Christopher and Michelle Fulton, *The Inheritance: Poisoned Fruit of JFK's Assassination,* Walterville, OR: Trine Day, 2018.

SECTION II: THE SHADOWS OF AMBITION

Chapter 11 End Notes:

140 Stone, Roger. *The Man Who Killed Kennedy*, New York, New York: Skyhorse, 2013, p.18.

141 Davis, John H. *Mafia Kingfish*, p. 82.

142 Hersh. Seymour. *Dark Side of Camelot,* p. 17.

143 Davis, Robert T. Interview in person with the authors on May 24, 2013. All of his information and quotes are attributed to this interview.

144 Katzenbach, Nicholas. *Memorandum to William Moyers*, November 25, 1963.

145 Summers, Anthony. *Official and Confidential: The Secret Life of J. Edgar Hoover*p. 335.

146 Gentry, Curt. *J. Edgar Hoover— The Man and His Secrets*, New York: W. W. Norton & Co., 1991, p. 552.

147 Davis, Robert T. *Memorandum to Texas Attorney General Waggoner Carr*, 1964.

148 Davis, Robert T. Interview.

149 Carr, Waggoner. *Personal letter to Texas*

Senator Lloyd Benson, September 9, 1975. Texas Tech Southwest Collections.

150 Davis, Robert T. Interview.

Chapter 12 End Notes:

151 Day, George. Interview in person with the authors on May 9, 2014. All of his information and quotes are attributed to this interview.

152 Day, George A. *Juanita Dale Slusher Alias Candy Barr,* Brownwood, Texas: ERBE Publishing Company, 2009, pp. 180-181.

153 Ibid. 177.

154 Ibid. 189

155 Ibid. 231.

156 Morrow, Judge William. Interview In-Person with the authors in 2010. All of his information and quotes are attributed to this interview.

157 Schwarz, Ted and Mardi Rustam. *Candy Barr,* New York: Taylor Trade Publishing, 2008 p. 48.

158 Ibid. p. 276.

159 Interview in person with authors by an anonymous source May 9, 2014.

160 Ibid.

161 Day. Interview.

162 Bowden, Tom. Interview with the authors via telephone on October 27, 2018.

163 Day. Interview.

164 Day, Mrs. George. Interview with the authors via telephone on July 14, 2017.

Chapter 13 End Notes:

165 Campbell, Iris. Interviews in person with the authors, September 28, 2013, June 12, 2014, August 20, 2014. All of her information and quotes are attributed to these interviews.

166 Campbell. Interview.

167 *Office Memorandum of FBI, United States Government,* October 18, 1956. From Price to Rosen.

168 Stone, Roger and Mike Colapietro. *The Man Who Killed Kennedy: The Case Against LBJ,* New York: Skyhorse Publishing, 2013, pp. 37-39. And, Haley, J. Evetts. *A Texan Looks At Lyndon,* Canyon, Texas: Palo Duro Press, 1964. pp. 21-54.

169 Campbell. Interview.

170 Woods, Randall B. *LBJ: Architect of American Ambition,* New York: Free Press, 2006, p. 361.

171 Curington, John and Mitchel Whitington. *H. L. Hunt—Motive & Opportunity,* USA: 23 House Publishing, 2018, p.85.

172 Campbell. Interview.

173 Russell. p. 169.

174 Margolis, Jay and Richard Buskin. *The Murder of Marilyn Monroe— Case Closed,* New York, New York: Skyhorse, 2014, p. 21.

175 Reid, Ed. *The Grim Reapers.* Chicago, Il: Bantam. 1969, p. 131.

176 Pietrusza, David. *LBJ vs JFK vs. Nixon, Somerville, Mass.:* Union Square Press, 2010, p. 268.

177 *United States Government Memorandum* (FBI) February 13, 1964, From Rosen to Belmont.

178 Campbell. Interview.

179 Thomas, Helen. p. 118.

180 Hershman, D. Jablow. *Power beyond Reason: The Mental Collapse of Lyndon Johnson,* New Jersey: Barricade Books, Inc., 2002, p. 13.

181 Campbell. Interview.

182 Busby, Horace. *Reflections On a Leader, The Johnson Presidency,* Edited by Kenneth W. Thompson, Lanham, Maryland: University Press of America, Inc., 1986, p. 253.

183 Lincoln, Evelyn. *Kennedy & Johnson,* New York: H. H. Rinehart and Winston, 1968, p. 161.

184 www.evtv1.com. Jack Parr show November 16, 1962.

185 Zirbel, Craig I. *The Texas Connection,* Scottsdale, Arizona: TCC Publishers, 1991.

186 Thomas, Dylan. *Do Not Go Gentle Into That Good Night,* PoemHunter.com

187 Mills, George. *Preview Poll: Kennedy Could Lose, LOOK Magazine,* New York: Cowles Magazine and Broadcasting, December 17, 1963, pp. 94-102.

188 Brussell, Mae. www.maebrussell.com *Articles/ Last Words of Lee Oswald.* pp. 1-5.

189 Ibid.

190 Brussell, Mae. www.maebrussells.com, *Articles, Last Word of Lee Oswald.*

191 Proctor,Grover, Jr. *The Raleigh Call and the Fingerprints of Intelligence,* www. groverproctor,us/jfk/

192 Davis, John H. *Mafia Kingfish, Carlos Marcello and the Assassination of John F. Kennedy,* New York: McGraw Hill, 1989. p.139.

193 Ibid.

194 Campbell. Interview.

195 Davis, John H. *Mafia Kingfish.* p. 126.

196 Campbell. Interview.

197 Ibid.

198 Nelson, Phillip F. *LBJ: From Mastermind to "The Colossus",* New York: Skyhorse Publishing, 2013, p. 264.

199 Turner, Nigel. *The Men Who Killed Kennedy*, *Episode 9, DVD*: England, November 2003

200 Pope, John. Johnpopenola.com

201 Reedy, George. *Lyndon B. Johnson*. New York: Andrews and McMeel, Inc., 1982. p. 35.

202 Campbell. Interview.

Chapter 14 End Notes:

203 Brown, Kyle. Interview with the authors via telephone on October 14, 2013 and June 15, and 28, 2015. All of his information and quotes are attributed to these interviews.

204 Mellen, Joan. *Faustian Bargains*, New York: Bloomsbury Publishing, 2016, p. 179.

205 Brown. Interviews.

206 McClellan, Barr. *Blood, Money, & Power*, New York: Skyhorse Publishing, 2011, p. 109.

207 Nelson, Phillip F. *LBJ: The Mastermind of the JFK Assassination*, New York: Skyhorse Publishing, 2013, p. 221.

208 Mellen. pp. 258-259.

209 Ibid. p. 257.

210 *Vice-President's Lyndon B. Johnson's Daily Diary*. Thursday, August 9, 1962.

211 Brown. Interviews.

212 Ibid.

213 Nelson, Phillip. *LBJ: From Mastermind to "The Colossus"*, New York: Skyhorse Publishing, 2013, p. 258.

214 Ibid. p. 259.

Chapter 15 End Notes:

215 Wright, Tommy. Interview in person on June 10, 2014. All of his information and quotes are attributed to this interview.

216 Amos, Gail. Interview with the authors via telephone March 2016. All of her information and quotes are attributed to this interview.

217 Milan, Michael. *The Squad-The U.S. Government Secret Alliance with Organized Crime*, New York: Shapolsky Publishers, Inc. 1989, Jacket blurb.

218 Amos, Jan. Oral History at the Sixth Floor Museum on July 14, 2015, Interview with her daughter on March 2016, and from Phillip Nelson's book *LBJ: From Mastermind to "The Colossus."*

219 Harvey, C.G. You Tube Interview by Scott and Any Alderton. Indianapolis. 1999.

220 Amos, Jan.

221 *Los Angeles Times*, August 14, 1985, p. 8.

SECTION III: RENDEZVOUS WITH DEATH

Chapter 16 End Notes:

222 Lewis, Dan. *The Kennedy Assassin Who Failed*, Smithsonian.com December 6, 2012.

223 Bowden, Layte. Interviews with the authors via telephone and emails February 5, and 14, 2016. All of her information and quotes are attributed to these interviews.

224 Campbell, Iris. Interviews in person with the authors, September 28, 2013, June 12, 2014, August 20, 2014. All of her information and quotes are attributed to these interviews.

225 Steinberg, Alfred. *Sam Johnson's Boy*, New York: MacMillan Publishing Co., Inc. 1968, p. 524.

226 DeseretNews.com. Quotes: *U.S. vice presidency*. Published: Sunday, September. 28, 2008.

227 Hersh. The *Dark Side of Camelot*, p.123.

228 Epstein, Edward Jay. *Esquire,* December 1966.

229 Baker, Bobby. *Wheeling and Dealing*. New York: W. W. Norton & Company, Inc., 1978. pp. 123-126.

230 Thomas, Helen. *Dateline: White House*, New York: Macmillan Publishing Co., Inc. 1975, p. 39.

231 Summers, Anthony. *Official and Confidential: The Secret Life of J. Edgar Hoover*. p. 272.

232 Bundren, Jim. Interview in person on April 30, 2016, and via telephone on May 14, 2016, May 5, 2017, via emails on June 13, 2016 and June 20, 2017 and with the authors. All of his information and quotes are attributed to these interviews.

233 Thompson, Doug. *Is Deception the Best Way to Serve Your Country?* March 30, 2006, OpEdNews.

Chapter 17 End Notes:

234 *El Paso Times*, September 21, 1963, p. 1.

235 Bundren. Interviews.

236 Hancock, Larry Howard. *The Man in the Middle. Kennedy Assassination Chronicles* Vol. 5 Issue 4, Winter 1999.

237 Bundren. Interviews.

238 *El Paso Times* September 21, 1963, Front p. 3A.

239 Bundren. Interviews.

240 Russell, Dick. *The Man That Knew Too Much*, New York, New York: Carroll & Graf Publishers, 1992, p. 2 and p. 475.

241 Bundren. Interviews

242 *El Paso Herald*, December 10 1963. Pg. 1 *"Says Bank Holdup Try 'Patriotic"*

243 Ybarra, Bob. *My Demons Were Real*, Houston, Texas: Arte Publico Press, 2010, p. 133.

244 Ibid. p.144.

245 Bundren. Interviews.

246 Goode, J. Interviews in person with the authors

on August 5, 2013, October 13, 2013, August 7, 2014, February 10, 2015, October 4, 2015. All of his information and quotes are attributed to these interviews.

247 Russell. Dick. p. 286.

248 Ibid. p. 2.

Chapter 18 End Notes:

249 Tim King. *Salemnews*.com November 22, 2013.

250 Warren Commission Hearing and Exhibits Deposition 1107. *FBI Gemberling Report, vol. XXII* p. 64.

251 Summers, Anthony. *The Kennedy Conspiracy*, New York: McGraw— Hill Book Co., 1980, p. 624.

252 *The Predictions of Joseph Milteer* (Mary Ferrell Foundation preserving the legacy).

253 Warren Commission Hearing and Exhibits Deposition 1347. *FBI Gemberling Report, v*ol. XXII, pp. 577-578.

254 Adams, Don. *From an Office Building with a High-Powered Rifle*, Walterville, OR: Trine Day LLC, 2012 pp. 41-42.

255 Ibid. p. 166.

256 Ibid. p. 102.

257 Douglas, James W. *JFK and The Unspeakable— Why He Died and Why It Matters*, New York: Simon & Schuster, 2008, pp. 202-203.

258 Ibid. p. 203.

259 Bridger, Mark. *Who Was Igor Vaganov…*The Dealey Plaza Echo, p.37.

Chapter 19 End Notes:

260 Smith, Matthew *JFK: Say Goodbye to America*, Mainstream Pub. Edinburgh and London. 2004, pp. 163-164.

261 Latell, Brian. *Castro's Secrets— The CIA and Cuba's Intelligence Machine*, New York: Palgrave MacMillan, 2012, p. 103.

Chapter 20 End Notes:

262 Marcades, Michael. Interview in person, via Telephone, and emails, with the authors on December 20, 2015, February 15 and 21, 2016. All of his information and quotes are from these various interviews.

263 Douglas, James. p. 247.

264 Mellen, Joan. *A Farewell to Justice,* New York: Skyhorse Publishing, 2013, p .206.

265 Albarelli, H. P. Jr., *A Secret Order,* Oregon: Trine Day, 2013, pp.94-98.

266 DiEugenio, Jim. *Rose Cheramie: How She Predicted the JFK Assassination,* Probe Vol. 6 No. 5, July-August 1999 p. 2.

267 Mellen. *A Farewell to Justice*. p. 207.

268 Albarelli. p. 97.

269 Fruge's testimony HSCA, JFK Record Number 180-10106-10014. April 7, 1978 p. 5. Michael Marcades (Rose Ceramie's son) interviews.

270 Marcades. Interviews.

271 Marcades. Interviews.

Chapter 21 End Notes:

272 Goode, J. Interviews

273 Plumlee, Tosh. Interview in person with the authors on November 21, 2014. All of his information and quotes are attributed to this interview.

274 Sindler, Bernie. *The Bernie Sindler Story*, Las Vegas, NV: 7 Wives Press, 2015, pp.77-78.

275 MacKenzie, Roderick. *The Men Who Don't Fit In, self-published, 2009.*

276 Ibid.

277 Bailey, Monzel. Interview with the authors in-person April 16, 2015.

278 Reston, James Jr., *The Lone Star: The Life of John Connally*: New York: Harper & Row, Publishers, 1989, p. 276.

279 Crawford, Ann Fears, and Jack Keever. John B. Connally— Portrait In Power, Austin, Texas: Jenkins Publishing Co., 1973, p. 299.

280 Ibid.

SECTION IV: IN THE SHADOWS OF DEALEY PLAZA

Chapter 22 End Notes:

281 St. George, Judith. *In the Line of Fire: Presidents' Lives at Stake,* New York: Scholastic Books, 1999, pp.72-73.

282 Joesten, Joachim. *Oswald: Assassin or Fall Guy,* New York: Iconoclassic Books, 2012, p.86.

283 Drenas, Bill. *An Overlooked Texas Theatre Witness*. www.billdrenas.com. 2009, p.2.

284 Curington, John and Mitchel Whitington. *H. L. Hunt—Motive & Opportunity*, USA: 23 House Publishing, 2018 p. 112.

285 Warren Commission Hearings and Exhibits, Exhibit 832 Hosty/Bookout, 11/23/63.

286 Brussell, Mae. *The Last Words of Lee Harvey Oswald.* Found in The People's Almanac #2, by David Wallechinsky and Irving Wallace, New York, Bantam Books, 1978 pp.47-52.

Chapter 23 End Notes:

287 Roussel, Henry. Interview via telephone on August 3, 2019. All of his quotes are attributed to this interview.

288 Botelo, James. Interview via telephone on August 3, 2019. All of his quotes are attributed to

this interview.

289 Lord, Bill. Interview with the authors via telephone on March 27, 2017. All of his quotes are attributed to this interview.

290 Warren Commission Hearings and Exhibits *(Billy Joe Lord, June 26, 1964)* vol. XXVI pg. 117.

291 Lord. Interview.

292 Lord, Bill. *Letter to President Jimmy Carter,* February 2, 1977. http://tekgnosis.typepad.com/tekgnosis/2013/12.

293 Warren Commission Hearings and Exhibits, *Document 1114.* Vol. X, p. 80.

294 Stern, David. *"Minsk's Fond Memories of Lee Harvey Oswald"*, BBC News, www.www.bbc.com/news/magazine. All quotes are from this article.

Chapter 24 End Notes:

295 Hall, Pat. Interviews in person with the authors on May 16, 2014 and November 22, 2015. All of her information and quotes are attributed to these interviews.

296 Warren Commission Hearings and Exhibits, Vol. 10. p.303.

297 This information from Pat Hall contradicts what Mary and Ray La Fontaine wrote in *Oswald Talked* when they quoted a Griffin-Hubert memo pgs. 6-8, stating that the Johnsons saw Oswald's picture on television at a different address, and called the police. The "different address" must have been the Johnson's Café. Even if they had a television set there, they could not have seen Oswald's picture on it because he was still in the police car on the way to the police station.

298 Hall. Interviews.

Chapter 25 End Notes:

299 Frazier, Buell Wesley. Interview in person with the authors on May 15, 2015 and via telephone on May 30, 2015 and Jan. 29, 2019. All of his information and quotes in this chapter are from these interviews.

Chapter 26 End Notes:

300 Johnson, Marilyn. Interview in person, via emails, and telephone with authors on March 10 2014, June 14, 2014 and March 2017. All of her information and quotes are attributed to these interviews.

Chapter 27 End Notes:

301 Ernest, Barry. Interview with the authors via telephone on July 1, 2016, and his book *The Girl on the Stairs.* Gretna, Louisiana: Pelican Publishing Co., 2013 p. 255. All of his information and quotes are attributed to his interview and when noted, his book.

302 Styles, Sandra. Interviews via telephone and emails with the authors on July 3 and 12, 2016. All

of her information and quotes are attributed to these interviews.

303 Ernest. Interview and book p.244.

304 *Four Days.* New York, New York: American Heritage Publishing Co., Inc. 1983 p.29.

305 Alyea, Tom to Kritzberg, Connie. *Secrets from the Sixth Floor Window*, pp. 39-46, http://www.jfk-online.com/alyea.html.

306 Ibid.

307 Brennan Howard. Warren Report testimony.

Chapter 28 End Notes:

308 Sneed, Larry A. Video Interview with L. D. Montgomery. 1998.

309 Jones, Richard. Interview in person with the authors on June 9, 2016. All of his information and quotes are attributed to this interview.

310 Dockray, Dr. Karl. Interviews with the authors via telephone, letters and emails on August 28, 2014, October 27, 2014, April 3 and 11, 2014. All of his information and quotes are attributed to these interviews.

311 Ibid.

312 Shaw, J. Gary. Interviews in person with the authors on July 25, 2014, March 19, 2015 and November 20, 2015, via telephone on November 3, 2013, and September 23, 2014, and through several emails from September 28 2015 to July 15, 2017. All of his information and quotes are attributed to these interviews.

313 Dockray, Dr. Karl. Interviews.

314 Huddleston, James. Interview with the authors via telephone on April 3, 2019.

Chapter 29 End Notes:

315 Sloan, Bill. Interview in person with the author on May 13, 2015 and from his book, *JFK: Breaking the Silence*, Dallas, Texas: Taylor Publishing, 1993, p.89. All of his information and quotes are attributed to this interview and when noted, his book.

316 Goldstrich, Elysse. Interviews via telephone on May 21 and 30, 2015. All of her information and quotes are attributed to these interviews.

317 Ibid.

318 Sloan. Interview and his book *JFK: Breaking the Silence*, p. 89.

319 Sloan. Interview and p. 96.

Chapter 30 End Notes

320 Wright, Tommy. Interview in person with the authors on June 12, 2014. All of his information and quotes are attributed to this interview.

321 Wright. Interview.

322 Parnell, W. Tracy. *The Exhumation of Lee Harvey Oswald and the Norton Report: Part Two-Paul Groody.* 2003

Chapter 31 End Notes:

323 *Dallas Morning News*, November 22, 2013.

324 Groody, Donald. Interview with the authors via telephone on July 21, 2015. All of his information and quotes are attributed to this interview.

325 Baumgardner, Allan. Interview in person and via telephone with the authors on July 28, 2014. All of his information and quotes are attributed to these interviews.

326 Williams, Gene. Interview in person with the authors on July 1, 2014. All of his information and quotes are attributed to this interview.

327 Groody. Interview.

328 Baumgardner. Interview.

329 Cochran, Mike. Interview via telephone with the authors on April 25 and July 22, 2017. All of his information and quotes are attributed to this interview.

330 Oswald, Marguerite. *Aftermath of an Execution: The Burial and Final Rites of Lee Harvey Oswald, as told by his Mother Marguerite*, typescript.

331 Frazier. Interviews.

332 Hall Interviews.

333 Groody. Interview.

Chapter 32 End Notes:

334 Brooks, Elston. *An Arrest He'll Never Forget*, The Fort Worth Star-Telegram, November 20, 1983, p. 20F, (Sunday special section: *Turning Point: The Assassination of JFK*).

335 Ibid. 20F.

336 Lane. M. Duke. *The Cowtown Connection*, 1993, p. 4.

337 Ibid.

338 Ibid.

339 Ibid.

340 Brooks. *Turning Point*, p. 20F.

341 Ibid.

342 Shaw, Gary, and Larry Ray Harris. *Cover Up: The Government Conspiracy to Conceal the Facts About the Public Execution of John Kennedy*, Cleburne, TX: Gary Shaw, 1976. p. 88. Interviews in person with the authors on July 25, 2014, March 19, 2015, November 20, 2015 and numerous emails and telephone interviews.

343 Horton, Charles. Interview with authors via telephone August 17, 2014. All of his information and quotes are from this interview.

344 Shaw, Gary. Interviews and *Cover Up*. p. 88.

SECTION V: LEE AND HIS SHADOWS

Chapter 33 End Notes:

345 Simpkin, John. Lee Harvey Oswald: Biography, *Spratacus Educational,* Interview of Marchetti by Anthony Summers.

346 Armstrong, John. *Harvey & Lee*, Arlington, Texas: Quasar, Ltd, 2003, p. 28

347 Armstrong. pp. 21-24.

348 Walker. p. 3.

349 Warren Commission Hearings and Exhibits, Vol XX (*affidavit of Byron Phillips*).

350 Smith, Genevieve. Interview in person with the authors in Vernon, Texas, March 10, 2014. All of her information and quotes are attributed to this interview.

351 Warren Commission Hearings and Exhibits. #1386.

352 Garrison, Jim. Notes from his Investigation. *Miscellaneous Investigative Reports and Memorandum (Oscar Delatte)*, April 21, 1967. www.archive.org.

353 Warren Commission Hearings and Exhibits. Document 179 (*James Spencer FBI report 12/13/63*).

354 Warren Commission Hearings and Exhibits. Document 144 (*FBI Report re: Oswald*) p. 25

355 Garrison, Jim. Notes from his Investigation. *Miscellaneous Investigative Reports and Memorandum (David Lousteau)*, April 5, 1967. www.archive.org.

356 Warren Commission Hearings and Exhibits. Vol. XIX, p. 399.

357 Baylor University Poage Library. *JFK/John Armstrong Collection*, Box 5, Notebook 3 & 5.

358 Garrison, Jim. *On the Trail of the Assassins*, New York: Warner Brothers, 1988, p. 60.

359 Poage Library, *JFK/John Armstrong Collection*. Box 5, Notebook 5.

360 Ibid. Box 9, Notebook 4.

361 Ibid.

362 SA Eugene Petrakis. (*FBI Interview with Daniel Thomas McGowan)* October 28, 1976.

363 Warren Commission Hearings and Exhibits. Vol. X (*Clifton M. Shasteen*) pp. 309-311

364 FBI SA J. Hale McMenamin interview with Lillie Cline March 14, 1964.

365 Spielbaurer, Bruce. Quora.com, March 1, 2019

Chapter 34 End Notes:

366 Interviews in person with associates of John Craig on August 1, 2015, and December 3, 2016. All information and quotes are attributed to these

interviews.

367 Craig, John R., Phil D. Rogers. *The Man on the Grassy Knoll*, New York: Avon Books, 1992, p. 147.

368 Ibid.

369 Ibid. p.163.

370 Ibid. p.163.

371 Gibson, Lois. Interview with the authors via telephone and through emails on December 3, 2016. All of her information and quotes are attributed to these interviews.

Chapter 35 End Notes:

372 Garrison, Jim p. 77.

373 Kittrell, Laura. *Letter to Robert Kennedy December 26, 1963 and a letter to the HSCA.*

374 Ibid.

375 Ibid.

376 Ibid.

377 Ibid.

378 Warren Commission Hearings and Exhibits (*Ruth Paine*)

379 Garrison, Jim pp. 74-77

380 HSCA. *Aldene Magee* 180-10109-10075.

381 Warren Commission Hearings and Exhibits, (*SA John M. Kemmy FBI Interview*) 4/30/1964.

382 Warren Commission Hearings and Exhibits. Vol. XI (*Edith Whitworth*) pp. 263-264.

383 Armstrong. p. 766.

384 Warren Commission Hearings and Exhibits. Document 2886 (*FBI Charles Arndt*) 11/26/63 p. 807.

385 Ibid.

386 Warren Commission Hearings and Exhibits, *WCD 950 (Curry letter May 19, 1964. Re: Oswald)* p. 29.

387 SA Lenn E. Silver and David S. Byerly. (*FBI Report Vern Davis),* DL 44-1639 OC 44-430.

388 Armstrong. p. 777.

389 Goltz, Earl. *Confidential: The FBI's File on JFK—Part Two.* Cover-Up, December 1992.

390 Fletcher, Clyde Linberg. Interview in person with the authors via telephone on March 28, 2018. All of his information and quotes are attributed to this interview.

391 SA Ben S. Harrison (*FBI Report Ralph Leon Yates),* DL 44-1639 and DL 89-43-1554, November 26, 19631.

392 Douglas, James W. *JFK and the Unspeakable*, New York, New York: Simon & Schuster, 2010, p. 352.

393 Ibid. p. 354.

394 Armstrong p. 780.

395 Armstrong. p. 781.

396 Myers, Dale. *With Malice*, Milford, MI: Oak Cliff Press, Inc., 2013, p.57.

397 Armstrong. p. 799.

398 Ernest, Barry. Interview with the authors via telephone on July 1, 2015 and his book *The Girl on the Stairs*, Gretna, Louisiana: Pelican Publishing Company, 2013, p.192. All of his information and quotes are attributed to this interview or when noted, his book.

399 Kurtz, Michael. *Crime of the Century: The Kennedy Assassination from a Historian's Perspective*, Knoxville, Tennessee: University of Tennesse Press, 1993, p.132.

Chapter 36 End Notes:

400 Marrs, Jim. Interviews in person with the authors on November 21, 2015 and his book, *Crossfire—the Plot That Killed Kennedy*, New York: Carroll & Graf, 1989, p. 353.

401 Carolyn Crowder. Interview in person with the authors on November 25, 2017.

402 Warren Commission Hearings and Exhibits. (*C. T. Walker*) April 8, 1964.

403 Marrs.

404 L. D. Stringfellow's Deposition/homicide report. John F. Kennedy Archive— Box 5.

405 Armstrong. p. 872.

406 Drenas, Bill. *An Overlooked Texas Theatre Witness.* www.billdrenas.com. 2009, p. 2.

407 Ibid. p.4.

Chapter 37 End Notes:

408 Johnston, James P., and Jon Roe. *Flight from Dallas*, Bloomington, Indiana: 1stbooks, 2003 p. 23.

409 Ibid.

410 Ibid. p.27.

411 Ibid. p.29.

412 Ibid. p.69.

Chapter 38 End Notes:

413 Warren Commission Hearings and Exhibits. Vol. X (Carlos Bringuier) pp. 39-42.

414 HSCA. (*Adrian T. Alba*) January 24, 1978, p. 4.

415 Carr, Waggoner. *Waggoner Carr's* Papers. Texas Tech Southwest Collections.

416 Hudkins, Alonzo. *Oswald Rumored as Informant for U.S.*, Houston Post. January 1, 1964.

417 McCone, John. *Confidential Memorandum to James J. Rowley.* March 3, 1964, pp. 1-2.

418 Garrison, Jim Interview with *Gerry P. Hemming*, May 8, 1968.

419 Warren Commission Hearing and Exhibits, Document 1905, pp. 55-56.

420 Warren Commission Hearings and Exhibits, *Gary Taylor*, vol. IX, p. 73, Vol. XI p. 470.

421 Warren Commission Hearings and Exhibits, *Dennis Hyman Ofstein*. Vol. X p. 195.

422 Warren Commission Executive Session Transcript. January 27, 1964 p. 192.

423 Mellen, Joan. *Our Man in Haiti: George de Mohrenschildt and the CIA in the Nightmare Republic*, Oregon: Trine Day LLC, 2012, p. 121.

424 Ibid. p.172.

425 Marrs, Jim. *Crossfire*, New York, New York: Carroll & Graf Publishers, Inc., 1989, p. 287.

426 Hosty, James P. Jr. *Assignment: Oswald*. New York: Arcade Publishing, 2011, p. 40.

427 McShane, Larry. *New York Daily News, Dallas Homicide Det. Jim Leavelle, Captured in Iconic Image of Lee Harvey Oswald being Shot, Recalls Investigation*. November 17, 2013.

SECTION VI: DALLAS IN BLUNDERLAND

Chapter 39 End Notes:

428 *Dallas Times Herald*. November 23, 1963.

429 Hardy, Jack. Interview in person with the authors on April 19, 2015. All of his information and quotes are attributed to this interview.

430 Palamara, Vincent. Interview with the authors via telephone on October 18, 2016, and his book *Survivor's Guilt*, Chicago, Walterville, Oregon: Trine Day LLC, 2013, p.131. All of his information and quotes are attributed to this interview and when noted, his book.

431 Hardy. Interview.

432 Ibid.

Chapter 40 End Notes:

433 Flemmons, Jerry. *Turning Point the Assassination of President Kennedy, Fort Worth Star Telegram* November 20, 1983 p. 6F.

434 Poston, Bill. Interview in person with the authors on May 13, 2015. All of his information and quotes are attributed to this interview.

435 Wright, Eva. Interview in person with the authors on June 12, 2014. All of her information and quotes are attributed to this interview.

436 Cheever, Susan. *The Drunken Truth About the JFK Assassination*, www.newsweek.com., November 17, 2015

437 Manchester, William. *The Death of a President*, New York: Harper & Row, 1967, p.121.

438 Ibid. p.36.

439 Flemmons. p.7F.

Chapter 41 End Notes:

440 Manchester. p.37.

441 Warren Commission Hearings and Exhibits, *(James J. Rowley)*, Vol. V, p. 449.

442 HSCA, *Final Assassination Report*, p.228.

443 Bowden, Layte. Interviews with the authors via telephone and emails February 5, and 14, 2016. All information and quotes are attributed to these interviews.

444 McKinney, William. *Interview with Col. Fletcher Prouty. 112th Army Unit Ordered to "Stand Down" in Dallas*. Commentary for March, 1986.

445 Manchester. p. 41

446 Curry, Jesse. *JFK— The Assassination File*, Dallas, Texas: American Poster & Publishing Co., 1969, p.9.

447 Sloan, Bill. Interview In person with the author on May 13, 2015 and from his book, *JFK Breaking the Silence*, p.113. All of his information and quotes are attributed to this interview and when noted, his book.

448 Palamara. Interview and p. 326.

449 Bowen, Walter S. and Harry Edward Neal. *The United States Secret Service*, Philadelphia, Penn.: Chilton Company, 1960, p. 131.

450 Palamara. Interview and p.312.

451 Manchester. p.32.

452 Manchester. p.10.

453 Palamara. Interview and p.130.

454 Palamara. Interview and p.441.

455 Palamara. Interview and p.132.

456 Horne, Douglas. *Inside The ARRB*. Self-published, 2009.

457 Palamara. Interview and pp.263-264.

458 Palamara. Interview and p.27.

459 Turner, Nigel. *The Men Who Killed Kennedy*, Episode 9, DVD: England. November 2003.

460 Sloan. Interview and pp. 113-114.

461 Palamara. Interview and p.335.

462 Palamara, Vincent. *Interviews with Sam Kinney during October 1992 and March-April1994.*

Chapter 42 End Notes:

463 Peters, Shirley. Interview in person with the authors on September 29, 2013 and February 15, 2015. All of her information and quotes are attributed to these interviews.

Chapter 43 End Notes:

464 Loucks, Gary. You-tube

465 Loucks, Gary. Interview with the authors via telephone on September 12, 2015. All of his information and quotes are from this interview.

466 O'Neill, Tip. *Man of the House*, New York: Random House, 1987, p.178.

467 Connally, Nellie. *From Love Field*, New York: Rugged Land, L.L.C., 2003 p.119.

468 Ibid. p.119.

Chapter 44 End Notes:

469 Wean, Gareth. *There's A Fish in the Courthouse*, Cave Junction, Oregon: Casitas, 1987, p. 580.

470 Wean, Dorothy. Interview via telephone with the authors on January 14, 2014. All of her information and quotes are attributed to this interview.

471 Wean, Gareth. p. 584.

472 Wean, Dorothy. Interview.

473 Ibid.

474 Campbell, Iris. Interviews in person with the authors, September 28, 2013, June 12, 2014, August 20, 2014. All of her information and quotes are attributed to these interviews.

Chapter 45 End Notes:

475 Reeks, Anne. *Turning Point*, p.21 F.

476 Palamara. Interview and p.117.

477 Sneed, Larry. *No More Silence*, Dallas, Texas: Three Forks Press, 1998, p.224.

478 E. Gibbs, Interview in person with the authors on September 9, 2015. All of her information and quotes are attributed to this interview.

479 Walters, Interview with the authors via telephone on September 14, 2015. All of his information and quotes are attributed to this interview.

480 Ibid.

481 Ibid.

482 Ibid.

483 Ibid.

484 Ibid.

Chapter 46 End Notes

485 Boone, Eugene and Charmaine. Interview in person with the authors on December 19, 2013. All of their information and quotes are attributed to this interview.

486 Warren Commission Hearings and Exhibits *(Lee Bowers)* Vol. VI, p. 288.

487 You Tube interview, *Assassination Witness Lee Bowers Tells Mark Lane about Dealey Plaza and the Picket Fence*. March 31, 1966.

488 Perry, Dave. *Now It Can Be Told— The Lee Bowers Story*, McAdamsposc.mu.edu/bowers.text.

489 Boone. Interview.

Chapter 47 End Notes:

490 Warren Commission Hearings and Exhibits *2169*, Vol. XXIV, p.829.

491 Warren Commission Hearings and Exhibits, Vol. XXIV, pp.829, 831.

492 Heindel, John Rene. *Affidavit*, May 19, 1964.

493 Warren Commission Hearings and Exhibits *773*, Vol. XVII, p.635.

494 Craig, Roger. *When They Kill a President*, 1971, p.16.

495 Boone. Interview.

496 Warren Commission Hearings and Exhibits, Vol X, pp. 645-646.

497 LaFontaine, Ray and Mary. *Oswald Talked*. 1996. Gretna, Louisiana: Pelican Publishing, p.374.

498 Warren Commission Hearings and Exhibits *3048*, Vol. XXVI, p.525.

499 Garrison, Jim. *On the Trail of the Assassins*, New York: Warner Books, 1988, p. 115

500 Warren Commission Hearings and Exhibits *3048*, Vol. XXVI, p.525.

501 Frazier, Buel Wesley. Interview in person with the authors on May 15, 2015 and via telephone on May 30, 2015. All of his information and quotes are attributes to these interviews.

502 Warren Commission Hearings and Exhibits, Vol. VII, p. 388.

503 Johnson, Tom. *Dallas Morning News*, July 16, 1963.

Chapter 48 End Notes:

504 Gower, Paul. Interviews in person, via telephone and emails with the authors on March 20, 2015, April 17 and 20, 2015, September 28, 2015. All of his information and quotes are from these interviews.

505 Warren Commission Hearings and Exhibits *(Vincent Drain)*, Vol. XXVI, pp.832-833.

506 Warren Commission Hearings and Exhibits *(Robert Frazier)*, Vol. X, p.550.

507 Gower.

508 Warren Commission Hearings and Exhibits, Vol. X pp.566.

509 Warren Commission Hearings and Exhibits *(Robert Frazier)*

510 Agent X. Interview with the authors via telephone on May 12, 2015.

Chapter 49 End Notes:

511 Peters, Danny. Interview in person with the

authors on September 29, 2013 and February 15, 2015. All of his information and quotes are attributed to these interviews.

Chapter 50 End Notes:

512 Warren Commission Hearings and Exhibits (*Glen D. King*). Vol. XX p.462.

513 Gibson, Lois. *Presentation of the Tramps*, You-Tube, May 16, 2014. Interview with the authors via telephone on December 16, 2016.

514 Brunson, Doyle. Interview with the authors via telephone on April 19, 2017. All of his information and quotes are from this interview.

515 HSCA, *Marvin Wise Testimony*, November 14, 1977.

516 Dallas Police Transcript of Dispatcher's Radio Log. All quotes involving this radio log were found in Waggoner Carr's papers, Waggoner Carr Collection, Texas Tech Southwest Collections.

517 Ibid.

518 Marrs, Jim. Interview November 21, 2015 and his book *Crossfire*, p.354.

519 Smith, Matthew. *JFK: Say Goodbye to America*. Edinburgh, England: Mainstream Publishing, 2004, p.182.

520 Ibid. p. 186.

Chapter 51 End Notes:

521 Hosty, James P. Jr., and Thomas Hosty. *Assignment: Oswald*, New York: Arcade Publishing, 2011, p. 21.

522 Ibid. p. 31.

523 Official statement by Ural E. Horton, Jr. to FBI Inspector J. Allison Conley, July 23, 1975, Buffalo, Wyoming, p. 2

524 Katzenbach, Nicholas. *Memorandum to William Moyers,* November 25, 1963.

525 Jones, Penn. Forgive My Grief Vol III. Midlothian, Texas: Midlothian Mirrow, Inc. 1976, p. 101.

526 Hoover, J. Edgar. *FBI Memorandum to Mr. Tolson, Mr. Belmont, etc*. Washington, D.C., November 29, 1963, p. 3.

Chapter 52 End Notes:

527 Gordon, Joyce McDonald. Interview in person with the authors on November 21, 2013, and via telephone on September 20, 2013. All of her information and quotes are attributed to these interviews.

528 Dallas Morning News. *Reunited with Ruby in mural*...November 1, 2009.

529 Gordon. Interviews.

530 Cartwright. p.85.

531 Covert History. http://coverthistory.blogspot.

com/2007/09/jack-ruby-stripper-jada.html, September 19, 2007, pp. 1-2.

532 Gordon. Interviews.

SECTION VII: THE SHADOWY WORLD OF JACK RUBY

Chapter 53 End Notes:

533 Cartwright, Gary. *Who Was Jack Ruby?* Texas Monthly, November 1975, p.84.

534 Joesten. p. 177.

535 Warrren Report Appendix XVI. *Biography of Jack Ruby*, p.462.

536 Joesten, Joachim. *Oswald: Assassin or Fall Guy,* New York: Iconoclassic Books, 2012, p. 174.

537 *The 20th Century— Through the Eyes of Texas*, Supplement to *the Dallas Morning News*, September 22, 1999, Section R.

538 Barney, Mel. Interview with the authors via telephone on November 17, 2016 and his book, *Four Wars,* Farmers Branch, Texas: Merit Books, 2011.pp. 171-172. All of his information and quotes are attributed to these interviews and when noted, his book.

539 Cartwright, Gary. *Who Was Jack Ruby?* Texas Monthly, November 1975, p.5.

540 Singsong, J. J. Interview in person with the authors on May 12, 2015 and via telephone and emails on July 25, 2014, May 20, 2015, and June 2, 2015. All of her information and quotes are attributed to these interviews.

541 Schwarz, Ted and Mardi Rustam. *Candy Barr,* New York: Taylor Trade Publishing, 2008, p. 48.

542 Ibid. p.49.

543 *Adam*, Winter 1962, Los Angles, California: Knight Publishing Corp. p. 39.

544 Ibid. p. 40.

545 Ibid p. 40.

Chapter 54 End Notes:

546 Stephenson, Duke. Interview with the authors via telephone on February 12, 2014. All of his information and quotes are attributed to this interview.

547 Thorpe, Milton. Interview in person with the authors on January 10, 2014 and via telephone March 14, 2016. All of his information and quotes are attributed to these interviews.

548 Stephenson. Interview.

549 Thorpe. Interviews.

550 Stephenson. Interview.

Chapter 55 End Notes:

551 Schwarz. pp. 48, 256, 278

552 Ibid. p.262.

553 Singsong. Interviews.

554 Taylor, George. *John Simpkin Spartacus Educational website*. June 11, 2011.

555 Singsong. Interviews.

556 Engleberg, Morris. *DiMaggio on Setting the Record Straight*, St. Paul, MN: Kroywen Associates, Inc., 2003, pp. 282-283.

557 Kantor, Seth. *Who Was Jack Ruby?* Everest House, 1978.

Chapter 56 End Notes:

558 Hall, Ralph. Interview with the authors via telephone on March 22, 2014. All of his information and quotes are attributed to this interview.

Chapter 57 End Notes:

559 Marrs, Jim. *Crossfire*, New York, New York: Carroll & Graf Publishers, Inc., 1989, p. 404.

560 FBI Interviews. Herbert B. Braden by SA Paul L. Scott Jr. File # DL-44-1639 November 28, 1963.

561 FBI Interviews. Raymond Lester, Jr., and Paul L. Scott, Jr. with Dorothy Markham and Billie Irene Hadley. File number # DL-441639. November 28, 1963.

562 FBI Airtel for SAC, San Francisco, California, (105-16814) RE: Lee Harvey Oswald, November 28, 1966.

563 Armstrong, John. *Harvey and Lee*, Arlington, Texas: Quasar, ltd, 2003 p. 555.

564 Statement from DPD H. M. Hart to Captain Gannaway December 3, 1963.

565 Marrs. p. 409.

566 Ibid. p. 406.

567 Abrams, Malcolm. *JFK Murder Hatched in Ruby's Club— Oswald was there. Midnigh*t. November 15, 1976.

568 Ibid.

569 Ibid.

570 Marrs. Jim. Author Interviews with *Ester Ann Mash* summer and fall 1988, pp. 408-409.

571 Armstrong. p. 554.

572 Bill Cherry. Interviews in person and via telephone with the authors on November 18, 2018 and December 13, 2018. All of his information and quotes are attributed to these interviews.

573 Ibid. p. 767.

574 Jones, Penn. *Forgive My Grief, Vol III*, Midlothian, Texas: Midlothian Mirror, Inc. 1976, p. 103.

575 Albarelli, H. P. Jr., *A Secret Order, Walterville*, Oregon: Trine Day, 2013, p. 97.

576 H. M. Hart to Captain W. P. Gannaway.

Criminal Intelligence Report December 2, 1963.

577 Armstrong. p. 789.

578 *Dallas Archive Police Report.*

Chapter 58 End Notes:

579 Worthington, Peter. *The Jack Ruby Mystery: Dubious Public Avenger*, Toronto Star Telegram, November 28, 1963, p. 3.

580 Wean, Gareth. *There's A Fish in the Courthouse*, Cave Junction, Oregon: Casitas Books, 1987, p. 567.

581 Messick, Hank. *Lansky*, London: Robert Hale & Co., 1973

582 Worthington.

583 Scheim, David. *Contract on America, the Mafia Murder of President John F. Kennedy*, New York New York: Shapolsky Publishers, Inc. 1988, pp. 94-98.

584 Warren Commission Document 84, pp. 91-92, and Scheim. pp. 98-99.

585 Curington, John, Mitchel Whitington. *H. L. Hunt— Motive & Opportunity*, USA: 23 House Publishing, 2018, pp. 111-112.

586 Ibid. pp. 115-116.

587 Ibid. pp. 116-117.

588 Ibid. p. 117.

589 Ibid. p. 122.

590 JFK ASSASSINATION SYSTEM IDENTIFICATION FORM, FILE # 62-9-12-290,291, p. 2.

591 Patoski, Joe Nick. *The King of Clubs*, April 2000, www.texasmonthly.com.

592 Scheim. p. 101.

593 Ibid. p. 97, and Moldea, *The Hoffa Wars*, pg.112, Brill, *The Teamsters* p. 131.

594 Malone, William Scott. *The Secret Life of Jack Ruby*, New Times. January 23, 1978. p. 51.

595 Fulson, Don. *Richard Nixon's Greatest Cover-Up: His Ties to the Assassination of President Kennedy*: surftofind.com/mob.

596 Stone, Roger. *The Man Who Killed Kennedy. The Case against LBJ,* New York: Skyhorse Publishing, 2013, p. 18.

597 Giancana, Sam and Chuck. *Double Cross,* New York: Warner Books, Inc., 1992, p. 287.

598 Stephenson. Interview.

599 Worthington. p. 3.

600 Intelligence Report April 11, 1956.

Chapter 59 End Notes:

601 Barney. Interviews and his book.

602 Sneed, Larry A. *Video interview with Al Maddox*, 1998.

SECTION VIII: THE DIXIE MAFIA: DEEP IN THE HEART OF TEXAS

Chapter 60 End Notes:

603 Hayworth, Jim. Interview in person with the authors on September 10, 2013. All of his information and quotes are attributed to this interview.

604 Dene Sheppard. Interview in person with the authors on September 2, and 8, 2013. All of her information and quotes are attributed to these interviews.

605 Dene Sheppard. Interview.

606 Weaver, Boosie. Interview in person with the authors on July 19, 2014. All of his information and quotes are attributed to this interview.

607 Dene Sheppard. Interview.

608 Ibid.

609 Ibid.

610 Weaver, Boosie. Interview.

611 Ibid.

612 Smith, Lonnie. Interview with the authors via telephone on July 3, 2014. All of his information and quotes are attributed to this interview.

613 Ibid.

614 Legal Document filed in District Court Howard County: *Complaint NO. 11,910* June 17, 1959

615 Ibid.

Chapter 61 End Notes:

616 Mitchell, Al. Interview in person with the authors on April 10, 2014. All of his quotes come from this interview.

617 Brouillette, Frenchy and Matthew Randazzov. *Mr. New Orleans*, no publisher listed, 2014, p. 346.

618 *B'Spring Victim in Dixie Mafia. Abilene Reporter News*, Oct 1, 1970.

619 Ewell, James. *Police Crackdown on Outsiders Set, Dallas Morning News*, November 6 1969, p. 12A.

620 Weaver, James. Interview in person with the authors on July 19, 2014. All of his information and quotes are attributed to this interview.

621 Mitchell. Interview.

622 Ibid.

623 *Big Spring Man Linked with 'Dixie Mafia' Gang. Dallas Morning News*, October 1 1970.

624 Currie, John. Interviews in person with the authors on March 29, 2014, and July 12, 2014. Interview via telephone on September 13, 2013. All of his information and quotes are attributed to these interviews.

625 Oliver, Beverly. Interview in person with the authors on March 29, 2014, Small group discussions on November 21, 2014, and her book, *Nightmare in Dallas*, Lancaster, Pennsylvania: Starburst Publishers, 1994 p.143. All of her information and quotes are attributed to these interviews and when noted, her book.

626 Currie. Interviews.

627 Brunson, Doyle. Interview with the authors via telephone on April 19, 2017. All of his information and quotes are from this interview.

628 Ibid.

629 Hart, Clifford. Interview in person with the authors on July 11, 2014. All of his information and quotes are attributed from this interview.

630 Ibid.

631 Mesker, Robert. Interviews in person with the authors on February 20, 2015, and September 12, 2015. All of his information and quotes are attributed to these interviews.

632 Ibid.

633 Special Agent Lansing's FBI interview with Warren Gammon. File # DL 44-1639 on December 17, 1983.

634 Oliver. Interviews and her book *Nightmare in Dallas*, pp. 151-152.

Chapter 62 End Notes:

635 Hayworth, Jim. Interview.

636 Oliver. Interview and *Nightmare in Dallas*.

637 Currie, John. Interviews.

638 Hayworth, Jim. Interview

639 Interview with Big Spring native "A" who insists on anonymity, via telephone with authors July 20, 2014. All of his information and quotes are attributed to this interview.

640 Etchison, Taylor. Interview in person with the authors on March 3, 2014. All of his information and quotes are attributed to this interview.

641 Hayworth. Interview.

642 Johnson, Jimmy. Interview in person with the authors on July 11, 2014. All of his information and quotes are attributed to this interview.

643 Mesker. Interviews.

644 Dene Sheppard. Interviews.

645 Ibid.

646 Weaver, James. Interview.

647 Weaver, Boosie. Interview.

648 Fulgham, Roe. Interview in person with the authors on December 19, 2013. All of his information and quotes are attributed to this

interview.

649 Currie. Interviews.

650 Big Spring native "A"Interview.

651 Ibid.

652 Currie. Interviews.

653 Mesker. Interviews

654 Huckabee, John. Interview in person with the authors on April 25, 2014. All of his information and quotes are attributed to this interview.

655 McMorran, San Jose Dick. *A Bad Day In Dallas*, Bankingwiththebeard.com.

656 Fulgham. Interview.

657 Reback, Storms. *From the Poker Vaults: Texas Boss Gamblers*, Poker News.com 2009 p. 3.

658 Big Spring native "A" Interview.

659 Hughes, Johnny, Hugh. *George McGann: Gambler, Con Man, Hit Man, Kennedy Assassin?* Virtuallubbock, 2007.

660 Mesker. Interview.

661 Big Spring native "A" interview.

662 Ibid.

663 Interview with Big Spring native "B" who insists on anonymity, via telephone with the authors on July 21, 2014. All of his information and quotes are attributed to this interview.

Chapter 63 End Notes:

664 Currie. Interviews.

665 Rogers, Nell. Interview in person with the authors on June 16, 2014. All of her information and her quotes are attributed to this interview.

666 Weaver, James. Interview.

667 Big Spring native "A" interview.

668 Tonn, Mona Lue. Interview in person with the authors on July 19, 2014. All of her information and quotes are attributed to this interview.

669 Hitchcock, Joe. *Lubbock Avalanche*, September 30, 1970.

670 Big Spring native "A" interview.

671 *Big Spring Herald*. October 1, 1970

672 Oliver. Interviews and *Nightmare in Dallas*.

673 *Big Spring Herald*. October 1, 1970.

674 Ibid.

Chapter 64 End Notes:

675 Dene Sheppard. Interview.

676 Big Spring native "B" interview.

677 Huckabee. Interview.

678 McGann, George. *Funeral Guest Book Registry*.

679 *Odessa American* October 6, 1970.

680 Hughes, Johnny. Virtuallubbock.

Chapter 65 End Notes:

681 Letter from John Judge to Ed Sherry. May 21, 2001. Radical.org/ratville/JFK/John Judge/sewerShot.html

682 Mesker. Interviews.

683 Hughes, Johnny. Virtuallubbock.

SECTION IX: THE WEST TEXAS CONNECTION

Chapter 66 End Notes:

684 McFadden, Robert D. *Billie sol Estes, Texas Con Man Whose Fall Shook Up Washington, Dies at 88.* The New York Times, May 14, 2013.

685 Lasky, Victor. *It Didn't Start With Watergate*, New York, New York: Dial Press, 1977, p. 76.

686 *San Angelo Standard-Times*. April 5, 1962.

687 Michaelis, Fred. *Stay Quiet and Live*. Unpublished memoir.

688 Harvey, Paul. *Crossfire, Pecos Independent and Enterprise*. June 25, 1962.

689 Mangham, Jim. Interview with the authors through emails on October 24, 2015. All of his information and quotes are attributed to these emails.

690 McSwain, Ross. Wornout Memories, Ballinger, Texas, 2011, p 79.

691 de Toledano, Ralph. *R.F.K. The Man Who Would Be President*. New York: Signet 1967, p. 223.

692 Goolsby, Sue. Interview with the authors via telephone on June 11, 2016. All of her information and quotes are attributed to this interview.

693 Interview in person with a person who insists on anonymity. September 20, 2015.

Chapter 67 End Notes:

694 Anonymous Editor. Interview in person with the authors July 18, 2015. All of her information and quotes are attributed to this interview.

695 Anonymous Editor. Interview in person with the authors July 18, 2015.

Chapter 68 End Notes:

696 Bretz, Ben. Interview in person with the authors on December 8, 2013. And Interview In-Person with Milton Thorpe on January 10, 2014. All of their information and quotes are attributed to these interviews.

697 Lee, Deb. Interview with the authors via telephone on September 2016 and emails October 12, 13, 24, 2016. All of her information and quotes are attributed to these interviews.

698 Bretz, Ben. Interview In-Person with the authors on December 8, 2013. And Interview In-

Person with Milton Thorpe on January 10, 2014.

699 Lee. Interview.

700 Interview in via telephone with an associate of Jim Bolden who insists on anonymity, October 1, 2018.

Chapter 69 End Notes:

701 White, Ricky and Tricia. Interview in person with the authors on July 26, 2014 and in various emails on July 30, 2014, August 29, 2015, august 25, 2015, May 19, 2017 and May 19, 2017. All of their information and quotes are attributed to this interview and the emails.

702 Ibid

703 McConnell, Nina. Interview with the authors via telephone on February 18, 2015. All of her information and quotes are attributed to this interview.

704 Ladd, Jack. Interview in person with the authors on April 18, 2014. All of his information and quotes are attributed to this interview

705 Weatherby, Ray. Interview via telephone with authors in June 2015. All of his information and quotes are attributed to this interview.

706 Shaw, J. Gary. Interviews in person with the authors on July 25, 2014, March 19, 2015 and November 20, 2015, via telephone on November 3, 2013, and September 23, 2014, and through several emails from September 28 2015 to July 15, 2017. All of his information and quotes are attributed to these interviews.

707 Cartwright, Gary. *I Was Mandarin*, Texas Monthly December 1990 p.13.

708 Luckie, J. D. Interview with the authors via telephone on October 18, 2017. All of his information and quotes are attrivuted to this interview.

709 Nagel, John M. *Video Taped Interview with Mike Robinson*, 1993.

710 Ibid.

711 Ibid.

712 Brown, Walt. *Treachery in Dallas,* New York: Carroll & Graff Publishers, Inc., 1995, p. 188.

713 Nagel, *Video Taped Interview with Mike Robinson, 1993.*

714 Smith, Suzahn. Interview via telephone on May 5, 2014. All of her information and quotes are attributed to this interview.

Chapter 70 End Notes:

715 All of the information from the newscasters are attributed to Suzahn Smith's interviews and to the actual newscasters' televised documentary series and transcript.

716 Ladd. Interview.

717 Smith.Suzahn. Interview.

EPILOGUE: SHADOWS From THE PAST

718 Hougan, Jim. Spooks, pp. 124, 130-131.

719 Giancana, Sam and Chuck. *Double Cross,* New York: Warner Books, Inc., 1992, p. 143.

720 Tarby, Russ. *JFK in Dallas: The Syracuse Connections*, Syracuse, New York: *New Times*, 2013.

721 Ibid.

722 Collier, Peter and David Horowitz. *The Kennedys: An American Drama*, New York: Warner Books, 1984, p. 319.

723 Evans, Peter. *Nemesis*, New York, New York: HarperCollins Publishers, 2004, p. 282.

724 Lincoln, Evelyn, *Secret Lives: Jackie*. Barraclough-Carey Productions for Channel Four and Discovery Communication, 1995.

725 Taraborrelli, J. Randy. *Jackie Ethel Joan*, New York: Warner Books, 2000, pp. 563-564.

726 Belzer, Richard and David Wayne. Hit List, New York: Skyhorse Publishiing, 2013, p. 145.

727 Janney, Peter. July 29, 2007, The Education Forum: *Mary Pinchot Meyer*.

728 Shaw, Mark. *The Reporter Who Knew Too Much*, Franklin, TN: Post Hill Press, 2016, p. 94.

729 Ibid. pp. 99-107.

730 Meros, Tom. *Interview with James Jenkins*. www.tommeros.com

731 Campbell, Iris. Interviews in person with the authors, September 28, 2013, June 12, 2014, August 20, 2014. All of her information and quotes are attributed to these interviews

732 Phillips, Donald T., *A Deeper, Darker Truth,* Illinois, DTP/Companion Books, 2009, p. 145.

733 Ibid.

734 Ibid.

735 Ibid. p. 146.

736 Thomas, Dylan. *The Hand That Signed the Paper*. www.poemhunter.com.

737 Coley, Jerry. Interview with the authors via telephone on April 26, 2017. All of his information and quotes are attributed to this interview.

INDEX

BIBLIOGRAPHY

Abrams, Malcolm. *JFK Murder Hatches in Ruby's Club—Oswald Was There,* Midnight. November 15, 1976.

Albarelli, H. P. Jr., *A Secret Order,* Waterville, Oregon: Trine Day, 2013.

Anderson, Christopher. *Jack and Jackie: Portrait of an American Marriage,* New York, New York: William Morrow and Company, Inc., 1996.

Armstrong, John. *Harry & Lee,* Arlington, Texas: Quasar, Ltd, 2003.

Arvad, Inga. *Papers of John F. Kennedy, Personal Papers. Correspondence, 1933-1950: Friends.* Arvad, Inga. Presidential Library and Museum: Boston, Massachusetts.

Baker, Judith. *David Ferrie,* Waterville, Oregon: TrineDay Publishers, 2014.

—*Me and Lee,* Waterville, Oregon: TrineDay Publishers, 2010.

Baker, Russ. *Family of Secrets,* New York, New York: Bloomsbury Press, 2009.

Barney, Mel. *Four Wars,* Farmers Branch, Texas: Merit Books, 2011.

Belzer, Richard. *Dead Wrong,* New York, New York: Skyhorse Publishing, 2012.

Beschloss, Michael R. *Taking Charge—the Johnson White House Tapes,* New York: Simon & Schuster, 1997.

Big Spring Man Linked with 'Dixie Mafia' Gang, Dallas Morning News, October 1, 1970.

B'Spring Victim in Dixie Mafia, Abilene Reporter-News, October 1, 1970.

Blaine, Gerald. *The Kennedy Detail,* New York, New York: Gallery Books, 2010.

Blakey, G. Robert. *Fatal Hour,* New York, New York: Berkley Books, 1981.

Bolden, Abraham. *The Echo from Dealey Plaza,* New York, New York: Three Rivers Press, 2008.

Bowden, Layte. *Under the Radar during Camelot,* Miami, Florida: Figleaf Ltd, 2013.

Bradford, Sarah. *America's Queen,* New York: Penguin Books, 2000.

Brooks, Elston. *An Arrest He'll Never Forget,* The Fort Worth Star-Telegram, November 20, 1983.

Brottman, Mikita. *Car Crash Culture,* New York, New York: Palgrave, 2001.

Bridger, Mark. *Who Was Igor Vaganov?* The Dealey Plaza Echo.

Brown, Madeleine Duncan. *Texas in the Morning,* Baltimore, MD: The Conservatory Press, 1997.

Brussells, Mae. www.maebrussells.com, *Last Words of Lee Oswald.*

Bugliosi, Vincent. *Reclaiming History,* New York, New York: W.W. Norton and Company, 2007.

Cameron, Gail. *Rose,* New York, New York: Berkley Publishing Corp., 1971.

Canal, John. *Silencing the Lone Assassin,* St. Paul, Minnesota: Paragon House, 2000.

Caro, Robert A. *Means of Ascent - Years of Lyndon Johnson,* New York: Alfred A. Knopf, 1990.

Carr, Waggoner. *Personal Letter to Texas Senator Lloyd Bentson September 9, 1975.* Texas Tech University Library, Southwest Special Collections.

Cartwright, Gary. *I Was Mandarin,* Texas Monthly, Texas Monthly Press, December, 1990.

—*Who Was Jack Ruby?* Texas Monthly, Texas Monthly Press, November 1975.

Chellis, Marcia. *The Joan Kennedy Story-- Living with the Kennedys,* New York, New York: Jove Publishing, 1986.

Cheever, Susan. *The Drunken Truth about the JFK Assassination,* www.newsweek. com., November 17, 2015.

Collier, Peter, & David Horowitz. *The Kennedys: An American Drama,* New York, New York: Warner Books, 1984.

Complaint No. 11, 910, District Court of Howard County, Big Spring, Texas, June 17, 1959

Connally, Nellie. *That Day in Dallas,* speech delivered in 2003 from website by Robert Rees.

—*From Love Field,* New York: Rugged Land, L.L.C., 2003.

Covert History. http://coverthistory.blogspot. com/2007/09/jack-ruby-stripper-jada.html, September 19, 2007.

Craig, John R., Phil D. Rogers. *The Man on the Grassy Knoll,* New York: Avon Books, 1992.

Craig, Roger. *When They Kill a President,* unpublished manuscript, 1971.

Crenshaw, Charles A., M.D., *JFK-- Conspiracy of Silence,* New York, New York: Signet, 1992.

Curry, Jesse. *JFK—The Assassination File,* Dallas, Texas: American Poster & Publishing Company, 1969.

Dallas Police Transcript of Dispatcher's Radio Log. Waggoner Carr Collection, Texas Tech University Library-- Southwest Collections.

Dallas, Rita and Jeanira Ratcliffe. *The Kennedy Case.* New York: Popular Library, 1973.

David, Lester and Irene David. *Bobby Kennedy, the Making of a Folk Hero,* New York: Dodd, Mead & Co., 1986.

Davis, John H. *Mafia Kingfish: Carlos Marcello*

and the Assassination of John F. Kennedy, New York, New York: McGraw Hill, 1989.

Davis, Robert T. Memorandum to Texas Attorney General Waggoner Carr, 1964, Texas Tech University, Library of the Southwest—Special Collections.

Day, George A. Juanita Dale Slusher Alias Candy Barr, Brownwood, Texas: ERBE Publishing Company, 2009.

De Toledano, Ralph. R.F.K.—The Man Who Would Be President, New York: Signet, 1967.

DiEugenio, James. Destiny Betrayed, New York, New York: Skyhorse Publishing, 2012.

—Reclaiming Parkland, New York, New York: Skyhorse Publishing, 2013.

—Rose Cheramie: How She Predicted the JFK Assassination, Probe, Vol. 6, No. 5, July-August, 1999.

Douglas, Gary. Regicide, Huntsville, Alabama: Monte Sano Media, 2002.

Douglas, James W. JFK and the Unspeakable— Why He Died and Why It Matters, New York: Simon & Schuster, 2008.

Drenas, Bill. An Overlooked Texas Theatre Witness, www.billdrenas.com, 2009.

Eddowes, Michael. The Oswald File, New York, New York: Clarkson N. Potter, Inc. 1977.

Elliott, Todd C. A Rose By Many Other Names: Rose Cherami and the JFK Assassination, Walterville, Oregon: TrineDay, 2013.

Engleberg, Morris. DiMaggio—On Setting the Record Straight, St. Paul, Minnesota: Kroywen Associates, Inc., 2003.

Epstein, Edward Jay. Inquest—the Warren Commission and the Establishment of Truth, New York: Bantam Books, 1966.

—Legend: The Secret World of Lee Harvey Oswald, New York, New York, McGraw Hill, 1978.

Ernest, Barry. The Girl on The Stairs, Gretna, Louisiana, Pelican Publishing Co., 2013.

Evans, Peter. Nemesis, New York, New York: HarperCollins Publishers, 2004.

Ewell, James. Police Crackdown on Outsiders Set, Dallas Morning News, November 6, 1969.

Farris, Scott. Inga, Guilford, Connecticut: Rowman & Littlefield, 2016.

Fiester, Sherry. P. Enemy of the Truth—Myths, Forensics, and the Kennedy Assassination, Southlake, Texas: JFK Lancer Productions & Publications, Inc., 2012.

Flemmons, Jerry. Turning Point: The Assassination of President Kennedy, Fort Worth Star-Telegram, November 20, 1983.

Fonzi, Gaeton. The Lost Investigation, New York, New York: Thunder's Mouth Press, 1993.

Fuhrman, Mark, A Simple Act of Murder, New York: William Morrow, 2006.

Fulsom, Don. Richard Nixon's Greatest Cover-up: His Ties to the Assassination of President Kennedy, surftofind.com/mob.

Galbraith, John Kenneth. Ambassador's Journal, Boston, MS.: Houghton Mifflin Company, 1969.

Gallagher, Mary Barelli. My Life with Jacqueline Kennedy, New York, New York: David McKay Company, Inc., 1969.

Garrison, Jim. On the Trail of the Assassins, New York, New York: Warner Books, 1988.

Gatewood, Jim. Captain Will Fritz and the Dallas Mafia, Garland, Texas: Mullaney Corp. 2004.

— Sheriff Bill Decker a Texas Legend, Garland, Texas: Mullaney Corp. 1999.

Gentry, Curt, J. Edgar Hoover—the Man and His Secrets, New York: W. W. Norton & Co., 1991.

Giancana, Sam and Chuck. Double Cross, New York, New York: Warner Books, Inc., 1992.

Gibson, Lois. Presentation of the Tramps, You-Tube, May 16, 2014.

Gillon, Steven M. Lee Harvey Oswald 48 Hours to Live, New York, New York: Sterling Publisher, 2013.

Golz, Earl. Confidential: The FBI's File on JFK— Part Two. Cover-Up, December 1992.

Groden, Robert J. The Killing of a President, New York, New York: Penguin Group, 1994.

—The Search for Lee Harvey Oswald, New York, New York: Penguin Group, 1995.

Groden, Robert and Harrison Livingson. High Treason, New York, New York: Berkley Books, 1990.

Haley, J. Evetts. A Texan Looks at Lyndon, Canyon, Texas: Palo Duro Press, 1964.

Hancock, Larry. The Man in the Middle. Kennedy Assassination Chronicles, Vol. 5 Issue 4, Winter 1999.

Harvey, Paul. Crossfire, Pecos Independent and Enterprise, June 25, 1962.

Haslam, Edward T. Dr. Mary's Monkey, Waterville, Oregon: TrineDay Publishers, 2007.

Hyde, Wayne. What Does a Secret Service Agent Do? New York: Dodd, Mead, and Co., 1962

Hersh Seymour. The Dark Side of Camelot, New York, New York: Little Brown, & Company, 1997.

Hershman, D. Jablow. Power Beyond Reason: The Mental Collapse of Lyndon Johnson, New Jersey: Barricade Books, Inc., 2002.

Heymann, C. David, Bobby and Jackie, New York, New York: Atria, 2009

Hill, Clint. Mrs. Kennedy and Me, New York, New York: Gallery Books, 2012.

Hinkle, Warren and William Turner. Deadly Secrets:

The CIA-Mafia War against Castro and the Assassination of J.F.K., New York, New York: Thunder's Mouth Press, 1992.

Holland, Brent. *JFK Assassination: From the Oval Office to Dealey Plaza*, Southlake, Texas: JFK Lancer Production and Publication, 2013.

Holm, Axel. *Nogales Woman Had Intimate Connection with Kennedy.* NogalesInternationa.com. November 22, 2013.

Horne, Douglas. *Inside the AARB.* Self-published, 2009.

Hosty, James P. Jr. *Assignment: Oswald*, New York: Arcade Publishing, 2011.

Hougan, Jim. *Spooks—The Haunting of America—The Private Use of Secret Agents.* New York: William Morrow and Company, Inc., 1978.

Hudkins, Alonzo. *Oswald Rumored as Informant for U.S.*, Houston Post, January 1, 1964.

Hughes, Johnny. *George McGann: Gambler, Con Man, Hit Man, Kennedy Assassin?*

VirtualLubbock, 2007.

Hyde, Wayne. *What Does a Secret Service Agent Do?* New York: Dodd, Mead, and Co., l962.

Jackson, Gayle Nix. Orville Nix: The Missing JFK Assassination Film, United States: Semper Ad Meliora Publishing, 2014.

James, Rosemary & Jack Wardlaw. *Plot or Politics? The Garrison Case and Its Cast*, New Orleans, Louisiana: Pelican Publishing, 1967.

Janney, Peter. *Mary's Mosaic*, New York, New York: Skyhorse Publishing, 2012.

Joestein, Joachim. *Oswald: Assassin or Fall Guy?* Iconoclassic Books, 2012.

Johnson, Tom. *Dallas Morning News*, July 16, 1963.

Johnston, James P. and Jon Roe, *Flight from Dallas*, Bloomington, Indiana: 1stBooks, 2003.

Jones, Penn, Jr. *Forgive My Grief III*, Midlothian, Texas: Midlothian Mirror, Inc. 1976.

Katzenbach, Nicholas. *Memorandum to William Moyer,* November 25, 1963.

"Listening In" The Secret White House Recordings of John F. Kennedy. New York, New York: John F. Kennedy Library Foundation Inc., 2012

Kessler, Ronald. *In the President's Secret Service*, New York, New York: Random House, 2010.

—*The Secret of the FBI*, New York, New York: Random House, 2012.

Kritzberg, Constance. *Secrets from the Sixth Floor Window*, www.jfk.online.com/alyea.html.

Kritzberg Constance and Larry Hancock. *November Patriots-- the Murder of John Kennedy*, Colorado Springs, Co: Undercover Press, 1998.

La Fontaine, Ray and Mary. *Oswald Talked*, Gretna, Louisiana: Pelican Publishing Co., l996.

Lambert, Patricia. *The Continuing Inquiry*, vol. 2, 1977.

Lane, Duke. *The Cowtown Connection*, mcadams. posc.mu.edu/Cowtown.txt, l993.

Lane, Mark. *Plausible Denial*, New York, New York: Thunder's Mouth Press, 1991.

—*Rush to Judgement*, New York: Holt, Rinehart, & Winston, 1964.

Lasky, Victor. *JFK: The Man and the Myth*, New York, New York: Macmillan Company, 1963.

—*It Didn't Start with Watergate*, New York, New York: Dial Press, l977.

Latell, Brian. *Castro's Secrets—The CIA and Cuba's Intelligence Machine*, New York: Palgrave MacMillan, 2012.

Law, William Matson with Allan Eaglesham. *In the Eye of History— Disclosures in the JFK Assassination Medical Evidence,* Southlake, Texas: JFK Lancer Productions and Publications, Inc. 2005.

Lawford, Patricia Seaton. *The Peter Lawford Story*, New York, New York: Jove Books, 1990.

Leaming, Barbara. *Jacqueline Bouvier Kennedy Onassis: The Untold Story*, New York, New York: Thomas Dunne Book, 2014.

David, Lester and Irene David. *Bobby Kennedy, the Making of a Folk Hero*. New York, New York: Dodd, Mead & Co. 1986.

Lewis, Dan. *The Kennedy Assassin Who Failed*, Smithsonian.com, December 6, 2012.

Lifton, David. S. *Best Evidence*, New York, New York: MacMillan Publishing Co., 1980.

Lincoln, Evelyn. *Kennedy & Johnson*, New York: H. H. Rinehart and Winston, l968.

—*Secret Lives: Jackie,* Barraclough-Carey Productions for Channel Four and Discovery Communications, 1995.

—Signed Firsthand Account Letter, RR Auction, October, 2013.

Livingstone, Harrison E. *High Treason 2*, New York, New York: Carroll and Graf Publishers, Inc. 1992.

—*The Radical Right and the Murder of John F. Kennedy*, Victoria B.C. Canada: Trafford, 2004.

McClellan, Barr. *Blood, Money and Power*, New York, New York: Skyhorse Publishing, 2011.

McDonald, Hugh C. *Appointment in Dallas,* New York, New York: Kensington Publishing, 1975.

McElwain-Brown, Pamela. *SS-100-X, Car Crash Culture*, New York: Palgrave editor Brottman, Mikita, 2001.

McFadden, Robert D. *Billie Sol Estes, Con Man Whose Fall Shook Up Washington, Dies at 88*, The

New York Times, May 14, 2013.

McKinney, William. Interview with Col. Fletcher Prouty. *112th Army Unit Ordered to 'Stand Down' in Dallas*, Commentary for March, l986.

McMillian, Priscilla Johnson. *Marina and Lee*, New York: Random House, 2013.

Mahoney, Richard D. *Sons & Brothers*. New York, New York: Arcade Publishing, 1999.

Malone, William Scott. *The Secret Life of Jack Ruby*, New Times, January 23, 1978.

Manchester, William. *The Death of a President*, New York: Harper & Row, l967.

Marcades, Michael. *Rose Cherami: Gathering Fallen Petals*, Southlake, Texas, JFK Lancer Productions and Publications, 2016.

Marrs, Jim. *Crossfire*, New York, New York: Carroll & Graf, 1989.

Martin, Ralph G. *A Hero for Our Time*, New York, New York: Ballatine Books, 1983.

Meagher, Sylvia. *Accessories After the Fact*, New York, New York: Skyhorse Publishing, 1967.

Mellen, Joan. *Faustian Bargains*, New York, New York: Bloomsbury Publishing, 2016.

—*Our Man in Haiti*, Walterville, Oregon: Trine Day LLC, 2012.

—*A Farewell to Justice*, New York: Skyhorse Publishing, 2013.

Messick, Hank. *Lansky*, London: Robert Hale & Co., 1973.

Michaelis, Fred. *Stay Quiet and Live!* Unpublished memoir. Undated.

Milan, Michael. *The Squad: The US Government Secret Alliance with Organized Crime*, New York, New York: Shapolsky Publishers, Inc. 1989.

Morrow, Robert. *First Hand Knowledge: How I Participated in the CIA/Mafia Murder of President Kennedy*, New York: S.P.I. Books, 1992

Myers, Dale. *With Malice*, Milford, Michigan: Oak Cliff Press, Inc., 2013.

Nagel, John M. *Video Taped Interview with Mike Robinson*, 1993.

Nelson, Phillip F. *LBJ: From Mastermind to "The Colossus"*, New York, New York: Skyhorse Publishing, 2014.

— *LBJ: The Mastermind of the JFK Assassination*, New York, New York: Skyhorse Publishing, 2013.

O'Donnell, Kenneth P. and David Powers. "*Johnny, We Hardly Knew Ye*", Boston, MA: Little, Brown & Company, 1970.

Oliver, Beverly with Coke Buchanan. *Nightmare in Dallas*, Lancaster, Pennsylvania: Starburst Publishers, l994.

O'Neill, Tip. *Man of the House*, New York, New York: Random House, 1987.

Oppenheimer, Jerry. *The Other Mrs. Kennedy*, New York, New York: St. Martin's Press, 1994.

Oswald, Marguerite. *Aftermath of an Execution: The Burial and Final Rites of Lee Harvey Oswald, as told by his Mother Marguerite*, typescript.

Palamara, Vincent. *Survivor's Guilt*, Chicago, Illinois: IPG, 2013.

Parmet, Herbert S. *Jack: The Struggles of John F. Kennedy*, New York, New York: Eastland Press, 1986.

Parnell, W. Tracy. *The Exhumation of Lee Harvey Oswald and the Norton Report: Part Two—Paul Groody*, 2003.

Perry, Dave. *Now It Can Be Told—The Lee Bowers Story*, mcadamsposc.mu.edu/bowers.text.

Pietrusza, David. *LBJ vs JFK vs. Nixon*. Somerville, Massachusetts: Union Square Press, 2010.

Popkin, Richard H. *The Second Oswald*, New York, New York: Avon Books, 1966.

Prouty, L. Fletcher. *JFK the CIA, Vietnam, and the Plot to Assassinate John F. Kennedy*, New York, New York: Skyhorse Publishing, 2011

Quinlan, Casey J. and Edwards, Brian K. *Beyond the Fence Line*, Southlake, Texas: JFK Lancer Productions and Publications, Inc. 2008.

Reback, Storms. *From the Poker Vaults: Texas Boss Gamblers*, PokerNews.com, 2009.

Reedy, George. *Lyndon B. Johnson*, New York: Andrews and McMeel, Inc., 1982.

Reeves, Richard. *President Kennedy, Profile of Power*, New York, New York: Simon and Schuster, 1993.

Reeves, Thomas C. *A Question of Character*, New York, New York: The Free Press, 1991.

Reid, Ed. *The Grim Reapers*. Chicago, Illinois: Bantam, 1969.

Reston, James, Jr. *The Lone Star: The Life of John Connally*, New York: Harper & Row Publishers, 1989.

Reunited with Ruby in Mural, Dallas Morning News, November 1, 2009.

Rike, Aubrey. *At the Door of Memory*, Southlake, Texas: JFK Lancer Productions and Publications, 2008.

Roemer, William F. Jr. *Man against the Mob*, New York: Random House, 1989.

Russell, Jan Jarboe. *Lady Bird*. Dallas, Texas: Taylor Trade Publishing, 1999.

Russo, Gus. *Live by the Sword: The Secret War against Castro and the Death of JFK*, Baltimore, MD: Bancroft Press, 1998.

Russell, Dick. *The Man That Knew Too Much*, New York: Carroll & Graf Publishers, 1992.

Scheim, David E. *The Mafia Contract on America: Murder of President John F. Kennedy,* New York, New York: Shapolsky Publishers, Inc., 1988.

Schwarz, Ted and Mardi Rustam. *Candy Barr,* New York, New York: Taylor Trade Publishing, 2008.

Shaw, J. Gary, and Harris, Larry Ray. *Cover Up: The Government Conspiracy to Conceal the Facts About the Public Execution of John Kennedy,* Cleburne, TX: Gary Shaw, 1976.

Shaw, Mark. *The Poison Patriarch,* New York, New York: Skyhorse Publishing, 2013.

Shaw, Maud. *Caroline Kennedy at 16, Ladies Home Journal,* November 1973, Vol. XC, No. 11.

Shenon, Philip. *A Cruel and Shocking Act.* New York, New York: Henry Holt and Company, 2013.

Sloan, Bill. *Breaking the Silence,* Dallas, Texas: Taylor Publishing, 1993.

—*The Other Assassin,* New York, New York: Tudor Publishing, 1989.

Sloan, Bill and Jean Hill. *JFK the Last Dissenting Witness,* Gretna, La.: Pelican Publishing Co., 1992.

Smith, Matthew. *JFK: Say Goodbye to America,* Mainstream Publications, Edinburgh and London, 2004.

Sneed, Larry A. *No More Silence,* Denton, Texas: University of North Texas Press, 1998.

St. George, Judith. *In the Line of Fire: Presidents' Lives at Stake,* New York: Scholastic Books, 1999.

Steinberg, Alfred. *Sam Johnson's Boy,* New York: MacMillan Publishing Company, 1968.

Stockton, Bayard. *Flawed Patriot,* Dulles, Virginia: Potomac Books, Inc, 2006.

Stone, Roger. *The Man Who Killed Kennedy-- The Case against LBJ,* New York, New York: Skyhorse Publishing, 2013.

Summers, Anthony. *Not in Your Lifetime,* New York, New York: Open Road Integrated Media, 2013.

—*Official and Confidential: The Secret Life of J. Edgar Hoover,* New York, New York: G. P. Putnam's Sons, 1993.

—*The Kennedy Conspiracy,* New York: McGraw-Hill Book Company, 1980.

Tarby, Russ. *JFK in Dallas: The Syracuse Connections,* Syracuse, New York: *New Times,* 2013.

Tereba, Tere. *Mickey Cohen: The Life and Crimes of L.A.'s Notorious Mobster,* Toronto, Canada: ECW Press, 2012.

Thomas, Dylan. *Do Not Go Gentle into That Good Night,* www.PoemHunter.com.

—*The Hand That Signed the Paper,* www.PoemHunter.com.

Thomas, Evan. *Robert Kennedy: His Life,* New York: Simon & Schuster, 2000.

Thomas, Helen. *Dateline: White House,* New York, New York: Macmillan Publishing Co., Inc. 1975.

—*Front Row at the White House,* New York, New York: Simon & Schuster, 1999.

Thompson, Josiah. *Six Seconds in Dallas,* New York, New York: Bernard Geis Associates, 1967.

Tosches, Nick. *Dino,* New York, New York: Delta, 1999.

Turner, Nigel. *The Men Who Killed Kennedy,* Episode 9, England. November, 2003. DVD

The 20th Century: Through the Eyes of Texas, Supplement to the *Dallas Morning News,* Section R, September 22, 1999.

United Press International. *Four Days: The Historical Record of the Death of President Kennedy,* New York, New York: American Heritage Publisher Inc., 1964.

Van Buren, Ernestine O. *Clint—Clinton William Murchison,* Austin, Texas: Eakin Press, 1986.

Von Post, Gunilla, and Carl Johnas. *Love, Jack,* New York: Crown, 1997.

Waldron, Lamar. *Legacy of Secrecy,* Berkeley, California: Counterpoint Press, 2009.

Walker, Daniel. *JFK: Vernon's Ties to a Tragedy,* The Vernon Daily, November 19, 2013.

Warren, Earl et al,. *Report of the Warren Commission: The Assassination of President Kennedy,* New York, New York: McGraw Hill Book Company, 1964.

Wean, Gareth. *There's a Fish in the Courthouse,* Cave Junction, Oregon, 1987.

Weisberg, Harold. *Oswald in New Orleans Case for Conspiracy with the CIA,* New York, New York: Canyon Books, 1967.

Widmer, Ted. *Listening In,* New York, New York: Hyperion, 2012.

Wills, Garry. *The Kennedy Imprisonment,* Boston, Massachusetts: Little, Brown & Company, 1982.

Willis, Gary and Ovid Demaris. *Jack Ruby-- The Man Who Killed the Man Who Killed Kennedy,* New York: New American Library, 1968.

Wolfe, Donald H. *The Last Days of Marilyn Monroe,* New York, New York: William Morrow and Company, Inc., 1998.

Woods, Randall B. *LBJ Architect of American Ambition,* New York: Free Press, 2006.

Worthington, Peter. *The Jack Ruby Mystery: Dubious Public Avenger,* Toronto Star-Telegram, November 28, 1963.

Ybarra, Bob. *My Demons Were Real,* Houston, Texas: Arte Publico Press, 2010.

Zirbel, Craig. *The Texas Connection,* Scottsdale, Arizona: TCC Publishers, 1991.

ACKNOWLEDGEMENTS

W e wish to thank our families for their support and encouragement. They acted as sounding boards during our investigation and listened patiently as we regaled them with fascinating stories concerning the many people we were fortunate to interview.

Fellow researchers offered invaluable advice, but three in particular were truly our mentors: J. Gary Shaw, Phillip Nelson, and Edgar Tatro. We cannot thank them enough for sharing their time, their research, and their personal experiences with us.

We also want to thank the many people willing to come forward and speak openly about President John F. Kennedy and/or his assassination, some for the first time. Their memories are the heart of *The Lone Star Speaks*.

A number of individuals were particularly helpful to the authors, among them: Kay Burns, David Denton, Kellye Green, Chuck Helppie, Richard Jones, Jared Larson, Deb Lee, Priscilla Lewis, J. D. Luckie, Lora Meyer, Shelia Morrow, Mary and Foster Murphy, Mark Oakes, Beverly Oliver, Dr. William Pulte, Harry Roux, Dene Sheppherd, Kim Ulmer, Betty Windsor, Midland College staff members: Horace Griffin, Richard McKee, Jaroy Roberts, Chris Hieb, Rebecca Bell, Dorothy Baird, Diane Chambers, Margaret Chavez, Darla Coffman, Katherine Curry, Stacy Egan, Dr. Paula Gray, Dr. Todd Houck, Dr. Pamela Howell, Charlotte Sweatt, Bob Templeton, Neli Valles, and Lynda Webb.

Sadly, some of the people whose voices were so helpful are no longer with us, but their contributions are greatly appreciated. We are especially grateful to have known Eugene and Charmaine Boone, Dorothy Cox, John Currie, Robert T. Davis, George Day, David Dennis, Steve Ely, Pam Estes, Sherry Feister, Sue Goolsby, Joyce Gordon, Sue Hardy, Clifford Hart, John "Huck" Huckabee, Jack Ladd, Jim Marrs, B. J. Mayfield, William Morrow, Ed "Treefrog" Sherry, James Tague, James Weaver, and Tommy Wright.

We would also like to thank Ben Rogers of the Baylor University Poage Library, Gail Loving Barnes and Charles Cotten of the Presidential Archives and Museum in Odessa, Texas, the Nita Stewart Haley Museum, the Pecos Historical Museum, Tammy Schrecengost of the Big Spring Heritage Museum, staff members of the Texas Tech University Southwest Collections, the Texas

Christian University Library, the Sam Rayburn Museum, the Mob Museum in Las Vegas, Nevada, Krishna Shenoy of the Sixth Floor Museum at Dealey Plaza, the Lyndon Baines Johnson Presidential Library, and the staff of the *Vernon Daily Record.*

K.W. ZACHRY   SARA PETERSON

ABOUT THE AUTHORS

Sara Peterson attended the University of La Verne in California, where she earned a Bachelor's of Arts Degree in Political Science and in History. After being told by her Political Science Department Chair that she could not do her senior thesis on the Kennedy assassination, she went ahead anyway, focusing on those planning, carrying out, and covering up Kennedy's murder . Among the most powerful, she decided, was Lyndon Baines Johnson, a former Texan senator and then U.S. Vice-President. Since then, she has continued her research on the assassination and why the Warren Report's "evidence" is, in her view, inaccurate, incomplete, and in some cases manufactured. She is currently employed at Midland College in Texas as the Coordinator of the Developmental Education Language Lab and Writing Center.

K. W. Zachry earned a Bachelor of Science in English and Political Science from McMurry College and a Master of Arts in English from the University of Texas at El Paso. Her interest in the Kennedy assassination began when her grandparents, who lived in Dallas on 11/22/63, shared with her all of the local newspapers from the assassination. Ever since, she has been reading, researching, and "digging for bits and pieces" from people with first-hand information about the events surrounding the president's murder. By combining information and sources with Sara Peterson, she discovered that many uninterviewed Texans possessed information about the greatest mystery of the twentieth century. She is currently employed at Midland College in Texas as a tutor in the Developmental Education Language Lab and Writing Center.